The Longwood Guide to Writing

FOURTH EDITION

Ronald F. Lunsford
University of North Carolina at Charlotte

Bill Bridges
Sam Houston State University

PEARSON

Longman

New York   San Francisco   Boston
London   Toronto   Sydney   Tokyo   Singapore   Madrid
Mexico City   Munich   Paris   Cape Town   Hong Kong   Montreal

Acquisitions Editor: Lauren A. Finn
Senior Supplements Editor: Donna Campion
Senior Marketing Manager: Sandra McGuire
Production Manager: Eric Jorgensen
Project Coordination, Text Design, and Electronic Page Makeup: Electronic Publishing Services Inc., NYC
Cover Design Manager: Wendy Ann Fredericks
Cover Designer: Nancy Sacks
Cover Art: *Outside the Box,* David Arsenault/Private Collection The Bridgeman Art Library International
Photo Researcher: Chrissy McIntyre
Senior Manufacturing Buyer: Alfred C. Dorsey
Printer and Binder: Von Hoffmann Graphics/MO
Cover Printer: Coral Graphic Services, Inc.

For permission to use copyrighted material, grateful acknowledgment is made to the copyright holders on pages C-1 to C-2, which are hereby made part of this copyright page.

Library of Congress Cataloging-in-Publication Data

Lunsford, Ronald F.
  The Longwood guide to writing/Ronald F. Lunsford, Bill Bridges.—[4th ed.]
    p. cm.
  Includes bibliographical references and index.
  ISBN-13: 978-0-205-55376-1 (pbk.)
  ISBN-10: 0-205-55376-1 (pbk.)
  1. English language—Rhetoric—Handbooks, manuals, etc. 2. English language—Grammar—Handbooks, manuals, etc. 3. Report writing—Handbooks, manuals, etc. 4. College readers. I. Bridges, Charles W. II. Title.
PE1408.L88 2008
808'.042—dc22   2007026771

Copyright © 2008 by Pearson Education, Inc.

All rights reserved. No part of this publication may be reproduced, stored in a retrieval system, or transmitted, in any form or by any means, electronic, mechanical, photocopying, recording, or otherwise, without the prior written permission of the publisher. Printed in the United States.

Please visit us at www.ablongman.com

ISBN 13: 978-0-205-55376-1
ISBN 10:   0-205-55376-1

2 3 4 5 6 7 8 9 10—VHO—10 09 08

Contents

Preface xiii

Part I Strategies for the Writing Process 1

Why Write? 1
How Does Writing Happen? 3
Stages in the Writing Process 3
Writing and Reading 5
Writing and Visuals 5
Computers and Writing 5

1 Invention: Finding Something to Say 9

Finding Topics 9
Keeping a Writer's Notebook 10 / Interest Inventory 11 / *Computer Tip* 13

Writing About an Assigned Topic 13

Exploring Topics 14
Brainstorming 14 / *Computer Tip* 15 / Freewriting 15 / *Computer Tip* 19 / Clustering 20 / Visualizing 22 / Asking Questions 24 / *Writing Strategy: Questions for Analysis* 26 / Application: The Fuzzwort Refining Company 27 / *Computer Tip* 31

Finding Information 32
Researching Information on the World Wide Web 32

Sample Student Process—Prewriting 36

From Inventing to Drafting 37

2 Shaping an Essay 41

Initial Shaping Strategies 41
Writing for a Reader 41 / Focus Statements 41

iii

Sample Student Process—Discovery Draft 44
Computer Tip 46

Developing an Essay's Structure 47
Shaping Strategies 47

Elements of an Essay 53
Writing a Thesis Sentence 53 / *Writing Strategy: When Should You Write a Thesis Sentence?* 55 / Introductions 55 / *Writing Strategy: When Should You Write an Introduction?* 58 / Paragraphs—Topic Sentences 58 / Paragraphs—Cohesion 62 / *Writing Strategy: Principles of Paragraph Development* 64 / *Writing Strategy: One Page, One Paragraph* 65 / Conclusions 65
Writing Strategy: Beating the Dreaded Writer's Block 68

3 Revising 71

Computer Tip: Adding, Deleting, and Moving Text Around 71

Revising Strategies 73
Getting Distance 73 / Revising for Meaning (Global) 74 / Revising for Audience (Global) 75 / Revising for Structure (Global) 77 / *Computer Tip* 78 / Revising for Words (Local) 78 / Revising for Sentences (Local) 81 / Peer Review (Global and Local) 89

Writer's Notebook: Responding to Readers' Comments 92

Editing Strategies 92
Computer Tip 94

Writing a Self-Assessment 95

Sample Student Process—Revision 95
Marisol Vargas, MIRROR IMAGE 100

Writing Strategy: Revision Tips 102

4 Responding to Readings 105

Sample Reading 106
Lee K. Abbott, THE TRUE STORY OF WHY I DO WHAT I DO 106

Reading Strategies for Texts 110
Before You Read 111 / *Writing Strategy: The Time It Takes* 112 / While You Read 113 / *Writing Strategy: On Paraphrasing* 121 / After You Have Read 122

Reading Strategies for Visuals 123
Reading a Visual Image 127 / Analyzing a Visual Image 128

Writer's Notebook: Dialogue Notes 129
Reading Notes 129 / Class Notes 129 / Dialogue Notes 131

Writing Paraphrases and Summaries 132
Paraphrase 132 / *Writing Strategy: Checklist for Writing a Paraphrase* 135 /
Summary 135

Steven Pinker, RACIST LANGUAGE, REAL AND IMAGINED 136

Writing Strategy: Checklist for Writing a Summary 140

Writing a Response 141

Sample Student Essay—Summary and Response 143
Christian Clark, EMOTION AND THE DEATH PENALTY: AN ANALYSIS OF JACLYN TALBERT'S "JUSTICE FOR THOSE WHO HAVE SHOWN US NO MERCY" 143

PART II *Writing Occasions* 147

Aims of Discourse 147
Modes of Discourse 150
Wedding Aim and Mode 150
Classifying Occasions 151

5 Personal Essays 153

Sample Essays 153
Datus Proper, DARK HOLLOW 154

Judith Ortiz Cofer, THE MYTH OF THE LATIN WOMAN:
I JUST MET A GIRL NAMED MARÍA 158

Charles McNair, MY FATHER'S CABIN 163

Christopher Fisher, SCARS 165

The Rhetorical Triangle 176
Writer 176 / Subject 176 / Reader 177

Distinguishing Features of Personal Essays 178
Conflict 178 / Dialogue 179 / Vivid Detail 180

Visuals and Personal Essays 181

Assignment and Guidelines for Writing 184
Assignment 184 / Choosing a Topic 185 / Collecting Information 185 /
Focus Statement 186 / Planning Your Essay's Structure 186 / Refining Your Writing 188

Sample Student Process 189
Chris Miller, GRINGOS ON SAFARI 197
Checklist: Critiquing a Personal Essay 200

6 Information Essays 203

Sample Essays 204
Elisabeth Kübler-Ross, ON THE FEAR OF DYING 204

Suzanne Smalley, THE PERFECT CRIME 208

Jay Chiat, ILLUSIONS ARE FOREVER 211

Arthur Rosenfeld, SHOULD ANYONE HAVE TO LIVE IN PAIN? 213

Gloria Naylor, MOMMY, WHAT DOES "NIGGER" MEAN? 216

Sandra Y. Govan, LISTENING TO THE WORD, OR 21st CENTURY READER'S AND THE SOULS OF BLACK FOLK 219

Elizabeth C. Gardner, TRANSFORMING A NATION, TRANSFORMING AN ENEMY 227

The Rhetorical Triangle 234
Subject 234 / Writer 235 / Reader 237

Distinguishing Features of Information Essays 238
Reader's Knowledge 238 / Clarity 239

Assignment and Guidelines for Writing 241
Assignment 241 / Choosing a Topic 241 / Collecting Information 242

Making Use of Visuals 242
Tables and Figures 242 / Focus Statement 247 / Planning Your Essay's Structure 248

Meir Shalev, IF BOSNIANS WERE WHALES 252

Thesis Statement 259 / Refining Your Writing 260

Sample Student Process 261
Michael Graham, ALL IN A DAY'S WORK: GENERALIZING, PROFILING, AND STEREOTYPING 267

Checklist: Critiquing an Information Essay 270

7 Essays *About* and *From* Literature 273

Sample Works of Literature 275
Joyce Carol Oates, SHOPPING 275

Aaron Gwyn, OF FALLING 285

Robert Frost, FOR ONCE, THEN, SOMETHING 295

Margaret Atwood, SPELLING 296
Sherman Alexie, THAT PLACE WHERE GHOSTS OF SALMON JUMP 298
Sherman Alexie, THE POWWOW AT THE END OF THE WORLD 300
Sherman Alexie, EVOLUTION 301

Sample Essays 303

Kendra Stead, THE MAKING OF SPELLS 303
Amy Wright, A QUEST TO RETURN TO THE GARDEN: PERCEPTION "OF FALLING" 306
Kendra Stead, NO EXCEPTIONS 310
Steve Stoeckel, WHAT ABOUT THE CUSTOMER? 313

The Rhetorical Triangle 316
Subject 316 / Writer 324 / Reader 325

Distinguishing Features of Interpretive Essays 326
Interpretation 326 / Theme 326 / Thesis and Support 326 / Beyond Summary 327 / Citing Sources 327

Assignment and Guidelines for Writing 328
Assignment 328

Writing *About* Literature 329
Collecting Information 329 / Focus Statement 330 / Planning Your Essay's Structure 330 / Refining Your Writing 331

Writing *From* Literature 331
Collecting Information 331 / Focus Statement 332 / Planning Your Essay's Structure 332 / Refining Your Writing 333

Sample Student Process 333
Kristina Geray, "HOW EXHAUSTING IT IS" TO KEEP UP APPEARANCES 341

Checklist: Critiquing an Essay About Literature 344
Checklist: Critiquing an Essay From Literature 345

8 Evaluation Essays 347

Sample Essays 349
Ellen Goodman, BEAUTY INDUSTRY ON RAMPAGE 349
Kathleen Hall Jamieson, SHOOTING TO WIN; DO ATTACK ADS WORK? YOU BET—AND THAT'S NOT ALL BAD 352
Bill Bridges, "NO THANKS"—A STEP BEYOND "JUST SAY NO" 358
Jennifer Pitman, BOOZE IT? LOSE IT!: AN EVALUATION OF NORTH CAROLINA'S DRUNK DRIVING LAWS 362
Amy Wright, THE DA VINCI CODE: A STUDY IN PRINT AND FILM 365

The Rhetorical Triangle 371
Subject 371 / Writer 371 / Reader 372

Distinguishing Features of Evaluation Essays 372
Evaluation Criteria 372
  Lou Jacobs, Jr., WHAT QUALITIES DOES A GOOD PHOTOGRAPH HAVE? 373
Writer's Judgment 376 / "Because" Support 378

Evaluating Visual Images 378
Political Cartoons 379 / Political Advertising 383

Assignment and Guidelines for Writing 386
Assignment 386 / Choosing a Topic 387 / Collecting Information 387 / Focus Statement 388 / Planning Your Essay's Structure 389 / Thesis Statement 389 / Sample Structure 389 / Refining Your Writing 390

An Exercise in Evaluation and the Internet 390
Using Search Engines 391 / Evaluating a Website 391 / Evaluating a Counterpoint 393

Portfolios 396
Putting the Reflection in Your Reflective Essay 396 / Sample Portfolio Assignments 397 / Sample Reflective Essays 399
  Jacqueline Cotter, GETTING IT RIGHT: FITTING MESSAGE TO AUDIENCE 399
  Steve Duran, STEVE WANTS AN A 402

Sample Student Process 404
  Bridget McCollam, ADULT AUDIENCES ONLY 408
    Checklist: Critiquing an Evaluation Essay 410

9 Position Essays 413

Sample Essays 413
  Michael Haley, THE RIGHT NOT TO LISTEN 414
  David Amante, TEACHING IS ALWAYS A POLITICAL ACT 420
  Stephen Jay Gould, NONOVERLAPPING MAGISTERIA 426
  Jennifer Pitman, EUTHANASIA AND THE RIGHT TO DIE 437

The Rhetorical Triangle 440
Reader 440 / Subject 441 / Writer 442

Distinguishing Features of Position Essays 446
Logical Arguments 446 / Ethical Stance 452

Assignment and Guidelines for Writing 452

Assignment 452 / Choosing a Topic 452 / Collecting Information 453 / Focus Statement 457 / Planning Your Essay's Structure 457 / Thesis Statement 464 / Checking for Logical Fallacies 464 / Refining Your Writing 473

Sample Student Process 473
Heather Hall, THE NEXT BIG WINNER IS . . . !! 479
Checklist: Critiquing a Position Essay 482

10 Persuasion Essays 485

Sample Essays 486
Michael R. Heaphy, DISMEMBERMENT AND CHOICE 486

Thomas Oliphant, EXPOSED IN THE SUPREME COURT: LIES ABOUT "PARTIAL BIRTH ABORTION" 490

Martin Luther King, Jr., I HAVE A DREAM 492

Richard Dawkins, WHEN RELIGION STEPS ON SCIENCE'S TURF: THE ALLEGED SEPARATION BETWEEN THE TWO IS NOT SO TIDY 497

Jaime Sherrill, ZERO TOLERANCE FOR ABUSE 501

Jaclyn Talbert, JUSTICE FOR THOSE WHO HAVE SHOWN US NO MERCY 504

The Rhetorical Triangle 507
Reader 507 / Subject 508 / Writer 509

Distinguishing Features of Persuasion Essays 510
Emotional Appeal 510 / Ethical Persuasion 511 / Persuasive Language 512

Assignment and Guidelines for Writing 516
Assignment 516 / Choosing a Topic 516 / Collecting Information 517 / Focus Statement 517 / Planning Your Essay's Structure 518 / Thesis Statement 518 / Refining Your Writing 519 / Using Visuals to Persuade 519

Sample Student Process 524
Alysia Tucker, NO MORE 530
Checklist: Critiquing a Persuasion Essay 533

11 Problem/Solution Essays 535

Sample Essays 536
William E. King, OUT OF HURRICANE'S WAY 536

Julie Titone, BALANCE OF POWER: CAN ENDANGERED SALMON AND HYDROELECTRIC PLANTS SHARE THE SAME RIVERS? 542

Andrew Overton, CHANGE 546

The Rhetorical Triangle   551
Reader 551 / Subject 551 / Writer 552

Distinguishing Features of Problem/Solution Essays   553
Well-Defined Problem 553 / Thorough Exploration of the Problem 554 / Best Solution 555

Assignment and Guidelines for Writing   555
Assignment 555 / Choosing a Topic 555 / Collecting Information 556 / Focus Statement 557 / Planning Your Essay's Structure 558 / Thesis Statement 559 / Refining Your Writing 560

Sample Student Process   560
Kristina Geray, THE PET OVERPOPULATION PROBLEM 568

Checklist: Critiquing a Problem/Solution Essay 571

PART III Research   573

12 Researching and Writing   577

Writing Strategy: Research Notebook 578

Topic Selection   579

Searching a Topic   580
Sources of Information 580 / Library Search 582 / *Computer Tip: Sample Listing of CD-ROM Databases* 583 / Field Search 585 / Internet Search 590 / *Computer Tip: Research Tool* 595 / *Computer Tip: More Useful Internet Sites* 597

Incorporating Material from Sources   598

Documenting Information   601
Initial Bibliography 602 / Final Bibliography 602

Citations   613

Sample Annotated Essays   618
Clarita Brown, THE AMERICAN INDIAN MOVEMENT AS A COUNTERCULTURE 618

Writing Assignment   624

Sample Student Process   624
Gardiner Rhoderick, YES, IT'S GRAFFITI. BUT IS IT ART? 630

Checklist: Critiquing a Research Essay 637

Contents   xi

PART IV Writing and Assessing   639

Assessment via Essay Exams   639

13 Essay Examinations   643

Packaging the Process   644
Writing Strategy: Summary of the Essay-Exam Process 646

Planning Your Essay's Content   646
Summary 647 / Synthesis 648 / Evaluation 651 / Interpretation 652

Planning Your Essay's Structure   655

Overlapping Terminologies   657

Essays That Ask for Practical Applications   658

Planning Sample Essays   660
Writing Strategy: Planning Essay-Exam Answers 661

PART V Preparing for Publication   663

Basic Grammar   665

Parts of Speech   665
Semantic Categories 665 / Function Categories 671

Phrases and Modification   672
Modifiers 673 / Types of Phrases 674

Sentence Functions   675
Subjects 675 / Predicate Nominatives 675 / Direct Objects 676 / Indirect Objects 677 / Secondary Objects 678 / Objects of Prepositions 678 / Substantives 679

Sentence Types   680
Simple Sentences 680 / Complex Sentences 681 / Compound Sentences 681 / Compound-Complex Sentences 681

Punctuation, Spelling, and Manuscript Mechanics   682

End Punctuation   682

Punctuation within Sentences   684

Spelling 696
Manuscript Mechanics 700
Capitalization 701
Abbreviations 702 / Numbers 702 / Italics 703 / Hyphens 703

Literary Credits C-1
Index I-1

Preface

In one sense, this book began well over thirty years ago, when the two of us met at Florida State University in a graduate-level rhetorical theory course taught by our mentor, James McCrimmon. Thanks to the many conferences we have attended together since then and to advances in technology that have allowed us all but immediate communication, we have collaborated more and more, eventually co-authoring several articles and three books. We even confer with each other in our teaching; these days, we scarcely take a new writing exercise to class that the other has not read, critiqued, and, ultimately, made better. Over the years that we have worked together, we have written and talked our way to the writing theory that provides this book's framework. We can best describe this theory as one in which writing is viewed as rhetorical, personal, and communal.

Writing as Rhetorical

Professor McCrimmon introduced us to the work of Kenneth Burke, and through Burke to Aristotle. The result is a heavy commitment to writing as rhetorical, that is, to the view that the quality of a piece of writing is judged by its effectiveness in achieving its writer's purpose for the intended reader. That commitment is made evident in our use of the rhetorical triangle as a means of structuring the chapters in Part Two that treat various writing occasions.

Writing as Personal

Good writing is personal; that is, it is steeped in the significance the writer sees in her subject. *The Longwood Guide to Writing* reveals our commitment to the personal nature of writing in our emphasis on significance in all types of writing. Whether a personal essay or a fully developed researched argument, good writing conveys the significance or meaning that matters for the writer.

Writing as Communal

Writing, as we have come to know it, is not a solitary act. Our work on this book—and on numerous projects before it—has taught us that good writing does not happen in a vacuum, or even in a writer's garret—unless that garret has an email connection. In our own writing, it is at times hard for us to know who is responsible for what. For example, one of us drafts a chapter, and the other responds, rewrites, and then ships it back to the other. From there, the chapter's initial writer revises. This back-and-forth process continues until, in the end, the product is a joint one. Through email, we have even worked with each other's students, serving as readers and editors at a distance. Our work together has helped us develop more and more collaborative exercises for our writing classes. We have included many of these exercises in this text.

DISTINCTIVE FEATURES OF THE LONGWOOD GUIDE TO WRITING

Writing as a Process

We have attempted to make writing process an integral part of this book without falling into the trap of acting as if there were only one writing process that all writers either do or should employ for all types of writing. What makes our approach distinctive is the availability of process throughout the text. We begin by devoting an entire section to writing process: Part I, with chapters on invention, shaping, revising, and reading. Further, in the first three of these chapters, we follow a student writer's process as she begins thinking and freewriting about her topic, then writes an initial discovery draft, and then revises that rough draft three more times until she completes the assignment. Then, in each of the writing occasion chapters in Part II, the attention to process continues with an Assignment and Guidelines for Writing section, which offers specific advice and activities to help students complete an essay assignment.

The Rhetorical Triangle

What is good writing? As a way of answering this question, think for a moment about the various situations in which writing takes place. We write notes to family and friends. We write grocery lists and to-do lists. We write terse letters to credit card corporations, asking to be taken off their mailing or telephone lists. Some of us write books. Many of us write email messages to our teachers, students, and friends. What do all of these writing situations have in common? Each involves a writer, a subject, and a reader. These elements are often referred to as the *rhetorical triangle:* This triangle suggests that good writing results from a process in which a

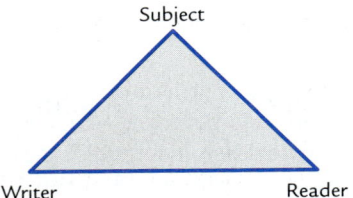

writer shares meaning with a reader. It also suggests that writing requires some sort of balance among writer, subject, and reader. The writer must fit the subject to the reader. The writer must identify with the audience in such a way as to predict what readers want to learn from the writing and what information they need as background before they can understand the essential information in the text. This is difficult enough when writing for one reader—for example, when one family member writes a note to another about how to program the VCR. It becomes increasingly difficult as the readers become more numerous and more varied in their interests and knowledge. In writing an instruction booklet that includes a section on programming a VCR, a writer must arrive at some concept of a typical reader in order to decide what information to include.

In Part II, we use the rhetorical triangle extensively. Each chapter in this part includes three sections corresponding to the corners of the rhetorical triangle: spotlighting the writer, spotlighting the subject, and spotlighting the reader.

Emphasis on Invention

We devote the first chapter of *The Longwood Guide to Writing* to invention and return to invention activities in the Guidelines section of each chapter in Part II. These activities range from the informal—for example, freewriting and brainstorming—to the formal—for example, a comprehensive set of questions for analyzing a topic, discovering insights or information to use in an essay, and shaping those materials into an essay. This set of questions is consistent with our commitment to a Burkean approach to rhetoric, for it derives from Burke's logological analysis.

Modes as Invention and Organizational Structures

We see modes as very powerful tools in the writing process. However, it seems wrong to us to equate types of writing with modes. In *The Longwood Guide to Writing*, we are careful to illustrate how each mode may be, and often is, employed in writing with any aim. For example, even though the overall structure of an informative essay will likely be provided by one of the expository modes, there is no one-to-one correlation between expository modes and informational or explanatory writing. In fact, informational writing may well make use of an argumentative thesis and employ narrative or descriptive modes. The same could be said for writing with any other aim; that is, the writer may well use any mode to help achieve any aim. In the Guidelines section of Chapter 6, we present modes as tools for generating and shaping material rather than as constraints or containers that limit writing.

Connections Between Writing and Reading

Writing and reading are very closely connected, and *The Longwood Guide to Writing* includes a chapter devoted to this connection. In Chapter 4, we focus on ways in which writing can help students understand what they are reading. This chapter offers a comprehensive range of reading and writing strategies students may use before they read, while they are reading, and after they have read to help them better understand a given text and then use that text in fulfilling a writing assignment.

Writing *About* and *From* Literature

In Chapter 7, we present two ways of responding to literature: writing *about* literature and writing *from* literature. Writing *about* literature requires the writer to analyze a piece of literature and write an interpretation of it, while writing *from* literature involves using a piece of literature as a springboard to an essay. These essays tend to be personal, but they can be argumentative or even informative. Both types of literature essays—writing *about* and writing *from*—begin with reading closely to derive an understanding of the literature at hand. Chapter 7 discusses how to develop this understanding.

Argument and Persuasion

We have chosen to deal with argument and persuasion in two chapters rather than one. In Chapter 9, we attempt to help students strengthen their abilities to think through an argument, both from their own perspectives and from the perspectives of those who would disagree with them. The writer's goal in this type of writing is not to persuade a person holding an opposite point of view to agree with him, but rather to gain the respect and understanding of those who disagree. To do so, the writer must show respect and understanding for those who hold an opposing point of view.

In Chapter 10, we follow two important tenets of Kenneth Burke. The first is that persuasion occurs only when writer and reader can identify with each other. This identification cannot occur when writer and reader begin with opposing positions on arguments that, in part, determine their identity. The second Burkean principle follows from the first, namely, that in persuasive writing the writer must carve out an audience that suits the topic of persuasion. Thus, if a writer wants to persuade readers to take some action to promote the goals of a controversial topic such as abortion, she must choose an audience that can be persuaded on this topic. To do otherwise is to do pretend, rather than real, writing.

Student Writing

We make ample use of student writing, featuring essays written by our students as examples in a number of chapters. In addition, each of the chapters in Parts II and III presents a piece of student writing in its entirety from prewriting to final draft. The collaborative nature of writing is emphasized and illustrated in these sample essays by the inclusion of actual peer reviews and teacher comments that students received during their writing processes, whether in prewriting and planning or between drafts.

Realistic Professional Models

We have chosen professional writing that can serve as models for student writing. Most of these essays are of comparable length to those essays written by our students. Thus, students should be able to see parallels between the structure of these essays and the essays they will be writing. The Questions for Review after each of these essays encourage students to reflect on the ways each essay illustrates the concepts being treated in the chapter in which it is presented.

NEW TO THE FOURTH EDITION

Introduction of Visuals

More and more, written texts and visuals appear together. Our students must be made aware of the effect visuals are having on them as they consume texts, and just as importantly, they must become proficient in using visuals in their own writing. To that end we have expanded five chapters significantly by adding treatment of visuals.

Reading Visuals   In Chapter 4: Responding to Readings, we introduce a unit that offers students a set of principles for interpreting visuals. Building on C. S. Peirce's triad for interpretation—*index, icon,* and *symbol*—we offer students three views of any image: they may view it as a *copy,* a *perspective,* or a *symbol*. We then perform an in-depth analysis of several visuals and offer a set of questions and activities designed to help students hone their abilities to interpret images.

Interpreting Visuals   We've often heard it said that a picture is worth a thousand words. There is a sense in which this is true. But it may take a thousand words, or more, for a writer to express what she sees in a picture. In Chapter 5: Personal Essays, we add a unit in which we explore the role that expressive writing can play in helping a person explore images. In our discussion, Bill uses a keepsake from his past, a guitar given to him by his father, to show students how writing can come from a visual. Bill creates the visual he writes about by taking two pictures of that old guitar, then describing the scenes on the guitar and speculating a bit about the guitar's meaning. We then offer guidelines and exercises that help students think about ways to use visuals as springboards for their own writing.

Using Visuals to Inform   We have added a section to Chapter 6: Information Essays in which we discuss the role that visuals can play in conveying information. In this section, we show how writers use various tables and figures to share information. Students are then encouraged to think of how they may use visuals as a means of collecting information on their topics. Finally, we present exercises that give students practice in evaluating visuals and in generating their own visuals to help clarify their writing.

Evaluating Visuals   Beginning with the second edition of *The Longwood Guide to Writing*, a mainstay of Chapter 8: Evaluation Essays has been evaluation of visuals. In that edition, Bill presented an essay, "No Thanks," in which he evaluates an antidrug advertisement that appeared in *seventeen* magazine.

The fourth edition retains Bill's essay and builds on it with a section in which we use the terms introduced in Chapter 4: Responding to Readings—*copy*, *perspective*, and *symbol*—to analyze political cartoons and political advertisements. Teachers encouraging students to write about issues raised in the 2008 political campaigns will find the analyses and exercises in this new section extremely useful.

Using Visuals to Persuade   Chapter 10: Persuasion Essays adds a section that builds on the information on visuals in Chapter 8: Evaluation Essays. Again, we use the three viewpoints—*copy, perspective,* and *symbol*—to analyze cartoons that are intended to sway readers. The two central cartoons analyzed in this section treat abortion, the topic argued by the first two essays in this chapter: "Dismemberment and Choice" and "Exposed in the Supreme Court: Lies About 'Partial Birth Abortion.'" After an in-depth analysis of these cartoons, we offer students exercises designed to give them practice in analyzing the role visuals play in persuasion.

Expanded Treatment of Paraphrase and Summary

We have expanded the treatment of summary and paraphrase in Chapter 4: Responding to Readings. We have done so in response to our own experience in the classroom that leads us to believe these skills demand much more of our students than the cursory treatment often given to them in composition classes would suggest. We have also heard from a good many users of our text who have called for more samples to help students with these tasks.

While many have come to use paraphrase and summary interchangeably, our treatment of the two terms stipulates a clear difference. Summary captures the gist of a work; paraphrase attempts to render the entire work in the words of the paraphraser. Thus, summary should be much shorter than the original, while paraphrase should be roughly the same length. Building on this foundation, we offer sample passages and then show various paraphrases and various summaries of these passages. We then explain in detail what makes for successful paraphrases and summaries. Finally, we offer exercises in which students can learn these skills by applying the principles we have explained.

Expanded Documentation and Citation

In Chapter 12: Researching and Writing, we have added text boxes that serve to annotate MLA and APA formats, both for documentation and in-text citations. We have also added an annotated essay that makes use of the MLA style. We have retained the current annotated essay that makes use of the APA style, so we now have two completely documented essays that illustrate both MLA and APA documentation. These annotations should help students more readily grasp the elements of these two styles of documentation and citations, thereby making the job of working with sources easier.

Thematic Threads in Readings

This edition of *The Longwood Guide to Writing* presents twenty-five professional essays, twenty-four essays written by students, two short stories and six poems. Of these readings, thirteen of the professional essays are new, one poem is new, and six student essays are new.

From our first edition, one of the earmarks of *The Longwood Guide to Writing* has been our belief that reading and writing are integrally connected. In our own teaching, we have always used reading as a springboard to writing, as we explain in detail in Chapter 4: Responding to Readings. From that first edition, it has been our goal to choose reading selections that would be of interest to our students and that would lead to the kind of personally significant writing we always encourage them to aim for. As we have moved from edition to edition, we have attempted to keep readings that seem to work well for those who use our text and replace others with readings that complement the ones we've kept. This process has led very naturally to some mini-themes that one can find in our readings. For the first time, we would like to call attention in this edition to some of the themes that have evolved to date.

Opposing Arguments

Abortion Issues:

> Michael R. Heaphy, "Dismemberment and Choice," p. 486
> Thomas Oliphant, "Exposed in the Supreme Court: Lies About 'Partial Birth Abortion,'" p. 490
> Mike Peters, "Judge Peers Over Bench at Woman," p. 520
> Brian Fairrington "Woman Holding Protest Sign," p. 521

Expressing Bias in Teaching:

> Michael Haley, "The Right Not to Listen," p. 414
> David Amante, "Teaching Is Always a Political Act," p. 420

Separation of Religion and Science

> Stephen Jay Gould, "Nonoverlapping Magisteria," p. 426
> Richard Dawkins, "When Religion Steps on Science's Turf: The Alleged Separation Between the Two Is Not So Tidy," p. 497

Essays Written About Specific Pieces of Literature or Other Texts

> Christian Clark, "Emotion and the Death Penalty: An Analysis of Jaclyn Talbert's 'Justice For Those Who Have Shown Us No Mercy,'" p. 143 (The analyzed student essay also appears in our text, p. 504.)

Amy Wright, "A Quest to Return to the Garden" (An analysis of Aaron Gwyn's "Of Falling"), p. 306

Kendra Stead, "No Exceptions" (An essay that responds to Marge Piercy's "A Work of Artifice"), p. 310

Steve Stoeckel, "What about the Customer?" (An essay that connects Stoeckel's experiences to his reading of Carl Sandberg's "Name Us a King"), p. 313

Kristina Geray, "'How Exhausting It Is' To Keep Up Appearances" (An analysis of Joyce Carol Oates', "Shopping"), p. 341

Amy Wright, "The *Da Vinci Code:* A Study in Print and Film" (A comparison of Michael Brown's book by that title and a film by the same title, directed by Ron Howard), p. 365

Other Themes

Racist Language:

Steven Pinker, "Racist Language, Real and Imagined," p. 136
Gloria Naylor, "Mommy, What Does 'Nigger' Mean?" p. 216

Humanitarian Service:

Marisol Vargas, "Mirror Image," p. 100
Chris Miller, "Gringos on Safari," p. 197

Spousal Abuse:

Jamie Sherrill, "Zero Tolerance for Abuse," p. 501
Alysia Tucker, "No More," p. 529

Art—What Is It and What Does It Do for (and to) Humans?:

Lee K. Abbott, "The True Story of Why I Do What I Do," p. 106
Robert Frost, "For Once, Then, Something," p. 295
Margaret Atwood, "Spelling," p. 296
Bridget McCollam, "Adult Audiences Only," p. 408
Gardiner Rhoderick, "Yes, It's Graffiti, But Is It Art?" p. 630

Gender and Society:

Judith Ortiz Cofer, "The Myth of the Latin Woman: I Just Met a Girl Named Maria," p. 158
Joyce Carol Oates, "Shopping," p. 275
Margaret Atwood, "Spelling," p. 296
Kendra Stead, "The Making of Spells," p. 303
Marge Piercy, "A Work of Artifice," p. 310

Kendra Stead, "No Exceptions," p. 310
Kristina Geray, "'How Exhausting It Is' to Keep Up Appearances," p. 341
Ellen Goodman, "Beauty Industry on Rampage," p. 349
Bill Bridges, "No Thanks," p. 358

Problems of Progress:

Datus Proper, "Dark Hollow," p. 154
Elisabeth Kübler-Ross, "On the Fear of Dying," p. 204
Sherman Alexie, "That Place Where Ghosts of Salmon Jump," p. 298
Sherman Alexie, "The Powwow at the End of the World," p. 300
Sherman Alexie, "Evolution," p. 301
William E. King, "Out of Hurricane's Way," p. 536
Julie Titone, "Balance of Power: Can Endangered Salmon and Hydroelectric Plants Share the Same Rivers," p. 541
Clarita Brown, "The American Indian Movement as a Counter Culture," p. 618

The Power of Language:

Jay Chiat, "Illusions Are Forever," p. 211
Elizabeth C. Gardner, "Transforming a Nation, Transforming an Enemy," p. 227
Michael Graham, "All in a Day's Work: Generalizing, Profiling, and Stereotyping," p. 267
Ellen Goodman, "Beauty Industry on Rampage," p. 349
Kathleen Hall Jamieson, "Shooting to Win; Do Attack Ads Work? You Bet—and That's Not All Bad," p. 352

Human Suffering and Modern Medicine:

Arthur Rosenfeld, "Should Anyone Have to Live in Pain?" p. 213
Jennifer Pitman, "Euthanasia and the Right to Die," p. 437

SUPPLEMENTS FOR *THE LONGWOOD GUIDE TO WRITING*

The Longwood Guide to Writing is supported by a variety of helpful supplements for instructors and students.

◆ The *Instructor's Resource Manual* we wrote contains an introductory section that provides sample syllabi for various courses in which *The Longwood Guide to Writing* can be used; a section in which we discuss each chapter individually, providing background information about what we hope students will achieve as they work through the material, as well as responses to many of the exercises in the text; and a theoretical section, in which we discuss, in three separate articles, the essential ingredients of a process approach to writing, various ways of giving students feedback about their writing, and the theories of Kenneth Burke that are the foundation of our text. Finally, a separate essay, written by Nancy Pfingstag, a member of the English Language Training Institute faculty at UNC Charlotte, deals with issues in teaching writing to students for whom English is a second language.

- *MyCompLab (www.mycomplab.com <outbind:///174/www.mycomplab.com>).* Putting writing at the center, the new release of MyCompLab — available for Fall 2008 courses — revolutionizes online composition resources. The new release offers a flexible and familiar writing space in which students can write and revise their papers; access interactive, in-context tutorials and exercises for grammar, writing and research topics; create a study plan and track their progress; do peer review; see instructor comments; get paper review help from Smarthinking's e-tutors; and create a portfolio of their work in MyCompLab's e-portfolio. Contact your local Pearson representative for a demo of this revolutionary new release.

ACKNOWLEDGMENTS

A project like this leaves us indebted to many more people than we can properly thank. We would like to begin with the many students we have taught and who have taught us through the years. We especially thank those whose essays are included in this text.

We thank Greg Wickliff, Associate Professor of English at the University of North Carolina at Charlotte, for serving as a consultant for all sections of the book dealing with the Internet.

We thank Longman for giving us the opportunity to write this book. We especially thank Eben Ludlow for believing in the project from the start. Now that he has retired to devote more time to supporting his beloved Yankees, we would like to thank Lauren Finn for her dedication to making a good book even better.

In this text, as in every professional endeavor we have undertaken since coming under his powerful and generous influence, we are indebted to our inspiring mentor, the late Dr. James McCrimmon.

Ron wishes to thank his mother, Reba, for her undying love; Nancy, for her love and support throughout this project, and Tamara and Christopher for continually making him proud to be a father.

Finally, Bill wishes to thank Mary Beth, for her loving support through it all, and their children, Mark and Suzie, David and Jennifer, and Matt and Corinne, in whom Bill and Mary Beth take great pride.

RONALD F. LUNSFORD
BILL BRIDGES

PART 1

Strategies for the Writing Process

WHY WRITE?

In the current computer-rich business climate, it seems that paper is on its way out, that the paperless office is increasingly taking over. Computers are replacing pen and paper as the medium of choice for writing. The implication is that writing will soon be unnecessary, for all we really need to do to communicate is pick up the phone and call or get on-line and send an email message. But the concept of the paperless office should not lead us to expect an end to writing, or even a lessening in its importance. Even though there may be less and less paper, there is, in fact, more and more writing. All of that work we do at keyboards is writing; any time we use words to compose our thoughts, using a medium that lets us review the words we have written and revise if we choose to, we are writing. So, despite the pervasiveness of telecommunications, writing will remain an important part of our attempts to communicate.

Writing will be crucial to your success after college, and you'll no doubt find many opportunities to hone your writing skills in college. You'll write essay exams, essays, research papers, and laboratory reports. You'll keep notes on reading assignments, class lectures, and lab experiments. You'll probably write for personal reasons as well—letters, journal or diary entries, to-do lists, to name but a few. Writing clearly has a number of purposes, including these:

Remember "Write it down—paper remembers." Even though paper is often replaced by a computer screen, there is a very real sense in which this old saying is still true. If we write a grocery or to-do list, we use writing to help us remember what we need to do. But writing can also help us remember important people, places, and events as we record them in journals or diaries. When we ask our students who keep journals why they do so, many tell us they want to remember what happened.

Record We use writing to record what happened in a given situation. Sometimes this written record may take the form of minutes of a meeting or a step-by-step description of what occurred during a biology lab. Creating such records is important because we often need to document an event; we need to create a history.

Understand and Think Critically As we write, we often pause to reflect and consider what we think about a particular person, event, or concept. Why did your boyfriend or girlfriend break up with you? Why did you pick the major you did? Why do you think you want to change your major? What were the principal causes of a historical event? Your writing can help you find answers to these and many other questions. Writing can be especially powerful when you analyze and interpret the ideas of others, that is, when you couple writing and reading. As you write about the ideas of other writers, you strengthen your own critical reading skills; you strengthen your abilities to summarize, analyze, and interpret.

Learn One of the most powerful uses of writing is to learn. As a physical act, writing seems to be connected directly with the mind; there's just something about consciously creating words and ideas on the page (whether we're using a ballpoint pen, a typewriter, or a word processor) that causes us to retain those words and ideas longer. We create knowledge by writing things down; at the same time, we transfer that knowledge from the page to the mind, from the page to the brain's idea warehouse.

Writing to learn begins when you take notes from your readings and from lectures and labs, and it continues as you write essays in response to formal writing assignments. As you review your notes (and even take notes on those notes), you'll work at learning their important parts. As you write to prepare for essay exams, you'll learn the subject matter better than you would otherwise and so improve your chances for a good grade. And, as you work through an extended essay assignment, you'll discover things you didn't know about the topic. In making such discoveries, you'll come to know the subject in more comprehensive ways.

Create Order We use language to bring order out of chaos. Think, for example, about a camper who hears the banging of garbage cans as something tries to knock off their lids and get at whatever scraps of food they contain. What's the effect of his saying, "Oh, that's just raccoons after bacon"? The mere naming of the noisemaker makes familiar the unfamiliar; it shrinks the two-headed beastie with twelve-inch claws and razor-sharp fangs to something much smaller and more manageable—raccoons after bacon. Although this example is simple, it illustrates how you can use language to create order in your world and so obtain more control over it.

The Longwood Guide is designed to help you explore the ways in which you can use writing to achieve these purposes.

HOW DOES WRITING HAPPEN?

Let's begin with this scenario: Late at night, the professional writer sits down to compose another masterpiece. She thinks for a bit, mulling over her day as she enjoys a cup of hot tea; then, out of nowhere, inspiration strikes! She grasps an idea, perhaps jots a note or two or a quick outline to make sure the idea doesn't escape, and then dashes off a poem, essay, short story, play, or novel effortlessly, without stopping, without making a mistake. She smiles contentedly as she prints a copy of the work. Then she either ships the text electronically to her agent or places it in an envelope for the next day's mail, confident of immediate publication and critical acclaim, if not a sale of movie rights.

Here's a second scenario: Having put off beginning his writing assignment until the absolute last minute, the student writer drags himself over to his writing desk and sits down. He dreads the laborious task he's about to undertake, but he knows he has to get it done. So he begins. He thinks up a topic. He thinks about this topic. He writes a thesis sentence. He writes an outline. He writes the essay. He reads the essay only once, correcting errors in spelling, grammar, and mechanics as he goes. He staples the pages together and stuffs the draft into his backpack. He smiles ruefully, knowing that he hasn't written a very good paper, but he does have something to hand in the next day.

While these scenarios seem overdrawn, the first reflects the ideal that many students aspire to, whereas the second reflects their actual writing practices. In our experience, however, writing is something much less magical than the first scenario implies and much less predictable than the second one does. Writing is a recursive process in which the writer engages in considerable trial and error, looping backward while moving forward. She may begin by freewriting or asking questions about her topic, then compose a rough outline for her essay, move to a draft, move forward to experimentation with words, trying to find the right word for a specific thought, then hit a snag in a certain passage and move back to freewriting about what seems to be bothering her in the passage, get some insight into an entirely new section that needs to be added, return to the rough outline and revise it to allow for this new section, and then write a second draft of her essay. Like the preceding sentence, the writing process is fluid and ongoing.

STAGES IN THE WRITING PROCESS

How can you manage something as seemingly chaotic as writing? One way is to break your writing task into several parts, or stages, each with specific activities you may complete along the way, rather than trying to deal with the assignment as a whole. Now, we really can't divide the writing process neatly into separate units, but it is useful and convenient to talk about three stages—prewriting, drafting, and revising—as if they were discrete units. This separation allows us to deal with smaller parts than the whole of the writing process. By thinking of your writing in terms of these stages, you can manage a writing project from start to finish.

Prewriting, which occurs before the writer produces the first rough draft, is a planning and preparation stage. In prewriting, the writer selects a subject and begins to discover what he wants to say about it and how best to present his thoughts to his intended audience. This stage provides the foundation for discovery; it is the germination, or gestation, period, the stage in which ideas begin to take shape. Our first chapter, Invention: Finding Something to Say, offers strategies for getting started on an essay and for finding things to say in your writing.

Drafting is the stage in which the writer produces a rough draft of the paper. Here the writer should concentrate on actually writing his ideas; he should not be overly concerned with such matters as finding exactly the right word, restructuring sentences or paragraphs, or correcting errors in spelling or punctuation. Too much attention to these matters may constrict or stop the flow of ideas, but the free flow of ideas is essential during this stage. Shaping an Essay, our second chapter, offers advice on how to structure your writing so that you can produce a rough draft from the information you generated during your prewriting.

Revising is that part of the process in which the writer takes stock of his draft and decides what he needs to do to strengthen and improve it. Revision is an important part of writing that is at times neglected by many writers. This stage requires the writer to make decisions that determine the final shape and effectiveness of his writing; thus, revising is fundamental.

We like to think of revision as a stage in which the paper is examined by a quality checker who has an idea of what the final paper should look like—or, more correctly, who will know it when she sees it. She may look at a draft and see that it needs only minor changes, a word here and there, or that it needs some tightening of sentence structure and some attention to editing conventions. In other cases, this quality checker will find big gaps in the paper, places that can be filled in only by more prewriting and drafting.

If a writer is to produce a piece of good writing, he must revise—deleting what doesn't fit in the final draft, making what remains stronger, creating new information that will clarify parts of the draft, leaving alone what is satisfactory, or discarding everything and starting again. Whatever the changes at this stage, they must come in light of decisions already made in the other stages of the process. The writer is not bound, however, by these previous decisions. Changes made at this stage reflect the writer's ability to see the previous stages of the writing process from a new vantage point. To revise is to see again and to change the paper as this "seeing again" dictates. Thus, revising is creating anew. Our third chapter, Revising, offers a number of strategies to help you revise and edit your writing.

As we stated earlier, it is not easy to make neat distinctions among the three stages of the writing process. Sometimes they come together. Think about your own writing. When you have been writing a rough draft or answering an essay examination, how many times have you combined writing and rewriting by scratching out a word, sentence, or paragraph and substituting a more appropriate choice? You've probably done so many times. In all likelihood, you've written sentences or paragraphs (drafting) in your exploration of a subject (prewriting) and revised them on the spot (revising) before incorporating them into a paper. The fact that these stages frequently occur simultaneously reinforces our statement that writing is a recursive process that involves considerable trial and error as the piece of writing unfolds and takes shape.

WRITING AND READING

Writing and reading are very closely connected, and good writers often make extensive use of readings before and while they write. They read to get ideas, to consider the ways other writers have written, and to enjoy someone else's insights and language. Responding to Readings, our fourth chapter, offers a number of comprehensive reading strategies and then suggests ways in which you may use reading as an important element of your writing process.

WRITING AND VISUALS

At first, it may seem a bit strange to talk about visuals in a textbook about writing. After all, aren't writing and visuals supposed to compete with each other? We've often been told that "a picture is worth a thousand words." Those in the other camp would agree with Samuel Johnson that "writing maketh a man exact." More recently, Margaret Atwood has pointed to the importance of the word in her poem "Spelling" (see pages 296–297) in which she says,

> A word after a word
> after a word is power.

But writing and visuals need not be seen as competitors. They may not be two sides of the same coin, but they certainly complement each other in the ways they capture and reflect meaning. A picture may be worth a thousand words, but it often takes a thousand words to express to someone else all the meaning that floods over a person as he experiences a picture. In Chapters 5, 8, 9, and 10, we present writing assignments that allow you to analyze the meaning you find in various visuals. On the other hand, a visual may help to make written data much clearer and understandable, as we will find in our section on visuals in Chapter 6.

COMPUTERS AND WRITING

Computers and word processing have had a profound impact on writing in many ways. Probably the most dramatic impact has been on the ease of revision. Before computers, writers relied on pencils, pens, and typewriters to produce their drafts. Changing more than a word or two of a handwritten or typed draft often meant redoing the entire thing, so many writers were reluctant to revise. Today, computers make it easy to revise. It takes very little effort to insert a word here, move a paragraph from one place in the draft to another, or import text from other files into a piece you're working on.

Computers hold other benefits for writers as well. They make storage of drafts and other materials, such as your prewriting, easy. And when you're ready to print and submit a final draft of a paper, you may print only that draft, so that all of your other materials reside on a single floppy disk. With access to the Internet, computers provide a powerful means of researching a topic and communicating with others through email. It's possible for you to sit at a keyboard in your room and retrieve information from a library located hundreds or thousands of miles from your school. And computers can help you produce a professional-looking paper, through the range of typefaces, fonts, and graphics typically available in most word-processing software packages.

How much you'll use a computer in your writing will depend on availability and on your level of comfort in using one. Throughout the first four chapters, and where appropriate in the rest of *The Longwood Guide,* we'll offer advice on using the computer while you write. Writing with a word processor and becoming computer-literate will be important for you, not only during your college career but once you graduate and enter the workforce.

Exercise

Computer Facilities

Does your campus have computer centers or clusters or labs, where machines are available to all students? If so, visit one, and find out the following:

> Hours—when is it open?
> Computers—how many are available? What kind (PC, Macintosh, both)?
> Printers—how many are available? What kind (laser, inkjet)?
> Staff—how many staff members are available to help you?
> Services—what instructional support is offered? Formal, credit-bearing classes? Tutorials? One-on-one help in response to specific questions?
> Costs—is the cost of your using the facility already supported by the fees you paid to register, or are there additional costs? If the latter, what are these?

Writing Center

Does your campus have a writing center designed to help students with their writing? If so, visit it, and find out the following:

> Hours—when is it open?
> Staff—how many staff members are available to help you? Will they work with you one-on-one or in small groups?

Services—what writing support is offered? Tutorials? Individual or small-group conferences with a tutor? Handouts?

Costs—is the cost of your using the center already supported by fees you paid during registration, or are there additional costs? If the latter, what are these?

Computers—are computers available for writing in the center itself? If so, how many and how readily available are they?

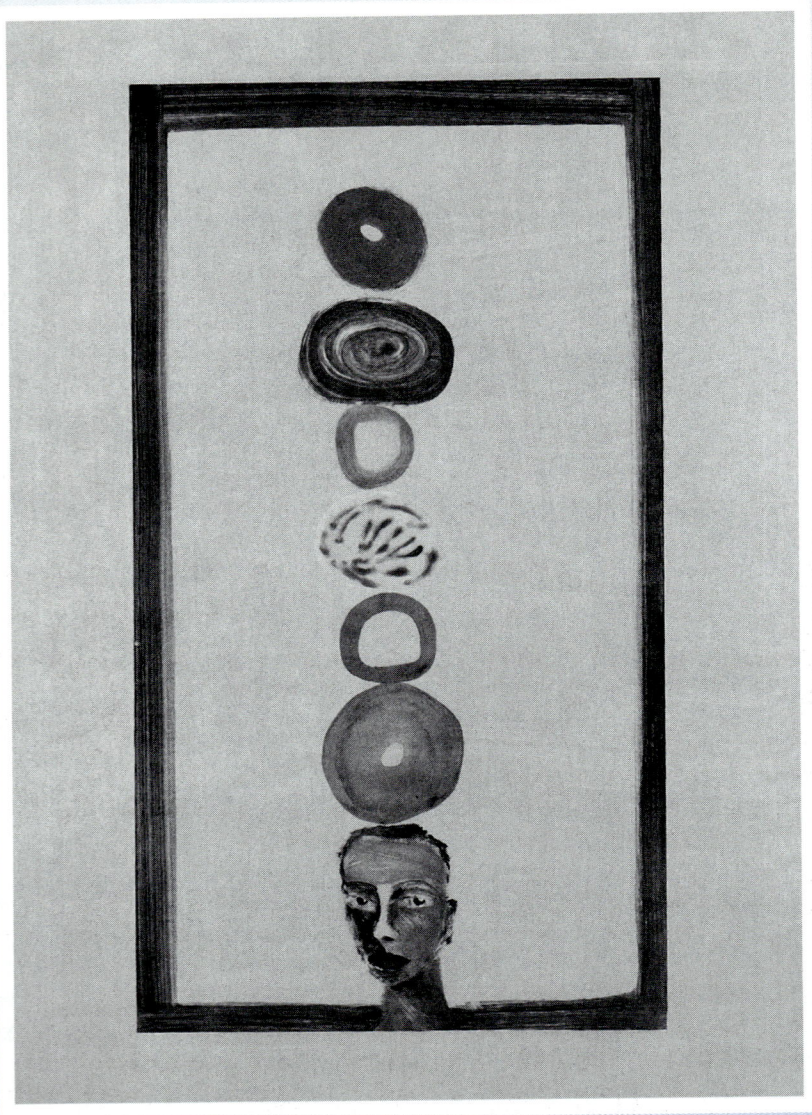

Francesco Clemente, "Untitled," 1986. Oil on paper (monotype 104), 49 × 32 in. Private Collection. Courtesy: Mary Boone Gallery, New York.

CHAPTER 1

Invention: Finding Something to Say

You sit in class, and your teacher assigns your first essay. What do you do now? Where, how to begin? Getting started on a writing assignment is not difficult, if you plan your route through the assignment carefully. When is the due date? What kind of essay does the assignment call for? What steps has your professor recommended or required you to follow? Learning to manage an assignment is an important part of learning to write well.

Whether you have been given an assignment or you have an idea to explore on your own, you may ask yourself three questions as you begin:

1. What do I know about my subject?
2. What else do I want or need to know?
3. What is important, interesting, or significant enough about this subject that I want to tell someone else about it?

This last question is of particular importance, because the best writing matters both to the writer and to the reader. That is, good writing is marked by a sense of significance, by a sense that the writer has something she wants to say and has taken particular care in presenting that something to a reader. Your job as a writer is to discover this significance, this something that you want to say, and then to discover the best ways to present that to a reader. In this chapter, we'll offer you some strategies that can help you find this significance. We suggest that you work through each strategy at least twice, so that you get a feel for how each can help you generate information to use in a paper.

FINDING TOPICS

Choosing a topic for your writing is important, and you need to take care to pick one that interests you and that you can make interesting for your reader. You'll live with an essay's topic from the time you begin until you submit your final draft, and you'll invest a good bit of time and energy in writing your essay. Writing requires you to make choices all along the way, from start to finish, and the better the choices you make, the better your writing is likely to be. To begin, then, select your topic; don't simply settle for one. Two things our students have found helpful in selecting a topic are a writer's notebook and an interest inventory.

Keeping a Writer's Notebook

Many writers keep a writer's notebook. Sometimes it's called a log or a journal, but whatever its label, the writer's notebook can serve you well. Think of it as a repository, a place to put such things as:

- ideas and observations
- remembrances
- clippings from newspapers or magazines
- doodles and sketches
- freewrites and notes taken in preparation to fulfill writing assignments
- responses to assignments
- responses to readers' comments about your writing
- lecture notes
- reading notes
- self-sponsored writing, including personal writing and reflections

Because it provides a place to keep your writing, a writer's notebook can help you maintain a complete record of your progress as a writer.

A writer's notebook can also form a very important part of your invention activities, for whatever you put in it can become the topic for a piece of writing. If you see something unusual, write about it. In your notebook, describe what you see; then speculate about what it was or why it occurred. If you read or hear something that intrigues or disturbs you, write about it. In your notebook, speculate about its intriguing or disturbing qualities. If you have an essay assignment for your writing class or another of your classes, write about it. In your notebook, freewrite about the topic, or pose questions that you may want your essay to answer. Then continue writing by answering the questions.

While there really isn't a correct formula for keeping a notebook, one defining feature is at work: discipline. If you're to use a writer's notebook to its fullest advantage, then you'll have to have or develop the discipline to write in it frequently, preferably every day. If you plan to keep a notebook, or if your teacher assigns one, use the following exercise to help you develop the discipline you'll need to write daily.

> **Exercise 1.1**
>
> Keep a writer's notebook for a ten-day period, writing in it daily. Ideally, you should let your topics choose you, but if you're stuck, then do either of the following:
>
> Answer such questions as these (one a day for ten days):
>
> 1. Why did you choose to enroll in college? Why did you pick your school?
> 2. What activities are available to you at your school? Do you intend to participate? Why or why not?
> 3. What is your major? Why did you choose it?
> 4. If you haven't chosen a major yet, which course of study appeals to you most? Why?
> 5. What questions do you have about your school?
> 6. What do you like most about your school? Least? Why?
> 7. If you could travel anywhere, where would you go? With whom? Why?
> 8. Where do you see yourself in ten years? Twenty?
> 9. How important are these in your life: friends, solitude, family, religion, politics? Why?
> 10. What's most important to you in life? Why?
>
> Designate a specific period each day as your time to write in your writer's notebook. Don't let anything else interfere with that time; do nothing then but write in your notebook. During this writing period, reflect on the day's activities, commenting on what happened and then on the importance of those events. Close each of these writing periods by writing a question you want answered (or that you want to answer) related to one or more of those events. [NOTE: we're not asking you merely to keep a diary in which you simply tell yourself what happened. Instead, we're asking that you write through those events, talking about what's most important to you, and why.]

Among the kinds of writing you may place in your writer's notebook, we listed "responses to readers' comments about your writing," "lecture notes," and "reading notes." We'll have more to say about using your notebook for the first of these purposes in Chapter 3, Revising, and for the second and third in Chapter 4, Responding to Readings.

Interest Inventory

Answer as fully as you can each question under at least five of the following six topic headings. This assignment is designed to help you select topics for your writing that are meaningful to you—there are no right or wrong answers, only *your* responses.

1. Community
   a. Where do you live?
   b. What type of community is your hometown or neighborhood?
   c. What especially interests or disturbs you about your community? Why?
   d. What particular places or events in your community do you enjoy? Why?
   e. What things about your community would you like to see changed? Why?
2. Family, Friends, and Acquaintances
   a. What about your family is unique?
   b. Which of your relatives are especially interesting or important to you? Why?
   c. What special customs does your family have? (For example, is there anything special about how you celebrate such events as birthdays, religious holidays, or Thanksgiving?)
   d. Which of your friends are especially interesting or important to you? Why?
   e. Do you know any unusual people? If so, what makes them unusual?
   f. Which of your neighbors are especially interesting or important to you? Why?
3. Education
   a. What type of educational background do you have? (Consider kindergarten, elementary school, and so on. Think about such things as class and school size, what you learned, and teachers who impressed you.)
   b. What types of courses have you taken or are you taking? Which are your favorites? Why? Which do you dislike? Why?
   c. If you could change anything about any of the schools you have attended, what would you change? How would you change it? Why?
   d. What informal (not strictly related to school) educational experiences have you had? How were they educational?
4. Jobs
   a. What types of jobs have you had? What about them interested or disturbed you? Why?
   b. What career do you hope to have? Why have you chosen this particular field?
5. Leisure
   a. What hobbies do you enjoy? What makes each enjoyable?
   b. What kinds of movies, music, and reading material do you like? Why?
   c. What types of vacations or travel do you enjoy? If you could travel anywhere, where would you go? Why?
   d. What types of extracurricular activities do you engage in? Why?
6. Attitudes and Issues
   a. Have you experienced a change in your attitude toward such things as politics, religion, school, family, or friends? If so, what was that change, and what caused it?

b. What events in the past year or so have interested you or disturbed you most? Why?
c. What types of issues (for example, political or environmental) interest you? Why? Identify one or two specific events that represent these interests.
d. Have the technological advances or changes you've seen been for the best? Why? What technological developments would you like to see take place? Why?
e. Have the societal changes you've seen been for the best? Why? What changes in society would you like to see take place? Why?
f. What particular social customs interest or disturb you? Why?

Your responses to these questions will, in all likelihood, reveal broader rather than more narrow interests. As you look to this inventory for topic ideas, keep in mind that you'll have to work with any topic you select, narrowing it and probing or exploring it until you discover a subject that's manageable in the context of your writing assignment.

COMPUTER TIP

Create a file named INTINV. Type in the first question of the Interest Inventory and answer it, then the next question, then the next, and so on until you've completed your Interest Inventory. Be sure to save your work frequently. When you finish answering the inventory's questions, print a copy and keep it available for handy reference, either in your writer's notebook or pinned to a bulletin board near your study desk. ✦

WRITING ABOUT AN ASSIGNED TOPIC

In many writing situations, your topic will be assigned. At times, the topic will be well-defined; at other times, less so. Your writing begins as you read the assignment to see what your instructor wants you to do. Consider this assignment, which we have taken from Chapter 5:

> Describe an event from which you learned something. Your job is to use your language to recreate the event so that your readers will feel that they have been at least observers of this important event with you, if not participants in it.

What does this assignment call for? One way to decide is to examine its key terms: "describe," "important event," "use your language to recreate." Your first step is to pick an event that you count as important. Once you have selected this event, you can begin to work with your language to recreate it for the reader. For all assigned topics, identify the key terms of the assignment and use those key terms as an initial guide in completing the assignment.

EXPLORING TOPICS

Once you have either selected or been assigned a topic, how can you explore it? How can you generate information or ideas about it? Five approaches that many writers find helpful are brainstorming, freewriting, clustering, visualizing, and asking questions.

Brainstorming

To brainstorm, list quickly any and all ideas that come to mind. As you brainstorm, do not censor any ideas; just list. Below is an example of brainstorming that Bill wrote in response to this prompt: Spend fifteen minutes listing every event you've participated in that comes to mind, no matter how serious or inconsequential.

> band at Tarleton
> trumpet in Joey's closet
> Jake & Dot's café
> Homer's thick milkshakes
> TSC dorms
> beating the drum—homecoming
> Lake Proctor
> Thanksgiving float trip
> Gus, Larry, Lynn, Harvey
> kicked PAT
> move from Tallahassee
> Ol' Mullet
> kids' cradle
> fishing—Sam Rayburn Res. (7 lb. bass)
> hiking and backpacking
> Three Rivers Camp (fell in river, wasps)
> Eagle projects
> Willow Creek—building step-down dams
> conservation work at Aguirre Springs
> setting up double-wide trailers
> FSU track—jogging
> Pittsburgh—early a.m. runs (park, llamas)
> Mark—worm
> Pirates/Expos game
> bus rides
> Dad's old red pickup
> van—hauling kids
> soccer—Roswell tourney

road trips—soccer, football, choir, Scouts
conference in Nashville (Opryland, Grand Ole Opry)
DFW airport

Note the informality of this list. Bill was not concerned with writing complete sentences, only with getting down whatever came to mind. He simply jotted down events he remembered until he had listed thirty-one possible topics for an essay. How many of these could serve as the basis for an essay? Each one could, depending on what Bill found important, and which topic or topics he thought might be worth exploring.

Computer Tip

Create a file named BRAIN or BRNSTRM. Use this file for at least one brainstorming session, as outlined in the following exercise. After you finish brainstorming, consider how using a computer affected the process. How does your computer-generated list compare to any you completed by hand? ✦

Exercise 1.2

Brainstorm about potential topics for an assignment. If your instructor has already made an assignment, then use this exercise to begin work on it. If you do not have an assignment yet, then brainstorm about significant events or about problems you have encountered since enrolling at your university. List every idea that comes to mind, whether you think it a good one or not. Do not censor any idea. Write for ten minutes or until you fill at least a page from top to bottom.

Freewriting

Freewriting is just what its name suggests—to freewrite, you simply write. Once you start, do not stop. Do not lift your pen or pencil off the page; do not lift your fingers off the keyboard—write! If you get stuck, if the thoughts will not come, then write a single word—"stuck, stuck, stuck"—or write a nonsense phrase—"wet ducks, wet ducks, wet ducks"—or write a sentence about your frustrations—"this is dumb, this is dumb, this is dumb." It doesn't really matter what you write, so long as you continue to write. Eventually, writing that word, nonsense phrase, or sentence should get you past your stuck point and back to what interests you. As you write, do not stop to correct grammar and spelling errors. Freewriting is designed solely to uncover ideas, so grammar and mechanics do not count, and worrying about them at this point in the writing process can cause you to lose focus on your subject and the ideas you will discover. The key thing to remember is this: Do not censor, do not correct, just write.

The following examples of freewriting were written by Arlene Yusnukis, a composition student at New Mexico State University (NMSU). Arlene began with a particular assignment: to write a personal essay about a place or event that affected her deeply. In the first freewrite, Arlene's job was to write about places and events that stood out in her mind.

> I remember being sprayed in the face with a chemical fire extinguisher at 2:30 in the morning, backpacking in the pecos wilderness the rams eating crackers, waterskiing for the very first time, cliff jumping, the green station house with the card rack when mom and I got off the train, riding my tricycle in circles around a big red ant, my grandmother dying of cancer & being there for a month going to school in Spokane, the hot lunch cart getting bronchitis and letters from dad c/o my aunt my cousins picking on my brother my grandfather and his horses. Flicka a horse bit my brothers hand. Meeting Kelli and Paul my boyfriend and the initiation into the band, going to Denver and freezing the huge Bronco football players, stepping on head phone, sleeping by the bathroom. Sneaking out to play frisbee in the middle of the night and getting caught cuz the frisbee was loud cuz we never caught it. trying to make poptarts quietly in the dark. My dog dying. Our toilet getting stuck flushing. Being in two accidents in less than a year seeing the front grill of the truck before it hit us. Physical therapy, migraines, pills for schizophrenics. The old age home and smell—

Is this a finished piece of writing? Obviously not. But it is a very good example of what an initial freewrite is supposed to do because it uncovered a number of topics that Arlene could have written about. How many topics are in this freewrite? At least a dozen. And note the range of things Arlene wrote about. Some of the topics she remembers from her childhood (riding the tricycle in circles around the ant), others from events that happened as recently as the preceding semester (the band trip to Denver). Some of the topics are very serious (her grandmother's death, being in two accidents), others far less so (making Poptarts). What is most important to note is that Arlene just wrote; she did not censor herself, did not judge any particular topic as better or worse than any other, did not stop to mull any topic over, did not scratch anything out, did not try to correct errors in grammar, spelling, or punctuation. She started writing and kept writing until the time allotted for freewriting was over.

Exercise 1.3

Pick an entry from your Interest Inventory or one of the topics you listed while brainstorming and freewrite about it for ten minutes. Once you get started, don't stop until time is up. Don't worry about grammar or spelling. Don't lift your pen or pencil off the page; don't stop writing—just write. When you finish, let the freewrite sit for a few minutes, then read through it. How many potential topics can you identify? Did anything of what you wrote surprise you? If so, why? Did you uncover something you didn't think you would? If so, what?

Next, Arlene selected one of the potential topics she had uncovered—"backpacking in the pecos wilderness the rams eating crackers"—and did a second freewrite to see whether she would be interested in writing an entire paper about it. At first, it may seem that such a small detail would hardly let Arlene develop a paper about a place or event that affected her deeply, but then that was her task as a writer—to show that the event or place was important to her. Here is her second freewrite:

Driving up there the road dirt for so long and our caddy not liking the drive but tolerating it. Trying to get everyones packs into the trucks and trunks. The storm clouds over the pecos mountains as we drove up. The quaint little town inside the canyon, Jack's creek. The beautiful campground at the top where we started from. Climbing up and up at a steep angle and looking down to my left at a vertical nearly drop. Switchbacks, losing my sleeping bag having to bring up the rear with Brad and Chip, fellow workers, up front slowpokers in back. Hard to get transportation. Chip not wanting to charge for gas. Rain in the late afternoon. The big highcountry meadow with posts to mark trail in snow. The smell, clear sky, critters heaviness of pack & Brad taking lighter stuff as trip goes on. Cold in rain. Finally stop near Pecos baldy lake. Small lake. Pecos baldy bald! Just flat rocks—shale? Wet, brad no warm clothes water cold to wash face in. Brad sick. Starting Svea stove quick! Finally getting all kids in tents in bed. Teresa & I talking for a long time. Boys growl whole camp awake. Sunny next morning. Better tempers cute people in morning messy hair, buffalo breath.

One ram one ewe big horn sheep come down embankment near camp. Ewe no hair on neck, radio collar rubbed off. Eat out of Ross hand knock over packs a camp away & eat crackers. Climbing saddle to leave PB area. Switchbacks a tight zipper. Relief on other side. Walk forever that day. Walking just behind storm. See hail everywhere but not on us. Worry that won't get out in time. Boys tell steve to eat skunk cabbage cabonions. Pest bad news hard to get in the swing of walking after them. Knives of pain on top of shoulder. hip strap much too big for me. Ross gets stuck between rock & log. Steve fell over one. Don't stop where we were supposed to. Have to go on Pretty golden meadow. Clumps of trees on mntn on either side. Narrow with stream in middle Horse Thief meadows. Finally stop to camp on top of flat hill base of mtn sparse trees no camp in meadow Steve sick. Cabbage poison could die. Gets dry heave scares us. We eat rest, massage shoulders me no hiking boots only tennies, no blisters yet. We eat wash up in red stream below. Notice old forbidden trails. Steve ok we sleep. Me with a stick in my middle. Go on. Next day.

See Stewart and Spirit lakes. Rain no fun my poncho—day-glo orange—rips. We know where we want to camp—by Santa Fe baldy. Some want to climb. I do. send rest to camp spot. Climb steep hill above timber line. Takes longtime. Big rocks. On top see into eternity rest on rocks. Marmits whistle at us. We see SFB lake—glacier lake Finally leave. Run down jumble insides, cow almost charges us. Join group and play. Sleep Rain.

Chip & Brad too anxious to leave. They go ahead. I take poky ones like me later. We catch up go to rondevous and wait for 1½ hrs. I told them no rush. rain. Mr Tatro watermelon yum. Ski basin pretty home. limp blisters cut open by bad surgeon. Relief bath. sleep.

Danielle Corder, a first-year writing student at NMSU, used freewriting in a different way. First, she generated a short list of potential topics for a persuasive essay. Then, she completed a freewrite about each of those topics to see what kind of interest she had in them.

Things I feel strongly about:

- Parents have a responsibility to bring their children up in a good way.
- Bringing a weapon to school is unjustifiable.
- Children should be encouraged to participate in extracurricular activities.
- A legal adult—can do anything but purchase and consume alcoholic beverages. Either the age of consumption should be lowered or the legal adult age should be raised. Maybe. Hmmm . . .
- I'm running out of ideas!
- Gender roles aren't a bad thing. Yes, men and women are different, but they should still have equal rights & privileges & etc.
- I can't think!

1. Parents and their responsibility to their children.
   First off, let me start by saying anyone mature enough to make the child should be prepared to raise and be there for that child throughout their life. I believe parents have the major and primary responsibility to be in that child's life. They have a responsibility to provide for the child emotionally and physically. Parents need to be role models for the next generation, avoiding drugs, excessive drinking, and mental and physical abuse. They need to be a large part of their children's lives.
2. Weapons at school.
   I understand that at times a person feels as if they need to defend themselves, so they bring a gun to school. It's still wrong. A gun is used for one thing—to kill. Not to wound, to kill. There are many other options. In the movie "Friday," a father says something to his son that should really hit home to the youth who find it necessary to bring weapons to school: You don't need a gun, when you have your fists and they're all you need. If you can't use those your a wimp. Yes, you lose some. Yes, you win some. The one thing is you're still alive and *that's* the most important thing.
3. Children in extracurricular activities. It's not too much of an outrageous statement to tell someone that children involved are children who stay out of trouble. I would even bet statistics say the same. Growing up is a difficult process. It's hard to find oneself and to find what you enjoy. Often times boredom and limited acquaintances lead children to other "not-so-nice" extracurricular activities. Encourage children to try new things. Thousands of

things are available. Schools alone offer tons of activities: club, organizations, sports. There's such a variety, it'd be hard to not find something for your child. The city and community also offer activities along with churches and other organizations. So don't let your child think there's nothing to do.
4. Legal adults not being able to drink.
   Okay, so my point is this: Why can an 18 year old do anything but drink. They take on all other responsibilities—why are they incapable of just this one. Yes, it is a big one and I know a lot of 18 year olds I wouldn't want drinking. I'm not very decided on this one.
5. Yuck! I don't even want to write about gender roles or gender discrimination.

For her essay, Danielle selected the third entry—children and extracurricular activities. Through freewriting, she found that she had enough interest in this topic to work with it as the basis for an entire essay.

COMPUTER TIP

Create a file named FREEWRITE. Use this file to complete the following exercise; then compare your computer writing to any freewriting you did by hand. ✦

Exercise 1.4

From your initial freewrite, identify a particular topic or idea that interests you. Then do a second freewrite about it, this time taking fifteen to twenty minutes to write.

In comparing the two examples of freewriting given here, we find that Danielle used her freewriting to decide whether she had enough interest in a particular topic to base an essay on it, whereas Arlene used her freewriting to discover a topic and then to generate a fair amount of detail about it. Danielle wrote in complete sentences; Arlene did not. Each writer used freewriting well, with each discovering a topic for her essay.

We want particularly to note the detail that Arlene began to generate about her camping experience in the Pecos Wilderness. She even implied what may have been significant about the experience when she wrote, "On top see into eternity." Note also how little attention Arlene paid to correctness. For example, how many sentence fragments did she write in the first paragraph alone? How many words are misspelled? Arlene generated a substantial amount of information, not all of which found its way into her final draft.

Exercise 1.5

Compare your two freewrites from Exercise 1.4. How detailed is the second? How does it relate to the first? Did any of what you wrote surprise you? If so, why? Did you uncover something you did not remember? If so, what? Did you discover any gaps in your knowledge, anything you either need or want to know more about? If so, what will you need to do to fill those gaps? Does any of this second freewrite point toward the significance of the topic? If so, identify it.

Clustering

Clustering can help you generate ideas and show potential relationships among them. You start by capturing your topic idea in a single word or short phrase and placing it in a box or circle in the center of a sheet of paper. Then, write down things about the topic that come to mind, circling each item and connecting it with a line to the main topic or to other circles, whichever connection seems more appropriate. You'll build individual clusters of ideas that relate to each other and to the main topic idea.

Clustering works on the principle of association. The more ideas you generate, the more ideas are likely to occur to you, and so you compile a group of ideas and show how they relate to one another. Seeing how things relate can help you discover the significance that is characteristic of good writing. And in showing specifically how different ideas relate, clustering can give you a visual representation of the relative importance of particular ideas—the more circles in a given cluster, the more important that cluster is likely to be. [For an extended discussion of clustering, see Gabriele L. Rico's *Writing the Natural Way* (Los Angeles: Tarcher, 1983).]

Figure 1.1 is an example of clustering Bill did with his children's literature class in connection with Frances Hodgson Burnett's *The Secret Garden*. You'll find the topic of the cluster, "gardens," in the middle of the page, with those things Bill associated with gardens connected to that term. But you'll also see that this exercise took him over a range of territory and subjects, some directly related to gardens, some only brought to memory by one of the other terms. Note the power of association this cluster shows—from the main topic, "gardens," to "backyard" (a reference to flowers in Bill's backyard), to "gladiolas (dead)," to "Altha, FL." Bill made the tie from gladiolas to Altha because Mary Beth, his wife, taught in Altha's elementary school. Gladiolas are grown around Altha, and Mary Beth's students often brought her armfuls of fresh-cut gladiolas.

How many papers could come from this single clustering? If we focus only on those clusters of three or more terms, then Bill could be interested enough in these topics:

chaperoning a junior/senior prom
the Alabama/Florida State football game (either 1974 or 1975)

Figure 1.1 Prewriting Strategy: Clustering

remembering Jimmy (his cousin who died from leukemia at the age of 52)
spending time at his grandmother's fish camp
Florida panhandle home cooking

Exercise 1.6

1. Pick an event that was important in your life. If you cannot think of a specific event immediately, look again at your Interest Inventory or at the events you listed in brainstorming. Then cluster that event, following the directions given for clustering. What major clusters or idea groups emerge? How do these point toward the significance of the event for you? Does your clustering point toward any gaps in your knowledge of the topic? If so, what do you need to do to fill them?
2. Cluster at least three of these topic ideas: fear, happiness, fifth grade, winner, pain, family, college, backyard, the future, today, the past, flying, running, racing. What major clusters or idea groups emerge? How do these point toward the significance these terms have for you? Does your clustering point toward any gaps in your knowledge of the topic? If so, what do you need to do to fill them?
3. Use your major as the key term for a cluster. If you haven't declared a major, then pick some topic you're interested in and use it as the key term for a cluster. What major clusters or idea groups emerge? How do these point toward the significance of the term you selected? Does your clustering point toward any gaps in your knowledge of the topic? If so, what do you need to do to fill them?
4. Select a topic that has at least some controversy surrounding it, such as a campus issue or a community or political issue, and use it as the key term for a cluster. What do you learn about the topic and your interest in it from completing this cluster?

Visualizing

Another effective technique for developing detail is visualizing. This technique helps you "see" your topic—create it in your mind so that it comes to life as much as possible.

Exercise 1.7

We invite you to travel in your mind to your favorite place. First, find a quiet spot, one in which you can relax as completely as possible. Throughout this exercise, be as still and as attentive as possible to the detail you will generate. Below is a set of directions for you to follow. Do not respond out loud to any of them—visualize first, then respond in writing. The first few times you try this, you may need to have a friend read the directions aloud so that you can work through the exercise completely. Eventually, with enough practice, you'll be able to do this exercise on your own.

1. Close your eyes and take several deep breaths. Sit very still in as comfortable a position as possible.
2. Identify the place, naming it in your mind.
3. Bring this place to life by recreating it in your mind's eye.
4. Stand in the center of the scene you have created. Turn very slowly in a complete circle, letting your eyes pan up and down like a camera taking in scenery. What do you see? What particular features dominate the scene? What colors stand out? When you have completed one turn, stop. Stand absolutely still.
5. Let your senses other than sight come into play.
    a. Is there a dominant odor in this place? Is it pleasant, sweet, acrid, faint, strong, pungent, foul? Identify its source.
    b. Is there a dominant sound? Is it loud, soft, pleasant, harsh, unpleasant, bright, muted? Identify its source.
    c. Is there anything you can touch? Does it feel cold, hot, wet, dry? What is its texture? Smooth? Rough?
    d. Does this place have a dominant taste, perhaps something in the air? Is this taste pleasant or unpleasant? Identify its source.
6. Is anyone with you in this place? If so, who? Name the person(s) there. What are you (both or all) doing? What kind of conversation is taking place—small talk, argument, important discussion? Try to capture as much of the conversation and action as possible.
7. What is the dominant mood of this place? Why is this place important to you? Why is it your favorite place?
8. Slowly, take one last look around, stopping to examine dominant or important aspects of this place in as much detail as you think necessary. When you are ready, leave this place and come back to where you are now.

Write a paragraph in which you detail this place. Your task is to write so that a reader can see that this place is meaningful to you without your having to say that. Do not use such words as "favorite" and "meaningful"; instead, let the detail you give the reader carry this message.

As you read over the paragraph you wrote, did you find any surprises? Did you remember anything about the place that you didn't think you would? Did anything startle or please you? Identify that element. Why does it stand out? Are there any noticeable gaps in your memory of the place? If so, what do you need to do to fill them?

Once you have completed this exercise, try it again; visualize your favorite place a second time. When you have written the second descriptive paragraph, compare it with your first, looking for similarities but also for differences, such as increased detail.

Exercise 1.8

Repeat the steps listed in Exercise 1.7 to help you visualize two or three of the following topics, and then write a paragraph detailing your visualization: your school's orientation or registration sessions, friendship (or a friend), patriotism (or a patriot), racism (or a racist), sexism (or a sexist).

You'll note that these topics lend themselves to writing that could be more argumentative than personal in nature. If, for example, you were to decide to write an essay examining problems you had with your school's registration system and proposing solutions to those problems, you could use visualization to relive your experiences and thus sharpen the focus of your writing. Visualization is one way to explore a topic, whether intensely personal or very public.

Asking Questions

One of the best ways to explore a topic is to ask questions about it, so we've developed a set of questions designed to help you generate a lot of information. It won't always be necessary to ask every question every time you use this technique, but until you get used to asking these questions about a topic, you should ask and try to answer all of them. Begin by identifying or defining your topic, either in a word or two (e.g., "college football") or in a phrase ("reintroducing wolves in New Mexico wilderness"). Then substitute your word or phrase for *"your topic"* in each question.

The questions are given in the present tense, but if your topic is an event that has already taken place, then consider varying the tense you use. For example, if you are writing about a football game you played a year ago, you can rephrase the question "What are the implications of the game?" to "What were the implications of the game?" But you can also use the present-tense form if you want to consider how your present-day view of the topic contrasts with that from the past. Similarly, if your topic is set in the future, you may want to ask several of the questions in the future tense.

Finally, a particular question may not seem to apply to your topic. If this occurs, then skip that question for a moment, but return to it later and try to see how it might fit.

Questions of association **enable you to**
define, state what something is
classify, sort, or group like things with like

compare, state how something is like something else
describe the physical attributes of something
create a context, place something in its environment

Each of these activities involves you in generating ideas you associate with your topic, things that go or fit with your topic. Here are questions based on association:

How do you define *your topic*? What is it?
What do you associate with *your topic*?
What are the physical elements or characteristics of *your topic*?
Where does *your topic* take place? In what context does it occur?
What has been written or said in favor of *your topic*?
How does *your topic* compare with other things like it?

Questions of opposition enable you to

look at opposites and opposition
contrast, see how something is unlike something similar
examine tensions, see how something does not fit with its surroundings
look for what does not quite add up, for what may be out of line with other things

Each of these activities requires you to consider those aspects of your topic that set it apart from other things. Here are questions based on opposition:

Who or what opposes *your topic*? Why? What is the nature of this opposition?
What has been written or said against *your topic*?
How is *your topic* unlike other similar things? What sets it apart from those things?
How does *your topic* stand out against its context?
What about *your topic* seems odd, incongruous, or unusual?

Questions of sequence enable you to

consider how something evolved
examine cause and effect
look at the order of something
consider the order of steps or stages from start to finish

Each of these activities asks you to examine the origin, order, or development of your topic. Here are questions based on sequence:

What is the specific sequence in *your topic*? What comes or happens first, then second, then third, and so on?
How did *your topic* come to be?
What are the causes of *your topic*?
What steps, if any, are involved in *your topic*?

***Questions of consequence* enable you to**

consider knowledge gained from exploring a topic
examine problems and solutions
ask "What if?" and "Why?"
make a value judgment

Each of these activities requires you to consider the worth or implications of your topic. Ultimately, these activities require you to assess your topic and so to discover your understanding of its significance. Here are questions based on consequence:

What did you learn from *your topic*?
What did you learn from your investigation of *your topic*?
What problems are inherent in *your topic*? What are their solutions?
What results from *your topic*?
What opportunities does *your topic* offer?
What are the implications of *your topic*?
What about *your topic* is good? Bad? Desirable? Undesirable? Necessary?
Should *your topic* be? Not be? Why or why not?

When should you use these questions? At any point as you work to generate ideas. You may use them as the starting point in working up a topic; you may select a topic from your Interest Inventory and begin asking the questions. You may also use them to continue exploration of a topic that was the basis for any brainstorming, freewriting, clustering, or visualizing you may have done. And you may use them as you revise an essay. Whenever it is necessary for you to generate detail and ideas, you may use the questions.

WRITING STRATEGY

Questions for Analysis

To explore a possible writing topic, ask yourself these questions:

Association
How do you define *your topic*? What is it?
What do you associate with *your topic*?
What are the physical elements or characteristics of *your topic*?
Where does *your topic* take place? In what context does it occur?
What has been written or said in favor of *your topic*?
How does *your topic* compare with other things like it?

Opposition
Who or what opposes *your topic*? Why? What is the nature of this opposition?
What has been written or said against *your topic*?

How is *your topic* unlike other similar things? What sets it apart from those things?
How does *your topic* stand out against its context?
What about *your topic* seems odd, incongruous, or unusual?

Sequence
What is the specific sequence in *your topic*? What comes or happens first, then second, then third, and so on?
How did *your topic* come to be?
What are the causes of *your topic*?
What steps, if any, are involved in *your topic*?

Consequence
What did you learn from *your topic*?
What did you learn from your investigation of *your topic*?
What problems are inherent in *your topic*? What are their solutions?
What results from *your topic*?
What opportunities does *your topic* offer?
What are the implications of *your topic*?
What about *your topic* is good? Bad? Desirable? Undesirable? Necessary?
Should *your topic* be? Not be? Why or why not?

Application: The Fuzzwort Refining Company

The following application focuses on a fictitious refining or smelting company, the Fuzzwort Refining Company (FRC). If you have ever seen a plant like a smelter in operation, its smokestacks probably stand out in your memory. Such stacks are large and, because of the smoke they emit, highly visible. Try to visualize the plant or plants you have seen as we proceed with our application of the Questions for Analysis to FRC. In the application, *"your topic"* in each question is replaced by the subject, "FRC." And the investigator of the topic, the student writer, is represented by "I."

Questions of Association

What is FRC?

It's a refining corporation that refines such metals as copper from raw ores. It's a heavy industry, with smelters capable of polluting its surrounding environment.

What do you associate with FRC?

Last year there was a big flap about the plant's smoke emissions. At the request of a concerned group of citizens, a team from the Environmental Protection Agency (EPA) inspected the plant and found that it was emitting at least twice the pollution allowed by EPA standards. Nearly every local newspaper covered the story, all of them praising the EPA's attempts to restrict this pollution. But nothing was done, thanks to court action brought by FRC attorneys. FRC seems to have little, if any, concern for the public's or the environment's well-being. Other things—the plant has a big payroll (I don't know how much) and pays a lot of local and state taxes. It employs a lot of people in all (I don't know how many).

What are the physical elements or characteristics of FRC?

The actual physical plant covers a number of acres, mostly devoid of plant life. It's a bleak place, grimy, with a large parking lot, usually full of the cars of commuting workers. It has several smokestacks, all in use twenty-four hours a day, the smaller ones up to 750 feet high, the largest one a 1,200-foot-high giant. At times these stacks belch a thick, black, sooty smoke that hangs over the countryside like a pall. Things to find out: What's the particulate composition of that smoke? What kinds of chemicals are those stacks putting into the air?

Where does FRC take place? In what context does it occur?

The context is a broad one. First is the immediate context, the countryside surrounding this plant. It's set in a rural area with cultivated fields on three sides. Within four or five miles of the plant are several small towns, each having a population under 5,000. Within thirty miles is a large city with a population of close to 1,000,000. Nearly all the workers at this plant commute from the city; only a small part of the workforce comes from the smaller nearby towns. A larger context involves the economical setting; that is, FRC is set in a context of industrialism and big business.

What has been said or written in favor of FRC?

Company officials ran a big ad campaign not too long ago—newspapers, radio, billboards. The general message was that FRC is the county's friend because it employs a lot of people, pays a lot of taxes, and produces materials vital to national security. All this put the company in a very positive light, presenting only the company's point of view. I need to find these and look at them again.

How does FRC compare to other things like it?

It's like other businesses that emit smoke and pollutants. In this sense, it's like chemical plants that release toxic wastes into rivers as well as into the air. It's also like power plants fueled by oil and coal. It's also like other businesses that employ large numbers of people; it contributes to the county's economy.

Questions of Opposition

Who or what opposes FRC? Why? What is the nature of this opposition?

Two years ago, a group of concerned citizens formed a special-interest group and became a watchdog of this plant. They called in the EPA inspection team, and since that team's visit this group has filed suit in the federal courts to force strict compliance by FRC with EPA guidelines. In addition, three local newspapers have begun writing about the plant's continued pollution and so have begun exposing FRC to public scrutiny. The group's and the papers' goal is to see the plant stop its pollution entirely or shut down. Lately, there has been much concern over the acid rains afflicting much of the northern United States, and great debate between environmentalists and businesspeople has ensued. Environmentalists offer much opposition, though not just to this plant.

What has been said or written in opposition to FRC?

All the local newspapers ran negative stories about the pollution. These stories discussed plants dying, greater incidence of respiratory illnesses the closer you got to the plant, and so on. Several investigative reporters really took company officials apart. I need to find copies of these articles. Then there are the articles on acid rain published by *National Geographic* and other environmentally oriented magazines. Because FRC has been accused of contributing to this problem, these articles might set the company's problems in a broader context. I need to locate these articles also.

How is FRC unlike other similar things?

Where can I find a refining plant that doesn't pollute the environment?

How does FRC stand out against its context?

The plant provides a stark contrast with the countryside immediately surrounding it. That countryside is lush and green and is characterized by cultivated fields seemingly carved out of forest. As far as standing out against the larger context of industrialism or big business, this particular plant does not; rather, it blends right in and is actually indistinguishable from other plants and similar businesses.

What about FRC seems odd, incongruous, or unusual?

There's a real incongruity at work, given the company's ad campaign (everything's just fine and dandy), in light of the reality of the plant itself. It looks like a plant in Eastern Europe.

Questions of Sequence

What is the specific sequence in FRC? What comes or happens first, second, third, and so on?

There's been something of a sequence at work as company officials responded to increasing criticism. At first, they simply ignored their critics. But as the media attention created increased concern, the officials' response escalated as well. I need to go back and look at the sequence of events here.

How did FRC come to be?

It began as a turn-of-the-century company, responding to the need to deal with raw ore being taken from the surrounding mountains. It grew up in an era when there was little concern for pollution standards, because the U.S. public seemed simply to want more and more material goods. The plant continued to expand until it reached its current size about thirty years ago. It has quadrupled in size since it was first built. It's a very profitable plant for its owners, hence the dynamic growth. Just how profitable is it? I don't know.

What are the causes of FRC?

A response here is implicit in the preceding question, where I talked about the need for a smelter and then the expansion in response to demand by the U.S. public.

What steps are involved in FRC?

I guess I could talk about the actual process of refining ore, tracing it step-by-step as it moves through the various stages of refining until an ingot of metal is produced.

Questions of Consequence

What did you learn from FRC?

How to put an advertising campaign together. Theirs was really a slick production designed to shift public concern away from the negative aspects of the plant so that the public would consider only the benefits (jobs, taxes, payroll).

What did you learn from your investigation of FRC?

The language of the ad campaign was incredibly manipulative. Its goal was to hide the pollution the plant produced, not to deal with the problem of the pollution itself. So I learned to be wary of big business and advertising—actually, I was already wary, so I guess my wariness got reinforced.

What problems are inherent in FRC? What are their solutions?

Obviously, the problem this plant poses is pollution of the countryside. Given the way tall stacks disperse pollutants into the atmosphere, FRC may pose an environmental problem to areas many miles away as well. The solutions are complex. The plant should either clean up its emissions or shut down. To clean up the emissions would require expensive scrubbers for the smokestacks; to shut down would result in the loss of jobs at the plant as well as the loss of business to those businesses that support the plant—a railroad, chemical suppliers, equipment suppliers, and companies subcontracted to perform maintenance at the plant.

What results from FRC?

Two primary products: the refined copper, which is beneficial, and the pollution, which is not. And, of course, accompanying the copper is the plant as an economic entity, with its jobs and so on.

What opportunities does FRC offer?

Another expansion is planned; so there will be more jobs, ranging from jobs for construction workers during the building of the expansion to jobs for more FRC workers to staff and run the expansion.

What are the implications of FRC?

Continued emissions at the present level will do the environment no good whatsoever. Continued operation of the plant will do the local and, by extension, the national economy much good.

What about FRC is good? Bad? Desirable? Undesirable? Necessary?

Okay, so I need to make a value judgment. That judgment is: The FRC plant is necessary, but at present not at all desirable. I could propose that the plant be required to install the scrubbers necessary to clean up its emissions and that antipollution devices and procedures be required in the new expansion so that the expansion will not aggravate the problem. Because of its importance to the local economy I don't want the plant to shut down, but I don't want it to continue polluting the environment.

Should FRC be? Not be? Why or why not?

Well, we have to have metals, and the only way to get them is to refine ore. So it's difficult to say that the company should shut down, especially since many people will be directly hurt economically by a shutdown. I guess the bottom line is what I said in the preceding question: The smelter has to clean up its emissions, or it has to shut down.

In examining FRC as the subject for a paper, we uncovered a great deal of material a writer could use in an essay. We also discovered aspects of this topic that called for more investigation. Were we to investigate them, we would generate still more information. Obviously, a writer could not use all this information, nor would he wish to. Instead, he would have to take a stance on the subject and then use only the information relevant to that stance. If, for example, the writer agreed with our value judgment, he could mention the benefits of the FRC plant, but he would focus on the problem of the plant's pollution and then on solutions to that problem.

COMPUTER TIP

Create a file named QUESTION. Use it to complete Exercise 1.9.

1. Type in the name of the first topic you select.
2. Type in each question and your response to it in turn.
3. When you complete the questions for your first topic, enter a page break or four to five line spaces; then type in the name of your second topic.
4. Type in each question and your response to it in turn.
5. Let your responses sit for a day; then reopen the file. Read your responses, and respond to the exercise's questions that ask you to consider the kinds of detail you generated. ✦

> **Exercise 1.9**
>
> Identify two topics, one more concrete (e.g., an event, a person, a place), the other more abstract (e.g., morality, ethics, government, religion). Write two or three sentences in answer to each of the Questions for Analysis. If a particular question doesn't seem to work, don't give up on it entirely; instead, skip it, leaving space in your responses to come back to it later. When you have finished, consider the kinds and amount of information you generated. How much detail did you generate? Did you find anything that surprised you? If so, what, and why was it a surprise? Did you remember anything that you didn't think you would? If so, what? What gaps in your knowledge did your use of the questions reveal? What will you need to do to fill them? And what kinds of statements did you make in response to the questions about consequence?

FINDING INFORMATION

Thus far, our focus on invention has been on helping you uncover what you know about a given topic. But in asking whether you found gaps in your knowledge of a topic you explored, Exercise 1.9 suggests a question that every writer must eventually answer: "Where do I find information to use in my writing?" One place is the writer's personal experience—what he already knows or can generate, for example, through firsthand observation, interviews, and questionnaires (see pages 585–589 for more detail about these). A second place is a library (see pages 582–585). Colleges and universities spend huge sums on subscribing to professional and popular journals, on buying books, on making various electronic and other nonprint media available to students, and on staffing libraries with people trained to assist students in their research. A third place, one increasingly popular with students, is the Internet. While we offer more information about using the Internet—the World Wide Web—in Chapter 12, Researching and Writing (see pages 590–598), we want to introduce you to the net early on as a potential source for your writing.

Researching Information on the World Wide Web

The Internet, one of the most useful and convenient research tools imaginable, brings a library of web pages to you at your workstation. However, remember that most documents on the web are short. While the web is a good source for summaries and overviews, you may find it difficult to locate extended critiques and comparisons of the kind that we find in professional journal articles and scholarly books. The printed texts of a real library are invaluable resources that can be supplemented but not replaced by Internet-based research.

Evaluating Website Quality You probably know a good deal about evaluating the quality of a printed source, but you may not have given careful thought to the question of the quality of a website. The quality of print sources often depends on the expertise of the author and how recent the information is, in light of changes in the subject. The same criteria can be applied to a website. The World Wide Web can be an excellent source for recent information. In fact, the standard for timeliness on the web is much shorter than for printed documents. For example, a website that hasn't been updated for two years is likely to be considered very out of date and, therefore, not very credible. By contrast, if a book were to be revised within a two-year interval, it would likely be considered recent and credible. For specific questions to ask in evaluating (1) a printed source, see pages 584–585 and (2) an Internet source, see pages 590–598.

The more problematic issue with the World Wide Web is the expertise of the authors represented. Because the web is a self-publishing forum, anyone with the money to purchase file space from an Internet Service Provider (ISP) can distribute his work electronically worldwide. The result has been a flood of electronic publishing. Unfortunately for student researchers like you, not everyone bothers to check information for accuracy and completeness before distributing it on the web. And not everyone is an expert on the subjects about which he writes. You should be especially wary of personal homepages in which individuals often present biased and even harmful information without identifying sources, themselves, or their credentials. Undated work is also not credible. So, for reliable sources, look for websites that:

- are not .com or .net sites that are trying to sell you a particular product
- identify the author or authors by name and credentials
- identify the audience for which the site is intended
- name the site's purpose explicitly
- include a recent date or the last update
- provide both overviews and detailed information
- include links to other reliable sources

Don't be overly impressed by websites that have animated graphic images or sound clips running in the background. If the animation or sound reveals something important about a topic (a simulation of walking though a proposed building design, perhaps), then you are right to value it. If the animation simply reveals that an obnoxious animal icon can bounce endlessly across the top of your computer screen, then you should question whether the authors have made other frivolous design or content decisions in building the website.

Using Search Engines   A search engine is an electronic index to the contents of the World Wide Web. These indices are built both by website authors who submit information to the search engines and by programs called spiders that search for new sites on the World Wide Web to add to their database.

There are many different search engines because there are many competing needs of the users of these engines. Some very fast search engines may search only the titles and descriptions of websites. Other more inclusive engines search all of the words in the first paragraph or set of paragraphs from web pages. Still others search out every word of every page of a website. Meta-engines search multiple search engines simultaneously. Of course, in general, the larger the electronic index, the more "hits" will be found for any particular search query. But when we are dealing with hundreds of thousands or millions of potentially relevant documents, more hits is not necessarily better. Search engines are most helpful when you know clearly what you're looking for, including key words, their synonyms, and perhaps even key phrases.

Structuring Boolean Searches   Boolean searches use logic to structure a query. Named after the nineteenth-century mathematician George Boole, the technique is one that expert searchers such as librarians use often. In electronic Boolean searches, key words can be grouped together or excluded to narrow the results quickly. Most search engines support some kinds of Boolean searches, although it may be necessary to click on the "advanced search" options to conduct a Boolean search. The following show the kinds of information a Boolean search may generate, depending on the key terms used in a query:

Query	Results
photography **or** *history*	Any web page in the search engine's database that contains the word *photography* or the word *history*, but not necessarily both words
photography **and** *history*	All web pages in the search engine's database that contain both terms *photography* and *history*. This should be a smaller set of results than the one above.
photography **and** *history* **not** *printing*	All web pages in the search engine's database that contain both the terms *photography* and *history*, except those that also contain the word *printing*. This should be an even smaller set of results.

Using Synonyms in Searches   To search effectively, it's also necessary for you to remember that a search engine isn't a person, even if, as is the case with "Ask Jeeves," the designers have projected human traits onto the computer tool. From one point of view, search engines don't really even search for words or terms, because the computer doesn't understand human language and its meanings. What the computer is able to do is to look quickly for strings of characters that match. From the computer's point of view, a search for "photography" and one for "sl66se24x" are equally logical and meaningful.

Thus, you can't count on the computer to understand or guess at what you meant to search for. If you misspell a word of your query, such as "photgraphy" the search engine will show you only the web pages where the key term is misspelled in the same way. And the search engine will not include "photograph," "photographs," "photographic," "photographer" or "camera" unless you tell it to. Often, you need to conduct a search for synonyms to find the best results for your query.

Searching for Exact Phrases   A potentially even more efficient way of narrowing your search is to structure your query around one or more exact phrases. If you put the query in quotation marks, the search engine looks for that specific phrase in its index. For example, a search for "nineteenth century American photography" will return far fewer results than any of the Boolean searches above. A combination Boolean and exact phrase search for "American and Civil War photography" would narrow the results even further.

Using Multiple Research Sources   Even should you be so lucky as to find multiple websites that take up exactly the issues you are interested in, you shouldn't necessarily stop your research there. Websites tend to be good for creating overviews and presenting summaries, but they seldom provide the whole text of longer, carefully detailed, and well-edited documents, such as books. In addition, personal interviews, surveys, direct observations, and your own memories are all potentially valuable ways to gather information about a topic. A "Works Cited" page is much more credible if it contains sources of various types, rather than a simple listing of the URLs you find by pointing and clicking.

Warning: Building User Profiles and Policing the Web   One of the ways that websites make money is by collecting and selling information about you to marketing and retail groups that are willing to pay for it. Look closely when a website asks you to reveal personal information about yourself before allowing you to browse the contents of the site. Even when you may not realize that you are revealing anything, a site, such as your favorite search engine, may be tracking the key terms of your queries. If you are searching for a used car and visit two or more websites on which automobiles are advertised, don't be surprised if the pop-up ads in your browser windows start enticing you to other used car sites. It may seem that there is an intelligence at work behind this—a person looking over your shoulder. In reality the software in place is simply finding ways to match key terms, which as we have noted above are simply strings of characters, with other key terms, so that guesses can be made as to what advertisements are likely to be appropriate for you.

For some types of queries, however, the obscene and illegal, such programs may also send a signal to a real person to investigate your browsing habits. Remember that if you're browsing from work or from school, the files that appear on your screen have moved through one or more file servers first. Each server creates a record of the files having been moved. In this way, browsing habits can be policed if organizations that own the computing equipment choose to do so. This means that if you call up a pornographic or other banned site on a university computer or on the computer you use in your job, the net may report that you have done so. Evidence of inappropriate browsing habits has cost many people their jobs and positions of responsibility. If the computer you are using to browse the web doesn't belong to you, then you are bound by the browsing policies of the owner, and it is your responsibility to become aware of university and corporate policies regarding Internet use and to act accordingly.

SAMPLE STUDENT PROCESS—PREWRITING

To illustrate how you may move from prewriting through writing to revising, we'll follow a first-year composition student's process from start to finish. Marisol Vargas was assigned to write a personal essay in response to this prompt, which is one of three we present in Chapter 5:

> Describe an event from which you learned something. Your job is to use your language to recreate the event so that your readers will feel that they have been at least observers of this event with you, if not participants in it.

Bill, Marisol's instructor, specified that the paper be 1,000–1,500 words long, about 4–6 pages.

Bill suggested that his students freewrite for fifteen minutes about important moments or events they remembered. But Marisol didn't do that; instead, she remembered immediately what she counted as a major turning point in her life and spent the entire fifteen-minute period on it.

Freewrite 1

I remember the changing point in my life. It was when I really began to realize that I did need other people, and that was when I became happy again. My friend Erika had been gone for an entire month in the summer and I missed her. That summer when she got back we did things. One of these days she called me to help her pack and visit a friend. I remember we went to visit Ed. I gave him a plant because it was his birthday. Erika and I had planned to go out to eat that day and to talk. After we made up an excuse to leave Ed's we got in the car to drive to the restaurant. I did not feel like myself that day. I felt somehow apart from everything and everyone. I was also extremely tired. I usually get that way before a huge storm, so I told her how I felt and she felt the same. We went out to eat and we talked forever about the past. About our broken hearts, lost loves. Both of us were trying to get some guys out of our heads. They had made an incredible impact in our lifes. These guys were so similar. I got out of the restaurant feeling refreshed. Then it came. The rain storm. We were so excited. We wanted to go the park to play. As I was driving it poured. The windows were open wide and we took it all in. We went to her house to change. Then to the park. It poured the afternoon for almost an hour. That is unusual for NM. We danced outside played on the swings, sang, and did belly slides. When it stopped raining I noticed a little D on my arm. I still don't know how I got it. It was crazy. I remember that day I felt like everything I thought was important didn't matter anymore. Broken heart was for nothing. It all was washed away by the rain. Erika was the only person who I know of who would go out in the rain with me like that. The next day I woke up feeling so clean. Like I had taken a hot bath in roses for hours. My thoughts were so clear. It was that day that I forgot about the past. I realized I had all I needed. I have never had a friend as wonderful as Erika and never will. She helped me realize that things aren't as important as the ones that stay. We moved. She is the one that I miss. I realize now that I need her friendship. It is because of her that I got out of my depression and I will never forget her or that day for that.

This freewrite clearly is not a polished piece of writing. But that's the nature of a freewrite. It's designed to help the writer get as much on the page about her thoughts as possible, and that's what Marisol did here. However, after considering whether she wanted to base her first essay on this freewrite, she decided to find another topic. So she produced a second freewrite, again without worrying about grammar or spelling.

Freewrite 2

I remember when I went with my mom to feed the homeless. When I first got there I was a little scared. I didn't really know what to expect. We got out of the car with pans of food. They all just looked at us. I tryed not to make eye connect. I remember when we got into the building we went into the kitchen, a small separated area. It was hidden from the dining area. I just wanted to stay in there, but the other volunteers sent me out with a fruit bowl. I had to ask people if they wanted fruit. I am a shy person so this was a hard job for me. But I did it. How they crowded me wanting the fruit. They asked for bananas especially for potassium they said. By the second bowl I felt better. I lifted my eyes from the bowl to make sure I got everyone and survey the area. There were family's in there. The children looked so sad. There were people with animals who were outside. They were really nice and thanked me so much for the fruit. I remember this one man who wanted some fruit. He reminded me of Santa Claus with a sweet rosy smile. He had coffee in his hand and plate. "Sir would you like some fruit," I asked. He looked at me as if to say where can I put it. With a shaky hand he took it with the hand of his coffee. Some of the coffee split. I think it burnt him. He just thanks me so sweetly and walked off clumsily. I'll never forget the way he looked. It was at that moment that I realized how stupid and selfish I was. I had tryed to hard not to make eye connect. What for it is not as though they were going to kill me with their eye. Homeless are just like everyone else and there is no reason that they should be viewed differently. We look business men in the eye. A homeless person could have once been a business man. Sometimes we treat the homeless worst than animals. At that moment I realized one day I could be in that position or maybe a friend or family member. I would be greatful of the person who took the time to look me in the eye and smile. There was an indian man who wanted a banana, but there were not more. When I got my new batch I found him to give him the banana. We are so lucky with what we have. Getting almost anything we want, the least we can give is a banana. I learned humility that day.

Marisol decided that this topic—volunteering at a homeless shelter—was one she wanted to work with, so she was then ready to work this freewrite into a longer, more detailed piece of writing. We'll continue working with Marisol's drafting process in Chapter 2.

FROM INVENTING TO DRAFTING

Once you have worked through one or more of these invention devices, you'll proceed to drafting. Your task will be to shape many of the details you generated into an initial draft of an essay. Keep in mind that you probably won't use all of the information you generated, but the writer's task is to choose the details that best represent her topic to her reader, which oftentimes means not using everything she generates. Just as a reminder here, look again at the details Arlene generated in her two freewrites about the backpacking trip. She discovered a lot of detail, but she wasn't able to use all of it in her final draft, simply because it didn't fit.

The next chapter, on shaping an essay, is designed to help you move from your inventing to writing a first rough draft of an essay.

Fernand Léger, "The Construction Workers," 1950. Musée National Fernand Léger, Biot. Photo: Gérard Blot/Réunion des Musées Nationaux/Art Resource, NY © 2008 Artists Rights Society (ARS), New York/ADAGP, Paris.

CHAPTER 2

Shaping an Essay

Once you've generated some ideas and information in your prewriting, your next job is to shape those ideas into a rough draft, one ready for peer review. In this chapter, we'll offer some practical strategies for drafting that should help you do this.

INITIAL SHAPING STRATEGIES

Writing for a Reader

As you begin writing your first draft, your discovery draft, consider who your audience may be. Who might want or need to read your paper? Identify your audience and then respond to these questions:

1. What do my readers already know about this topic?
2. What do I want them to know, understand, or learn from reading my writing?
3. Why do I want them to know this?

Writing answers to these questions can help you focus your drafting by identifying things you want to cover and why you want to cover them. Your job at this point is not to write a final draft for this initial audience; instead, it's to find out as much as you can about your topic and what you think and feel about it. When we move to a discussion of revising, you'll work with your audience more extensively. For now, it's enough for you to speculate about who your audience might be and what information you'll need to present to those readers.

Focus Statements

To develop an initial focus for your paper, consider what you might want readers to learn from your paper and why you want them to learn it. As you speculate about what and why, you should be able to develop a tentative focus statement for your paper. This statement, which should be at least three sentences long, is an initial speculation about purpose, about what you think you want your essay to accomplish or do. Here is an example of a focus statement for an essay on a meaningful event:

> The event I want to write about is the time I failed to pass a swimming merit badge class at Scout camp. I want to talk about the experience of failing the class. I learned that it's ok to fail. I didn't learn it at that time; instead, I came to realize it only a couple of years after the fact. And I learned that it's ok to fail, as long as you try, and I want my readers to see that failure isn't always a bad thing.

A writer using this statement would have several tasks to accomplish: (1) to describe the class, what he did, how he came to fail, which parts of the class worked for him and which did not; (2) to describe what it felt like to fail; and (3) to talk about what he eventually realized from having experienced that failure.

Writing a focus statement can suggest an initial structure or direction for a paper. In this example, the writer could divide the paper into three major sections, one for each of the tasks listed: first, a description or narration of the events of the class; second, a description of that key moment when he learned that he had failed and how that felt; third, a discussion of what he eventually learned. Although hardly a detailed blueprint of the essay's structure, this three-part division could serve as an initial look at that structure.

Another way to use a focus statement is to project what a potential reader would need to know about your topic. Below are two statements, the first by Katherine Ozment, the second by Adam Castoreno, both first-year composition students at New Mexico State University. These statements were developed as essay proposals that identified a topic and then stated an initial position on it at the drafting stage in a researched essay assignment. During class, these students circulated their statements to members of their peer groups, who asked questions raised by the statements.

Katherine's Focus Statement and Her Readers' Questions

> I would like to write my paper on a recent proposal to the education system—inclusion. Inclusion refers to classrooms that have a wide variety of students or, more specifically, completely integrating special ed students into regular ed classrooms. I would like to oppose this idea.

In this brief statement, Katherine identifies her topic (first sentence), defines it (second sentence), and then takes a stance or position on it (third sentence). The members of Katherine's group posed these questions in response:

1. Why do you oppose inclusion?
2. What are the implications for approving or disapproving inclusion?
3. What's a detailed definition of inclusion?
4. What is wrong with the current system?
5. What is wrong with inclusion?
6. What would happen if the two systems were integrated?

Adam's Focus Statement and His Readers' Questions   Adam's focus statement is more fully developed, more detailed, than Katherine's. But at this point, Adam doesn't know whether he thinks gene therapy (the topic of his paper) is a good idea or not. There is a tentative nature to his third paragraph, especially in the last sentence, that suggests he will use the assignment to explore the topic so that he can determine what he feels or thinks about gene therapy. He would like to be positive about it, but he needs to work through this paper to help him decide whether he can be. Here's his focus statement:

> Imagine one day possessing the knowledge, the ability to alter the human DNA and correct serious genetic defects in a developing fetus. By performing "Gene Therapy," a particular gene can be taken out, altered or cloned, and placed back into the DNA, where it can perform as "programmed." According to many critics, this type of brilliant technology is not without flaws. Do we have the right to manipulate the human DNA? How far is genetic research going to take us? Can we one day develop the technology to make human beings "superhuman," possessing only superior genes or those deemed acceptable?
>
> These kinds of philosophical questions carry some validity. However, the knowledge and information we can gain from carrying on with genetic research is enormous. Disease and genetic disorders could become dilemmas of the past. We must remember that the driving force behind gene manipulation is not to create further problems for society, but to help solve some.
>
> Gene therapy is a serious issue facing our society which needs to be considered more deeply. As it stands currently, the knowledge base in the field of genetics is doubling every five years and will continue to increase at an even faster rate. Researching an argument in favor of my possible career choice is essential if I ever want to work in the field with any strong convictions.

The members of Adam's group posed these questions:

1. What has been done with this so far?
2. What positive things can come from this research?
3. What negative things can come from this research?
4. Are you in favor of this process? If not, how can this research be stopped or prevented? If so, how do we make sure people don't try to form "superhumans"?
5. What are the ethical problems/questions?
6. What is the procedure?
7. Could this result in more bad than good? Could someone abuse this technology?

Both Katherine and Adam created expectations in their potential readers, as reflected in the questions their group members asked. These questions helped Katherine and Adam generate still more ideas as they thought about the kinds of information potential readers would need and want. These questions also helped them consider various arguments they might have to respond to or questions they might have to answer in their papers.

Once you've developed a focus statement, either ask someone else to read and respond to it by asking several questions, as in the examples here, or prepare your own questions, listing what you would want to know if you were the intended reader of the essay. These questions can point the way to specific elements you should include in your writing and thus can help you organize your paper.

SAMPLE STUDENT PROCESS— DISCOVERY DRAFT

Your writing task now is to produce a *discovery draft*—a tentative first draft, one that probably will not be nearly as complete or as fully developed as the final draft you write. A discovery draft continues the exploration of the topic you began in your prewriting, connecting the bits and pieces of insights and information you created or uncovered while prewriting into a larger piece of writing, an essay. To begin, use your initial consideration of audience and your focus statement as reminders of what you want to cover and for whom. You may also want to develop a quick outline or list of the points you want to make. As you write, don't be concerned with grammar and mechanics, with finding the exact word, or with creating a perfectly structured final essay. Instead, concentrate on getting as much information on the page as possible. Your goal is to produce a draft that you may then revise into a rough draft for review.

Below we continue working through the drafting of Marisol Vargas's essay on her experience helping at a homeless shelter. After completing the two freewrites you read in Chapter 1, Marisol felt that she wanted to base her essay on her experience at the homeless shelter. As she moved from her second freewrite toward a discovery draft, she wrote an initial audience analysis and a focus statement to provide guidance for her writing.

Initial Audience Analysis

My audience is the members of this English class, so it's a group of 21 NMSU students, most freshmen, different majors and hometowns. Probably a good cross-section of NMSU's student body.

1. What do my readers already know about this topic?

Like me, they probably don't have too many good feelings about the homeless, because of what we've all seen—beggars, street persons pushing shopping carts, dirty, raggedy. Television also shows this stereotype as well.

2. What do I want them to know, understand, or learn from reading my writing?

That the homeless can be just about anybody and that meeting and dealing with them isn't bad.

3. Why do I want them to know this?

Because homelessness is a problem in this country. The more we stay away from the homeless, the more they'll stay faceless. And that just keeps the problem from being solved.

Focus Statement

I want my readers to understand how I felt at the beginning and the end of the day I spent at the homeless shelter. I want them to see what I thought and felt. In order to do this I must be very descriptive. I have to describe the area, the way people looked, the families. I have to show the emotion I felt while I was serving the fruit. I have to show the other people's reactions. I have to show my change in thought.

Discovery Draft

It is the experience that stands out in my mind the most.

The stop light turned red and as the car slowed to a halt, I opened my eyes to my surroundings. I had been asleep for most of the journey and now the change in the car's momentum awakened me. As I looked around I noticed groups of people walking.

The steady momentum, rhythm of my life changed when I went with my mother to feed the homeless. Through this experience I learned to view people in a different light. Feeding the homeless made me realize that others people's suffering may be greater than my own. Therefore, I have learned to be more considerate.

The light turned green and we turned heading for in the same direction as the crowd.

"We're here," my mom said. I remember thinking that it wasn't as large as I expected. In front of us was a small grey building surrounded by an old chain like fence. It reminded me of a warehouse.

This was the first time I had come with my mother to feed the homeless. She had asked me many times before, but because the comfort of my bed in the early morning, I had always declined. This time, however, I worked up the energy to go.

We got out of the car with casseroles and bags of fruits. As we walked toward the shelter, I felt as though everyone was watching us and I tried not to make eye connect. "Just look straight," were the only thoughts in my head.

We entered the building through narrow doors and went toward the kitchen, a small area hidden from the rest of the cafeteria. I helped some of the other volunteers warm the food that everyone had brought. I decided that if I stayed in the seclusion of the kitchen I would be "safe."

Then we were called out to the dining area for a short breakfast prayer. I went out nervously. When it was over I hurried to the kitchen and started to serve the food, but the volunteers had a different job for me. They wanted me to go out with a bowl full of fruit and offer it to everyone. I am a shy person so the thought of having to approach unfamiliar faces scared me.

As I filled up my dish, I prepared myself for the worst. I got up, clenched my fruit bowl and slowly walked out to the dinning area. As I looked around all of my foolish thoughts and fears diminished.

Many people crowded around me waiting to get their fruit. They were very polite, thanking me with smiles and kind words. When the bowl was empty I raced back into the kitchen to refill it and I hurryed back out.

The room was filled with people of different gender and race. There were families, and single men and women, and outside there were people with animals.

Watching the families made me sad. There were little girls who's dresses were loose from hunger and the stresses of living of the street. Their eyes resembled that of an older person with lines of stressful days and sleepless nights.

As I walked outside one man caught my eye. He reminded me of Santa Claus because of his sweet eyes and big rosy cheeks. "Sir would you like some fruit," I asked. He looked at me and smiled bashfully. He looked down at his hands. He was holding coffee and an empty plate. He looked back at the fruit, he was wondering if he had room in his hands to carry it. He carefully took it into the hand that held his coffee. It split from his shaky, nervous movements. Then he thanked me sweetly and slowly walked away.

At that moment I realized how foolish I had been. Fear had kept me away so long. As I walked around I couldn't quiet figure out what it was that I feared. The people I was looking at could have easily been me or a family-member. I was lucky to have my comfortable warm bed to sleep in at night and wake up to in the morning. I couldn't imagine how it would be to have a sidewalk for a bed.

As we walked out of the shelter that day, I made it a point to look people in the eye and smile, a genuine smile. As we drove away that morning I remember my mom saying, "I think we fed over a hundred people today." All I could do was think of the faces I had seen, and I realized how much they looked like me.

How tightly structured is this essay? Not very. For example, the first six paragraphs jump back and forth between the narrative (the story Marisol wants to tell) and Marisol's commentary on it. Further, this draft lacks a good bit of detail; what she saw and felt just doesn't come alive on the page. But it serves its purpose—in drafting it, Marisol got her thoughts about that day at the homeless shelter on the page. Keep in mind that this is not her final draft; in fact, Marisol wrote another rough draft and then revised it into an essay to submit. Finally, she revised her essay one last time, following the recommendations of Bill, her instructor. We'll present these three drafts in Chapter 3.

COMPUTER TIP

When you have finished your discovery draft, save it as *draft 1*, or *discodft* (short for "Discovery Draft"). When you return to begin your next draft, retrieve your discovery draft and create a new file, *secdraft*. And when you move the next draft, retrieve *secdraft*, and create a new file, *thrdraft*, or *final*. How many files of each paper should you have? It depends. If your teacher requires a set number of drafts of your paper, then you should have a file for each of these drafts. If that isn't the case, you should have a file for each time you have attempted to look at your paper as a whole and to make changes that bring that whole closer to the final product you want to produce. These drafts will make it much easier for you to reflect on your drafting process if your teacher requires a portfolio and reflective essay at the end of the course. ◆

DEVELOPING AN ESSAY'S STRUCTURE

All of the elements of an essay come together as you work to develop a discovery draft, that tentative first draft we mentioned at the start of this chapter. Once you establish at least an initial focus, either in a focus statement or a thesis sentence, you'll need to develop a structure—a shape or form—to guide you in writing your discovery draft. What follows are some practical suggestions for developing a structure. Again, keep in mind that your goal is not to produce a finished paper at this stage but to use your writing to explore your topic further. Developing an initial structure can help you in that exploration.

Shaping Strategies

Gilbert Highet offers this insight on the need for a piece of writing to have a shape, a form:

> The next thing is to devise a form for your essay. This, which ought to be obvious, is not. I learned it for the first time from an experienced newspaperman. When I was at college I earned extra pocket- and book-money by writing several weekly columns for a newspaper. They were usually topical, they were always carefully varied, they tried hard to be witty, and (an essential) they never missed a deadline. But once, when I brought in the product, a copy editor stopped me. He said, "Our readers seem to like your stuff all right, but we think it's a bit amateurish." With due humility I replied, "Well, I am an amateur. What should I do with it?" He said, "Your pieces are not coherent; they are only sentences and epigrams strung together; they look like a heap of clothespins in a basket. Every article ought to have a shape. Like this" (and he drew a big letter S on his pad) "or this" (he drew a descending line which turned abruptly upward again) "or this" (and he sketched a solid central core with five or six lines pushing outward from it) "or even this" (and he outlined two big arrows coming into collision).
>
> I never saw the man again, but I have never ceased to be grateful to him for his wisdom and for his kindness. Every essay must have a shape. You can ask a question in the first paragraph, discussing several different answers to it till you reach one you think is convincing. You can give a curious fact and offer an explanation of it. You can take a topic that interests you and do a descriptive analysis of it: a man's character [. . .], a building, a book, a striking adventure, a peculiar custom. There are many other shapes which essays can take; but the principle laid down by the copy editor was right.
>
> Gilbert Highet, *Explorations*

That principle is a simple one: Every essay you write should be shaped or structured for a purpose. You can use the following strategies to marshal support for your focus statement, to shape your essay's content.

Listing   Read your focus statement, and look back over the information you generated while inventing. Then develop a list of the important ideas, topics, or points you want to include in your paper. Your list can be as elaborate or as sparse as necessary. Its sole function is to guide you through your writing by reminding you of what you wanted to cover. Try these steps:

1. Write down all of the points about your topic that seem important to you. Derive these from your prewriting, from whatever freewriting, clustering, visualizing, or questioning you may have done to get started. It's important not to censor yourself while making this list. Don't argue with yourself; don't worry about the order in which you list the points—simply list.
2. Number the points in the sequence in which you think they will appear in your paper. You may, for example, rank your entries in order of importance, from most to least important or from least to most important. Or you may place your entries in chronological order, taking a first-to-last approach.
3. Look again at your list, considering its completeness in light of your focus statement. If something needs to be added or deleted, then do so. If you think it would be helpful at this point to recopy the list, putting each entry in order, then do so. Otherwise, start writing.
4. As you write, refer every now and then to your focus statement and list to see whether you're covering what you thought you needed to. If you aren't, don't be too concerned, because you may well discover a new focus as you write this discovery draft.

If you find while writing that you need to add a point not on your list, then add it. And if you decide while writing that something on the list doesn't fit after all, then delete it.

Topic Outlines A topic outline is a listing of the topics, or subjects, and the order in which you think they will appear in a paper. It is most helpful when you let it serve as a tentative itinerary for your trip through the paper. That is, you will need to be flexible enough to depart from your outline if your writing calls for you to do so. To develop your topic outline, identify the main idea in your focus statement and then order the support for that idea in an outline format.

Below is a topic outline for a paper on assisted suicide for people with terminal illnesses.

Thesis sentence: A terminally ill patient should have the legal right to ask for death or help in dying without legal repercussions.

I. Introduction (include thesis)
II. History of euthanasia
    A. Greeks: acceptance of suicide and death
    B. Modern: accepting death
III. Issues, views
    A. Right-to-die
    B. Right-to-life
    C. Physicians' dilemma

IV. Legal aspects
   A. Past laws
   B. Current laws
   C. Future laws
V. Conclusion

The entries marked by Roman numerals represent major sections of the paper, and the entries under these represent paragraphs and topics to support and develop the thesis. (See pages 53–55 for discussion of thesis sentences.) This is not a detailed outline; instead, it presents an overview of the paper's structure. It identifies the main points of an essay and support for them, and it provides a guide for drafting and then, later, a checklist for completeness.

Blocking   Blocking enables you to create "bins" to hold the content of the various sections of your essay. Each block represents a major section of the paper and will probably contain several paragraphs. To begin, identify the main idea from your focus statement and then draw several blocks. Into each block, jot notes of support for the main idea you generated in prewriting. If you wish, you can subdivide larger blocks to create a block for each paragraph.

Were you to write about the problem of inadequate lighting on your campus, you could block your essay as shown in Figure 2.1.

Blocking can give you an overview of the essay's structure, representing that structure as a whole (the biggest block) divided into its parts (the smaller blocks).

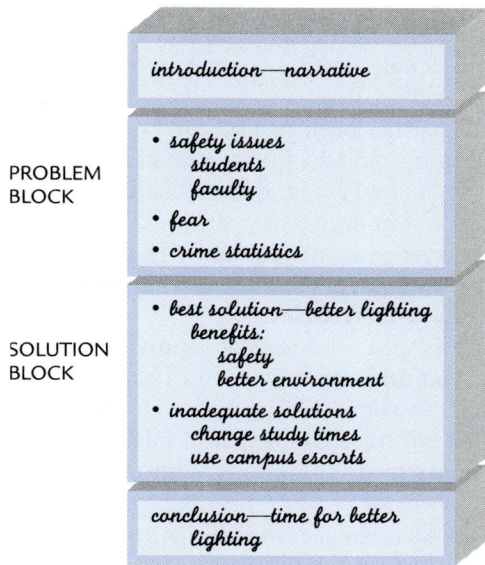

FIGURE 2.1   Organizing Strategy: Blocking

Such a representation can help you see how the various parts of the essay fit together. Blocking is useful at two points in your writing. Early on, it can help you shape a discovery draft by providing you with places to put the information you generated while exploring your topic. Think of a block as a bin into which you place information related to the subject of that block. In the case of the problem/solution essay presented in Figure 2.1, all information generated about the problem during prewriting would go into the problem block, or bin, and all information about the solution would go into the solution block. Later, as you revise, blocking can help you examine your draft's structure for consistency. To use blocking for this second function, summarize each paragraph's content in a phrase and place these summaries in the appropriate blocks. You may well find that a paragraph is out of place and that you need to move it or delete it altogether.

Mapping   Mapping is similar to clustering (see Chapter 1), in that the writer uses clusters of ideas to direct, or map, the essay. Daniel Martinez, a first-year composition student at NMSU, developed the map in Figure 2.2 to guide his writing of an essay on deadbeat parents. As the map suggests, Daniel's essay involved interviews of two people, a young man who hadn't paid child support and a young mother who wasn't receiving child support. Daniel made notes in each of the blocks, creating a list of what to include. This map will probably seem chaotic to you, but it's a personal guide that Daniel used effectively.

Drawing   Another way to structure a paper is to draw a shape for it. Mike Tietsworth, a writing tutor at NMSU, has his students use a fish skeleton (see Figure 2.3) to help them remember structure. In this skeleton, the head represents the introduction and the tail the conclusion, with the ribs ready to hold the supporting details, so that the writer puts meat on the bones of the essay.

Another visual aid that has been helpful for some students is a bookshelf. In Figure 2.4, the bookends represent the introduction and conclusion, and the books represent either individual paragraphs or major sections of a paper.

Or you could think of your essay as a pearl necklace, with each pearl a paragraph or major section of your essay tied tightly to the next. When the clasp is closed, the necklace forms a circle, so that the end connects to the beginning and completes the circle, as shown in Figure 2.5.

Skeletons, bookshelves, and pearl necklaces provide ready-made representations of structure, and you may use them for just about any paper you need to write. But you may also draw your own figure for a given paper. Here's an account of one such drawing that Bill created to help him solve a structural problem with a formal essay he was preparing to submit for publication:

> Committing to a shape is a technique I use for arranging the material generated
> in my prewriting, and I've found that drawing my paper is a very good way of

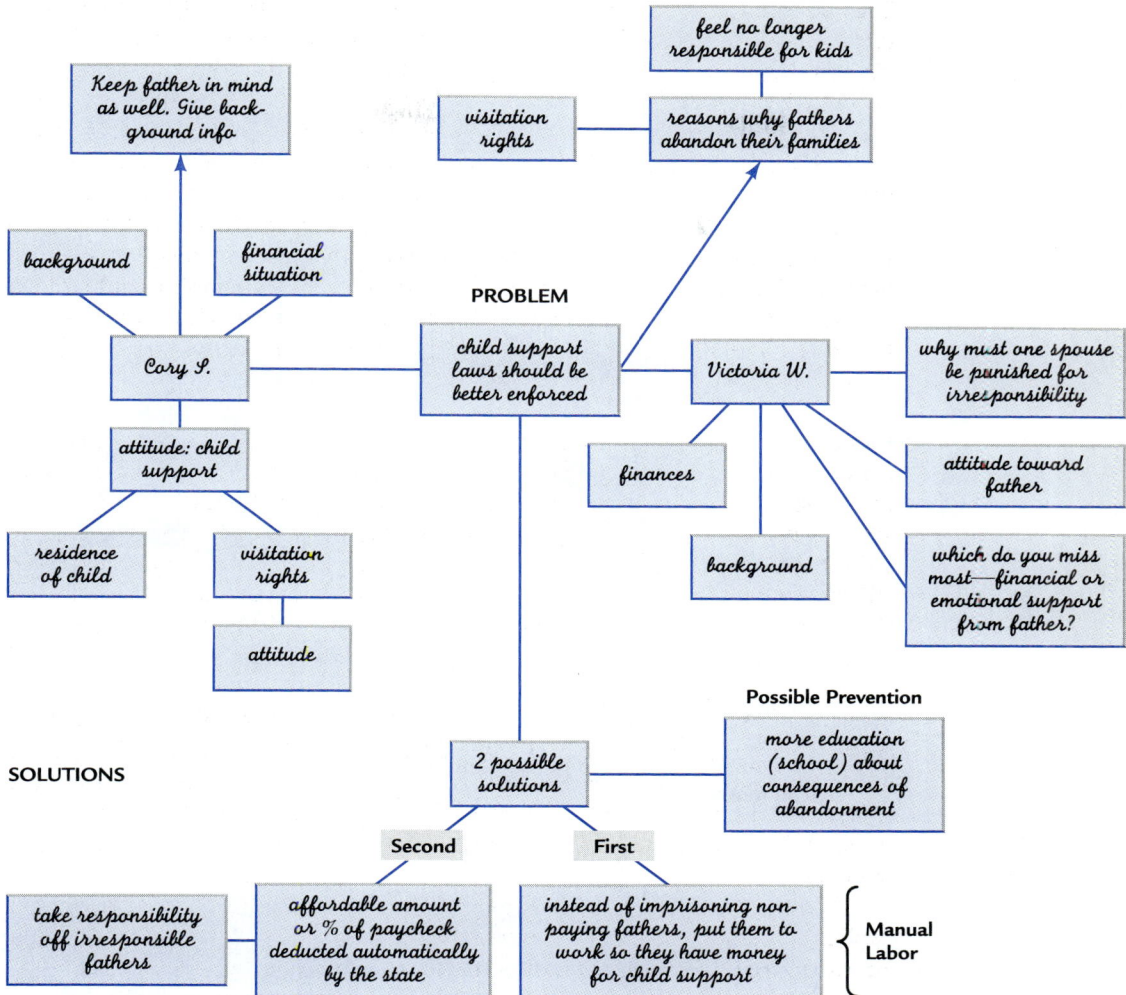

FIGURE 2.2 Organizing Strategy: Mapping

finding a shape. Recently, I was stuck on discerning a workable shape for a paper describing the rationale and then the structure of a course I teach designed to prepare teachers of writing. The course has several strands, which derive from a central theme—that by employing the best we know of theory and research on writing, we create a student-centered class—and I was having trouble organizing discussion of the strands. I tried drawing a hamburger, but that suggested there was a central meaty issue, with the other elements being simple garnishes for that issue. The breakthrough came when, in one of those heavy rains rare to New Mexico, I saw the paper's shape as an umbrella, with the

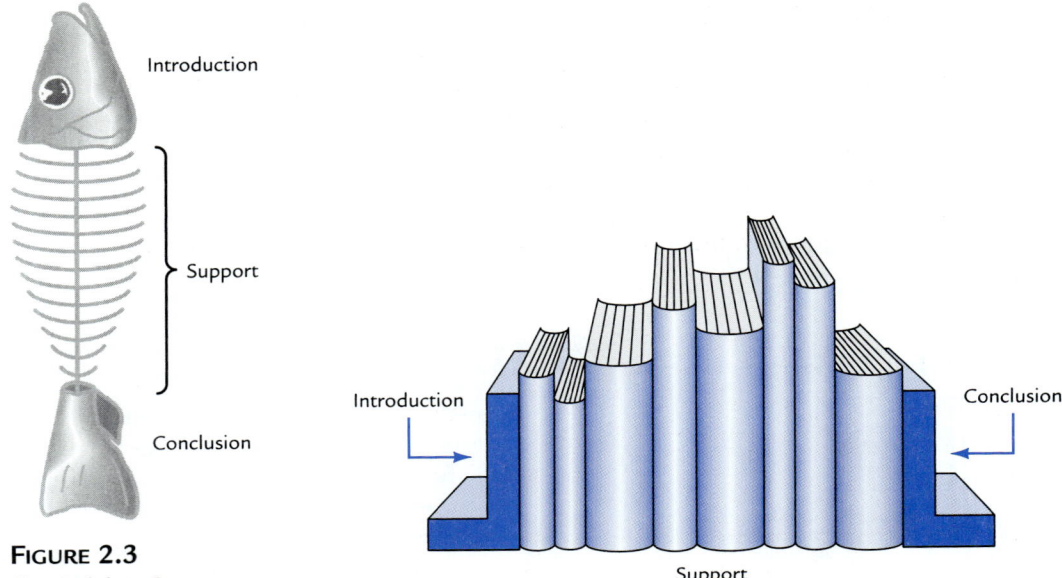

FIGURE 2.3 Organizing Strategy: Fish Skeleton

FIGURE 2.4 Organizing Strategy: Bookshelf

umbrella providing the overall rubric and each strand represented by raindrops streaming from the umbrella. This drawing worked by letting me see the parts of my course as equally important and necessary, with each deriving from the central theme.

Figure 2.6 shows the drawing Bill made.

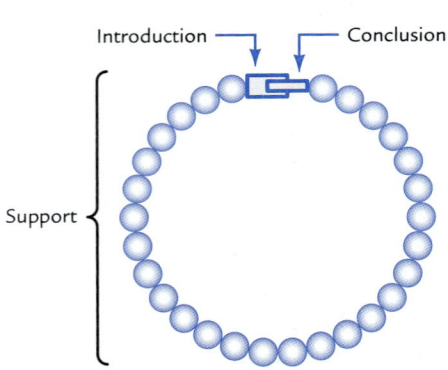

FIGURE 2.5 Organizing Strategy: Pearl Necklace

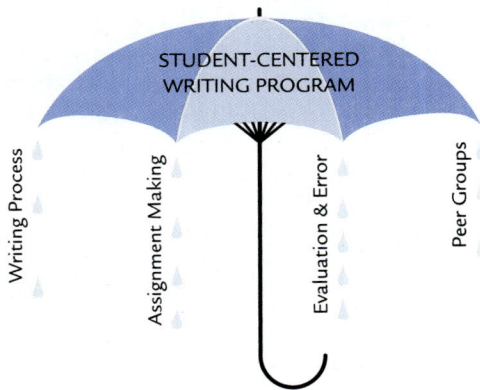

FIGURE 2.6 Organizing Strategy: Umbrella

ELEMENTS OF AN ESSAY

For our purposes, we define an *essay* as a sequence of paragraphs that support and develop the essay's main idea. Similarly, each paragraph is a sequence of sentences that develop the paragraph's main idea. We can view the elements of an essay as pieces of a puzzle, with sentences working together to build paragraphs—sections of the puzzle—and paragraphs working together to build the essay—the complete picture. We will discuss several of the specific puzzle pieces that are elements of an essay: thesis sentences, introductions, paragraphs, and conclusions.

Writing a Thesis Sentence

The thesis sentence provides a center of gravity for the paper, capturing its significance in a single sentence. This sentence can do a number of things, including

1. make an assertion: "Clearly, the current pandering of politicians to lobbyists and political action committees for contributions shows that campaign laws must be reformed."
2. issue a call to action: "Somewhere in New Mexico a sanctuary for the Mexican gray wolf must exist, and I urge you to actively support its reintroduction to the Gila Wilderness."
3. direct a reminiscence: "That summer I spent in Ireland continues to be vivid in my memory nearly twenty years later."
4. offer an evaluation: "*Grumpier Old Men* is one of those rare sequels that works; it is funnier than *Grumpy Old Men*."

By capturing the writer's thinking on the essay topic in a single sentence, the thesis provides direction for the reader. And it makes promises to the reader that the writer must keep. It differs from the focus statement in both length and wording. Whereas a focus statement should be a minimum of three sentences long, a thesis sentence is a single sentence. Although a focus statement may suggest the writer's stance or position on the subject, a thesis sentence clearly reveals the writer's stance. In showing that position, the thesis sentence promises the reader the specific direction the writer intends to take.

Look again at Katherine Ozment's and Adam Castoreno's focus statements (pages 42–43). Katherine states a position on her topic of inclusion: "I would like to oppose this idea." Compare this statement with her paper's thesis sentence: "Regardless of the degree of severity [of a student's handicap], inclusion is an educational policy that does more harm than good and should be stopped." Katherine's focus statement is a fairly simple statement of opposition, whereas her thesis sentence makes specific assertions that Katherine has to support in the rest of her essay. What promises does Katherine's thesis imply? What expectations does it create about the kinds of support that Katherine will develop?

Although Adam hints at his position on gene therapy in the last sentence of his focus statement—"Researching an argument in favor of my possible career choice is essential if I ever want to work in the field with any strong convictions"—he doesn't state a specific position. A reader could infer from the focus statement that although Adam might think he approves of gene therapy, he is still undecided and will use this essay to explore this topic. The thesis sentence from Adam's essay—"Gene therapy is a vital technology which should be researched further, enabling numerous doors to be opened with regard to a plethora of ailments which plague our society"—shows that he is in favor of research into gene therapy. In this thesis sentence, Adam takes a specific stance; he asserts that gene therapy has great potential and should be the subject of further research. What expectations about essay direction and supporting details does this thesis create for you as a potential reader of Adam's essay?

Where does a thesis sentence appear in an essay? It can appear anywhere, but most often it appears near the beginning, as part of the introduction. Certain kinds of essays may have a different thesis placement. For example, an essay presenting the writer's solution to a problem could fairly neatly divide into two parts: a section for discussion of the problem and a section for discussion of the solution. The statement of the solution would be the essay's thesis, and it would probably come at the beginning of the second part. So in this case, the thesis would appear near the middle of the essay.

Should every paper have a thesis? Most will, because in the thesis the writer makes commitments to the reader. Although three of the four examples at the beginning of this section would appear in persuasive essays, a thesis statement is also useful in essays that explain, as this thesis illustrates: "As health care becomes more and more expensive and as our health care delivery system becomes more and more complicated, many individuals in our society find that the quality of their health care becomes worse and worse." As we discuss in Chapter 6, a thesis that states an argument may well be used in informative writing, because it allows the writer to make her promises to the reader clear. Personal essays, however, often do not have a specific sentence that can be identified as a thesis. Instead, the writer uses his language to present an event or a person to the reader and lets the reader infer the importance of that event or person for the writer. But a personal essay needs direction just as much as any other essay, and a clearly written focus statement can provide this direction.

It's important to remember that you may change your thesis to fit the paper as it develops. If the thesis does not fit the paper as you proceed with your writing, then either the paper or the thesis has to change. Having a clearly stated thesis can provide you with a helpful revision tool as you make sure during revising that your essay fully develops your thesis.

WRITING STRATEGY

When Should You Write a Thesis Sentence?

Some writers develop a thesis sentence early in their drafting and use it as a guide throughout their writing. Others will write a tentative statement that doesn't qualify as a thesis sentence as we've defined it. Only when these writers have written their way to discovering exactly what they want to say will they write a thesis sentence, one that truly reflects the essay's purpose. So the answer to the question about when you should write a thesis sentence is this: It depends. You may write one at the start of your process; then again, your thesis may not come to you until you're in the middle of or perhaps nearly finished with your drafting. If you can't develop a strong thesis sentence right at the start of your drafting, don't worry. Just write a statement to point the way you think you want to go, and then follow it until you have a firmer understanding of what you want your writing to say.

Introductions

An introduction forms the reader's entrance into the paper. This introduction, which may consist of a single paragraph or several paragraphs (depending on the essay's length and the writer's purpose), plays an important role in the essay. It prepares the reader for the essay that follows. It orients the reader to the paper, laying out the paper's general topic and suggesting, if not stating clearly, the writer's position on or attitude toward that topic. It catches the reader's attention. It may present a thesis sentence; then again, it may not, for as we have noted, a thesis sentence may appear anywhere in an essay. Below we present four introductions. After reading each, respond to these questions:

1. What is the essay's general subject? What is the writer's position on or attitude toward this subject?
2. How effectively does each introduction catch your attention? What information or details does the writer present to do so?
3. What expectations does the introduction create in you? What promises does it make that its writer must keep?
4. If a thesis sentence is presented, how effective is it? What does it reveal of the writer's purpose? If a thesis sentence is not presented, does its omission hamper the introduction? Why or why not?

The first introduction, by Datus Proper, opens his personal essay "Dark Hollow." In this introduction, Proper raises the question of ownership of a trout stream and points toward potential conflict.

> Fish a place long enough and it becomes a homestead, a personal stretch of boulders and water and trout. I've been proving my claim on Dark Hollow Run

for twenty years now, so I wondered about the other car parked on Skyline Drive, right where I always start my hike down to the stream. Maybe the visitor was just the usual refugee from the city, out for a stroll on the Appalachian Trail, but then again I might find a fisherman ahead of me. I hurried down the mountainside with my rod and rucksack.

The visitor was easy to catch. "Hill's getting hard to pull," she said. Her hair was more gray than red where it fell over the lace collar of her dress. Her name was Betty Cave and her only burden was a bunch of flowers, but it established a claim 200 years older than mine. I read the names of her family when we got to what used to be the Dark Hollow settlement.

There were more headstones in the clearing than Betty had flowers to decorate—rough fieldstones, big ones and little ones, lots of little ones. One of the unmarked stones was for the Cave who brought the family's red hair from Ireland to the Blue Ridge long ago. The oldest legible marker was for John G. Cave of the Virginia Light Artillery, C.S.A. Near it were stones for Betty's parents and her sister Lula Belle.

Not far away was a fireplace, stones chinked with mud, standing lonely in the woods. Betty Cave had stories to go with that old hearth. It had been part of her family's cabin once, and she remembered the days when her mother tended the fire and her father came home with food.

The second example, by Camille Paglia, opens "Rape and Modern Sex War," a piece of persuasive writing, with a strong, startling statement:

Rape is an outrage that cannot be tolerated in civilized society. Yet feminism, which has waged a crusade for rape to be taken more seriously, has put young women in danger by hiding the truth about sex from them.

Gloria Naylor begins "Mommy, What Does 'Nigger' Mean?" by identifying the subject of her essay as language, but not specifically the language of racism.

Language is the subject. It is the written form with which I've managed to keep the wolf away from the door and, in diaries, to keep my sanity. In spite of this, I consider the written word inferior to the spoken, and much of the frustration experienced by novelists is the awareness that whatever we manage to capture in even the most transcendent passages falls far short of the richness of life. Dialogue achieves its power in the dynamics of a fleeting moment of sight, sound, smell and touch.

I'm not going to enter the debate here about whether it is language that shapes reality or vice versa. That battle is doomed to be waged whenever we seek intermittent reprieve from the chicken and egg dispute. I will simply take the position that the spoken word, like the written word, amounts to a nonsensical arrangement of sounds or letters without a consensus that assigns "meaning." And building from the meanings of what we hear, we order reality. Words themselves are innocuous; it is the consensus that gives them true power.

Stacy Birch, a first-year composition student at NMSU, opens her essay considering the potential effectiveness of a new legal program by summarizing it, providing the reader with information about the program.

On October fifteenth of this year [1997] a new project, called Project Amnesty, was adopted throughout the state of New Mexico. Project Amnesty has been specifically designed to decrease the number of parents, especially fathers, who do not pay child support or provide medical insurance for their children. These parents who are not currently financially supporting their sons and daughters have now been given a forty-five day amnesty period to make child support payments, or at least provide health care insurance. If no action is taken during this amnesty period, penalties, including heavy fines and even arrest, could and will be levied. Project Amnesty will be an overall benefit to the children of New Mexico because it will force deadbeat parents to provide money and insurance that rightfully belongs to their children.

Each of these introductions does its job differently.

Proper: Proper structures his introduction as a narrative that establishes the place (Dark Hollow Run in the Appalachians), but it also establishes potential conflict with the introduction of Betty Cave, who has a much longer "claim" to the land Proper fishes.

Paglia: Paglia opens with a very strong statement, first with a definition of rape ("an outrage that cannot be tolerated"), and then with an intriguing assertion: "feminism [. . .] has put young women in danger by hiding the truth about sex from them." This assertion is hardly what we expect to hear because of the feminist movement's strong advocacy of women's rights.

Naylor: By offering a statement of her topic—"Language is the subject"—Naylor provides something of a scholarly counterpoint to her essay's title. Naylor forecasts the thrust of her essay in the last sentence of her introduction, focusing on what gives words their "true power."

Stacy: Stacy gives a quick synopsis or summary of Project Amnesty's main provisions—that deadbeat parents have to make arrangements to pay up or be prepared for legal sanctions—and then her evaluation of this project.

Three of these introductions contain a thesis sentence, an assertion that the essay will support or attempt to prove.

Paglia: Yet feminism, which has waged a crusade for rape to be taken more seriously, has put young women in danger by hiding the truth about sex from them.

Naylor: Words themselves are innocuous; it is the consensus that gives them true power.

Stacy: Project Amnesty will be an overall benefit to the children of New Mexico because it will force deadbeat parents to provide money and insurance that rightfully belongs to their children.

Having made an assertion, each writer then had to offer arguments, examples, anecdotes, and other kinds of support for that statement.

Proper's is the only introduction that doesn't contain a thesis sentence. But Proper does provide a sentence that helps structure the remainder of his essay: "Betty Cave had stories to go with that old hearth." Proper builds his essay around several of Betty Cave's stories about her family, alternating her stories with his own story of his day fishing Dark Hollow Run. Near the end of the essay, Proper makes an assertion that reveals a significant dilemma when he comments on the meaning he's gleaned from his fishing and from listening to Betty Cave: "Something beautiful had been saved for me—and taken from the Caves."

Although these sample introductions are varied, each achieves its primary purpose—to identify the topic and the writer's stance on it and to bring the reader into the paper.

WRITING STRATEGY

When Should You Write an Introduction?

Although some writers may begin writing by composing the introduction, we suspect that most do not. In order to start at the beginning and proceed straight through the essay to its end, a writer would have to have thought through her writing completely and so know fully everything she wanted to say in the essay before actually composing it. Some writers find this possible, but most do not. Thus, in many cases, the introduction will be one of the last sections the writer composes.

Exercise 2.1

Select an essay in another chapter in this text, and look at its introduction. How effective is that introduction? What does the introduction do for the reader? How well does it establish a context for the essay it introduces?

Paragraphs—Topic Sentences

A well-written paragraph displays a certain logic; it has a tight structure that leads the reader through the development of its content. One element of this logic is the topic sentence, which makes a statement that the paragraph then develops, explains, or supports. The topic sentence is a signal to the reader that identifies what the paragraph is about and so directs or guides the reader through the paragraph's content.

Most often, the topic sentence appears at the beginning of the paragraph, but it can occur anywhere in the paragraph. We've underlined the topic sentence of each of the following paragraphs. After you read each paragraph, respond to the questions that follow.

This paragraph appears in Susan Jacoby's essay "Common Decency," which offers a counterpoint to Camille Paglia's "Rape and Modern Sex War":

> The immorality and absurdity of using mixed signals as an excuse for rape is cast in high relief when the assault involves one woman and a group of men. In cases of gang rape in a social setting (usually during or after a party), the defendants and their lawyers frequently claim that group sex took place but no force was involved. These upright young men, so the defense invariably contends, were confused because the girl had voluntarily gone to a party with them. Why, she may have even displayed sexual interest in *one* of them. How could they have been expected to understand that she didn't wish to have sex with the whole group?

1. What focus does the topic sentence provide? What promises does it make? How well does the paragraph develop this focus and so keep its promises?
2. How well does the topic sentence guide you through the paragraph?

In this paragraph, Jacoby derides one of the more prevalent defenses offered in cases of gang rape. The language she chooses—"the immorality and absurdity" of the mixed-signals defense—focuses the reader immediately on her attitude toward this defense. The paragraph then develops the attitude implicit in the topic sentence through irony, if not outright sarcasm. Jacoby labels the accused rapists "upright young men" with whom the rape victim had gone "voluntarily" to a party. Continuing her attack, Jacoby uses conversational language that has a sneering quality to it: "Why, she may have even displayed sexual interest in *one* of them. How could they have been expected to understand that she didn't wish to have sex with the whole group?" Jacoby, then, presents a well-structured paragraph that develops its topic sentence well, showing clearly the "immorality and absurdity" of a mixed-signals defense for gang rapists.

In this paragraph from "Clean Up or Pay Up," Louis Barbash places a topic sentence near the middle:

> The athlete's first priority is to play pro ball. Forty-four percent of all black scholarship athletes, and 22 percent of white athletes, entertain hopes of playing in the pros. That's why they will play four years for nothing. But in fact, the lure of sports that keeps kids in school is a false hope and a cruel hoax. "The dream in the head of so many youngsters that they will achieve fame and riches in professional sports is touching, but it is also overwhelmingly unrealistic," says Robert Atwell, president of the American Council on Education. The would-be pro faces odds as high as 400–1: of the 20,000 "students" who play college basketball, for example, only 50 will make it to the NBA. The other 19,950 won't. Many of them will wind up like Tom Scates, in minimum wage jobs, or like Reggie Ford, who lost his football scholarship to Northwest Oklahoma State after he injured his knee and now collects unemployment compensation in South Carolina.
>
> Louis Barbash, "Clean Up or Pay Up"

1. Do you agree or disagree with our designation of this paragraph's topic sentence? Why?
2. What focus does the topic sentence provide? What promises does it make? How well does the paragraph develop this focus and so keep its promises?
3. How well does the topic sentence guide you through the paragraph?
4. What is the function of the sentences preceding the topic sentence?

Barbash wishes to decry the common belief among college athletes that they'll make it to the NFL or NBA. To do that, he has to show that this is indeed a prevalent belief—hence the statistics he cites in the first sentence. The topic sentence focuses on the "false hope and [. . .] cruel hoax" of athletes believing they will eventually play in the pros, which Barbash implies is the primary reason many student-athletes stay in college. Having made this statement, Barbash must support it, and he does so through statistics and by quoting an authority in the field. To make his assertion even more convincing, Barbash closes the paragraph by referring by name to two athletes whose experience in collegiate sports didn't send them into professional sports. Barbash has written an effective, convincing paragraph that develops its topic sentence well.

Our third sample paragraph is from Julie Titone's "Balance of Power: Can Endangered Salmon and Hydroelectric Plants Share the Same Rivers?" Titone places her topic sentence at the paragraph's end.

> In the early 1900s, as many as 16 million wild salmon traveled up the Columbia River and its tributaries each year. Today there are only 2 million, all but 300,000 of which are from hatcheries. As salmon sport-fishing declined in recent decades, many Idaho riverside communities lost an important source of income. Now the misery is flowing downstream, as fishing communities on the Lower Columbia and along the Pacific coast face up to rough new harvest restrictions. <u>The fish just aren't there.</u>

1. Do you agree or disagree with our designation of this paragraph's topic sentence? Why?
2. What focus does the topic sentence provide? What promises does it make? How well does the paragraph develop this focus and so keep its promises?
3. How well does the paragraph lead to the topic sentence?
4. Titone could well have opened her paragraph with the last sentence. What would she have lost or gained by doing so?

By placing the topic sentence at the end of the paragraph, Titone uses her writing to accomplish two goals. First, she creates some suspense by layering detail upon detail, showing the impact of the severe decline in the number of salmon initially on upstream "riverside communities" and now on "fishing communities" downstream. As readers, we want to know the writer's interpretation of all the details. Titone makes us wait, withholding her interpretation until the end, so that it has a greater impact than it would have at the beginning of the paragraph. Second, by leading us from one detail to the next, Titone forces us to make sense of those details with her, enabling us to recognize more clearly the validity of her interpretation. The placement of this topic sentence is effective.

Although a paragraph may sometimes not contain a topic sentence, each paragraph should develop what we call a topic idea. A paragraph without a topic sentence must nonetheless contribute to the essay's development, and it may do so by developing an extended example or by developing an idea from a preceding paragraph in more detail. The following excerpt from "Politics and the English Language" illustrates this point. In this essay, George Orwell talks about defending the English language from those who misuse it. He closes one paragraph dealing with various minor misuses and ways to remedy them with this statement: "The defence of the English language implies more than this, and perhaps it is best to start by saying what it does *not* imply." Orwell then goes on to this paragraph:

> To begin with, it has nothing to do with archaism [. . .] or with the setting up of a Standard English which must never be departed from. On the contrary, it is especially concerned with the scrapping of every word or idiom which has outgrown its usefulness. It has nothing to do with correct grammar and syntax [. . .] or with the avoidance of Americanisms, or with having what is called a "good prose style." On the other hand it is not concerned with fake simplicity and the attempt to make written English colloquial. Nor does it even imply in every case preferring the Saxon word to the Latin one, though it does imply using the fewest and shortest words that will cover one's meaning. What is above all needed is to let the meaning choose the word, and not the other way about.
>
> George Orwell, "Politics and the English Language," *Shooting an Elephant" and Other Essays*

This paragraph has no topic sentence. Instead, it is guided by the last sentence in the preceding paragraph, and it develops that sentence. Note Orwell's use of pronouns to connect the two paragraphs. If you write a paragraph that does not carry a topic sentence, you must make very clear connections between that paragraph and the idea that guides it.

Exercise 2.2

Select an essay in another chapter of this text and examine each paragraph of the body for its topic sentence. What idea does the topic sentence imply the paragraph will develop? How well does the paragraph develop this idea? Where does the topic sentence appear? Is it where it should be? If a paragraph does not have a topic sentence, does it develop a topic idea expressed in a preceding paragraph? If not, should it have its own topic sentence? Why or why not?

Paragraphs—Cohesion

A well-written paragraph hangs together; it consists of related sentences that further the point the writer wants to make. We can talk of this hanging together as cohesion. A well-written paragraph is cohesive; its sentences fit together, one sentence working with the next and the next and then the next until the paragraph is structured. Three important cohesive devices, illustrated below, are repetition of key terms, repetition of sentence structure, and transition.

Repetition of Key Terms
A key term is an important word or phrase that adds meaning to a paragraph and essay. In the following paragraph, Loren Eiseley repeats key terms, which we've underlined, to create cohesion. How effective are they?

> Some years ago the old elevated railway in Philadelphia was torn down and replaced by a subway system. This ancient El with its barnlike stations containing nut-vending machines and scattered food scraps had, for generations, been the favorite feeding ground of flocks of pigeons, generally one flock to a station along the route of the El. Hundreds of pigeons were dependent on the system. They flapped in and out of its stanchions and steel work or gathered in watchful little audiences about the feet of anyone who rattled the peanut-vending machines. They even watched the feet of crowds who gathered between trains. Probably very few among the waiting people who tossed a crumb to an eager pigeon realized that this El was like a food-bearing river, and that the life which haunted its banks was dependent upon the running of the trains with their human freight.
>
> Loren Eiseley, "The Brown Wasps," *The Night Country*

Repetition of Sentence Structure
Repeating a particular sentence structure works to create cohesion, as the upcoming two sample paragraphs will illustrate. In the first paragraph, from "Clean Up or Pay Up," Louis Barbash repeats a sentence pattern we may label subject-verb-complement (SVC). That is, Barbash begins a sentence with a subject and follows that immediately with the sentence's verb and then the complement, the rest of the predicate. The subject in the second, third, and fourth sentences is the pronoun "it"; the verb is "is"; the complement is cast as a noun clause beginning with "that." How well do you think this paragraph hangs together?

> One scarcely knows where to start in on a statement like that. It's appalling that an accredited state university would admit a functional illiterate, even recruit him, and leave him illiterate after four years as a student. It's shocking that it would do all this in order to make money from his unpaid performance as an athlete. And it is little short of grotesque that an educator, entrusted with the education of 20,000 young men and women, would argue that the cynical arrangement between an institution of higher learning and an uneducated high school boy was, after all, a fair bargain.

In the next paragraph, a bread maker and aspiring cookbook writer repeats a sentence structure that uses an introductory clause (the "if" clause at the start of the sentence) and an explanatory clause (the "because" clause at the end of the sentence) to emphasize the relationship among the paragraph's sentences. How effectively does this repetition work to create cohesion?

> As you make bread, experiment with adding various ingredients to enhance the flavor and nutritional value of each loaf. If you add honey instead of sugar as a sweetener, your bread will taste better, because honey adds its own distinctive flavor as well as sweetness. If you add wheat bran, your bread will be more healthful, because the bran fiber adds the bulk necessary for proper digestion. And if you add wheat germ, your bread will be more nutritious, because wheat germ adds vitamins. What you choose to add to your bread dough determines whether what you bake will be merely bread or B*R*E*A*D.

Use of Transitional Words and Phrases Transitional words and phrases are the connectors we all use in speaking and writing. Here is a partial list of transitions and the relationship each signals:

> *addition*—and, also, in addition to, further, furthermore, similarly, not only/but also, both/and, moreover, either/or, another, like
> *contrast*—but, contrary to, yet, still, in opposition to, however, notwithstanding, although, whereas, while, neither/nor, on the other hand
> *example*—for example, that is
> *time*—when, as, already, then, after, afterwards
> *sequence*—next, then, soon, after, afterwards, following, since, first, second, finally
> *result*—thus, therefore, since, so, because, for

Writers use transitional words and phrases to connect parts of sentences, to connect sentences within a paragraph, and to connect paragraphs within an essay. In the following passage, the various transitions are underlined. How effectively do they create cohesion within the paragraph?

> One recourse we do have is to teach our daughters how to talk back to and make fun of the mass media. This is especially satisfying <u>since</u>, thanks to Nickelodeon, we sometimes see them watching the same stuff we grew up with. In an episode of *Lassie* my daughter and I watched one morning, a ranger comes to the house to warn the mom that there are some mountain lions in the area. <u>As</u> he tries to show her, on a map, where they'd been spotted, she demurs, confessing that she can't read maps <u>and</u> they just confuse her. <u>Then</u>, on her way to meet Dad and Timmy at a Grange dinner, she gets a flat—which, of course, she hasn't a clue how to change—<u>and then</u> gets caught in one of the traps set for the mountain lions. Lassie—a dog—has more brains than she does <u>and</u> has to save her. Such scenes provide the feminist mom with an opportunity to impart a few words of wisdom about how silly and unrealistic TV can be when it comes to women.
> <u>But</u> this was an exception. I don't want to monitor my daughter's TV viewing on Saturday morning, I want to go back to bed. How many mothers have the time or the energy for such interventions? Why should such interventions be so constantly necessary? <u>And</u> even the most conscientious and unhurried mom can't compensate for the absences, the erasures, of what their daughters don't see, may

never see, about women and bravery, intelligence, and courage. And this is just what little white girls don't see. What of my little girl's best friend, who is Asian? She will confront even more erasures, and more glib stereotypes. Of one thing I am certain. Like us, our daughters will make their own meanings out of much that they see, reading between the lines, absorbing exhortations to be feisty side by side with exhortations to be passive. Like us, they will have to work hard to fend off what cripples them and amplify what empowers them. But why, after all these years, should they still have to work so hard and to resist so much?

Susan Douglas, *Growing Up Female with the Mass Media*

Exercise 2.3

Select an essay in another chapter of this text and examine its paragraphs for unity and coherence. Does each paragraph follow the direction established by its topic sentence? If a particular paragraph does not contain a topic sentence, does it develop a topic idea, perhaps an idea stated in a preceding paragraph? If so, how well does it develop that idea? Mark any transitional words and phrases used. Are these appropriate? Why or why not? Mark any repetition of key terms. Are these appropriate? Why or why not?

WRITING STRATEGY

Principles of Paragraph Development

To check the development of your paragraphs, keep these principles in mind:

1. A paragraph is a sequence of content-related sentences that develops an idea in some detail.
2. A paragraph usually contains a topic sentence. This sentence serves to guide both writer and reader through the paragraph's content. The topic sentence can occur anywhere in the paragraph, though it usually comes at the beginning.
3. In some cases, a paragraph may not have a topic sentence, developing instead a topic idea stated in a preceding paragraph. (If you find that you have written a paragraph without a topic sentence, check to be sure that the paragraph does develop some aspect of your paper's purpose, some topic idea. Be sure to identify where that topic idea is stated.)
4. Paragraphs should be unified; each should develop one particular aspect of an essay's main thesis.
5. Paragraphs should be coherent; the sentences in each should be logically connected by transitional words and phrases, by repetition of key terms, and/or by repetition of sentence structure.

WRITING STRATEGY

One Page, One Paragraph

Some of our students have found it helpful to give each paragraph a separate page for drafting. Here is how this works:

1. At the top of a sheet of paper, place a topic idea or topic sentence, something that represents support for the essay topic you want to write about. This idea may come from your focus statement, or it may be an entry on an outline or a list. (For discussion of topic sentences, see pages 58–61.)
2. Write a paragraph that explores this topic idea or sentence. As you write, do not stop to worry about the appropriateness of what you are writing or whether what you are writing will find its way into the final essay—just write.
3. When you have completed a first draft of each paragraph, you will have several individual sheets of paper. Arrange these in what appears to be their logical or most effective order. (As you revise these paragraphs to form a whole paper, you will have to be sure to provide an introduction, a conclusion, and appropriate transitions between the paragraphs to tie them together.)

Students who have used this technique report that having to concentrate on developing only one paragraph at a time helps them manage writing the whole essay better, because focusing on only one part seems less worrisome than trying to focus on that one part and the rest of the essay at the same time.

Conclusions

There is quite a difference between ending an essay and merely stopping it. The ending, or conclusion, of an essay is the final section; it completes the background against which the material in the body is to be placed and, thus, helps shape the overall meaning of the essay. It is more than a simple summary, though it may include a summary in certain situations, especially when the essay is long and involved.

Below are the conclusions to the essays from which we took the introductions given earlier (see pages 55–58). As you read these conclusions, keep these questions in mind:

1. How effectively does the writer provide insight into his or her purpose for writing the essay? Is there a statement or implication of the paper's significance for the writer?
2. What is the nature of the conclusion—a summary, a call to action, a reiteration of the thesis?
3. How effective does the conclusion seem? (Although we have not presented the entire essay, speculate about this effectiveness.)

Datus Proper structures his essay as something of a dialogue with Betty Cave, alternating one of her stories with a narrative of part of his day's fishing. He repeats this structure throughout the essay and ends the essay by describing the significance Dark Hollow holds for him, following his talk with Betty Cave. Here is the conclusion of his essay, with Proper's commentary in regular type and Cave's final story in italics:

> Change would have come to the settlement in time, even if the old families had been allowed to stay in their homes. Somebody would have driven a car to the cabins and the world would have followed, one vehicle at a time. People who had been part of nature would have erected television antennas in the heart of Dark Hollow.
>
> With humans gone, the original vegetation returned, and if the young hardwoods drank some of the stream's water, they also protected the watershed from erosion. The trout were not big, but they were doing better here than in most parts of their ancestral range. I expected to find the native wildlife waiting for me as long as I could manage the hard pull.
>
> Something beautiful had been saved for me—and taken from the Caves.
>
> *When they first built Skyline Drive, I would hike up there and sell little paper flowers. Mama made 'em for me. I'd charge a dime, but some of the guests would stop their cars and give me a dollar. I was five years old.*
>
> *After awhile, the government pushed us off our land and made it part of Shenandoah National Park. That was before the war started—1939 or the edge of '40, I think. Daddy got a dollar an acre. Friends gave us use of a house outside the Park—they knew we couldn't pay rent. We wanted to go back to Dark Hollow, but the government burnt down all eight cabins. Burnt the church, too.*
>
> *Daddy didn't have any work. All he knew was farming and hunting and fishing. I remember him sitting outside every evening, cryin' and cryin'.*

By following his statement of the significance Dark Hollow holds for him with Betty Cave's story about the impact of having to leave the Hollow on her family and particularly on her father, Proper creates a powerful ending for his essay. By continuing the pattern of alternating stories, he maintains the essay's cohesion. And through his use of "hard pull," he echoes Betty Cave's words in the introduction, providing a thread that helps tie the introduction and conclusion together.

Camille Paglia closes "Rape and Modern Sex War" by repeating her theme of the truth about sex.

> As a fan of football and rock music, I see in the simple, swaggering masculinity of the jock and in the noisy posturing of the heavy-metal guitarist certain fundamental, unchanging truths about sex. Masculinity is aggressive, unstable, combustible. It is also the most creative cultural force in history. Women must reorient themselves toward the elemental powers of sex, which can strengthen or destroy.
>
> The only solution to date rape is female self-awareness and self-control. A woman's number one line of defense is herself. When a real rape occurs, she should report it to the police. Complaining to college committees because the courts "take too long" is ridiculous. College administrations are not a branch of the judiciary. They are not equipped or trained for legal inquiry. Colleges must

alert incoming students to the problems and dangers of adulthood. Then colleges must stand back and get out of the sex game.

Paglia's conclusion maintains the stark, terse tone established by her essay's introduction. Given that her purpose was to upbraid feminism for failing young women while maintaining a pro-women stance, Paglia's conclusion works. Whether readers will agree with her stance or not, Paglia offers a provocative essay, framed by a strongly worded introduction and conclusion.

Following discussion of the various contexts in which she heard the term "nigger" used, Gloria Naylor explains how blacks she knew—her family and her family's friends—defused the term:

> I don't agree with the argument that use of the word "nigger" at this social stratum of the black community was an internalization of racism. The dynamics were the exact opposite: the people in my grandmother's living room took a word that whites used to signify worthlessness or degradation and rendered it impotent. Gathering there together, they transformed "nigger" to signify the varied and complex human beings they knew themselves to be. If the word was to disappear totally from the mouths of even the most liberal of white society, no one in that room was naive enough to believe it would disappear from white minds. Meeting the word head-on, they proved it had absolutely nothing to do with the way they were determined to live their lives.
>
> So there must have been dozens of times that the word "nigger" was spoken in front of me before I reached the third grade. But I didn't "hear" it until it was said by a small pair of lips that had already learned it could be a way to humiliate me. That was the word I went home and asked my mother about. And since she knew that I had to grow up in America, she took me in her lap and explained.

Throughout her essay, Naylor has explained the various contexts in which she has heard the term "nigger" applied. In exploring these contexts, Naylor supports the assertion of her thesis sentence: "It is the consensus that gives [words] true power." Her conclusion maintains this position. But by presenting the ultimate context in which "nigger" was discussed—her grandmother's living room—Naylor brings to life the abstract concept of the consensus generating true power, claiming, "the people in my grandmother's living room took a word that whites used to signify worthlessness or degradation and rendered it impotent." So in her conclusion Naylor returns to her introduction, providing a final example in support of her thesis's asssertion.

In her conclusion, Stacy Birch acknowledges the speculative nature of her evaluation of Project Amnesty.

> Since Project Amnesty has only begun, we cannot gauge its final outcome. It is Project Amnesty's goal to at least double the amount of child support payments currently being paid in New Mexico. I believe that the amount of child support payments will increase, maybe even meet that goal, because of this program. If payments do increase, if children do benefit from this program, then the effort to push the program forward will have been worth it, even if some deadbeat parents are fined or jailed for not supporting their children.

At the time Stacy wrote the paper, Project Amnesty had been in effect only a short time, so she really couldn't say with any certainty that it would work. However, her conclusion derives quite logically from her essay; the evidence and support Stacy presented throughout the essay led her to believe that Project Amnesty would be effective and that, ultimately, children in New Mexico would benefit from the program. Her conclusion, then, forms an effective ending for her paper.

Exercise 2.4

Read the essays by Datus Proper and Judith Ortiz Cofer in Chapter 5 and draw a structure for each. What did you draw? How effectively does your drawing represent the structure for each? What do your drawings suggest to you about potential structures for your own writing?

WRITING STRATEGY

Beating the Dreaded Writer's Block

Sometimes you'll get stuck while writing, and no matter how long you stare at the page or computer monitor before you, the words just won't come. How to get unstuck? Try any of these:

1. Go back to the beginning of your essay and read through to your stuck point.
2. Look back at your focus statement to see how much of it you've developed and what's next.
3. Use invention techniques—brainstorm, freewrite, cluster, visualize, ask questions.
4. Freewrite about why you're stuck—what you want the essay to do, where you want it to go, why you can't seem to get there.
5. Map your essay—where you began, where you think you are, where you think you want to go. Then write about how you can get to your destination.
6. Talk it out with your roommate, a classmate, or your instructor. Email a friend or your instructor and ask for a response.
7. Read something related to your topic.
8. Take a break—walk the dog, throw a load of clothes in the washer, mow the lawn, make a grocery list, fix a glass of iced tea, watch a couple of innings of a baseball game. Sometimes a short break can help you refocus when you return to your writing.
9. Let it sit for a day. If all else fails, then leave your writing alone for at least twenty-four hours. This is especially helpful if you're tired.

Judy Cotton, "Crossing the Desert" (detail), 2000. Encaustic on panel, 48 × 127 in. Courtesy James Graham & Sons, New York, NY.

CHAPTER 3

Revising

The myth: The writer sits down, turns on the faucet, and writing pours out—clean, graceful, correct, ready for the printer.

The reality: The writer gets something—anything—down on paper, reads it, tries it again, rereads, rewrites, again and again.

Donald M. Murray, *The Craft of Revision*

What does it mean to revise a piece of writing? It means rethinking, reviewing, reseeing, and reconsidering what you have placed on the page. It means looking at each aspect of the paper, from its purpose to individual words, sentences, and paragraphs. It means reworking the paper you have written, whether you change only a word or two or start your writing process all over again with an entirely new topic. Ultimately, your goal in revising is to make sure that you have said to your reader what you intended to say.

Don Murray is absolutely right—the reality of writing is that the writer must revise. Revising is one of the most important parts of the writing process, so important that many composition instructors will tell you that writing is revising, that in order to write successfully the writer must rewrite. When you revise, you must be ruthless, ready to cut out and throw away what must be cut and thrown. It may be hard for you to eliminate words you struggled to find and whole paragraphs you labored to write, but if those words and paragraphs don't fit, they have to go—you have to give them up.

COMPUTER TIP

ADDING, DELETING, AND MOVING TEXT AROUND

One of the advantages of computers is that they make revising easy. To add text, you simply place the cursor at the appropriate location, make sure the Insert function is on (if necessary), and then type in the additional text. You can also add text by typing entire paragraphs or sections in a different file and then using the Insert function to combine the two files. You can move existing paragraphs or sections from one place to another by using the Copy function. And you can delete words, sentences, and paragraphs by highlighting them and then pressing the Delete key. ✦

Even the best writers must learn to delete lengthy passages that aren't working to achieve their purposes. For example, in one part of a manuscript he was working on, Aldous Huxley (author of *Brave New World*) scratched out an entire passage three paragraphs long and began a revision of it in the margin, but scratched that out, too.

James Jones (author of *From Here to Eternity*) had a different revision problem. An original passage from one of Jones's novels read:

> Solid and dense, sweeping away to the foothills in the distance, it might have been an ancient avalanche of green lava which had rolled down from some volcano to form this flat-topped plateau a hundred feet high.

The revised version reads this way:

> Solid and dense, sweeping away to the foothills in the distance, it might have been an ancient green lava flow laid down by some volcano centuries ago to form this flat-topped plateau a hundred feet high.

Jones made few revisions in this sentence, but those he made strengthened the sentence and thereby the entire passage in which it appears. Consider the change in the verb "rolled." Jones listed four choices in the margin before he decided to change "rolled" to "laid." By choosing "laid," he attributed an active role to the volcano—the lava didn't merely flow from it; instead, the volcano assumed a life of its own and laid the lava down to form the plateau. It's important to note that Jones didn't stop while writing to find the right term but returned to the draft to work on it only after he had gotten his thoughts down on the page.

These two examples illustrate two approaches to revision. Huxley engaged in what we may call global revision—that is, revision of fairly extensive proportions. Global revision may involve such activities as reorganizing an entire piece of writing, considering the development of ideas as a whole, or, as Huxley did, discarding a lengthy passage and starting over again. Jones engaged in local revision, that is, revision of smaller details. Local revision may involve working with individual sentences, working with diction (individual word choice), as Jones did in the second example, or editing. Your focus in revision, whether global or local, will be on strengthening your writing, on deciding whether to rework longer passages, perhaps even the entire essay, or to reconsider individual word choice to ensure that you present your reader with the right word rather than one that is almost right.

Global and local revision may take place at any point in the writing process, but global revisions tend to be made relatively early on. A typical writing process may resemble the following scenario: Following some prewriting, the writer composes a first draft—a discovery draft—and puts it aside for a short while to get some distance from it. She returns to the draft and reads it, probably making a few local revisions, tinkering with a sentence here, a word there, perhaps correcting a misspelled word or two. She then sets the draft aside for a longer period, perhaps as long as an entire day. Next, she considers global revisions—matters of overall meaning and structure, for example—to produce a second draft. She repeats this process with the second draft, getting a little distance before considering local revisions and then more distance before attempting global revisions. She continues this process until she completes the draft.

We need to say again that, in practice, you cannot separate global and local revision. We have separated them in our discussion to encourage you to be sure to incorporate global revision in your process. All too often, the only kind of revision that takes place is local. Unless you are an exceptional writer, failure to consider global revision will undermine the quality of your writing.

To help you work through both kinds of revision, we present several strategies that focus on these specific aspects of revision: distance, meaning, audience, structure, sentences, words, and peer review.

REVISING STRATEGIES

Getting Distance

To begin revising, get some distance from your writing. When a writer rewrites immediately after completing a draft, he more often than not reads what he intended to write rather than what he actually wrote. To help you guard against this tendency, we offer the following advice:

1. Finish the paper at least two days before its due date. Meeting this deadline will require you to have the discipline to begin your writing well ahead of time to avoid the "night before the due date" rush to write the entire paper.
2. Once you have completed it, set the paper aside for at least a day before you turn to revising it.
3. After that period passes, read the paper at least twice. The first time through, read without marking anything in your draft. Take the time to review your writing as a whole before considering reworking its parts. The second time through, mark places in the paper that you think are particularly strong as well as those that you think may need work.
4. Read the paper aloud. Reading aloud will cause you to slow your reading down so that you will have a better chance to find places that need work.
5. Focus first on broader concerns—whether the meaning you intended is clear and well supported, whether you have written for your audience, whether the overall structure of the paper and the structure of each paragraph provide an effective framework for your ideas.

6. Focus next on matters of style and diction—whether each sentence effectively represents your thinking, whether each word carries the precise meaning it should.

Revising for Meaning (Global)

You already have good starting points for considering whether your paper says what you meant in your focus statement and your thesis sentence, both of which make promises to the reader (see Chapter 2). Your job at this point is to decide what promises you made and how well you kept them. As you think about your paper's content, write a short response to each of these questions:

1. What is the purpose of your paper?
2. What parts of the paper develop that purpose? How do they do so?
3. Are there any parts of the paper that do not specifically develop your purpose? If so, what will you need to do to remedy this (e.g., add more detail to those parts or simply delete them)?
4. What details have you provided to support your purpose?
5. Identify your thesis sentence. What promises does it make? Point to places in the paper that have kept those promises. How effectively have you kept your promises to the reader?
6. What are the major points you wanted to make to support your thesis sentence? Which of these have you made? Which have you not made? If there are points you haven't made, do you need to add them, or will your paper stand without them?
7. What is the significance you want your writing to carry? How clearly does this significance come through? What parts of the paper keep it obscured or hidden? What do you need to do to clarify the significance you intended?

Steve Duran, a first-year writing student at NMSU, wrote this assessment of his essay "The Intricacies of an Idiot," an evaluation of Homer Simpson as a funny cartoon character. Although he didn't write in strict response to the questions above, Steve nonetheless addressed most of them.

> The purpose of my essay is to evaluate why I think Homer Simpson is the most entertaining cartoon character on TV. I believe my paper gives good examples of the intricacies of this particular idiot, although to truly understand why Homer is so funny, one must watch the show. That is another goal of this paper; to get an Anti-Simpsonite to watch the show and laugh at one man's stupidity. It's great fun. I think the introduction is a good description of Homer and different views of him. The conclusion shows that although Homer is insanely incompetent, it is funny because somehow he comes out on top. He gets through life on dumb luck, and sometimes we can all use luck instead of skill (i.e., pulling a Homer). I believe the part of the audience that still doesn't like Homer might not understand my concluding sentence, my semi-idolization of Mr. Simpson.

I couldn't come up with any blanket criteria about what makes all cartoon characters funny, so my criteria was basically any reason why I think Homer is funny. I used many quotes from different shows, although there are so many different episodes that I couldn't include (or remember) all that I would like to have included in this paper. Many of the situations that I think are just hilarious would not have been good to include in this paper because they are either all in the animation, or are too complicated to write in less than forty pages. I hope I used quotes and situations that accurately show Homer's stupidity and comedic value. But, alas, I am a biased writer, so pretty much everything involving Homer is funny as hell to me.

The language I used was hopefully humorous and descriptive. The language will be good for those who watch the Simpsons, but I am not sure about how well the language fits the non-Simpsons watching audience. I tried to relate it to them, but I'm not sure how well I did that. (I have a friend in Texas who doesn't like Homer or the rest of the Simpsons, and I tried to aim this paper at her, to convince her that the Simpsons are worth watching.) I think my language is good for my purpose, if it is descriptive and funny enough.

I already gave my paper a title after the discovery draft. I like using a big word like "intricacy" with a smaller word that also starts with an "I," "idiot." It shows exactly what Homer is like. He is an idiot, yet he tries to be smart. Although, it was very hard trying to find all kinds of different words for "stupidity." (As I am writing this, I just remembered a perfect example of one of Homer's funniest moments. So, I am going to add something, and print out yet another draft of this paper.)

Steve discovered something very important from writing this statement—he remembered another example that would support his analysis of Homer Simpson, so he stopped his assessment and returned to his essay to add the example. As Steve's experience illustrates, revision can occur at any point during the writing process, even when the writer thinks he's finished.

Revising for Audience (Global)

Earlier, we advised you to pick an initial or tentative audience for your paper and use that audience to help provide direction for your discovery draft. As you revise that draft and continue writing, you need to give greater attention to audience. You can gain much insight into the form and details of your paper by clarifying who your reader will be. Begin to do so by writing about your audience in response to such questions as these:

> Who are your intended readers? Who would benefit from reading your paper?
> What are these readers' tendencies in matters of politics and social beliefs?
> What social class(es) do your readers come from?
> Where do your readers live—in one particular region or type of community (e.g., rural, urban, or somewhere else)?

What kinds of work might your readers do?
What types of reading do your readers do? What magazines, books, or newspapers might they be familiar with?
What kinds of issues might particularly concern your readers?

Although this list is not exhaustive, these questions can help you begin to define your audience. And with this initial understanding of your readers, you can begin to develop the kinds of information you need to use in your writing. The better you understand your readers, the better your chance at presenting them with an effective piece of writing.

For an essay entitled "Vim," which details her positive experiences with yoga, Marisol Vargas wrote this initial definition of audience:

> My audience will be a group of people who wonder how I can get up so early to go to yoga. They already will know a little about this exercise from others, but have never experienced it, or heard a detailed description. They are open-minded about yoga and are likely to respond to its effectiveness. How it combines mind, body, and soul.

Because she assumed a receptive audience, Marisol shaped her draft as more of an informative than an argumentative essay, relying on specific examples to develop an assertion that yoga is an effective exercise because it's holistic, focusing on "mind, body, and soul."

Once you have defined your audience, respond to these questions about your paper and your readers:

1. What do you want your readers to understand or gain from reading your paper?
2. What attitudes are your readers likely to have toward your topic? What aspects of those attitudes have you addressed in your paper?
3. What do your readers already know about your topic? What do they need to know?
4. What questions will your readers have about your topic? How effectively have you answered them?
5. What particular action do you want your readers to take, if any? Is your writing compelling enough to make them want to take this action? Why or why not?
6. Is there any part of your paper in which your readers may disagree with your thinking? If so, how effectively have you prepared them for this material?
7. Is there any aspect of your paper that is likely to surprise your readers? If so, does this surprise serve your purpose? If not, how may you more effectively prepare your readers for this material?

After completing a draft, Marisol wrote this response to the questions:

> 1. I want my reader to gain a better understanding of yoga and how its combinations are effective.

2. My reader has a positive attitude and is open-minded about this exercise.
3. My reader only knows what he has heard secondhand. He knows a little about the yoga postures, but needs clarification on how they work and their benefits.
4. My reader will wonder how it has affected me as well as how it can help with ailments.
5. I would like my reader to go to a yoga class; my thoughts are too jumbled to be clear.
6. Since my reader is open-minded, he won't reject the information given to him.
7. The meditation contemplation may be a surprise. I think explaining it fully will help him to better understand this concept.

Three points derive from this second analysis:

1. Marisol's realization that she needed to clarify yoga's postures for the reader (3) led her to add detail to her discussion of those postures as she moved from her rough draft to her final draft.
2. Her statement "my thoughts are too jumbled to be clear" (5) was important; Marisol identified a problem in her paper and revised accordingly.
3. Marisol's understanding that the reader could be surprised by the "meditation contemplation" aspect of yoga (7) led her to make sure to provide enough detail so that the reader would understand it.

If you can, get someone to assume the role of an intended reader and to read from that perspective. Ask this person to point to places in your draft that work as well as to those that do not. Having an outside reader—someone other than yourself or your teacher—can help you identify which parts of your writing you can keep and which you need to rework.

Revising for Structure (Global)

In Chapter 2, we talked about paragraph cohesion. The structure of your writing sends important messages to your readers. As you look at the overall structure and how the various parts of your essay fit, consider such questions as these:

1. What shape did you intend for your paper? Did you draw it? If so, how effectively does the paper follow that shape? If you didn't draw it, do so now. Does this shape seem appropriate for your purpose and audience? Why or why not?
2. What transitional words and phrases have you used to move the reader smoothly through the paper? How effectively have you used them?
3. How unified and coherent is the paper overall? How well does it develop one primary point? How effectively does each paragraph develop that point? Are there any paragraphs that do not develop the point? If you need to keep such paragraphs, what do you need to do to ensure that they develop part of the paper's purpose?

4. In what order have you presented your support? Have you presented your strongest or most important first? Last? How effective is this order likely to be? Why?

> ## Computer Tip
>
> Your computer has functions that help with global revisions, such as
>
> *Cut and Paste*: move blocks of text around in your essay
> *Insert*: add text from another file
> *Delete*: highlight and delete portions of text that must be cut out
>
> Be sure to provide a transition that ties any moved or inserted text tightly to the rest of the essay. ✦

Revising for Words (Local)

Each word you use should be chosen carefully. First consider your readers. Who constitutes your projected audience? What kind of language (e.g., formal or informal) would be appropriate for them? Consider also your topic. If you're writing about a serious topic, then your language will probably be more formal than colloquial. The diction you choose—the language you use—will depend on your purpose, topic, and audience.

Finding the right word for a given situation will often involve choosing one word from three or four that are very close in meaning. For example, you could characterize a conversation between two people as "conversing," "talking," or "chatting," since these three words have relatively similar meanings. And these are not the only possible choices, of course. Depending on the situation and your purposes in writing about the conversation, you could also use such words or phrases as "confab," "powwow," "meeting of the minds," "tête-à-tête," and "dialogue" to represent what is taking place between the two people. So how do you choose? If you have a firm grasp of the various subtle differences in meaning that careful and skilled readers will take from these words, you can make the proper choice to convey your intended meaning. The differences are, to be sure, subtle, but they do exist. For example, as we move from "conversing" to "talking" and then to "chatting," there is a movement from somewhat formal to informal to very informal. We *converse* with important people in important situations, but we usually don't *converse* with friends in a bar.

We see other subtle differences in meaning when we look at the second group of words. In "confab," "powwow," and "tête-à-tête," there is some hint that the matter being talked about is a problem or issue of some sort. But "confab" implies that the two parties communicating are working together toward the resolution of the problem for the issue. Thus, if you and a friend are trying to decide how best to get your roommate to clean up the bathroom, you might have a *confab* about the matter. Both "tête-à-tête" and "powwow," however, allow for some possible conflict, as might happen when the two people on either side of an issue meet with each other. Thus, if you talk with your roommate directly about the issue, the two of you might have a *tête-à-tête* or a *powwow*. Note that even though the element of conflict is here, there is also a very strong sense that you and your roommate are talking to each other and hearing each other. To have a *tête-à-tête* or a *powwow* about an issue is very different from having a *confrontation* about the issue.

Denotation and Connotation   These examples lead us to two terms that you're probably already familiar with, *denotation* and *connotation*. If so, you know that the denotative meaning of a word is the meaning found in a dictionary, whereas the connotative meaning is the meaning we associate with a word because of the various situations, or contexts, in which we have encountered that word. The connotative meanings of words often reveal the writer's attitude toward a person or situation. For example, if you receive a gift that didn't cost very much and you're not happy with it, you may refer to it as "cheap." However, if you like the gift, you may deem it "inexpensive." A person who is careful with her money is "frugal," if you like her, "cheap" or "tight" if you don't. If a person is on your side in a negotiation, he is "firm" or "resolute"; if not, he is "obdurate" or even "pigheaded."

If you look some of these words up in a dictionary, you will find that what we are calling a connotative meaning has made its way into the dictionary definition as a third or fourth possible meaning for the word. This makes us face two important facts: First, language is always changing, though that change tends to be very slow. Second, the line between a word's denotation and connotation is sometimes difficult to draw.

Exercise 3.1

1. For each of the sets of words below, state what you see as the shared denotative meaning. Then, determine which words you would label positive, which neutral, and which negative. On what do you base your labeling? Write sentences that cause readers to see the words as you do. In addition to these positive/negative differences, what other differences do you see between these words? Are these additional differences denotative, connotative, or both?

   thin, scrawny, lean, gaunt, slender, lanky, scraggy

   rash, heady, impetuous, hasty

2. For each of the words below, develop a set of synonyms. Then, rank your words from most positive to most negative. If you were to use each word to describe someone or something, how would your attitude toward that person or thing change as your language changed?

   lazy, small, satirical, sweet, large, motive, feisty

General and Specific As you examine the words you choose, think about who you are writing for—and why. That will help you decide just how specific your writing needs to be. If you are writing an informal email response to a friend who has written to ask what you did this weekend, it may be perfectly appropriate to respond with "the usual stuff." Assuming your friend knows you (and your weekend rituals) very well, this language may tell her all she needs to know. But in a more formal writing situation, more care in word selection will be needed. After all, "reading novels in your residence hall," "visiting your parents," "going to a football game," and "attending an opera" could all fall under this very general category of "stuff." As you revise your essays, look for this kind of vague language— nouns such as "something," "thing," and "stuff," adjectives such as "nice," "big," and "lovely"—and decide whether you should be more specific, and if so, what words will more clearly convey your meaning to the readers of your essay.

Technical Language and Jargon Using jargon can keep readers from understanding what you're trying to tell them. Of course, there are situations in which technical language (*jargon* is the term people usually use when they believe language is too technical or obscure) is perfectly appropriate, even helpful. The more we know and can assume our readers know about a given topic, the more shortcuts technical language affords us. Individuals trained in language studies find it very hard to converse with one another without such terms as "clause," "t-unit," "free-modifier," and "modality." Those in health care could not do their work without such terms as "cardiovascular system," "CAT scan," "EKG," and "PET." Individuals trained in computer science find useful such terms as "modem," "bit," "byte," "ROM," and "RAM."

We must keep in mind, however, that one person's technical language is another person's jargon. Shortcuts do not help those who do not have the knowledge to understand the shortcuts. And there is another potential problem with jargon. People often use technical language to make their writing sound more impressive than it would had they used ordinary language. As you examine your language, ask yourself whether you need the technical language you are employing. For example, don't use such language as "personal communication device" when "cell phone" is what you mean. However, if you're talking not just about cell phones, but about cordless phones, beepers, and room monitors for infants, as well as cell phones, then "personal communication device" may, in fact, be the technical term you need to convey your meaning.

Clichés and Trite Expressions If you don't step lively, clichés and trite language can undercut and undermine your written expressions to the point that when you come up for air, you find that your writing products are on their last legs, or to put the matter more correctly, that they are, in fact, deader than a doornail, so dead that they literally smell to high heaven. Okay, you get the point. This is bad writing. But why? And what exactly is a cliché? What makes writing trite? Let's start with triteness. When we say something is trite, we mean that it is absolutely predictable. It's as if the writer is no longer really thinking about what he is saying—he is just letting one word dredge up the next. In fact, trite writing often makes use of parallelism and items in a series. Look at the first sentence in this section: *undercut and undermine*. Why do we need both of these words? What does the second add to the first, other than a sense of rhythm and flow? w*ritten expressions*—Why not "writing"? *written products*—Why not "writing"?

Now let's turn to clichés. At their core, clichés are often examples of metaphor. In the passage above, we are comparing a writer to someone who is literally walking or running ("stepping lively"); we are comparing clichés and trite language to forces of nature or to humans, a thing or a person that could be said to undercut and undermine some other thing. Literally to undercut or undermine is to get underneath something in such a fashion as to take its foundation away from it. And there's much more here—*coming up for air, last legs, deader than a doornail, smell to high heaven*. You may have been encouraged to enliven your writing with metaphors. Why, then, should the writer avoid clichés, when, in fact, they are often so metaphorical? The guiding principles are originality and accuracy. First, ask yourself if your metaphorical language is original. If you're using metaphors that you've heard over and over, your reader would probably rather hear what you have to say in your own words. Then ask whether your metaphors create humor. If they do and if you're not attempting to write a humorous piece, then you may want to find more exact and original language.

In looking at the words you have chosen to represent your thinking, consider such questions as these:

1. How vivid is the detail that you have presented to your reader? Are there are any bland or overused words or metaphors that don't convey your thinking clearly?
2. How accurate is the language you have used? How accurately have you interpreted events or data?

Revising for Sentences (Local)

A large part of the meaning in any writing comes about as the result of the ways in which we put words together into sentences. Let's begin with a simple sentence:

> The firefighter slumped into her bunk at the end of a long run.

Clear enough, right? We have an image of a firefighter who is tired after having fought a fire for quite a while (the "long run"). But let's add the word "exhausted" to the sentence. Where may we place it? These are some possibilities:

> Exhausted, the firefighter slumped into her bunk at the end of a long run.
>
> The exhausted firefighter slumped into her bunk at the end of a long run.
>
> The firefighter, exhausted, slumped into her bunk at the end of a long run.
>
> The firefighter slumped, exhausted, into her bunk at the end of a long run.
>
> The firefighter slumped into her bunk, exhausted at the end of a long run.
>
> The firefighter slumped into her bunk at the end of a long run, exhausted.

What's the effect of moving that single word "exhausted" to different positions in the sentence? Which sentence has more emphasis? (We would argue it's the first, because we're focused immediately on the firefighter's state of tiredness.) Which is least emphatic? (Probably the second, because there "exhausted" is in the usual position for an adjective, the one that draws least attention to it.) Clearly, this example shows that part of the meaning of any sentence comes from how the writer puts words together to form that sentence.

Combining Sentences   Just as the arrangement of words within a sentence contributes to the meaning of that sentence, the way we put sentences together affects the meaning of those sentences. To see what we mean, consider the meaning of these two sentences:

>That Studebaker pickup has a lot of character.
>
>It has a lot of dings from hard use.

Each of these sentences conveys a meaning to us. We are saying something positive about the truck in the first sentence—it may be old, but it's a good kind of old. In the second sentence, we're saying something about the condition of the truck's body—it has dents in it, perhaps from rocks, doors of other vehicles, or shopping carts hitting it. About the only relationship we can assume is that the two sentences refer to the same thing, an old Studebaker pickup. But if we combine the two sentences, we begin to build more comprehensive meaning. Consider these combinations:

1. That Studebaker pickup has a lot of character; it has a lot of dings from hard use.
2. Even though that Studebaker pickup has a lot of character, it has a lot of dings from hard use.
3. Its many dings from hard use give that Studebaker pickup a lot of character.

How does the meaning of each sentence differ? Sentence 1 presents the dings as neutral, as simply part of the truck's description. Sentence 2 presents the dings as negative, as part of the truck that works against its character and, probably, its value. Sentence 3 presents the dings in a more positive light, as things that contribute to the truck's character.

Now let's look at the various techniques we used to combine the original sentences. Sentence 1 represents a joining of the two original sentences through *coordination*; that is, the two original sentences are presented as having equal status. We show such status through punctuation (the semicolon is used most often to join two independent clauses or sentences) and through coordinating conjunctions (*and, but, yet, or, for, nor, so*—That old truck has character, *and* it has a lot of dings. That old truck has character, *but* it has a lot of dings).

If we want to show that one of the sentences is more important than the other, we use *subordination*. There are two types of subordination. In the first, we transform one of the sentences (the one we want to make of lesser importance) into a subordinate or dependent clause. Thus, the sentence "It has a lot of dings from hard use" becomes "Because it has a lot of dings from hard use." To change a sentence into a subordinate clause, we introduce that sentence by means of a subordinating conjunction. Below are some of the common subordinating conjunctions:

after	before	now that	until
although	even though	since	when, whenever
as far as	how	so that	where, wherever
as soon as	if	though	whether
as if	in that	till	while
because	insofar as	unless	

Note that the subordinated clause may precede the main clause, as in sentence 2 above, or it may come after the main clause: "That Studebaker pickup has a lot of character, because it has a lot of dings from hard use."

A second type of subordination involves putting one sentence inside another one—a process called embedding. We see this technique at work in sentence 3 above, "The fact that it has a lot of dings from hard use gives that Studebaker pickup a lot of character." Embedding enables the writer to insert a major component of one sentence into another, with the inserted element becoming so integral to the new sentence that removing it would destroy the new sentence. There are many reasons for using embedded structures, but a simple explanation would be to say that they allow the writer to move her writing at a much faster pace. Rather than saying that the truck had character and that it had dings, we can make both assertions at the same time. Of course, as we noted above, we are also implying that the dings are part of the reason for the truck's character.

As you become efficient at combining sentences, your sentences will tend to become longer. This is not to say that a longer sentence is better than a short one. There are times when a very short sentence, usually in the company of several long sentences, adds tremendous power to one's writing. But, in general as your writing style improves, your sentences will become longer and more varied in structure.

Exercise 3.2

Combine the following pairs of sentences using the principles of coordination and subordination (including embedding). How does the meaning of each new sentence you create change depending on how you combine the original sentences?

1. The boy ran from the house at full speed. His sister chased after him.
2. The mayor lost her bid for reelection. She ran a campaign without using negative advertising.

Cumulative and Periodic Two additional sentence strategies are the *cumulative sentence* and the *periodic sentence*:

Cumulative
The man and woman sat at the red light in complete resignation, his hands still dirty from a long day's work, her back still bent from hours of stooping to pick row after row of beans.

Periodic
His hands still dirty after a long day's work, her back still bent from hours of stooping to pick row after row of beans, the man and woman sat at the red light in complete resignation.

As these sentences illustrate, the cumulative sentence presents the sentence's main idea at or very near the beginning—the man and woman sat in complete resignation—and then adds supporting detail so as to build as complete an image as the writer intends. Standing opposite the cumulative sentence, the periodic sentence withholds its main idea until the end. Presenting supporting details before arriving at that main idea, the periodic sentence causes the reader to hold those details in mind till the writer reveals her primary point. Thus, periodic sentences create a kind of suspense or anticipation in the reader.

Three key elements characterize both cumulative and periodic sentences: *participial phrases* (that is, *-ing* or *-ed* phrases), *appositives,* and *absolutes.* These words may sound complicated, but the processes they refer to are not. In creating a participial phrase, you simply incorporate a sentence with an *-ing* or *-ed* verb into another sentence:

The man stayed up all night.

The man was listening to the jazz musicians.

becomes

The man stayed up all night listening to the jazz musicians.

or

Listening to the jazz musicians, the man stayed up all night.

The *appositive* is one of the most useful tools you can employ in your writing. It provides you the opportunity to rename some word or phrase in a sentence and then add more detail about this word or phrase. In the following examples, the appositive is in bold, and the word the appositive renames is underlined.

Franco gave the keys to the boy.

The boy was a small figure.

He was seen against the overwhelming massiveness of a truck.

He was about to drive the truck.

becomes

Franco gave the keys to the boy, a small **figure** seen against the overwhelming massiveness of the truck he was about to drive.

The School Board President gave Jenny a prize.

She was the last person so honored in that old high school.

becomes

The last **person** so honored in that old high school, Jenny was given a prize by the School Board President.

The last strategy we'll discuss here is the *absolute phrase*. An absolute structure is a combination of one independent sentence and a second assertion that is made by a subject and a verbal—a present or past participle. This sounds much more complicated than it is. Consider these examples:

His hands were waving frantically.

Federico approached the car hurriedly.

becomes

His hands waving frantically, Federico approached the car hurriedly.

In this example, the verbal is a present participle, the *-ing* form of a verb. In an absolute phrase, which must have a subject and a participle, some comment is made on some aspect of the information in the main part of the sentence. As an illustration, in the examples below the subjects are in bold and the participles (in this case, past participles) are underlined.

Their **hopes** dashed, the members of the team left the arena.

They seemed ashamed, **eyes** fastened on the ground.

Exercise 3.3

Below are several model sentences formed by using the strategies just presented. Under each of these models is a series of sentences that can be combined to form a sentence with the structure of the model sentence. Produce that sentence. Then create a sentence of your own with the same structure.

1. One of my favorite teachers, a choral director, died recently.

    The man ran to help the boy.

    The man was large.

    The man was a firefighter.

2. Eyes darting, nostrils sniffing the air, the deer stood frozen in the clearing.

   His legs were pumping.

   His lungs were gasping for air.

   The cyclist seemed fixed in his determination.

3. Her hands gesturing gently in the air, my grandmother told her story.

   The fire truck's siren pierced the silence.

   The fire truck rounded the corner.

4. They last saw him on Friday, swimming fearlessly in the high waves and waving to them in utter glee.

   The mayor arrived at noon.

   The mayor was shaking hands with everyone in sight.

   The mayor was kissing every baby he could find.

In looking at your sentences, consider such questions as these:

1. How long are your sentences? In a given paragraph, what is the longest sentence? The shortest? If all of your sentences are approximately the same length, how might you combine sentences to vary the length?
2. How much sentence variety is at work? Do you rely too heavily on sentences that consist of only one simple clause with a subject and verb? Do you make use of introductory phrases and clauses and a variety of sentence types? How might you combine sentences to create more variety in your writing?
3. Identify any sentence fragments in your paper. Did you intend to write each one for emphasis? How effective is each intended fragment?
4. What kinds of transitions do you use between sentences?

The following revision of a paragraph by Chris Miller deals primarily with sentences and words. In the essay from which this paragraph is taken, Chris talks about the problem of cyclists riding on sidewalks at New Mexico State University. This particular paragraph offers discussion of a similar problem and an attempted solution to it. First, we present the paragraph as it appeared in Chris's paper; next, we see how it was revised during a whole-class discussion of revision; finally, we offer the revised paragraph.

> This has also been a problem in places other than college campuses. The city of Albuquerque, for example, recently had a problem with bicycles and pedestrians having accidents on sidewalks. Their solution to the problem was to ban all bicycles on its sidewalks. This ended up causing more problems and accidents than it solved. The people who still ride their bikes are left with two choices: ride on the sidewalk and break the law, or ride in the street with the cars. The ones

who ride on the sidewalk are stopped by the police and even ticketed. The ones who ride in the street are put in a much greater danger than accidents with pedestrians ever cause. Many of Albuquerque's streets have no bike lanes so the cyclists are forced to ride in the right hand lane. This has caused many accidents. Cars speed down the road going 45 or 50 m.p.h., not expecting to see a bike. If they turn a corner and suddenly there is one going 10 m.p.h. they can't do anything except swerve into the next lane and pray there isn't a car there. Unfortunately, many times there is a car there and they hit each other. It has happened time and time again. Cars have even hit the bikes. Since the onset of this law, the number of accidents has decreased, but the seriousness has increased. This is another example of a failed way to solve this problem.

Bill, Chris's teacher, photocopied the paragraph on an overhead transparency and, with Chris's permission, based a revision workshop on it. The sentences in the version below are numbered, to make discussion easier. To begin, we'll note that about half of the paragraph's sixteen sentences consist of one simple clause with only one subject and finite verb (sentences 1, 2, 3, 9, 10, 13, 14, and 16).

Following an initial reading, the students in the class made these comments on the paragraph:

1. It's wordy. What's said here can be said more concisely. Try to tighten things up.
2. It plods along; it has too much of the same kind of sentence structure. Try some sentence combining to make it read more smoothly.
3. The language seems a little bland in a couple of places. Think about verbs like "wreck" for "hit each other" in sentence 12. Try to cut such expressions as "there are" and "this is" if you can.
4. The paragraph has a few grammatical errors in it that need fixing, including a problem with parallelism (sentence 5), a couple of comma errors (8 and 12), and a dangling modifier (sentence 10).

With these comments as a guide, the class revised the paragraph. The handwritten annotations in the following version are the revisions recommended by the class.

(1) This has also been a problem in places other than college campuses. (2) The city of Albuquerque, for example, recently had a problem with ~~bicycles and~~ pedestrians ~~having accidents~~ [cyclists running into] on sidewalks. (3) ~~Their~~ [Albuquerque's] solution to the problem ~~was~~ to ban all bicycles on ~~its~~ sidewalks. (4) ~~This ended up~~ caus[ed] more problems and accidents than it solved. (5) ~~The people who still ride their bikes are left with~~ [In effect, cyclists have] two choices: ride on the sidewalk and break the law, or ride in the street ~~with the cars~~ [and take their chances]. (6) ~~The ones~~ [Those] who ride on the sidewalk are stopped by the police and even ticketed, [but those] ~~(7) The ones~~ who ride in the street are ~~put in a~~ [in] much greater danger ~~than accidents with pedes~~

|| ism = parallelism problem
dm = dangling modifier
ℓ = delete indicated material

~~trians over cause.~~ (8) Many of Albuquerque's streets have no bike lanes, so the cyclists are forced to ride in the right hand lane, which ~~(9) This~~ has caused many accidents. (10) Cars ~~speed down the road going 45 or 50 m.p.h.~~ travel at a normal rate of speed, their drivers, dm not expecting to see a bike. (11) If they turn a corner and suddenly ~~there is~~ come up behind one going 10 m.p.h., they can't do anything except swerve ~~into the next lane~~ and pray ~~there isn't a car there.~~ for a clear lane (12) Unfortunately, many times ~~there is a~~ they meet another car ~~there~~ and they ~~hit each other.~~ crash ~~(13) It has happened time and time again.~~ (14) Cars have even hit the bikes. (15) Since the onset of this law, the number of accidents has decreased, but their seriousness has increased, ~~(16) This is~~ another example of ~~a failed way to solve the problem.~~ this solution's failure.

Here's a summary of the specific revisions the class suggested:

1. Reword sentence 2 to focus on cyclists hitting pedestrians—"cyclists and pedestrians having accidents" isn't as forceful or quite as accurate as "cyclists running into pedestrians."
2. Combine 3 and 4 to decrease wordiness; create emphasis by setting off the definition of the solution with dashes.
3. Open 5 with transition ("in effect"); use fewer words; clear up parallelism problem at the end of the sentence.
4. Combine 6 and 7; repeat "those" for emphasis; delete unnecessary words.
5. In 8, add comma after "lanes" to work with the coordinating conjunction "so" to clear up the comma error; combine 8 and 9 (9 becomes a relative clause subordinate to 8).
6. Add a subject ("drivers") to the participial phrase in 10 to clear up the dangling modifier ("dm")—cars can't expect to see a bike, but drivers can.
7. Reword 11 to delete repetition of "there"; set off introductory clause with a comma.
8. In 12, add a comma after "car" to work with the coordinating conjunction "and" to clear up the comma error; reword to delete repetition of "there."
9. Delete 13 because it really doesn't add much to the paragraph.
10. Combine 15 and 16; delete unnecessary words.

Here's a clean copy of the revised paragraph. This version has 11 sentences and a total of 198 words, compared to 240 words in the original version. It contains five simple sentences and six complex sentences. How effective do you think these revisions are? Why?

> This has also been a problem in places other than college campuses. The city of Albuquerque, for example, recently had a problem with cyclists running into pedestrians on sidewalks. Albuquerque's solution—to ban all bicycles on sidewalks—caused more problems and accidents than it solved. In effect, cyclists have two choices: ride on the sidewalk and break the law, or ride in the street and

take their chances. Those who ride on the sidewalk are stopped by police and even ticketed, but those who ride in the street are in much greater danger. Many of Albuquerque's streets have no bike lanes, so cyclists are forced to ride in the right hand lane, which has caused many accidents. Cars travel at a normal rate of speed, their drivers not expecting to see a bike. If they turn a corner and suddenly come up behind one going 10 m.p.h., they can't do anything except swerve and pray for a clear lane. Unfortunately, many times they meet another car, and they crash. Cars have even hit the bikes. Since the onset of this law, the number of accidents has decreased, but their seriousness has increased, another example of this solution's failure.

Peer Review (Global and Local)

In peer review, someone else reads your writing and comments constructively on it. At times, you'll be able to call on another writer or group of writers in the class for which you're writing. When this is the case, that person or group will be aware of your paper's context and so should be able to give you an idea of how well you have fulfilled the assignment. At other times, you may ask someone unfamiliar with the paper's context to review it for you. In either case, you have a responsibility to provide your reviewer with more than the paper itself. You should give your reviewer a quick assessment of how well you think the paper works and where you think there are trouble spots. To prepare this assessment, write a note to the reviewer in which you

1. state your intended purpose and audience,
2. identify those parts of the paper that you think work well, and
3. ask for help.

If you think there is a trouble spot in the paper but don't know quite how to fix it, then point to it and ask the reviewer to pay particular attention to that spot.

One principle to keep in mind concerning any form of peer review is that ultimately, you, the writer, are responsible for deciding which pieces of your reviewers' advice to heed and which to ignore. Your readers are expressing their opinions about your paper and offering support for them, but the final decision about how to revise your writing is yours to make.

Working One-on-One Working with another person one-on-one, you may each read the other's paper silently, paying attention to the writer's assessment (see above) and responding in writing to the parts that worked as well as to those that didn't. Next, you should talk through your reactions to the piece of writing, one at a time, focusing on both strengths and weaknesses. After such a peer-review session, your job is to consider your reviewer's comments and decide which ones you want to use to guide your revising.

Another one-on-one strategy requires each of you to read the other's paper aloud, so that the writer hears her words in someone else's voice. The writer listens but may not comment. As you read your partner's essay aloud, mark in the margins where you think the writing works and where it doesn't work, so that you and the writer may discuss these sections later. Once you've finished reading the paper, talk with the writer about the parts you've marked. The writer's role is to listen, to take notes, and to ask questions, but not to argue with your reading of the essay.

Working with a Group Working with a group of students in your writing class is a good way to get several opinions about your writing. To make this strategy work, groups need guidelines to follow. Your instructor may provide these guidelines, or she may prefer that you establish your own guidelines as a group. If you are creating your own guidelines, begin the process by discussing these basic principles for working successfully in a group:

1. *Attending group meetings.* Attendance is obviously crucial, since group meetings are not possible if the members don't attend.
2. *Being prepared.* If you don't have your rough draft ready for your group workshop, then you can't get the help you need.
3. *Being helpful, not hypercritical.* If your group is to work, you have to be willing to critique your peers' papers honestly. But all group members need to remember what we call the Golden Rule of Peer Criticism: Nobody says or does anything designed to hurt another person.
4. *Being receptive to group critiques.* Receiving criticism is also an important aspect of working with a group; you have to accept your group members' assessments of your work in the same spirit in which you critique their work. The ability to receive criticism is one you'll have to cultivate.

Your group may wish to incorporate these four principles, along with others you may devise, into a contract that each member helps to write and then signs. Should your group not function as well as you would like, consult with your instructor about how to make it work better.

Once you have the principles in place, you're ready for group sessions. It's important to structure these sessions carefully so that all writers receive the maximum benefit from them. To conduct a review session, follow these steps:

1. Before reading any of the essays of the group members, read through the directions your instructor provides. Your instructor may provide a critique sheet—a list of specific questions and directions to use in a review session—or may want you to develop your own. To do so, you may use several of the strategies for revision presented above and focus on the following aspects of a paper:
    a. *Purpose.* What is the essay's purpose? How effectively has the writer achieved it?
    b. *Strengths.* What is particularly effective about the paper? Identify at least two aspects of the essay that work well and tell the writer why you think they're effective.
    c. *Weaknesses.* What seems ineffective? Identify at least two places where the essay needs work and make specific suggestions for revision.

d. *Essay structure.* Identify the paper's beginning, middle, and end, describing what the writer has done in each section. How effective is each section? What makes it so? Make specific suggestions for revision.
   e. *Paragraph structure.* How effectively is each paragraph structured? Does each have a topic sentence? How effectively is that topic sentence supported? Make specific suggestions for revision.
   f. *Sentence structure.* How varied are the sentences (length, word order)? How effectively does each sentence fulfill the writer's purpose? How effectively has the writer used such devices as transition and repetition of key terms to create connections between and among sentences? Make specific suggestions for revision.
   g. *Details and word choice.* How effective are the details the writer has chosen? Are there specific words or phrases that don't support the writer's purpose? Make specific suggestions for revision.
   h. *Overall assessment.* When you've finished responding to the various parts of the paper, write a statement giving your final impressions of the paper, summarizing its strengths and offering the writer suggestions for improvement.
2. Read a given paper once without marking anything on it. Read it as a whole, paying attention to its impact on you. Then read it again, this time marking your responses to the critique sheet on the paper itself.
3. After this second reading, respond in writing to the various parts of the critique sheet.
4. When all the papers presented have been read and critiqued, talk with the writer. The writer's drafts are returned, along with all written criticism from the group, and then each group member tells the writer his or her impressions of the essay. The writer isn't to quibble or argue about these points but to consider them as attempts to be helpful.

Note that different instructors may suggest different group procedures. For example, Ron often has a writer distribute a copy of an essay to each group member and then read the paper aloud twice before the group begins work on it. During the first reading, group members simply listen. During the second reading, they make notes on the draft where there is something they want to discuss with the writer.

Each of these strategies is designed to provide a means for peers to offer you insights that might help make your paper better. But once you have their thoughts, what do you do with them? How much of the group's criticism do you use? Whatever you think is helpful. If a majority of your group members mark a place in the paper as needing work, then you should consider making revisions at that point. If only one member marks a place as needing work, you should consider that criticism as well, though it may not carry as much weight in your mind as it would if the majority had commented on that place. Remember that, ultimately, you are responsible for your writing, and decisions about what to revise and what to let stand are yours to make.

WRITER'S NOTEBOOK: RESPONDING TO READERS' COMMENTS

One of the best ways to respond to any spoken or written comments you may receive is to write about them in your writer's notebook. By reflecting on these comments in writing, you may come to understand better what they mean, and you can plan a way to use them, perhaps by taking notes toward revisions, perhaps by rejecting the advice they carry. Keep in mind that even though a reader makes a suggestion, you still own the piece of writing. That is, you, the writer, are responsible for the final draft that you submit. Before you decide not to use a piece of advice from a reader, however, try writing about it to make sure that you don't want or need to use it as you revise.

You may also write in response to any evaluative comments your teacher may make. In all likelihood, your teacher will write notes in your essay's margins (sometimes called "marginalia") calling your attention to aspects of your writing that are strong or that need work. He may also write a note after he's finished as a final wrap-up, a note that offers an evaluative overview or summary of your essay's effect on him as your reader. Write in response to such comments. If you don't understand part of the marginalia, make a note that you need clarification and ask for that clarification in a conference. If there's some part of the final comment by your teacher that you don't understand, write about it, again raising questions that you want to ask in a conference. Keep all your responses in your writer's notebook.

EDITING STRATEGIES

Although *editing* and *revising* are often used interchangeably, we make an important distinction between the two terms. *Revising* is a much broader term than is *editing*. In revision, you consider substantive changes to every aspect of your paper. Editing involves carefully proofreading and then making those final changes in grammar and mechanics (e.g., spelling and punctuation) that make for a finished product. Some successful proofreading strategies include reading backwards, spotlighting problems, and using a word processor.

Reading Backwards Often, writers read their best intentions instead of what they actually put on the page. To counteract this tendency, read each word from the last to the first, so that you read each out of its context.

Spotlighting Problems If you tend to make a particular grammatical or mechanical problem, then spotlight that problem during proofreading. If, for example, your instructor has called comma splices to your attention then look at every comma you use in your essay. If a comma separates two independent clauses without being accompanied by a coordinating conjunction, then you've committed a comma splice and need to decide how best to fix it. Or, if you tend to write sentence fragments that are relative clauses, then you need to look at every relative pronoun; if that pronoun opens a clause, then you need to make sure that the clause is attached to a sentence rather than standing alone.

Using a Word Processor One very effective tool for proofreading and editing is a word processor. You should always use the Spellcheck function before you submit a draft for peer review or to your instructor. A word of caution, though—spelling checkers aren't totally reliable because they don't check to make sure you've written the right word and they don't distinguish between homophones (words that sound alike but differ in meaning and sometimes in spelling). Here's a paragraph that a spelling checker considered correct:

> Its vary clear that the computer can bee a useful tool, butt you half two read draughts carefully too ensure their correct. Other ways, you mite assume you're draughts are all together finished and sew ready too bee handed inn for grating. How ever, you're teacher cud get the idea that you should of proof red a printed copy, to.

The Search function (sometimes known as Seek or Replace) can prove valuable for editing. If you have trouble with homophones, you may find each instance of these in your paper to make sure you have the right word. Common homophones include "to," "too," "two" and "there," "their," "they're." You can also use the Search command to help locate and correct grammatical problems. For instance, if you have a tendency to write dangling modifiers, you can type "ing" in the Search For box, because most dangling modifiers have an *-ing* verbal as part of their structure. Here's an example:

> While pitching wide to the trailing halfback, the ball popped loose and was recovered by the defense.

The dangler in this sentence is the introductory phrase "While pitching wide to the trailing halfback." In its position in the sentence, the introductory phrase must modify the sentence's subject, in this case, "ball." But the ball cannot pitch itself; someone (probably the quarterback) has to do the pitching. So the modifier (the introductory phrase) is said to dangle because it does not refer clearly to the subject. Here is one possible revision to correct this problem:

> While pitching wide to the trailing back, the quarterback was hit by a linebacker, and the ball popped loose, only to be recovered by the defense.

In this revised sentence, it is clear who was doing the pitching, so the introductory phrase no longer dangles. If you can identify each instance of an *-ing* verbal in your paper, then you have the chance to correct the ones that are dangling.

You can use the Search function to identify other problems with your writing that may need attention as well. If you tend to use such listless constructions as "There is" and "There are" in your writing, finding and replacing them will make your writing stronger. If you tend to overuse such verbs as "have" and "be" (including "to be," "been," "was," "is," "are," and "were"), find them and consider whether you can substitute a more lively verb. The Search function will facilitate your editing by enabling you to find quickly and easily every occurrence of a word or phrase that you know gives you trouble.

COMPUTER TIP

Your word-processing program offers you a wide range of features that will help you prepare a professional-looking manuscript.

HEADERS AND/OR FOOTERS

Use the Header/Footer command to create headers and/or footers. You may include an identifying label for your paper in a header or footer and continuous page numbers as well. A header for Marisol Vargas's essay might be one of these:

Vargas—p. 2
Vargas, "Mirror Image," 2
"Mirror Image"—p. 2.

MARGINS

The default margin of word processors is usually one inch for the top, bottom, and both sides. But you can change the margins if you need to. For instance, you'll want to change the left-hand margin if you need to inset a quotation that is more than four lines long.

FONTS

Word processors offer a number of fonts and type sizes. For your writing, you should select one of the common text fonts. Typical fonts for essays include Times New Roman, Courier, and Arial. You shouldn't use a fancier font, such as an Old English, or a script font, such as ShellyVolante, for your papers, though such fonts work well when you're creating a certificate or when you're trying to create a special effect in your paper. Also, select a point size (size of type) of either 10 or 12, as these are standard sizes. Use larger or smaller sizes only when you're trying to create a special effect.

Be sure your papers conform to the specifications your teacher requires for manuscript preparation. If you have any questions about format, consult your instructor. ✦

WRITING A SELF-ASSESSMENT

One way to become a better writer is to become a better reader of your own writing. To do so, you need to focus on your writing as both interested reader and critic. Writing a self-assessment requires you to step outside yourself as writer and read with a critic's eye. As you write this assessment, focus first on what you think to be strong in a given piece of your writing then on where you think your writing could be strengthened. The following checklist will help you assess your writing:

1. What is the purpose of your essay? To what extent does your draft fulfill that purpose? What revisions do you think will be necessary?
2. How well does the introduction work? What, specifically, did you intend the introduction to do? Is it appropriate for your audience and topic? If not, what should you do to make it appropriate?
3. How well does the conclusion work? What, specifically, did you intend the conclusion to do? Is it appropriate for your audience and topic? If not, what should you do to make it appropriate?
4. How appropriate is the language you've used in the paper? Is the tone appropriate for your audience and topic? If not, what should you do to make it appropriate?
5. What level of detail have you used? Are the words you've used concise and exact enough to convey your meaning? Are there any words that may cause difficulty for your readers or keep them from understanding your meaning?
6. What sentence strategies have you used? Are your sentences primarily all of one type (e.g., short or long, cumulative or periodic)? Is there enough variety in your sentences to keep your writing from being choppy?
7. Are your paragraphs unified and coherent? Does each paragraph develop some aspect of your thesis sentence?
8. What grammatical or mechanical errors do you see?
9. What title will you give your paper? What word, phrase, or sentence do you think will best represent your paper to your reader?
10. What parts of the essay gave you the most trouble? How did you solve these problems?

SAMPLE STUDENT PROCESS—REVISION

We'll continue working with Marisol's personal essay here, focusing on the revisions she made, particularly in light of advice she received from her writing group and from Bill, her teacher. Marisol began revising by reading back over her discovery draft, identifying parts she thought needed work, and then revising, producing the rough draft that follows. As you read this draft, identify three or four changes that Marisol made. How effective do you think they are? How much did she change the essay? Did she strengthen or weaken it? What's the basis for your response?

Rough Draft

The steady rhythm of my life changed when I went with my mother to feed the homeless.

Through this experience I learned not to take things for granted. For what may seem common to me, may be a luxury for another. It is this occurrence that stands out in my mind the most.

The stop light turned red and as the car slowed to a halt, I opened my eyes to my surroundings. I had been asleep for most of the journey and now the change in the car's momentum awakened me. As I looked around I noticed groups of people walking. The light turned green and we turned, heading in the same direction as the crowd.

"We're here," my mom said. I remember thinking that it wasn't as large as I expected. In front of us was a small grey building surrounded by an old chain-link fence. It reminded me of a warehouse.

This was the first time I had come with my mother to feed the homeless. She had asked me many times before but, because of the comfort of my bed in the early morning, I always declined. This time, however, I worked up the energy to go.

We got out of the car with casseroles and bags of fruits. As we walked toward the shelter, I felt as though everyone was watching us and I tried not to make eye contact. "Just look straight," was the only thought in my head.

We entered the building through narrow doors and went directly toward the kitchen, a small area hidden from the rest of the cafeteria. I helped some of the other volunteers warm the food that everyone had brought. I decided that if I stayed in the seclusion of the kitchen, I would be "safe."

Then we were called out to the dining area for a short breakfast prayer. I went out nervously. When it was over, I hurried to the kitchen and started to serve the food, but the volunteers had another job for me. They wanted me to go into the dining area and offer fruit to everyone. I am a shy person, so the thought of having to approach unfamiliar faces scared me.

As I filled up my dish, I prepared myself for the worst. I got up, clenched my fruit bowl and slowly walked out to the dining area. As I looked around, all of my foolish thoughts and fears diminished. Many people crowded around me waiting to get their fruit. They were very polite, thanking me with smiles and kind words. When the bowl was empty, I raced back into the kitchen to refill it and I hurried back out.

The room was filled with people of different gender and race. There were families, and single men and women. Outside there were people with animals. Watching the families was heart breaking. There were little girls whose dresses were loose from starvation and the stresses of living on the street. Their eyes resembled that of an older person, with lines of stressful days and sleepless nights.

As I walked outside one man caught my eye. He reminded me of Santa Claus, because of his sweet eyes and big rosy cheeks. "Sir, would you like some fruit," I asked. He looked at me and smiled bashfully. He looked down at his hands. He was holding coffee and an empty plate. He looked back at the fruit, wondering if he had room in his hands to carry it. He carefully took it into the hand that held his coffee. It spilt from his nervous, shaky movements. Then he thanked me and slowly walked away.

At that moment I realized how foolish I had been. Fear had kept me away so long. As I walked around I couldn't quite figure out what it was that I feared. The people I was looking at could have easily been a family member or me. I was lucky to have a comfortable bed to sleep in at night and wake up to in the morning. I couldn't imagine having to use a concrete sidewalk as my bed.

As we drove away that morning, I remember my mom saying, "I think we fed over a hundred people today." All I could do was think of the faces I had seen, and I realized how much they looked like me. 13

Marisol provided each member of her review group with a copy of this rough draft. Over two class meetings, group members read, marked, and responded to the questions on the following review sheet:

Follow these instructions in reviewing the essays from your group members: (1) Before you read any essays, read the questions below. (2) Read each essay through once without marking anything. (3) Read the essay again, this time marking places in the paper that you think are strong and that you think need work. (4) Using the markings from 3 as a guide, respond in writing to the questions below. (5) Talk about your reading of the essay with its author.

Above all else, remember the Golden Rule of Peer Review: Nobody says or does anything designed to hurt another person.

1. What event is the essay about?
2. What did the writer learn from having experienced the event; that is, what is the significance the writer sees in the event? How clearly does this significance come through? Make specific suggestions for revision.
3. Identify two places you think are particularly strong. What makes them strong?
4. Identify two places you think need work. What, specifically, should the writer do to strengthen these?
5. How effective is the detail the writer has written? On what do you base your assessment? If you see the need for revision, make specific suggestions to help the writer.
6. What is your overall assessment of the essay's effectiveness? Remember that your job is to help the writer make the essay better.

One group member commented:

1. The essay is about the time she went with her mother to feed the homeless.
2. She extinguishes any fear of the homeless she once had through this experience. Not quite sure what fear was (shyness, fear of them, etc.)? Might be helpful to expand on feelings of fear. Staying in kitchen—¶7—keeps her "safe" from what?
3. One great part is ¶11—the description of the "Santa Claus." She uses great imagery. Great description. Helped me see the man in my head. Another great part is the last sentence. If you do decide to expand closing, from my point of view the last sentence is a great closing thought.
4. A couple areas I would like to see more description is your time spent in kitchen away from homeless. More of your thoughts/images/actions. Why fearful. Maybe the conclusion and opening ¶s could be expanded. I would like it if opening, you worked way toward shelter. Maybe not come right out and state essay about feeding homeless. I love your usage of "steady rhythm of life" in the first sentence.
5. I loved the details you recalled about "Santa Claus." It would be great if you could talk about other people with that detail. Overall the detail used to describe things was good. I could get the picture in my head of this place.

6. The essay is very effective. It is a very positive reflection to read. Good essay to read even if you don't want to make any changes.

A second member commented:

1. About the time the author went to feed the homeless.
2. The writer learns not to take for granted the luxuries she has. I don't think it comes through very clear, though, because it seems to me that she learned more about humanizing the homeless, than really appreciating material objects. She learns not to fear them and that are just like you & me. very little writing is given to appreciating what she has.
3. I really like the last sentence of the 7th paragraph. It conveys the author's insecurities very well, and by putting "safe" in quotations it also shows how she feels those insecurities were silly, now. I also liked the first sentence, or rather the part I underlined. It starts off the essay with a bang. It says "this is an extremely important event in my life" and it makes you want to read on.
4. I think if the author really wants to convey the lesson of not taking things for granted, she should expand on this paragraph, but like I said it seems to me the greater lesson was humanizing the homeless.
5. Her detail is wonderful, I think. for example, the 11th paragraph about Santa Claus is detailed very well and I particularly liked the description of the little girls at the end of paragraph 10.
6. I believe it is an effective essay and she writes well and I've already harped on my one concern enough in comments 2 & 4.

These comments are typical of first reading sessions. You'll note that the readers are a bit reluctant to say very much that's openly critical, and they tend to overpraise the essay's effectiveness. This is not to say that Marisol's writing at this point isn't effective. Instead, we're saying that the essay, however much promise it may show, still is not a finished piece of writing. And both group members point to places that need revising.

Draft for Instructor Evaluation

Taking into consideration her group's advice, Marisol revised her rough draft, creating the essay that follows.

One Sunday morning my mother invited me to volunteer with her at a homeless shelter. Volunteering at a shelter taught me that no one can be excluded from poverty. It is not prejudice towards race, gender, or age. This realization changed the steady rhythm of my life. 1

The stop light turned red and as the car slowed to a halt, I opened my eyes to my surroundings. I had been asleep for most of the journey and now the change in the car's momentum awakened me. As I looked around I noticed groups of people walking. The light turned green and we turned, heading in the same direction as the crowd. "We're here," my mom said. I remember thinking that it wasn't as large as I expected. In front of us was a small, warehouse-like building surrounded by an old chain-link fence. 2

My mom and I unloaded casseroles and bags of fruits from the car. We entered the building through narrow doors and went directly toward the kitchen, a small area, secluded from the rest of the cafeteria. Our food was combined 3 with that of the other volunteers, making a diverse potluck. My first job was to help warm the food. Then we were called out to the dining room for a short breakfast prayer. I went out nervously, not knowing what to expect. When the prayer was over, I hurried to the kitchen and started to serve the food, but the volunteers had another job for me. They wanted me to go into the dining area and offer fruit to everyone.

As I filled up my dish, I prepared myself for my task. I got up, clenched my fruit bowl and slowly walked out to the dining area. Many people crowded around me waiting to get their fruit. They were very polite, thanking me with smiles and kind words.

The room was filled with people of different gender and race. There were families, and single men and women. Outside there were people with animals. There were little girls whose dresses were loose from starvation and the stresses of living on the street. Their eyes resembled that of an older person, with lines of stressful days and sleepless nights.

As I walked outside one man caught my eye. He reminded me of Santa Claus, because of his sweet eyes and big rosy cheeks. "Sir, would you like some fruit," I asked. He looked at me and smiled bashfully. He looked down at his hands. He was holding coffee and an empty plate. He looked back at the fruit, wondering if he had room in his hands to carry it. He carefully took it into the hand that held his coffee. He spilt from his nervous, shaky movements. Then he thanked me and slowly walked away.

Outside animals greeted me. There were beautiful dogs who seemed to be unaware of their misfortune. Some of the people took care of their animals' hunger before their own. One man had a litter of puppies that needed homes. He tried to convince me to take one with me. His puppies were playful and healthy. They seemed very content.

After breakfast was over, I helped the crew clean everything. It was then that I realized my fortune. I had a comfortable bed to sleep in at night and wake up to in the morning. I never had to be tortured by the rumbling growls of hunger in my stomach. I could not imagine having to use a concrete sidewalk as my bed or a cardboard box as my home.

As we drove away that morning, I remember my mom saying, "I think we fed over a hundred people today." All I could do was think of the faces I had seen, and I realized how much they were like mine.

Marisol submitted this draft to Bill for his evaluation. After he read it, Bill wrote this comment:

> Marisol—thanks for this essay. It's a quiet affirmation of you, and I appreciate your letting me see it. You need more; it needs to be longer so that the details become sharp and clear. Let's have a conference before you revise it.

The draft wasn't long enough to meet the minimum length requirement specified in the assignment (4–6 pages, 1,000–1,500 words), and it had some grammatical errors. The more important consideration was that Marisol hadn't provided enough detail for a reader to truly understand her feelings and her experience. In conference Bill suggested that she consider working with the introduction to detail her reluctance to go with her mother, and that throughout the essay she pay attention to these three words: detail, detail, detail. Marisol subsequently submitted this revised final draft of her essay.

Revised Final Draft

MARISOL VARGAS

MIRROR IMAGE

"Please come with me tomorrow," my mother begged as we wrapped up the chicken casserole preparing it for its journey to the homeless shelter. It wasn't the first time my mother asked me to accompany her, and my argument always was the same: I can't get up. I don't want to go. I just can't peel myself out of bed that early in the morning. As if anticipating these words, my mom quickly said, "You can sleep in the car on the way."

Defeated, I shrugged my shoulders, and reluctantly answered, "Okay."

The next morning when my alarm rang, I quickly turned it off and tried to resume slumber, hoping my mother would forget about the agreement we made the night before. I could hear her rummaging through the kitchen. Soon the sound of her movements headed toward my room. The door creaked open. "Wake up, Marisol, I made you breakfast," she said. A human alarm clock whose words forced me to arise. I reluctantly dragged myself out of bed, and stumbled into the kitchen, where my breakfast was neatly placed. Although grateful for her generous gestures, I still wanted to return to my warm, comfortable bed. Instead I ate in silence. As I put my empty plate on the kitchen sink, I saw my mom frantically preparing for our trip. I wanted to beg off, to tell her I'd go with her next week, even though I knew I wouldn't want to. But she looked so energetic and happy that I could not bear to disappoint her, so I sluggishly picked up a bag of fruit, headed for the car, and plopped myself onto the front seat. My mom swiftly placed the casserole on my lap, and we were off. My eyes slowly began to close, and I nodded off.

A red stop light caused the car to slow to a halt, and I opened my eyes to my surroundings. I had been asleep for most of the journey, and now the change in the car's momentum awakened me. As I looked around, I noticed a variety of people walking. People of different genders, races, and ages. The light turned green and we turned, heading in the same direction as the crowd. "We're here." my mom said. I remember thinking that it wasn't as large as I expected. In front of us was a run-down, grey, warehouse-like building surrounded by asphalt and an old chain-link fence. For some reason, I thought it would look more like a restaurant. Instead, it reminded me of an elementary school cafeteria.

My mom and I unloaded the casserole and bags of fruit. We entered the building through narrow doors and went directly to the kitchen, a small area, secluded from the rest of the cafeteria. Combining our food with that of the other volunteers, we concocted a diverse potluck filled with a variety of casseroles, enchiladas, beans, and tortillas, as well as desserts and fruit. The volunteers split up the work of preparation, and my job was to warm the food.

Then we were called out to the dining room for a short prayer. I went out nervously, not knowing what to expect. I imagined the homeless as they are portrayed on TV—crazy people with rotten teeth who talk to themselves on street corners. I realized my ignorance and slowly walked out. Scanning the room, I noticed people of all different shapes and sizes, yet none looked crazy nor foamed at the mouth. I stood by my mom and waited for the opening prayer, a universal blessing that was written as not to favor any one religion. When it was over, I hurried to the kitchen and began serving the food, but the volunteers had another job for me. They wanted me to go into the dining area and distribute fruit.

As I filled the large plastic bowl with apples, oranges, bananas, and the odd peach or two, I prepared myself for the task. How would I approach or address them? "Mom," I whispered. "What do I say to them? Can't somebody else do this?" She shook her head. "Just treat them like people, Marisol, just treat them like you'd treat anybody else." I got up, clenched my fruit bowl tightly, and left the kitchen. Many people crowded around me waiting to receive their fruit. They were very polite, thanking me with smiles and kind words, "Thank you, ma'am," or "God bless you" immediately dissolved all of my tension. It was almost a shock to hear so many grateful words. I felt uplifted with the loss of my fears.

Again I looked around the room, but this time I saw more than just "people." Families, single men, and women filled the room. Little girls whose dresses were loose from starvation and the stresses of living on the street, their eyes resembling those of an older person, with lines of stressful days and sleepless nights. Women and men whose appearances could easily hide their poverty, and others who looked tired and weak. Smiling faces headed outdoors to get a whiff of the morning air and converse with others.

I began to walk outside with my fruit bowl, when one man caught my eye. He reminded me of Santa Claus, because of his sweet eyes and big rosy cheeks. "Sir, would you like some fruit?" I asked. He looked at me and smiled bashfully. He looked down at his hands. He was holding coffee and an empty plate. He looked back at the fruit, wondering if he had room in his hands to carry it. Carefully, he took a banana into the hand that held the coffee, and spilled it with his nervous movements. He thanked me and slowly walked away.

Sorrow stricken, I continued to walk outside and was greeted by jumping dogs, beautiful dogs that seemed to be unaware of their misfortune. The owners satisfied their dogs' appetites before their own. One man had a litter of puppies that needed homes. He tried to convince me to take one, but they seemed very content there, with him.

After breakfast was over, I helped the crew clean. As we washed the empty casserole bowls and pots, my mind began to wander. It was then that I realized my fortune. I had a comfortable bed to sleep in at night and wake up to in the morning. I never had to be tortured by the rumbling growls of hunger. I could not imagine having to use a concrete sidewalk as my bed or a cardboard box as my home. Volunteering that day taught me that poverty can come for any of us—it is not prejudiced towards race, gender, or age. This realization changed the steady rhythm of my life. 11

As we drove away that morning, I remember my mom saying, "I think we fed over a hundred people today." All I could do was think of the faces I had seen, and I realized how much they looked like mine. 12

Exercise 3.4

Revisit each draft of Marisol's essay. How effectively does the revised final draft fulfill the promises Marisol makes in her discovery draft (pages 45–46)? In her freewriting (pages 36–37)? Point to at least two places in the revised final draft that you think are particularly strong. Why do you think these are effective? Point to at least two places in this draft that you think need revising. Why do you think these are less effective? What advice would you offer Marisol, were she to revise this paper for her portfolio?

WRITING STRATEGY

Revision Tips

Get some distance. Give yourself enough time to let the paper sit at least twenty-four hours before you begin revising.

Revise for meaning. Decide whether you've kept the promises your focus statement and thesis sentence made.

Revise for audience. Try to read from your reader's perspective, or ask someone else to read your essay from that perspective.

Revise for structure. Look at the overall structure or shape of the essay first, then at the structure of each paragraph.

Revise for sentences. Consider the variety of your sentences, including sentence type and length.

Revise for words. Make sure your words are accurate and appropriate.

Use peer review. Participate in review sessions with your classmates.

Edit. After you've worked through all these revision strategies, proofread your paper to correct problems in spelling, grammar, and mechanics.

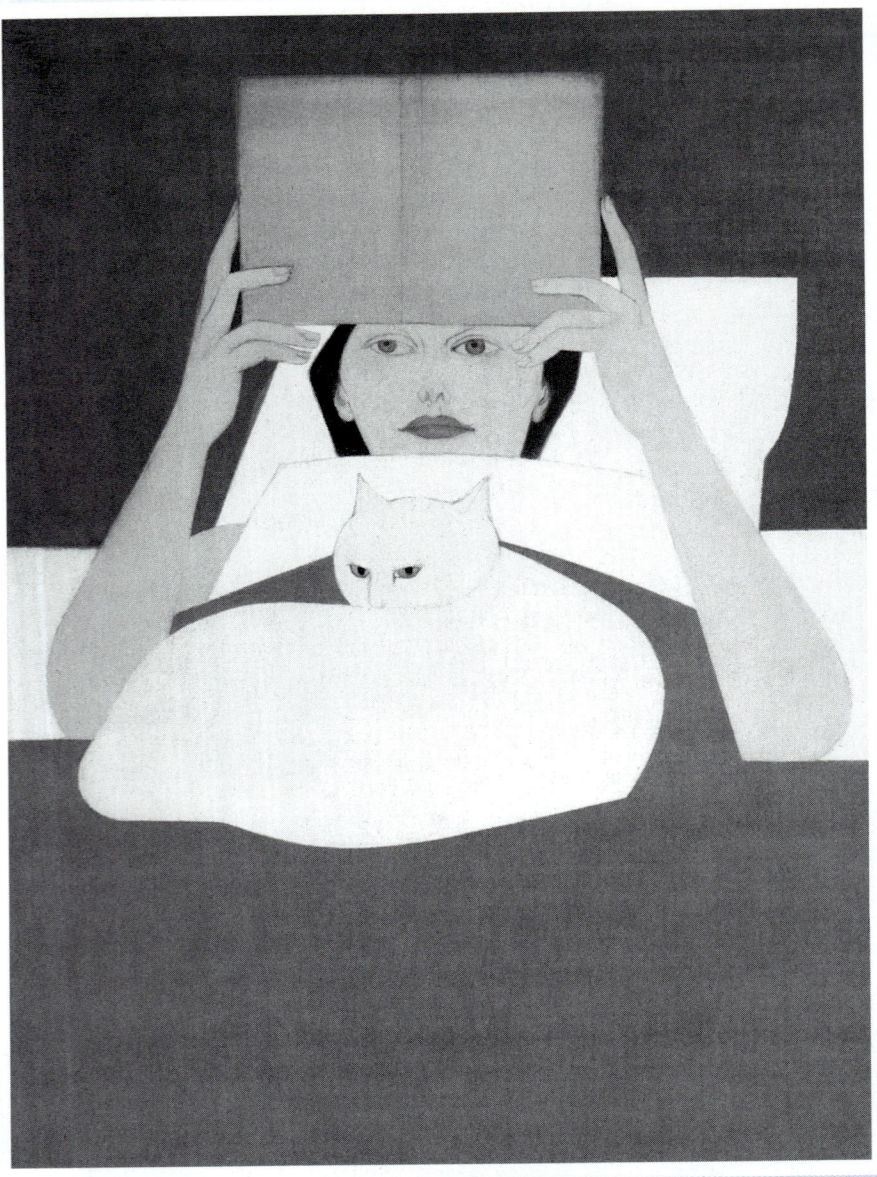

Will Barnet, "Woman Reading," 1965. Oil on canvas, 45 × 35 in. Courtesy Alexandre Gallery, New York. © Private collection/Will Barnet/Licensed by VAGA, New York, NY.

CHAPTER 4

Responding to Readings

Many students approach reading as though it were a spectator sport. You can see this by watching them move from their written homework to the reading they have been assigned. While they write, they generally sit at a desk or table. But when it comes time to read, they move to a soft chair or even a bed and get comfortable—they take off their shoes and kick back, reclining into what looks like a very passive state in which the only thing that moves is their eyes. It's no wonder that reading has often been prescribed as a cure for insomnia. But your reading process, just like your writing process, should be far more active than this.

In "How to Mark a Book," Mortimer J. Adler advocates reading actively and explains how the active reader can come to "own" the books she reads:

> There are two ways in which one can own a book. The first is the property right you establish by paying for it, just as you pay for clothes and furniture. But this act of purchase is only the prelude to possession. Full ownership comes only when you have made it a part of yourself, and the best way to make yourself a part of it is by writing in it. An illustration may make the point clear. You buy a beefsteak and transfer it from the butcher's icebox to your own. But you do not own the beefsteak in the most important sense until you consume it and get it into your bloodstream. I am arguing that books, too, must be absorbed in your bloodstream to do you any good.

To get what you're reading "into your bloodstream," you have to become an active reader. And as Adler suggests, one of the best ways to own a book, or any other kind of reading, is through writing in it and about it. (A disclaimer here: You may have been told repeatedly not to mark in your books, so actually writing in a text may not be an easy thing for you to do. A little later in this chapter, we'll suggest some alternatives to writing in the text itself. See page 114.)

Reading and writing are so tightly connected that we can say they're intertwined, so much so that your ability to write is strengthened by your ability to read, and vice versa. And although we may argue that writing is the most powerful learning tool we have, we could also argue for the powerful ways we learn by reading. Reading gives us information that we would not have access to otherwise. However—and here the inseparability of reading and writing becomes clear—we often learn more by writing about what we read. Many of your teachers in college will require you to write about the readings they assign because they believe that you will retain more of the readings by writing about them. Obviously, you should complete these assignments as thoroughly as possible. But even when you aren't given such a writing assignment, you'll find it helpful to write about assigned readings. For one thing, you'll engage a given text more actively by writing about it than by simply reading it and closing the book until your next class meeting. For another, you may find that you can expand your ideas for writing on a topic by reading and responding to what others have said about that topic.

Reading thoroughly and well will be extremely important for you during your college career. Take the time necessary to read and respond to class readings, whether written response is assigned or not. You'll strengthen your reading and study skills, and that should lead, in turn, to improved grades. In this chapter, we'll discuss specific reading and writing strategies that should help you strengthen your abilities to use writing while reading and then reading while writing.

SAMPLE READING

Read the following personal essay and consider the questions that follow it. Lee K. Abbott is a professional author and teacher of creative writing. His essay first appeared in *Puerto del Sol,* a literary magazine published by New Mexico State University's Department of English.

LEE K. ABBOTT

THE TRUE STORY OF WHY I DO WHAT I DO

1   All stories are true stories, especially the artful lies we invent to satisfy the wishful thinker in us, for they present to us, in disguise often and at great distance, the way we are or would want to be. Told to us in a lingo as unique as a fingerprint, they address our up-and-down, our here-and-now. They come, I think, from a desire, as irresistible as love itself, to fix on the page a moment, suffered or made up, when something—one puny thing or idea or person—revealed itself and so turned off the Boom-Boom-Boom which usually deafens us to ourselves. Happily-ended or not, stories are the truth we leave behind, like crumbs, to say how we've come and what was there to see.

2   To be inspirational, as high-minded and upward-looking as the foolish half of me mostly aims to be, I have to tell you about my father—as crazed, driven and cross-hearted a hero as I have ever known. His analogues have appeared in dozens of my stories: he's the gentleman, in golf togs or business suit, throwing the epic tantrum, careening hither and thither in a men's locker or banker's office; he's the

one, in the fiction I invent, with the outraged moral intelligence, the one who hectors and harangues, the one telling another (usually me, you can guess) how to behave and when to beware and what is likely to be the dry end of things we love.

In fiction, he is imperious, forbidding as a Puritan God, sharp-minded as an out-of-town lawyer, stiff as pig bristle, wiry and unforgiving; in fiction, the made-up landscape I am a sometime citizen in, he suffers and is redeemed (or he is not), does the wrong thing and is shamed (or is not), comes to insight and is crushed (or is not). In fiction, given its unities and shape and its epiphanies, I comprehend my father. I know exactly what he meant when he told me that you could tell a gentleman by his hand shake and his shoe shine. I know, and can articulate, what significance there is in the properly mowed lawn, what wisdom there is in the order of dried dishes. In fiction, I know—maybe as Flannery O'Connor did—why the heathen rage.

In life, however—which, messy and improbable and ephemeral, is not good fiction—I had no idea what made his world spin round and round. The facts were clear to me, not the flesh. He went to Dartmouth, I knew. He pole-vaulted cross-handed. One brother died on the Bataan Death March; his sister in a boating accident on Lake Sasebo in Maine. His father went blind in the last years of his life; his mother squandered an inheritance of at least one million dollars. He was a roué, I heard, a slick-haired rake who hung out on the pier at Old Orchard Beach and went down to Miami in the winter. He married my mother, the over-pampered daughter of a Canadian insurance executive, in Harlingen, Texas, while he was at gunnery school in VMI. They lived in Panama, where I was born. He ran the National Guard in Illinois, where my brother was born. He played one year of professional golf. He became a career military man, went to England, Korea, Germany, resigned his commission twice because somebody, or something, infuriated him.

If it is true, as Willa Cather says, that the "basic material a writer works with is acquired before the age of fifteen," then by the time I was a sophomore in high school in Las Cruces, New Mexico, already telling my teachers and myself that I was going to be a writer, the material I had acquired I'd got from him: a duke's mixture of soirees, of country clubs and officers' clubs, of colorful compadres named Red and Goonch and Uncle Inches—the whole of it tragic and tearful to the aggressively poetic kid I was then. My mother was a drunk, institutionalized when I was twelve; my father was a drinker.

He had psoriasis on his knobby knees and knobby elbows, he smoked like the dickens, he threw a wedge at the TV, he dressed in pink polkadots for the Club Championship, he banished me to my room forever, he expected my brother and me to know the truth and speak it invariably—this was my material, a hodgepodge of goo and muck and human blah-blah-blah the responsibility for which I was absolutely unaware of until the inspirational summer afternoon I am partly here to yap about.

Once upon a time (Isn't this the rhetoric, in truth, that opens every fairytale we survive and want to write about?), my father and I found ourselves alone at home. I want to say it was a Sunday, for in my memory the day, if not the events themselves, have a liturgical, quasi-holy "feel." In my memory, that attic atop the shoulders where everything truly felt is found, there is that Sunday light, crooked and mote-filled and lazy, and that Sunday time, heavy and ever in danger of wobbling to a halt. My father, in his bermuda shorts and golf shirt, is in the TV room, drinking the rum thing he preferred; he had the habit, annoying I think now, of dumping his half-used ice cubes back in the freezer, a habit the girl who became my wife told me was disgusting every time I made her a Coke and it tasted like hooch. I am in the living room, I think, listening to records; more likely, I am reading—*Sports Illustrated,* the *National Geographic, Life* magazine.

My taste in those days ran to the quick, the immediate—prose of the slash-and-burn kind. *Mila 18* by Leon Uris, *The Naked and the Dead* (still an excellent book, by the way), Alistair MacClean's high seas adventures. I saw myself writing a book like those one day—a book, conceived out of testosterone and *Nugget*-style macho, a book as pithy and direct as a dust jacket blurb: "Mr. Abbott," the endorsement would run, "writes like an assassin. He's the 'Aaarrgghh' the yellow yammer when they spy the vast What-Not opening to greet them." I had, I thought then, no experience (this was long before I realized that Henry James was correct when he said that "experience was an atmosphere of the mind"). I was just a kid, after all. Skinny, with a flat-top and fifteen pimples, half my mind tilted toward girls, the other half tilted toward glory (which would, in the reasoning I was the victim of, get me girls). 8

The hours passed that Sunday afternoon as they always do when I cast myself back into the dangerous tides that are my past: the clock above the antique writing desk chiming on the quarter-hour, the father wandering between the refrigerator and liquor cabinet, Pee Wee Reese or Dizzy Dean saying in the TV room what the Dodgers were doing; the son in another room cobbling together in his fertile but screwy imagination a tale of swashbuckling and hair-raising, a narrative of guns and grateful bimbos and nick-of-time derring-do. We were in our elements, him and me: one, the older, tuned to the stupid clatter of the exterior world; the other, the younger flesh of him, tuned to the twilight interior world of fetch-and-keep, of fantasy. Then he burst into the living room, eyed me as if wondering for the last time whether I was up to the burden he was about to pitch my way, and said, a little drunkenly, "Come with me." 9

He had been thinking about himself, it is clear now. An inventory, check mark after check mark after check mark, had been taken: three heart attacks, a fist-sized hunk of his lung removed at William Beaumont General Hospital in Ft. Bliss, the yips on the putting green, Homeric-like anger, frustration at a life twisted which-away, hopes high as heaven he believed in, bitterness at being less than the hero he'd promised himself he'd be. I didn't know this at the time I followed him outdoors and into the utility rooms at the end of the car port. I knew only that he was semi-sloshed. I knew only that he was fifty-six years old, gray-headed and tough. I knew he hated going to work at the post office, his job in those days, where he supervised and inspected and, unhappiest of all for him, had to tattle on those who stole money or stamps or swiped somebody's *Playboy* magazine. 10

"See this, Kit?" he said. He was standing in the center of the utility room, lawn mower here, gas can there, the walls hung with tools I never got the sense of. Golf clubs were in there, a bucket of practice balls, cans of oil, greasy rags, a hoe, a rake, a cheap hardware store of goodies that smelled old and used and too sweet. "You want to be a writer, huh," he said, sweeping his arms, then pulling me after him. He snarled the word; it was sound which scorned ignorance and innocence. Against the wall, high as the ceiling, were stacked his footlockers and steamer trunks, from the Army of the United States and from the regiments that were the families of his own father, innkeeper Layman Kittredge Abbott of Portland, Maine. I like to think now that I knew we were coming to something, my father and me, that he was going to say words to me and I, perhaps for the first time, was going to understand him precisely. I like to think now that I was smart enough to know that I was in the presence of a truth grander than the two of us, a truth the price of which we go on paying forever, a truth more dire than the knowing that we die and do not rise. This is the moment, I like to think of myself thinking then, when you discover how hard the world is, when what you've cleaved to is cleaved from you with a broadaxe.

Then he assaulted those lockers and trunks. In a fury, huffing and puffing, he snatched them down, one by one, hollering "Timber!" when the uppermost went tumbling. They crashed and banged, and I tried backing up a little, as he flung one behind him and scrambled over another to reach a third. He was hollering, you have to know, all the New England notes of his voice echoing in that now cramped room, and maybe I was some scared. This was the temper I'd witnessed elsewhere—on the golf course, behind the wheel of his Ford, in the living room when someone in the big world made a ding-a-ling out of himself. But there was more than anger here: there was pain, the particular kind of which was personal and buried deep in his bones, pain for which there is no Latin name or medicine or machine, other than fiction, to account for.

"Write it all down!" he was shouting. "Write it all goddam down!"

And it was here, from a certain X-spot in the world, 1855 Cruse, that my father, teetering from booze and the awful weight of his own life, was taking seriously, in a manner I couldn't yet, what purpose writing ought to have. Here it is, he was in effect saying. Crated and stored, catalogued and preserved, year by used-up year, place by rotten place. Here it is: the come and go of it, the building and collapse of it, the joy and weep of it. Here it is, he was saying. All the tissues and nerves and human jingle-jangle, that want and excess of it, the rigamarole and whirling, damaged creatures we are. And all you have to do, son and boy, is write it down. Write it all goddam down.

This, I submit, is the inspirational part. If we write for any larger purpose than a simple good time—and, believe me, there is nothing at all wrong with a good time—it is, I think, because we all feel, less and more, the obligation we have to our fathers, to our mothers, to all the folks, linked by biology or not, who have raised us; an obligation, as essential to our moral natures as our hearts are to long life, to the places we were raised in and to the knowledge we learned there. We want, I hope, because there is no other way to do it, to write it down, to transform it, to set it straight. At our best, we do not write for the money alone, though money is nice; nor do we write for fame, though fame is likewise nice. We write, beginner and professional alike, because, though half-frightened, we want to know what is in the trunks and lockers we lug forward through time, what vital secrets they can be sprung to reveal.

◆ QUESTIONS FOR REVIEW

1. How effectively does Abbott's essay develop the promise of its title?
2. Identify two or three instances of vivid language that you noticed as you read. What makes these passages noteworthy or interesting?
3. How effectively does Abbott use specific examples in his essay?
4. Were any parts of the essay confusing? If so, which ones? What reading strategies did you use to understand them?

Exercise 4.1

How did you read Abbott's essay? Think back for a moment to your reading and write a brief description of your reading process. Where did you read it? What did you do while you read? Did you make any notes? How many times did you read it?

READING STRATEGIES FOR TEXTS

In this section, we offer a good bit of advice about how you can make your reading more productive than it might be otherwise. In general, you should start your reading by giving yourself enough time to read.

Far too many students leave reading assignments to the last minute, thinking that saving them until the eleventh hour will mean that the material will be fresher in their minds. This is a shaky rationalization at best. You may be able to remember enough details to get through a test, but waiting until the last minute is like cramming—you may retain information in the short run but not over the long term. And long-term retention of facts and ideas should be your goal. So the first piece of advice is to give yourself enough time to complete the reading assignment. That means you'll have to plan your reading time carefully, perhaps dividing a longer assignment into manageable chunks.

Second, try to read assignments more than once. This seems absolutely untenable to many students. They have reading assignments in all their classes, and for each class major assignments and tests seem to be due within a week of one another. And it may not be possible to read longer assignments (e.g., a novel) twice. But when you can, plan your time so that you read assignments at least twice. You really can't expect to uncover all (or even most) of a text's meaning on the first reading. Complex texts, those rich in ideas or data, take time to absorb and digest, and a single reading just won't provide enough exposure to a given text to "get it into your bloodstream," to use Adler's analogy.

The following are ten specific reading strategies that you may use. We don't want to prescribe exactly how you should read, and we recognize that you probably won't use all of the strategies we suggest every time you read an assigned text. However, we do suggest that you try them all at least once. When you've done this, then you may choose those strategies you think work best for you. To illustrate the kinds of information you can generate using these various strategies, Bill applied each strategy in turn to Abbott's essay, "The True Story of Why I Do What I Do." Each application appears immediately following discussion of the strategy it represents.

Before You Read

1. Jot down some of the expectations you bring to the kind of reading you have been assigned. What kind of reading have you been assigned—a piece of fiction, an autobiography or biography of a historical figure, a poem, a chapter in a chemistry textbook, an essay from your composition textbook? What expectations do you have for the reading? For example, if you have been assigned to read a novel, consider what you know about fiction (about characters, plot, and conflict, to name three elements of fiction) that will inform your reading. If you have been assigned to read a biography of a major historical figure, what do you expect to learn from reading that text? What do you already know about that figure? What do you want to learn from reading about the person? If you have been assigned a chapter from your chemistry text, what do you expect to learn from this reading? How will the reading fit with your work in the chemistry classroom or laboratory?

Expectations

personal essay, so I expect some kind of statement Lee will make about learning something or coming to realize something important from personal experience.

author—Lee K. Abbott. I know a little bit about him, having met him on several occasions. He's a graduate of Las Cruces H. S. and NMSU, got an MFA in creative writing, published several collections of short stories (e.g., *The Heart Never Fits Its Wanting*—good stories). currently a faculty member in the English department at Ohio State. Abbott gives very good readings of his stories.

2. Preview the assigned reading, jotting brief responses to the following questions. Before you begin reading, take a look at the text's title, subtitle, headings, and any graphics (i.e., visual aids) and their captions. What orientation to the text do these elements offer? What does the title tell you about the text to come? How does the subtitle expand or clarify the title? How do the headers break up the text itself? What do they suggest about how the text is structured? What graphics—tables, charts, maps, diagrams, drawings, photographs—are present? How do they support the text? What is their purpose?

When you have finished this initial survey, read the first section of the text and then the last. What is the content of each section? What does the writer say in each? What material does the writer present in each? What does the first section suggest about the rest of the text? What is the writer's purpose? What is the writer's attitude toward the subject and toward the reader? What does the last section tell you about the writer's purpose? How does the writer end the text?

From this preview, write a statement of purpose or a summary of what you think the text's main idea is. Also write two or three questions you want the text to answer or write about two or three aspects of the text you find interesting or curious.

Preview

15 ¶s, so it's not very long. no headers or graphics, just the title: "The True Story of Why I Do What I Do." "true story" might seem oxymoronic, perhaps ironic, since stories are sometimes made up, a fiction. reminds me of a line from a country and western song: "That's my story, and I'm stickin' to it."

first section—read first ¶. Abbott talks about "true stories" as being "artful lies." They reveal things to us. They're the "truth we leave behind." So stories—"artful lies"—are important

How can "true stories" be "artful lies"? terms a bit incongruous, at odds.

last section—¶15. Abbott says, "This . . . is the inspirational part." What's the "this" that's "inspirational"? He says we have an "obligation" to those (parents & others) who "raised us," to the "places we were raised in" & the "knowledge we learned there." He closes by saying we write to understand, to know what our past & experiences mean.

main idea? I expect Abbott to talk about why he's a writer or a teacher of writing and why he has to write.

WRITING STRATEGY

The Time It Takes

How much time should you devote to studying? We tell our students that, in general, they should allot two hours outside class for each hour in class, so that your sixteen-hour load would require thirty-two hours of study time in addition to the time spent in class and labs. Although this may seem like an inordinate amount of time, you need to treat your schoolwork as you would a job—you have to put in the time to get out of it what you should.

While You Read

3. Consider the sequence—the text's beginning, middle, and end. One way to think about the flow of a text is to see it as proceeding from a beginning, through a middle, and to an end. As you read, identify these three parts of the text. How does the writer begin the text? What information or material does the writer provide in the introduction? Where does the beginning move into the middle, and what does the writer present in that middle? Where does the middle move into the ending, and what does the writer do to end the text? What transitions does the writer use to make moving from beginning to middle to end smooth and clear? How does each part support the others?

Beginning, Middle, End

Beginning—¶s 1–6. Once I got into the essay, I had to change my mind about the first section. It actually consists of the first six paragraphs, not just the first paragraph as I'd originally thought. Abbott talks about writing, stories, artful lies. talks about his father (a complex man), understandable in fiction but not life. writer's material comes from early experience (Cather).

Middle—¶s 7–14. tells story of an afternoon when he was about 16 and his father showed him what it meant to be a writer, what the writer's job is—to "write it all down."

End—¶15. Abbott draws conclusions about why he writes and why other writers write. He's compelled, they're compelled to write; writers are obligated to see what "vital secrets" their writing may reveal.

4. Pause at natural breaks to write about what you have read. As the writer moves from one major section of the text to the next, stop reading and write a one- or two-sentence summary of what you have just read or write one or two questions you have about your reading. Are there aspects of what you've read that have made you curious or that you don't understand? If so, write a note or a question about these.

Natural Breaks

first major break comes between ¶s 6 & 7 as Abbott moves into the narrative of the afternoon. "inspirational" appears again (second time)—but it's shifted slightly in meaning. question: Is "inspirational" a key term? Why the shift in meaning?

second major break comes between ¶s 14 & 15 as Abbott ends the story about the afternoon with his dad and begins the conclusion. And there's "inspirational" again. And it's shifted in meaning again, seems broader in scope here than before. question: How do the three instances of "inspirational" work together? What do the shifts in meaning signal?

5. Mark and annotate the text as you go, preferably on your second reading. Highlight or underline (or mark in some other way) important passages while you're reading. If you simply cannot stand to mark a book, make your notes on index cards or on pieces of paper that are slightly smaller than the pages of your book and insert them between pages themselves, so that you have everything together. Jot a quick note in the margins of the text to create a topic index or to indicate an important section. If you're just not a text marker, then use small, stick-on note strips to create this index, and write on each strip why the section is important.

A word of caution—don't mark everything. Some parts of a text are more important or carry more weight than others. How do you decide what to mark? Look for words and ideas that are repeated. Look also for parts you found interesting, you agreed with, or you disagreed with. Mark these, and return to them later; these sections may provide a starting point for your written response.

The following is a sample annotation of Lee Abbott's "The True Story of Why I Do What I Do." What would you mark and comment on that we didn't? Why?

Lee K. Abbott

THE TRUE STORY OF WHY I DO WHAT I DO

All stories are true stories, especially the artful lies we invent to satisfy the wishful thinker in us, for they present to us, in disguise often and at great distance, the way we are or would want to be. Told to us in a lingo as unique as a fingerprint, they address our up-and-down, our here-and-now. They come, I think, from a desire, as irresistible as love itself, to fix on the page a moment, suffered or made up, when something—one puny thing or idea or person—revealed itself and so turned off the Boom-Boom-Boom which usually deafens us to ourselves. Happily-ended or not, stories are the truth we leave behind, like crumbs, to say how we've come and what was there to see.

To be inspirational, as high-minded and upward-looking as the foolish half of me mostly aims to be, I have to tell you about my father—as crazed, driven and cross-hearted a hero as I have ever known. His analogues have appeared in dozens of my stories: he's the gentleman, in golf togs or business suit, throwing the epic tantrum, careening hither and thither in a men's locker or

[margin annotations:]
1 *true stories = lies?*

what stories are (truth left behind)?

compare to ¶s 6 & 15

2 *what's role of Lee's father?*

banker's office; he's the one, in the fiction I invent, with the outraged moral intelligence, the one who hectors and harangues, the one telling another (usually me, you can guess) how to behave and when to beware and what is likely to be the dry end of things we love.

In fiction, he is imperious, forbidding as a Puritan God, sharp-minded as an out-of-town lawyer, stiff as pig bristle, wiry and unforgiving; in fiction, the made-up landscape I am a some-time citizen in, he suffers and is redeemed (or he is not), does the wrong thing and is shamed (or is not), comes to insight and is crushed (or is not). In fiction, given its unities and shape and its epiphanies, I comprehend my father. I know exactly what he meant when he told me that you could tell a gentleman by his hand shake and his shoe shine. I know, and can articulate, what significance there is in the properly mowed lawn, what wisdom there is in the order of dried dishes. In fiction, I know—maybe as Flannery O'Connor did—why the heathen rage. 3 *vivid language similes* / *repetition "I know"*

In life, however—which, messy and improbable and ephemeral, is not good fiction—I had no idea what made his world spin round and round. The facts were clear to me, not the flesh. He went to Dartmouth, I knew. He pole-vaulted cross-handed. One brother died on the Bataan Death March; his sister in a boating accident on Lake Sasebo in Maine. His father went blind in the last years of his life; his mother squandered an inheritance of at least one million dollars. He was a roué, I heard, a slick-haired rake who hung out on the pier at Old Orchard Beach and went down to Miami in the winter. He married my mother, the over-pampered daughter of a Canadian insurance executive, in Harlingen, Texas, while he was at gunnery school in VMI. They lived in Panama, where I was born. He ran the National Guard in Illinois, where my brother was born. He played one year of professional golf. He became a career military man, went to England, Korea, Germany, resigned his commission twice because somebody, or something, infuriated him. 4 *a man given to sensual pleasure*

¶s 2–6 describe Lee's father—quite a complex man

If it is true, as Willa Cather says, that the "basic material a writer works with is acquired before the age of fifteen," then by the time I was a sophomore in high school in Las Cruces, New Mexico, already telling my teachers and myself that I was going to be a writer, the material I had acquired I'd got from him: a duke's mixture of soirees, of country clubs and officers' clubs, of colorful compadres named Red and Goonch and Uncle Inches—the whole of it tragic and tearful to the aggressively poetic kid I was then. My mother was a drunk, institutionalized when I was twelve; my father was a drinker. 5

legacy

He had psoriasis on his knobby knees and knobby elbows, he smoked like the dickens, he threw a wedge at the TV, he dressed in pink polkadots for the Club Championship, he banished me to my room forever, he expected my brother and me to know the truth and speak it invariably—this was my material, a hodgepodge of goo and muck and human blah-blah-blah the responsibility for which I was absolutely unaware of until the inspirational summer afternoon I am partly here to yap about.

legacy

truth—compare to ¶s 1, 6, 11, & 15 (3rd time to appear)

Once upon a time (Isn't this the rhetoric, in truth, that opens every fairytale we survive and want to write about?), my father and I found ourselves alone at home. I want to say it was a Sunday, for in my memory the day, if not the events themselves, have a liturgical, quasi-holy "feel." In my memory, that attic atop the shoulders where everything truly felt is found, there is that Sunday light, crooked and mote-filled and lazy, and that Sunday time, heavy and ever in danger of wobbling to a halt. My father, in his bermuda shorts and golf shirt, is in the TV room, drinking the rum thing he preferred; he had the habit, annoying I think now, of dumping his half-used ice cubes back in the freezer, a habit the girl who became my wife told me was disgusting every time I made her a Coke and it tasted like hooch. I am in the living room, I think, listening to records; more likely, I am reading—*Sports Illustrated*, the *National Geographic*, *Life* magazine. 7

why this fairytale opening in the middle of the essay?

why quasi-holy?

inspirational—compare to ¶s 2 & 15

My taste in those days ran to the quick, the immediate—prose of the slash-and-burn kind. *Mila 18* by Leon Uris, *The Naked and the Dead* (still an excellent book, by the way), Alistair MacClean's high seas adventures. I saw myself writing a book like those one day—a book, conceived out of testosterone and *Nugget*-style macho, a book as pithy and direct as a dust jacket blurb: "Mr. Abbott," the endorsement would run, "writes like an assassin. He's the 'Aaarrgghh' the yellow yammer when they spy the vast What-Not opening to greet them." I had, I thought then, no experience (this was long before I realized that Henry James was correct when he said that "experience was an atmosphere of the mind"). I was just a kid, after all. Skinny, with a flat-top and fifteen pimples, half my mind tilted toward girls, the other half tilted toward glory (which would, in the reasoning I was the victim of, get me girls). 8

highly stylized language—young boy's infatuation with words

The hours passed that Sunday afternoon as they always do when I cast myself back into the dangerous tides that are my past: the clock above the antique writing desk chiming on the quarter-hour, the father wandering between the refrigerator and liquor cabinet, Pee Wee Reese or Dizzy Dean saying in the TV room 9

"that Sunday afternoon"—something important to happen?

what the Dodgers were doing; the son in another room <u>cobbling together in his fertile but screwy imagination</u> a tale of swashbuckling and hair-raising, a narrative of guns and grateful bimbos and nick-of-time derring-do. <u>We were in our elements,</u> <u>him</u> and <u>me</u>: one, the older, tuned to the stupid clatter of the exterior world; the other, the younger flesh of him, tuned to the twilight interior world of fetch-and-keep, of fantasy. Then he <u>burst</u> into the living room, eyed me as if wondering for the last time whether I was up to the <u>burden</u> he was about to pitch my way, and said, a little drunkenly, "Come with me."

10   He had been thinking about himself, it is clear now. An inventory, check mark after check mark after check mark, had been taken: three heart attacks, a fist-sized hunk of his lung removed at William Beaumont General Hospital in Ft. Bliss, the yips on the putting green, Homeric-like anger, <u>frustration at a life twisted which-away,</u> <u>hopes high as heaven he believed in,</u> <u>bitterness at being less than the hero he'd promised himself he'd be.</u> I didn't know this at the time I followed him outdoors and into the utility rooms at the end of the car port. I knew only that he was semi-sloshed. I knew only that he was fifty-six years old, gray-headed and tough. I knew he hated going to work at the post office, his job in those days, where he supervised and inspected and, unhappiest of all for him, had to tattle on those who stole money or stamps or swiped somebody's *Playboy* magazine.

catalog —

11   "See this, Kit?" he said. He was standing in the center of the utility room, lawn mower here, gas can there, the walls hung with tools I never got the sense of. Golf clubs were in there, a bucket of practice balls, cans of oil, greasy rags, a hoe, a rake, a cheap hardware store of goodies that smelled old and used and too sweet. "You want to be a writer, huh," he said, sweeping his arms, then pulling me after him. He <u>snarled</u> the word; it was sound which scorned ignorance and innocence. Against the wall, high as the ceiling, were stacked his <u>footlockers and steamer trunks,</u> from the Army of the United States and from the regiments that were the families of his own father, innkeeper Layman Kittredge Abbott of Portland, Maine. I like to think now that I knew we were coming to something, my father and me, that he was going to say words to me and I, perhaps for the first time, was going to understand him precisely. I like to think now that I was smart enough to know that I was in the presence of a <u>truth</u> grander than the two of us, a <u>truth</u> the price of which we go on paying forever, a <u>truth</u> more dire than the knowing that we die and do not rise. This is the moment, I like to think of myself thinking then, when you discover

compare to ¶*s 12 & 15*

truth repeated again—see ¶s 1, 6, & 7

how hard the world is, when what you've cleaved to is cleaved from you with a broadaxe.

compare to ¶s 11 & 15

Then he assaulted those lockers and trunks. In a fury, huffing and puffing, he snatched them down, one by one, hollering "Timber!" when the uppermost went tumbling. They crashed and banged, and I tried backing up a little, as he flung one behind him and scrambled over another to reach a third. He was hollering, you have to know, all the New England notes of his voice echoing in that now cramped room, and maybe I was some scared. This was the temper I'd witnessed elsewhere—on the golf course, behind the wheel of his Ford, in the living room when someone in the big world made a ding-a-ling out of himself. But there was more than anger here: there was pain, the particular kind of which was personal and buried deep in his bones, pain for which there is no Latin name or medicine or machine, other than fiction, to account for.

"Write it all down!" he was shouting. "Write it all goddam down!"

climactic (key) moment

And it was here, from a certain X-spot in the world, 1855 Cruse, that my father, teetering from booze and the awful weight of his own life, was taking seriously, in a manner I couldn't yet, what purpose writing ought to have. Here it is, he was in effect saying. Crated and stored, catalogued and preserved, year by used-up year, place by rotten place. Here it is: the come and go of it, the building and collapse of it, the joy and weep of it. Here it is, he was saying. All the tissues and nerves and human jingle-jangle, that want and excess of it, the rigamarole and whirling, damaged creatures we are. And all you have to do, son and boy, is write it down. Write it all goddam down.

stuff of writing

This, I submit, is the inspirational part. If we write for any larger purpose than a simple good time—and, believe me, there is nothing at all wrong with a good time—it is, I think, because we all feel, less and more, the obligation we have to our fathers, to our mothers, to all the folks, linked by biology or not, who have raised us; an obligation, as essential to our moral natures as our hearts are to long life, to the places we were raised in and to the knowledge we learned there. We want, I hope, because there is no other way to do it, to write it down, to transform it, to set it straight. At our best, we do not write for the money alone, though money is nice; nor do we write for fame, though fame is likewise nice. We write, beginner and professional alike, because, though half-frightened, we want to know what is in the trunks and lockers we lug forward through time, what vital secrets they can be sprung to reveal.

compare to ¶s 2 & 6 (3rd time to appear) writer's obligation

tell the truth? ¶s 1, 6, 7, & 11

why writers write ¶s 11 & 12

6. Consider the context of words and terms. Often, you'll find that the meaning of a word or term will shift, so that the word or term takes on a meaning you may not ordinarily associate with it. Abbott uses the word "inspirational" three times, in paragraphs 2, 6, and 15. But each time, the meaning of this term shifts. In paragraph 2, "inspirational" suggests that Abbott's been asked to write a piece that offers insight into writing and the life of the writer and so is "inspirational" for the reader. In paragraph 6, Abbott shifts the meaning of this term away from the reader and uses it to describe the summer afternoon and its events that inspired him to write, so "inspirational" becomes more personalized. And in paragraph 15, Abbott shifts the meaning slightly once again, so that "inspirational" remains personalized but also takes on a larger meaning, one that suggests the true nature of the writer's inspiration to write: "the obligation we have to our fathers, to our mothers, to all the folks, linked by biology or not, who have raised us; an obligation, as essential to our moral natures as our hearts are to long life, to the places we were raised in and in the knowledge we learned there." Although the shifts in meaning are subtle, they are nonetheless important. The larger meaning of the last use of "inspirational" is particularly important for the aspiring writer. "Inspirational" is customarily used to describe something that is positive, something that helps motivate us to think better thoughts or to do good works—"this morning's talk was not only informative but inspirational." But in this last use, Abbott suggests that the writer is driven to write by his past—not simply motivated to write but driven by obligation. So in this last use, "inspirational" takes on less positive connotations. And in taking on those less positive connotations, the term expands in meaning, so that it becomes more comprehensive in its meaning than it was when we first encountered it in the second paragraph.

Terms That Shift Meaning in Context

inspirational—appears in three ¶s (2, 6, & 15). It's significant that it appears at the juncture of the beginning and middle and then of the middle and end.

7. Take note of places where your knowledge of history, language, culture, or some other specialized subject (e.g., music or mathematics) helps you create meaning with the author. Writers depend on our knowing a great deal. They must do so, because they simply don't have enough time and space to tell us everything we might need to know in support of their writing. But even if they could do so, they wouldn't, because part of the pleasure of reading is working to figure out what the writer means. For example, Abbott writes:

> The hours passed that Sunday afternoon as they always do when I cast myself back into the dangerous tides that are my past: the clock above the antique writing desk chiming on the quarter-hour, the father wandering between the refrigerator and liquor cabinet, Pee Wee Reese or Dizzy Dean saying in the TV room what the Dodgers were doing; the son in another room cobbling together in his

fertile but screwy imagination a tale of swashbuckling and hair-raising, a narrative of guns and grateful bimbos and nick-of-time derring-do. We were in our elements, him and me: one, the older, tuned to the stupid clatter of the exterior world; the other, the younger flesh of him, tuned to the twilight interior world of fetch-and-keep, of fantasy.

This passage offers two allusions that help contrast Abbott and his father. By naming Pee Wee Reese and Dizzy Dean and the Dodgers, Abbott identifies his father's interest in baseball and identifies the particular time of the passage. (Reese and Dean were television announcers for baseball from the mid 1950s to the early 1960s.) By alluding to the adventures at work "in his fertile but screwy imagination," Abbott reveals his own romantic nature as a hero wannabe, one who overcomes overwhelming odds to rescue "grateful bimbos," always at the risk of great personal danger, always threatened by gunfights and the like. Abbott assumes that the reader has some knowledge of baseball in the first instance and of escapist fiction in the second; he thereby invites the reader to share particular scenes from his previous experience to help heighten the contrast between father and son that he is drawing.

Specialized Knowledge

Abbott refers to three prominent American writers of this century: O'Connor, Cather, and James. As an English teacher, I understand their importance and know that each wrote about the writer's craft. I particularly remember one of James's statements from "The Art of Fiction": "Try to be one of the people on whom nothing is lost." seems to me that that's what Abbott's father was telling him.

Flannery O'Connor (¶3)—short-story writer who lived in Georgia. wrote also about the writer's craft

Willa Cather (¶5)—American novelist who wrote about the Midwest, also wrote *Death Comes for the Archbishop* (a novel set in NM)

wedge (¶6)—golf club used for hitting high, arcing shots from within 75 yards or so of a green

Nugget (¶8)—a men's magazine, lots of nudity, cheesecake

Henry James (¶8)—American novelist and short-story writer. sometimes called the father of psychological realism, so he got into his characters' heads as much as possible.

Pee Wee Reese & Dizzy Dean (¶9)—professional baseball players in the '40s and '50s who also were a popular team as sports announcers in the '50s. broadcast the Falstaff Game of the Week every Saturday.

8. Take note of particularly creative uses of language. Paraphrase these; that is, put them into your own words. We expect poets to use such devices as metaphor, simile, and personification to convey meaning to their readers. However, prose (whether fiction or nonfiction) can be just as rich as poetry in these devices. For example, Datus Proper uses personification (attributing human qualities to an inanimate object) in "Dark Hollow": "The fly rights itself, shimmies its peacock body at the trout, and flashes you a V-for-victory sign with white wings." (see page 145). Using the verbs "rights," "shimmies," and "flashes," Proper attributes purposeful action to a fishing fly, making the fly come to life and seem to be a conspirator with Proper against the trout. Another example from Proper's essay involves a description of the size of a sycamore tree: "The trunk was as thick as four Dark Hollow girls standing back to back, pale toes wriggling down into the pool." Just how big is this tree? A rough paraphrase might be "The sycamore tree's trunk was about three feet in diameter, and its roots were down into the water." What is lost in such a paraphrase? As you consider that question, you'll be developing insight into one of the most significant characteristics of good writing.

Creative Uses of Language

Lots of such uses, and here's a sampling of things I marked—

Boom-Boom-Boom (¶1)—the noise of daily life that can deafen us to what we need to hear

The description of the father particularly stands out (¶3)—lots of adjectives (imperious, forbidding), similes (stiff as pig bristle). And the structure of the first sentence is pretty much vintage Abbott.

moment of discovery (¶13)—"when you discover how hard the world is, when what you've cleaved to is cleaved from you with a broadaxe." play on "cleaved" works, says life's lessons don't come easy.

WRITING STRATEGY

On Paraphrasing

To paraphrase is to restate a piece of writing (e.g., a sentence or a paragraph) in your own words, so that you accurately rephrase its content. A paraphrase should be approximately the same length as the original passage on which it's based.

As a reading strategy, paraphrasing can help you understand a difficult passage more clearly, because it forces you to read the passage carefully. As a writing strategy, paraphrasing can help you make things easier for your reader to understand. In essence, when you paraphrase, you translate the language of the original passage into terms your reader may more readily grasp.

When you paraphrase, whether only a sentence or a longer passage, you must document your source; that is, you must cite the source in the text of your writing and then document it as part of a "Works Cited" page. For more information on documenting sources, see pages 601–618. For an extended treatment of paraphrasing, see pages 132–135.

Exercise 4.2

Writing a paraphrase means rewriting a passage in other words. A paraphrase is a complete rendition of the original passage and generally approaches the original's length. Although paraphrases are most often used in connection with research, the following exercise is designed to help you focus on the power of creative uses of language.

What images are evoked by the following examples of figurative language? After you read each example, paraphrase it. What differences do you notice between the original and your paraphrase?

> And on this afternoon, the sense of illness lay so heavy you could have gathered it in your hands like snow and rounded it into balls to throw.
> Henry Louis Gates, Jr., "Change of Life," *Colored People*

> She moved quickly, darting through the field like a rabbit startled by a hunter.

> The cat moved sideways as it approached the mouse, looking for all the world as if a stiff wind were blowing it into the helpless prey.

> By "language using" here I am referring to the employment of any system of symbols in order to make sense of the world—the primary means by which all of us run order through chaos, thereby giving ourselves the identities we have.
> William E. Coles, Jr., *Seeing Through Writing*

After You Have Read

9. Write answers to the questions you raised; write responses to the curiosities you identified; or write a response to the writer about points of interest, agreement, and/or disagreement (see 2, 4, and 5 above). How did your reading answer your questions? How did those curiosities you identified figure in the text? At what points did the writer truly pique your interest? On what points did you agree or disagree? Why?

Answers to Questions Raised Earlier

I understand the essay's title—it's appropriate, "true stories" can be "artful lies." The key here is "artful." Abbott says the writer writes out of "obligation" and writes "to write it all down, to transform it, to set it straight" (¶15). The "it" here is experience, and Abbott says the writer needs to write but also to "transform" that experience and "set it straight." Transforming requires changing things, perhaps selecting only the key details instead of telling every mundane detail. To select one detail means not to select another, so that's one way the whole story may not get told. There's also embellishment by writers (by all of us, to make a good story better?) as they select details. Look at the picture Abbott draws of his father—his father ranges over the spectrum from good to bad, positive to negative.

10. Index the text's key terms. Just as the index of a book captures the book's important concepts, you may create your own index by identifying a text's key terms and then writing about the meaning of each and how it supports the writer's purpose. In a novel, for example, you may identify particular symbols or characters that are important. What are these, and why are they important? In a chapter in a physics text, you may identify concepts (e.g., heat transfer or masses in motion) that are important. Define these concepts, and speculate about why they are important to the chapter.

How do you identify a key term? Look for terms that appear frequently in the text. Look for terms used in the title, subtitle, and headers that recur in the body of the text. Such repetition often signals that terms are key terms. Also look for terms that appear in an essay's thesis, topic sentences, introduction, and conclusion and reappear throughout the essay.

Key Terms

Lee Abbott—"I" first person narrator throughout. reports himself as a skinny, pimply, testosterone-driven, 15–16-year old aspiring writer

father—mercurial, drinker, anger, pain, unpredictable

footlockers & steamer trunks—literal lockers and trunks in ¶s 11 & 12; figurative or metaphorical meaning in ¶15. literal meaning—holders or containers of stuff, of physical reminders of life, of past, of keepsakes. metaphorical meaning—holders or carriers of significance, things remind us of significant events and people

writing, purpose of writing (specific references in ¶s 1, 5, & 8)

inspirational (¶s 2, 6, & 15)

write it all down (¶s 13 & 14)—advice from Abbott's father that eventually proved true and inspirational

truth (¶s 1, 6, 7, & 15)

READING STRATEGIES FOR VISUALS

If we are to be good readers in today's world, we have to learn to read more than texts. We live in an increasingly visual world. Think about all the signs you see every day, signs that give you vital information without using any words. For example, we encounter signs such as the ones on the following page every day.

Both of these images have a clear meaning that we can interpret at a glance. But interpreting images isn't always a simple or easy process. Before we say more about how you can improve your ability to read visual images, let's explore what we mean by the term *image*. In the broadest sense, an image is

Sign image from the Manual of Traffic Signs <http://www.trafficsign.us/> This sign image copyright Richard C. Moeur. All rights reserved.

something that represents something else. And images aren't limited to the visual. If you have ever tasted a watermelon, your brain found a way to represent what that taste was—that is, it created an image of watermelon. If you didn't have such an image in your brain, you would not be able to pass a blindfold taste test in which you identify watermelon, as opposed to cantaloupe or some other melon. Or you wouldn't be able to taste two different kinds of chewing gum and say which of the two was peppermint and which was watermelon.

An image, then, is an attempt at representation. A visual image is an attempt to create a copy that someone's eyes can interpret as the thing being represented. If one wants to represent himself to someone else, he can use a technologically advanced camera to take a picture and then send that picture via the internet thousands of miles away. And the person who looks at that representation can feel that she is looking at him. The likeness can be so exact that a viewer can make very precise judgments about the looks of the person being represented. For example, when Ron's son, Christopher, was studying in London, he sent a picture of himself to Ron, who promptly informed Christopher that he needed a haircut. Ron hadn't seen Christopher's hair; in fact, he hadn't seen Christopher at all. But he had seen a very realistic representation of the way Christopher looked at that moment. Of course, visual representations need not be that exact. The figure on the next page is a cartoon representation of a joke that circulated in various forms shortly after it became clear that Nancy Pelosi would become the first female Speaker of the House. If a cartoonist wants to draw a cartoon in which a man talks to a woman about this issue, she can represent each of these people with rudimentary stick figures such as the ones on the following page.

Here, the key information that the cartoonist wants us to have is that one of these characters is masculine and the other is feminine, because the humor in the exchange between the two hinges on gender stereotypes. That is, the stereotypical male won't stop and ask for directions should he be lost, but the

stereotypical female will. The political implications of this cartoon are that Congress has been lost and has needed to ask for directions. But most times, those who create images want us to have more information than would be conveyed by gender. In some cases, they want us to see as exact a copy of the subject as humanly possible—as would be the case if you were sending a picture of yourself to a friend.

Or would it? Have you ever had to choose a photo of yourself to send to a friend or to send to a newspaper doing a piece about you for a local interest story? In such cases, would you decide on the basis of which of those pictures most clearly represents how you look? Or would you choose the one that makes you look the best?

Fortunately, you don't have to answer this question out loud. But we'd bet that if you answered honestly you'd say that you'd choose the picture that makes you look good. But how is this possible? Doesn't a camera represent what is really there? And if so, why would one picture make you look better than another? Of course, you know the answer to this question. In photography, perspective is everything. We look different from different perspectives, and some of those perspectives make us look better than others. Just as words have denotations and connotations—would a young teenager rather be called a young woman (or man) or an adolescent?—images have more than one type of meaning. We can get some insight into how this is so by thinking about the full meaning of the word *represent*. At the core of this word is a verb, *present*. An image presents one view of a particular person, place or thing. In doing so, it must leave out all other views that could be presented. To get a complete picture of a person, we would need a composite of all angles from which that person could be viewed. One particular picture affords us only one angle.

Steve Nease

From perspective, it is a short leap to opinion and evaluation. When we look at an image, we immediately form opinions of the people, places and things presented in that image. In some cases, for example, in political cartoons, those opinions are carefully orchestrated by those who create the images. As a case in point, let's look at the cartoon above, drawn by Steve Nease during the oil crisis in 2005.

Nease's opinion seems clear: driving a hybrid makes more sense than driving an SUV. How does he convey this opinion to us? One way he does so is by his use of perspective. There are many perspectives from which one might view a hybrid or an SUV; that is, there are many features of body style and interior design of both vehicles on which one could focus his attention. But Nease has chosen one feature for his focus: size. The hybrid looks tiny and the SUV looks huge. If Nease were using a camera, he could choose a perspective—for example, taking the shot with the grill of the SUV very close to the camera and the hybrid distant in the background—that would make the real difference in size seem even greater than it is. But as a cartoonist, Nease has even more tools of distortion at his disposal; he can focus on a feature of these vehicles and exaggerate it beyond any realistic possibility. The SUV in the cartoon stands at least three times taller than its driver, whereas the hybrid is slightly shorter than its driver, and the two drivers are approximately equal in height.

This kind of cartoon employs the technique of caricature; that is, it uses distortions of perspective to create humor and to evaluate and criticize various people and ideas in the culture. Let's look more fully at the message being conveyed in this caricature. Gas prices are listed as "LOTS" for Regular, "MORE" for Plus, and "DON'T ASK" for Super. And those prices are listed under the heading of "GA$," so that a dollar sign substitutes for the "S" in "GAS." Nease clearly implies that gas prices are exorbitant. The license plates for both vehicles also are telling. Nease has given the hybrid a plate reading "HI-BRD," which we can say is a neutral description. But the plate for the SUV reads "THIRS-T," an obvious comment on the fuel economy of the SUV. Both vehicle owners are gassing up. The hybrid owner, with a smile on her face (her dog is also smiling), is whistling, while the SUV owner, standing on tiptoes to put the nozzle in his vehicle, looks irritated and says "OH SHUT UP!" Nease uses caricature to underscore his point about SUVs versus hybrids in a gas crisis.

Reading a Visual Image

This brief consideration of perspective, opinion, and evaluation leads us to still another way in which we learn to read images: as symbols. Just as words may be interpreted denotatively, connotatively, or metaphorically, images have something like literal or denotative (representational), connotative (presentational) and associational (symbolic) meanings. Let's return to Nease's cartoon. We didn't really say anything about it as a representation, skipping that stage to talk about its connotative or evaluative elements, that is, the view that the SUV is too large and wasteful in comparison with the hybrid. But this evaluation grows out of a real representation of a scene that happens all too often in our everyday lives: we pull our cars up to gasoline pumps and stand beside the vehicles while gasoline is being pumped into our tanks.

There is yet a third way we can approach this cartoon, and that is by looking for its associational, or symbolic, meaning. What do we associate with hybrids? Many of us would associate environmentally aware people with these cars. Of course, if we see those people in a negative light, we might call them "tree-huggers." What, or who, do we associate with large SUVs? Depending on the viewpoint of those doing the talking, we might find such associations as people with large families, soccer moms, wealthy people, and people with little concern for the environment. How we used those associations would depend on the message we want to get across. If, for example, we were creating an advertisement intended to encourage people to take care of their environment, we would be much more likely to include a picture of a hybrid than one of an SUV, unless we were taking a negative tack or stance.

Given the different ways in which images convey messages to us, you should train yourself to analyze and recognize the key elements in images. Below is a summary of the strategies you may find helpful in doing so. To begin, we present three views of image: image as copy, image as viewpoint; and image as association.

Image as Copy (Representation): The first thing we do when presented with an image is to determine what it represents; that is, we look for the literal meaning in the image. For example, is this image a copy or depiction of a human being, and if so, is it a specific human being? Or of a place, or of a thing? Even though there was no attempt at realistic representation, Nease's cartoon does depict a real scene in which people are found doing things we do in everyday life.

Image as Viewpoint (Perspective): Next we begin to interpret the image, that is, to decide what meanings the image creates for us by means of the perspectives it offers. What features of the people, places, and/or things in an image does the creator use to express his ideas or opinions? In the case of Nease's cartoon, the relative size of the vehicles is a key element in getting his message across. Of course, there's more to this cartoon than this one feature. The driver of this SUV is presented as being in a very bad mood, as is obvious from the irritated expression on his face. The driver of the hybrid is presented as happy; she's whistling as she pumps the gas into her car, and even her dog has a pleasant expression on its face.

Image as Association (Symbol): Finally, we consider the symbolic meaning of the image. Some associations will be very clear because of the culture in which we live. It has often been said that, in America, bigger is better. In our consumerist society, there's a push for more and better, e.g., increasingly bigger television screens. However, here the large size of the SUV is associated with excessive oil prices that cause much pain for American consumers. A simple but fairly accurate summary of this cartoon's message is to say that the hybrid symbolizes a smart and effective way to deal with this economic situation while the SUV symbolizes an inefficient, wasteful and painful approach.

Analyzing a Visual Image

As you analyze an image, you may find the following questions and activities helpful:

1. What are your initial impressions of the image? Write a brief description of the image and decide its purpose.
2. How does the image work with any caption or title given? Does that caption or title help explain the image or set a context for it? If there are other words in the image itself, how do they work with the graphic elements?
3. In what context does the image appear? E.g., is it on the editorial page of a newspaper or on a billboard on the side of an interstate highway? What impact or influence does the context have on the image?
4. How is the image designed? What catches your eye first, second, and so on? Why is your eye drawn to these elements in this order?
5. Is the image created (e.g., a cartoon or clip art) or is it a photograph? How does this affect your understanding of the image or how it represents its subject?
6. How does the image resonate with other images you've seen before?
7. What associations do you have with the image? Are these positive? Negative? Why?
8. What is your overall impression of the image? How effective is it in its context? How does it affect you as a viewer?

> **Exercise 4.3**
>
> Images frequently supplement and so help us understand a written text, and their symbolic value cannot be underestimated. In many venues, writing and visuals cannot be separated, as they work together to create meaning. We can illustrate this point in the following exercise.
>
> A. Go to the following websites: www.chevrolet.com/silverado
> www.fordvechicles.com/f150
> How do any pictures or drawings communicate with you, the reader? Is there sound (e.g., music or speaking) at work on the site? What is the impact of that sound? What size and style of font or fonts are present in each? How does a particular font support the website's theme or message?
> B. Find two or three newspaper or news magazine articles that incorporate visual elements. What elements are used? How effectively do these elements supplement the article's main theme or point?
> C. On the following page are two images that are similar in their composition. Write a brief comparison of the two, focusing on what each represents, on the perspective of each, and on what each symbolizes.

WRITER'S NOTEBOOK: DIALOGUE NOTES

Another reading strategy is to create a section in your writer's notebook titled "Dialogue Notes." As you keep these notes, you'll create a conversation with yourself about your reading, and you may extend this strategy to include class, lecture, and lab notes and your responses to them.

Reading Notes

To begin, divide a page vertically into halves. On the right-hand side of the page, take notes on your reading, using any or all of the strategies listed in the While You Read section above. When you finish reading, go back through your notes and comment on them in the left-hand column. Raise questions; answer questions; identify curiosities; list points of interest, agreement, disagreement. Take this notebook to class and write additional clarifying notes in the left-hand side as points are discussed. Keeping this notebook will provide a record of your understanding of a text, as well as a record of class discussions of particular points.

Class Notes

You may also devote part of your writer's notebook to class notes and your response to them. In the right-hand column, take notes during discussions, lectures, laboratories, and the like. Review your notes in preparation for your next class meeting, writing responses to them in the left-hand column. If there are points

Thomas E. Franklin/The Bergen Record/Getty Images

Bill Schorr: ©United Feature Syndicate, Inc.

you don't understand, formulate a question or two to raise during class, or simply comment on what you found interesting or important. Reviewing your notes in this manner will not only help you prepare for class discussions and other activities (such as tests) but will also help you get a more comprehensive or thorough grasp of the course's materials.

Dialogue Notes

Below is an example of dialogue notes for Abbott's "The True Story of Why I Do What I Do."

Response to Notes	**Reading Notes**
Quite a style at work in here, lots of vivid language. key terms: true stories, artful lies, Boom-Boom-Boom, truth	¶1 Abbott talks about role and value of literature, especially stories. They're "true stories," "artful lies."
What's the role of Abbott's father in this? key term: inspirational	¶2 Abbott's purpose—to be "inspirational." introduces his father as a major figure
key term: In fiction . . . I comprehend my father.	¶3 description of father as he appears "in fiction" (Abbott's fiction). lots of vivid language
key term: roué, mother an over-pampered daughter	¶4 contrast: father "in life" v. "in fiction." Facts of father's life
hint of father's importance to Abbott as writer? key terms: mother a drunk, father a drinker	¶5 points toward legacy of material, based on quote from Willa Cather
key terms: this was my material, a hodgepodge of goo and muck and human blah-blah-blah, inspirational, truth (again)	¶6 legacy idea continues. 2nd time "inspirational" appears (meaning shifted?)
This ¶ seems to provide transition; it seems to set up the essay's significance, what Abbott wants to tell us about why he writes. key terms: truth (again); liturgical, quasi-holy "feel"	¶7 opens with "Once upon a time," a curious thing to see in the middle of an essay. Sets up contrast between Abbott as a teenaged aspiring writer and his father
language is vivid, especially the book jacket bit. funny	¶8 description of Abbott as budding writer, "just a kid"
key term: that Sunday afternoon	¶9 presents a contrast of father and son, interests, actions. sets up conflict to come
key terms: frustration, bitterness	¶10 father takes Abbott to utility room in the carport.
key terms: footlockers and steamer trunks, truth (repeated again—see ¶s 1, 6, & 7)	¶11 shows Abbott footlockers and trunks, repositories of the father's stuff (i.e., his life)
father's angry, pent-up fury and rage rule key terms: lockers and trunks, anger, pain	¶12 father throws lockers and trunks to ground at Abbott's feet.
key term: "Write it all down!"	¶13 only a sentence long. seems like the essay's climax, like that of a story (an artful lie?)

This ¶ moves toward an end, a conclusion of the essay. key terms: X-spot, purpose of writing, "Write it all goddamn down."	¶14 Abbott tells us father's message—what the purpose of writing ought to be, the "stuff" of writing
What's the lesson? Why do writers write? Because they want to understand themselves and the (mental) baggage they carry around? key terms: inspirational, obligation, set it straight (synonym for truth?), trunks and lockers (see ¶s 11 & 12)	¶15 essay's final ¶. Abbott sums up what he learned that day (perhaps only in retrospect), and it's a major lesson for a writer. Inspirational appears for a third time, changed in meaning again.

Exercise 4.4

Write a dialogue notebook entry for an article from a weekly magazine, such as *Newsweek, Time,* or *Sports Illustrated,* that has both text and graphic elements. You may use any of the reading strategies provided here, but be sure to preview the article (strategy 2), looking particularly at its graphic elements. What do you think of the article? What's your response to it?

WRITING PARAPHRASES AND SUMMARIES

Paraphrase and summary are essential to reading and writing, for we make meaning of the texts that we read by paraphrasing and summarizing them. And these paraphrases and summaries are then available to be used in our own writing.

Paraphrase

Although the terms *paraphrase* and *summary* are sometimes used interchangeably, it is useful to distinguish between the two. When you paraphrase, you attempt to capture what a text says in your own words; that is, you try to translate most of the content words in a passage, the nouns, verbs, adjectives, and adverbs, into your own language. This is especially important when those content words are not commonly used.

But just as important as the words in your paraphrase are the sentence structures you employ. If you are to capture your understanding of what the writer is saying in your own language, you must separate the author's meaning from the sentence structures in which she presents that meaning. As we'll see on the next page, your paraphrase must be more than a slot and filler exercise in which you reach into the writer's sentences and replace certain key words you find there with your words.

Exercise 4.5

In an essay titled "How They Chose These Words," Walter Isaacson discusses the edits that Benjamin Franklin made on Jefferson's first draft of the Declaration of Independence. Below is a paragraph from that essay and four different paraphrases of that paragraph. Order these paraphrases from worst to best. Then write a paragraph in which you explain your ranking.

The Passage

Franklin's other edits were less felicitous. He changed Jefferson's "reduce them to arbitrary power" to "reduce them under absolute despotism," and he took out the literary flourish in Jefferson's "invade and deluge us in blood" to make it more sparse: "invade and destroy us." And a few of his changes seemed somewhat pedantic. "Amount of their salaries" became "amount and payment of their salaries."

Paraphrase #1

Franklin's other changes were less helpful. He rephrased Jefferson's "reduce them to arbitrary power" to "reduce them under absolute despotism," and he replaced the high sounding language in Jefferson's "invade and deluge us in blood" to make it clearer: "invade and destroy us." And some of his other changes were pedantic. "Amount of their salaries" became "amount and payment of their salaries."

Paraphrase #2

Franklin made other changes that did not improve the text. "Reduce them to arbitrary power" was rewritten as "reduce them under absolute despotism"; the ostentatious phrase "invade and deluge us in blood" was rendered in the simple phrase "invade and destroy us." Some of the changes Franklin made seemed rather pedantic. "Amount of their salaries" was rewritten as "amount and payment of their salaries."

Paraphrase #3

Other revisions weren't as good. "Reduce them to arbitrary power" became "reduce them under absolute despotism." The powerful language of "invade and deluge us in blood" lost that power: "invade and destroy us." And then there were the stylistic changes that seemed designed to make the text sound more learned: "Amount of their salaries" was changed to "amount and payment of their salaries."

Paraphrase #4

Franklin made some other changes that were not so good. He took out some literary flourishes and he made some phrases more pedantic.

We would rank #4 as the least successful paraphrase; in fact, this is much closer to summary than to paraphrase. As we'll see below, a summary gives the overall import of a text; a paraphrase, on the other hand, offers a rewording of a text. For that reason, a paraphrase is likely to be about the same length as the text it is paraphrasing, while a summary will be considerably shorter.

After #4, the least successful paraphrase is #1. Compare the language of #1 with that of the original text. Below, we present paraphrase #1 with blank spaces representing the places where the writer changed the wording of the original text:

Franklin's other _____ were less _____. He _____ "reduce them to arbitrary power" to "reduce them under absolute despotism." And he _____ the _____ _____ _____ in Jefferson's "invade and deluge us in blood" to make it _____: "invade and destroy us." And ___ ____ of his _____ changes _____ _____ pedantic. "Amount of their salaries" became "amount and payment of their salaries."

The writer of #1 seems to approach the art of paraphrasing as if it were an exercise in replacing some of the words in original text with synonyms. To be sure, the paraphrase's writer has captured most of the meaning of the text. However, he has not captured that meaning in his own words. Although several nouns and verbs have been changed, the basic sentence structures of the original passage remain the same. If you are going to use such a high percentage of the words and sentence structures from the original text, you should quote the text in its original format.

From Paraphrase #1 we move to #2. Clearly, this writer attempts to capture the meaning she finds in that original in her own words and sentences. But there are problems with her paraphrase. Let's begin with the first sentence. Isaacson says that Franklin's other edits were "less felicitous." What he is saying is that the changes discussed in this paragraph are not as successful as the ones that he discussed in a previous paragraph. If you were to say that you were not as successful last semester in your chemistry class as you were in your history class, would it be correct to assume that you were not successful in chemistry? That is the assumption that this paraphrase makes. The writer takes the phrase "less felicitous" (where felicitous means happy, good, or successful) and makes it mean something quite different. Later, this writer replaces "literary flourish" with "ostentatious phrase." What is a literary flourish? According to the "Your Dictionary," "flourish" may have the following meanings:

1. A dramatic or stylish movement, as of waving or brandishing: *"A few . . . musicians embellish their performance with a flourish of the fingers"* (Frederick D. Bennett).
2. An embellishment or ornamentation: *a signature with a distinctive flourish.*
3. An ostentatious act or gesture: *He bowed deeply from the waist, doffing his hat with a flourish of obvious disdain.* http://www.yourdictionary.com/

Our writer has chosen a legitimate translation for flourish, but in this context it is not the best translation. If the language in the original document had been ostentatious, then something sparse might have been better. But Isaacson is criticizing Franklin for taking away the literary flourish in this passage—remember this whole paragraph is about changes that weren't as successful as they might have been. Thus, it isn't likely that Isaacson meant for the reader to see these literary flourishes as "ostentatious."

This brings us, then, to Paraphrase #3, which we see as the most successful. Here, the writer has transformed the original into her own words and sentence structures. Every assertion that is made in the original is represented by an assertion here. Clearly, this paraphrase does not say exactly the same thing as the original; anytime we change the words or the arrangement of words, we change the meaning in some sense. But this rephrasing is about as close to an original as possible. If one wants to be more faithful to the text than this, then one wants a quotation, not a paraphrase.

Exercise 4.6

Below is a passage from Mortimer Adler's "How to Mark a Book." After you've read it:

1. Paraphrase this passage and then write a paragraph in which you discuss any difficulties you had in this process.
2. Compare your paraphrase with that of a classmate. What do you learn about the original and the art of paraphrasing by comparing these two paraphrases?

The Passage

Confusion about what it means to "own" a book leads people to a false reverence for paper, binding, and type — a respect for the physical thing — the craft of the printer rather than the genius of the author. They forget that it is possible for a man to acquire the idea, to possess the beauty, which a great book contains, without staking his claim by pasting his bookplate inside the cover. Having a fine library doesn't prove that its owner has a mind enriched by books; it proves nothing more than that he, his father, or his wife, was rich enough to buy them.

WRITING STRATEGY

Checklist for Writing a Paraphrase

1. Is your paraphrase about the same length as the original?
2. Have you written the paraphrase in your own words, or have you simply done a fill-in-the-blank exercise?
3. Have you kept to the original intent of the writer?
4. Have you provided appropriate documentation? If you use information from your summary as part of your own writing, remember that you must document it; that is, you must provide both a citation in the body of your essay and a reference to the source as part of a "Works Cited" page. (For more information about documenting sources, see pages 601–618.)

Summary

Like paraphrase, summary is a powerful reading and writing tool. In paraphrasing, you restate, in your own words, the meaning of a text. In summary, you reduce and capture the essential meaning of a text. To do so, you identify the important parts of the text and then create an overview of it.

Your goal in summarizing is to report the text's main idea or ideas accurately, so that someone who hasn't read the text can gain an overview of it just from reading your summary. How long should a summary be? Generally, the length is determined by the length of the piece being summarized. A 500-word passage should be summarized in only a few sentences, but an entire book probably can't be summarized well in fewer than 500 words.

Follow these steps in writing a summary:

1. Read the text carefully, using some or all of the reading strategies we've presented so far.
2. Look back through the text, taking note of what you've marked as important, and write a brief list of the text's major points. If you don't understand something, jot down a couple of questions to ask when your class discusses the reading or in conference with your teacher.
3. Write a sentence or two giving your impression of the text's purpose or significance.
4. Write a sentence in which you capture each of the main points in the text.
5. Using the sentences you wrote in #3 and #4, draft an initial summarizing paragraph, being sure to connect these sentences with transitions that capture the major relationships between these ideas.
6. Let this paragraph sit awhile; then return to it and revise it for accuracy, completeness, and style.
7. In your final draft, include the author's name, the text's title, and complete publication information.

Exercise 4.7

Read the following essay, which deals with racist language.

February 2, 1999, *New York Times*

STEVEN PINKER

RACIST LANGUAGE, REAL AND IMAGINED

Last week David Howard, an aide to the Mayor of Washington, resigned after a staff meeting in which he called his budget "niggardly." A colleague thought he had used a racial epithet, though in fact "niggard" is a Middle English word meaning "miser." It has nothing to do with the racial slur based on Spanish for "black," which came into English centuries later.

This is not the first time the inaccurate parsing of an innocent remark has led to confusion. Remember, in "Annie Hall," how Woody Allen thinks he has been the target of an anti-Semitic slur from two people on a New York street? One person had asked, "Dj'ou eat yet?" and his companion had replied, "No, dj'ou?"

Last week's misunderstanding was of a different sort. "Niggardly" may be unexceptionable on etymological grounds, but given what we know about how the mind deals with language, the word was a disaster waiting to happen.

Most words and parts of words have many meanings, and when we listen to someone speak, our brains have to find the right ones. Some recent laboratory experiments indicate that this is a two-stage process.

First, all the meanings of a word, including inappropriate ones, light up willy-nilly in the brain. When we hear about "spiders, roaches and bugs," the thought of surveillance devices flashes through our minds for a few hundredths of a second—until that misinterpretation is repressed by our analysis of the context.

Thus it is impossible for anyone to hear "niggardly" without thinking, if only for a moment, of the ethnic slur.

Worse, the context is of little help in squelching the wrong meaning. Everyone is an amateur linguist, and we all strive for a logical – though sometimes incorrect— parsing of what we hear. This is why folk etymologies are rampant in dialects, like "sparrowgrass" (asparagus) and "very-close" (varicose) veins.

Many phrases have become standard English, like chaise lounge (from the French chaise longue or "long chair"), cockroach (from the Spanish cucaracha) and bridegroom (originally bridgome, Middle English for "bride man").

"Niggardly" is easy to mis-parse. English grammar allows a "d" or "ed" to be stuck on a noun to form an adjective (as in "hook-nosed" and "left-handed"), and it allows "ly" to be put on an adjective to form an adverb.

Thus we get "absent-mindedly," "good-humoredly," "half-heartedly," "markedly," "otherworldly," "pointedly," "shame-facedly" and "single-handedly."

The "a" is not much help, because "ar" often substitutes for "er"—as in "beggar," "burglar," "hangar" and "scholar."

Worst of all, the deducible meaning makes all-too-good linguistic sense. Terms for stinginess and duplicitousness are among the most common examples of racist language: "to gyp" (probably from gypsy), "to welsh" (perhaps from Welsh), "Dutch treat," "Indian giver."

Does this mean a perfectly innocent word is doomed? It would not be the first time. Words are often sacrificed when they take on secondary, emotionally charged meanings. "Queer," for example is now problematic, and many animals (like donkeys) are losing their fine old Anglo-Saxon names.

If you find yourself vaguely offended thinking of the other words I could have included here, you should have some sympathy for David Howard's audience.

Still, Mr. Howard should get his job back. Though "niggardly" begs to be misunderstood, the misunderstanding can be overruled. After the various associates of a word light up in the mental dictionary, the rest of the brain can squelch the unintended ones, thanks to the activity that psycholinguists call "post-lexical-access processing" and that other people call "common sense."

1. Write a brief summary of Pinker's essay, then compare your summary to the one on the next page. (Before the summary, we present our list of the main points of the essay.) How would you characterize the difference between your summary and ours?

2. Examine the transitions in our summary. Write a paragraph in which you explain how the transitions help to identify the focal points in the essay.

Main Points in the Text

Howard called the mayor of Washington's budget "niggardly."
Howard resigned.
"niggard" is a Middle English word meaning "miser".
It is not etymologically related to the racial slur.
Most words and parts of words have many meanings.
Recent lab experiments indicate that when our brains try to understand a word, they go through a two-step process: various meanings of the word "light up" in the brain; context helps us suppress wrong meanings and favor right meanings.
Folk etymologies abound when the context does not make it clear that a word is not related to a given sound.
Niggardly is a prime example of what can go wrong. The meaning of the two words, "niggard" and "nigger" and the processes by which nouns are made into adjectives conspire to make it seem that "niggardly" is derived from "nigger."
Sometimes such happenstances cause us to have to give up an otherwise perfectly good word.
Howard should be given his job back.

Summary of "Racist Language, Real and Imagined"

In "Racist Language, Real and Imagined" (*New York Times*, 2 Feb. 1999), Steven Pinker takes the occasion of the resignation of David Howard, an aide to the Mayor of Washington, D.C., to explain the way the brain processes words. Pinker says that while Howard should not lose his job for using the word "niggardly" in reference to the mayor's budget, there are certain words that have to be removed from our vocabularies because our brains may tend to misunderstand them. While the words "niggardly" and "nigger" have very different etymologies, the normal functioning brain will always think of the word "nigger" when it hears the word "niggardly." This kind of thing happens with a word like "bug," which will, for a second, be associated with an insect and with a surveillance device any time it is processed. However, unlike the two meanings of "bug," which will always be used in very different contexts, the two meanings of "niggardly" and "nigger" share certain negative associations which may well cause certain people to think there is an etymological connection between the words. Thus, this word will always have the potential of causing problems we would want to avoid.

We chose Pinker's essay for this summary because, even though it is short, it is not easy to summarize. Because Pinker begins his essay by talking about David Howard and what happened to him when he inadvertently used the word "niggardly," and then ends by asserting that Howard should not lose his job, it is very tempting to write a summary that makes this essay about Howard. We could easily imagine a summary something like the following:

In "Racist Language, Real and Imagined," Steven Pinker tells the story of what happened when David Howard, an aide to the mayor of Washington, D.C., used the word "niggardly." Pinker says that Howard's use of this word should not cause Howard to lose his job, and he explains how Howard's use of "niggardly" could have been misunderstood by people who were not paying close attention to what this word really means.

It would be easy to write such a summary as this, but to do so would be to misread Pinker's essay. The essay is not about David Howard; rather it is about language and the way language works. Pinker uses what happened to Howard as a pretext to teach his readers something about the way language works and to suggest that when we understand fully how it works, we will know that at times we have to give up perfectly good words because of the associations they occasion. A careful reading of this essay will produce a summary that focuses on language and the way language works, not on Howard's situation.

Exercise 4.8

The two summaries below were written for an essay that appears in Chapter 6, pages 216–218, "Mommy, What Does 'Nigger' Mean?" Examine the two summaries and then write a paragraph in which you explain why one of these is a more effective summary than the other.

Summary A

Although she begins her essay, "Mommy, What Does 'Nigger' Mean?" by announcing her refusal to enter the debate concerning the role of language in shaping reality, Gloria Naylor makes it clear that she believes humans can, and should, control language, rather than allowing it to control them. Naylor recounts the story of how she first heard the word "nigger" in the third grade, when a fellow student used it to insult her. She then recounts that even though the term "nigger" had been used in her presence by her parents and relatives many times prior to this insult, she had not understood it as derogatory because of the contexts and inflections within which it had been set. She then details the various positive meanings the term had been given in those various contexts. Naylor acknowledges that some might see her family's use of this term as a case of "internalization of racism," but she argues that racism would exist even if the specific word "nigger" went away. In Naylor's view her family's "transformation" of the meaning of this word was an act of defiance against those who would try to deny them their full humanity.

Summary B

In "Mommy What Does 'Nigger' Mean?" Gloria Naylor supports the use of the word "nigger." She tells about the first time she heard the word; a classmate in the third grade used it to insult her, though she didn't really know what it meant at that time. Naylor recounts how she had to ask her mother what the word meant at the time, but in refection she now knows that she had often heard the word used in many positive ways by members of her extended family: in the singular, it referred to a man who had done something good; with the possessive and used by a woman, it was a term of endearment; in other contexts, the word represented "the pure essence of manhood." It could also have a negative meaning in the plural, describing a group of people who had "overstepped their bounds." So when Naylor's mother took her into her lap and explained the meaning of the word, "nigger," she was explaining that blacks could, and should, use the term to mean very good things about themselves but that when whites used it against blacks, it was always used as an insult.

WRITING STRATEGY

Checklist for Writing a Summary

1. Have you given the author's name, the text's title, and complete publication information?
2. What is the text's main idea? How accurately have you reported it?
3. Have you directly quoted key words or terms, perhaps even entire sentences? If so, have you identified direct quotations by placing them in quotation marks?
4. If you have included specific details (e.g., data or examples), is the information absolutely essential for the summary to make sense?
5. How long is it? If you've summarized a shorter piece, does your summary run more than 120–200 words? If you've worked with a longer piece, is your summary long enough to capture the spirit and content of that text?
6. Have you provided appropriate documentation? If you use information from your summary as part of your own writing, remember that you must document it; that is, you must provide both a citation in the body of your essay and a reference to the source as part of a "Works Cited" page. (For more information about documenting sources, see pages 601–618.)

Exercise 4.9

1. Select two or three items from a weekly magazine such as *Newsweek, Time,* or *Sports Illustrated* and write a summary of each. Bring the articles with you to class, and exchange one article and summary with a classmate. Read your classmate's article and summary, and discuss with him his summary's accuracy.
2. Read and summarize an essay selected by your instructor from one of the chapters in this textbook. Exchange your summary with those of two of your classmates. How are their summaries similar to yours? Different? How do you account for any differences you find? How accurate do you think their summaries are, even though they may be different from yours?

WRITING A RESPONSE

Writing a response to a text requires you to go beyond summarizing to interpreting the material you read. In reading to understand a text, you need to be able to tell not only what it was about but also what you think it means. Such interpretation is crucial to critical reading, and it's important that you decide and write about the worth or value of what you read. Responding to a text begins with summary and then continues with a value judgment of some kind about the reading. Why should you summarize a text before responding to it? Writing a summary oftentimes gives you insight that you might not get otherwise, because you have to be engaged with the text to summarize it. And checking your summary against the text by rereading both can help you gauge the accuracy of your summary; it can help you identify portions of the text that you haven't understood clearly and so need to reconsider.

To make a value judgment is to consider the quality of the text you read. This judgment may take the form of a fairly straightforward statement of like or dislike. Or you may want to argue or take issue with the writer on one or more aspects of the reading. Several of the questions based on consequence in the Questions for Analysis (see pages 26–27) can guide you in writing a response:

> *What did you learn from the text?* What new information did the writer present to you? Do you count it valuable or not? Why?
>
> *What did you learn by investigating the topic of the text?* If the reading inspired you to do some reading or other kinds of investigation into the topic, what did you learn? Do you count it valuable or not? Why?
>
> *What problems are inherent in the topic? What are their solutions?* Did the author identify problems to which you might respond? Do you agree or disagree with the author's solutions? Or did the reading raise problems for you? What in the reading is potentially problematic for you? Why?
>
> *What about the text is good? Bad? Desirable? Undesirable? Necessary?* Would you recommend this reading to a friend? Why or why not? To what extent was the reading helpful to you in the context of any assignment that required you to read it? Why?

Answering such questions as these can help you find a focal point—something about the text that intrigued or angered or irritated or amused you—to use as the center of your response. Once you have a focal point, you may then decide what you want your response to do. It may

1. argue with the text's author—you may find points of agreement or disagreement, and you may write either to support the author's points or to disagree with, perhaps even debunk, them.
2. evaluate the text—you may evaluate the effectiveness of the text as a whole or of some particular aspect of it. How clearly did the author write? How effective was her argument, how effectively supported? How fairly did the author treat her subject?

3. comment on the text's meaning or importance to you—to what extent does the text ring true in your own experience? What did it say that you count important to you personally?

Whether arguing, evaluating, or commenting, you should begin your written response with a summary of the text, so that your reader will have a concise, accurate overview of the text. Next, present your opinion of the text, and then support that opinion with enough detail from the text to let your reader understand your point of view.

Your goal in writing a response is to provide a quick evaluation of the reading at hand. Not everyone will respond to a piece of writing in the same way. The following sample responses to Lee Abbott's "The True Story of Why I Do What I Do" should illustrate this point, that is, that different readers won't see the same things in a given piece of writing. Before you read the responses, review both the dialogue notes we gave for this essay (pages 131–132). How accurately do the summaries reflect the contents of the essays? How does each response differ from the others? With which response(s) do you agree? Disagree? Why?

Response #1

"The True Story . . ." is a fine piece of writing. I like the way Abbott chooses just the right word to get his meaning across. His language is vivid, his sentence structure delightfully comprehensive, sometimes even convoluted, but always fun to read. I like the description of him and his father—one "tuned to the stupid clatter of the exterior world" and the other "tuned to the twilight interior world of fetch-and-keep, of fantasy." Abbott makes some important points about what it means to be a writer. The writer's obligation, Abbott says, is to write out the truth as he knows it from within himself, to let the writing flow from within so that he creates a record of that truth for others to see. It's a good lesson for any aspiring writer.

Response #2

I got lost in reading this essay. I think there's a lot of worthwhile stuff in here, and I think Abbott's right about the writer's purpose to "write it all down." That was the lesson his father taught him by throwing all his old Army trunks and footlockers around. But it's sometimes a difficult piece to read—I got lost in a couple of sentences and had to go back to figure them out. When I did get them figured out, I thought it was worth my time to do so, and I think the essay speaks the truth about the writer's job.

Response #3

There's just too much busy-ness going on in here to suit my tastes. Abbott certainly likes to play with words. Just look at "Boom-Boom-Boom" and the "hodgepodge of goo and muck and human blah-blah-blah." Seems a little overdone at times. Abbott's a skillful writer, no doubt about it. And the theme he wants me to get—the purpose of writing—well, I get it. But I think I want more directness in what I read.

SAMPLE STUDENT ESSAY—SUMMARY AND RESPONSE

Christian Clark, a first-year writing student at Sam Houston State University, wrote the following essay to evaluate the effectiveness of another piece of student writing in *The Longwood Guide*. Christian blends summary and response in his analysis of Jaclyn Talbert's "Justice for Those Who Have Shown Us No Mercy," which you'll find on pages 504–506. Read Jaclyn's essay first, then Christian's evaluation of it.

CHRISTIAN CLARK

EMOTION AND THE DEATH PENALTY: AN ANALYSIS OF JACLYN TALBERT'S "JUSTICE FOR THOSE WHO HAVE SHOWN US NO MERCY"

1   Capital punishment is a controversial topic of discussion that frequently forecasts impassioned debate. The nature of the topic does not generally allow one to hold a neutral position, but instead evokes a strong opinion either for or against the death penalty. Between these opposing black and white stances is a multiplicity of arguments to convince others that one opinion is superior to the other. Jaclyn Talbert, the author of the essay "Justice for Those Who Have Shown Us No Mercy," offers several arguments in hopes of persuading her audience that her pro death penalty stance is one that we should all adopt.

2   Although the intent of the essay is not fully revealed until paragraph seven, the process by which Talbert arrives at that point proves to be a successful method of engaging the reader on the subject of capital punishment. Talbert begins her persuasive message by sharing a personal account from her life that has undoubtedly influenced her opinion on this matter: only two days after celebrating her sixteenth birthday, Talbert's cousin became the sixth victim of a murderer who, after being apprehended and diagnosed insane, was exiled to "a home for the mentally ill, where he continues to live in peace and quiet" (Talbert 504). She continues by describing the daily turmoil experienced by her aunt and uncle and the rest of her family as they try desperately to recover from the loss of their beloved daughter and cousin.

3   Talbert continues by recounting additional detailed and sobering stories to draw the audience into her thoughts before revealing the purpose of the entire essay. First is the story of Susan Smith, a woman who killed her own two children by driving her car into a lake with the precious cargo still inside. Talbert's

drawing on this incident is effective because it was sensational and made national news at the time it occurred. Many people were probably aware of the details and had formed an opinion similar to Talbert's prior to reading the essay, so this helps her readers recall the unsettling thoughts they encountered when they first heard about the mother. Moreover, people universally see children as being completely innocent, so there is absolutely no excuse that permits sympathy for someone who brings harm to a child. Talbert's next example involves Matthew Heikka, an adopted son who murdered his loving parents "for money and the car" (505). From prison, he writes to his girlfriend that his one regret was not killing her when he had the chance.

All three of these examples lay the groundwork for Talbert's thesis by implying that the criminals in these cases have not been adequately punished. They have committed inexplicable crimes against humanity, yet they sit comfortably in jail while the families of the victims suffer great sorrow and loss knowing that they will never again see their child, or mother, or brother. By appealing to the emotions of the reader Talbert is trying to convince her audience that the emphasis of concern should fall on the victim and the victim's family rather than on the murderer, who with a plea of insanity could contentedly spend the rest of his life "in a state supported hotel" (505). After presenting these examples, Talbert clearly states her position:

> The murderer is not the one who deserves our pity. The victim and the victim's family should be our primary concern.
> The murderer should die. (506)

Although she has significant personal reasons for taking a strong stance on the topic, she never depicts capital punishment as a form of revenge. She makes it clear that her pro death penalty position has nothing to do with inflicting torture upon the killer, nor is she seeking revenge; she simply wants murderers removed from society so that there will never be the possibility that they might repeat their crime. By revealing the account of the son who only wished that he had killed his girlfriend when he had the chance, Talbert stresses that not only is the convicted man not sorry for his gruesome actions, but would have gone even further given the opportunity. This individual planned the murder months in advance, admitted that he knew his parents adored him, yet still proceeded to shoot his mother in the head as she told him that she loved him. Knowing that he could plead insanity and avoid the death penalty, he even went so far as to indicate that he would continue his killing spree after being released in twenty years. Talbert is trying to persuade the reader that a more substantial sentence is required for such a criminal. Her point is this: reality suggests that had this vengeful man been sentenced to death, there would be no chance for him to take the life of his girlfriend; therefore, there is no other solution.

Talbert's knowledge on the subject of capital punishment does not arise from statistics or scientific studies, but rather from a wholly emotional right versus wrong standpoint. In all of the aforementioned situations, Talbert expresses her belief that murderers should not be afforded the luxury of living in a jail or psychiatric hospital. Should they be allowed to have familial visits, while their victim's family is required to go to a cemetery to visit their loved one? Talbert does not think so, and her objective in this essay is to show why she feels this way. She effectively provides a number of relevant points while introducing and supporting her view in favor of capital punishment. Even from the title, the reader becomes instantly aware of the tone that will be utilized throughout the work. Talbert purely desires justice for the families of murder victims, nothing more, nothing less.

It is unlikely that Talbert will persuade those opposed to the death penalty, those who feel that capital punishment is inhumane, to adopt her point of view. Instead, the audience that Talbert attempts to reach consists of readers who may be neutral or have pro death penalty leanings but have not been moved to act on those feelings. The compelling approach by which she presents her message should, at least, cause her readers to question their own thoughts on the death penalty. In doing so, Talbert succeeds in convincing others to consider her opinion in support of capital punishment.

Work Cited

Talbert, Jaclyn. "Justice for Those Who Have Shown Us No Mercy." *The Longwood Guide to Writing*, Fourth Edition. Ronald F. Lunsford and Bill Bridges. New York: Longman, 2005. 504–506.

✦ WRITING OPPORTUNITY

Select another essay in *The Longwood Guide*. Read it, using several of the reading strategies presented in this chapter. Write both a summary of and a response to it; then write an evaluation based on the information you've generated with the reading strategies, your summary, and your response. ✦

Exercise 4.10

Locate an essay on the Internet. Read it on-line, and complete a reading log entry for it, including summary and response. How is this experience different from reading and responding to a hard-copy text? Which do you prefer? Why?

PART II

Writing Occasions

In Part II, we present seven occasions for writing. Of course, there will be thousands of occasions on which you will write during the course of your life, and they will all differ in certain ways. But they will also share similarities. Our seven chapters on writing occasions represent our attempt at very broad categories that capture some of these similarities and differences.

Before we discuss these occasions, however, we need to explain two terms that we use in talking about them: *aims of discourse* and *modes of discourse*.

AIMS OF DISCOURSE

Central to the concept of aims of discourse is the rhetorical triangle (see page xiv). This triangle allows us to analyze any writing situation according to three key elements: a writer, a subject, and a reader. Another way of looking at this is that in any writing situation, someone is saying something to somebody. This is rather basic and obvious. All three elements would have to exist, or there would be no reason for writing. But the elements may be seen as being more or less important in various writing situations—and this is where rhetorical aims come in.

Rhetorical aims allow us to look at the three elements in the rhetorical triangle as if they were rings in a three-ring circus. If you've ever been to a circus, you know that it's virtually impossible to attend to the action occurring in all three rings at once. The ringmaster proudly announces what is in the center ring, for instance, and the circus spotlight shines down on this ring in such a way as to move what is going on in the other two rings to the background. Our attention is captured by the spotlighted act.

This is not to say that the acts in the other two rings are no longer there or no longer worth paying some attention to. It wouldn't be a three-ring circus without them. And if one of those acts is particularly interesting to you for some reason—perhaps you're learning to juggle and there is a juggling act in the ring on the right—you may resist the pull of the center ring and fasten your attention on the other ring instead. Whether you do or not, it is still there. The same is true with writing. All three rings are always there—writer, subject, and reader—but in some writing situations, the spotlight is on the writer. In other situations, the subject is spotlighted, and in still other situations, the reader is spotlighted.

Think for a minute about three very different types of writing you might do. Have you ever had an experience that was so powerful, exciting, or unusual that you wanted to capture something of that experience in writing? Perhaps you wrote about it in your journal or diary. Or you may have simply written a letter to yourself in which you recounted some of its high points and some of your feelings about it.

Now consider another very different type of writing. Have you ever written a note or a letter telling a friend how to find your house? Perhaps your friend lives in a different city and has never visited your home. You begin with some landmark close to you that you assume your friend will pass, and then you direct your friend point by point to find your home from there.

Finally, consider a situation in which you bought a product, used it for a short time, and found it defective in some way. You attempted to return it to the local store that sold it to you, but because the normal time for returns had passed and you did use the product for a brief time before finding it defective, you were told that you could not return it for the purchase price. The clerk suggested that you check into the warranty and have the product repaired for a reasonably low cost. However, you feel that the product was defective and should be replaced or your money refunded. So you want to write the company and convince its customer service office of your point of view.

What will be the focus in these three types of writing? In the first, in which you try to capture an important experience, you will no doubt focus on what this experience meant to you. Ten or twenty years from now, you may well be able to remember or reconstruct the itinerary of an important trip, but you will probably not be able to remember the specific details of what you did on one particular afternoon or the way a particular sunset affected you. Your focus in writing about this experience is on yourself as experiencer—and writer.

You'll have a different focus in the writing situation in which you offer directions to a friend who intends to visit you. Most likely, you will spend time going over the route in your mind. If Ron were writing these directions for Bill, he might proceed by thinking: "Okay, Bill's going to get to my house by beginning at the intersection of I–85 and Highway 73. So, when he gets off the interstate and turns left, how far will he have to go before he gets to the Circle K, where he'll turn right? I travel that road every day, but I haven't really measured the distance. What would I guess it to be? And then he turns right onto Trinity Church Road and goes—now how far is that? And then it's a right onto Orphanage Road and about—what? One or two miles, before he turns left onto—what is the name of that little road?" Your focus here is on the subject, on giving accurate directions.

And for the final piece of writing, the one in which you'll attempt to get a replacement or a refund for a defective product, you'll have yet another focus—this time, on the reader. You may begin by asking for a policy statement from the company so that you can read about the procedures for returns. After studying that document, you may reason along these lines: Technically, you kept the product a bit longer than prescribed in the document. But, after all, you bought the lawnmower at the end of the mowing season, so, although you have had it for six months, you have effectively just bought it. Furthermore, you meet all of the other criteria for returns—you have a sales receipt, you have all the packaging the product came in, and so forth.

How does all this relate to the rhetorical triangle? In the first writing situation—writing about an exciting trip or event—you focus on yourself as writer. In the second situation, writing directions to your friend, you focus on the subject. And in the third situation, in which you are attempting to get your money back, you focus on the company representative who will decide on your claim—your reader. Every writing situation will require all three elements of the rhetorical triangle. In writing about your personal experience, you must have a subject to write about—the events of the trip in this case. And there is a reader, even if that reader is only yourself ten or twenty years from now. But your spotlight is on yourself as experiencer (and writer). As you ponder what word or phrase to use in capturing an exhilarating moment, your focus is on capturing what this trip meant to you.

Similarly, in giving directions to a friend, you still exist as writer and your friend is your reader. But the subject is spotlighted as you sit to write. What are you thinking about? To some degree, you will have to be aware of what your friend knows about the area you live in, but right now, first and foremost, you have to get down what you know about it. In our example, Ron has to ask: How far is it from I–85 to the Circle K? What is the name of that little street that intersects with Orphanage Road? If he cannot come up with satisfactory answers to these questions, he will find himself making the drive from I–85 to his home and focusing on those things he looks at every day but never "sees." He is clearly spotlighting the subject—the path he takes from I–85 to his house.

And in the letter about the defective product, you certainly exist as writer, and you have something to say, but the spotlight is on the reader. You want something from this reader—your money back. And if you don't get it, your writing will not have been successful—no matter how well you know your subject. As you sit down to write this letter, you focus on your reader and the rules under which your reader is operating. Your task is to show that the rule you have broken—keeping the product too long before returning it—is a minor technicality and that in all other respects you are operating within the guidelines the company has set down; thus, your reader should refund your money.

These are the aims, then, that form the major divisions within Part Two:

Spotlight on Writer	Chapter 5, Personal Essays
Spotlight on Subject	Chapter 6, Information Essays
	Chapter 7, Essays *About* and *From* Literature
Spotlight on Reader	Chapter 8, Evaluation Essays
	Chapter 9, Position Essays
	Chapter 10, Persuasion Essays
	Chapter 11, Problem/Solution Essays

MODES OF DISCOURSE

You may already know the term *modes of discourse*. In the past, you may have used modes of discourse to label writing situations. If you were asked to write a paper based on modes, you understood that in a narrative, you tell a story; in a description, you describe a person, place, or thing; in an exposition, you explain something; and in an argument, you defend an assertion.

Whether or not you have worked with these modes, you can no doubt see the logic here. But the logic does not hold up. If you examine some of the writing in our occasional chapters, you will find that most writing employs more than one mode. In a personal essay, you will no doubt narrate *and* describe, and you may well *explain* certain things. We call an essay "personal" not because it uses narration, but because the writer's aim is to focus attention on his experiences. We call an information essay by that name not because it tends to use explanatory modes—such as comparison and causality—but because the writer's aim is to focus attention on the subject about which he is writing.

WEDDING AIM AND MODE

To summarize, then, a writer's aim is determined by which of the elements in the rhetorical triangle he wishes to spotlight. In spotlighting any one element, he may well use several modes to order, or structure, his essay. In a sense, when we know the writer's aim, we know *what* he is writing about. When we examine the various modes he employs, we gain insight into *how* he accomplishes his aim. The following list identifies the key question a writer will ask for each of the expository modes. As the writer answers these questions, the structure of his essay will unfold.

Mode	Key Question That Provides Structure
Narration	What happens next?
Description	How does my topic look, smell, taste, feel, and/or sound?
Process	How do I do this, or how does this thing work?
Comparison	How are these things alike or different from one another?
Causality	How does one of these things derive from or lead to the other?
Classification	How are the things in this group like each other and different from things in similar groups?
Definition	What names will be assigned to any one item (or the various items) in the group(s) I have identified?
Analysis	How do the elements of this thing or event fit together to form the whole?

CLASSIFYING OCCASIONS

We are now ready to return to the writing occasions. There is nothing magical about the seven writing occasions we have chosen to present. Our choice of these occasions is itself an example of the use of classification. Since the criteria by which we have developed this classification are ours—and not those of the writers of these essays—it should be expected that some of the essays seem to fit our categories better than others do. For example, Michael Haley's essay, "The Right Not to Listen," seems to fit our concept of the position essay very well. Stephen Jay Gould's "Non overlapping Magisteria," however, fits less well. But we decided that it more nearly fit a position occasion than a persuasion occasion and thus included it in the position essay chapter.

As you work through these chapters and read the various sample essays in them, remember that we offer our classification to help you analyze and emulate some of the strategies these writers use. Above all else, these essays are examples of people taking the time to share their thoughts on various subjects with their readers. In the end, that should be the goal of your writing.

Ernest L. Blumenschein, "Sangre de Christo Mountains," 1926. Oil on canvas, 50 1/8 × 60 in. Courtesy of The Anschutz Collection, Denver. Photo: William J. O'Connor.

CHAPTER 5

Personal Essays

The personal essay is close to the writer's self. The writer often begins by trying to gain personal insight into a situation or event but then looks beyond and shapes her writing so that readers can share her experience. Your goal as a writer of a personal essay is to structure your thoughts so that your reader can experience, insofar as possible, what you experienced.

Why write a personal essay? Such an essay can serve you in a number of ways. It can help you gain perspective on a meaningful time in your life so that you come to understand that time in deeper ways than you had before. It can help you explore an important shaping or defining moment of your life. Or it can help you rediscover a significant experience, so that you may relive that experience, albeit from a distance.

Writing this essay can help you with other college courses, because you'll be strengthening your writing skills as you work through this assignment. It will help you practice using details, a skill you'll need in informative and persuasive writing. While other kinds of writing provide practice in using such materials as statistics and facts, a personal essay allows you to hone the narrative and descriptive skills that help provide substance and support in expository and argumentative writing situations.

SAMPLE ESSAYS

Read the following examples of personal essays, and respond to the questions that follow each. As you read, keep in mind that each essay carries significance for its writer. Try to identify that significance, or importance, and decide how the writer presents or reveals it to you.

Our first sample essay was written by Datus Proper, a travel writer with a national reputation. This particular essay, which focuses on an event Proper experienced while he was fishing a favorite stream, appeared in *Field & Stream*.

Datus Proper

DARK HOLLOW

Fish a place long enough and it becomes a homestead, a personal stretch of boulders and water and trout. I've been proving my claim on Dark Hollow Run for twenty years now, so I wondered about the other car parked on Skyline Drive, right where I always start my hike down to the stream. Maybe the visitor was just the usual refugee from the city, out for a stroll on the Appalachian Trail, but then again I might find a fisherman ahead of me. I hurried down the mountainside with my rod and rucksack.

The visitor was easy to catch. "Hill's getting hard to pull," she said. Her hair was more gray than red where it fell over the lace collar of her dress. Her name was Betty Cave and her only burden was a bunch of flowers, but it established a claim 200 years older than mine. I read the names of her family when we got to what used to be the Dark Hollow settlement.

There were more headstones in the clearing than Betty had flowers to decorate—rough fieldstones, big ones and little ones, lots of little ones. One of the unmarked stones was for the Cave who brought the family's red hair from Ireland to the Blue Ridge long ago. The oldest legible marker was for John G. Cave of the Virginia Light Artillery, C.S.A. Near it there were stones for Betty's parents and her sister Lula Belle.

Not far away was a fireplace, stones chinked with mud, standing lonely in the woods. Betty Cave had stories to go with that old hearth. It had been part of her family's cabin, once, and she remembered the days when her mother tended the fire and her father came home with food.

Daddy used to bring a leather pouch with trout spilling over the top. He caught 'em on worms—big fish, like this—a foot long, some of 'em. They was real pretty. Mama cleaned 'em all and kept 'em cool in a stone jar in the springhouse. The meat was pink when she cooked 'em. They tasted awful good.

I strung up my rod, tied on a little dark-water fly, and worked upstream making backcasts when I could, but otherwise just pushing the line out. This sounds impossible—like pushing a string—but you get good at pushcasting on Dark Hollow Run. When there is brush behind, you just pile line on the water at your feet, hold the rod straight up, and make half a roll-cast, the forward half. It's not a way to break distance records. The line goes where the rod tip points, though, and the fish are not far away. The little fly rights itself, shimmies its peacock body at the trout, and flashes you a V-for-victory sign with white wings. You hold the rod tip high so that the line does not get caught in the fast water at the tail of the pool. You want the fly to take life easy, like a big trout.

7   Watching a good fly is like watching a bird dog that knows what it's doing. You have faith. Almost every pool has at least a small fish—in the middle, where a trout can hold in slow water and foray into the current for a passing snack, or in the calm patch above a boulder, or in little eddies at the head of the pool. When the fly dallies over just the right spot, the fish responds. A little one is a sparkle, making up its mind and pouncing in the same instant. A big trout is a shadow, a lovely lazy rise without fuss.

8   The oldtimers all say that the fish used to run larger than they do now. Betty Cave tends to understatement, like most of the mountain people, so you must not dismiss her foot-long trout as yarn-spinning. I don't know what has changed the ecology of the stream. Acid rain is probably involved and so are the young oaks and maples, which drink up moisture that used to reach the Run. There was more water for the fish when the Caves lived in Dark Hollow.

9   *We had 400 acres, all grass but for the orchard and the hemlocks around the house. We kept the brush cut down till the government made us leave. We grazed six heifers and a horse and two milk cows, and Mama stored the butter in the springhouse.*

10 *Grandma planted that snowball bush, too. It blooms every June and the apple trees still set fruit, but the pears and peaches are shaded out now. Mama used to can all the fruit. Mama and Daddy worked hard, but we weren't hungry.*

11 I worked hard, too, sneaking up to the tails of pools, sitting on a rock to keep my head below the trout's line of sight, and planning before each cast. The brook trout that took the fly were two-year-olds about 7 inches long. None of the big three-year-olds would rise to my fly. The concentration was tiring, more so than the walk down the mountain. I was relieved to reach the Lunch Pool, sit on a patch of moss, and pull out my food.

12 The Lunch Pool is one of those places that just grew around me over the years. Maybe it was in the middle of my homestead water because I deserved a break, or maybe I staked my claim knowing that the pool was available. The sycamore tree beat me there by a long time, anyhow. It may have been growing even in the days of Great-grandfather Cave. The trunk was as thick as four Dark Hollow girls standing back to back, pale toes wriggling down into the pool.

13 I ate each of my rye crackers with a sardine dripping oil on it and halfway through lunch there was a grumble over the ridge to the south. Dark clouds moved overhead fast but the thunder stayed lazy. A few raindrops made rings in the pool while I rushed through my apple, and then there was another ring made from below the water. I stripped line off the reel and covered the fish with one false cast, not standing up. The trout drifted under the fly and took it and pulled with a strength almost unseemly on such a small battlefield. Then the fish gave up and lay in my left hand. Both its mouth and its girth were big for its length of $9\frac{1}{2}$ inches and its belly was the deep red-orange of a maple tree. This was a three-year-old, survivor of two spawning seasons but programmed by its genes to die before another. It died instead for my wife's dinner.

The shower was steady by then, and I wasted no time. Another good fish took my fly in the next pool but the hook lost its grip. I changed to a fly with more clearance between point of hook and fat herl body, and in the two pools upstream I caught two more big fish, which meant that both my wife and I could have dinner. That's how it goes on Dark Hollow Run: you can fish for hours without a venerable trout, but the first shower gives you satisfaction.

The old fish hide when the water gets low. Then the rain comes and they move out, chase the small fry away from the best spots in the pools, and lie in wait, tails moving, eyes looking up. Even the first few raindrops revive some genetic recollection of the wetter, colder climate Betty Cave describes.

I let the cat out one time and it froze in the snow before it got back in. I cried and cried. My Daddy hiked down to the old copper mine for work in winter. He didn't have no boots—had to put socks over his shoes and tie them up with tar strings. The snow was so deep that his clothes was froze up to his waist when he got home. We were happy to get the money.

There was eight cabins in Dark Hollow then, and the church. They was awful good people, good Christian people. Daddy went around with a lantern in the snow when the diphtheria came. He visited the houses of sick people to pray. Two children died the same day. Daddy had to cut up a church bench to make a coffin for them.

The climb back up through the woods to Skyline Drive was slow, my excuse being that I wanted to take an inventory of my homestead. Rain made that easier, too. The violets stood straighter, the wild geraniums glowed pink-purple, and the first white trilliums began to open. In what was left of the orchard at Betty Cave's old place, a mountain pheasant twisted off through gray trunks. We call them ruffed grouse now. I saw no woodcock, but farther along the path a gray squirrel darted to the back side of its tree and I wondered why it was so spooky till a goshawk buzzed me. Its nest must have been nearby, with young hungry for small game.

Two bunches of deer, on the other hand, stood watching me tamely. Recently deer have become too abundant for their forage—a problem common in the National Parks. Hunting is not allowed and there are not enough big predators to control populations.

I don't remember deer in the '30s. Never heard Daddy name a deer, but he hunted mountain pheasants here in the hollow and walked to Big Meadow to shoot wood hens. They was funny little birds with long bills and round heads and big eyes.

We heard a mountain panther screamin' and hollerin' like a baby one time, and our dog was so scared we let him inside. I looked out the window and saw the panther coming closeter and closeter. It had eyes like a piece of fire.

A bear broke into our smokehouse one night and stole a ham. Daddy tracked the bear down but he told me he didn't kill it, because I didn't like anything to get hurt. We had plenty of ham left, I remember. Wonder if some of it come from that bear.

Daddy tracked rabbits and squirrels with his little dog, and they did smell good when Mama cooked 'em. I remember she baked raccoons, too, with potatoes and carrots from the garden. We ate the mushrats and sold their hides. We didn't eat 'possums, but some folks did—fattened them up and cooked 'em.

Change would have come to the settlement in time, even if the old families had been allowed to stay in their homes. Somebody would have driven a car to the cabins and the world would have followed, one vehicle at a time. People who had been part of nature would have erected television antennas in the heart of Dark Hollow.

With humans gone, the original vegetation returned, and if the young hardwoods drank some of the stream's water, they also protected the watershed from erosion. The trout were not big, but they were doing better here than in most parts of their ancestral range. I expected to find the native wildlife waiting for me as long as I could manage the hard pull.

Something beautiful had been saved for me—and taken from the Caves.

When they first built Skyline Drive, I would hike up there and sell little paper flowers. Mama made 'em for me. I'd charge a dime, but some of the guests would stop their cars and give me a dollar. I was five years old.

After a while, the government pushed us off our land and made it part of Shenandoah National Park. That was before the war started—1939 or the edge of '40, I think. Daddy got a dollar an acre. Friends gave us use of a house outside the Park— they knew we couldn't pay rent. We wanted to go back to Dark Hollow but the government burnt down all eight cabins. Burnt the church, too.

Daddy didn't have any work. All he knew was farming and hunting and fishing. I remember him sitting outside every evening, cryin' and cryin'.

◆ QUESTIONS FOR REVIEW

1. What is the point or significance of this essay? How effectively does Proper reveal it to you?
2. How does Proper structure his essay? Identify its beginning, middle, and end.
3. Proper's use of Betty Cave's dialogue with him is a bit unusual. How effective do you think it is? Why does Proper place Cave's words in italics instead of the usual quotation marks? How does Proper ensure that he can juggle what essentially are two narratives—his and Cave's—yet maintain a unified, coherent essay?
4. Identify at least two places in the essay where Proper uses vivid description. How effective are these descriptions?
5. At first, it seems as though the essay's title, "Dark Hollow," simply identifies the locale or scene of the essay. What else does this title suggest to you, now that you've finished the essay?
6. What kind(s) of conflict or tension does Proper create in this essay? How effectively does he use it?

> ◆ **WRITING OPPORTUNITY**
>
> Write about a confrontation you had with somebody. What was the conflict? How was it resolved? ◆

Our second essay is by Judith Ortiz Cofer, who writes about prejudice and racial bias. This essay appears in Cofer's collection of essays and poems titled *The Latin Deli*.

JUDITH ORTIZ COFER

THE MYTH OF THE LATIN WOMAN: I JUST MET A GIRL NAMED MARÍA

1   On a bus trip to London from Oxford University where I was earning some graduate credits one summer, a young man, obviously fresh from a pub, spotted me and as if struck by inspiration went down on his knees in the aisle. With both hands over his heart he broke into an Irish tenor's rendition of "María" from *West Side Story*. My politely amused fellow passengers gave his lovely voice the round of gentle applause it deserved. Though I was not quite as amused, I managed my version of an English smile: no show of teeth, no extreme contortions of the facial muscles—I was at this time of my life practicing reserve and cool. Oh, that British control, how I coveted it. But María had followed me to London, reminding me of a prime fact of my life: you can leave the Island, master the English language, and travel as far as you can, but if you are a Latina, especially one like me who so obviously belongs to Rita Moreno's gene pool, the Island travels with you.

2   This is sometimes a very good thing—it may win you that extra minute of someone's attention. But with some people, the same things can make *you* an island—not so much a tropical paradise as an Alcatraz, a place nobody wants to visit. As a Puerto Rican girl growing up in the United States and wanting like most children to "belong," I resented the stereotype that my Hispanic appearance called forth from many people I met.

3   Our family lived in a large urban center in New Jersey during the sixties, where life was designed as a microcosm of my parents' casas on the island. We spoke in Spanish, we ate Puerto Rican food bought at the bodega, and we practiced strict Catholicism complete with Saturday confession and Sunday mass at a church where our parents were accommodated into a one-hour Spanish mass slot, performed by a Chinese priest trained as a missionary for Latin America.

4   As a girl I was kept under strict surveillance, since virtue and modesty were, by cultural equation, the same as family honor. As a teenager I was instructed on how to behave as a proper señorita. But is was a conflicting message girls got, since the Puerto Rican mothers also encouraged their daughters to look and act like women and to dress in clothes our Anglo friends and their mother found too "mature" for our age. It was, and is, cultural, yet I often felt humiliated when I appeared at an American friend's party wearing a dress more suitable to a semi-formal than to a playroom birthday celebration. At Puerto Rican festivities, neither the music nor the colors we wore could be too loud. I still experience a vague sense of letdown when I'm invited to a "party" and it turns out to be a marathon conversation in hushed tones rather than a fiesta with salsa, laughter, and dancing—the kind of celebration I remember from childhood.

5   I remember Career Day in our high school, when teachers told us to come dressed as if for a job interview. It quickly became obvious that to the barrio girls, "dressing up" sometimes meant wearing ornate jewelry and clothing that would be more appropriate (by mainstream standards) for the company Christmas party than as daily office attire. That morning I had agonized in front of my closet, trying to figure out what a "career girl" would wear because, essentially, except for Marlo Thomas on TV, I had no models on which to base my decision. I knew how to dress for school: at the Catholic school I attended we all wore uniforms; I knew how to dress for Sunday mass, and I knew what dresses to wear for parties at my relatives' homes. Though I do not recall the precise details of my Career Day outfit, it must have been a composite of the above choices. But I remember a comment my friend (an Italian-American) made in later years that coalesced my impressions of that day. She said that at the business school she was attending the Puerto Rican girls always stood out for wearing "everything at once." She meant, of course, too much jewelry, too many accessories. On that day at school, we were simply made the negative models by the nuns who were themselves not credible fashion experts to any of us. But is was painfully obvious to me that to the others, in their tailored skirts and silk blouses, we must have seemed "hopeless" and "vulgar." Though I now know that most adolescents feel out of step much of the time, I also know that for Puerto Rican girls of my generation that sense was intensified. The way our teachers and classmates looked at us that day in school was just a taste of the culture clash that awaited us in the real world, where prospective employers and men on the street would often misinterpret our tight skirts and jingling bracelets as a come-on.

6   Mixed cultural signals have perpetuated certain stereotypes—for example, that of the Hispanic woman as the "Hot Tamale" or sexual firebrand. It is a one-dimensional view that the media have found easy to promote. In their special vocabulary, advertisers have designated "sizzling" and "smoldering" as the adjectives of choice for describing not only the foods but also the women of Latin America. From conversations in my house I recall hearing about the harassment that Puerto Rican women endured in factories where the "boss men" talked to

them as if sexual innuendo was all they understood and, worse, often gave them the choice of submitting to advances or being fired.

It is custom, however, not chromosomes, that leads us to choose scarlet over pale pink. As young girls, we were influenced in our decision about clothes and colors by the women—older sisters and mothers who had grown up on a tropical island where the natural environment was a riot of primary colors, where showing your skin was one way to keep cool as well as to look sexy. Most important of all, on the island, women perhaps felt freer to dress and move more provocatively, since, in most cases, they were protected by the traditions, mores, and laws of a Spanish/Catholic system of morality and machismo whose main rule was: *You may look at my sister, but if you touch her I will kill you.* The extended family and church structure could provide a young woman with a circle of safety in her small pueblo on the island; if a man "wronged" a girl, everyone would close in to save her family honor.

This is what I have gleaned from my discussion as an adult with older Puerto Rican women. They have told me about dressing in their best party clothes on Saturday nights and going to the town's plaza to promenade with their girlfriends in front of the boys they liked. The males were thus given an opportunity to admire the women and to express their admiration in the form of *piropos*: erotically charged street poems they composed on the spot. I have been subjected to a few piropos while visiting the Island, and they can be outrageous, although custom dictates that they must never cross into obscenity. This ritual, as I understand it, also entails a show of studied indifference on the woman's part; if she is "decent," she must not acknowledge the man's impassioned words. So I do understand how things can be lost in translation. When a Puerto Rican girl dressed in her idea of what is attractive meets a man from the mainstream culture who has been trained to react to certain types of clothing as a sexual signal, a clash is likely to take place. The line I first heard based on this aspect of the myth happened when the boy who took me to my first formal dance leaned over to plant a sloppy overeager kiss painfully on my mouth, and when I didn't respond with sufficient passion said in a resentful tone: "I thought you Latin girls were supposed to mature early"—my first instance of being thought of as a fruit or vegetable—I was supposed to *ripen*, not just grow into womanhood like other girls.

It is surprising to some of my professional friends that some people, including those who should know better, still put others "in their place." Though rarer, these incidents are still commonplace in my life. It happened to me most recently during a stay at a very classy metropolitan hotel favored by young professional couples for their weddings. Late one evening after the theater, as I walked toward my room with my new colleague (a woman with whom I was coordinating an arts program), a middle-aged man in a tuxedo, a young girl in satin and lace on his arm, stepped directly into our path. With his champagne glass extended toward me, he exclaimed, "Evita!"

10   Our way blocked, my companion and I listened as the man half-recited, half-bellowed "Don't Cry for Me, Argentina." When he finished, the young girl said: "How about a round of applause for my daddy?" We complied, hoping this would bring the silly spectacle to a close. I was becoming aware that our little group was attracting the attention of the other guests. "Daddy" must have perceived this too, and he once more barred the way as we tried to walk past him. He began to shout-sing a ditty to the tune of "La Bamba"—except the lyrics were about a girl named María whose exploits all rhymed with her name and gonorrhea. The girl kept saying "Oh, Daddy" and looking at me with pleading eyes. She wanted me to laugh along with the others. My companion and I stood silently waiting for the man to end his offensive song. When he finished, I looked not at him but at his daughter. I advised her calmly never to ask her father what he had done in the army. Then I walked between them and to my room. My friend complimented me on my cool handling of the situation. I confessed to her that I really had wanted to push the jerk into the swimming pool. I knew that this same man—probably a corporate executive, well educated, even worldly by most standards—would not have been likely to regale a white woman with a dirty song in public. He would perhaps have checked his impulse by assuming that she could be somebody's wife or mother, or at least *somebody* who might take offense. But to him, I was just an Evita or a María: merely a character in this cartoon-populated universe.

11   Because of my education and my proficiency with the English language, I have acquired many mechanisms for dealing with the anger I experience. This was not true for my parents, nor is it true for the many Latin women working at menial jobs who must put up with stereotypes about our ethnic group such as: "They make good domestics." This is another facet of the myth of the Latin woman in the United States. Its origin is simple to deduce. Work as domestics, waitressing, and factory jobs are all that's available to women with little English and few skills. The myth of the Hispanic menial has been sustained by the same media phenomenon that made "Mammy" from *Gone with the Wind* America's idea of the black woman for generations; María, the housemaid or counter girl, is now indelibly etched into the national psyche. The big and the little screens have presented us with the picture of the funny Hispanic maid, mispronouncing words and cooking up a spicy storm in a shiny California kitchen.

12   This media-engendered image of the Latina in the United States has been documented by feminist Hispanic scholars, who claim that such portrayals are partially responsible for the denial of opportunities for upward mobility among Latinas in the professions. I have a Chicana friend working on a Ph.D. in philosophy at a major university. She says her doctor still shakes his head in puzzled amazement at all the "big words" she uses. Since I do not wear my diplomas around my neck for all to see, I too have on occasion been sent to that "kitchen," where some think I obviously belong.

One such incident that has stayed with me, though I recognize it as a minor offense, happened on the day of my first public poetry reading. It took place in Miami in a boat-restaurant where we were having lunch before the event. I was nervous and excited as I walked in with my notebook in my hand. An older woman motioned me to her table. Thinking (foolish me) that she wanted me to autograph a copy of my brand new slender volume of verse, I went over. She ordered a cup of coffee from me, assuming that I was the waitress. Easy enough to mistake my poems for menus, I suppose. I know that it wasn't an intentional act of cruelty, yet of all the good things that happened that day, I remember that scene most clearly, because it reminded me of what I had to overcome before anyone would take me seriously. In retrospect I understand that my anger gave my reading fire, that I have almost always taken doubts in my abilities as a challenge—and that the result is, most times, a feeling of satisfaction at having won a convert when I see the cold, appraising eyes warm to my words, the body language change, the smile that indicates that I have opened some avenue for communication. That day I read to that woman and her lowered eyes told me that she was embarrassed at her little faux pas, and when I willed her to look up at me, it was my victory, and she graciously allowed me to punish her with my full attention. We shook hands at the end of the reading, and I never saw her again. She has probably forgotten the whole thing but maybe not.

Yet I am one of the lucky ones. My parents made it possible for me to acquire a stronger footing in the mainstream culture by giving me the chance at an education. And books and art have saved me from the harsher forms of ethnic and racial prejudice that many of my Hispanic *compañeras* have had to endure. I travel a lot around the United States, reading from my books of poetry and my novel, and the reception I most often receive is one of positive interest by people who want to know more about my culture. There are, however, thousands of Latinas without the privilege of education or the entrée into society that I have. For them life is a struggle against the misconceptions perpetuated by the myth of the Latina as whore, domestic or criminal. We cannot change this by legislating the way people look at us. The transformation, as I see it, has to occur at a much more individual level. My personal goal in my public life is to try to replace the old pervasive stereotypes and myths about Latinas with a much more interesting set of realities. Every time I give a reading, I hope the stories I tell, the dreams and fears I examine in my work, can achieve some universal truth which will get my audience past the particulars of my skin color, my accent, or my clothes.

I once wrote a poem in which I called us Latinas "God's brown daughters." This poem is really a prayer or sorts, offered upward, but also, through the human-to-human channel of art, outward. It is a prayer for communication, and for respect. In it, Latin women pray "in Spanish to an Anglo God / with a Jewish heritage," and they are "fervently hoping / that if not omnipotent, / at least He be bilingual."

◆ QUESTIONS FOR REVIEW

1. What is Cofer's point in writing this essay? What is its significance? How effectively does Cofer reveal it to you?
2. How well does Cofer support such assertions as the one about culture versus chromosomes?
3. What is the tone of this essay? How does the tone support the essay's significance?
4. How many personal anecdotes does Cofer give? How effective are they in developing her theme?
5. According to Cofer, what is the media's role in creating stereotypes? To what extent is she right?

◆ WRITING OPPORTUNITY

1. Have you ever been in a situation that involved issues of race or of prejudice? Describe it. What was the outcome?
2. Are there problems with prejudice on your campus? How might these problems be solved? ◆

The third sample essay, "My Father's Cabin," is by Charles McNair. In it, McNair talks about his father having found "a place of peace." As you read, think about similar places in your experience.

CHARLES MCNAIR
MY FATHER'S CABIN

About 16 years ago, my father went down. A coronary, at age 54, put him in a hospital bed at the University of Alabama at Birmingham with bypasses around his heart and a zipper of sutures up his chest and both legs.

My mother and I drove him home from the hospital to Dothan, in the southeastern corner of Alabama. His body convalesced quickly. In less than a month, the stitches mended, the overhauled heart rocked along. He ate well and went back to work, cruising acres of timberland he owned.

But through the smokescreen of hard work, it became plain to us in the family that a different kind of healing seemed sadly lacking. My father was suffering a long depression. The condition is not uncommon to robust men who get an early wake-up call. But it is inexplicable. At times my father raged at those around him, or else sank deep into a sleepless chair with his fists clenched, staring out blank windows in the brooding night.

A hundred-year-old pine-log cabin seemed like the most unlikely cure in the world. Found moldering on a farm near Pilgrim's Rest Church, the old place hadn't known a human breath in decades. Rain fell clear through the roof. Ghosts cracked their knuckles in every corner when the wind blew.

To the great surprise of the family, my father bought the weed-strangled old ruin for $500. Helped by hired hands and my younger brothers, the patriarch of our family took apart the double log structure—two simple rooms with a dogtrot through the center—and moved it to property near home. There, he reassembled the cabin meticulously, plank by plank, log by log, driving nails and pegs himself. He and his crew used blown-down pines to replace logs softened black by the years.

Late that spring, my father settled into a straight-back chair on the cabin's newly restored porch. A tin roof gleamed in the sunlight, and two brick chimneys rose over the bright metal. The turpentine of pines filled the breeze. He had found a place of peace.

Years later, I asked him about the restoration. He grew talkative—a rare state for this flinty old businessman. He described the stone-hardness of old pine logs, the dimensions of the limestone and iron-ore rocks supporting the house, what kind of split-wood shingles once covered the roof. The kitchen, he said, stood off from the house a ways so a cookfire wouldn't threaten the living quarters. He pointed out that the house may even have held two families, one on each side of the dogtrot.

In that conversation, my father let slip the one thing that made me understand, with laser clarity, what had made fixing the cabin—this resinous jumble of logs—so important to him during that delicate time.

"You know, my mama was born in a cabin just like this," he said. "I've got a picture when she was a little girl standing in front of it!"

The angels took his mother when my father was only 13. But he had something now that connected him to her in an indescribable private way—a plain log cabin that rumbled when you walked across the porch. And a mansion in glory too. A sense of place, of connection, too deep for any explanation.

Someday, sooner than I'll ever be ready, this father of mine will pass away. And when I come to remember him, I'll sit on the porch of the cabin he saved, under those same whispering trees.

I will remember the way he looked, and how he got up and down steps, and   12
the way he poured sweat in the summers when he worked. I'll recall the train
songs he sang to me when I was a very little boy, and the rough sketches he drew
to entertain me, on notebook paper with a stubby knife-sharpened pencil.

And I'll remember that one of the best drawings he made, even long ago,   13
was a simple cabin in the woods.

◆ QUESTIONS FOR REVIEW

1. What is the focal point of this narrative?
2. How does McNair reveal the importance of the cabin? How effectively does he do so?
3. We could divide this essay into two parts: ¶s 1–6 and ¶s 7–13. What does each section of the essay do? How effectively do they work together to reveal the essay's significance?
4. Other than in ¶4, McNair doesn't use a great deal of figurative language. On what does he rely to detail the importance of the cabin for his father?

◆ WRITING OPPORTUNITY

Write about an object that's important to you. Describe it; then talk about its importance. ◆

Our final essay was written by Christopher Fisher while he was a student at Sam Houston State University. He is now completing an MFA in Creative Writing at The University of Southern Maine's Stonecoast Program for Writers.

CHRISTOPHER FISHER
SCARS

I. Strangers

Here's a dare. Next time you're out in a crowd, pick a spot to sit, or just   1
stand still. Then watch, really look at the faces of the strangers who pass you by.

Try to ignore the things you'd normally notice first—eyes, hair, lips. You want to focus, instead, on the skin. Look deep, right down to the lines and wrinkles.

Now, find one face—just one—that doesn't carry a scar.

I've been doing this off and on for eighteen years in airports and shopping malls, libraries and church auditoriums. I've never found one. And I don't think you can, either. Oh, you might have to look hard, but the scar is there.

Every face is scarred, and behind each scar is a story.

It's the story behind the scar that has always fascinated me. Sometimes after noticing a particularly interesting one, I'll give in and ask a stranger how he got his. If you're polite about it, most people are more than willing to tell. The stories are almost always of childhood injury—a fall from the front porch, a bike wreck. I guess we all have to kiss the dirt a few times before we learn what hands are for. Or maybe young skin scars easier.

My scar is a pencil-thin line, barely noticeable, tracing my left cheekbone. It has faded through the years, so much that unless I pointed it out, you might not even notice it. I once worked up a story—in case someone asked—about a pack of wild dogs and a barbed wire fence. No one ever asked, so I never got to tell it. The story I'll tell you is different, though. Not as exciting as seven Cujos chasing me into a fence, but pretty good. And true, too.

II. A Gift from Dad

When I was a boy, I lived with my parents and two sisters on an Oklahoma farm. This was not a *real* farm—we didn't grow crops or breed livestock for a living—but we had several farm animals. Pets, actually. By the time I was twelve we had owned at one time or another four horses, two goats, one large sow, a couple dozen rabbits, a flock of ducks, and maybe fifty chickens.

Let's talk about chickens. Chickens begin as eggs, of course. They bust out of their shells all smelly and sticky. Not a pretty sight. Within a few hours, though, their feathers are clean and fluffy and yellow. All baby chicks are yellow. At least that's the way I remember it.

One winter night when I was six, Dad brought home a box of chicks from the feed store. My sisters and I crowded around him, nudging in close as he set the box on the kitchen floor and hung a lamp over its side. Inside, seven or eight clean, yellow chicks huddled together, chirping under the warm light.

Whenever a new litter of puppies or kittens arrived, it was my childhood custom to pick a favorite—usually the runt, or the one with the spot or the longest ears. Looking over the tiny balls of feather, I found picking a chick would be difficult. They were all identical.

I leaned over the box for several minutes, crinkling my nose at the smell of cardboard and chicken crap baking in the heat of the lamp. When I finally reached inside, the chicks scurried away—all but one. I picked it up and lifted it to my face. It chirped, then pecked hard at my nose.

"It kissed me," I said with a smile.

My younger sister, Amy, asked, "What are you going to name him?" I peeked between the chick's legs but saw no evidence that it was a him. Years later, I would hear of a man who made six figures sexing chickens for poultry farms—two hundred thousand dollars a year for peeking between the legs of baby chicks. To a seven-year-old child, however (and to most normal adults for that matter), there is no visible difference between a baby rooster and a baby hen. In the end, I ignored the usual rules of observation and trusted Amy's intuition. The chick would be a him, and I named him Sunshine, for his bright, yellow feathers.

III. Little Sister

I can't speak of scars without mentioning my sister, Amy. There was a time, way back there, when we were very close, but somewhere around the age of five, probably due to my constant bullying, Amy got very mean and very tough. She could whip all of my younger male cousins, and she could even whip me from time to time, if I turned my back on her. Half the scars on my body can be attributed to Amy. My scalp alone she split with a lamp, a steel pipe, and even a shovel.

She was tough.

I was fifteen and Amy was thirteen when Dad left Mom and moved to the city. My older sister, Kim, was married by then. So only Mom, Amy, and I were left on the farm. The three of us took the news like a shovel over the head. And though that blow left no physical mark, the emotional scars went deep. Mom lost her mind for the next two years. She went through counseling and overdosed on sleeping pills a couple of times. I claimed God as father, in the absence of my own, and locked myself in my bedroom like a monk in his cell. And Amy, that tough little girl, began to look more and more each day like a cancer victim. She wore the wound on her face like a steel frown behind a thin, plastic smile.

IV. Jesus and Zen

I have this friend who speaks of Christ, Tao, and Zen Enlightenment in the same sentence. He calls himself a Christian mystic, but not a Christian. "Modern Christianity is a neutered religion. An emasculated faith. It's Christ with all smiles and no scars."

Being men, we speak often of women. "There's a reason they're called the weaker sex, you know. And it's not meant as an insult. Just ask any woman if she would rather be strong or pretty. Strength is the pride of a man; beauty is that of a woman."

I've seen what he's talking about. Men wear their scars like badges, pointing them out with pride. *Look! I have been bloodied in battle, and I am still here*. I've never felt uncomfortable asking a man about his scars, because I know he *wants* to tell. But with women . . .

Women cover their scars with make-up.

V. A Good Bird

I spent a lot of time with Sunshine those first few weeks. As the other chicks ate grain from the bottom of their box, I fed Sunshine from my hand. I set him on my shoulder and took him for walks around the house while he nibbled at my earlobe. I lay on the carpet as he scratched around on my chest. Sometimes, I would even sing for him. He in turn would peck playfully at my nose.

Weeks passed. The days grew longer. Trees began to bud. Time for the chicks to go outside, Mom said. That spring I learned to ride a bicycle without the training wheels, and our Doberman bitch had puppies. I didn't spend much time with Sunshine after that. A chicken has nothing on a puppy or a bicycle.

Sunshine, who turned out to be a rooster after all, didn't mind my absence, for it was about this time that he discovered the hens. Full grown, he still had most of the yellow feathers for which he had been named, making him stand out next to the black and white hens. Occasionally, he would jump on one of their backs and flap his wings wildly.

"Stop fighting with her, Sunshine!" I would shout. Being the good bird he was, he hopped off and pecked at the ground while I turned to chase a puppy across the yard.

By the following autumn, my rooster and I were no longer on friendly terms. He fought more and more with the hens and no longer obeyed my commands. Once, I tried to feed him out of my hand and he just squawked and flew off across the yard.

I knew what the problem was. He was angry about the puppy. He'd been jealous of that puppy all along. Even after all the puppies—including my favorite—were sold at the end of summer, Sunshine held a grudge. Mom said it wasn't good to hold grudges, that I should forgive my sisters if they did something against me. So I decided the bird should be the one to apologize, and I would not speak to him until he did.

One afternoon, while I was playing under the big elm that shaded our house, I noticed Sunshine strutting with the hens nearby. I paid no attention, shunning him as usual. Suddenly, I heard a swooshing sound and looked up to find Sunshine hovering right in front of me.

I'd never seen a chicken hover, and never have since. But there he was, flapping his wings in a steady, graceful beat—floating effortlessly in place, just inches from my face.

VI. Scar Face

I have a rather old face. Not wrinkled, really. Not yet. Just serious—even angry— and a little worn. Always has been. I've never had trouble buying liquor thanks to this face, though that might have more to do with my facial hair.

I started shaving at thirteen. At the time, I was afraid my family, and especially Amy, would tease me about it. So I didn't tell them. For two years. Eventually, the whiskers became too thick to hide, like sixty grit sandpaper that grew back every eight hours. I let it grow out for a week then told Dad I wanted to start shaving. He held my chin in his hand, turning my face in the light. "Maybe it *is* time we get you some razors."

The idea seemed silly to me, the two of us in front of the mirror wearing white, foamy beards, and me feigning ignorance as he showed me how it was done. But the next day, Dad came home from the drug store, handed me a pack of Bics and a can of Barbasol, then sat down in front of the TV.

It's funny. There wasn't a thing he could have taught me. But I resented him for not trying.

VII. Sunshine

Sunshine hovered in front of me, and it was all so clear what the rooster wanted. He was coming to make amends, to apologize for behaving so selfishly. A smile stretched across my face, and in my heart, I forgave him that instant. In a tone of welcome and wonder, I said, "Sunshine!"

Sunshine. That's all I got out before he stretched out his claw and dragged a spur across my face. I screamed, horrified at the sting of pain and betrayal. The rooster squawked and flew off over my head. With one hand to my cheek— where the scar remains to this day—I turned to see him flapping clumsily across the yard. He landed near the hens and started scratching at the dirt as if nothing had happened.

My vision blurred with tears, and I wailed, "Maw-muh!" Mom came running out the door and, seeing my face wet with tears and blood, shrieked, "What happened? What happened?" I ran to meet her and latched on, pressing my bleeding face into her belly. All I could do was point and sob, "Sunshine, Mama! Sunshine!"

Mom brought me inside and cleaned me up. The scratch had already stopped bleeding, so she put peroxide on it but not a Band-Aid; it was long, but not at all deep. She gave me a cookie and some juice, and fifteen minutes later I was outside playing again.

VIII. Of a Boy

Strength is the pride of a man. And of a boy. Especially a boy.

I remember one night, just before the divorce, Amy and I were in Tulsa at an outdoor concert, right on the banks of the Arkansas River. Dad and Mom were also there, a couple of seats down. Some man, half-drunk and half-stoned, sat down next to us and tried to sell us a joint. Dad overheard the proposition and knocked the guy on his ass before we could even "just say no." I'll never forget Dad's face as he watched that drunk cower off to the other side of the amphitheater, the hardness radiating like waves of heat from his eyes, the muscles in his jaw flexing and releasing in time with the music. Even as the roar of the band and the murmur of the crowd swarmed around me and echoed back off the water, I thought I heard Dad's teeth grinding against each other, like the crunching of bones. This is my favorite memory of Dad, the moment he was hell-bent on shedding blood to protect us. I have never been so proud of my father.

A few months after that night, Mom and Dad separated. One morning soon after, I rode into town with my Grandfather, Mom's father.

Talk about *scars*. Grandpa was a walking scar, and the strongest man I've ever known. He worked thirty years in a steel casting plant—a place closer to Hell than any I've seen. His arms, neck, and face were freckled with tiny white scars, where molten metal had popped onto his skin like bacon grease. But he never complained. He was just happy to keep his kids fed and in shoes.

Driving me to town, Grandpa talked about the separation, how bad it was, how hard it was going to be for me. "You're the man of the house now, Chris. Whether you like it or not. You're gonna have to look after your Mom and sister."

Shoulders back, chin up, I nodded in silent agreement. I was a man at fifteen. Grandpa said so.

IX. Sunshine

By the time Dad came home, I had almost forgotten about the fight with Sunshine. I forgave the bird. But it could not end so simply. Dad took one look at my face then shot a glance to my mother. "What happened to him?"

Mom shook her head. "That damn rooster flogged him."

Dad inspected the scratch on my cheek, holding my chin in his hand and turning my face into the light. I felt the heat coming off his eyes and heard the grinding of his teeth as he stared at the long, red line. And I knew even at that innocent age that something terrible, something violent was about to happen. He looked me in the eye and said, "Go help your mother peel some potatoes."

That phrase apparently had some secret meaning to my mother, who nodded slowly and led me to the kitchen. She put me at the table and set a peeler, a paper sack, and a big pot of potatoes down in front of me. But my eyes followed Dad, who walked into the bedroom and came out with his .22 pistol. He walked around a corner into the living room. I heard the front door open. Then shut.

I looked up at Mom, but she wouldn't look me in the eyes.

"Kim and Amy can help, too," she said, then went off to find them.

As soon as she left the kitchen, I dropped the potato peeler and rushed to the window. A moment later my jaw dropped open.

Dad stomped toward the barn, holding Sunshine upside down by the feet as the rooster flapped its wings wildly, trying to escape. When they were a good distance from the house, Dad stopped. Taking Sunshine's head in his free hand, he twisted it all the way around about three times. Then he took the pistol out of a pocket and shot the bird in the l head—twice.

When Mom and my sisters returned to the kitchen, I was back at the table shedding tears and potato peels into the paper sack.

X. Man Of The House

The Christian God is a God of love, as you may have heard, a Father who loves all his sons and daughters. But that's not the whole truth. The same book that says God is Love also tells us that He hates. This is only one of those contradictions in scripture that has had theologians arguing for the past two thousand years. I confess I'm not comfortable with the idea of a God who hates. Who could be? But if you spend as many hours hiding in an open Bible as I did after Dad left, you'll find it's undeniable. If you are to believe the Bible, there are at least forty-five things God hates. And one of these, with few exceptions, is divorce. "Putting away," the prophet Malachi calls it, which in many divorces is an excellent description, calling to mind the way you might carelessly reshelve a book after you've laid bare all its secrets, studied all its naked pages, gotten out of it all you wanted.

When a marriage ends the way my parents' did, when one spouse just puts away the other after more than twenty years, it's as devastating as throwing a live grenade on the living room rug and running out the door. The one left behind gets all the shrapnel, along with anyone else who happens to be in the house, like the children And those scars are for life.

I didn't really need to read the Bible to know the evils of "putting away." All I had to do was watch what the separation did to my mother. The loss of emotional control. The constant crying. The pulling at her hair—I mean literally ripping it from her scalp. Living through that, I could not imagine a God who could smile on such a thing. I still cannot. But if Mom wasn't proof enough, I had my little sister as further evidence.

Amy's scar became more pronounced each year, despite her efforts to hide it. It was painful watching her hurt like that. I tried my best to help her. But, unfortunately, my idea of help was reading her my own list of the things she was doing which God hated. As you can imagine, my judgment and Sunday School solutions did nothing to heal her wound. So she sought other cures. Sex, drugs, alcohol . . . sex. Sex especially.

I worked all through high school, and one rainy winter night I came home late. Mom was out—she was gone a lot around that time—but Amy's car was parked outside. As I walked inside, shivering and wet, Amy came out of her bedroom and shut the door, her back firmly against it.

"Hey. How was work?" she asked.

"Fine," I said. She must have really thought I was stupid. "I'm gonna make a sandwich," I said, then turned to the kitchen. She darted into her room and shut the door behind her. I waited twenty seconds, then walked down the hall, opened her door, and asked, "Do you want a sandwi— " That last word trailed off as I saw what was going on.

Some kid I had never seen lay on the far side of Amy's tousled bed, pulling on his pants. Amy stood at the raised window, fighting to get the screen off so the boy could sneak out. The three of us froze solid, waiting, wondering what I would do. I think they were certain I would lose it, grab him by the hair and throw him through the window myself. And that's what I *felt* like doing. Only not through the window. Through the wall. But I could see this was no case of rape—not even statutory. The kid looked at least a year younger than Amy.

I held it in and said with a steely voice, "Get your clothes on and get the hell out of my house."

As it turned out, the boy didn't even drive. Amy had brought him to the house in her car. She offered to take him home. "No," I said, not trusting her. "I'll take him." Amy insisted on coming along, and it's a good thing she did. Her presence may have spared him a few scars of his own.

Not a word was spoken the whole drive, apart from an occasional "turn here." When I pulled up in front of his house, he got out quickly. I put the car in park and followed him, leaving Amy alone in the back seat. I stood with that boy in the freezing rain for fifteen minutes—me talking, him nodding emphatically. It was a long lecture, but basically all I said was, "If I ever see you around my sister again I'll rip your head off and hide it where it will never be found."

Never saw him again.

The drive home—with Amy—was quieter than the drive there. I couldn't think of anything to say to her. And I knew one of my sermons would accomplish nothing. I may have scared this one away, but she would have another boyfriend in a week. All I could think during that long drive was how unfair it was for me to even be in this position. It was not my job. I wasn't her father. I wasn't even a man, despite all my proud pretending. I was just an eighteen-year-old kid, wishing his father was there. I needed him, and I loved him. But I also hated.

XI. To Give Than To Receive

Hurt people hurt people

I hate to admit it, but after three long years as the "man of the house," I gave up on Amy. I had school. I had work. I had grass to cut in the summer and wood to split in the winter, and I had no more time or breath to preach to Amy about how she should live. She never listened to my sermons anyway. So I "handed her over to the devil" like I was taught to do with reprobates and hopeless causes.

What a thing to do to your own blood.

Still, I managed to enjoy my senior year. I was an actor in high school, and a notorious prankster. There was a cast party one night, after we finished the last of seven showings of "A Midsummer Night's Dream." The whole cast was there, from Oberon to the very least of his fairies. But the one I remember now is Steven—a quiet, slightly effeminate junior. A good kid. He played Snug and the Lion. We were all high on stage adrenaline, eager to do something crazy. Someone suggested we go hiking through the woods in the dark. Oooh, scary!

Maybe it was to them, but I was used to being in the forest at night. We set out into the dark, and after ten minutes of watching these city kids trip over roots and swing flashlight beams through the treetops, I had an idea for a prank that would have made Robin Goodfellow proud.

Quietly, I split from the group, turned off my flashlight, and crept a good distance away. Once I was far enough so they couldn't hear, I sprinted through the dark woods in a wide circle, coming around in front of them. Then I stopped and, panting from the run, waited for their approach. As soon as I saw the nervous beams flickering ahead, I grabbed a dead branch, stood up, and yelled, "Y'all kids get off my land!"

They ran, flashlights bobbing in rhythm with their retreat. I pursued, yelling the whole way and beating the stick on tree trunks. My blood rushed. My head filled with an endorphin-charged high, a furious exhilaration that felt like fist fighting, cliff diving, and French kissing all at the same time. I caught up with them in a clearing, where I threw myself on the ground in laughter. They didn't know whether to kiss me or kill me, so they took turns cursing me and laughing at themselves.

That's when I noticed Steven. He stood quiet, away from the group, his hand pressed to his face. The white T-shirt he always wore under his costume now sported a black oak-leaf design on the front. When I turned my flashlight on him, the black leaf turned red.

They had come to a barbed wire fence; that's why they had stopped in the clearing. Steven ran smack into the top wire and caught a barb just a centimeter under his right eye and didn't say a word to anyone. You can never tell just by looking who the strong ones are.

Steven took seven stitches that night. Within a couple of months, the scar healed remarkably—a gray thread the only evidence of the gash that almost took his eye. But for those weeks while it healed, I couldn't look Steven in the face. I felt sick each time I saw that swollen pink scar, convinced he would live out his years disfigured because of my foolishness, queasy with the knowledge that, at the moment I was having the time of my life, his tender skin was learning the cruelty of rusted steel.

XII. A Good Bird

Mom plucked Sunshine in the kitchen sink, dropping fistfuls of bright yellow feathers into the sack of potato peels. She cut his body into pieces, rolled the pieces in flour, and then dropped them in a pan of hot grease. Sunshine popped and sizzled in the grease, and I slouched off to my bedroom to cry.

Soon the house filled with the smell of Sunshine frying in the kitchen, and to my shame, my mouth watered even as the tears flowed. I vowed then that I would not eat. How could I even think of it? It would be obscene, even cannibalistic. When the table was set, Mom called us into the kitchen. I choked down my tears, set my jaw, and took my seat at the table.

For half an hour I sat with my arms folded and watched my family feast on mashed potatoes, peas, corn, hot biscuits, and fried Sunshine. My stomach rumbled. My mouth watered. Icy cold sweat rose up on my forehead and, to my horror, I saw my own trembling hand reach across the table. A voice inside my head screamed, "Fight it! Don't give in! He was your friend!" But I was young and unaccustomed to such powerful temptation. Despite all my efforts to resist, my fingers grasped a warm, crispy drumstick and pulled it toward my plate.

XIII. Beauty for Ashes

I wonder what my Zen friend would say about my eating Sunshine. "You absorbed your enemy and used his energy to heal the wound he gave you." Something like that. He would be right, except for one detail. The rooster was also my friend, once.

But Sunshine's energy went far and the wound healed well. You wouldn't even see it unless I pointed it out. I hardly see it myself anymore, only when I'm shaving. But I love to see it. It reminds me of a time when I knew Dad loved me and would fight to protect me.

I love him for killing that bird.

And that other wound? I still feel the sting from time to time. When it comes, I let it. I pray. I cry. I write as if great drops of blood fell from my brow. And in the fevered exhaustion that follows, I find that the pain is eased—absorbed. The scar is still there, deep down. But I don't wear it on my face.

Amy does. Her scars have faded some, but like mine they have a funny way of coming back. When it gets really bad, she has a dinner of prescription painkillers, followed by a vacation in a private hospital. This has happened three times, I think.

She made her own choices, I know, but there is a stinging suspicion that just maybe I could have done more. I could have refrained from judging and tried to understand what watching Dad walk out the door did to her. I could have at least spared one slap for that boy in her bedroom, and maybe a black-eyed ex-boyfriend could have been for her what a dead rooster became for me, proof that someone loved her enough to protect her. If nothing else, I could have simply wept with her, which might have been the thing she needed most. Instead, I played the Pharisee and watched her drown.

Sometimes it makes me sick to look at her, as sick as I felt when I looked at that scar on Steven's face. And I hope Dad feels the same way when he sees his daughter. I hope he still loves her enough to hurt for her. And to *hurt* for her.

If I had the hands of Christ, I would erase the hard years, wipe the worried lines from my sister's face like chalk from a blackboard, and every plastic surgeon in Beverly Hills would stand in awe. She would be that beautiful.

XIV. One He Never Gave

When I was a boy, almost a man, I came home from school to see that Dad had come to visit. He did this occasionally, after the separation and before the divorce. Just dropped by to talk to Mom. I didn't know then what they had left to talk about, though now I think I do.

Anyway, Mom and I got into it over something—God only knows what. Before long, we were screaming at each other, while Dad sat passively at the table. I've already said that Mom was insane at this point, and it's no exaggeration. She started swinging her fists at my face, intent on bringing blood. I blocked her blows, but she kept coming, backing me into a wall. I had to do something to stop her before she really did hurt me.

I grabbed her wrists. That's all I did. Grabbed her wrists and pushed her back a couple of feet.

Dad was up and on me in a beat. He snatched a fistful of my shirt and shoved me backward over a chair, pinning me upside down. His other fist came up, cocked and ready to slam into my mouth.

I'll never forget what went through my head at that moment, suspended in the grip of violence. Sure I was scared. Scared to death. My eyes watered under the heat from his stare. My whole frame melted at the sight of that flexing jaw, the noise of those grinding teeth. Still, part of me could have cried with joy, realizing that he still loved her. Thank God, he still loved her! But Dad's face relaxed. He lowered his fist. He let go of me and turned away.

I wish he had hit me.

Hard.

I would have worn the scar like a medal.

♦ QUESTIONS FOR REVIEW

1. In his essay, Chris recounts events in his life that range from early childhood to present day. What is the significance of the essay?
2. Chris uses scars as a unifying motif or symbol in his essay. What kind or kinds of scars does he focus on primarily? How effectively does he use the terms "scar" or "scars" to help unify the essay?
3. Chris has written what's called a braided essay. That is, he weaves several narratives to form one extended narrative essay. Identify the various narratives he uses. How well does the header work for each narrative? How does Chris move from one narrative strand to the next? What is the effect on you of this structure?
4. Identify at least two places where Chris uses vivid description. How effective are these descriptions?

5. How much dialog does Chris use in this essay? Should he have used more, or is the dialogue presented effective? Why?
6. How much conflict is at work in "Scars"? How effectively does Chris use it?

◆ WRITING OPPORTUNITY

1. Have you ever had to assume responsibility in a situation? What was the situation? What happened? How did you feel? What was the outcome?
2. Identify three or four turning points in your life. How connected are they? Sketch out several shorter narratives about each turning point to see whether they might work in a braided essay. ◆

THE RHETORICAL TRIANGLE

Writer

It's your job to engage in honest exploration of a topic that matters to you, to treat that topic seriously and in depth. You and what you learned from your experience will figure as the most important aspects of a personal essay. For example, if you choose to write about a significant event, then you'll work to identify an event that taught you something important. Each of us has such experiences, but we may not realize their importance until much later, when we take the time to reflect on them and try to puzzle out their meaning. Your job, then, will be to consider past events you count meaningful, to select one of them to write about, and then to probe and explore it thoroughly. You'll relive the event through recounting it, first for yourself and then for another reader. Ultimately, your job is to capture the meaning or significance of this event and then, using your language, to help your reader experience the event as you did.

To help your reader understand the significance of the topic for you, you'll work to recreate the topic's scene and events so that you bring them to life. Note that we're not asking you to write a piece of fiction, nor are we asking you simply to tell about something that happened to you. Instead, you'll need to select the most important details and events and then use your language to reveal their importance. You'll focus on these, so that your reader can say, "I understand," after having read your essay.

Subject

Let's assume that the subject for your essay will be an event that you count significant, one that taught you something about yourself. Now, *significance* can sometimes be a troublesome term, because many student writers think they've never had a truly significant experience. The kind of significance we're talking about here may be earth-shattering; then again, it may not. We think an event has significance if it helped you understand something about yourself, if it changed your mind or your actions in some way, or if it helped you see someone else in a different way. For example, if you ran for a student government office while in high school but didn't win, what did that experience teach you about your own feelings and your abilities to cope with disappointment? If you were active in a high school or other organization, how did your experiences in that organization affect you? If you've ever been supported at a critical moment by someone you thought an enemy, how did that affect your opinion of that person? If you've ever been betrayed by a friend in a critical situation, how did that affect your view of that friend? Recognizing that your experience has affected or changed you in some way is the first step in seeing that experience's significance to you.

The topic for your personal essay will involve an event in which you participated, one that affected you more than superficially. Datus Proper's topic—a chance encounter with a former tenant of land he likes to fish—gave him a sense of history of the Cave family and of the land, causing him to see the land in a very different light. Thus, he gained a new, deeper appreciation for Dark Hollow. From her experiences, Judith Ortiz Cofer presents a goal for each of us: to examine our own prejudices and fight against them. Charles McNair's topic—his father's cabin—gave him insight into his father that he would not have had otherwise. In each of these topics, the writer figured as a participant. As you consider a topic for your writing, focus on events you have participated in that hold very real significance for you, even if you can't articulate that significance at first.

Reader

Initially, you'll serve as the primary audience for your personal essay. You'll write to make sense of your experience in the attempt to reach a deeper understanding of your essay's subject and its importance to you. But keep in mind that you'll also shape a final draft for an audience beyond yourself. You should assume that your readers will be sympathetic to you and interested in what you have to say. Your job will be to help your readers relive the experience with you, so you'll have to make sure that the detail you choose captures as exactly as possible what happened and how you felt about it. As you work to make those insights clear for your readers, you'll invite them to come along with you as you reexperience the topic of the essay, to make sense of things just as you did in exploring the topic.

Look again at "Dark Hollow." Proper is not merely capturing his experience of meeting Betty Cave on a fishing trip to the hollow; he is shaping that experience to make it meaningful for his readers. One of the primary themes of this essay is ownership, and Proper raises the question, "Just who owns Dark Hollow; whose property is it?" Early in the essay, he establishes this theme, using the terms "homestead," "personal stretch," and "claim" in the first two sentences. How does his use of "claim" in the second paragraph qualify these terms in the first paragraph? And how do these images of Proper's ownership compare to or contrast with "something beautiful" (paragraph 26) and "our land" (paragraph 28)?

Add to these images of ownership what Betty Cave says about her father as she talks with Proper. In each of the first four episodes, he is seen as a strong man fully capable of taking care of family and community affairs. In paragraph 5, he catches fish to feed his family; in paragraph 10, he works hard (as does her mother), so that his family won't go hungry; in paragraphs 16–17, he hikes to work in the copper mines in winter and offers comfort to the sick and dying in Dark Hollow; in paragraphs 20–23 he hunts game to feed his family. How do these images contrast with the last we see of her father (paragraph 29)? What is the impact of this image?

We don't know when Cave told Proper about her father's response to having left the hollow, but we do know that Proper was very purposeful in leaving the reader with the image of the father "sitting outside every evening, cryin' and cryin'." Thus, Proper shaped the events of his trip to Dark Hollow to have the greatest possible impact on his readers. He selected the events, the language he used to present them, and their position in the essay to create the meaning he intended his readers to understand.

DISTINGUISHING FEATURES OF PERSONAL ESSAYS

Conflict

Writers use narrative to shape events in a fashion that reveals their significance. These events constitute the plot of the narrative. Like the plot (what happens) in fiction, the plot of a personal narrative may be based on conflict. That narrative often depends on the writer's creating conflict and then resolving it. Think about the structure of a television situation comedy. Characters get themselves into and out of various situations, some comical, some serious, each one marked by conflict of one kind or another. Each conflict comes to a head, usually just before a commercial so that you'll want to keep watching to see how the conflict will be worked out. Right after the commercial, the conflict gets resolved, but then another conflict presents itself, which gets resolved, which is followed by more conflict and more resolution, until the half hour is filled and the plot's major climax is reached. What keeps us absorbed as viewers? If we're interested in the characters, we want to know how things turn out, we want to see how the conflict is resolved.

Writers of nonfiction narratives also may create interest in their writing by creating conflict or tension that the reader wants to see resolved. In "Dark Hollow," at least three kinds of tension are at work. Initially, Datus Proper wonders who is ahead of him on the stream and feels that, in a sense, "his" stream has been usurped by this intruder. At the end of the essay, a more significant tension is at work in the conflict between the Caves and the government that moved them from the land; we may say that this conflict is between people like the Caves and U.S. society at large. Finally, there is the internal tension Proper feels. His empathy for the Caves and others like them is countered by his pleasure at having land like Dark Hollow preserved for people like him.

As you consider various events for your own narrative, look for those marked by conflict (whether real, implied, potential, or threatened). Oftentimes, our experiences teach us their lessons as we struggle with others, our environment, or ourselves; they teach us as we are engaged in conflict. These experiences are the stuff of narrative, the stuff of the personal essay.

Dialogue

The more detail you include in a particular scene or event in your paper, the more importance that scene or event will assume for your readers. One way to provide this kind of detail is through dialogue. If you want your readers to remember the specifics of a particular event that involves key characters, try telling the event by means of a conversation between those characters.

Below are two versions of the same event, one a summary, the other a detailed account of the event given in dialogue. How do they differ? In what circumstances would each be appropriate for an essay?

> **Version 1**
> Linda had a heated argument with John, her father, that resulted in her being grounded.
>
> **Version 2**
> "I'm tired of always being last!" Linda shouted. Her face started to flush, and she clenched her fists.
> John, her father, paused a moment before replying, seeming to weigh his words carefully. "Honey," he began, "I know it can seem that your sister, being the youngest, gets favored, but . . ."
> "Seems like? Seems like! Don't patronize me, Dad. It's absolutely true, and you know it!" Linda's words echoed in the spacious den. "You're so unfair," she whined, "You always let Beth do whatever she wants, but not me. Oh, no! I have to do all the work around here—wash the dishes, cut the grass, walk the dog, haul Beth around in my car burning my gas—doesn't matter what it is. Nope, sweet little ol' Bethie just lounges around while I do everything!"
> "All right now, Linda," John muttered through clenched teeth, "best you'd be careful. You're pushing it, young lady."
> Linda saw her father's set jaw and knew what that meant. She was flirting with disaster, dangerously close to losing her freedom. But that didn't matter; heedless of the consequences, she pressed on. "I'm not your 'young lady'; I'm not a child! I'm 16 years old, Dad, and I'm sick and tired of being treated like I'm 8. It's so unfair!"
> "That's it, kiddo." (She hated it when her father called her "kiddo.") Both of them had lost sight of the original bone of contention; both knew what was coming; both knew they'd both lost. "You're grounded." John pronounced the punishment solemnly, like a judge sentencing a criminal. "You're grounded till next Wednesday."

"A whole week!" Linda exploded, outraged. "But, but, but I have a date this weekend!" she sputtered. She stopped, pondering her options. "Aw, come on, Dad, please let me just apologize. Please don't embarrass me like that. I'll just die if I have to break my date. Please, Dad, please?" she begged.

"I'll think about it," John said. "But for now, go to your room."

Linda turned on her heels and stalked down the hallway, slamming her door in reply.

> **Exercise 5.1**
>
> Identify the verbs that report who said what in the conversation between Linda and her father. How many times does "said" appear? Write your own dialogue between two characters, paying particular attention to verbs, especially those used to report who said what and how they said it.

Vivid Detail

Details carry freight. "The person entered the room" may be a grammatically correct sentence, but it doesn't reveal anything about the person, the person's actions, or the room. Consider these sentences, each of which involves a person entering a room:

> Exhausted, the junior high teacher stumbled into her principal's office, muttering, "I just can't stand it any longer."

> His coattails flapping in the breeze, little Johnny Wilson, the ten-year-old terror of the neighborhood, wheeled his skateboard to a skidstop just inside the door to Mrs. Smith's kitchen, his wheels marking tracks on the freshly waxed linoleum floor.

> Sgt. Sally Johnson, undercover policewoman extraordinaire, crept stealthily into the crack house, leading her infamous team—The Drugbusters—on yet another raid to rid her town of dope, druggies, drug dealers, and other sundry undesirable elements.

Although somewhat facetious, these examples should illustrate the point that your description—the language you use to detail the events of your writing—is all that is available for the reader to consider. Your job is to bring those events to life, to use your language to ensure your reader's understanding of the significance of those events.

You can also create detail by using lists, sometimes called *catalogs,* that present a string of details, naming things. Here's a passage from Lee K. Abbott's "The True Story of Why I Do What I Do" that shows how cataloging can help create an image in the reader's mind:

> "See this, Kit?" he said. He was standing in the center of the utility room, lawn mower here, gas can there, the walls hung with tools I never got the sense of. Golf

clubs were in there, a bucket of practice balls, cans of oil, greasy rags, a hoe, a rake, a cheap hardware store of goodies that smelled old and used and too sweet.

Abbott depicts a cluttered utility room and emphasizes clutter by describing the room's contents as almost a jumble. The detail "lawn mower here, gas can there" in the second sentence emphasizes the random placement of items, with this randomness underscored by the layering of detail in the next sentence. Abbott keeps adding details one by one until the reader sees the scene Abbott wants her to see.

VISUALS AND PERSONAL ESSAYS

Visuals, in the form of personal images, may be used as the basis for a personal essay. A personal image is one with some special meaning for the writer. Such images may recall a particular event, time, person, or object from the writer's life, something the writer found important or significant. For example, we all have memorabilia or keepsakes of one type or another—a ticket stub or program from a favorite group's concert; a family heirloom; a souvenir from a vacation; a scrapbook; an elementary, middle, or high school yearbook; a photo of friends, family, or a place important to us. Each of these may constitute a personal image. Such an image represents more than its physical presence; it carries meaning. A personal essay based on a personal image explores that meaning.

    The significance a personal image carries derives from the principle of perspective (see page 128 for more discussion of this concept). Perspective has to do with the particular vantage point from which we view something. Applied to a personal image, perspective allows us to look at the image, to focus on one or two particular aspects of what it represents for us, and then to write about those aspects. In relating this sense of images to the rhetorical triangle, we can say that images viewed from the angle of perspective correspond to a focus on the writer. When you write about a personal image, you're actually exploring the significance the image holds for you, perhaps what you learned from the experience it recalls for you. As an example of how perspective works as a way to explore a personal image, we offer the following example, one in which Bill talks about this old guitar handed down to him by his father.

    Here's Bill's story about it:

> Early June, 1966, my 20th birthday was approaching, and I was headed to Philmont Scout Ranch to work for the summer. I wanted a guitar, though I didn't know how to play, but I wanted to learn. So when Dad asked me what I might want as a birthday present, I immediately replied, "A guitar." He made me a deal. "Bill," he said, "you can have my old guitar and this." And he held out to me a 20 gauge, Winchester Model 12 shotgun. I didn't hesitate a lick; I took him up on it, thinking to buy my own guitar at the end of the summer, so that I'd then have two guitars and a shotgun to boot. At the time, I was more enthralled with the shotgun, knowing its value. Model 12s were in short supply 40 years ago, and they're even more rare now. But so is Dad's old guitar. I just didn't know it at the time.

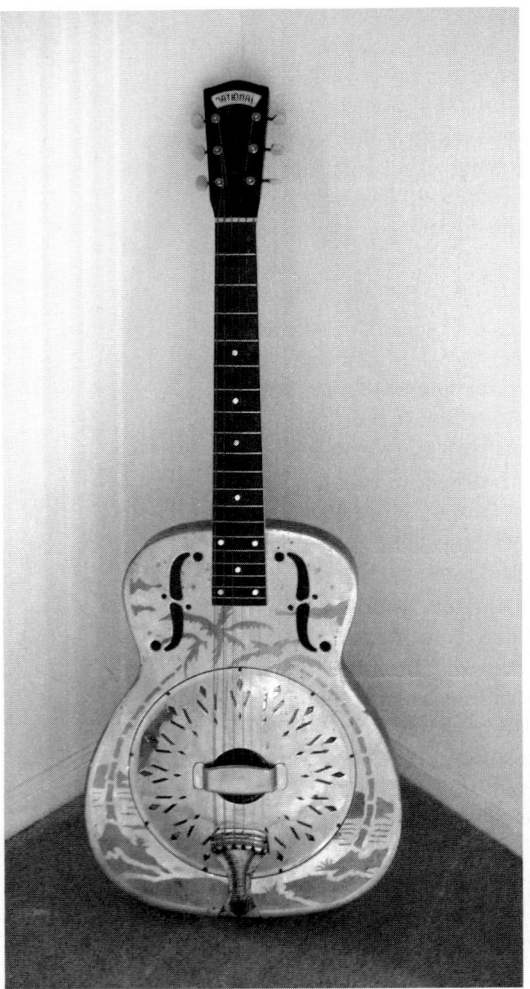 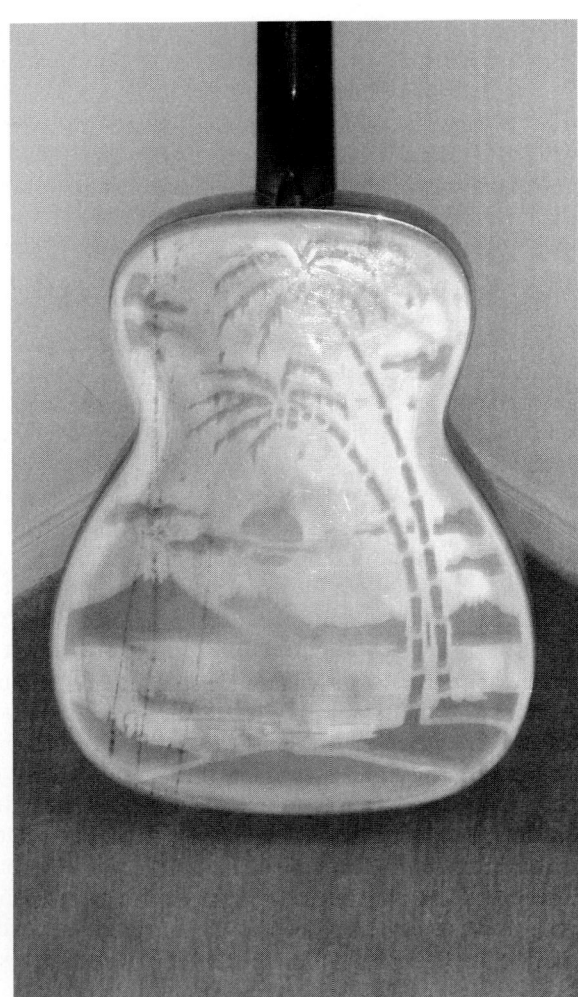

Courtesy of the author

It's a National Style O, a metal-bodied guitar with a sounding board called a cone about nine and a half inches in diameter. It has a shiny nickel plating, with an island scene sandblasted onto the surface, front and back. It was built between 1929 and 1935 by the National Guitar Company, and it became the preferred guitar by blues players and bands wanting a Hawaiian sound, popular at the time. It's loud as the cone really projects the sound, and it sounds a lot like a steel guitar in today's country and western music. On the front, palm trees frame the resonator, and the plate over the cone has plenty of vents to let the sound out. On the back is an island scene, reinforcing the Hawaiian theme of the guitar's legacy. In the background are island mountains (perhaps volcanoes), in the foreground an island beach scene, complete with palm trees and a canoe with two people in it on the water (near the bottom, just above the island beach). The moon, split by clouds, is in the middle. It's hard to see the canoe, as that part of the back has been worn a bit. And there are vertical streaks on the back, because it needs a good cleaning, if not a complete restoration. Don't know what that would do to its value, but restoring it to original quality would make it look simply outstanding. So I may have that done at some point.

I strung it up with nylon strings (a sacrilege that I wasn't aware of at the time), as the steel strings on it were rusted and would have killed my fingertips. I suspect Dad hadn't played it in at least 10 years, and I remember him playing it only once, one night when he played rhythm guitar while Mother played some honkeytonk tunes on the piano. Dad had been in a band when he was in his late teens, and that's the music he played. At the end of that summer, I bought an Epiphone six-string flattop jumbo (made by Epiphone before Gibson bought the company, so it's another valuable instrument). And I put Dad's guitar aside for a long while.

At some point, I began to piece together the story behind it, though I think I got most of the information from my mother. Dad and I just didn't talk much about such things. In 1933, when he was 16, Dad left school to go to work in the Civilian Conservation Corps (CCC). The CCC was a works project designed to give employment to men during the Depression. Dad made $25.00 a month and was required to send $20.00 of that home, so that he was actually helping support his family back in the Florida Panhandle. That left him $5.00 a month for his own personal needs. And from the $5.00 each month, he scrimped and saved till he had the $60.00 he needed to buy the guitar. That was some kind of sacrifice he made, to save that amount of money during the depths of the Depression. He wanted that guitar badly, and he got it without any help—no layaway plan, no credit card, no outside money. For he was on his own at the age of 16. I didn't have that kind of resolve when I was 16. Guess I didn't have to, but he did.

I haven't played it much, a little, though I still have designs on doing so. This past Christmas, Matt (my youngest son, now 25) played it when he was home. While Matt owns three guitars himself and plays quite a bit, it was the first time I remember him picking up Dad's guitar. Matt's an excellent guitarist, and I imagine that eventually I'll hand it on to him.

Obviously, this isn't a finished piece of writing, but it has the makings of an essay that could focus on the guitar's meaning as well as the relationship Bill had with his father. The guitar has become a personal image for Bill, and it provides several perspectives, several opportunities for exploration. One such perspective involves what the guitar meant to his father. Another would involve what it has come to mean for Bill, including some reflection on his relationship with his father. Were Bill to work this initial story—an extended freewrite by any other name—into an essay, he would need to do more research. One avenue is the Internet, to find information about National guitars. Another is his family. Three of his aunts (his father's sisters) are still living, and they may know more about the guitar's history and about his father's life during the Depression.

Exercise 5.2

A. What personal images do you have that are important to you? Pick a keepsake or an object that carries significance for you. Describe it physically; then write about what it means for you. Respond to such questions as these:
   1. How long have you had it?
   2. When did you get it?
   3. What were the circumstances of your getting it? What was the scene or context?
   4. Why have you held on to it?
   5. Would you ever give it up? If so, to whom, and under what circumstances? If not, why not?
B. As you look for a topic for your personal essay, consider writing about a personal image.

ASSIGNMENT AND GUIDELINES FOR WRITING

Assignment

As you begin your personal essay, you may use one of the four writing prompts listed below or a prompt provided by your teacher. Remember that, ultimately, your task is to discover and then reveal the significance in your topic to your readers.

1. Describe an event from which you learned something. Your job is to use your language to recreate the event so that your readers will feel that they have been at least observers of this important event with you, if not participants in it.
2. Describe a favorite place, one that's significant for you. What makes it a favorite? What makes it significant? Your job is to depict this place so that your readers will see clearly its importance to you. Option: Use this place as the setting for an essay about a significant event that occurred there.
3. Write about a person who has been significant in your life or about an object that's important to you. Be sure your focus is on why this person or object is significant to you; your language should help the reader see that significance.
4. Base your essay on one of the Writing Opportunity assignments to which you responded earlier in this chapter. Choosing this option will likely lead you to write about an event, place, person or object. Whatever your topic, be sure your essay's focus is on the personal significance you find in the topic.

Choosing a Topic

If you've already settled on a potential topic for this essay, move to Part B of these instructions. If you're undecided about a topic, try any or all of the activities in Part A.

Part A

1. Take a look again at your responses to the Interest Inventory (pages 11–13). Look especially for topics about events, places, and people you know well. Pick two or three and write about each for ten minutes. Why did you pick these particular potential topics? What's important about them? Why do they stand out or appeal to you?
2. Develop an Important List, a list of people (family, friends, teachers), places (home, favorite places, work, school), ideas (family values, family history, your desires and dreams, your goals), or things (awards, events, personal objects) that are significant or meaningful for you. Write two or three sentences about each entry on your list. Then, select the ones you think are most important, and write three or four more sentences about each of those. Why did you select these particular entries? [We adopted this activity from *Paideia*, edited by Kristina Fury and Kimberly Whitehead (New York: Forbes Custom, 1998). For an example of its use, see Chris Miller's prewriting, pages 190–193.]
3. Freewrite for fifteen minutes about your memories of events, places, and people. Start with "I remember" and jot down all the events, places, and people that come to mind. Write nonstop for fifteen minutes. Don't censor any thoughts that come to mind; don't worry about grammar, mechanics, or sentence structure—just write.

From these writings, select a topic that you think you may want to use as the basis for your essay.

Part B

Now that you've identified a possible topic, freewrite for at least fifteen minutes about it. Again, don't stop during the entire period; don't censor any thoughts that come to mind; don't worry about grammar, mechanics, or sentence structure—just write.

After you've finished this fifteen-minute writing period, look back over what you've written. What is beginning to emerge as the focal point of your topic? If you don't see anything just yet, you may want to continue with another fifteen-minute freewrite, followed by reflection on what you write. This process may be repeated until you find a topic.

Collecting Information

Reader. You may use your reader as a means of generating details for your writing. Write a short statement describing someone you imagine will want to read your essay. What will make the experience come alive for that person? What details will you need to present to enable your reader to understand the significance of the topic for you?

Visualization. Another way to generate material is to visualize your topic (see the visualization exercise, pages 22–24). When you've finished your visualization, write down everything you remember about the exercise as quickly as you can. Just as with freewriting, don't worry about anything except writing.

Talking. Talking is another good way of generating information for this assignment. Find a sympathetic listener and tell her your story, or find someone who was part of your topic and reminisce with that person about it. Use a tape recorder; take notes during your conversation, or write down as much of the discussion as you can remember immediately following it.

Freewriting. Return to freewriting. If you get stuck, then freewrite to get started again. Select one aspect of your topic and write about only that aspect for ten minutes. If you need more information about a certain part of your topic, freewrite about it.

Focus Statement

As you generate information for your paper, look back over your freewriting and then write a brief statement about the focal point of your essay. Keep in mind that this will be a tentative statement. You may phrase it something like this:

> *Personal object (response to Exercise 5.2.A., Page 184).* My topic is my Dad's old guitar that he gave to me. It's a National that he bought in 1934 with money he saved from working in a CCC camp. I'll have to describe the guitar physically (Dobro-type metal body, Hawaiian scene etched into the finish, four-digit serial number), what it's worth, how I got it, memories I have as a child of him playing it (Mom on the piano, both singing), what it now means to me. I want my readers to come away with a sense of just how much I value the guitar. (Maybe I'll quote from a song by John Denver about his old guitar.)

Use this statement as a very general guide to getting started. It should begin to address the significance you want your writing to carry, and it can point the way toward the kind of details you'll have to present in the essay: In order to fulfill your focus statement, what will you have to do; what details (and in what order) will you have to present?

Planning Your Essay's Structure

The primary structuring principle of the personal essay is chronology, which shows the relationship of events, places, and people in time. The significance is revealed gradually through the layering of details the writer presents, so that when the reader finishes, he has a sense of having gradually come to understand the writer's intent.

It's not enough, however, to tell what happened in a "first this, then this, then this" sequence. Instead, you'll need to make it clear to your reader how one part of your writing leads to the next, and that to the next, and so on until you make your point or show how the events form an important or significant whole.

Typically, chronology is straightforward, though occasionally a writer will use a flashback, moving backwards in time to tell a part of the story that comments on the story line that's developing. Chris Fisher's "Scars" is a braided essay, consisting of 14 sections. The essay opens in the present, but the second section (II. A Gift from Dad) moves back in time to an incident when Chris was a boy. The third section (III. Little Sister) returns to the present but includes elements of the past. The fourth section (IV. Jesus and Zen) is in the present, but the fifth section (V. A Good Bird) flashes back to the same timeframe of that of the second section. Here's a summary of the timeframe for the remaining sections of "Scars":

   VI. Scarface—the present
  VII. Sunshine—the past, same time as the fifth section (V. A Good Bird)
 VIII. Of a Boy—the past, when Chris was a teenager in high school (about ninth grade)
   IX. Sunshine—the past, same timeframe as sections V and VII.
    X. Man of the House—the past, two to three years later than section VIII.
   XI. To Give Than To Receive—the past, Chris' senior year of high school
  XII. A Good Bird—the past, same timeframe as sections V, VII, and IX.
 XIII. Beauty for Ashes—the present
  XIV. One He Never Gave—the past, when Chris was in high school

Chris closes his essay with a brief, present-day reflection of the significance of the confrontation with his father he describes in XIV.

Datus Proper's narrative takes a different approach to using chronology as a structuring device. Proper takes us through a day's fishing from start to finish, moving from one event to the next in order. At the same time, he weaves Betty Cave's narrative into his, so that they comment on each other. But the point here is that Proper takes us through the events of his day of fishing in the order in which they happened.

Did any of the authors write everything that happened during the events they reported? Clearly not. Their job was to present the most important details to the reader and to shape those details so that the reader would come to understand the significance they wanted the reader to understand. Selecting details is an important consideration for a writer of personal essays.

Make a list of the details you think will be important in your essay. Then, create an order for them. Is this order absolutely chronological, or are there reasons to tell things out of sequence in places? Why? Using this ordered list as a guide, write a draft of your essay.

> **Exercise 5.3**
>
> "Dark Hollow" is arranged chronologically, with Proper taking us with him as he walks from his car to the stream, encounters and converses with Betty Cave, and then fishes the stream. He doesn't tell everything that occurs on that trip; instead, he selects events that are important to the significance he's trying to present to his readers. Are there events that don't seem to be important enough to warrant inclusion in the essay, or does each event that Proper reports contribute something to the essay? Which events could, or should, have been deleted? Pick two events or details from this essay that carry special significance for you and explain what they contribute to it.

Refining Your Writing

After you've written your essay and taken some time away from it, revise it, keeping the following principles in mind:

Selection of detail. Select only the key moments, the ones that your paper must have to make sense. Focus on those moments that create conflict or tension.

Amount of detail. Give important moments more space or detail. The more time your reader spends with a given section of your essay, the more importance it will assume.

Quality of detail. Provide sufficient detail to help the reader see the scene you're writing about. The more vivid the image—the more descriptive the language—the more likely your reader will be to grasp its importance to you.

Dialogue. Use dialogue to help bring characters to life. Letting a character speak instead of summarizing or reporting what she said can give that character immediacy and importance in the paper. Two notes: (1) Be sure to pay attention to the conventions of punctuation at work with dialogue (e.g., quotation marks); (2) try to help readers hear how a speaker sounds by describing how he utters his words. It is fine to use "say" or "said" sometimes, but keep in mind that speakers often "reply," "retort," "respond," "exclaim," "utter," "whisper," "whimper," "comment," "cry," and "shout."

> **Exercise 5.4**
>
> 1. Look again at one or two of the essays in the first part of this chapter. How does the writer feature or emphasize the important moments in his or her essay? Identify any parts of each essay that you think are extraneous. Why do you think so? How vivid is the detail each writer provides? Is this detail sufficient to help you see the event? Why or why not? To what extent and how effectively does each writer use dialogue?

2. Identify the key moments you remember about your topic. How can you feature or emphasize them? Why do they figure as key or important? In what order do you think you should present them to your reader? Which event or events do you think you'll give more space to? Why? What kind of detail will help bring these moments to life? Does any event lend itself to dialogue? If so, what will you have each character say?

SAMPLE STUDENT PROCESS

In this section, we present a student writer at work from start to finish. Chris Miller, a first-year student at NMSU, began his essay by doing several prewriting exercises. He then tried out two potential topics to see which might be the more promising, picked one, changed his mind, and then wrote and revised a draft of his essay. We've reproduced Chris's writings exactly as he wrote them—abbreviations, spelling errors, mechanical errors, and all. These examples make it clear that Chris followed our instructions not to worry about correctness until the final draft.

Prewriting

Chris began by writing an "I remember" list of places, people, and events (see A.3., page 185). His job was to list everything that came to mind—not to censor anything, simply to list.

I remember...
50-miler backpack trip
mountain climbing
my house
Silver Jack
OA Greagor
Key Club convention
State cross-country meet
Oak Grove Elementary
vacations in Washington, Oregon, California
Mexico w/ Habitat for Humanity
working at Kirtland
Amy
Philmont
continuation
Mrs. Woelfel, Mr. Brown, Mrs. Brice, Mrs. Winkler
academic decathlon
White Sands
Montrose
Grand Junction—Beth
Christmas w/ my family

Lassie
He-man
my brother breaking his arm
NJHS trip
BSA Jamboree
50-miler in Utah
Eagle Court of Honor
getting in trouble with police
Game Boy
grandparents
woodcutting
Kayla/Misty
the countryside
getting Gina
my great-grandma
my biology test

The second prewriting exercise Chris completed was an Important List of people, places, and ideas (see A.2., page 185). Again, Chris was not to censor but to name, then to expand his initial list, and then to discuss the expanded list.

Name
People—groups, teachers, family
Places—home, travel, work
Ideas—ethics & morality, goals & desires, self-respect

Expand
People—
    groups: Scouts and Key Club
    teachers: elementary, middle, and high school
    family: mom and dad
Places—
    home: Montrose, Albuquerque
    travel: Scouts, Mexico
    work: fast food, OA Greagor, Kirtland
Ideas—
    ethics & morality: Scouts, importance
    goals & desires: help, happiness, learning
    self-respect: originality, drinking

Discuss
People—
    Many groups have influenced my life. The biggest influence has definitely come from scouts. I've been influenced with scouts since I was about six in Cub Scouts. My mom helped w/ my pack and volunteered at my elementary school. She definitely had a big influence on my life at this time. I feel like I had a good start on life thanks to her. When I joined Boy Scouts, the influence shifted to my father, who soon became scoutmaster. Many experiences

that I had in Boy Scouts influenced me, but few changed me as much as being on staff at our council's scout camp, OA Greagor. I learned and changed more from being on staff for two summers than at any other time.

Places—[*Since Chris misplaced this portion of his prewriting, it can't be reproduced here.*]

Ideas—

If I could narrow down the basis of my life and who I am to one thing, it would be my ethics. I consider them in everything I do. The main source of my ethics was scouts. I learned to value honesty and truth. Today I base my life on these beliefs. I am also very concerned with my self-respect. It is very important to me. My personal code is very strict. I don't smoke or drink. Sometimes it is hard, but it's well worth it. My goals for my life are to be happy, to help others, and to learn as much as I can.

Focus Statement

Having chosen to write about a significant place—the OA Greagor Scout Camp—Chris wrote this focus statement designed to give him some direction for his drafting:

My purpose is to educate readers about a favorite place of mine. I will tell about its significance to me, and what I learned from it.

describe the place
tell about experiences
tell about significance
what I learned
who I met
how it affected me
The place is OA Greagor and I worked there for two years.

Chris submitted his focus statement to his peer group (three other students in his first-year composition class), and they raised these questions:

Why is this place so significant to you? How has it influenced your life to make you who you are today?
What is OA Greagor? What did you do while you worked there?
What types of work did you do—fun, strenuous? How does this job mean more to you than perhaps others in the past? What is it that you hope the readers will gain? Experiences, hardships, etc.?

Knowing what his peer-group readers would want to learn from reading the paper, Chris began to write a narrative about his experiences at this camp, producing this draft:

OA Greagor

When I think back on my life before I moved to Albuquerque, age 15, there are many memories. I was a typical kid. I had my friends, with whom I spent a great deal of time <u>playing with.</u> I was involved in a <u>few activities,</u> and I had worked doing babysitting or mowing people's lawns. All these things hold memories for me, but none stand out as much as OA Greagor Boy Scout Camp. The first time I ever rode up the rutted, dirt road leading to the camp, I was 10 and had just joined Boy Scouts. I didn't know any one, and I got my <u>first horrible taste of homesickness</u>. I spent the week either physically ill or depressed, and despite the <u>five merit badges I earned</u>, I swore I would never go back. ~~The next year~~ Early the next year my father ~~took~~ agreed to take over the ~~scoutmaster position~~ troop from our handicapped scoutmaster. He boosted the troop membership and got many younger kids to join.

You'll note that Chris underlined several phrases to remind himself to return to these places later and add detail. He also scratched out some words, substituting others he thought more appropriate. And he stopped very short of producing a first or discovery draft. For whatever reasons, Chris didn't like the way this essay was developing, so he did a very smart thing—he changed topics. He returned to the prewriting he'd done earlier and selected as his new topic a trip to Mexico that he'd mentioned in both prewriting exercises.

Having picked this new topic, Chris made a prewriting list of specific things he recalled from a trip to Nogales, a border town in both Arizona and Mexico, to do volunteer work for Habitat for Humanity.

Mexico
Habitat house
stories—Mexican prison
Nogales—US
Nogales—Mexico
Nogales habitat house
Chano
work sites
Doña Chuy
dinners at houses
marketplace
poverty
factories
pickaxing
moving rocks
hauling & leveling dirt
showers & bathrooms
food
sleeping
Dos X's
strip poker
border crossing
video camera
writing
Tucson
trying to speak Spanish
Bueno, lame, Gringos on Safari
show examples (cheese thing)

Chris then wrote this outline of the points he wanted to make in a draft:

I. Mexicans have little or no money
   A. houses
   B. food
   C. inflation—reason
      2 ~~1.~~) Makiladores—machines
      1 ~~2.~~) cheese & other prices
II. They are happy and kind
   A. family
   B. friends
   C. food—give up what they have
   D. Chano
   E. worksites
   F. house materials

Note that this isn't a traditional outline; it is more a list of things to remember to include than a structure for the paper to come. Chris then wrote part of a draft before stopping for a breather:

> It was approaching midnight when Chano, our ~~Mexican~~ translator, finally lead us into what would become our home for the next week. It was a small rectangular ~~concrete~~ building with one half serving as an office and the other as two bedrooms ~~and the~~ divided by the bathroom. ~~Standing in the center of the bathroom I could reach both my hands out and touch the opposing walls. It~~ We piled our bags in the corner and then, to tired to do anything else, stumbled into the bedrooms and ~~went to~~ fell asleep.
>
> Six short hours later, ~~we~~ after some asking, reminding, and finally threatening, ~~by our chaperones~~, we grudgingly got out of bed. ~~The only food~~ We hadn't been to a grocery store yet, so the only food we had for breakfast was leftover bread and some apples. We ate this while listening to Chano explain what was to happen. "Today we will begin working. We ~~are going to a~~ will be ~~helping with a house~~ working on a house

Chris stopped this draft here but returned to it later and completed it. He submitted the draft that follows for his peer group to review.

Rough Draft for Peer Review

> It was approaching midnight when Chano, our translator, finally lead us into what would become our home for the next five days. It was a small rectangular building with one half serving as an office and the other as two bedrooms divided by the bathroom. We piled our bags into the corner and then, too tired to do anything else, stumbled into the bedrooms and fell asleep.
>
> Six short, uncomfortable hours later, after some asking, reminding, and finally threatening, we grudgingly got out of bed. There hadn't been time to go to a grocery yet, so the only food we had for breakfast was leftover bread and some apples. We ate this while listening to Chano.

"Thank you for coming. Habitat for Humanity appreciates your help. We will leave for the first work site in about half an hour." Chano's English was grammatically flawless and had only a slight Spanish accent, the result of working with "gringos" for the last ten years. He was the director of Habitat for Humanity in the Nogales area. Under his guidance the organization had built over one hundred houses and donated thousands of hours to help the local residents. Because our group of teenagers and two chaperones contained only three people who had ever been to Mexico, we had been dubbed "Gringos on Safari" by our friends in Albuquerque, and it stuck, becoming the name of our expedition.

We loaded the van with shovels, picks, rakes, axes, and several other tools that we had been told we would use. It was a thirty minute drive to the work site on the outskirts of Nogales. This drive was my first real introduction to Mexico. I knew it was a poor nation, but I hadn't even imagined this much poverty could exist. The houses we saw were smaller than many of friend's living rooms. They were built with wood, dirt, cardboard, or whatever else was available. It seemed like a strong wind would blow Nogales over. As we advanced further from the city the road became worse. Soon the van had to be put into four wheel drive. Chano explained that the city had not been built for cars, since less than ten percent of the population owned one.

Finally we got to the work site. It consisted of a small, flat plot of dirt that was going to be a house foundation and a large pile of dirt a short distance away. We spent the first five hours moving dirt from the pile to the flat foundation. By about 11:00 the blistering sun had warmed the area to almost 90 degrees and it kept getting hotter. The twelve of us worked along with Chano and the six people that would eventually occupy the house. They had a deal with Habitat, so that they helped build the house in exchange for paying less for it. I couldn't imagine one person living in a house this size much less six. Finally the lunch break arrived. We struggled over to the van and got our lunch out. Then we dropped to the ground in the only shade at the site, provided by a small, dying tree. The break ended far to soon and it was back to work for five more hours. The only comfort came from the fact that it gradually cooled off as the afternoon wore on. Finally we hauled the last load of dirt to the foundation. It was almost six by then and we had added a foot to the entire 20 x 20 foot plot. We celebrated the end of the day by dragging ourselves into the van and collapsing. I had three blisters, a sprained ankle, and a sore back to show for my ten hours of work. When we arrived back at the house the chaperones prepare dinner while the rest of us cleaned up. Their was no water pressure in this part of Nogales, because no one could afford it. To shower, we poured water over our heads and washed off as best we could. We ate a quick dinner and then, to tired to do anything else, went straight to sleep.

Once again we had to be forced out of bed. We devoured a slightly larger breakfast to give us energy for the long day ahead and then piled into the van. The new site was only about ten minutes away, but it led us to an even worse part of town. Here the houses were sometimes made of tires or even old trash. There were dogs running around the streets and filthy, naked babies playing in trash. The house we were working on was made of wood on the three sides it had. The owner had run out of money after building three sides of it and had been living there with no back wall for two months. He had finally saved enough money to buy the forty tires which he was going to use as a wall since they were cheaper than wood. We started by splitting into two groups. One group started filling dirt into the first layer of tires along the back wall, while the other began picking a hole that would serve as an outhouse. I started out with a pick ax and began working on the outhouse. We worked for about four hours, picking into the rocky, hard ground until we were exhausted, and dug the hole almost three inches deep. During lunch we sat back admiring our accomplishment until Chano informed us that the hole needed to be at least six feet deep. The owner couldn't afford to hire a jackhammer. We switched jobs after lunch and worked for another four hours. Our moral was much better on this day despite the intense heat and new blisters. That evening we had the honor of eating with some local Nogales residents. We divided into three groups and each went to a different house. Our group went to the house of Doña Chuy, a native of Nogales. She was 47 years old and lived in a two room shack with her husband, three kids, and her oldest daughter's boyfriend. They survived on what the husband and son made at the maquilas. Literally translated maquila means machine, but in Nogales it refers to the huge American owned factories. The companies open factories in Mexico because the labor is much cheaper. Over eighty percent of Nogales works in the maquilas, often for incredibly little money and no benefits. Doña Chuy told us about the maquilas as well as she could in broken fragmented English.

"My husband, once he work for Phillips. He work for five years, then one day he go there and there is no on in the maquila. There is a sign says the company close and leave. He lucky one and get a new job but many others have to leave Nogales." Chano later explained that Phillips had a factory in Nogales, but cheaper labor was available in the Philippines, so overnight they closed the factory and left. They used a legal loophole to avoid paying the people their severance pay and it left about 1200 people out of a job. Most of them were forced to move out of Nogales, because they couldn't get another job. Doña Chuy cooked homemade tortillas for us, and then stuffed them with chicken, rice, and cheese. She also gave us some of her homemade pineapple beer, usually reserved only for religious holidays and birthdays. After a long day of work it tasted better than any gourmet meal I've ever had. We later found out that this one diner cost the family more than they usually spend on food in a week. To the people of Mexico it is a huge honor to have guests and they sacrifice a lot of personal comfort for them. This wasn't the first time that Mexico's generosity would impress me. We reluctantly left Doña Chuy's house, filled with her delicious food and the warmth of her kind and generous attitude toward us.

The next day dawned with the promise of a surprise after lunch. We worked hard all morning fueled by anticipation of the surprise and dug the outhouse hole to an impressive seven inches. At twelve thirty we all crowded inside the house and ate while speculating on the surprise. Just as we finished eating Chano came in and told us that since we had worked so hard and had done so well, we were going to take the afternoon off. He also explained that because we had skipped some of the tourist attractions and had saved money on food, we each had ended up with a sixty dollar refund. We took the money and began to drive to the marketplace. About half way there, however, we changed our minds. After seeing the lifestyles of the people of Nogales, we couldn't just rashly waste sixty dollars on some tourist junk. Instead we took the money to Doña Chuy and the women who fed the other two groups. They were speechless and, after some crying, gratefully accepted the money. We talked with them some more and then drove back to the marketplace to buy a few more groceries. (Three weeks after we got back from the trip, we got a postcard from Chano which said, among other things, that the women had used the money to buy clothes for almost twenty families in Nogales.) On the way we saw a schoolhouse with the children playing at recess. The school was too poor to afford playground equipment, so the kids made up games of their own using whatever they could find. That seemed to be a common theme in Mexico—Do the best you can with what you can find. We spent almost two hours in the marketplace comparing prices to American products. By the time a typical Mexico worker had worked enough hours to buy a pound of cheese, it's price was equivalent to $60.00. The outrageous inflation would be intolerable in America, but to the Mexico people it was accepted as a way of life. I had noticed throughout the trip that the people seemed happier and more content than most people I knew in America. They came to rely more on family and less on money. It was not uncommon to see three generations of family living happily together in one house. It was like the poverty and inflation and working conditions and houses didn't matter to them. They didn't let it depress them. I had always been told that money couldn't buy happiness, but I never believe it until I went to Mexico.

Our last day was another work day. We toiled for about nine hours with a short lunch break and then drove back to the house for one last time. We sadly said our good-byes to Chano and his family, and then loaded our van to leave. I spent the drive home thinking about what I had learned and how I had grown. I thought of Doña Chuy and all the other people we met. I also thought about the poverty and all the problems with Nogales, but when I think back on the trip today what I remember is the generosity and kindness of the people. I saw the actual value of money and the real power of love on the trip and it has made a dramatic difference in my life. I am more content with what I have and less materialistic than before. I also value my friends and family much more. These have all made me a happier person and I can't imagine a better learning experience.

Chris's peer group read, marked, and commented on the draft. They felt that it was an effective first draft but that Chris needed to pay attention to these things:

1. It tells an awful lot. It's over 1,800 words long (too long for the assignment, a max of 1,500 words), so it needs to be cut down and shaped.
2. The paragraphs are too long, need to be split into more logical units.
3. It has some grammatical errors—but it's a draft, so these aren't bad unless you don't fix them in a final draft.
4. The ending is a bit much; it makes too many unsupported assertions.
5. The attempt at humor (digging the pit—one inch in one day?) doesn't quite work, so it needs to be revised or maybe deleted.

6. Some of the paragraphs have choppy sentence structure, so these need to be smoothed out.
7. More dialogue in a place or two would help bring this piece more to life.

Taking into account his group members' comments (and those of Bill, his teacher), Chris then produced the final draft that follows. As you read it, consider the differences between it and the rough draft. Do you think the changes Chris made are effective? Why or why not?

Final Draft

Chris Miller
GRINGOS ON SAFARI

1   Near midnight, Chano, the Director of Habitat for Humanity for the Nogales area, finally led us into what would become our home for the next five days—a small rectangular building with one half serving as an office and the other as two bedrooms divided by the bathroom. Piling our bags into the corner and then, too tired to do anything else, we stumbled into the bedrooms and fell asleep. For all but three of us, this was a first trip to Mexico, so our friends in Albuquerque had dubbed us "gringos on safari." We were ready for adventure.

2   Six short, uncomfortable hours later, after some asking, reminding, and finally threatening, we grudgingly got out of bed. Because we'd had no time to shop, we munched on leftover bread and some apples while Chano very concisely laid out the day's itinerary. "Thank you for coming. Habitat for Humanity appreciates your help. We will leave for the first work site in about half an hour."

3   We loaded the van with shovels, picks, rakes, and axes, tools that none of us used very often. The half-hour drive to the work site was my first real introduction to Mexico. I knew it was a poor nation, but I hadn't even imagined this much poverty could exist. The flimsy houses we saw, smaller than many of my friends' living rooms, were built with wood, dirt, cardboard, or whatever else was available. A strong wind could blow Nogales over.

4   The work site consisted of a small, flat plot of dirt that would form a house's foundation and a large pile of dirt a short distance away. "Your job is to move this dirt," Chano pointed at the large pile, "to the foundation, spread it out evenly, and pack it tight." My friend John and I looked at each other and rolled our eyes. Some safari. Some adventure.

5   Five hot, grueling hours later, we dropped gratefully to the ground to have lunch in the only shade available, provided by a small, dying tree. Another hot, grueling five hours later, we stood back to admire our handiwork. We had raised the foundation a foot, and we celebrated by dragging ourselves into the van and

collapsing. I had three blisters, a sprained ankle, and a sore back to show for my ten hours of work.

I also had a new appreciation for the term "sweat equity." Our work crew this day had included the family of six who would occupy the house. We didn't talk with them very much because none of us knew more than a year of textbook Spanish, and they spoke no English. But at the end of the day, we understand their repeated "*Muchas gracias*" well enough. We were bound by blisters, sweat, and dirt.

Next morning, our chaperones had to pry us out of the sack. This day's site was a house with only three sides made of wood. The owner had run out of money before he could complete it and had been living there with no back wall for two months. He had finally saved enough money to buy the forty tires to form this wall since they were cheaper than wood. We split into two groups, one to fill the first layer of tires with dirt, the other to pick a hole in what seemed like solid rock that would serve as an outhouse. Outside of Scout camps and portapotties, none of us had much experience with outhouses.

We were amazed by the poverty that surrounded us. Dogs ran in packs in the streets; filthy, naked babies played in the trash. A man saved for two months just to buy forty used tires to keep out the weather. Most of us had an allowance that would buy that much in a week. Six people would live in a 400 sq. ft. house. Most of us lived in four-bedroom, 3500 sq. ft. brick homes, palaces by comparison.

That evening we had the honor of dining in the homes of some local Nogales, Mexico, residents. My group dined with Doña Chuy, a 47-year-old woman who lived in a two-room shack with her husband, three kids, and her oldest daughter's boyfriend. They survived on what the husband and son made at the *maquilas*. Literally translated *maquila* means machine, but in Nogales it refers to the huge American-owned factories. The companies open factories in Mexico, attracted by cheap labor. Over eighty percent of Nogales works in the *maquilas*, often for incredibly little money and no benefits. Doña Chuy told us about the *maquilas* as well as she could in her fragmented English.

"My husband, once he work for Phillips. He work for five years, then one day he go there and there is no one in the *maquila*. There is a sign says the company close and leave. He lucky one and get a new job but many others have to leave Nogales." She did not seem angry about this; instead, she seemed to accept it as something that just happened. Chano later explained that Phillips had a factory in Nogales, but cheaper labor was available in the Philippines, so overnight they closed the factory and left. They used a legal loophole to avoid paying the people their severance pay and left about 1200 people out of a job. Most were forced to leave Nogales. No work.

Doña Chuy cooked homemade tortillas for us, then stuffed them with chicken, rice, and cheese. She also served homemade pineapple beer, usually reserved only for religious holidays and birthdays. After a long day of work those tortillas tasted better than any seven-course gourmet dinner I've ever had. We later found out that this one meal cost the family more than they usually spent on food in a week. But for the people of Mexico it is a huge honor to have guests, and they sacrifice a lot of personal comfort for them. Reluctantly, we left Doña Chuy's house, filled with her delicious food and the warmth of kindness and generosity.

The next day Chano surprised us after lunch. "You've worked hard, and I thank you. So you get the afternoon off. And because you've toured less and worked more, you've saved some money. Each of you gets a $60.00 refund."

"Sixty bucks apiece? Wow! Anybody for the *mercado*?"

"Yessir! I want a sombrero and maybe some sandals and a sarape to hang on the wall."

"Not me. I want about a gallon of Coke."

Halfway there, we changed our minds. After seeing the lifestyles of the people of Nogales, we couldn't just rashly waste sixty dollars on some tourist junk. Instead we took the money to Doña Chuy and her friends. They were speechless but gratefully accepted the money. (Three weeks later, we got a postcard from Chano which said, among other things, that the women had used the money to buy clothes for almost twenty families in Nogales.)

We did drive to the *mercado* for groceries and spent almost two hours there comparing prices to American products. By the time a typical Mexican worker had worked enough hours to buy a pound of cheese, its price was equivalent to $60.00 US. Such outrageous inflation would be intolerable in America, but the Mexican people accepted it as a way of life. I had noticed throughout the trip that the people seemed happier and more content than most people I knew in America. They relied more on family and less on money. They had to, to survive. It was not uncommon to see three generations of family living together in one house. The poverty and inflation and working conditions and ramshackle houses didn't seem to matter to them. They didn't let it depress them. I had always been told that money couldn't buy happiness, but I never believed it until I went to Mexico.

Our last day was another work day. We toiled another nine hours with a short lunch break and then drove back to our headquarters one last time. We sadly said our goodbyes to Chano and his family, then loaded our van to leave. I spent the drive home thinking about Doña Chuy and all the other people we had met, about the poverty and all the problems in Nogales we had seen. But when I think back on the trip today what I remember most is the generosity and kindness of the people. I saw the actual value of money and the real power of love on the trip and it has made a dramatic difference in my life. I am more content with what I have and less materialistic than before. I also value my friends and family much more. Sometimes, when you go on safari, you come back with less but more than you expected.

CHECKLIST: CRITIQUING A PERSONAL ESSAY

1. Which of the assignment options does the essay respond to? In a sentence, summarize the significant statement the essay makes.
2. Identify places in the paper you think worked well. What makes these places effective?
3. Identify places in the paper you think need work. What revisions need to be made?
4. How effective is the paper's organization? Consider the beginning, middle, and end. Does the introduction catch the reader's attention? If so, how? If not, what revisions need to be made?
5. Does the paper adhere to conventions of usage, mechanics, and format? Correct any errors you find.

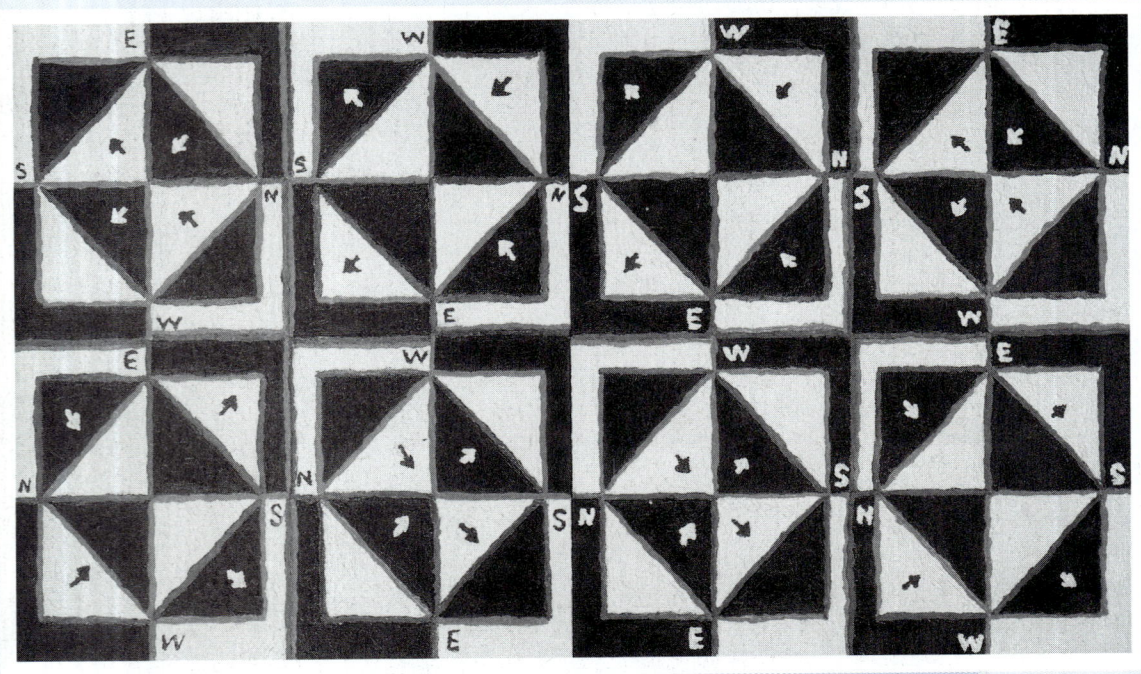

Alfred Jensen, "Correspondence in Function of Magnet & Prism," 1961. Oil on canvas, 50 × 84 in. Courtesy PaceWildenstein, New York. Photo: Ellen Page Wilson © 2008 Estate of Alfred Jensen/Artists Rights Society (ARS), New York, NY.

CHAPTER 6

Information Essays

The following quotations make it clear that the word "information" has a broad range of meanings.

Bob:	When Betty and I got home last night, she put on a cd and I could see she was in a romantic mood, so . . .
Bill:	Too much information . . .
Mr. Smith:	I need to know whether my son has been attending class regularly
Dean:	I'm sorry, Mr. Smith, but federal regulations prohibit me from giving out that information.
Bob:	Do you have the Jones's number?
Sally:	No, why don't you try calling Information.
Advertisement:	We live in an information age.
Catalogue:	Our Information Technology degree combines the most modern technologies with time-honored principles of rhetorical theory.

Despite the very real differences in the meaning of the term *information* in these quotations, there is, in each case, a reference to a transaction between one who possesses (in a nonphysical sense) some knowledge that he or she could share with someone not in possession of that knowledge. This ability to share information is one of the most important skills humans have. All of us give and receive information every day of our lives, as the following exercise should help illustrate.

Exercise 6.1

In how many different situations have you shared information with others during the last week? In how many situations have you received information from others during this week? Group these different occasions. How many different groupings do you come up with? What did the situations have in common? What role, if any, did writing—and here we include any type of keyboarding—play in your giving or receiving information?

Although there are many types of informative occasions, you should have found some common characteristics they all share. The key, whether you are offering information or receiving it, is understanding; that is, informative writing must translate ideas into language that will communicate meaning to the intended readers.

SAMPLE ESSAYS

The following sample essays provide readers with various types of information and differ in many ways. But, as pieces of informative writing, they also have important similarities, as we shall see in our discussion of informative occasions.

Our first sample essay was written by Elisabeth Kübler-Ross, a physician who has spent her lifetime dealing with the issues surrounding death and dying. This essay, "On the Fear of Dying," has become a classic in the literature on the subject.

Elisabeth Kübler-Ross
ON THE FEAR OF DYING

1 The ancient Hebrews regarded the body of a dead person as something unclean and not to be touched. The early American Indians talked about the evil spirits and shot arrows in the air to drive the spirits away. Many other cultures have rituals to take care of the "bad" dead person, and they all originate in this feeling of anger which still exists in all of us, though we dislike admitting it. The tradition of the tombstone may originate in this wish to keep the bad spirits deep down in the ground, and the pebbles that many mourners put on the grave are left-over symbols of the same wish. Though we call the firing of guns at military

funerals a last salute, it is the same symbolic ritual as the Indian used when he shot his spears and arrows into the skies.

I give these examples to emphasize that man has not basically changed. Death is still a fearful, frightening happening, and the fear of death is a universal fear even if we think we have mastered it on many levels.

What has changed is our way of coping and dealing with death and dying and our dying patients.

Having been raised in a country in Europe where science is not so advanced, where modern techniques have just started to find their way into medicine, and where people still live as they did in this country half a century ago, I may have had an opportunity to study a part of the evolution of mankind in a shorter period.

I remember as a child the death of a farmer. He fell from a tree and was not expected to live. He asked simply to die at home, a wish that was granted without questioning. He called his daughters into the bedroom and spoke with each one of them alone for a few minutes. He arranged his affairs quietly, though he was in great pain, and distributed his belongings and his land, none of which was to be split until his wife should follow him in death. He also asked each of his children to share in the work, duties, and tasks that he had carried on until the time of the accident. He asked his friends to visit him once more, to bid good-bye to them. Although I was a small child at the time, he did not exclude me or my siblings. We were allowed to share in the preparations of the family just as we were permitted to grieve with them until he died. When he did die, he was left at home, in his own beloved home which he had built, and among his friends and neighbors who went to take a last look at him where he lay in the midst of flowers in the place he had lived in and loved so much. In that country today there is still no make-believe slumber room, no embalming, no false makeup to pretend sleep. Only the signs of very disfiguring illnesses are covered up with bandages and only infectious cases are removed from the home prior to the burial.

Why do I describe such "old-fashioned" customs? I think they are an indication of our acceptance of a fatal outcome, and they help the dying patient as well as his family to accept the loss of a loved one. If a patient is allowed to terminate his life in the familiar and beloved environment, it requires less adjustment for him. His own family knows him well enough to replace a sedative with a glass of his favorite wine; or the smell of a home-cooked soup may give him the appetite to sip a few spoons of fluid which, I think, is still more enjoyable than an infusion. I will not minimize the need for sedatives and infusions and realize full well from my own experience as a country doctor that they are sometimes life-saving and often unavoidable. But I also know that patience and familiar people and foods could replace many a bottle of intravenous fluids given for the simple reason that it fulfills the physiological need without involving too many people and/or individual nursing care.

The fact that children are allowed to stay at home where a fatality has stricken and are included in the talk, discussions, and fears gives them the feeling that they are not alone in the grief and gives them the comfort of shared responsibility and shared mourning. It prepares them gradually and helps them view death as part of life, an experience which may help them grow and mature.

This is in great contrast to a society in which death is viewed as taboo, discussion of it is regarded as morbid, and children are excluded with the presumption and pretext that it would be "too much" for them. They are then sent off to relatives, often accompanied with some unconvincing lies of "Mother has gone on a long trip" or other unbelievable stories. The child senses that something is wrong, and his distrust in adults will only multiply if other relatives add new variations of the story, avoid his questions or suspicions, shower him with gifts as a meager substitute for a loss he is not permitted to deal with. Sooner or later the child will become aware of the changed family situation and, depending on the age and personality of the child, will have an unresolved grief and regard this incident as a frightening, mysterious, in any case very traumatic experience with untrustworthy grownups, which he has no way to cope with.

We would think that our great emancipation, our knowledge of science and of man, has given us better ways and means to prepare ourselves and our families for this inevitable happening. Instead the days are gone when a man was allowed to die in peace and dignity in his own home.

The more we are making advancements in science, the more we seem to fear and deny the reality of death. How is this possible?

We use euphemisms, we make the dead look as if they were asleep, we ship the children off to protect them from the anxiety and turmoil around the house if the patient is fortunate enough to die at home, we don't allow children to visit their dying parents in the hospitals, we have long and controversial discussions about whether patients should be told the truth—a question that rarely arises when the dying person is tended by the family physician who has known him from delivery to death and who knows the weaknesses and strengths of each member of the family.

I think there are many reasons for this flight away from facing death calmly. One of the most important facts is that dying nowadays is more gruesome in many ways, namely, more lonely, mechanical, and dehumanized; at times it is even difficult to determine technically when the time of death has occurred.

Dying becomes lonely and impersonal because the patient is often taken out of his familiar environment and rushed to an emergency room. Whoever has been very sick and has required rest and comfort especially may recall his experience of being put on a stretcher and enduring the noise of the ambulance siren and hectic rush until the hospital gates open. Only those who have lived through this may appreciate the discomfort and cold necessity of such transportation which is only the beginning of a long ordeal—hard to endure when you are well, difficult to express in words when noise, light, bumps, and voices are all too much to put up with. It may well be that we might consider more the patient under the sheets and blankets and perhaps stop our well-meant efficiency and rush in order to hold the patient's hand, to smile, or to listen to a question. I include the trip to the hospital as the first episode in dying, as it is for many. I am putting it exaggeratedly in contrast to the sick man who is left at home—not to say that lives should not be saved if they can be saved by a hospitalization but to keep the focus on the patient's experience, his needs and his reactions.

When a patient is severely ill, he is often treated like a person with no right to an opinion. It is often someone else who makes the decision if and when and where a patient should be hospitalized. It would take so little to remember that the sick person too has feelings, has wishes and opinions, and has—most important of all—the right to be heard.

Well, our presumed patient has now reached the emergency room. He will be surrounded by busy nurses, orderlies, interns, residents, a lab technician perhaps who will take some blood, an electrocardiogram technician who takes the cardiogram. He may be moved to X-ray and he will overhear opinions of his condition and discussions and questions to members of the family. He slowly but surely is beginning to be treated like a thing. He is no longer a person. Decisions are made often without his opinion. If he tries to rebel he will be sedated and after hours of waiting and wondering whether he has the strength, he will be wheeled into the operating room or intensive treatment unit and become an object of great concern and great financial investment.

He may cry for rest, peace, and dignity, but he will get infusions, transfusions, a heart machine, or tracheotomy if necessary. He may want one single person to stop for one single minute so that he can ask one single question—but he will get a dozen people around the clock, all busily preoccupied with his heart rate, pulse, electrocardiogram or pulmonary functions, his secretions or excretions but not with him as a human being. He may wish to fight it all but it is going to be a useless fight since all this is done in the fight for his life, and if they can save his life they can consider the person afterwards. Those who consider the person first may lose precious time to save his life! At least this seems to be the rationale or justification behind all this—or is it? Is the reason for this increasingly mechanical, depersonalized approach our own defensiveness? Is this approach our own way to cope with and repress the anxieties that a terminally or critically ill patient evokes in us? Is our concentration on equipment, on blood pressure our desperate attempt to deny the impending death which is so frightening and discomforting to us that we displace all our knowledge onto machines, since they are less close to us than the suffering face of another human being which would remind us once more of our lack of omnipotence, our own limits and failures, and last but not least perhaps our own mortality?

◆ QUESTIONS FOR REVIEW

1. What is the thesis of Kübler-Ross's essay? Does it appear in the essay? If so, where? How does she develop (or support) her thesis?
2. In ¶5, Kübler-Ross narrates the story of the death a farmer. With the exception of the last sentence, ¶5 is devoted to narrating this experience. How is the last sentence different from the other sentences in the paragraph? What purpose does it serve?
3. What audience might Kübler-Ross be writing for? Is this audience likely to see this as a controversial topic? Are there any indications in her text that Kübler-Ross thinks readers may take an opposing point of view?
4. What information did you possess on this subject before reading Kübler-Ross's essay? What information in her essay was particularly interesting to you? Were you surprised by any of the information in this essay? If so, what was it? Did you disagree with Kübler-Ross on any points? What were they?

◆ WRITING OPPORTUNITY

Kübler-Ross's essay has become a classic. Of course, since it was written thirty years ago, there have been many changes in our treatment of death and dying in this country. Write a brief essay in which you discuss any changes you know of in today's practices as compared with the practices outlined in Kübler-Ross's essay. What practices have remained essentially the same? ◆

In our second sample essay, "The Perfect Crime," Suzanne Smalley provides some important information about a drug being used in hundreds of recent cases of rape.

SUZANNE SMALLEY

THE PERFECT CRIME

After two Whisky and Cokes, Patricia White decided to call it a night. The 47-year-old mother of three had been talked into helping her boss, Lorenzo Feal, celebrate his birthday with several colleagues. As she was leaving, Feal handed White a bottle of water, she says. She took a big gulp and spit the rest out because it tasted salty. Three hours later, White woke up in Feal's bed, naked and nauseated: she'd been drugged and raped. 1

White fled and called the police from her cell phone. Doctors found traces of gamma hydroxybutyric acid (GHB)—a recreational drug that is fueling a growing number of rapes—in her system. She's one of the lucky ones. Most women don't have proof that they've been dosed with GHB—because it exits the body within six to 12 hours. "Sexual predators are hunting with GHB," says prosecutor Christopher Frisco, who convicted Feal of using an anesthetic substance in carrying out White's rape. (Feal claimed the sex was consensual.)

"It's ideal for predators and tough for prosecutors." Another prosecutor, Timothy Walsh, calls GHB—fueled sex assaults the "perfect crime" since the liquid poison is colorless, odorless and frighteningly easy to use. And without toxicological evidence, it can be difficult to prove that the rape victim didn't willingly consent to sex. GHB, long popular among clubgoers, has been illegal since 2000, but it can be manufactured in the kitchen sink using commonly available chemicals. Most victims wake up hours later with little or no memory of what has happened.

GHB's use has been growing for almost a decade, but recently doctors, advocates for rape victims, and toxicologists called in to testify in sex-assault cases have seen a large surge in reports of GHB-fueled sex assaults. In just the past couple of weeks, both coasts have featured sensational GHB cases. In San Diego, Andrew Luster, a Max Factor cosmetics heir, went on the lam in the midst of his trial for multiple rapes; prosecution tapes show Luster having sex with snoring girls. And in New York, a Hofstra University student pleaded guilty to the 2001 murder of another student who was doped on GHB at the time of his death. As recently as 1994—when the drug was still relatively new—there were only 56 GHB-related emergency-room visits nationwide. By 2001 that number had spiked to 3,340, according to the Substance Abuse and Mental Health Services Administration.

Alarmed, colleges are taking an active role in protecting women. More than 40 universities and thousands of bars have ordered coasters that detect the drug by turning blue when exposed to GBH (women splash their drink onto "test spots"). But activists are already warning women not to rely solely on the coasters, since they don't test for increasingly popular, easy-to-obtain—and still legal—GHB knockoffs like GBL and l,4BD.

The DEA is so concerned about the rise in GHB—facilitated sexual assaults that officials have been meeting with representatives from the Rape, Abuse & Incest National Network (RAINN) to heighten awareness of GHB and other "predatory" drugs—an unusual move for an agency typically focused on interdiction. In November, the DEA announced that it will double the number of predatory-drug investigations it undertakes. Perhaps the agency was inspired by a recent success: in September authorities announced the arrests of 115 people in 84 cities for peddling GHB on the Internet.

The DEA's attention to the problem couldn't come at a better time. Some RAINN centers are reporting as much as a 50 percent uptick in GHB—fueled rapes in the past year. Trinka Porrata, a 25-year veteran of the Los Angeles

Police Department and founder of Project GHB, has been flooded with messages from flummoxed cops trying to learn how to investigate rapes featuring this quickly vanishing drug.

And victims are helping to spread awareness. "You don't get over rape," 8 White tells *Newsweek*. She now counsels victims and says she is talking publicly so that others know what she didn't about GHB. With this drug, the more you know the safer you are.

◆ QUESTIONS FOR REVIEW

1. What is the thesis of Smalley's essay? Does it appear in the essay? If so, where? How does Smalley develop (or support) her thesis? What is the relationship between the title of her essay and her thesis?
2. What device does Smalley use to introduce her essay? Is her introduction effective? Why, or why not?
3. What audience might Smalley's essay be written for? Since we've placed this essay in our information chapter, obviously, we think she wishes to inform this audience. What other aim could characterize her purpose for writing to this audience?
4. What information did you possess about this topic before reading Smalley's essay? What additional information would you like to have about this topic?

◆ WRITING OPPORTUNITY

Although Smalley's essay makes it abundantly clear just how serious a threat GHB can be to unsuspecting women, our culture is replete with jokes about men using "aids" to encourage women to have sex with them. Stories about various substances that can be put into drinks abound, and we even hear "humorous" ditties such as: "Candy is dandy, but liquor is quicker." Clearly such "humor" is sexist and degrading to women. Can you think of similar types of humor that degrade men? If so, compare those attempts at humor with the ones noted above. If not, speculate on the reasons for this disparity. ◆

Our next essay is written by the founder (in 1967) of the Chiat/Day advertising agency, one of the most prestigious agencies in the United States. He has created some of the most successful advertising campaigns in history, notable among them the battery ads featuring the Energizer Bunny.

Jay Chiat

ILLUSIONS ARE FOREVER

I know what you're thinking: That's rich, asking an adman to define truth. Advertising people aren't known either for their wisdom or their morals, so it's hard to see why an adman is the right person for this assignment. Well, it's just common sense—like asking an alcoholic about sobriety, or a sinner about piety. Who is likely to be more obsessively attentive to a subject than the transgressor?

Everyone thinks that advertising is full of lies, but it's not what you think. The facts presented in advertising are almost always accurate, not because advertising people are sticklers but because their ads are very closely regulated. If you make a false claim in a commercial on network television, the FTC will catch it. Someone always blows the whistle.

The real lie in advertising—some would call it the "art" of advertising—is harder to detect. What's false in advertising lies in the presentation of situations, values, beliefs, and cultural norms that form a backdrop for the selling message.

Advertising—including movies, TV, and music videos—presents to us a world that is not our world but rather a collection of images and ideas created for the purpose of selling. These images paint a picture of the ideal family life, the perfect home. What a beautiful woman is, and is not. A prescription for being a good parent and a good citizen.

The power of these messages lies in their unrelenting pervasiveness, the twenty-four-hour-a-day drumbeat that leaves no room for an alternative view. We've become acculturated to the way advertisers and other media-makers look at things, so much so that we have trouble seeing things in our own natural way. Advertising robs us of the most intimate moments in our lives because it substitutes an advertiser's idea of what ought to be—What should a romantic moment be like?

You know the DeBeers diamond advertising campaign? A clever strategy, persuading insecure young men that two months' salary is the appropriate sum to pay for an engagement ring. The arbitrary algorithm is preposterous, of course, but imagine the fiancée who receives a ring costing only half a month's salary? The advertising-induced insult is grounds for calling off the engagement, I imagine. That's marketing telling the fiancée what to feel and what's real.

Unmediated is a great word: It means "without media," without the in-between layer that makes direct experience almost impossible. Media interferes with our capacity to experience naturally, spontaneously, and genuinely, and thereby spoils our capacity for some important kinds of personal "truth." Although media opens our horizons infinitely, it costs us. We have very little direct personal knowledge of anything in the world that is not filtered by media.

Truth seems to be in a particular state of crisis now. When what we watch is patently fictional, like most movies and commercials, it's worrisome enough. But it's absolutely pernicious when it's packaged as reality. Nothing represents a bigger threat to truth than reality-based television, in both its lowbrow and highbrow versions—from *Survivor* to A&E's *Biography*. The lies are sometimes intentional, sometimes errors, often innocent, but in all cases they are the "truth" of a media-maker who claims to be representing reality.

The Internet is also a culprit, obscuring the author, the figure behind the curtain, even more completely. Chat rooms, which sponsor intimate conversation, also allow the participants to misrepresent themselves in every way possible. The creation of authoritative-looking Web sites is within the grasp of any reasonably talented twelve-year-old, creating the appearance of professionalism and expertise where no expert is present. And any mischief-maker can write a totally plausible-looking, totally fake stock analyst's report and post it on the Internet. When the traditional signals of authority are so misleading, how can we know what's for real?

But I believe technology, for all its weaknesses, will be our savior. The Internet is our only hope for true democratization, a truly populist publishing form, a mass communication tool completely accessible to individuals. The Internet puts CNN on the same plane with the freelance journalist and the lady down the street with a conspiracy theory, allowing cultural and ideological pluralism that never previously existed.

This is good for the cause of truth, because it underscores what is otherwise often forgotten—truth's instability. Truth is not absolute: It is presented, represented, and re-presented by the individuals who have the floor, whether they're powerful or powerless. The more we hear from powerless ones, the less we are in the grasp of powerful ones—and the less we believe that "truth" is inviolable, given, and closed to interpretation. We also come closer to seeking our own truth.

That's the choice we're given every day. We can accept the very compelling, very seductive version of "truth" offered to us daily by media-makers, or we can tune out its influence for a shot at finding our own individual, confusing, messy version of it. After all, isn't personal truth the ultimate truth?

◆ QUESTIONS FOR REVIEW

1. There is a sense in which Chiat's essay makes advertisers look manipulative, if not sinister. What purpose can you imagine an advertising executive might have for writing such an essay as this? Do you think the essay is successful in achieving that purpose—why or why not?
2. In his first sentence, Chiat addresses the reader directly. How do you respond to this tactic? Do you find his introduction effective—why or why not?

3. Chiat uses an extended example in his sixth paragraph. Does this example help him achieve his overall purpose? How do you respond to this example?
4. Surely, you as reader already know much about advertising in our society. What, if anything, was information to you in this essay? Why, or how, might this information be useful to you?

♦ WRITING OPPORTUNITY

In paragraph 11 of his essay, Chiat tells us that "Truth is not absolute." He goes on to say that if we understand that, we may "come closer to seeking our own truth." What does Chiat mean by *truth* in these two different contexts? Does the distinction he is making seem useful to you? ♦

Our fourth essay was written by the author of *The Truth About Chronic Pain,* a book that explores the problems those who have chronic pain have in finding effective treatments.

ARTHUR ROSENFELD

SHOULD ANYONE HAVE TO LIVE IN PAIN?

"Often it feels as if my arm, my leg and the left side of my face are on fire," says Esther Reiter of Chicago. "When that pain starts, it doesn't stop, though I can block it when I sleep." Reiter, 60—who has a brain condition called thalamic pain syndrome—is one of an estimated 50 million Americans who cope daily with pain—often disabling. Many suffer needlessly and lead unnecessarily restricted lives because they do not get the relief they need. 1

Chronic pain takes over lives. Reiter calls pain "an adversary I must continually fight in order to function." While she has access to the strong medications she needs to cope, her pain never goes away completely. For 19 years it has ruled her daily activities. "I'm in extreme pain when I wake up," she says. "If I have to be somewhere at 9 a.m., I have to get up at 5:30 or 6, take medication, rest while the medication takes effect, then get up again and shower." 2

Pain is a key factor in her relations with others. "I have to be careful," she says. "Talking about it with friends carries the danger of burdening the friendship. People feel badly when you're in pain. It can become a barrier. 3

Reprinted by permission of PARADE and Arthur Rosenfeld. Copyright © 2003 by Arthur Rosenfeld.

"It's an enormous part of who and what I am," she adds. "That bothers me. I don't want to be 'the person in pain.' I don't want to be pitied."

Hal E. Garner Jr., 41, of North Logan, Utah, was a promising player with the NFL's Buffalo Bills when a spinal injury ended his football career and propelled him into the world of a chronic-pain patient. Garner lived with severe pain for 12 years before he found effective therapy. He felt pressure to adopt a stoic posture. "Everyone gets sick of hearing how much you hurt," he says. "I had to paint a smile on my face every day."

He felt harshly judged: "People think you're making it up. They want you to see a psychiatrist. But this pain is real. It comes from rods in my back and scar tissue from surgeries pressing on nerves. It was hard to sleep, to get out of bed in the morning, go to work day to day and make a living—and keep everybody happy."

Today, Garner has a pump that delivers strong medication directly into his spine. A specialist helps him to manage his pain. "Now," he says, "I don't have to put on a smile or make excuses for myself."

Why pain patients don't get better treatment. Ideally, alleviating chronic pain should be a straight-forward exercise of human kindness. Instead, "pain management" has become a battleground of conflicting agendas and priorities among doctors, patient advocates, government regulators and insurance companies. A key issue is the pervasive fear of addiction.

"Hooked" on painkillers? The medications that help Reiter and Garner are called *opioid analgesics*. Related to morphine, one of the strongest painkillers known, they are generally safe and effective. They're not for everyone, but for many, these drugs are a godsend. (Treatments such as hypnosis, biofeedback, surgery, physical therapy and acupuncture also can help.)

Yet not everyone who needs these drugs gets them. Many doctors are reluctant to prescribe opioids for fear that their patients will become addicts. Addiction is a serious disease with psychological, social and probably genetic roots. Dependence is an unavoidable side-effect. While pain patients may become physically *dependent* on medications, research shows that addiction is uncommon unless there is a previous history of substance abuse. The pain patient depends on the drug the way a diabetic depends on insulin. Misunderstanding this difference creates problems.

"When you tell somebody you take an opioid," say Reiter, "they look at you like, 'Oh, my goodness, she's going to become addicted!' But I don't use drugs; I take medication. I'm not addicted; I'm dependent. And I monitor myself carefully."

"I ran into prejudices at every job I went to," says Garner. "I was seen as addicted to medications."

Some doctors withhold or underprescribe opioid painkillers because they are wary of scrutiny by state medical boards (some states set dosage limits for these drugs) and the Drug Enforcement Agency. In the climate created by the "war on drugs," a person reporting pain whose cause cannot be determined may be suspected of seeking a prescription for a controlled substance.

"They thought I was faking pain." Mathew Rudes, 17, of Northridge, California, was born with severe infantile Marfan syndrome, an often lethal connective-tissue disease that also affects the heart, blood vessels, eyes and skin. Multiple surgeries and other procedures saved his life, but Rudes had recurrent episodes of severe spinal pain that doctors could not diagnose. Many didn't believe it was real. "They'd do scans, X-rays and other tests, and they'd come up negative," Rudes says. "The doctors then thought I was faking it. That made me really angry."

He is now under the care of a pain specialist, who prescribes effective medications and monitors his dosage weekly. Mathew is an 11th grade honor student. "I have a 4.0 grade average," he says. 15

The cost of relief. Finding the best treatment often requires a trial-and-error process. Few treatments are cheap, and health plans may put caps on how much they will pay and for how long. A patient who needs a costly medication for a lifetime may be covered for only six months. 16

What needs to change. If chronic pain is to be defeated, say pain-care experts, people need to understand that pain can have wide-ranging effects and hidden causes. We need to be clear on the difference between addiction and dependence. The romance with stoicism must go. Above all, more compassion is needed—from doctors, legislators, insurers and everyone else—so that chronic pain receives as much attention as drug abuse. We must stop judging sufferers and see pain for what it is: a part of life. It could happen to any of us. 17

◆ QUESTIONS FOR REVIEW

1. What is the thesis of Rosenfeld's essay? If the thesis is stated in the essay, identify it. If not, write a thesis statement for the essay. Then explain how Rosenfeld develops this thesis.
2. Divide the essay into its beginning, middle, and end. Then, discuss the rhetorical strategies Rosenfeld uses to structure his essay.
3. One of Rosenfeld's assertions, that the medical community could do a better job of combatting chronic pain, could be seen as argumentative. Does Rosenfeld seem to anticipate opposition to this assertion from readers? Explain your answer.
4. Before reading Rosenfeld's essay, had you thought about the distinction he makes between drug "dependence," and drug "addiction"? Do you find this a useful distinction—why or why not?

◆ WRITING OPPORTUNITY

In his final paragraph, Rosenfeld argues that in our society chronic pain should receive as much attention as drug abuse. Write a brief response in which you agree or disagree with Rosenfeld's assertion. ◆

In our fifth essay, novelist Gloria Naylor explains what the word "nigger" meant to her as a child and reflects on the ways in which words come to have the power to inflict pain.

GLORIA NAYLOR

MOMMY, WHAT DOES "NIGGER" MEAN?

Language is the subject. It is the written form with which I've managed to keep the wolf away from the door and, in diaries, to keep my sanity. In spite of this, I consider the written word inferior to the spoken, and much of the frustration experienced by novelists is the awareness that whatever we manage to capture in even the most transcendent passages falls far short of the richness of life. Dialogue achieves its power in the dynamics of a fleeting moment of sight, sound, smell and touch.

I'm not going to enter the debate here about whether it is language that shapes reality or vice versa. That battle is doomed to be waged whenever we seek intermittent reprieve from the chicken and egg dispute. I will simply take the position that the spoken word, like the written word, amounts to a nonsensical arrangement of sounds or letters without a consensus that assigns "meaning." And building from the meanings of what we hear, we order reality. Words themselves are innocuous; it is the consensus that gives them true power.

I remember the first time I heard the word "nigger." In my third-grade class, our math tests were being passed down the rows, and as I handed the papers to a little boy in back of me, I remarked that once again he had received a much lower mark than I did. He snatched his test from me and spit out that word. Had he called me a nymphomaniac or a necrophiliac, I couldn't have been more puzzled. I didn't know what a nigger was, but I knew that whatever it meant, it was something he shouldn't have called me. This was verified when I raised my hand, and in a loud voice repeated what he had said and watched the teacher scold him for saying a "bad" word. I was later to go home and ask the inevitable question that every black parent must face—"Mommy, what does 'nigger' mean?"

And what exactly did it mean? Thinking back, I realize that this could not have been the first time the word was used in my presence. I was part of a large extended family that had migrated from the rural South after World War II and formed a close-knit network that gravitated around my maternal grandparents. Their ground-floor apartment in one of the buildings they owned in Harlem was a weekend mecca for my immediate family, along with countless aunts, uncles and cousins who brought along assorted friends. It was a bustling and open house with assorted neighbors and tenants popping in and out to exchange bits of gossip, pick up an old quarrel or referee the ongoing checkers game in which my grandmother cheated shamelessly. They were all there to let down their hair and put up their feet after a week of labor in the factories, laundries and shipyards of New York.

Amid the clamor, which could reach deafening proportions—two or three conversations going on simultaneously, punctuated by the sound of a baby's crying somewhere in the back rooms or out on the street—there was still a rigid set of rules about what was said and how. Older children were sent out of the living room when it was time to get into the juicy details about "you-know-who" up on the third floor who had gone and gotten herself "p-r-e-g-n-a-n-t!" But my parents, knowing that I could spell well beyond my years, always demanded that I follow the others out to play. Beyond sexual misconduct and death, everything else was considered harmless for our young ears. And so among the anecdotes of the triumphs and disappointments in the various workings of their lives, the word "nigger" was used in my presence, but it was set within contexts and inflections that caused it to register in my mind as something else.

In the singular, the word was always applied to a man who had distinguished himself in some situation that brought their approval for his strength, intelligence or drive:

"Did Johnny really do that?"

"I'm telling you, that nigger pulled in $6,000 of overtime last year. Said he got enough for a down payment on a house."

When used with a possessive adjective by a woman—"my nigger"—it became a term of endearment for husband or boyfriend. But it could be more than just a term applied to a man. In their mouths it became the pure essence of manhood—a disembodied force that channeled their past history of struggle and present survival against the odds into a victorious statement of being: "Yeah, that old foreman found out quick enough—you don't mess with a nigger."

In the plural, it became a description of some group within the community that had overstepped the bounds of decency as my family defined it: Parents who neglected their children, a drunken couple who fought in public, people who simply refused to look for work, those with excessively dirty mouths or unkempt households were all "trifling niggers." This particular circle could forgive hard times, unemployment, the occasional bout of depression—they had gone through all of that themselves—but the unforgivable sin was lack of self-respect.

A woman could never be a "nigger" in the singular, with its connotation of confirming worth. The noun "girl" was its closest equivalent in that sense, but only when used in direct address and regardless of the gender doing the addressing. "Girl" was a token of respect for a woman. The one-syllable word was drawn out to sound like three in recognition of the extra ounce of wit, nerve or daring that the woman had shown in the situation under discussion.

"G-i-r-l, stop. You mean you said that to his face?"

But if the word was used in a third-person reference or shortened so that it almost snapped out of the mouth, it always involved some element of communal disapproval. And age became an important factor in these exchanges. It was only between individuals of the same generation or from an older person to a younger (but never the other way around) that "girl" would be considered a compliment.

I don't agree with the argument that use of the word "nigger" at this social stratum of the black community was an internalization of racism. The dynamics were the exact opposite: the people in my grandmother's living room took a word that whites used to signify worthlessness or degradation and rendered it impotent. Gathering there together, they transformed "nigger" to signify the varied and complex human beings they knew themselves to be. If the word was to disappear totally from the mouths of even the most liberal of white society, no one in that room was naive enough to believe it would disappear from white minds. Meeting the word head-on, they proved it had absolutely nothing to do with the way they were determined to live their lives.

So there must have been dozens of times that the word "nigger" was spoken in front of me before I reached the third grade. But I didn't "hear" it until it was said by a small pair of lips that had already learned it could be a way to humiliate me. That was the word I went home and asked my mother about. And since she knew that I had to grow up in America, she took me in her lap and explained.

♦ QUESTIONS FOR REVIEW

1. What is the thesis of Naylor's essay? Does it appear in the essay? If so, where? How does she develop (or support) her thesis?
2. Read the material having to do with classification on pages 256–257. Then examine how Naylor uses classification to sort the ways in which the word "nigger" was used by the adult community she was reared in. How does classification help Naylor structure this essay?
3. What audience might Naylor's essay be written for? Is her audience likely to see the topic as controversial? Are there any indications in her text that Naylor thinks readers may take an opposing point of view? If so, what are they? If not, why not?
4. What information did you possess on this subject before reading Naylor's essay? What information in this essay did you find particularly interesting? Were you surprised by any of the information in this essay? If so, what was it? Did you find yourself disagreeing with Naylor on any points? If so, what were they?

◆ WRITING OPPORTUNITY

Have you had an experience in which a particular word held the power to hurt you or someone you knew? Discuss this situation and the word itself. What stands out in your memory of this experience? What, if anything, did this experience teach you about language? ◆

In our sixth essay, "Listening to the Word, or 21st Century Readers and *The Souls of Black Folk*," Sandra Y. Govan, Professor of English at the University of North Carolina at Charlotte, discusses what modern students can learn about style from one of the masters of style at the turn of the twentieth century.

SANDRA Y. GOVAN

LISTENING TO THE WORD, OR
21st Century Readers and *The Souls of Black Folk*

[1] Unless you've taken a class, a special seminar or workshop focused on African American literary history or upon African American social/political thought in America (or perhaps you have been preparing for a College Bowl IQ contest or a "Jeopardy" appearance), you are unlikely to have met W. E. B. Du Bois, or Dr. William Edward Burghardt Du Bois. Given how tentatively the majority of our public schools still approach race issues in America, it is the rare college student who has previously met Dr. Du Bois in high school readings or through some other educational setting. The student, therefore, is often shocked and surprised to find that a Negro or Black intellectual the caliber of Du Bois even existed prior to the mid-century Civil Rights Movement and the advent of Dr. Martin Luther King, Jr. Yet scholars of the African American literary canon have recognized *The Souls of Black Folk*, Du Bois's penetrating collection of essays first published in 1903, as one of the most influential books in the African American literary canon; it has been hailed as both a literary masterpiece and a cornerstone of Black intellectual thought.[1] His voice has been praised as one of the most powerful and effective on the American scene and he has been judged one of the most brilliant, most astute, men of his age and beyond. Indeed, Henry Louis Gates and Nellie McKay describe Du Bois as the "Renaissance man of African American letters during the first fifty years of the twentieth century" because as historian, social scientist, poet, novelist, editor, columnist, public

speaker and evocative writer, Du Bois served as an unceasing advocate for the full human rights of Black people around the globe.²

Though I would encourage my reader to take time to come to know this entire collection, I have time here for only a few matters. Because we are so far removed from the rhetorical practices that marked the prose of the late nineteenth century, I'd like to help you listen to, and actually hear, his nuanced, evocative, often lyrical prose. And while we're examining his prose style, we will spend some time examining two key concepts introduced in *Souls*.

We begin with one of those key concepts that has echoed and reverberated since the book was published. When Du Bois announced that "the problem of the Twentieth Century is the problem of the color-line," he demonstrated an insight and an acumen more telling than any of his day could have realized. After this announcement, Du Bois moved to a second powerful insight, describing the American Negro as affected by a binding "double-consciousness." Once Du Bois identified this debilitating psychological phenomenon, his insight suddenly became a truth self-evident to thoughtful readers everywhere. Since Du Bois coined the term, double-consciousness became a perennial motif among African American writers. It appears in such novels as James Weldon Johnson's *Autobiography of an Ex-Colored Man* (1912), Ralph Ellison's *Invisible Man* (1952), and Toni Morrison's *Song of Solomon* (1977), and it resonates in countless additional texts—be they fiction, poetry, or drama.³

Today, however, because important concepts and ideas are too often presented in abbreviated televised sound bites, or in short simplistic sentences in newspapers, journals or magazines, a general audience is unaccustomed to meeting with Du Bois's rhetorical grace. My students often struggle with his elaborate, often elevated sentence structure, his distinctive diction, and his use of various other stylistic devices. I tell my students their efforts will be richly rewarded, for when they are able to adjust to the pitch of Du Bois's style, they will be able to experience, at a heightened level, the message that is forged in his images, metaphors, allusions, and flowing syntax.

Du Bois calls his readers' attention to the effort required of them in the first page of his book, a preface titled "The Forethought." This deceptively simple page not only serves as a prefatory note but it actually functions as an elaborate table of contents. Here Du Bois outlines his intentions as interlocutor or interpreter and announces what he expects from his anticipated reader as well. "Herein lie buried many things which if <u>read with patience</u> [a phrase I emphasize for my classes] may show the strange meaning of being black here in the dawning of the Twentieth Century" (3). Astute readers also note that this introductory paragraph concludes with the prophetic phrase that reverberates throughout the entire text— "the problem of the Twentieth Century is the problem of the color-line" (3).

This phrase appears throughout Du Bois's text, making it one of the most important assertions in this book. My students are always impressed by its demonstrable accuracy. When I raise questions about it, my students generally relate racial incidents drawn from their individual experiences or from family history. They cite experiences at other schools, or information they have learned about overt racial violence or more subtle forms of racism. Non-European students coming from around the world may also have had experience with issues of color or caste, with segregation or the legacy of colonization, and so they too have had brushes with "the problem."

In any racially diverse class I always ask my students to think back and try to determine when they "discovered" race, at what point they found out that skin color still matters in America. The reader may want to ask of himself or herself the questions I ask of my students: Was your skin tone ever at issue? At what point did you become aware of your racial or ethnic identity? How? Did you become conscious of this identity, or the fact of your skin color, through some family member teasing you about your color? Or, as too often happens still, were you targeted by someone else—a child or an adult—*because* of your skin color, your identity as a person of color? Such questions, and their answers, should make it clear just how prophetic Du Bois's pronouncement was. There is no question that Du Bois was right in saying—"the problem of the Twentieth Century is the problem of the color-line." It isn't yet clear, however, whether he was right in limiting the scope of the problem to one century.

Du Bois teases the reader with this "problem" in his "Forethought"; he doesn't return to the statement until he gets to the second chapter of *Souls*, where he explores his premise fully. However, in his initial chapter, "Of Our Spiritual Strivings," he illustrates and personalizes these issues, portraying himself as a *problem*. "And yet, being a problem is a strange experience, —peculiar even for one who has never been anything else save perhaps in babyhood and in Europe" (7). Du Bois describes his revelation of just how constricting racial distinctions can be by telling the story about a white child's refusal of his offer of a Valentine's Day card simply because of his identity. Du Bois reconstructs the moment of his recognition in two sentences that capture both his alienation and his determination: "Then it dawned upon me with a certain suddenness that I was different from the others; or like, mayhap, in heart and life and longing, but shut out from their world by a vast veil. I had thereafter no desire to tear down that veil, to creep through; I held all beyond it in common contempt, and lived above it in a region of blue sky and great wandering shadows" (8).

Students' first response to a sentence such as this may well be fear and/or intimidation. However, when we examine it more closely, they come to appreciate the way in which Du Bois's style reflects his substance. I noted above that this passage consists of two sentences. These two sentences represent the separate worlds of whites and blacks. In the first sentence, Du Bois realizes that he is shut out from white society; in the second, he commits himself to not only living separate, but living above (superior to) this white society.

But there's more. Let's examine the syntax of the first sentence. Its first clause contains the first realization that he is "different from the others;". After this semicolon and before we move to the determination found in the higher level of the second sentence, we head down another path, perhaps hoping for a reversal of the first dire realization. Here Du Bois understands that while he is like the whites in "heart and life longing," any hope that shared commonality may suggest is shattered by the intervention of a "but" that introduces the cold, hard reality that he is "shut out from their world by a vast veil."

We are not finished yet—not even close. Look at the alliterative phrases in these sentences: "certain suddenness," "vast veil," and "common contempt." What does alliteration do? It pleases our ears, of course, but if that's all it did, it would not be very important rhetorically. It does much more. With "certain suddenness," we feel (through our ears) the speed with which this realization pervaded Du Bois's consciousness. And with the alliterative "vast veil," Du Bois introduces, in Biblical tones, the powerful metaphor for white/black separation. And finally, with "common contempt," we draw attention to the two-sided nature of Du Bois's solution to this problem. We can actually feel the syntax pulling us in a way emblematic of the pull of society on Du Bois. Look closely at the phrase "common contempt." The phrase "in common" is what linguists call a collocation. That means that the two words go together; when we see "in," we will often see "common." And when we see the two, we expect them to pair together to create a meaning, as in the following sentences:

> Derrell and Kiesha found they had much in common.
> Tyrone has something in common with Jamie: they both like hot dogs.

So, when Du Bois says that he "held all beyond it in common . . ." a reader might be led to interpret this first as a collocation; we think that Du Bois is going to say something about what he and the white culture hold "in common." However, the alliteration that follows, "common contempt" pulls us away from this collocation and focuses our attention on Du Bois's reaction to the way white culture has shunned him. He will hold that culture in "common contempt." And what does "common" mean in this phrase? It does double duty. He has raised himself above them and thus looks on them as "common," that is, beneath him. At another level, though, "common" may refer to the fact that the "contempt" goes both ways; they have contempt for him, and he has contempt for them.

We mentioned above that "vast veil" introduces an organizing metaphor for this whole book. By referring to the veil in the Biblical temple that separated God and humans before the coming of Christ, Du Bois is drawing attention to the seemingly insurmountable wall between white and black societies.

Having made segregation absolutely personal, Du Bois introduces his readers to the psychological concept of double-consciousness, a concept he formulated to capture the psychological profile of African Americans as an entire people about to enter the twentieth century but bringing with them a history and a legacy of living with the stigma of race. In complex, balanced, and rhythmic evocative prose, Du Bois links the paradoxical psychological position of the American Negro to other distinguished nationalities who have held the world's center stage. "After the

Egyptian and the Indian, the Greek and the Roman, the Teuton and Mongolian, the Negro is a sort of seventh son, born with a veil, and gifted with second-sight in this American world,— a world which yields him no true self-consciousness, but only lets him see himself through the revelation of the other world. *It is a peculiar sensation, this double-consciousness, this sense of always looking at one's self through the eyes of others, of measuring one's soul by the tape of a world that looks on in amused contempt and pity. One ever feels his two-ness,—an American, a Negro; two souls, two thoughts, two unreconciled strivings; two warring ideals in one dark body, whose dogged strength alone keeps it from being torn asunder"* [emphasis added] (8–9).

15 It is critically important that contemporary readers understand Du Bois's remarkable passage for the insight it provides. Not only does the passage articulate in precise parallel constructions the conflicting psychological tensions and stresses (racial joined to a national identity, duality, assumptions about an alleged inferiority, denial of opportunity based upon assumptions of capability, internalization of self-hate yet a strong determination to prove one's self an equal) affecting African Americans at the dawn of the twentieth century, its essential truth remains a constant throughout the twentieth century and into the twenty-first. Without a true self-consciousness or self-awareness, without the ability to see one's self as a fully competent and equal contributor to American society and culture, individuals within the group may fall victim to the persistent stereotypical images (poor, ignorant, lazy, comical, criminal, or violent) that, despite a Martin Luther King, a Colin Powell, or a Marian Wright Edelman, still attempt to define Black character in the popular culture.[4]

16 Before moving to a detailed discussion of the role the Negro played in the world's history and American history, Du Bois concludes his discussion about consciousness, framing the issue so that it can in no way be misunderstood. To live successfully in this country as a full participant in its largesse *does not mean that Negroes want to be white*. Nor does it mean that America should become black. Racial heritage should not be seen as a negative but rather as a positive identity. It should be possible, as Du Bois argues, "for a man to be both a Negro and an American, without having the doors of Opportunity closed roughly in his face" (9).

17 Although the resonant double-consciousness passage may at first appear difficult, when the reader pauses to listen to its language, to hear the rhythms of its prose, and to follow as it defines terms, it is not that hard to decipher. Du Bois not only enlists balanced parallel constructions ("the Egyptian *and* the Indian, the Greek *and* the Roman"), he returns to the "veil" image first evoked in "The Forethought" and used in various ways throughout *Souls;* but here he adds the flavor of the mystical. Using a flowing alliterative assonance (". . . the Negro is a sort of seventh son, born with a veil"[5]) Du Bois posits that Black folk have a unique gift, that of "second-sight," or prophetic vision; yet that veil blocks or conceals any true self-consciousness; thus historically, Black folk have only seen themselves in terms of their standing or their relationship to "the other world." Hence, the "peculiar sensation," the feeling of "double-consciousness," the "sense of always looking at one's self through the eyes of others . . . " (8).

The opening sentence in "Of the Dawn of Freedom," the second chapter in *Souls,* returns readers to Du Bois's essential thesis, "The problem of the Twentieth Century is the problem of the color-line, —" (16). Here, however, readers should note the position of the statement has changed. In contrast to its position as the final emphatic declarative phrase of a complex sentence in "The Forethought," in this second chapter it serves as an introductory clause to a richer more complex definition in context. The full sentence adopts a global stance, accurately predicting forthcoming changes in world race relationships.[6] Thus, the full sentence declares, "The problem of the Twentieth Century is the problem of the color-line,— the relation of the darker to the lighter races of men in Asia and Africa, in America and the islands of the sea." As historian, Du Bois wants to locate the immediate issue with respect to deeper questions; in his estimation, the Civil War was not a conflict about preserving the union or about states rights; slavery was the real reason for the war. The rest of the chapter then turns to the Civil War and its aftermath, framing for readers the historical period 1861–1872. Du Bois acquaints us with "the dawn of Freedom" for former slaves and with the successes and the failures of the Freedmen's Bureau, the under-funded government agency established to help smooth freedmen's path. Using the rhetorical strategies of exposition, description, definition, argument, allusion, narrative, and irony, this chapter stands as one of the most explicit summaries of this period ever written. Here Du Bois capsulizes the bitterness of both sides following the war; he makes clear the origins of the "forty-acres and a mule" (land ownership for Black people) promised to every freedman and explains how the freedmen were to be bitterly disappointed (25–29).

In the conclusion of this chapter, Du Bois turns again to the poetic images and metaphors that are central to his style. He places himself in the role of an observant traveler moving through a historical continuum; he then paints a very expressive illustration of the changes the country will face following the end of slavery. This final paragraph comes full circle, employing Du Bois's well-honed techniques of assonance and alliteration, of allusion and metaphor, of stylistic repetition with variation for emphasis. And finally the chapter concludes where it began. It began with that celebrated clause as an introduction; it now concludes with that clause as a declarative statement that stands alone as an assertion of fact.

> I have seen a land right merry with the sun, where children sing, and rolling hills lie like passioned women wanton with harvest. And there in the King's Highway sat and sits a figure veiled and bowed, by which the traveller's [sic] footsteps hasten as they go. On the tainted air broods fear. Three centuries' thought has been the raising and unveiling of that bowed human heart, and now behold a century new for the duty and the deed. The problem of the Twentieth Century is the problem of the color-line (35).

Endnotes

[1] In his essay, "Slavery and the Literary Imagination: Du Bois's *The Souls of Black Folk*," Arnold Rampersad addresses the controversy the book initially provoked but notes that even its critics could not "deny its originality and beauty as a portrait of the Afro-American people" (104). Rampersad cites several prominent African American writers and critics, among them Benjamin Brawly, J. Saunders Redding, Langston Hughes, and James Weldon Johnson. Brawly regarded *Souls* as "the most important work in 'classic English'" and felt that it showed "the passion of a mighty heart." Redding said the text was more "history making than historical." Hughes compared his reading and appreciation of *Souls* as a young man to his reading of the Bible, and Johnson argued in *Along this Way* (1933) that *Souls* "had produced a greater effect upon and within the Negro race in American [sic] than any other single book published in the country since *Uncle Tom's Cabin*." Rampersad also includes the comments of Du Bois scholar Herbert Aptheker, noting that Aptheker saw *Souls* as "one of the classics in the English language." Concluding this recitation of perspectives with his own observation, Rampersad declares, "Among black intellectuals, above all, *The Souls of Black Folk* became a kind of sacred book, the central text for the interpretation of the Afro-American experience and the most trustworthy guide into the grim future that seemed to loom before their race in America" (104–105). Novelist and essayist John Edgar Wideman, who edited a Vintage Books edition (1990) of *Souls*, wrote as the opening sentence in his introduction, "If I could put one and only one book into the hands of students to whom I was teaching post-Civil War American history, I would choose without hesitation *The Souls of Black Folk*."

[2] Gates and McKay also assess Du Bois's writing, commenting that he wrote "not as a detached social scientist but as a cultural interpreter, a historian, advocate, an oracle of his people." See the introduction to the selection on Du Bois in *The Norton Anthology of African American Literature* (606–07).

[3] In drama, for instance, I think of Lorraine Hansberry's 1959 classic, *A Raisin in the Sun* or August Wilson's *Fences*, which won for Wilson a Tony Award and a Pulitzer Prize.

[4] Martin Luther King, Jr. was a revered leader in the Civil Rights Movement of the 1960s; Colin Powell served as the Secretary of State (the first African American to do so) during George W. Bush's first term as President; and Marian Wright Edelman, an attorney, is most often associated with the Children's Defense Fund, a children's rights advocacy organization she founded.

[5] The legend of the "seventh son" is apparently ancient and curious. The seventh son of a seventh son is purportedly a healer, the "chosen one," who is gifted with second sight and magical powers. By birthright, he is a "maker of things" with the ability to predict the future. While he is supposedly "lucky," he is also "cursed by the good and evil forces battling for his eternal soul" (http://www.mysticalworldwideweb.com).

> ⁶One could argue that not only does Du Bois predict the failure of western European colonial power where Europeans had destroyed or usurped local governments or authorities to establish territorial privilege in non-white Third World counties, but that the anti-western rise of Islamic fundamentalism, led by men of color from the Arab world, is the other shoe dropping.

◆ QUESTIONS FOR REVIEW

1. What is the thesis of Govan's essay? Does it appear in the essay? If so, where? How does she develop (or support) her thesis?
2. In the second paragraph of her essay, Govan says that she intends to outline two basic concepts found in *The Souls of Black Folk*. State those two concepts in your own words. Then reflect on any particular words or phrases that you found difficult to paraphrase. Can you explain why these words or phrases prove troublesome?
3. Divide the essay into beginning, middle, and end. What rhetorical and/or stylistic devices help form these divisions?
4. What audience might Govan's essay be written for? What information on this topic does Govan assume her audience has? Does Govan make it clear why she believes her audience will want (or should want) this information?
5. What information did you possess on this subject before reading Govan's essay? What information in her essay was particularly interesting to you? Were you surprised by any of the information in this essay? If so, what was it? Did you disagree with Govan on any points? If so, what were they?

◆ WRITING OPPORTUNITY

1. According to Govan, Du Bois's phrase about the problem of the color line is one of the most important, and most prophetic, assertions in his book. For support for this claim, one has only to examine the history of the Civil Rights Movement in the U.S. Some people claim that movement began with the tragedy of Emmit Till. Do some research on this case and then write a brief discussion of what you learn about the "problems of color" in the U.S.
2. In a passage that Govan does not refer to, Du Bois makes the following observation about the South: "It is usually possible to draw in nearly every Southern community a physical color-line on the map, on the one side of which whites dwell and on the other Negroes." As you reflect on the community(ies)

you were reared in, to what degree do you see a color line that separates the dwellings of various races and ethnicities? Write a brief essay in which you explore whether your community had such a line of separation and what factors account for the existence (or non-existence) of such a line. ◆

Our final essay, which discusses the role that cartoons played in the propaganda leading up to World War I, was written by Elizabeth C. Gardner while she was a student at UNC Charlotte. Elizabeth is currently working on her Ph. D. in English at the University of St. Andrews in Scotland.

Elizabeth C. Gardner

TRANSFORMING A NATION, TRANSFORMING AN ENEMY

Attacked by a German submarine, the British liner *Lusitania* sank to the depths of the ocean in only eighteen minutes, taking over 1,000 people to their deaths, 128 of whom were Americans (Trueman pars. 9–10). The accounts of the torpedoing of the ship served as the pivot point for American neutrality: Germany was no longer fighting fairly, and American sentiment began to turn. History records that Germany's use of unrestricted submarine warfare prompted America's entry into World War I. However, while the *Lusitania* sank on May 7, 1915, America did not enter the war officially until two years later, on April 6, 1917. During those two intervening years, America remained neutral and reelected Woodrow Wilson, who ran successfully on a policy of neutrality.

America had maintained a seemingly strict isolationist stance as the war broke out in Europe. In fact, Woodrow Wilson called for neutrality in an address to Congress in August of 1914:

> The United States must be neutral in fact, as well as in name, during these days that are to try men's souls. We must be impartial in thought, as well as action, must put a curb upon our sentiments, as well as upon every transaction that might be construed as a preference of one party to the struggle before another. ("President Wilson's Declaration of Neutrality" par. 1)

Yet in 1917, less than a year after winning reelection, Wilson asked Congress for a formal declaration of war. In his speech, he called the German submarine attacks against commercial vessels "a warfare against mankind," and citing Germany's use of unrestricted submarine warfare as the precipitating factor, Wison made this statement:

> With a profound sense of the solemn and even tragical character of the step I am taking and of the grave responsibilities which it involves, but in unhesitating obedience to what I deem my constitutional duty, I advise that the Congress declare the recent course of the Imperial German Government to be in fact nothing less than war against the Government and people of the United States; that it formally accept the status of belligerent which has thus been thrust upon it, and that it take immediate steps not only to put the country in a more thorough state of defense but also to exert all its power and employ all its resources to bring the Government of the German Empire to terms and end the war. ("President Woodrow Wilson's War Message" par. 6)

Wilson is certainly not the first president to take actions contrary to campaign promises, but because he had run on his platform of neutrality, many Americans were not ready to plunge headlong into war with Germany. Following his declaration, Wilson needed to find a way to bolster America's willingness to fight. Aaron Delwiche states,

> The absence of public unity was a primary concern when America entered the war on April 6, 1917. In Washington, unwavering public support was considered to be crucial to the entire wartime effort. On April 13, 1917, Wilson created the Committee on Public Information (CPI) to promote the war domestically while publicizing American war aims abroad. Under the leadership of a muckraking journalist named George Creel, the CPI recruited heavily from business, media, academia, and the art world. The CPI blended advertising techniques with a sophisticated understanding of human psychology, and its efforts represent the first time that a modern government disseminated propaganda on such a large scale. (par. 1)

Delwiche is surely right that the U.S. use of propaganda leading up the WWI is unprecedented in scale; however, the history of propaganda use extends backwards in history for centuries.

An early record of propaganda as a means of propagating or spreading the word comes from the Roman Catholic Church's College of the Propaganda, which was established in 1622 by Pope Gregory XV to oversee foreign missions ("propaganda"). "Propaganda" derives from the Latin root, *propago*, which means "to set forward, extend, enlarge, spread, increase . . . to generate, procreate, engender, propagate" (Lewis 662), reminding the historian that propaganda is more than a mere selling campaign. In fact, in setting forward its message, propaganda may engender unity in a society. Propaganda occurs in a multitude of forms, and it continues to evolve as new situations allow the use of new technologies.

Although newspapers were not a new source of propaganda at the beginning of the twentieth century, the industry had undergone some technological advances, such as telegraph communication and new papermaking techniques, that allowed for a larger readership (Gorman and McLean 7). Telegraphs, being able to transmit reports very quickly over long distances, allowed for more consistent and more timely news reporting. New papermaking techniques involving making paper from wood pulp instead of rags reduced the cost of newspaper production. And this technology was further enhanced by the Second Industrial Revolution, which introduced steam power and the cylinder press, thereby increasing the speed of production.

Of course, none of these technological advances would mean much if there was not sufficient readership for these papers. Before the late nineteenth century, literacy could not be assumed. But in the last decades of that century, universal free schooling made a basic education the norm for the white population of the United States. John Faragher, et al., claim that "by the turn of the century more than 4,000 [public school kindergartens] throughout [America] enrolled children between the ages of three and seven. The number of public high schools increased from 160 in 1870 to 6,000 by the end of the century" (381). This increase had a direct impact on the readership of newspapers during the first decades of the twentieth century. Speaking of the period before World War I, Stewart Ross says, "America was increasingly a literate society, a direct result of universal, compulsory free education" (12). Ross goes on to speak of "an almost unnoticed communications revolution that paralleled the more boisterous industrial revolution of the nineteenth century" (12). With an increasingly literate public to read newspapers and with the impact of the new technologies for gathering and printing the news, America's newspapers stood poised to have an impact on public opinion.

One major element in this communications revolution is certainly the *New York Times*, and the *Times* provides a useful, complete record to examine the use of propaganda in political cartoons. In 1913, the year in which Kaiser Wilhelm celebrated his silver jubilee, the *Times* depicted the Kaiser in very positive ways. In a Sunday special section, the *New York Times* regaled the leader of Germany as the "chief peacemaker," enlisting letters from Theodore Roosevelt and William Taft. As an example of the laudatory words, Roosevelt wrote, "The Emperor, personally, was of real aid in helping induce Russia to face and come to an agreement with Japan" (in "Kaiser" 1). These words should be especially striking, given Roosevelet's later rallying for war against Germany. Taft's praise for Wilhelm was even broader and more sweeping in its acclaim of the ruler: "He has been, for the last quarter of a century, the greatest single individual force in the practical maintenance of peace in the world" (in "Kaiser" 1). Accompanying these words of praise was an illustration (see Figure 6.1) featuring a kind-eyed gentleman, whom these leaders embraced with "high opinion of his word in behalf of peace and progress" ("Kaiser" 1).

In the years immediately preceding America's entry into the War, images of the Kaiser in the *Times* changed.

The most apparent examples of conditioning of American readers occur before the war. After the sinking of the *Lusitania*, even though Wilson was imploring the American public to remain neutral, editorial cartoons delivered a different message. On June 6, 1915, the *Times* presented a depiction of Uncle Sam advising Kaiser

FIGURE 6.1   Kaiser Wilhelm. "Kaiser, 25 Years a Ruler, Hailed as Chief Peacemaker," *New York Times,* Special Supplement (8 June 1913) 1. © 2008 by The New York Times Co. Reprinted with permission.

Wilhelm about America's policy on unrestricted submarine warfare (see Figure 6.2).

Towering over the Kaiser, Uncle Sam, with his striped pants and goatee, points to a representation of the first correspondence following the sinking of the *Lusitania*. Kaiser Wilhelm sits, shoulders slumped and head bowed, in deference to the document and Uncle Sam. With the caption, "Lest He Forget: U. S.—You'd better read that part of my note over again, Wilhelm," Americans readers were made to understand that, while America stood for peace, it would not condone the policy of unrestricted submarine warfare.

During this time period, special attention was focused on non-native-born Americans. The census of 1910 revealed that a significant percentage of America's population consisted of German immigrants. According to Fredrick Luebke, "First- and second-generation Germans, numbering well over eight million persons, were by far the most numerous immigrant group in the United States in 1910" (30). These individuals found their loyalties vacillating between their homeland of Germany and their new home, America. By means of its editorial cartoons, the press sought to influence these German immigrants. In one particularly chilling cartoon, published in the *Times* on May 16, 1915, only a month after she was sunk, the *Lusitania* reaches from its watery depths to demand that immigrants declare their partiality to a country (see Figure 6.3).

FIGURE 6.2   "Lest He Forget: U.S.—You'd better read that part of my note over again, Wilhelm," *New York Times* (6 June 1915) sec. 4, 24. © 2008 by The New York Times Co. Reprinted with permission.

The cartoon features a huge arm reaching to grasp the hyphen between "German" and "American." This arm reaches out of water in which we see the nameless faces of the sinking ship's noncombatant victims, women and babies, floating in their graves. The caption makes its demand crystal clear: "Removing the Hyphen: Now It Must Be Either One or the Other." German-Americans seem forced to shoulder the guilt of Germany's unrestricted submarine warfare. To absolve themselves of this guilt by association,

14

FIGURE 6.3 "Removing the Hyphen: Now It Must Be Either One of the Other," *The New York Times* (16 May 1915) sec. 5, 24. © 2008 by The New York Times Co. Reprinted with permission.

German-Americans had to choose their new home over their heritage.

15   Even at this point, however, President Wilson implored the American public to follow a peaceful course. Two days after the attack on the *Lusitania*, Wilson made the following plea: "The example of America must be the example not merely of peace because it will not fight, but of peace because peace is the healing and elevating influence of the world and strife is not" ("America" par. 1). Despite Wilson's admonitions, on June 3, 1917, the *New York Times* ran a cartoon that reflected an America no longer so eager to embrace peace (see Figure 6.4).

FIGURE 6.4 "Find the Man Who Has Just Made a Pacifist Speech," *The New York Times* (3 June 1917) sec. 6, 15. © 2008 by The New York Times Co. Reprinted with permission.

16   A lone man, representing those who would attempt a peaceful solution in the then-current world situation, seeks safety from a riotous crowd by climbing to the top of a pole. By throwing rocks at him, the crowd expresses disdain for pacifist ideology. In the background, a sign proclaims, "Your country needs you: Join Now." The threatened man drops his belongings, including a book titled, "Peace." The caption, addressed to the reader, reveals the sentiments of the crowd: "Find the Man Who Has Just Made a Pacifist Speech." By early in 1917, America's sentiments toward the war seem to be shifting. To be a pacifist was to face the rebuke of fellow Americans.

17   As these cartoons indicate, American citizens were prepared to accept a view in which Germany was its enemy. Capitalizing on these earlier efforts, George Creel and the CPI easily transformed Germans into barbarians. Once depicted as a kind-eyed gentleman, Kaiser Wilhelm underwent a radical transformation in the media. In fact, the CPI demonized the German leader in movies and print. One striking example is a CPI-published Army recruitment poster, drawn by H.R. Hopps, that depicts the Kaiser, identifiable by his spiked helmet, as a gorilla with fierce teeth and wielding a club of Kultur (see Figure 6.5). The "mad brute" carries Lady Liberty and encroaches on the shores of America. No longer a peacemaker, the Kaiser threatens the very existence of liberty and America.

FIGURE 6.5   H.R. Hopps, "Destroy This Mad Brute," 24 February 2007 <http://www.hrc.utexas.edu/collections/art/holdings/poster>. Harry Ransom Humanities Research Center. The University of Texas at Austin.

18   Historians attribute America's entry into the First World War to Germany's policy of unrestricted submarine warfare. While this policy was a motivating factor, the American public needed more emotional appeals to cause them to want to go to war against Germany. One important agent in generating these appeals involved cartoons in the *New York Times*. While propaganda can be overt, as illustrated in the "Mad Brute" Army recruitment poster, the subtle but always powerful seeds of propaganda sown in the editorial cartoons of the *New York*

Times tell an important part of the story of how this country moved from trying to remain neutral to being prepared to wage war against Germany.

Works Cited

Delwiche, Aaron. "The Committee on Public Information." *propaganda* (29 Sept. 2002): 8 pars. 18 Jan. 2007 <http://www.propagandacritic.com/articles/ww1/cpi/html>.

Faragher, John Mack, et al. *Out Of Many: A History of the American People*. New Jersey: Prentice Hall, 2000.

"Find the Man Who Has Just Made a Pacifist Speech." *New York Times*. 3 June 1917, sec. 6, 15.

Gorman, Lyn and David McLean. *Media and Society in the Twentieth Century: A Historical Introduction*. Massachusetts: Blackwell Publishing, 2003.

Hopps, H.R. *Destroy This Mad Brute*. 24 Feb. 2007 <http://www.hrc.utexas.edu/collections/art/holdings/poster/>.

"Kaiser, 25 Years a Ruler, Hailed as Chief Peacemaker." *New York Times*, 8 June 1913, Special Supplement.

"Lest He Forget: U.S.—You'd better read that part of my note over again, Wilhelm," *The New York Times Magazine*. 6 June 1915, sec. 4, 24.

Lewis, C.T. *Elementary Latin Dictionary*. Oxford: Oxford U Pr, 1977.

Luebke, Fredrick C. *Bonds of Loyalty: German-Americans and World War I*. Dekalb: Northern Illinois University Press, 1974.

"propaganda." *The Oxford Dictionary of English* (revised edition). Ed. Catherine Soanes and Angus Stevenson. Oxford University Press, 2005. *Oxford Reference Online*. Oxford University Press. Sam Houston State University. 23 February 2007 <http://www.oxfordreference.com/views/ENTRY.html?subview=Main&entry=t140.e62021>.

"Removing the Hyphen: Now It Must Be Either One of the Other." *The New York Times Magazine*. 15 May 1915, sec. 5, 24.

Ross, Stewart Balsey. *Propaganda for War: How the United States Was Conditioned to Fight the Great War of 1914–1918*. Jefferson, NC: McFarland and Company, 1996.

Trueman, Chris. "The Lusitania." History Learning Site. 15 pars. 18 Jan. 2007 <http://www.historyleariningsite.co.uk/lusitania.htm>.

Wilson, Woodrow. "America Must Be a Special Example." *The World War I Document Archive* (2 Feb. 1996): 1 par. 24 Feb. 2007 <http://net.lib.byu.edu/~rdh7/wwi/1915/amexamp.html>.

———. "President Wilson's Declaration of Neutrality." *The World War I Document Archive* (Feb. 1996): 4 pars. <http://net.lib.byu.edu/~rdh7/wwi/1914/wilsonneut.html>.

———. "President Woodrow Wilson's War Message." *The World War I Document Archive* (Oct. 2002): 17 pars. <http://net.lib.byu.edu/~rdh7/wwi/1917/wilswarm.html>.

◆ QUESTIONS FOR REVIEW

1. What is the thesis of Elizabeth's essay? Does it appear in the essay? If so, where? How does she develop (or support) her thesis?
2. Divide Elizabeth's essay into beginning, middle, and end. What rhetorical and/or stylistic devices help form these divisions?
3. What audience might Elizabeth's essay be written for? Is this audience likely to see this as a controversial topic? Are there any indications in her text that Elizabeth thinks readers may take an opposing point of view? If so, explain.
4. What information did you possess on this subject before reading Elizabeth's essay? What information in her essay was particularly interesting to you? Were you surprised by any of the information in this essay? If so, what was it? Did you disagree with Elizabeth on any points? If so, what were they?

◆ WRITING OPPORTUNITY

1. Elizabeth Gardner's essay suggests that the cartoonists in the U.S. helped to turn the U.S. public against the Germans during the years immediately before World War I. How much can a cartoonist's renderings of a political or public person shape and how much do they reflect the public's opinions of that person? What would the public's reaction be to a very unflattering drawing of someone who was revered by the people seeing that drawing?
2. In her essay, Elizabeth demonstrates how certain cartoonists' drawings of Kaiser Wilhelm changed as America drew closer and closer to war with Germany. But in the last 60 years, Americans' opinions of Germany (its leaders and its people) have changed dramatically from very negative to very positive. Germany and the U.S. are allies in many endeavors on the world's stage. But during this time, other countries have come to be regarded as the enemies of the U.S. and of what the U.S. and its allies refer to as "the free world." Choose one of these countries and write an essay in which you explore the role that the U.S. media have played in shaping the opinions of U.S. citizens regarding that country and its citizens. ◆

THE RHETORICAL TRIANGLE

Subject

Almost any subject can be approached from an informative perspective. But some topics are more difficult than others to treat in an essay with an informative aim. Subjects such as gun control and abortion can shade into argumentation almost before you know what has happened, since you're likely to have an opinion on these topics and to allow that opinion to color the information you're attempting to convey. By the same token, most readers approach essays on such topics as these with strong opinions that tend to make them read to see whether the writer agrees or disagrees with them rather than what information the writer may have to share on this subject.

Other topics, however, do not tend to strike an argumentative note with most readers. In writing about these subjects, you may structure your writing as "argument" without writing a paper with an argumentative aim. For example, Elisabeth Kübler-Ross ("On the Fear of Dying") asserts that our fear of death is one of the causes of all the attention we give to medical technology in treating the dying; Jay Chiat asserts that advertising "robs us of the most intimate moments in our lives . . ." and Arthur Rosenfeld asserts that the "conflicting agendas and priorities among doctors, patient advocates, government regulators and insurance companies" are causing many people to live in pain unnecessarily.

Gloria Naylor's "Mommy, What Does 'Nigger' Mean?" deals with a subject that is potentially very controversial. No one would argue that the word "nigger" should be used in its usual derogatory sense, but Naylor argues that the use of this term by blacks is a way of diffusing the word's power to hurt. However, she is assuming an audience that wants to be informed about the ways in which language works, not one that will want to resist what she is saying about the way this hateful word has been used.

In summary, we can say that the most likely subjects for informative essays are ones that do not lend themselves to controversy. However, if you're careful to focus your essay on information that your audience does not have and if you structure your essay in a nonargumentative fashion, you can write an informative essay on almost any topic.

Writer

Before writing, you will want to have a solid base of information, whatever topic you choose. For example, Kübler-Ross, a physician and long-time advocate for the rights of patients, has obviously given much thought to the treatment of dying patients in U.S. society. Likewise, Chiat has spent his entire career in the field of advertising.

You may not be able to bring the kind of professional expertise to a topic that these writers have developed over many years. But like the student writers whose essays are featured in this chapter, you do know a great deal about a number of topics. Elizabeth Gardner's essay, "Transforming a Nation, Transforming an Enemy," shows that she has given much thought to the ways propaganda works in war time, and Michael Graham—whose essay, "All in a Day's Work: Generalizing, Profiling, and Sterotyping" is our student sample at the end of this chapter—has worked as a security guard in a large department store. As a part of his job, he has learned how to profile people who might steal from the store, and as his essay makes clear, he has spent a good bit of time reflecting on the positives and negatives of this practice. Like Michael, you may well choose to write about a subject that you would not ordinarily associate with formal, or academic, writing. Don't limit yourself to academic subjects: write about topics you really know and care about. You may have had a job that has given you information that your readers will not have. Or you may have acquired information as a member of the 4-H club or from trips you have taken to visit other countries. Or you may have information as a result of your interest in some art or craft. Any subject that interests you and about which you know a good deal can be suitable for an informative essay.

Of course, you may not have a wealth of information about your topic when you choose it for an information paper. In such a situation, your task is to make yourself more knowledgeable about a topic of interest to you. But how do you obtain this information? You may want to begin with the traditional sources of information, often divided into two types: library and field searches. Library searches are no doubt already familiar to you. If you need a refresher on the various sources available to you in the library, you may want to turn to Chapter 12, pages 582–585. You may have also done some type of field search in your writing. For additional information on various field searches—interviews, surveys, questionnaires, and observations—turn to Chapter 12, pages 585–590. The last resource that we will mention here may well be the first one that came to your mind. The Internet provides us with information about nearly any subject known to humankind. For more on the ways in which your searches may use the Internet, see Chapter 12, pages 590–598. For information on the basic tools that will assist you in using the internet, see Chapter 1, pages 32–35.

As a result of their knowledge about their topics, writers of informative prose speak with confidence. They need not, in fact, should not, be arrogant or high-handed, but they approach the reader with the assumption that what they say is worthy of the reader's attention.

How do writers exhibit this confidence and demonstrate their authority? One key characteristic of informative writing is the writer's willingness to generalize. The writer may, and often does, deal in specifics, but she is willing and able to move from those specifics to the general principles they illustrate. Gloria Naylor ("Mommy, What Does 'Nigger' Mean?") begins her essay in generalities. She tells her reader that she considers "the written word inferior to the spoken, and much of the frustration experienced by novelists is the awareness that whatever we manage to capture in even the most transcendent passages falls far short of the richness of life." Note that Naylor uses the first person here, but she does not say, or imply, that this is only her opinion. Her experience with and knowledge of the subject have given her information that is generalizable and sharable.

Probably the most authoritative writing in our sample essays is in Kübler-Ross's "On the Fear of Dying." In the first paragraph of her essay, she offers historical information that establishes her knowledge about rituals having to do with death and dying. Then, in the first sentence of the second paragraph, she assumes the authority to say that "man has not basically changed," in regard to the fear of death. Near the end of her essay, Kübler-Ross attempts to help her reader see what makes people want to rely so heavily on the technologies of modern medicine:

> Those who consider the person first may lose precious time to save his life! At least this seems to be the rationale or justification behind all this—or is it? Is the reason for this increasingly mechanical, depersonalized approach our own defensiveness? Is this approach our own way to cope with and repress the anxieties that a terminally or critically ill patient evokes in us? Is our concentration on equipment, on blood pressure our desperate attempt to deny the impending death which is so frightening and discomforting to us that we displace all our knowledge onto machines, since they are less close to us than the suffering face of another human being which would remind us once more of our lack of omnipotence, our own limits and failures, and last but not least perhaps our own mortality?

Kübler-Ross structures the preceding passage with a series of questions. In general, asking questions rather than making assertions can make a writer seem less authoritative, but Kübler-Ross's passage is an exception to this rule. Note how she reveals her authority in asking these questions. She labels the modern approach to medicine as one that is "increasingly mechanical, depersonalized"; she calls reliance on this technology a "desperate attempt to deny the impending death" of the patient, and she asserts that modern practice allows us to "displace all our knowledge onto machines." Her authority and confidence come through even when she is asking questions about this very complex issue.

This last point brings us to another characteristic of successful informative writers: They know enough about their subject matter to avoid oversimplifying. As we see here, despite all her misgivings about modern medicine, Kübler-Ross, in the end, asks a series of questions that point to the difficulty of determining exactly why we rely so much on technology. We may well be using this technology to mask our fears of death, but it is clear also that at times this technology saves us from death. Kübler-Ross is much too knowledgeable to suggest a simplistic solution, such as returning to the practices of her childhood.

Reader

Readers of informative writing are assumed to be receivers of information. By this, we mean something a bit more specific than being able to read and process the words on a page. Readers of informative writing meet the following minimal criteria:

1. They have some reason for being interested in the topic. That reason may vary considerably—from a real need to know something about the topic to a curiosity about what interests the writer.
2. They are willing and able to assume the position of one being instructed; that is, they do not feel they know more about the topic in question than the writer.
3. They do not take an opposing position on the topic from that of the writer. (It is the writer's responsibility to know his topic and his reader well enough to ensure that this is the case. If it is not, the writer must write a different kind of essay.)

> **Exercise 6.2**
>
> Examine two of the professional essays presented at the beginning of this chapter. Before looking to see where they originally appeared (this information is provided in the Acknowledgments at the end of the book), give some thought to who the writers' intended readers may have been. What cues in the texts help you gain insight into potential readers? How successful will the writers be in getting their points across to the intended readers? Finally, consider whether you are a suitable reader for each of these texts. If you are not, reflect on what elements in the text do not work for you. Is there anything you could do to make yourself a suitable reader for the text?

DISTINGUISHING FEATURES OF INFORMATION ESSAYS

In an information essay, the focus is on the information that is transferred from writer to reader. If the reader doesn't receive the information, for whatever reason, the writing is not successful.

Reader's Knowledge

It is essential that the writer have a clear sense of what his reader knows about the topic in question, since the reader's knowledge is the foundation on which the information essay is built. If the writer assumes a foundation that does not exist, the reader will not understand what the writer is trying to say; to continue our foundation metaphor, the structure will fall in on itself. This passage is from a recent book on linguistics:

> Propositional content conditions or rules are the most textual: they concern reference and predication (the propositional act). A propositional content rule for promises, for example, is the predication of a future act (A) by the speaker. Preparatory conditions or rules are varied; they seem to involve background circumstances and knowledge about S [speaker] and H [hearer] that must hold prior to (and then be altered by) the performance of the act. A preparatory condition for promises, for example, concerns H's preference about S's doing of an act (A).
>
> Deborah Schiffrin, *Approaches to Discourse*

The writer of this text, Deborah Schiffrin, wants to tell us something about "propositional content conditions." She begins by assuming that we will know the linguistic meaning of such terms as "textual," "reference," "predication," "propositional act," and "preparatory condition." By "linguistic meaning," we are referring to what such a term as "preparatory condition" means in linguistics as opposed to what the two words mean in ordinary conversation. Readers not familiar with these terms will have great difficulty in understanding the information the writer wants to give us.

This difficulty should not lead us, however, to think that a good information essay will explain all terms. To do so would be to slow down and bore—and probably irritate—readers who know the terms. The linguistic students for whom Schiffrin intends her text will know these terms; if she attempted to define all of her terms, Schiffrin would slow the pace of instruction far too much to be effective for her student readers. The following text begins as if it may well attempt to define all of its terms:

> Verbs and their subjects must agree in person and number. By "agree," we mean to indicate that there are patterned changes, or correspondences, between these two elements in a sentence. If "I" is the subject, and a form of the verb "be" is the verb, then the pattern will be "I am." If "he" is the subject and a form of the verb "be" is the verb, then the pattern will be "He is." Here we see patterned agreement in "person." But what about agreement in number? If "I" is the subject and a form of the verb "be" is the verb, then the pattern will be "I am," as we saw above. However, if "we" is the subject and a form of the verb "be" is the verb, then the pattern will be "We are." Here we see patterning in number.
> Ron Lunsford

Are you asleep yet? If not, it probably wouldn't take too much more of this kind of writing to induce sleep. Why? You already know everything Ron is attempting to tell you. You may not know everything Ron could tell you about grammar—such as the basic difference between a gerund and a participle or what constitutes an elliptical adverbial clause—but before you get to this material, you are likely to have quit paying attention to the text. In terms of our metaphor, the writer is attempting to build a foundation that already exists.

Clarity

Clarity is the watchword in information essays. You may be tempted to ask why we need to say this here. Shouldn't clarity be the aim in all writing? To answer this question, we ask you to imagine a situation in which a teenager must inform her parents that she has wrecked the family car and that she was at fault. Which of the versions of this incident, given as A, B, and C below, would she prefer her parents receive? Which is clearer? Which is better suited to informative writing?

> **A.** The car in front of me stopped while I wasn't looking at it. When I saw the car, it was too late to avoid hitting it. The police officer gave me a ticket for following too closely.
>
> **B.** All I can say is that I am glad that no one was hurt, and I am amazed at how simplistically a police report has to treat a very complicated situation. I never speed, and I was not speeding today. I was paying attention to my driving, as I always do, and trying to be alert to the various possible hazards that might endanger my life—and the lives of those in the car with me—when, in the corner of my eye, I saw a car in a parking lot to my left start to dart out in front of me—or so it seemed. The driver must have managed to stop before I got to him—since I never saw him again—but by the time my gaze returned to the road, the car in front of me had

screamed to a stop at a caution light that any experienced driver would have gone through. I talked to the police officer afterward, and he agreed with me that inexperienced drivers—and this kid driving the car in front of me had only had his permit for two weeks—do sometimes stop for caution lights that an experienced driver would, and should, go on through. But the police officer was not there and could not document exactly how it had happened. The officer also told me that at times paying attention to what happens in our peripheral vision can save our lives. He said that if he (or anyone else who might serve as an unbiased witness) could verify that a car had nearly pulled out in front of me, he could write this incident up as a "no fault," which it clearly was. However, given the rules he had to work with, he had to give me a ticket for following too closely. The good news, of course, is that no one was hurt and that the damage to both cars was minimal.

C. Car B hit car A from behind at the intersection of Fifth Street and Irwin Avenue. Car A was heading east on Irwin and had stopped at a red light at Fifth. The tire marks and damage to cars indicate that car B was traveling at a rate of speed of between 29 and 37 miles per hour before the incident. The driver of car B reported that a car had nearly darted out in front of her—from the parking lot of the business on the southwest corner of the intersection. No corroboration of this claim was possible.

We would guess that she would prefer her parents receive the account in example B. In this account, the reader finds the basic information—that there was a wreck and that she was found to be at fault; however, the reader also feels with her how complicated this situation was and how easy it is for a wreck to happen when a driver is doing everything possible to drive safely. Her purpose in giving her parents this account would be to help them view this event as she views it.

Exercise 6.3

Our example above makes the point that writers can have multiple purposes. The writer of passage C, the police officer, wants to present as factual and as clear an account of this event as possible. The writer of passage B, the young driver of the car, wants to tell what happened but also wants to draw attention to the complexities of the situation. This account has strong leanings toward persuasion; thus, clarity is not as important as is capturing a full accounting of all the factors in this situation. Look back at the sample essays at the beginning of the chapter and analyze them from the standpoint of purpose. Obviously, the writers intend to give their readers information. Can you discern other goals these writers are attempting to achieve in their essays? Are some of them more purely informational than others? How high a priority do the writers give to clarity in their writing?

The preceding exercise is intended to help you explore the fact that no one piece of writing is exactly like another in its purposes, or aims. For that reason, no two pieces of writing will have exactly the same commitment to clarity. When we say, then, that the hallmark of information essays is clarity, we are mindful of the fact that various writing situations and purposes will call for, or allow, various degrees of clarity. In general, we can say that information essays should be as clear as purpose and situation will allow them to be. Four principles may help you achieve this clarity:

1. Strive to draw attention to your subject, rather than to yourself as writer or to your reader's response to the writing.
2. Choose words that express rather than impress. That is, if a simple word will convey the information you wish, then use it.
3. Make your sentence structures as direct and readable as possible. Avoid overly complicated sentences that the reader will have to reread to understand.
4. Make your overall organization as clear as possible early in the essay. Write a thesis sentence that gives readers insight into the order of your essay. If your essay is long, consider headings that make the relationship of the parts of your essay clear to the reader.

ASSIGNMENT AND GUIDELINES FOR WRITING

Assignment

Write a paper sharing information you have with an audience that is receptive to that information. For this essay, you should identify a topic about which you already know a great deal or about which you would like to know more.

Choosing a Topic

Part A

1. Select three or four subjects that you know a great deal about. If you need help choosing, refer to the information in your Interest Inventory (see pages 11–13); you may also find a suitable topic in one of your responses to the "Writing Opportunity" assignments in this chapter. Then, freewrite on each of these subjects for ten minutes or so.
2. Reread the freewrites you did in 1 above and circle words or phrases that seem particularly interesting to you. Then choose two or three of these circled items as the beginning point for five- to ten-minute focused freewriting sessions. (In a focused freewrite, you start from a word or phrase and write whatever comes to mind, attempting to focus on ideas that are in some loose sense related to the phrase you started from—see Michael Graham's freewritings at the end of this chapter.)
3. After you have done the exercises in 1 and/or 2 above, begin to consider a possible topic for your paper by answering the following questions:
    a. What word or phrase best captures a potential topic for your paper?
    b. Why is this topic interesting to you?
    c. Is this a topic that many people know a great deal about? If so, what special knowledge do you have about this topic? If people do not know a lot about this topic, why? Is it difficult? Is it not interesting to most people? Or is there some other reason?

Part B
1. Select a topic that you would like to know more about. Freewrite for five to ten minutes, exploring what interests you about this topic and trying to capture what you already know about this topic.
2. List the ways in which you can obtain information about this topic.
3. Do some preliminary investigation to see what you can find about this topic.

Part C
Pick one topic that you came up with in doing the exercises in Part A or Part B above. Briefly describe an audience that might be interested in what you have to say about this topic. How would you reach this audience? Where might your essay be published, or where might you speak to this audience? Describe a typical reader's or listener's dealings with, and knowledge about, this topic.

Collecting Information

You probably already know a great deal about this topic, as your freewrites should have made clear; however, you may gather more information in the following ways:

> *Questions for Analysis.* Ask the questions of association, opposition, sequence, and consequence presented in Chapter 1 (pages 24–31).
>
> *Brainstorming/clustering/mapping.* Use any of these strategies (and others introduced in Chapter 1) to generate additional material about which to write.

Making Use of Visuals   As you collect information for this assignment, explore the various types of information that may be presented in tables and figures. Think of the role that visuals often play in informative writing. When you write to provide a reader with information, it's often helpful to support your words with a visual representation of those words. It's often easier to assemble a bicycle or to set up a computer, for example, by referring to a diagram (a visual image) that shows how the handlebars on the bike fit into the frame or which cable plugs in where on the computer than it would be if all we had to guide us were words. Such diagrams help clarify and so supplement the text they accompany.

In writing informational essays, we often present information that is essential but difficult to absorb quickly. In such instances as these, if we can present a visual image that will supplement our explanation in the text, then we can help the reader grasp what we're saying more readily. Among the primary visual images used in informational writing are tables and figures.

Tables and Figures   On the following pages we examine the various types of tables and figures you may find helpful in organizing and presenting information.

TABLE 6.1 Analysis of the 12 Readers' Focuses of Commentary

	Number	Percentage
Ideas	736	29
Development	351	14
Global structure	313	12
Local structure	107	4
Wording	275	11
Correctness	144	6
Extra-textual comments	603	24
TOTAL	2529	100

Source: Richard Straub and Ronald F. Lunsford, *Twelve Readers Reading: Responding to Student Writing* (Cresskill, NJ: Hampton Press, 1995), p. 182.

Tables Any data that is presented via ordered rows and columns may be referred to as a table. We can illustrate the function that a table can play in providing information by means of a table used in a book that Ron wrote with the late Richard Straub: *Twelve Readers Reading: Responding to College Student Writing*. In that book Rick and Ron asked twelve well-known college composition teachers to respond to a group of essays as they would if they were actually teaching the students who wrote the essays. Rick and Ron's book, then, was informative in aim, in that it intended to provide information about these twelve teachers' responding styles to an audience of college writing teachers. After they had examined these marked essays carefully, Rick and Ron came up with a list of categories that teachers' comments could be placed in, according to what issues these teachers were responding to in a specific comment. For example, a student might write a paper explaining how to get a pilot's license. If a teacher responds, "I never knew how much work it takes to become a pilot," it is clear that the teacher is responding to the *ideas* in that student's paper. On the other hand, if the teacher says, "This sentence is confusing," she is talking about what Rick and Ron call *local structure*. It isn't necessary for you to understand all the categories that Rick and Ron devised in order to see how a table such as Table 6.1 above provides interesting information to teachers of writing.

This table shows that two types of comments—those that deal with ideas in the text and those that deal with matters not referred to expressly in the text, such as the classroom instruction the teacher would like the student to apply to the paper in question—account for more than half of the comments made by these teachers. The twelve readers, then, spent more time responding to ideas and content than to mechanical errors.

Figures Several types of figures can help you find and relay information to your readers. The first of these is the graph. You no doubt remember the graphs you drew in charting the various figures you studied in geometry. A line graph is a visual representation of the relationship between any two sets of data. As an example, let's look at gas price data taken from a website created by Robert Sahr of Oregon Sate University (<http://oregonstate.edu/dept/pol_sci/fac/sahr/sahr.htm>). This graph

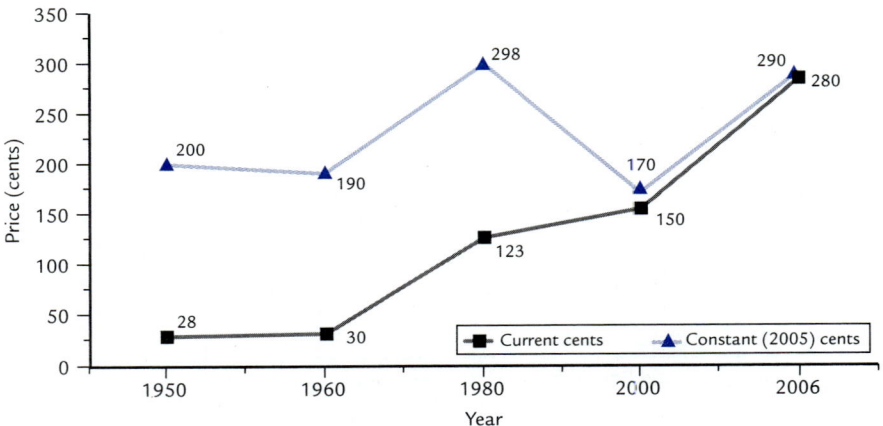

FIGURE 6.6   Graph of United States Gasoline Prices 1950 to 2006 in Current and Constant (Year 2005) Cents per Gallon. Robert Sahr, 25 Feb. 2007
<http://oregonstate.edu/dept/pol_sci/fac/sahr/sahr.htm>.

charts the price of gasoline in the U.S. from 1950 to 2006 in terms of the actual pennies per gallon in a given year and the constant price those pennies represent as based on the economic index of 2005.

What does this graph show us? At a glance we can see a few striking facts. The first is that there was relatively little rise in gasoline prices from 1950 until about 1964. Then we see rather significant increases in current prices from 1971 until 1981 and from 1998 until the present. But when we look at the constant price of gas—that is, the real price as measured against inflation (with a base year of 2005)—we find that the only real increases in gasoline prices occurred between 1960 and 1982 and between 2002 and the present. Even so, we see that the real rise in the cost of gasoline over the course of the last 56 years has been less than 30 percent—a beginning of $2.00 per gallon (in terms of 2005 prices) and an ending price of $2.80. All of this can be said in words as we have just done. However, if you want your reader to get the full impact of your claim that what appears to be an unremitting rise in gas prices from 1950 to the present is, in fact, a rather modest rise in real cost, nothing will provide that impact more quickly or more effectively than a line graph like the one in Figure 6.6 above.

The bar graph is another type of graph that can be very effective in conveying information. Figure 6.7 on the following page presents the information in Table 6.1 (see page 243) in the form of a bar graph.

Such a graph as this is particularly effective when we want to have a visual representation of the differences between several numbers. When we see the numbers in Table 6.1, we can interpret them so as to understand that the 736 comments made about *ideas* is a much larger number than the 107 made about *local structure*. But when we see Figure 6.7, we don't need to compute numbers: we "see" the

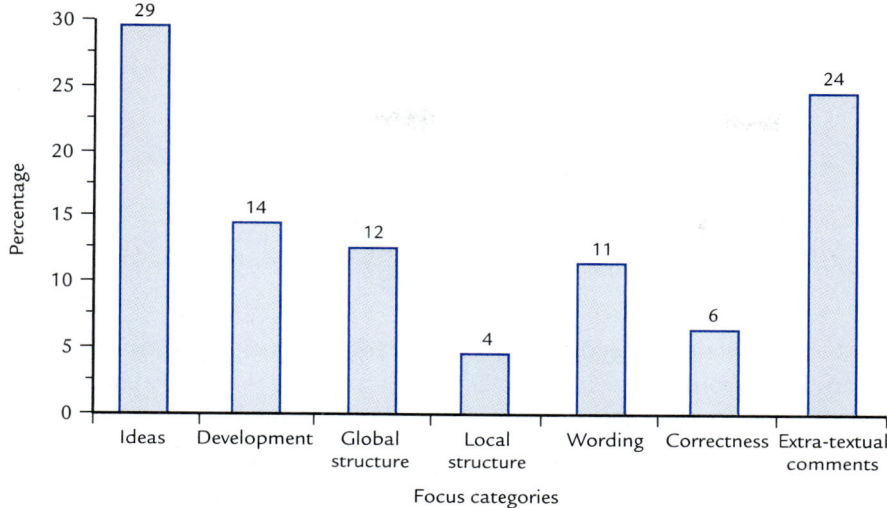

FIGURE 6.7   Readers' Focus Profile. Richard Straub and Ronald F. Lunsford, *Twelve Readers Reading: Responding to Student Writing* (Cresskill, NJ: Hampton Press, 1995) 182.

relationship between *ideas* and *local structure* in the same way that we "see" two people and immediately know something about their relative heights.

A second type of figure is a pie chart. We can illustrate the function that this kind of chart can play in providing information by means of a pie chart that presents the information in Table 6.1.

In Figure 6.8, all the items having to do with content have been grouped into what Rick and Ron labeled as Global issues. The items having to do with sentence structure, word choice and correctness are labeled Local issues. Extra-textual issues include teacher comments that do not refer to the text at hand but serve to create a conversation between teacher and student, e.g., "My brother is a pilot." When the reader looks at Figure 6.8 on the following page, certain information leaps out at her, namely, the fact that these teachers spend much more time responding to content (that is, global issues) than to other items.

Figures can do much more for us than represent numbers. As a case in point, let's look at one final example from *Twelve Readers Reading*. One of the most interesting findings of the book was the fact that the twelve readers did not limit themselves to comments about the text they were reading. In fact, Rick and Ron found five different categories of response depending on what they came to refer to as the five contexts for response:

Context	Sample Comment
Textual	This paragraph could be developed more fully.
Writing Process	You might want to do more prewriting in the future.

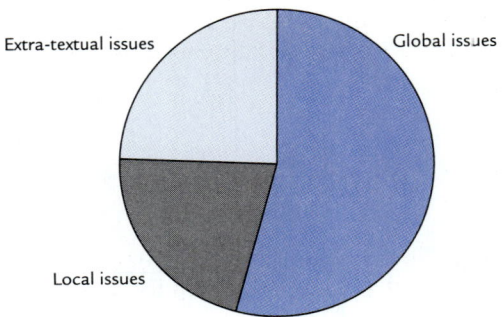

FIGURE 6.8   Major Categories of the 12 Readers' Focuses of Commentary. Extrapolated from information in Richard Straub and Ronald F. Lunsford, *Twelve Readers Reading: Responding to Student Writing* (Cresskill, NJ: Hampton Press, 1995).

Rhetorical Context	I wonder if your readers will know what this word means.
Personal Context	Have you written about this experience before?
Social Context	This topic doesn't seem to work well for an argument assignment.

Figure 6.9 below attempts to capture these five contexts. Note that each of the contexts is represented as encompassing all the other contexts before it, so that the rhetorical context envelops the textual context, the personal context envelops

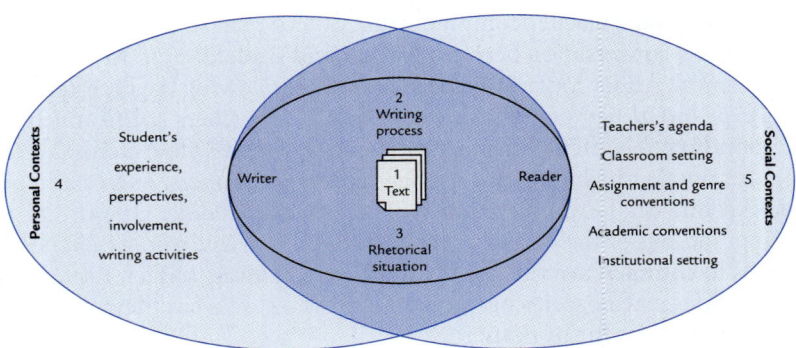

FIGURE 6.9   The Five Contexts of Student Writing. Richard Straub and Ronald F. Lunsford, *Twelve Readers Reading: Responding to Student Writing* (Cresskill, NJ: Hampton Press, 1995) p. 165.

the rhetorical and the textual, and so on. In doing so, the figure captures the central nature of the student's text, and, at the same time, shows how all the other contexts radiate out from that text.

Exercise 6.4

1. Search the web and other sources (e.g., one of your textbooks) for informative writing that makes effective use of visuals. Find at least three different visuals that work particularly well and write an analysis of each explaining its effectiveness.
2. Find some information for your Information Essay that lends itself to a table or figure. Represent this information in as many different visuals as you can. Then, choose the visual that works best for your audience and write a brief explanation of why it is the best.

Exercise 6.5

Take a short poll of your classmates to gather the following kinds of information:

a. Number of students in a high school graduating class:
   (1) less than 20, (2) 20–50, (3) 50–100, (4), 100–200, (5) 200–500, (6) 500+.
b. Distance between students' hometowns and your school:
   (1) less than 5 miles, (2), 5–25 miles, (3) 25–50 miles, (4) 50+ miles, (5) out-of-state, (6) international.

Display the information you generate in at least one table and two different types of figures. Which type of visual image provides the clearest picture of that information? Explain. What inferences can you make about the information you generate? If your class can be seen as representing a typical crosssection of your student body, what does the information say about your school's student population?

Focus Statement

Compose a focus statement for your essay. Below is the focus statement that Michael Graham wrote for his essay, "All in a Day's Work: Generalizing, Profiling, and Stereotyping" (pages 267–269).

> I want to write about the time when I profiled someone. I then want to discuss the use of profiling and its advantages and disadvantages. I also want the reader to see the comparison between profiling and stereotyping. I will concentrate on race, gender, and social status. I want to show why groups profile.

Michael's focus statement is a workable start. It allowed him to move on to his next draft. Note that he is a long way from the clear thesis that he eventually constructs (page 264), but that thesis will come only after he has written about the matters he has put on the table in this focus statement.

Planning Your Essay's Structure

One way to think about the shape of your essay is by using one or more of the modes of discourse.

Modes of Discourse   One key to the overall shape of your essay will be the mode of discourse you employ in your writing. You will remember from our discussion in the introduction to Part Two that *mode* refers to the structuring devices we use to organize our thoughts about a topic. Although a writer may make use of several different modes in one essay, one will provide the overall structure for any piece of informative writing.

Process   *Process* is the word we use for an organizational strategy based on chronology. In Chapter 5, we said that chronological connections are at the heart of narration. How, then, may we differentiate process from narration? It's not always easy, but as a rule narration sets up a sequence of events that develops a story, whereas process sets up a sequence of events that provide information. In the following excerpt, John Holt uses a sequence of events detailing how we might teach children to learn to speak—if indeed we did teach them—in order to give us information about how children actually do learn language.

> Bill Hull once said to me, "If we taught children to speak, they'd never learn." I thought at first he was joking. By now I realize that it was a very important truth. Suppose we decided that we had to "teach" children to speak. How would we go about it? First, some committee of experts would analyze speech and break it down into a number of separate "speech skills." We would probably say that, since speech is made up of sounds, a child must be taught to make all the sounds of his language before he can be taught to speak the language itself. Doubtless we would list these sounds, easiest and commonest ones first, harder and rarer ones next. Then we would begin to teach infants these sounds, working our way down the list. Perhaps, in order not to "confuse" the child—"confuse" is an evil word to many educators—we would not let the child hear much ordinary speech, but would only expose him to the sounds we were trying to teach.
> Along with our sound list, we would have a syllable list and a word list.
> When the child had learned to make all the sounds on the sound list, we would begin to teach him to combine the sounds into syllables. When he could say all the syllables on the syllable list, we would begin to teach him words on our word list. At the same time, we would teach him the rules of grammar, by means of which he could combine these newly learned words into sentences. Everything would be planned with nothing left to chance; there would be plenty of drill, review, and tests, to make sure that he had not forgotten anything.

Suppose we tried to do this; what would happen? What would happen, quite simply, is that most children, before they got very far, would become baffled, discouraged, humiliated, and fearful, and would quit trying to do what we asked them. If, outside of our classes, they lived a normal infant's life, many of them would probably ignore our "teaching" and learn to speak on their own. If not, if our control of their lives was complete (the dream of too many educators), they would take refuge in deliberate failure and silence, as so many of them do when the subject is reading.

John Holt, *How Children Learn*

If we look closely at this passage, it is clear that chronological connections provide much of its structure. Holt tells us that if we taught children to speak, "*First,* some committee of experts would [....]" Two sentences later, the chronological connections continue with "*Then* we would begin to teach infants these sounds [...]" until we have the whole story.

We should not, however, be misled into assuming that structuring by means of process is a simple, straightforward task. Just as the writer of a narrative must choose his details consciously and carefully in order to make the story mean what he wants it to, process requires the writer to keep an astute eye on his reader to determine how much and what kind of detail is needed to promote understanding. For example, if Ron wanted to tell a friend how to get to his home, how would he begin? Depending on the knowledge of the person for whom he was writing, he could begin with either of the following:

1. As you leave the university, turn right onto Highway 49. Stay on 49 until you get to the first stoplight, about two-thirds of a mile. Immediately after going under this light, take a right onto Harris Boulevard West. Travel west on Harris for about a mile and a half until you get to I–85. Take I–85 north and travel 10 miles to Highway 73.
2. Turn right off Interstate 85 at Highway 73.

The first set of directions would be written for someone who knows very little about Charlotte and its surroundings. Ron would be attempting to give this person the detail needed to find his home, starting at the UNC Charlotte campus. The set of directions that begins with the sentence in 2 would be written for someone who knows something about the northeast section of Charlotte. For a person who knows where Highway 73 intersects with Interstate 85, the four steps Ron wrote telling how to get from the university campus to this intersection would be unnecessary. Thus, even though the writer using the process knows that his basic connectors will involve chronology, he is doing more than simply filling in the blanks with what happens next. His choice of how to connect the various parts of the process and, indeed, his sense of what to include in the process are guided by his overall purpose in this writing situation.

Comparison   In our discussion below, we will use comparison in the broad sense in which it can refer to both likenesses and differences. In order to see how basic the recognition of similarities and differences is to learning, you need

Exercise 6.6

Compare the directions on a household product, such as a packaged food, with those for a prescription medicine. How do the sets differ? What is the purpose of each? Is the information given in each set equally clear?

Exercise 6.7

Although many essays use process as a major ordering device, many others make use of process as one means of order. For example, look at the role process plays in Kübler-Ross's essay at the beginning of this chapter. A major part of her essay is the comparison of the process by which we used to handle death and dying with the typical process today. Reflect for a few minutes on the role process may play in your essay. What, if any, processes will you need to inform your readers about? Sketch these now as a means of generating material for your essay.

only observe a young child as she attempts to make sense of her world. She sees a small, fur-covered animal that has two eyes, a nose, a mouth, four legs, and a tail—among many other characteristics that might escape the child's notice. Her parents inform her that this strange-looking creature is a "doggie." Then the child sees another small animal and exclaims, "Doggie." Her parents will be pleased, but they may not fully realize what a feat this child has accomplished. The child recognizes the second dog even though she has never seen it before and even though it is not exactly like anything she has ever seen before. This dog's coat is not exactly the same color as that of the first dog, its weight is not the same, its nose is not the same length, and so forth. But the child has learned to recognize this animal as a dog by means of comparison. Of course, the child may also "recognize" several cats as dogs for a time, but as her ability to make comparisons sharpens, she will reach a point at which she knows what a dog is. She could never do so without mastering the comparative mode of thinking.

What exactly does comparison entail? It involves us in sizing up a subject. In some cases, this sizing up is literal. For example, if someone tells you, "There is a very large bug on your foot," the word "large" must be understood in the context of "bug" and "foot." How large can the bug be if it is on your foot? What does the word "large" mean in this context? That is the crucial question, isn't it? When you hear that a bug is large, you automatically assume a comparative context. You think about this bug's size in terms of the usual bug's size. If this bug is big, then it will be larger than that usual size. A big bug is still very small in comparison with an average-sized elephant.

Of course, at times the sizing up that we do is not literal at all. For example, consider the following excerpt from Jonathan Kozol's *Savage Inequalities*:

New York City's public schools are subdivided into 32 school districts. District 10 encompasses a large part of the Bronx but is, effectively, two separate districts. One of these districts, Riverdale, is in the northwest section of the Bronx. Home to many of the city's most sophisticated and well-educated families, its elementary schools have relatively few low-income students. The other section, to the south and east, is poor and heavily nonwhite.

The contrast between public schools in each of these two neighborhoods is obvious to any visitor. At Public School 24 in Riverdale, the principal speaks enthusiastically of his teaching staff. At Public School 79, serving poorer children to the south, the principal says that he is forced to take the "tenth-best" teachers. "I thank God they're still breathing," he remarks of those from whom he must select his teachers. [. . .]

In order to find Public School 261 in District 10, a visitor is told to look for a mortician's office. The funeral home, which faces Jerome Avenue in the North Bronx, is easy to identify by its green awning. The school is next door, in a former roller-skating rink. No sign identifies the building as a school. A metal awning frame without an awning supports a flagpole, but there is no flag.

In the street in front of the school there is an elevated public transit line. Heavy traffic fills the street. The existence of the school is virtually concealed within this crowded city block. [. . .]

Beyond the inner doors a guard is seated. The lobby is long and narrow. The ceiling is low. There are no windows. All the teachers that I see at first are middle-aged white women. The principal, who is also a white woman, tells me that the school's "capacity" is 900 but that there are 1,300 children here. [. . .]

Two months later, on a day in May, I visit an elementary school in Riverdale. The dogwoods and magnolias on the lawn in front of P.S. 24 are in full blossom on the day I visit. There is a well-tended park across the street, another larger park three blocks away. To the left of the school is a playground for small children, with an innovative jungle gym, a slide and several climbing toys. Behind the school there are two playing fields for older kids. The grass around the school is neatly trimmed. [. . .]

The school serves 825 children in the kindergarten through sixth grade. This is approximately half the student population crowded into P.S. 79, where 1,550 children fill a space intended for 1,000, and a great deal smaller than the 1,300 children packed into the former skating rink; but the principal of P.S. 24, a capable and energetic man named David Rothstein, still regards it as excessive for an elementary school.

Kozol gives us a good deal of insight into the problems of funding of public education by means of this stark comparison. In a sense, he is using comparison to size up those problems.

Comparison is natural. No one has to encourage a child to compare his allowance to a friend's allowance or his curfew to that of his classmates. Of course, if the comparisons do not produce information that is useful—that is, if he finds his allowance is bigger or his curfew is more lenient than that of his friends—he may keep that information to himself. It is instructive, though, that he knows what types of comparisons might prove useful. He does not bother to compare himself with children reared in a distant part of the country or with children whose socioeconomic status is very different from his. It is not likely to be useful to a young child to know that children of extremely wealthy parents have allowances that are three times the amount of his. However, if Andy across the street has an allowance that is 10 percent larger, it may be time to renegotiate.

This brings us to a basic principle of comparison. There must be essential similarities between the subjects we are comparing if our comparisons are to produce useful information. As subjects become more and more similar, we must look closer and closer to discover features that distinguish between them. If you have ever tried to get into the wrong automobile in a large parking lot (and had a burglar alarm scream at you for doing so), you have probably discovered some rather subtle features that allow you to distinguish your car from others of the same make and model. The fact that there are many automobiles very similar to yours has made you look more carefully at yours.

We should note here, however, that in saying that subjects of comparison should be similar, we do not mean to imply that this rule should be followed slavishly. At times, writers break it for specific purposes. For example, consider the following very brief essay, which is structured by means of comparison.

MEIR SHALEV
IF BOSNIANS WERE WHALES

1. Wherever I go, I always visit the zoo. That's where I get my preconceived notions about the human race.

2. Not long ago, I visited a marine zoo, the aquarium of Baltimore. The place was lavish and attractive, full of sharks, octopuses, eels and many other fish and varieties of marine life that I did not recognize at first, since they look so different on the grill. The aquarium's planners had obviously realized that a few of the exhibits would whet appetites, for despite the adage "no talking of charcoal in the sheep pen," here and there they'd placed mouth-watering gastronomic descriptions of seafoods.

3. Unlike sea bass and flounder, swordfish and lobster, there are some sea creatures whose flesh Americans refuse to consider edible. In the U.S., quoting the recipe for whale steak from "Moby Dick" is like offering ham braised in butter to a Jew on Yom Kippur. A proud Baltimorean (her mouth stuffed with clams) recently told me of a whale that had drifted too close to shore. It was immediately fished out, resuscitated and flown—at taxpayers' expense—to the Baltimore Aquarium, where it underwent extensive medical treatment, including psychological rehabilitation.

4. Anyone who remembers the whale stuck off Alaska a few years back that had to be freed by an icebreaker and several million dollars will find it difficult

to shake the feeling that whales have simply learned to know a sucker when they see one.

My visit to the aquarium ended with the dolphin pool. The trainers talked to us about the social lives of marine mammals (most complex), about their emotional virtues (they are full of love) and especially about their astonishing intelligence. The brain of the dolphin, for those who don't yet know it, is larger, more complex and, in particular, deeper than the Silly Putty found in the human cranium. Indeed, while we stupid land mammals sat in the bleachers munching popcorn, these gifted marine mammals were performing complex somersaults in midair. Then we were told that dolphins have highly sophisticated "communications systems." As proof, one of them let out a few shrill shrieks for a reward of two mackerel. (The mackerel, as we all know, is not a marine mammal, but a fish and may therefore be eaten.)

We next heard a diatribe against the cruel Japanese tuna fishermen who trap and kill innocent dolphins in their nets. We released a collective moan. It seems that the dolphins have better P.R. people than the tuna: No one asked why it's O.K. to kill tuna.

At the end of my visit, I made a donation to save the dugong and the rain forests and then hurried back to my host's house to watch a movie about the large primates of Africa on the Discovery Channel. It was nice. Especially the end. As a gorilla vanished into the bush, the narrator said, "We have to make this world a better place for the mountain gorilla."

Then he, too, vanished, never realizing that with these words he had articulated the solution to the problem of U.S. intervention in Bosnia. It would, after all, be a bit difficult to convince the public that the Bosnians are marine mammals. But if it were possible to convince them that they are a land species in danger of extinction—a fact not far from the truth—then it might be possible to make this world a better place for the Bosnians, too.

News reports haven't helped the Bosnians. Or the Somalians. Americans have no energy for yet more images of murder, suffering and torture. If I were the leader of the Bosnians, I would kick all the news teams out of Sarajevo and invite the guys from "Survival" to make a nature film about my people. A documentary about the domestic habits of the Bosnians, their mating dances, territorial marking practices, the way they hollow out their lairs, would do the trick.

For a conclusion, the narrator could read: "Only a short time ago, millions of Bosnians grazed the mountainsides of Yugoslavia. Now, only a scant few remain. We have to make this world a better place for the Bosnians." Then, and only then, would the world awaken.

We generally don't think of people and whales as similar. Shalev is using their obvious dissimilarities to illustrate the point that while we have much concern and empathy for certain animals that are very different from us in many respects, we may, at the same time, turn our backs on the suffering of fellow human beings.

Discussion of Shalev's essay brings us to a second basic principle of using comparison—comparison should be purposeful. In comparing your car with other similar cars, you helped ensure that you could find your car in a crowded parking lot. In comparing the way we treat whales with the way we treat suffering Bosnians (the real comparison being made in his essay), Shalev helped raise our awareness of the ongoing crisis in Bosnia and, perhaps, caused us to rethink what the United States was doing to assist in this crisis. Kozol's comparison is also intended to move us to action that would change the dire circumstances of students in inner-city schools.

Exercise 6.8

Comparison is so essential to thinking that you are likely to find it helpful in writing about any information topic. Think of several comparisons relevant to your topic and use them to generate material for your essay. After you have done so, reflect on what purposes these comparisons might serve in your essay.

Causality   When we use causal thinking, we are attempting to see through things, to look in depth at what causes certain phenomena or what effects they have. Causal thinking is fundamental to modern science, of course. But it also pervades our daily existence. We are constantly attempting to figure out the causes for the actions of people in our lives and to determine what the effects of our decisions and actions will be. But causal analysis is not limited to actions and behaviors; we often ponder the causes of our very thoughts and ideas. As an example, in the following exercise we ask you to reflect on some of the causes for your thinking.

Exercise 6.9

Consider the following passage from Jonathan Kozol's "The Human Cost of an Illiterate Society":

> Illiterates cannot read the menu in a restaurant. They cannot read the cost of items on the menu in the window of the restaurant before they enter. Illiterates cannot read the letters that their children bring home from their teachers. They cannot study school department circulars that tell them of the courses that their children must be taking if they hope to write a letter to the teacher. They are afraid to visit in the classroom. They do not want to humiliate their child or themselves.

In this sample passage, Jonathan Kozol outlines some of the ways in which illiteracy affects people. Can you think of additional effects illiteracy might have on a person? Brainstorm for a few minutes, noting every possible effect of illiteracy you can think of. After you have written your list, look over the list on page 255, from the rest of Kozol's essay; then answer these questions: How does your list compare with Kozol's? What significant effects did you see that Kozol did not mention? What effects did Kozol mention that you did not imagine? After you have answered these questions, consider the implications of your findings. What caused you to see things that Kozol did not see? What caused you to overlook effects that Kozol saw?

> Other things that people who are illiterate cannot do, according to Jonathan Kozol in "The Human Cost of an Illiterate Society":
>
> read instructions on prescription medicine
> understand the written details on a health insurance form
> read waivers they sign before surgical procedures
> read lease agreements
> manage checking accounts
> use mail
> read notices from welfare offices and the IRS
> look up numbers in the telephone directory
> read the admonition on a pack of cigarettes
> identify no-name (and thus cheaper) products, since illiterate people depend on pictures and logos
> distinguish between products with similar labels
> read instructions for cooking food
> travel freely, because they can't read traffic signs, street names, and bus schedules
> read TV programming information

In the preceding exercise, we asked you to examine the causes of something very abstract: your thought processes. Why do you suppose you listed the things you listed? Did you leave out what now seem to you to be significant effects? Why? Perhaps you feel that Kozol's analysis of potential causes and effects is problematic. If so, what makes you feel this way? Could Kozol be guilty of exaggerating? What motivations might he have for doing so?

Exercise 6.10

Generate more material for your essay by exploring the role of causality in your thinking. You may want to return to the sequence and consequence questions in our questions for analysis (pages 24–32). We do not want to confuse chronological relations with causal relations—and hence be guilty of a logical fallacy (see pages 467–470). However, whenever one event follows another, it is worth asking whether there is a causal relationship between the two events.

Analysis   Analysis is a process by which we break something into components, or parts, to see how they fit together to function as a whole. For example, we can divide a personal computer (PC) system into CPU (central processing unit) and peripherals (e.g., monitor, printer, scanner, modem). To analyze those components further, we can look at the makeup of each. What kind of "brain" does the motherboard have—what kind of chip, what kind of graphics support, what kind of ports, what kind of BIOS? how much memory (RAM) does it have? Once we begin to break a subject into its parts, we can examine each in detail based on the criteria we have established for this scrutiny.

An essay in our book that uses analysis very effectively is Kendra Stead's "The Making of Spells" (pages 303–306). Kendra divides the poem she is writing about, Margaret Atwood's "Spelling" (pages 296–297), into six sections and then discusses each of these sections in detail. At the end of her analysis, Kendra comes to feel that Atwood's poem is "an intricate, muti-layered poem . . . [that] speaks of the historical suppression of women's language, . . . [and also] screams of progress." Her analysis of the structure of this poem is crucial to her ability to understand and explain the meaning of this complicated poem.

> **Exercise 6.11**
>
> Generate more material for your information essay by using analysis. If your topic can be seen as a whole, break it into its parts. If not, find some aspect of your topic that can be analyzed into its parts. Then discuss what you learn about your topic by means of this analysis.

Classification   Classification requires grouping like things with like to determine in which class a particular thing belongs. The following are classes into which students in your college may be placed:

  major
  college or school (e.g., College of Arts and Sciences, School of Business and
    Economics, Graduate School)
  gender
  ethnicity
  class (e.g., freshman, graduate student)
  residence status (in-state, out-of-state, foreign)
  admission status (e.g., provisional, probationary, regular)

A given student could fit in any of these classes; for example, a student could be described as an in-state, female, Hispanic, junior English major with regular status in the College of Arts and Sciences.

We form classes by looking at several different things and finding certain ones that share important traits or characteristics. Once we have enough items sharing important attributes, we can form a class and say that all items possessing these attributes belong in that class. As an example, consider the following lists. Which elements of each list are similar enough to be grouped together? What is the basis of your decision; that is, what is the principle on which you based your classification?

> marlin, sailfish, shark, manta ray, largemouth bass
> Ford Mustang, Saturn, Honda Civic, Lincoln Town Car, Buick Skylark, Honda Accord, Cadillac DeVille, Toyota Corolla, Ford Thunderbird

The first list consists of fish. While the largemouth bass is a freshwater fish, all the others live in saltwater. So all but the bass can be grouped, with the basis of the grouping being what kind of water the fishes live in. Of course, someone very knowledgeable about fish might find other ways of grouping those entries. The second list consists of various types of automobile, and its entries may be grouped in several ways. For one, they could be grouped by manufacturer: the Ford Mustang, Ford Thunderbird, and Lincoln Town Car are made by Ford; the Cadillac DeVille, Saturn, and Buick Skylark by General Motors; the Honda Civic and Honda Accord by Honda; the Toyota Corolla by Toyota. Further, they could by grouped by U.S. and non-U.S. car companies. Or they could be grouped in still other ways: the DeVille and Town Car are relatively expensive and luxurious; the Mustang and Thunderbird are sporty; the Skylark and Accord are relatively inexpensive full-sized cars; the Saturn and Corolla are more economical autos.

A powerful process, classification helps us create order by enabling us to identify some new aspect of our experience as being like something we've already experienced. For example, you were able to get started in your college classes because you've been a student for a number of years already. Although college classes differ from high school classes, there are enough similarities (e.g., a teacher, textbooks, homework, and classmates) that you could feel at least some comfort in knowing that a new course would be like other courses you had taken.

In her essay, Gloria Naylor used classification to sort out the ways the word "nigger" was used by the adults in her childhood community. To create each class, Naylor reflected on the many times she had heard the term used and grouped those that had important similarities; in doing so, she was able to gain insight into this community. This process can be an important tool for order and insight in your writing.

Exercise 6.12

Try classifying key objects or concepts in the paper you're writing. Can you find more than one basis on which to form these classes? Will these classifications help you convey your information to your readers? Why or why not?

Definition In defining, we often make use of both classification and comparison. Classical definition is a natural process we use when we try to give a concise statement of what a particular thing or concept is. We first place the term to be defined in a class and then modify it with some type of phrase or clause, usually an implied comparison or contrast between the item to be defined and other items in the class. For example, we might define a *peninsula* (term to be defined) as a body of land (class) surrounded by water on three sides (modifying phrase, which contrasts peninsulas with other bodies of land, such as islands and continents).

Definition can play an important role in structuring an essay, as we can see by looking at the thesis of Arthur Rosenfeld's "Should Anyone Have to Live in Pain?" (page 214).

> Addiction is a serious disease while dependence is an unavoidable side effect.

Rosenfeld's basic argument is that failure to understand the difference between these conditions, addiction and dependence, is at the center of the confusion that keeps many sufferers from getting the relief that is available to them.

There is a second type of definition, known as stipulative definition. This kind of definition is one that stipulates or establishes a particular meaning for a term, and it is used to make readers aware of the specific definition the writer will use in talking about a term that is potentially ambiguous. For example, in an essay about education, a writer may stipulate that for her purposes "satisfactory progress" will be defined as "work that has been judged at the 'C' level or above." By stipulating such a definition, the writer works to clarify the information for her reader.

> **Exercise 6.13**
>
> Use both classical and stipulative definitions to clarify the meaning of key terms in your essay. Which method of defining proves more helpful? What makes it effective?

Mode as a Tool for Shaping Even though any piece of expository writing will likely contain several modes of discourse, we can usually point to a dominant mode that provides the primary structure of that writing. As we saw in Chapter 5, narration and description often provide the overall structure for essays that spotlight the writer and her experiences. In essays focusing on the subject, the expository modes—process, comparison, causality, analysis, classification, and definition—provide structure.

As an example, let's look at the structure of the sample essay presented at the end of this chapter, "All in a Day's Work: Generalizing, Profiling, and Stereotyping" (pages 267–269). The writer, Michael Graham, begins with a narrative about an event that happened one Friday while he was working on his job at a retail store. As he reflects on what happened that day, he begins to analyze his experience and define what he did that day as "profiling." From there he moves, in paragraph two, to more analysis of what he does on a daily basis in his job at that store. In doing so, he makes use of causal reasoning as he attempts to decide what causes him to profile certain people in one way and others in another way. As he moves to his third paragraph, Michael begins to compare the type of profiling he does on his job with the profiling he does in his daily life.

It should be clear that Michael is making full use of the modes of discourse. He has moved from a narrative (which in this case is the "process" he went through to check people out) to analysis, definition, causal analysis, and comparison. What has he omitted? Oh yes, classification. But not really, since the act of profiling has involved comparing various people and putting them into classes of people in order to determine which classes are more likely to shoplift.

But what is the overall structuring mode of Michael's essay? In order to answer this question, we have to determine his overall aim for writing this essay. As we look carefully at this essay, we see that he wants to examine the right ways and wrong ways to profile people. In order to do so, he has to define carefully two types of profiling—generalizing and stereotyping. Thus, the major structuring device for Michael's essay is definition: his essay will serve as a definition of the three key terms that appear in his subtitle.

Exercise 6.14

Now that you have seen our overview of the structure of "All in a Day's Work," try your hand at doing such an analysis of one of the other essays presented in this chapter or of some other essay selected by your instructor. What is (are) the controlling mode(s) for this essay?

As you no doubt discovered in the preceding exercise, modal analysis is not an exact science. Our purpose in suggesting that you attempt an analysis is to illustrate that a writer's selection of modes is connected to her aim. There is a sense in which we are always unsure of claims we might make about the purposes of other writers. However, we can be sure of our own purposes. And that is the point of this discussion—to help you connect your sense of purpose to the overall structure of your essay. As you plan your essay, you may find it useful to determine which modal structure provides the overall shape of your essay.

Thesis Statement

At this point, you are ready to write a tentative thesis statement for your essay. As we discussed in Chapter 2, your thesis may or may not appear in the final draft of your essay. For now, state your thesis so that it reveals the basic structure of your essays. For example, the following are possible thesis statements for three of the essays presented at the beginning of this chapter.

> The natural human *fear* of death is part of the *cause* of the dehumanized treatment of patients in modern hospitals.
> Elisabeth Kübler-Ross, "On the Fear of Dying"

> The meaning (and power) of words *is caused* by the ways in which communities use those words.
>   Gloria Naylor, "Mommy, What Does 'Nigger' Mean?"

> Addiction to painkillers and dependence on painkillers are two very different conditions.

Of course, none of these sentences actually appears in the essays in question. We have framed the sentences so that they reveal the writers' structuring devices. In the body of her essay, Kübler-Ross makes much use of comparison, juxtaposing the way terminal patients used to be treated with the ways they are treated in modern hospitals, but the key structuring device of her essay is cause—the fear of death partly *causes* the impersonal treatment of the dying in our culture. Like Kübler-Ross, Naylor uses cause as the primary structuring agent of her essay—the various meanings of words come about as a result of (*are caused by*) the ways in which people use language. There is, of course, much reliance on definition and classification in the body of Naylor's essay where she outlines these various meanings. In "Should Anyone Have to Live in Pain?" Rosenfeld spends much time narrating the suffering of individuals who would have no quality of life without proper pain medication. However, the main thrust of his essay is to define the key terms "dependence" and "addiction," so that his readers can understand why doctors sometimes refuse pain medications to those who need them.

Refining Your Writing

After you've written a draft of your essay and taken some time away from it, revise it, keeping the following principles in mind.

> *Audience.* How appropriate is your chosen audience for this paper? Check to see that you have not assumed any knowledge this audience will not have and that you have not included material they will already know.
>
> *Organization.* Which mode provides the overriding organization for your paper? For example, do you rely more heavily on process than on comparison or perhaps more heavily on causality than on process? Make a list that describes the primary mode at work in each paragraph. How effectively does this structure work with your topic? With your reader?
>
> *Thesis.* How effectively does your thesis provide insight into the order of your essay; that is, how effectively does your thesis reveal or predict your essay's structure as a guide for your reader?
>
> *Clarity.* How appropriate is the language for your audience? Identify any jargon you may have used. How clearly will that jargon communicate to a reader who isn't as familiar with the topic as you are? Would headings be helpful in guiding your reader through the essay?

SAMPLE STUDENT PROCESS

The essay below was written by Michael Graham, a first-year writing student at UNC Charlotte. Below we present Michael's freewriting, his focus statement, his discovery draft, his thesis statement, and the draft he turned in to Ron for the information assignment, labeled *Second Draft*. The last draft presented below, which we have labeled as *Final Draft,* was Michael's revision of his information essay for his end-of-course portfolio.

Prewriting

Michael began his paper with an in-class freewriting. The first writing below was done in response to Part A.1. on page 241.

Judging or Profiling People

I hate watching Americans who profile or judge people because of what they wear or the color of their skin. I work at a large department store as a security officer and standing back and looking on the requirements of that job or any law enforcement job I can tell why they profile or judge people but I also have the side that says that it is wrong. Most Americans point to the cops and so forth as the ones who commit this unjust act but all American practice this judgment on people. When children go to school they are judge by their classmates on who their friends are and what they like and what they wear. Social groups are formed for either dislike or interest in something. However other groups are formed to judge those groups. Adults do the same thing. At work people talk about what others have done recently or in the past and then pass judgment on them. I don't know . . . thinking . . . Race is another way of judging people because if a minority is walking down the road the amount of . . . .

Next Michael did Part A.2. on page 241. As suggested he began by focusing on an idea found in his first freewriting. The underlined phrases in the passage above are passages that Michael had circled. He began with the last underscored phrase, Race is another way of judging people and did a five-minute freewrite.

Race as a Judging Factor

Race is used by every single ethnic group as a way of judging people based on their skin. Granted that within different ethnic groups there are cultural differences. However people in todays world judge people by stereotyping them into what they may like or what they may do, based on their race. If a child is raised to believe that a certain minority or ethnic group is bad for example then they will feel this way about every one of that group. Basically they take a single action and change it into a generalization where people are stereotyped. This leads to problems in the past causing people today to be stereotyped or judge . . . I don't know what to say, thinking, . . . People today are expected to talk, act, and dress depending on their ethnic group and if they don't then they are not normal and are judged. This is wrong. People should have the freedom to be what they want. Just because person wears certain . . . .

Focus Statement

After doing these freewrites, Michael wrote the following focus statement for his paper:

> I want to write about the time when I profiled someone. I then want to discuss the use of profiling and its advantages and disadvantages. I also want the reader to see the comparison between profiling and stereotyping. I will concentrate on race, gender, and social status. I want to show why groups profile.

Discovery Draft

At this point, Michael wrote a discovery draft. Since he still had not settled on a thesis for his paper, this draft is somewhat like a focused freewrite.

1   I work at a local retail store as a security associate and my job is to prevent unpurchased merchandise from leaving the store, as well as to assist the undercover associates in preventing theft. I remember it was a normal day at work, the usual busy Friday. Customers were entering the store one after the other and I was in my normal robotic sense of thinking. I was tired of standing on my feet for eight hours answering the same questions over and over, "Yes ma'am I work here." As people came into the store I watched them and alerted the undercover security officials if I saw anyone suspicious. One day this normal task caught me off guard. I became suspicious when I noticed a man enter the store wearing holy jeans and a dirty t-shirt. I discovered that I was profiling him as to whether or not he had the potential to steal. All Americans, either for positive or negative purposes, have profiled people based on their gender, race, and social status.

2   Stealing is just one of the many ways Americans form generalizations about people. I began to wonder that day why I profile people by their differences, but more importantly why other Americans do it everyday. I began to notice that I would call my associates more frequently if the "suspicious" customer was a male rather than a female. "Why did I do this?" I asked myself. Rationale tells me that in the business that I am in, males have been caught shoplifting more frequently than females. However, is it because they are watched more, or is it just because males steal more? I do not profile based on gender alone, but ponder the possibilities of what a person would steal based on their gender. Women, for example, would be more susceptible to steal clothing, or to change the prices of clothing. Males are more willing to steal higher priced merchandise that usually comes from the electronics department. Age in any situation is a factor to how people are profiled. A juvenile female is more likely to steal cosmetics, whereas a juvenile male is more likely to steal a compact disc. In a way I was fascinated by how much I thought about people unconsciously. I never want to judge a person by their gender, but the demands of the job cause me to be alert.

3   If Americans were more alert they would notice that they profile as much as a security officer. A person's generalizations are built upon how they perceive a person's characteristics or actions in a particular environment. "This is changing," you may say. It has been changing since the beginning of time yet it still serves a

useful purpose. For example, if a young lady was walking her dog and noticed a man stumbling down the street towards her carrying a beer bottle, she would become frightened and quickly enter the house. By generalizing this man's characteristics she successfully avoided a potentially threatening situation. On the other hand if a young lady was walking her dog in the same conditions and became frightened by the sight of a man walking down the street, then the lady had generalized men as threatening. In the previous example, generalizing is used in a specific reference to a set of characteristics, whereas, in the second example an entire gender is generalized without the threatening characteristics. The second example is a stereotype, where men are placed into a group that represents danger, therefore, creating a negative perspective of men. Generalizing, like profiling, can cause either positive or negative connections between how people are acting and the intent of their actions.

Race is an area where cultural groups are viewed as being a reflection of their characteristics. I can remember working with an individual who gave me the sense of racism in his voice. It happened one day, when a female was caught stealing by one of our security associates. Her husband, who was with her, was the one who placed the merchandise in her purse. We are only allowed to apprehend customers if the merchandise is on them, therefore, we could not have apprehended the husband. My associate later stated to me that he wished we could have apprehended the husband instead of the wife. This would not have bothered me except for the fact that the couple was interracial. I asked myself, "Did he do this because the male is of a different race, or because he put the merchandise in the purse?" I was terrified of working with an individual that people called a racist.

Racism is a social undercurrent that affects every individual, whether they know about it or not. A large majority of racism is caused by the simple fact that ethnic groups get blamed because of a select few. It is unbelievable that when one member of an ethic group is being racist towards another cultural group, then the whole ethnic group is labeled as racists. Racism will always be evident, because every individual has his or her own beliefs, but racism committed consciously is another matter. I would hate to be in an ethnic group that had to experience racial discrimination on a daily basis. However, profiling serves a purpose if used correctly. In a given moment it is impossible to survey everyone; therefore, certain characteristics must be evident in order to provide attention. On the other hand, this system also may be used to create stereotypes of ethnic groups, where one is seen as a higher risk than others. For example, if an African American came into a store and displayed characteristics of a thief, such as walking quickly to one area or looking around repeatedly, a security office would become suspicious. However, if an African American entered the store and did not display these characteristics and the security officer felt as if the person was suspicious, then that officer has generalized that person in a negative way. It becomes a negative practice when people believe that all members of an ethnic group share similar characteristics.

An expectation in one's social status is an area that I find is a large factor in my profiling at work. It is expected that people who dress or act as if they are in a high social position do not have the need to steal. However, a person who is of the lower social class is seen as a potential thief. I have experienced this concept to be true in some occasions when people did not have enough money to pay for the merchandise. There was one night that I was working when a group of young adults entered the store. By the way they were dressed, I imagined that they were well off. It turned out that they got caught for shoplifting. Profiling is a way for people in my profession to narrow down the suspects, because they cannot monitor everyone. However, this situation makes the system look as if it is not reliable and trustworthy, which is not true.

Society's system of profiling does not involve trying to protect a company's assets; it involves personal opinions. When I am at work I strive not to make personal opinions about people. However, society has developed the concept that if a person is not in the upper class then they have failed in life. This trend causes assumptions that if you observed two individuals walking beside each other, but one had on an expensive business suit, whereas the other individual had on faded jeans and a t-shirt, you would suspect the businessman to be more successful. This can be destructive generalization for anyone to experience and it can also be rewarding. A person can take this generalization in one of two ways. First they could say to themselves, "I will work hard and try my best to succeed." In doing so they have overcome the negative aspect of this generalization, which is to say, "I am not as important because I do not live a luxurious lifestyle." Social status can either be used as a way to move upward in society by trying harder or it can be used to limit ones opinion of success. I view social status as this: parents want their children to do, and go far beyond, what they did, and not go through the hard times they encountered. However, the cycle has to start over sometime, and for some the beginning is harder, or at a lower point.

In society generalizations can serve two purpose, to promote a sense of being a part of a unique group or to limit a person's progress in life. It hurts to be a part of an American wide epidemic that has infested itself in our society. However, this epidemic can have a positive treatment or it can be used to kill.

Michael's teacher (Ron) wrote the following comment at the end of this draft:

Michael,
As I said in class, this is certainly a workable topic. To this point, you haven't been able to make your overall purpose clear. Let's have a conference and talk about where you want to take the paper.

In their conference, Ron and Michael discussed specifically the need for a stronger thesis sentence than he had provided, one that would focus on the potential usefulness of profiling. Following the conference, Michael devised this thesis: "Although the acceptability of profiling depends on one's purposes for using it, profiling can be a useful tool." Michael then produced the following draft and submitted it to satisfy the course requirement that he write an information essay.

Thesis Sentence

Although the acceptability of profiling depends on one's purposes for using it, profiling can be a useful tool.

Second Draft

I work at a local retail store as a security associate and my job is to prevent exposed un-purchased merchandise from leaving the store, as well as to assist the undercover associates in apprehending dishonest individuals. I remember it was a normal day at work, the usual busy Friday. Customers were entering the store one after the other, and I was in my normal robotic sense of thinking. I was tired of standing on my feet for eight hours answering the same questions over and over, "Yes ma'am I work here." As people came into the store I watched them and alerted the undercover security officials if I saw anyone suspicious. One day I noticed a man enter the store wearing holey jeans and a dirty t-shirt and I immediately became suspicious. I discovered that day I had profiled that man as to whether or not he had the potential to steal. All Americans, either for positive or negative purposes, have profiled people based on their gender, race, and physical appearance.

People profile on the basis of many different factors; one's honesty is but one of these bases. I began to question why I profile people at work and the way in which I profile people, but more importantly I questioned why Americans do it every day. I began to notice that I would notify my co-workers more frequently if the "suspicious" customer were a male rather than a female. "Why did I do this? I asked myself. Rationale tells me that in the business that I am in, males have been caught shoplifting more frequently than females. Does this occur because security officers watch males more frequently and ignore females or does it occur because males just simply steal more? When I am at work, I use generalizations about a person's gender, based on prior experiences, as the basis of my profiling. Women, for example, would be profiled as being more susceptible to steal clothing, or to change the prices of the clothing. Males are more willing to steal higher priced merchandise that usually comes from the electronics department. Generalizations concerning age are always a factor in how a person is profiled. A juvenile female is viewed as being more likely to steal cosmetics, whereas a juvenile male is viewed as being more likely to steal a compact disc. In a way, I was fascinated by how much I thought about people unconsciously. I never want to judge a person by their gender, but the demands of the job cause me to be alert.

Americans profile in many different situations and as noted above, profiling may be positive or negative. Profiling is in essence a type of generalization. A person's generalizations about some group of individuals are based on characteristics or actions of a small number of individuals in that group, or in some cases of only one individual. For example, if a young lady walking her dog notices a man stumbling down the street toward her carrying a beer bottle, she would flee. She has no doubt seen enough stumbling men with beer bottles to make a generalization that all stumbling men with beer bottles should be avoided. On the other hand, what if the young lady walking her dog saw a well-dressed and completely sober young man, and was immediately frightened of him? We would see no reason for her to be frightened and we would say that she has stereotyped men as bad. We would say this even though she may have had bad experiences with one (or even several) men. One should not label an entire gender on the basis of the actions of a few members of that gender. But isn't that what I was doing when I was "profiling" all men as more likely to steal than women? Or is it? Is profiling always stereotyping, or can it be a legitimate type of generalization?

A person's race is often believed to predict an individual's or a group's actions and the individuals within each race are believed to share common characteristics. This is where the difference between stereotyping and profiling is established. I once worked with an individual who gave me the feeling that he was a racist because of the way he talked about different races. My awareness of my co-worker's racism occurred one day when a female was caught stealing but her husband was the one who placed the merchandise in her pocketbook. Although he placed the merchandise in her purse, my company's policy only allows us to apprehend the individual who has the merchandise concealed. After the incident was over my co-worker stated to me that he wished we could have apprehended the husband instead of the wife. This statement would not normally bother me because it is a frustrating situation to be in, but the couple was interracial and the male was of a different race than my co-worker. Judging by the tone of his voice and the fact that he whispered it to me, I believed that the basis of his statement was because of the difference in race. I became terrified of working with this individual because if a person thought he was making racist comments then they would associate his job with racism. I would now become stereotyped as being a racist because we shared one thing in common, our job.

Racism affects how each person views other individuals, or groups of individuals in society. Profiling can serve a useful purpose because in a given moment it is impossible to watch everyone, therefore, certain characteristics must be displayed to provoke attention. If a person's alertness to a potential problem is based on characteristics associated with the problem, then profiling is being used effectively. However, this same system often runs into the problem mentioned above, which is people make connections between individuals and larger groups, in particular racial groups. If a person's alertness to a potential problem is based on a common racial group instead of an individual's characteristics, then profiling is being used as a way of stereotyping groups of people. For example, if an African American came into a store and displayed common characteristics of a thief, such as, walking quickly to one area or looking around repeatedly, then a security officer may pay attention to that person. In this situation, profiling was used to help pick this person's threatening characteristics out of a crowd of people and have some basis for watching this individual. However, if the same African American entered the store and did not display these characteristics and the same security officer pays close attention to this individual, then that security officer has used a personal stereotype and not a set of common characteristics as the basis of their investigation. Profiling becomes a negative process when individuals stereotype all members of an entire group as having similar negative characteristics.

Generalizing people by their physical characteristics or how people are dressed is often used to profile how people will act. For example, if an individual dressed in a business suit entered a retail store, they could be viewed as having a low risk of stealing, based on their appearance. However, if the individual stated above entered the retail store wearing dirty jeans and a holey shirt, then that individual could be viewed as having a higher risk of stealing. Profiling used to predict a person's actions based on their physical appearance can be used in a positive way. If a security officer were in a situation where two individuals acted as if they were going to attempt to steal, then profiling would be a vital tool to decide which individual should be watched. The use of profiling in the above situation is used effectively because there was an obvious need to profile the individuals. However, when the security officer profiles every individual on the basis of his or her physical appearance, then it is no longer profiling, but becomes stereotyping. Stereotyping people based on their physical characteristics causes negative assumptions about every single member of a distinct group.

In society, generalizations can be used to profile a person by their characteristics or generalizations can be used to stereotype an entire group of people as having a common set of negative characteristics. The purpose behind the generalization can have a positive effect, profiling, or can have a negative effect, stereotyping. But, all Americans form some type of generalization of people based on that individual's gender, race, or physical appearance. 7

Michael submitted this paper as the final draft for the assignment. Ron reviewed the draft and offered these comments:

> Michael,
> You have done a good job of revising here. Your essay's focus is tighter; overall, it seems more unified and coherent than your rough draft did. You may want to revise this essay for your portfolio. If you do, be sure to pay attention to word choice and sentence structure.

Michael decided to continue working on the essay and revised it for his end-of-semester portfolio, submitting the following draft:

Final Draft

Michael Graham
ALL IN A DAY'S WORK: GENERALIZING, PROFILING, AND STEREOTYPING

I work at a local retail store as a security associate and my job is to prevent theft. I also assist the undercover associates in apprehending shoplifters. I remember it was a normal day at work, the usual busy Friday. Customers were entering the store one after the other, and I was in my normal robotic state. I was tired of standing on my feet for eight hours answering the same questions over and over: "Yes ma'am, I work here." As people came into the store I alerted the 1 undercover security officials if I noticed anyone suspicious. That day a man entered the store wearing holey jeans and a dirty t-shirt, and I immediately became suspicious. Something else happened that day. As I reflected on what I was doing, I discovered that I had profiled that man as to whether he had the potential to steal. I was using profiling as a tool for doing my job, but I now realize that all of us use it in our everyday lives. Honesty is but one of the characteristics that we may attempt to determine by means of profiling. There are many others. And we may use various strategies to create these profiles.

That day I began to question why, and how, I profile people at work. I began to notice that I would notify my co-workers more frequently if the "suspicious" customer were a male rather than a female. But why? My experience in the business has made it clear that males are caught shoplifting more frequently than females. But does this occur because security officers watch males more frequently and ignore females, or do males just simply steal more? This is a difficult question to answer, but some differences between males and females seem rather clear. For example, females are more likely to steal clothing or to change the prices of the clothing. Males are more willing to steal higher priced merchandise that usually comes from the electronics department. Generalizations concerning age combine with those about gender to provide profilers with useful information. A juvenile female is more likely to steal cosmetics, whereas a juvenile male is more likely to steal a compact disc. As I reflected on this profiling, I was fascinated by how much I "knew" about people as a result of these factors. I never want to judge a person on the basis of gender or age, but the demands of the job force me to be alert.

As I thought about this issue, I realized that I also use profiling in my everyday life. We all do. It can be a good and useful thing or it can be very damaging, depending on our purposes and our criteria for profiling. In essence, profiling involves generalizing. A person's generalizations about a particular group of individuals are usually based upon characteristics of only a few individuals within that group. But some generalizations are more acceptable than others. For example, if a young lady walking her dog noticed a man stumbling down the street towards her carrying a beer bottle, she would flee. She has no doubt seen enough stumbling men with beer bottles to make a generalization that all stumbling men with beer bottles should be avoided. On the other hand, what if the young lady walking her dog saw a well-dressed and completely sober young man, and was immediately frightened of him? We would see no reason for her to be frightened, and we would say that she has stereotyped men as bad. We would say this even though she may have had unpleasant experiences with one man, or even several men. One should not label an entire gender on the basis of the actions of a few members of that gender. But isn't that what I was doing when I was "profiling" all males as more likely to steal than females? Or is it?

If we want to establish differences between stereotyping and profiling, issues of race provide a good starting point. Sometimes people believe that one's race is indicative of his characteristics or actions. I once worked with an individual who made me uncomfortable in the way he talked about different races. His racism began to become apparent one day when a female was caught stealing. As it turned out, her husband actually placed the merchandise in her pocketbook, but even though we knew that, we knew that we could only charge the individual who had the merchandise concealed. After the incident was over, my co-worker said that he wished we could have apprehended the husband instead of the wife. This statement would not normally bother me, because this is a frustrating situation to be in. But in this case I was troubled by the fact that the husband, in the interracial couple, was African-American while my co-worker was white. My co-worker's tone, together with the fact that he was whispering to me, convinced me that his comments were racially motivated. I no longer wanted to work with this individual, for fear that I would be associated with his racism.

Racism prevents people from seeing each other as individuals. We must avoid racism, and it would be good if we could always treat other people as individuals. But there are times and situations when this is not possible. In the work-related situations I have discussed above, it is not possible to watch every person all the time. In these situations, profiles can serve a useful purpose; however, problems arise when people use shortcuts such as race. For example, if a person from a minority race came into a store and displayed common characteristics of a thief, such as walking quickly from one area to another or looking around repeatedly, then a security officer might pay attention to that person. In this situation, the person is profiled according to his characteristics, that is, the way he is behaving. However, if the same minority person entered the store without exhibiting these behaviors and was singled out for attention on the basis of his minority status, the person profiling him would be guilty of racial stereotyping. Profiling becomes a negative process when individuals stereotype all members of an entire group as having similar negative characteristics.

Profilers often use appearance as a basis for generalizing. For example, if an individual dressed in a business suit entered a retail store, he might be seen as unlikely to steal. However, if the same individual entered the retail store wearing dirty jeans and a holey shirt, he might seem much more likely to steal. There is nothing inherently wrong with this kind of profiling, if it is done with care. If a security officer were in a situation where two individuals exhibited behaviors associated with theft and if one of them was clean and well-dressed and the other was not, the profiler might decide which person to focus his attention on based on appearance. However, profilers should avoid stereotyping as dishonest all people who cannot afford to dress expensively.

Generalizing can be a very useful tool when used wisely, as is the case in the kinds of profiling I have discussed above. However, generalizations that are used as shortcuts have the effect of labeling all members of a group on the basis of the negative actions of a few members of that group. This kind of generalization is called stereotyping because it tends to type people according to their gender, race, or physical appearance.

CHECKLIST: CRITIQUING AN INFORMATION ESSAY

1. What is the essay's topic?
2. What assertion does the writer make about this topic; what is the essay's thesis? Summarize the thesis in your own words. How effectively does the thesis make its assertion?
3. How clear is the essay's organization? What mode provides the overall structure for the essay? Are transitions clear and effective? Are paragraphs unified and cohesive? Are the introduction and conclusion effective?
4. Who is the audience for the essay? Will the essay's information be interesting to and/or needed by this audience? Is the language of the essay appropriate for this audience?
5. Identify places in the paper you think are particularly strong. What makes them effective?
6. Identify places in the paper you think need work. What revisions need to be made?
7. Does the paper adhere to conventions of usage, mechanics, and format? Correct any errors you find.

Jacob Lawrence, "Strike," 1949. Howard University Gallery of Art, Washington, DC. © 2008 the Jacob and Gwendolyn Knight Lawrence Foundation, Seattle/Artists Rights Society (ARS), New York, NY.

CHAPTER 7

Essays *About* and *From* Literature

Why do we read literature? What does it do for us? We may read for pleasure—for the adventure of a technothriller, for the love story of a popular romance, for the humor in an intentionally funny story. We may read to learn, to gain insight into the life and times the writer depicts. And we may read to wonder, to ponder what the writer may be trying to tell us about how we should be. When we read serious literature, our task is to attempt to understand what the writer is saying to us.

Exercise 7.1

In the title essay of *The Philosophy of Literary Form,* 3rd edition (Berkeley: University of California Press, 1973), Kenneth Burke uses the word "poetry" to stand for all types of literature. He defines poetry as "any work of a critical or imaginative cast" (page 1). Poetry in this broad sense encompasses not only poems, but also short stories, novels, plays, and even nonfiction prose. Later in his essay, Burke says that poetry is "produced for purposes of comfort," that it is "equipment for living," and that it "would protect us" (page 61). In a short response, explain what Burke might have meant in saying that literature might comfort us. How might it protect us?

What pieces of literature have you read that you might think of as "equipment for living"? How did they comfort or protect you?

Burke's definition of literature as "equipment for living" includes writing that invites interpretation and that deals with important issues people face. In this sense, his definition would not encompass such escapist writing as a technothriller or a romance. We don't mean to say that we always know where to draw the line between serious literature and escapist writing; it's probably better to think of works as arranged on a continuum than to think of discrete categories.

We also don't mean to say that escapist works aren't worth reading. However, literature that we would deem worthy of study in the classroom tends to require more (rather than less) interpretation and tends to deal with important issues humans face. A detective novel may hold you spellbound, but in reading it, you're engaged in trying to figure out "who done it." Once you solve the mystery, you've satisfied your curiosity and been entertained, but you haven't necessarily learned anything about your life or the lives of other people. On the other hand, a poem by Robert Frost, a short story by Joyce Carol Oates, or a novel by Rudolfo Anaya is more likely to engage you in trying to figure out what the writer meant or what that piece of literature means to you. By writing in response to such works, you'll be engaged in this process of determining their meaning and, thus, in equipping yourself with knowledge that can help you live your life.

How do we respond to literary texts? As the title of this chapter reveals, we'll consider two primary ways of responding: writing *about* literature and writing *from* literature. Writing *about* literature results in an interpretive essay, a formal paper in which the writer offers and supports her opinion of what a work means. On the other hand, writing *from* literature allows a writer to use the text as a springboard to a paper that is really about her or some event or situation in her life. In such an essay, the literary text provides the context in which the essay is set, but the essay's focus in on a topic beyond the text.

What shape will this paper take? One kind of essay *from* literature is akin to the personal essay we discussed in Chapter 5. Have you ever read a poem or story and realized that you have had an experience similar to that of one of the characters? Have you found any help from a poem or story in solving a problem? Have you applied some aspect of a poem or story to your dealings with other people? An essay written *from* a piece of literature will move from the literature to your experience, talk about the problem situation and how it worked out, or offer a narrative account of your dealings with others, presenting your experiences in light of those presented in the literature from which you are writing.

Other kinds of essays *from* literature are possible as well. If a literary text correlates with a situation in your community, for example, you could write an essay in which you evaluate some event or situation. Or your essay could involve you in solving a problem. Let's assume that one of your favorite teachers is under attack because his teaching style is quirky, unorthodox, or even radical. If you've read Louanne Johnson's *My Posse Don't Do Homework* (the book on which the movie *Dangerous Minds* was based), then you might point to Johnson's experiences as evidence that out-of-the-ordinary teaching and unusual responses to student needs sometimes work better than more traditional methods of instruction. And you could draw on this book as a resource in writing a defense of your teacher as

1. a personal essay, in which you recount and then assess his influence on you,
2. an essay evaluating the quality of his teaching, or
3. an essay that examines the problems he confronts (e.g., a lawsuit-wary school board or an unimaginative principal or department chair) and then offers a

solution (e.g., comprehensive evaluation of teaching by a committee of teachers instead of a single administrator).

Although you will most often write *about* literature during your college career, both types of responses are valid. Whether writing *from* or *about,* you will begin with the piece of literature, reading the text closely and then working with it to see what it means to you. At the end of this chapter, we'll offer two options for a formal essay: one writing *about* literature, the other writing *from* literature. Whichever option you choose, you'll begin by reading a piece of literature carefully and then analyzing it to see what it says or means to you.

SAMPLE WORKS OF LITERATURE

In this section, we present literary selections. Specifically, we have included two short stories and five poems. These works represent a range of good writing and may serve as topics for essays *about* and *from* literature. As you read these literary works, refer back to the reading strategies we offer in Chapter 4 to help you explore the meaninig in each text.

Our first story, "Shopping," is by Joyce Carol Oates, a noted American fiction writer.

JOYCE CAROL OATES
SHOPPING

An old ritual, Saturday morning shopping. Mother and daughter. Mrs. Dietrich and Nola. Shops in the village, stores and boutiques at the splendid Livingstone Mall on Route 12. Bloomingdale's, Saks, Lord & Taylor, Bonwit's, Neiman-Marcus: and the rest. Mrs. Dietrich would know her way around the stores blindfolded but there is always the surprise of lavish seasonal displays, extraordinary holiday sales, the openings of new stores at the Mall like Laura Ashley, Paraphernalia. On one of their Mall days Mrs. Dietrich and Nola would try to get there at midmorning, have lunch around 1 P.M. at one or another of their favorite restaurants, shop for perhaps an hour after lunch, then come home. Sometimes the shopping trips were more successful than at other times but you have to have faith, Mrs. Dietrich tells herself. Her interior voice is calm, neutral, free of irony. Ever since her divorce her interior voice has been free of irony. You have to have faith.

2   Tomorrow morning Nola returns to school in Maine; today will be a day at the Mall. Mrs. Dietrich has planned it for days. At the Mall, in such crowds of shoppers, moments of intimacy are possible as they rarely are at home. (Seventeen-year-old Nola, home on spring break for a brief eight days, seems always to be *busy*, always out with her *friends*—the trip to the Mall has been postponed twice.) But Saturday, 10:30 A.M. they are in the car at last headed south on Route 12, a bleak March morning following a night of freezing rain, there's a metallic cast to the sky and no sun anywhere in the sky but the light hurts Mrs. Dietrich's eyes just the same. "Does it seem as if spring will ever come?—it must be twenty degrees colder up in Maine," she says. Driving in heavy traffic always makes Mrs. Dietrich nervous and she is overly sensitive to her daughter's silence, which seems deliberate, perverse, when they have so little time remaining together—not even a full day.

3   Nola asks politely if Mrs. Dietrich would like her to drive and Mrs. Dietrich says no, of course not, she's fine, it's only a few more miles and maybe traffic will lighten. Nola seems about to say something more, then thinks better of it. So much between them that is precarious, chancy—but they've been kind to each other these past seven days. Mrs. Dietrich loves Nola with a fierce unreasoned passion stronger than any she felt for the man who had been her husband for thirteen years, certainly far stronger than any she ever felt for her own mother. Sometimes in weak despondent moods, alone, lonely, self-pitying, when she has had too much to drink, Mrs. Dietrich thinks she is in love with her daughter—but this is a thought she can't contemplate for long. And how Nola would snort in amused contempt, incredulous, mocking—"Oh *Mother!*"—if she were told.

4   Mrs. Dietrich tries to engage her daughter in conversation of a harmless sort but Nola answers in monosyllables, Nola is rather tired from so many nights of partying with her friends, some of whom attend the local high school, some of whom are home for spring break from prep schools—Exeter, Lawrenceville, Concord, Andover, Portland. Late nights, but Mrs. Dietrich doesn't consciously lie awake waiting for Nola to come home: they've been through all that before. Now Nola sits beside her mother looking wan, subdued, rather melancholy. Thinking her private thoughts. She is wearing a bulky quilted jacket Mrs. Dietrich has never liked, the usual blue jeans, black calfskin boots zippered tightly to mid-calf. Mrs. Dietrich must resist the temptation to ask, "Why are you so quiet, Nola? What are you thinking?" They've been through all that before.

5   Route 12 has become a jumble of small industrial parks, high-rise office and apartment buildings, torn-up landscapes—mountains of raw earth, uprooted trees, ruts and ditches filled with muddy water. There is no natural sequence to what you see—buildings, construction work, leveled woods, the lavish grounds owned by Squibb. Though she has driven this route countless times, Mrs. Dietrich is never quite certain where the Mall is and must be

prepared for a sudden exit. She remembers getting lost the first several times, remembers the excitement she and her friends felt about the grand opening of the Mall, stores worthy of serious shopping at last. Today is much the same. No, today is worse. Like Christmas when she was a small child, Mrs. Dietrich thinks. She'd hoped so badly to be happy she'd felt actual pain, a constriction in her throat like crying.

"*Are* you all right, Nola?—you've been so quiet all morning," Mrs. Dietrich asks, half-scolding. Nola stirs from her reverie, says she's fine, a just perceptible edge to her reply, and for the remainder of the drive there's some stiffness between them. Mrs. Dietrich chooses to ignore it. In any case she is fully absorbed in driving—negotiating a tricky exit across two lanes of traffic, then the hairpin curve of the ramp, the numerous looping drives of the Mall. Then the enormous parking lot, daunting to the inexperienced, but Mrs. Dietrich always heads for the area behind Lord & Taylor on the far side of the Mall, Lot D; her luck holds and she finds a space close in. "Well—we made it," she says, smiling happily at Nola. Nola laughs in reply—what does a seventeen-year-old's laughter *mean*?—but she remembers, getting out, to lock both doors on her side of the car. The smile Nola gives Mrs. Dietrich across the car's roof is careless and beautiful and takes Mrs. Dietrich's breath away. 6

The March morning tastes of grit with an undercurrent of something acrid, chemical; inside the Mall beneath the first of the elegant brass-buttressed glass domes, the air is fresh and tonic, circulating from invisible vents. The Mall is crowded, rather noisy—it *is* Saturday morning—but a feast for the eyes after that long trip on Route 12. Tall slender trees grow out of the mosaic-tiled pavement, there are beds of Easter lilies, daffodils, jonquils, tulips of all colors. Mrs. Dietrich smiles with relief. She senses that Nola too is relieved, cheered. It's like coming home. 7

The shopping excursions began when Nola was a small child but did not acquire their special significance until she was twelve or thirteen years old and capable of serious, sustained shopping with her mother. This was about the time when Mr. Dietrich moved out of the house and back into their old apartment in the city—a separation, he'd called it initially, to give them perspective—though Mrs. Dietrich had no illusions about what "perspective" would turn out to entail—so the shopping trips were all the more significant. Not that Mrs. Dietrich and Nola spent very much money—they really didn't, *really* they didn't, when compared to friends and neighbors. 8

At seventeen Nola is shrewd and discerning as a shopper, not easy to please, knowledgeable as a mature woman about certain aspects of fashion, quality merchandise, good stores. Her closets, like Mrs. Dietrich's, are crammed, but she rarely buys anything that Mrs. Dietrich thinks shoddy or merely faddish. Up in Portland, at the Academy, she hasn't as much time to 9 shop but when she is home in Livingstone it isn't unusual for her and her girlfriends to shop nearly every day. Like all her friends she has charge accounts at the better stores, her own credit cards, a reasonable allowance. At the time of their settlement Mr. Dietrich said guiltily that it was the least he could do for them—if Mrs. Dietrich wanted to work part-time, she could (she was trained, more or less, in public relations of a small-scale sort); if not, not. Mrs. Dietrich thought, It's the most you can do for us too.

Near Bloomingdale's entrance mother and daughter see a disheveled woman sitting by herself on one of the benches. Without seeming to look at her, shoppers are making a discreet berth around her, a stream following a natural course. Nola, taken by surprise, stares. Mrs. Dietrich has seen the woman from time to time at the Mall, always alone, smirking and talking to herself, frizzed gray hair in a tangle, puckered mouth. Always wearing the same black wool coat, a garment of fairly good quality but shapeless, rumpled, stained, as if she sleeps in it. She might be anywhere from forty to sixty years of age. Once Mrs. Dietrich saw her make menacing gestures at children who were teasing her, another time she'd seen the woman staring belligerently at *her*. A white paste had gathered in the corners of her mouth.... "My God, that poor woman," Nola says. "I didn't think there were people like her here—I mean, I didn't think they would allow it."

"She doesn't seem to cause any disturbance," Mrs. Dietrich says. "She just sits—Don't stare, Nola. She'll see you."

"You've seen her here before? Here?"

"A few times this winter."

"Is she always like that?"

"I'm sure she's harmless, Nola. She just *sits*."

Nola is incensed, her pale blue eyes like washed glass. "I'm sure *she's* harmless, Mother. It's the harm the poor woman has to endure that is the tragedy."

Mrs. Dietrich is surprised and a little offended by her daughter's passionate tone but she knows enough not to argue. They enter Bloomingdale's, taking their habitual route. So many shoppers!—so much merchandise! Nola speaks of the tragedy of women like that woman—the tragedy of the homeless, the mentally disturbed—bag ladies out on the street—outcasts of an affluent society—but she's soon distracted by the busyness on all sides, the attractive items for sale. They take the escalator up to the third floor, to the Juniors department where Nola often buys things. From there they will move on to Young Collector, then to New Impressions, then to Petites, then one or another boutique and designer—Liz Claiborne, Christian Dior, Calvin Klein, Carlos Falci, and the rest. And after Bloomingdale's the other stores await, to be visited each in turn. Mrs. Dietrich checks her watch and sees with satisfaction that there's just enough time before lunch but not *too* much time. She gets ravenously hungry, shopping at the Mall.

18 Nola is efficient and matter-of-fact about shopping, though she acts solely upon instinct. Mrs. Dietrich likes to watch her at a short distance—holding items of clothing up to herself in the three-way mirrors, modeling things she thinks especially promising. A twill blazer with rounded shoulders and blouson jacket, a funky zippered jumpsuit in white sailcloth, a pair of straight-leg Evan-Picone pants, a green leather vest. Mrs. Dietrich watches her covertly. At such times Nola is perfectly content, fully absorbed in the task at hand; Mrs. Dietrich knows she isn't thinking about anything that would distress her. (Like Mr. Dietrich's betrayal. Like Nola's difficulties with her friends. Like her difficulties at school—as much as Mrs. Dietrich knows of them.) Once, at the Mall, perhaps in this very store in this very department, Nola saw Mrs. Dietrich watching her and walked away and when Mrs. Dietrich caught up with her she said, "I can't stand it, Mother." Her voice was choked and harsh, a vein prominent in her forehead. "Let me go. For Christ's sake will you let me go." Mrs. Dietrich didn't dare touch her though she could see Nola was trembling. For a long terrible moment mother and daughter stood side by side near a display of bright brash beachwear while Nola whispered, "Let me go. *Let me go.*"

19 Difficult to believe that girl standing so poised and self-assured in front of the three-way mirror was once a plain, rather chunky, unhappy child. She'd been unpopular at school. Overly serious. Anxious. Quick to tears. Aged eleven she hid herself away in her room for hours at a time, reading, drawing pictures, writing little stories she could sometimes be prevailed upon to read aloud to her mother, sometimes even to her father, though she dreaded his judgment. She went through a "scientific" phase a while later—Mrs. Dietrich remembers an ambitious bas-relief map of North America, meticulous illustrations for "photosynthesis," a pastel drawing of an eerie ball of fire labeled "Red Giant" (a dying star?) which won a prize in a state competition for junior high students. Then for a season it was stray facts Nola confronted them with, often at the dinner table. Interrupting her parents' conversation to say brightly: "Did you know that Nero's favorite color was green?—he carried a giant emerald and held it up to his eye to watch Christians being devoured by lions." And once at a large family gathering: "Did you know that last week downtown a little baby's nose was chewed off by rats in his crib?—a little *black* baby?" Nola meant only to call attention to herself but you couldn't blame her listeners for being offended. They stared at her, not knowing what to say. What a strange child! What queer glassy-pale eyes! Mr. Dietrich told her curtly to leave the table—he'd had enough of the game she was playing and so had everyone else.

20 Nola stared at him, her eyes filling with tears. Game?

21 When they were alone Mr. Dietrich said angrily to Mrs. Dietrich: "Can't you control her in front of other people, at least?" Mrs. Dietrich was angry too, and frightened. She said: "I *try.*"

22 They sent her off aged fourteen to the Portland Academy up in Maine and without their help she matured into a girl of considerable beauty. A heart-shaped

face, delicate features, glossy red-brown hair scissor-cut to her shoulders. Five feet seven inches weighing less than one hundred pounds—the result of constant savage dieting. (Mrs. Dietrich, who has weight problems herself, doesn't dare to inquire as to details. They've been through that already.) Thirty days after they'd left her at the Portland Academy Nola telephoned home at 11 P.M. one Sunday giggly and high telling Mrs. Dietrich she adored the school she adored her suite mates she adored most of her teachers particularly her riding instructor Terri, Terri the Terrier they called the woman because she was so fierce, such a character, eyes that bore right through your skull, wore belts with the most amazing silver buckles! Nola loved Terri but she wasn't *in* love—there's a difference!

Mrs. Dietrich broke down weeping, *that* time.

Now of course Nola has boyfriends. Mrs. Dietrich has long since given up trying to keep track of their names. There is even one "boy"—or young man—who seems to be married: who seems to be, in fact, one of the junior instructors at the school. (Mrs. Dietrich does not eavesdrop on her daughter's telephone conversations but there are things she cannot help overhearing.) Is your daughter on the Pill? the women in Mrs. Dietrich's circle asked one another for a while, guiltily, surreptitiously. Now they no longer ask.

But Nola has announced recently that she loathes boys—she's fed up.

She's never going to get married. She'll study languages in college, French, Italian, something exotic like Arabic, go to work for the American foreign service. Unless she drops out of school altogether to become a model.

"Do you think I'm fat, Mother?" she asks frequently, worriedly, standing in front of the mirror twisted at the waist to reveal her small round belly which, it seems, can't help being round. She bloats herself on diet Cokes all day long. "Do you think it *shows*?"

When Mrs. Dietrich was pregnant with Nola she'd been twenty-nine years old and she and Mr. Dietrich had tried to have a baby for nearly five years. She'd lost hope, begun to despise herself, then suddenly it happened: like grace. Like happiness swelling so powerfully it can barely be contained. I can hear its heartbeat! her husband exclaimed. He'd been her lover then, young, vigorous, dreamy. Caressing the rock-hard belly, splendid white tight-stretched skin. Mr. Dietrich gave Mrs. Dietrich a reproduction on stiff glossy paper of Dante Gabriel Rossetti's *Beata Beatrix*, embarrassed, apologetic, knowing it was sentimental and perhaps a little silly but that was how he thought of her—so beautiful, rapturous, pregnant with their child. She told no one but she knew the baby was to be a girl. It would be herself again, reborn and this time perfect.

"Oh, Mother—isn't it *beautiful*?" Nola exclaims.

It is past noon. Past twelve-thirty. Mrs. Dietrich and Nola have made the rounds of a half-dozen stores, traveled countless escalators, one clothing department has blended into the next and the chic smiling saleswomen have become indistinguishable and Mrs. Dietrich is beginning to feel the urgent need for a glass of white wine. Just a glass. "Isn't it beautiful?—it's *perfect*," Nola says. Her eyes glow with pleasure, her smooth skin is radiant. As Nola models in the three-way mirror a queer little yellow-and-black striped sweater with a ribbed waist. Punk style, mock-cheap, Mrs. Dietrich feels the motherly obligation to register a mild protest, knowing that Nola will not hear. She must have it and will have it. She'll wear it a few times, then retire it to the bottom of a drawer with so many other novelty sweaters, accumulated since sixth grade. (She's like her mother in that regard—can't bear to throw anything away.)

"*Isn't* it beautiful?" Nola demands, studying her reflection in the mirror. 31

Mrs. Dietrich pays for the sweater on her charge account. 32

Next, they buy Nola a good pair of shoes. And a handbag to go with them. 33 In Paraphernalia, where rock music blasts overhead and Mrs. Dietrich stands to one side, rather miserable, Nola chats companionably with two girls—tall, pretty, cutely made up—she'd gone to public school in Livingstone with, says afterward with an upward roll of her eyes, "God, I was afraid they'd latch on to us!" Mrs. Dietrich has seen women friends and acquaintances of her own in the Mall this morning but has shrunk from being noticed, not wanting to share her daughter with anyone. She has a sense of time passing ever more swiftly, cruelly.

She watches Nola preening in a mirror, watches other shoppers watching 34 her. My daughter. Mine. But of course there is no connection between them—they don't even resemble each other. A seventeen-year-old, a forty-seven-year-old. When Nola is away she seems to forget her mother entirely—doesn't telephone, certainly doesn't write. It's the way all their daughters are, Mrs. Dietrich's friends tell her. It doesn't *mean* anything. Mrs. Dietrich thinks how when she was carrying Nola, those nine long months, they'd been completely happy—not an instant's doubt or hesitation. The singular weight of the body. A trancelike state you are tempted to mistake for happiness because the body is incapable of thinking, therefore incapable of anticipating change. Hot rhythmic blood, organs packed tight and moist, the baby upside down in her sac in her mother's belly, always present tense, always *now*. It was a shock when the end came so abruptly but everyone told Mrs. Dietrich she was a natural mother, praised and pampered her. For a while. Then of course she'd had her baby, her Nola. Even now Mrs. Dietrich can't really comprehend the experience. *Giving birth. Had a baby. Was born.* Mere words, absurdly inadequate. She knows no more of how love ends than she knew as a child, she knows only of how love begins—in the belly, in the womb, where it is always present tense.

The morning's shopping has been quite successful but lunch at La Crêperie 35 doesn't go well for some reason. La Crêperie is Nola's favorite Mall restaurant—always amiably crowded, bustling, a simulated sidewalk café with red-striped umbrellas, wrought-iron tables and chairs, menus in French, music piped in overhead. Mrs. Dietrich's nerves are chafed by the pretense of gaiety, the noise, the openness onto one of the Mall's busy promenades where at any minute a familiar face might emerge, but she is grateful for her glass of chilled white wine. She orders a small tossed salad and a creamed-chicken crepe and devours it hungrily—she *is* hungry. While Nola picks at her seafood crepe with a disdainful look. A familiar scene: mother watching while daughter pushes food around on her plate. Suddenly Nola is tense, moody, corners of her mouth downturned. Mrs. Dietrich wants to ask, What's wrong? She wants to ask, Why are you unhappy? She wants to smooth Nola's hair back from her forehead, check to see if her forehead is overly warm, wants to hug her close, hard. Why, why? What did I do wrong? Why do you hate me?

Calling the Portland Academy a few weeks ago Mrs. Dietrich suddenly lost control, began crying. She hadn't been drinking and she hadn't known she was upset. A girl unknown to her, one of Nola's suite mates, was saying, "Please, Mrs. Dietrich, it's all right, I'm sure Nola will call you back later tonight, or tomorrow, Mrs. Dietrich?—I'll tell her you called, all right?—Mrs. Dietrich?" as embarrassed as if Mrs. Dietrich had been her own mother.

How love begins. How love ends.

Mrs. Dietrich orders a third glass of wine. This is a celebration of sorts isn't it? Their last shopping trip for a long time. But Nola resists, Nola isn't sentimental. In casual defiance of Mrs. Dietrich she lights up a cigarette—yes, Mother, Nola has said ironically, since *you* stopped smoking *everybody* is supposed to stop—and sits with her arms crossed, watching streams of shoppers pass. Mrs. Dietrich speaks lightly of practical matters, tomorrow morning's drive to the airport, and will Nola telephone when she gets to Portland to let Mrs. Dietrich know she has arrived safely?

Then with no warning—though of course she'd been planning this all along—Nola brings up the subject of a semester in France, in Paris and Rouen, the fall semester of her senior year it would be; she has put in her application, she says, and is waiting to hear if she's been accepted. She smokes her cigarette calmly, expelling smoke from her nostrils in a way Mrs. Dietrich thinks particularly coarse. Mrs. Dietrich, who believed that particular topic was finished, takes care to speak without emotion. "I just don't think it's a very practical idea right now, Nola," she says. "We've been through it haven't we? I—"

"I'm going," Nola says.

"The extra expense, for one thing. Your father—"

"If I get accepted, I'm going."

"Your father—"

"The hell with him too."

Mrs. Dietrich would like to slap her daughter's face. Bring tears to those steely eyes. But she sits stiff, turning her wine glass between her fingers, patient, calm, she's heard all this before; she says, "Surely this isn't the best time to discuss it, Nola."

Mrs. Dietrich is afraid her daughter will leave the restaurant, simply walk away, that has happened before and if it happens today she doesn't know what she will do. But Nola sits unmoving; her face closed, impassive. Mrs. Dietrich feels her quickened heartbeat. Once after one of their quarrels Mrs. Dietrich told a friend of hers, the mother too of a teenage daughter, "I just don't know her any longer, how can you keep living with someone you don't know?" and the woman said, "Eventually you can't."

47 Nola says, not looking at Mrs. Dietrich: "Why don't we talk about it, Mother?"

48 "Talk about what?" Mrs. Dietrich asks.

49 "You know."

50 "The semester in France? Again?"

51 "No."

52 "What, then?"

53 "You *know*."

54 "I don't know, really. Really!" Mrs. Dietrich smiles, baffled. She feels the corners of her eyes pucker white with strain.

55 Nola says, sighing, "How exhausting it is."

56 "How *what*?"

57 "How exhausting it is."

58 "What is?"

59 "You and me—"

60 "What?"

61 "Being together—"

62 "Being together how—?"

63 "The two of us, like this—"

64 "But we're hardly ever together, Nola," Mrs. Dietrich says.

65 Her expression is calm but her voice is shaking. Nola turns away, covering her face with a hand, for a moment she looks years older than her age—in fact exhausted. Mrs. Dietrich sees with pity that her daughter's skin is fair and thin and dry—unlike her own, which tends to be oily—it will wear out before she's forty. Mrs. Dietrich reaches over to squeeze her hand. The fingers are limp, ungiving. "You're going back to school tomorrow, Nola," she says. "You won't come home again until June 12. And you probably will go to France—if your father consents."

66 Nola gets to her feet, drops her cigarette to the flagstone terrace and grinds it out beneath her boot. A dirty thing to do, Mrs. Dietrich thinks, considering there's an ashtray right on the table, but she says nothing. She dislikes La Crêperie anyway.

67 Nola laughs, showing her lovely white teeth. "Oh, the hell with him," she says. "Fuck Daddy, right?"

68 They separate for an hour, Mrs. Dietrich to Neiman-Marcus to buy a birthday gift for her elderly aunt, Nola to the trendy new boutique Pour Vous. By the time Mrs. Dietrich rejoins her daughter she's quite angry, blood beating

hot and hard and measured in resentment, she has had time to relive old quarrels between them, old exchanges, stray humiliating memories of her marriage as well, these last-hour disagreements are the cruelest and they are Nola's specialty. She locates Nola in the rear of the boutique amid blaring rock music, flashing neon lights, chrome-edged mirrors, her face still hard, closed, prim, pale. She stands beside another teenage girl looking in a desultory way through a rack of blouses, shoving the hangers roughly along, taking no care when a blouse falls to the floor. As Nola glances up, startled, not prepared to see her mother in front of her, their eyes lock for an instant and Mrs. Dietrich stares at her with hatred. Cold calm clear unmistakable hatred. She is thinking, Who are *you*? What have I to do with *you*? I don't know *you*, I don't love *you*, why should I?

Has Nola seen, heard?—she turns aside as if wincing, gives the blouses a final dismissive shove. Her eyes look tired, the corners of her mouth downturned. Anxious, immediately repentant, Mrs. Dietrich asks if she has found anything worth trying on. Nola says with a shrug, "Not a thing, Mother."

On their way out of the Mall Mrs. Dietrich and Nola see the disheveled woman in the black coat again, this time sitting prominently on a concrete ledge in front of Lord & Taylor's busy main entrance. Shopping bag at her feet, shabby purse on the ledge beside her. She is shaking her head in a series of annoyed switches as if arguing with someone but her hands are loose, palms up, in her lap. Her posture is unfortunate—she sits with her knees parted, inner thighs revealed, fatty, dead white, the tops of cotton stockings rolled tight cutting into the flesh. Again, streams of shoppers are making a careful berth around her. Alone among them Nola hesitates, seems about to approach the woman— Please don't, Nola! please! Mrs. Dietrich thinks—then changes her mind and keeps on walking. Mrs. Dietrich murmurs isn't it a pity, poor thing, don't you wonder where she lives, who her family is, but Nola doesn't reply. Her pace through the first door of Lord & Taylor is so rapid that Mrs. Dietrich can barely keep up.

But Nola's upset. Strangely upset. As soon as they are in the car, packages and bags in the backseat, she begins crying.

It's childish helpless crying, as though her heart is broken. But Mrs. Dietrich knows it isn't broken, she has heard these very sobs before. Many times before. Still she comforts her daughter, embraces her, hugs her hard, hard. A sudden fierce passion. Vehemence. "Nola honey. Nola dear, what's wrong, dear, everything will be all right, dear," she says, close to weeping herself. She would embrace Nola even more tightly except for the girl's quilted jacket, that bulky L. L. Bean thing she has never liked, and Nola's stubborn lowered head. Nola has always been ashamed, crying, frantic to hide her face. Strangers are passing close by the car, curious, staring. Mrs. Dietrich wishes she had a cloak to draw over her daughter and herself, so that no one else would see.

◆ QUESTIONS FOR REVIEW

1. Oates presents a mother and daughter who are very much at odds with each other. What is the source of their conflict? Do you like either of these characters? Why or why not?
2. The physical setting for this story is the Livingstone Mall, which we may assume is a typical suburban U.S. mall. What does it represent (or symbolize), other than a place to go shopping?
3. What does this story say about the Dietrich family? How might this family represent others in our society?
4. Identify two or three places where Oates's use of language is particularly effective. What makes these passages effective?
5. What is your overall assessment of this story? Did you like it? Why or why not?

◆ WRITING OPPORTUNITY

Write about a conflict you've had with a family member. What was the situation? The outcome? ◆

Our next short story, "Of Falling," was written by Aaron Gwyn, a member of the English creative writing faculty at UNC Charlotte.

AARON GWYN

OF FALLING

1 GEORGE CRIDER WAS seven when Freddy was born, fifteen before his brother grew old enough to sit a horse. In the autumn, after their chores were done, the boys would ride bareback across the pasture to a persimmon grove, spend their afternoons climbing the thin trees for fruit.

2 One day the animal they were riding stepped in a sinkhole and bucked. George caught hold of its mane, but his brother was behind him and fell to the ground. The boy's arm broke the skin, and the bone jutted into dirt. He developed tetanus and in two weeks was dead. George blamed himself for this, as did his parents, and at the funeral, when he climbed into the grave and sought to open the casket, his father lost two teeth trying to retrieve him.

Three years later, grown to well over six feet, he slid a razor in his hip pocket, a change of clothes in his knapsack, and without saying good-bye, walked forty miles through the Quashita forest until he came to Highway 3, hitching across Oklahoma in the back of a cattle truck. He went to work in the oil field and bought a new car, kept a shotgun underneath his seat, sawed at the stock and barrel. One night he left for Louisiana and returned a week later with a Cajun woman, named Sadie, whom he had taken to wife.

Everyone thought George unflappable. He was tall and lean, with a hard, lean face and expressionless eyes. He did not talk about himself or his brother or his parents back in Shinewell, pastors of a Pentecostal church. He was quiet and felt no need to speak. The men he worked with respected him, for they knew he was strong and stubborn, and they would not have wanted to face him in a fight, fair or otherwise.

Then, in 1933, working the eighth floor of an oil derrick in Pontotoc County, scaffolding gave way and George fell 116 feet onto the bank of a saltwater pit.

He did not remember this. Not the fabric blowing against his limbs or the girders moving past or the platform where he'd stood traveling into sky. It took him nearly four seconds to reach the ground, but he could not recall them. For him there was only the eighth floor and the earth.

Through the years to follow, he would recount the incident for his wife: the stares of the men who found him, the ambulance and hospital, the doctor who examined him from top to toe as if he were a puzzle. He would tell her about watching the clouds change to ceiling tile, the sun to bright lamps and mirrors. He would tell about sandstone pressing into his back like shards of bone and then the cool of the sheets, the anesthetic.

Yet, stretched beneath the shadow of the derrick, George's first thoughts were not of family or friends, the condition of his soul, or whether he would be able to one day move his legs. His thoughts were not of the porch standing unfinished, the clothesline needing repair, the foundation wall that had shown signs of flaking just the day before. His thoughts were not of what he would lose in this world, gain or lose in the world hereafter.

Lying there with the sky weighing down and the wind moving over and across him, George had considered only the boards that had snapped beneath his feet. With his lower lip clenched between his teeth, he watched himself walk to where they lay at the side of the derrick and kick them to splinters.

THE FALL HAD broken both his arms, his legs, six of his ribs at their connecting points. His skull was fractured, and his sternum snapped in half. The doctor who admitted him said he would not live through the night.

He lived regardless. Through that night and the night after and the night after that.

The surgeons said it was a wonder; they said it was a phenomenon. One stood in the middle of his hospital room and pronounced it a miracle. And though he said George would never walk, he thought he might, one day, have a life of some kind.

In two years George was walking. In two more he had returned to work. By the time he reached his midthirties, George was spry as any roughneck in the state. He was promoted to foreman, and through the depression years, when many left to seek work elsewhere, George and his wife began to build a collection of antique glassware. If he chose, he could retire young, live comfortably off his pension and what he had invested in glass rarities.

George seemed much the same as before the fall. To see him pull to the curb in his burgundy Pontiac, step out and approach an antique shop—a tall, slender man, graceful as a dancer, with jet-black hair and eyes like drops of oil—you would not have thought he had fallen in his life. Not even from the height of a chair.

IT WAS ALONG this time, along the time George stacked his crutches in the rear of the closet and poured his vial of laudanum down the sink, that the dreams came.

They were not, as one would think, dreams of falling, the body released from its federation with the earth and betrayed to gravity. Neither were they dreams of impact. The dreams that visited George after his fall were of stillness.

In them, he would be lying in a field, feeling drops of sweat run into his eyes and pool around the sockets. When he attempted to raise his hand and wipe them, he could not. His ears itched, his face and neck. His body burned. He lay among the blades of grass, blinking into sky.

Soon there was a cloud. It was small at first. If he had been able, George could have retrieved a quarter from his pocket, held it at arm's length, and eclipsed the cloud entirely. But as it grew, he would have needed a fifty-cent piece, a silver dollar, and then, even with both hands outspread and extended in front of his face, wisps of gray would have bled the edges of his fingers.

There was nothing about the cloud to warrant fear. It was not boiling and black, or streaked with light. There was no rumbling and it gave no sound. This was not the type of cloud from which angels or prophets descend.

Only, lying there beneath it, George came to know death in the stillness of wide and all but empty sky.

He awoke screaming. He awoke on the floor. The doctors said such dreams were common among those who had fallen. They gave him pills of all sizes, but the dreams did not stop.

Then one night he awoke running through the house, glassware rattling the mahogany furniture. Sadie watched him from their doorway.

"Crider," she called, "you'll break everything we own."

She was right; several vases lay broken already.

When he wakened and was asked what he'd been dreaming, George went to his car and fell asleep across the seats. The next morning, he was sitting on the front stoop of Woolworth when the owner unlocked the doors.

GEORGE PURCHASED FOUR belts, fastened each to the other, and threaded them between his mattress and box springs. Each night he brought the ends together and buckled himself beneath his quilts.

Years passed in this way, with George awaking early every morning strapped to his bed. His wife began sleeping across the hall and, when they stayed in motels, made him reserve nonadjoining rooms.

Visitors seldom came, but when they did, Sadie would take them on a tour of their home. By then every surface in the house—sideboard, dining and coffee table, ottoman, divan—was covered in antique glass. Sadie had acquired the largest collection in Perser and was slowly overtaking Herbert Nasser and his wife, Vinita, who made claim of the largest in Oklahoma.

Her guests would follow her through the small, dark house, through the smell of must and old wood. There were two bedrooms, a bath, a small kitchen crowded with dining table and stove. None of the window blinds or curtains were open; Sadie feared those passing on the sidewalk would see inside. The worth of her collection was estimated at thirty thousand dollars.

"This piece is very old," she would tell her visitors, pointing to a candy dish. "I found it in a filling station outside Shreveport."

They nodded, ran their hands along its rim.

"And this piece," Sadie said, "I didn't think the man would part with it."

They nodded again, looked to their watches.

She would conclude her tour by showing George's room, the straps on his bed. The guests looked at her husband. They wanted to know how long it had been, if he would mind telling the story of his fall.

He would tell it. He knew it by rote: the platform, the derrick, the hospital, the dreams. It took him only fifteen minutes.

When he finished, his audience shook their heads. Often they reached to squeeze his hand or touch him on the arm. Sometimes they turned to Sadie and forced a smile.

She smiled back, gestured to George.

"This is what I have to live with," she would tell them.

• • •

IT WAS THEN 1957, the year Oral Roberts took a tent across the Midwest, bringing his revival to the lost and infirm. Sadie heard on the radio testimonies of those treated by Roberts. Some who had never walked made claim to walk. Some who had never seen claimed to see. Sharon Stilman was carried into his tent on a sheet and soon thereafter began a ministry of her own.

Sadie told her husband of this, and they drove 120 miles to a small town outside Tulsa, where for the past week Roberts had held a tent revival. They arrived late and sat toward the back.

George found much of the service consonant with what he had known from his childhood. There was a low stage and a choir on it, men in folding chairs dressed in ties and slacks and white shirts. There were rows of similar chairs for the audience, stapled pages containing a few hymns, sawdust on the floor, carpets down the aisles. Midway through, paper buckets with crosses stenciled on them were passed for offering. 41

After Roberts delivered a brief sermon, he asked those in need of healing to form a line to the left of the stage. He told them it did not have to be physical healing. 42

"There are three kinds of healing," he told them. "There is physical healing and emotional healing and healing of the spirit." He said God could perform all three. 43

Sadie leaned over, whispered to George. He shook his head. When she went to lean again, he rose from his seat and stepped in line. 44

Roberts sat at the edge of the stage with a handkerchief in one hand and a bottle of olive oil in the other. He was a young man: long nose, a long, smooth face. His hair was combed with tonic and laid back on his head. He wore a plain white shirt, a tie, gray slacks, polished black shoes. Between his legs stood a microphone tilted toward his mouth, positioned low on its stand. 45

Folks came and stood in front of the stage, handed one of Roberts's assistants an index card on which was written their names and the names of their afflictions. These in turn were handed to Roberts. 46

George examined the blank card and the pencil he had been passed moments before. He looked to the evangelist who was addressing an elderly woman with braces on her legs. 47

"How long have you had this, sister?" 48

"I been this way since I was twenty-two," the woman told him. 49

Roberts dabbed oil into the palm of one hand and told her to come close. He leaned over the edge of the stage, put the hand to her cheek, and lifted the other toward the ceiling, praying into the microphone. 50

"Lord," he prayed, "deliver her." 51

The woman began to shiver; then her body became rigid and she fell backward to the ground. A man in a dark suit came and covered her legs with a blanket. Another member of the audience approached, handed up her card. George watched all this, feeling of a sudden as if someone had hollowed him. 52

He started to turn, but just then one of Roberts's assistants happened down the line. He noticed George's card was blank and touched him on the elbow, inquiring after his affliction. 53

George shook his head, tried to step around the man, but found himself blocked by a row of card tables piled with books and pamphlets. 54

The man looked askance, leaned toward him, and George quickly told the story of his fall. When he finished, the other's face had an amazed look. He took George by the arm, parted the crowd, and led him onto the stage. They stood to 55 the side while Roberts prayed, and then the man went to the evangelist and whispered into his ear.

Roberts turned. He rose, took the microphone from its stand, and walked to George. The crowd quieted. Roberts's voice in the microphone was wet and very loud.

"Tell these people your name."

George shifted from one foot to the other. He brought a hand from behind his back and scratched at his nose. "George Crider," he said.

"And you had an accident?" Roberts asked.

"Yes."

"You fell?"

"Yes."

"How far?"

"One hundred sixteen feet."

Many in the crowd gasped; some called to God.

"And you were hurt?"

"Yes."

"How many bones did you break?"

"All of them," George said.

The preacher put his hand on George's shoulder.

"And what did the doctors say?"

George paused, looked down. "They told me I would never walk again."

There were a few moments of silence. Then the crowd began to stir and then to applaud. They cried in loud voices, and most all raised their hands. One man left his seat and began to run the aisles.

Roberts turned to face them. "Do you hear that?" he said. "The God that did this can do the same for you. The same God who caused this brother to walk after breaking every bone in his body can grant you your deliverance."

More folk left their seats and stepped in line. The preacher stood above them like an auctioneer.

George was led from the stage. He saw Sadie waiting for him near the ramp.

As he was about to walk away, the man who had discovered him asked if he would return the next night to give his testimony. George shook his head, took his wife by the arm, and escorted her from the tent.

IT WAS MORE than twenty years before he would visit another faith healer. By then George had retired from his job and begun to collect his pension. He and Sadie traveled most the year, attending antique shows, conventions, fairs and galleries. They acquired piece after piece, and in the 1969 edition of *Carnival Glass Anthology*, there was a black-and-white photo of his wife standing next to a bookcase full of depression-era teacups.

But, however great Sadie's satisfaction, George's condition grew worse. His hands would often shake and occasionally his vision blur. The man slept only two or three hours a night, and at times would go days on no sleep at all, walking through his afternoons with a glazed look. He did not talk about the dreams or the ailments that made him unfamiliar to his body. He refused to go back to the doctors or turn to the God of his father. He refused to take the shotgun from under the seat of the car and place the barrel in his mouth. Regardless, he found himself polishing the weapon once or twice a month, breaking it over at the dining-room table to check the shells.

In Denton, Texas, one night, Sadie forced him into a revival meeting held by the Reverend R. T. Shorbach. She told George that life with him had caused her to need healing of the spirit. George watched his wife leave her seat, walk the aisle, and take her place at the end of Shorbach's prayer line. He retrieved a hymnal from beside his chair and began to flip the pages. 79

Shorbach was an older gentleman from Tyler, Texas, who clothed his body in immense black suits. He had fat features and a welcoming face, thick eyebrows, a sweep of gray hair. The preacher smelled of strong cologne and sweat. 80

He stood down from the platform with a microphone, laying hands on those who came through his line. In front of each, he would pray loudly, examining the ceiling as people fell away from his thick fingers to the arms of an assistant. 81

After a while, George could no longer watch. He walked to the lobby, found a rest room and then a vending machine. He put quarters in, but the candy caught in a loop of the wire that held it. When he came back to the auditorium, his wife stood before the massive preacher. George crossed his arms and watched from the wings. 82

His wife seemed small from the distance. She was a petite woman still, her silver hair pinned in an elaborate bun. George watched as Shorbach's hand came to her forehead, watched Sadie's arms rise. He continued watching as her body went suddenly rigid and she fell backward into the arms of Shorbach's assistant. She was laid on the ground, covered with a blanket. 83

"Slain," Shorbach said over the swell of the organ, "slain in the Spirit." 84

The next night Sadie persuaded George to return to Shorbach's meeting, where she again approached the prayer line and soon lay sprawled on the floor. 85

A month later, in Biloxi, Mississippi, George would watch his wife fall from the hands of the Reverend Shorbach, and two months later in Little Rock, and six later in Atlanta. Sadie began keeping two schedules on her refrigerator, one of antique conventions, one of Shorbach's camp meetings. And several years later, when Sadie stepped from the prayer line in front of the man of God, he held the microphone away from his face and asked where he knew her from. 86

Sadie smiled, raised both hands, and braced herself for the fall. 87

YEARS PASSED. Numb years of sickness and pain. Sadie continued seeing Shorbach when the preacher came within driving distance of Perser. If George was too ill to take her, Sadie would phone a nephew to do so, and when he could not oblige, the woman closed the door to her bedroom and watched the broadcast on TBN. 88

In the past, George had been a quiet man; now he was utterly silent. He did not answer his wife's questions, and when visitors called, he would retreat to his work shed behind the house. He was in considerable pain but took nothing for it. His lower back had deteriorated, his shoulders and hips. Some mornings it would take him upward of an hour to rise from bed. The dreams, as ever, continued to shake him, and he spent much time weighing the benefit of life and death.

Then one evening, Sadie fell from the back porch. She was putting out bread for squirrels, and she slipped, snapping her leg below the knee. From the shed, George heard his wife's screaming. He managed to position her in the backseat of the car, drive her to the hospital. When they sent her home with a cast and crutches, it was George who helped her to bathe, brought her meals, took her from place to place.

"George," Sadie would say. "I need to go."

George would trundle in, assist her to the bathroom, stand outside the door waiting.

It was late that summer when the First Pentecostal brought in Leslie Snodgrass, an evangelist of fifteen, already known across Oklahoma and much of Missouri. People said amazing things of the boy. They claimed signs and wonders, miracles and healing and salvation of the lost. He preached repentance, prayed over the hopelessly ill. The young man came from a small town outside Tishomingo and had been preaching since the age of six. He was short and fair, very thin, but his voice was that of a man three times his years, and audiences watched him with an amazed look. The elders in the crowd would shout and sing, and sinners sat with whitened faces, sinking quietly in their seats. When Snodgrass ended his sermons, old and young alike would fall into the altars to seek mercy. He knelt among them and, when moved, stood to his feet and walked about, laying hands on the sick and troubled of spirit.

Sadie soon heard of this and began asking George to take her to one of these meetings. She wanted to see her leg heal quickly.

George had decided some time before he could not endure another service; he told his wife to find someone else. But Sadie was persistent, and in a matter of nights George found himself sitting along the rear wall of the church, listening to the young evangelist's words.

He watched with an expression no less amazed than those around him. It was indeed a sight to astonish. The boy moved like one possessed, his eyes tightly shut, wads of tissue clenched in his fists. There were hard men who had heard him preach and could not return to their former lives, but by this point George believed only in anguish, for that, he felt, was the truth of the world, and though entranced by the young man pacing the platform above him, he did not recover his faith.

The boy's sermon ended with an altar call, and the altars were soon full. George sat with open eyes, staring over the bowed heads. People knelt, wrestling with their spirits. Occasionally, an elder among them would raise his voice in travail. All prayed for what seemed a very long time, and then Snodgrass rose, approached the platform, and asked those in need of healing to come forward. Sadie began tugging at George's sleeve, wanting him to help her there.

George pulled her to her feet, positioned the crutches beneath her arms. 98 She hobbled out into the aisle and began inching toward the altar, her husband following a few steps behind. They reached the row of people standing along the front of the sanctuary, found themselves a place at the far right. George made sure of Sadie, then leaned against the wall to take the weight from his back.

He watched Snodgrass make his way down the line. The boy had no micro- 99 phone, no handkerchief or oil. He would stop and speak quietly with each, bow his head and whisper, sometimes laying a pale hand to the person's shoulder, his demeanor one of tranquillity, calm.

George was shocked to see the people remain standing. They did not fall; 100 they did not quake or run the aisles. They stood their places with broken looks, the wise looks of the condemned.

George noticed his wife was also watching the boy, but her face held a bitter 101 expression, more so the closer Snodgrass came. She seemed to understand that the evangelist would not lay hands to her forehead. He would not send her to the carpet, and no assistant would stand waiting with arms and a blanket. Sadie would leave just as she came, and realizing this, George began to chuckle quietly.

The boy came closer and Sadie's face grew harsher, and as Snodgrass was 102 praying for the man next to her, she spun suddenly from the line, casting George derision as she turned.

George watched his wife go up the aisle, past the pew where they'd formerly 103 sat, out the double doors into the lobby, A louder laugh escaped his lips, and when he turned back around, his face was cracked from smiling. Snodgrass stood in front of him.

George's laughter died, and he watched the evangelist with an anxious look, 104 failing for a moment to blink or breathe. The boy was utterly ashen, and he walked sternly up, raised his hand, and placed it to the old man's chest, closing his eyes to mumble a few words. George did not catch them. Only, the moment they left the boy's lips, the audience beheld George Crider fall like lightning.

It did not seem so to George. To him his descent seemed to take a very long 105 time. At first there was the feeling his legs had given way, his limbs wilted to nothing. He sensed his arm go numb and a terrific burst go off in his chest just to the left of where the boy had touched him. He felt warm there and very still and the air that buzzed about his ears was like fire.

There was time for George to consider many things before he struck the 106 ground, to consider a time before dreams troubled his sleep, before an injury placed him in a hospital bed. He considered walking forty miles through the Quashita forest, under the pines and cedars of southeast Oklahoma, and then the time of his boyhood under the dense trees, before his brother had fallen, before he had a brother at all. He considered when it was only he and his mother and his father, when they would pick him off the ground, only a child of four years then, place him in the center of a patchwork quilt, and lift him, allowing him to leave the fabric for a moment before he sank back to its folds. They repeated this for what seemed like hours—though it could not have been so long—the thin child rising and falling, caught up, snapped into the air.

It was weightless, that sense, the stomach a rush, face and arms and legs prickling, the heart feeling as if it might split. Rising and falling, and again, and over. If it had always been like that, there would have been point in nothing else but to live in the instant when gravity first took hold and pulled you to its center.

George considered this of all things as he abandoned himself to the fall, unaware he would expire some sixteen inches above the carpet, that his body would strike the floor with a hollow sound.

◆ Questions for Review

1. Gwyn narrates the entire life of a man, George Crider, in a short story. How does Gwyn keep the story from reading like a summary of the events that happened in Crider's life; that is, how does Gwyn make readers feel as if they come to know Crider in this very brief recounting of his life?
2. Great literature is always connected to strong conflicts. Identify two or three major conflicts in this story and explain how they are connected to the overall theme of the story.
3. What is the point of view of this story? Is it an effective point of view for telling this story? Why? How would the story change were it told from a different point of view?
4. One way to describe the main character in this story, George Crider, would be to call him stoic. What would one mean in using this term to refer to him? Explain. Can you think of another word that captures a different quality you see in Crider? If so, what is that term?
5. At the end of the story, how do you, as a reader, feel about Crider? Do you pity him, have sympathy for him, like him, dislike him? Something else? How does your view of Crider connect with the overall meaning you take from the story?

◆ Writing Opportunity

1. Literature often acts as a vehicle for social commentary. What does "Of Falling" have to say about the role of religion in some parts of society?

2. Clearly the title of this short story "Of Falling" is connected to the role that "falling" plays as a symbol in this short story. Write a brief essay in which you discuss the role this symbolism plays in the overall meaning you take from this story. ◆

The first poem we present is by Robert Frost, one of the most famous and best-liked of American poets.

ROBERT FROST
FOR ONCE, THEN, SOMETHING

Others taunt me with having knelt at well-curbs	1
Always wrong to the light, so never seeing	
Deeper down in the well than where the water	
Gives me back in a shining surface picture	
Me myself in the summer heaven, godlike,	5
Looking out of a wreath of fern and cloud puffs.	
Once, when trying with chin against a well-curb,	
I discerned, as I thought, beyond the picture,	
Through the picture, a something white, uncertain,	
Something more of the depths—and then I lost it.	10
Water came to rebuke the too clear water.	
One drop fell from a fern, and lo, a ripple	
Shook whatever it was lay there at bottom,	
Blurred it, blotted it out. What was that whiteness?	
Truth? A pebble of quartz? For once, then, something.	15

◆ QUESTIONS FOR REVIEW

1. How much of Frost's poetry have you read? Do you like his poetry? Why or why not?
2. How does this poem compare with others by Frost that you have read?
3. What questions does this poem raise for you? (For example, who are the "Others" Frost opens the poem with? Why is "Once" italicized in line 7?)
4. Is there a conflict at work in this poem? If so, what is it? How does Frost resolve it?
5. Mark the poem's key terms. Why did you select these terms as important?

6. What point or points do you think Frost is trying to make in this poem? What is Frost trying to say? What is the poem's theme?
7. What is your overall assessment of this poem? Did you like it? Why or why not?

◆ Writing Opportunity

1. How does Frost use images from nature to develop his theme?
2. Have you ever been criticized by people who didn't understand what you were trying to do? Write about this criticism and how you responded to it. ◆

The next poem is by Margaret Atwood, a contemporary poet who has also written novels and collections of essays. This poem appeared in *True Stories*, a collection of Atwood's writing published in 1981.

MARGARET ATWOOD

SPELLING

My daughter plays on the floor
with plastic letters,
red, blue & hard yellow,
learning how to spell,
spelling,
how to make spells

and I wonder how many women
denied themselves daughters,
closed themselves in rooms,
drew the curtains
so they could mainline words.

A child is not a poem,
a poem is not a child
There is no either/or.
However.

I return to the story
of the woman caught in the war
& in labour, her thighs tied

together by the enemy
so she could not give birth.   20

Ancestress: the burning witch,
her mouth covered by leather
to strangle words.

A word after a word
after a word is power.   25

At the point where language falls away
from the hot bones, at the point
where the rock breaks open and darkness
flows out of it like blood, at
the melting point of granite   30
when the bones know
they are hollow & the word
splits & doubles & speaks
the truth & the body
itself becomes a mouth.   35

This is a metaphor.

How do you learn to spell?
Blood, sky & sun,
your own name first,
your first naming, your first name,   40
your first word.

◆ QUESTIONS FOR REVIEW

1. How powerful is language and the ability to use it, according to Atwood? Point to three or four images or lines to support your response.
2. What is the metaphor Atwood mentions in line 36? What does it represent?
3. Identify two or three places where you think Atwood's language is particularly effective. What makes these passages effective?
4. What is the theme of this poem?
5. What is your overall assessment of this poem? Is it a piece of good literature? Why or why not? Did you like it? Why or why not?

◆ WRITING OPPORTUNITY

1. How does Atwood use the word "spell" in this poem?
2. Have you ever felt repressed or known anyone who was? What happened? How was language involved? What was the outcome? ◆

The next three poems are by Sherman Alexie, a member of the Spokane/Coeur d'Alene tribe. Alexie is the author of several volumes of poetry (including *The Business of Fancydancing* and *Old Shirts & New Skins*) and fiction (including *The Lone Ranger and Tonto Fistfight in Heaven* and *Reservation Blues*). In addition, Alexie's movie, *Smoke Signals,* was released during the summer of 1998. After you have read these poems, decide how well each poem succeeds individually and then how effectively they complement or provide a comment on each other.

SHERMAN ALEXIE

THAT PLACE WHERE GHOSTS OF SALMON JUMP

Coyote was alone and angry because he could not find love.   1
Coyote was alone and angry because he demanded a wife

from the Spokane, the Coeur d'Alene, the Palouse, all those tribes
camped on the edge of the Spokane River, and received only laughter.

So Coyote rose up with his powerful and senseless magic   5
and smashed a paw across the water, which broke the river bottom

in two, which created rain that lasted for forty days and nights,
which created Spokane Falls, that place where salmon traveled

more suddenly than Coyote imagined, that place where salmon swam
larger than any white man dreamed. Coyote, I know you broke   10

the river because of love, and pretended it was all done by your design.
Coyote, you're a liar and I don't trust you. I never have

but I do trust all the stories the grandmothers told me.
They said the Falls were built because of your unrequited love

and I can understand that rage, Coyote. We can all understand   15
but look at the Falls now and tell me what you see. Look

at the Falls now, if you can see beyond all of the concrete
the white man has built here. Look at all of this

and tell me that concrete ever equals love. Coyote,
these white men sometimes forget to love their own mothers   20

so how could they love this river which gave birth
to a thousand lifetimes of salmon? How could they love

these Falls, which have fallen farther, which sit dry
and quiet as a graveyard now? These Falls are that place

where ghosts of salmon jump, where ghosts of women mourn   25
their children who will never find their way back home,

where I stand now and search for any kind of love,
where I sing softly, under my breath, alone and angry.

◆ QUESTIONS FOR REVIEW

1. This poem has strong narrative elements in it. Identify those elements and comment on their effectiveness.
2. Identify two or three places where Alexie's use of language is particularly effective. What makes these passages effective?
3. What is the tone at the beginning of this poem? At what point does it change? How does this change affect the poem's meaning?
4. The poem's narrator addresses "Coyote." Who is Coyote? Why does the narrator call him a liar? Why does the narrator not trust Coyote? How important is Coyote's role in the poem?
5. What is the theme of this poem? What comment does the poem seem to make about contemporary society? About the place of Native Americans in that society?
6. What is your overall assessment of the poem? Did you like it? Why or why not?

◆ WRITING OPPORTUNITY

1. What environmental issues are at work in your town, city, or state? For example, is the environment being helped or damaged by a particular project? Write an assessment of this project.
2. Have you ever felt displaced or powerless? Write about that time and its outcome. ◆

Sherman Alexie

THE POWWOW AT THE END OF THE WORLD

I am told by many of you that I must forgive and so I shall
after an Indian woman puts her shoulder to the Grand Coulee Dam
and topples it. I am told by many of you that I must forgive
and so I shall after the floodwaters burst each successive dam
downriver from the Grand Coulee. I am told by many of you
that I must forgive and so I shall after the floodwaters find
their way to the mouth of the Columbia River as it enters the Pacific
and causes all of it to rise. I am told by many of you that I must forgive
and so I shall after the first drop of floodwater is swallowed by that salmon
waiting in the Pacific. I am told by many of you that I must forgive and so I shall
after that salmon swims upstream, through the mouth of the Columbia
and then past the flooded cities, broken dams and abandoned reactors
of Hanford. I am told by many of you that I must forgive and so I shall
after that salmon swims through the mouth of the Spokane River
as it meets the Columbia, then upstream, until it arrives
in the shallows of a secret bay on the reservation where I wait alone.
I am told by many of you that I must forgive and so I shall after
that salmon leaps into the night air above the water, throws
a lightning bolt at the brush near my feet, and starts the fire
which will lead all of the lost Indians home. I am told
by many of you that I must forgive and so I shall
after we Indians have gathered around the fire with that salmon
who has three stories it must tell before sunrise: one story will teach us
how to pray; another story will make us laugh for hours;
the third story will give us reason to dance. I am told by many
of you that I must forgive and so I shall when I am dancing
with my tribe during the powwow at the end of the world.

◆ Questions for Review

1. This poem has strong narrative elements in it. Identify those elements and comment on their effectiveness.
2. Identify two or three places where Alexie's use of language is particularly effective. What makes these passages effective?
3. What is the theme of this poem? What do you think Alexie is saying in it? How does this theme compare with that of "That Place Where Ghosts of Salmon Jump"?

4. What is the tone of the poem? How effectively does the tone support Alexie's theme? How does the tone of this poem compare with that of "That Place Where Ghosts of Salmon Jump"?
5. Images of water, food, and life clearly conflict with the dams Alexie mentions in this poem. How might "The Powwow at the End of the World" work with Julie Titone's essay "Balance of Power" (see pages 541–544) to form a comprehensive comment about dams and salmon fisheries in the Northwest?
6. What is your overall assessment of "The Powwow at the End of the World"? Did you like it? Why or why not?

◆ WRITING OPPORTUNITY

1. What kind of impact—positive or negative—has a public works project had on your community? Pick one such project and write a brief essay about it.
2. Have you been in a situation in which you've had to offer forgiveness to someone you didn't want to? Write about this situation and its outcome. ◆

SHERMAN ALEXIE

EVOLUTION

Buffalo Bill opens a pawn shop on the reservation   1
right across the border from the liquor store
and he stays open 24 hours a day, 7 days a week

and the Indians come running in with jewelry
television sets, a VCR, a full-length beaded buckskin outfit   5
it took Inez Muse 12 years to finish. Buffalo Bill

takes everything the Indians have to offer, keeps it
all catalogued and filed in a storage room. The Indians
pawn their hands, saving the thumbs for last, they pawn

their skeletons, falling endlessly from the skin   10
and when the last Indian has pawned everything
but his heart, Buffalo Bill takes that for twenty bucks

> closes up the pawn shop, paints a new sign over the old
> calls his venture THE MUSEUM OF NATIVE AMERICAN CULTURES
> charges the Indians five bucks a head to enter. 15

◆ QUESTIONS FOR REVIEW

1. We can talk about the structure of this poem in a couple of ways. First, it consists of five three-line stanzas. Second, the poem consists of three sentences. How does the structure of the poem contribute to the poem's overall meaning?
2. Examine the items that the Indians bring to Buffalo Bill. How does Alexie use these items to create the overall meaning of the poem?
3. Alexie is clearly making much use of symbol and metaphor in this poem. Find one key symbol and one key metaphor and discuss the meaning they create for you.
4. The last line of this poem is central to the powerfully ironic tone of this poem. What makes this line so ironic?
5. What is the theme of this poem? What is Alexie saying about the historical relationships between Native Americans and the European settlers who immigrated to this country?

◆ WRITING OPPORTUNITY

1. Alexie opens his poem by referring to Buffalo Bill. Many people would call Buffalo Bill a hero, but others would see him in a much less positive light. Some would call him an anti-hero or a villain. Do some research on the historical character that the legend of Buffalo Bill is based on and discuss what you learn about him and about American history in the process.
2. What do you make of Alexie's choice of "Evolution" to name this poem? Think of the ways this word "evolution" is used: as a name of a theory of the development of life on earth; as a word meaning the changes that take place as anything develops from its beginning point to later stages of its development. Is Alexie alluding to either (or both) of these meanings in this poem? Write a brief essay in which you explore the meaning he creates with this title.
3. How do the three poems given here by Sherman Alexie comment on or complement each other? ◆

SAMPLE ESSAYS

Below we present four essays written *about* and *from* literature. Three of the four essays are written by students and the fourth by a musician who writes a column for a local newspaper. The first two of these essays may be classified as writing *about* literature, since in each essay the writer's overall goal is to analyze and explain the meanings of the literary work she is writing about. In the last two essays, the writers use works of literature as touchstones for exploration of their lives and experiences. Thus, we would label these two essays as writing *from* literature.

Our first essay was written by Kendra Stead when she was a first year writing student at the University of North Carolina at Charlotte. Kendra is now studying law at Northwestern University.

KENDRA STEAD

THE MAKING OF SPELLS

1   In "Spelling," Margaret Atwood examines the relationships between words and power as they pertain to women. Atwood uses structure, word play, and historical allusion to convey her belief that the subordination of women throughout history is closely linked to the suppression of women's words.

2   The poem is divided into six sections, each one closely related to the others, with each introducing a new, distinct idea or serving a clear structural purpose. In the first of these stanzas, the narrator describes her daughter spelling out words on the floor with plastic letters. Atwood then breaks to a new section to ponder the history of women writers–women who chose not to have children so they could "mainline words" (line 11). This is likely an allusion or a reference to Virginia Woolf's novel, *A Room of One's Own*, which focused on female authors' need to find privacy in order to create works of genius. Atwood then acknowledges history's habit of making parenting and writing mutually exclusive paths for women.

3   The third section breaks from narrative into a reflection: "A child is not a poem, / a poem is not a child. / There is no either/or" (lines 12–14). This is further commentary on the difficulties female authors face in pursuing writing or child rearing exclusively: "A child is not a poem" (line 12) and therefore cannot fulfil one's desire to write; "a poem is not a child" (line 13) and therefore cannot satisfy the desire for a family. While Atwood claims that "there is no either / or" (line 14), she warns the reader that she is about to present some type of conflicting relationship between the two with her one-word sentence: "However" (line 15).

4   After this suggestion, Atwood begins a new section. Here she relates a story of a woman whose legs are bound to prevent her from giving birth to her child.

The second stanza of section three tells the story of an "ancestress," a word coined for obviously feminist purposes. Burned at the stake for witchery, this woman has been gagged to keep her from uttering any spells towards her persecutors. Note that both the coming baby and the coming words are stifled in the same way; by joining these two stanzas in the same section, Atwood capitalizes on the parallels to emphasize the historical subjugation of women. Atwood then states: "A word after a word / after a word is power" (lines 24–25). The ancestress cannot utter word after word to assert power, but Atwood and other women can. In this section, we have a stanza after a stanza after a stanza (each stanza a sequence of words, each word a sequence of letters), suggesting that the act of writing is an assertion of power, that this poem is an assertion of power.

The fifth section of the poem contains two stanzas, the first a series of metaphors, the second a simple sentence: "This is a metaphor" (line 36). The metaphors of the first stanza relate nature and language: the flesh becomes language "[a]t the point where language falls away / from the hot bones . . ." (lines 26–27), " . . . the rock breaks open and darkness / flows out of it like blood . . ." (lines 28–29), " . . . & the body / itself becomes a mouth" (line 35). There is a circular complexity to this stanza in that it seems to be saying that our language cannot get at the truths that come to us by means of metaphor, while, at the same time, illustrating that language is metaphor and metaphor is language. Atwood has already told the reader that words are power, and here she demonstrates that power.

In section six Atwood returns to the one-stanza form. This compact form allows for a sense of conclusion. In this stanza Atwood poses the question "How do you learn to spell?" (line 37) and presents her seemingly obtuse answer: "your own name first, / your first naming, your first name / your first word" (lines 39–41). By focusing on names and naming as part of "Spelling," Atwood echoes findings from sociology. Researchers in this field have examined naming and have noted that "the more emphasis a society places on the difference between girls and boys, the more carefully it will distinguish their names" (Bates, et al. 221). Atwood thus comments on the ways language marks and restricts women from birth onward and encourages a reevaluation of naming (and the larger reclaiming of language as a whole).

Atwood's word choice is interesting because she uses double meanings to create a multi-layered poem. In stanza one the narrator describes her daughter's games: "with plastic letters / red, blue & hard yellow" (lines 2–3). Red, blue, and yellow are the primary colors, emphasizing that letters are the primary units of language. The second stanza presents another interesting word choice: "so they could mainline words" (line 11). The word "mainline" has a well-known slang meaning of intravenous narcotic injection. To describe these women's commitment to writing, Atwood uses language that can be read as descriptive of an addict's compulsive behavior: "denied themselves daughters / closed themselves in rooms / drew the curtains / so they could mainline words" (lines 8–11). Atwood suggests that for women writers, the love of words was so powerful, so all consuming that it was impossible to ignore. In comparing women who write with drug addicts, Atwood emphasizes the sacrifices these writers make for their art and the power that working with words holds over them.

The most important word use in the poem is Atwood's play on the word "spell." Stanza one ends with: "spelling. / how to make spells" (lines 5–6). Because "Spelling" is the poem's title, the reader should pay special attention to it and its variations. Spelling in the sense of forming letters into words is not "how to make spells"; it is how to make words. Atwood is leading the reader to pay special attention to this word and contemplate other possible meanings. Section four tells the story of a gagged "ancestress" burned at the stake for witchery. The woman was gagged "to strangle words" (line 23) and so prevent her from casting spells, because "A word after a word / after a word is power" (lines 24–25). The idea of spells in the sense of the supernatural enhances this assertion that words are indeed powerful.

Section six closes "Spelling" by circling back to section one, as the narrator connects the spelling her daughter learns with "red, blue & hard yellow" letters (line 3) with the colors of nature she gives near the poem's end: "Blood, sky, & the sun" (line 38). In making this connection, the narrator connects her daughter to the women she celebrates in this poem, to those women who spell words and who use their language to cast spells.

The casting of spells throughout "Spelling" develops a historical allusion that advances the feminist theme of the poem. The depth of this allusion is striking. Historically, those who cast spells—witches—have been persecuted and often put to death, as Atwood notes in the fifth stanza. Witch hunts, which grew out of the Inquisition, primarily targeted women (Guiley 371). The term "witch" comes from the Old English word *wicca*, "wise woman." "Still another Old English term, *wican*, means 'to bend'" (Guiley 359). "Witch," then, becomes a woman-centered word that denotes the power to shape or transform things. There is a fascinating relationship here: women, who are labeled literally as powerful and wise, have been historically persecuted. It isn't difficult to see that Atwood is using witchery to extend the abilities of witches, such as wisdom and the power to "bend" or transform things, to all women, especially since she ties it to the young girl playing on the floor, transforming letters that are the primary colors of blood, sky, and sun into words, "learning how to spell" (line 4).

"Spelling" is an intricate, multi-layered poem. It speaks of the historical suppression of women's language, but it also screams of progress. The narrator's daughter is playing with letters: to make something into a toy, one must have power over it. By its very existence this poem is an assertion of power: a woman's writing about women, a reclaiming of all those stifled words. Atwood's rich use of language makes the poem accessible not simply through structure, word choice, and historical allusion, but rather through a complex interweaving of these elements.

Works Cited

Atwood, Margaret. "Spelling." *True Stories*. New York: Simon and Schuster, 1981. 63–64.

Bates, Ülkü Ü., et al. *Women's Realities, Women's Choices: An Introduction to Women's Studies*. New York: Oxford UP, 1983.

Guiley, Rosemary Ellen. *The Encyclopedia of Witches & Witchcraft*. Second Edition. New York: Checkmark Books, 1999.

◆ QUESTIONS FOR REVIEW

1. How does Kendra's reading of "Spelling" help you to understand this poem? How does her reading square with your own? On what points do you agree with her? Disagree? Why?
2. Identify Kendra's thesis statement. Where does it appear? How effectively does she support it?
3. Kendra works through the poem from start to finish, explicating the lines she thinks important. Does this help you to understand the poem better? Why or why not?
4. How effective is the essay's introduction? Conclusion? Why?
5. How well does Kendra incorporate information from sources other than the poem to support her interpretation?

Our second student essay is by Amy Wright, a writing student at Sam Houston State University. Amy's essay presents an interpretation of Aaron Gwyn's "Of Falling"; thus, Amy's essay represents writing *about* literature.

AMY WRIGHT

A QUEST TO RETURN TO THE GARDEN: PERCEPTION "OF FALLING"

1   Aaron Gwyn's short story "Of Falling" recounts different characters' experiences with and reactions to the experience of falling. The major characters in the story perceive falling differently. Even though none of the characters fully

understands the significance of their "falls," Gwyn creates an atmosphere in which the act of falling takes on symbolic and religious meanings. At the same time that falling represents a threat to one's life, it also represents, ironically, a quest for life. Gwyn treats falling as a natural and inescapable part of human experience that can take on symbolic meanings depending on the ways in which one perceives and interprets his or her fall.

In the story's first account of a fall, George Crider's eight-year-old brother Freddy is thrown from a horse and subsequently dies of an infection. George survives the incident and believes that he should have been able to save Freddy as well. The tragedy almost destroys the fifteen-year-old George, who jumps into the open grave at Freddy's funeral. In the following years, George lives in a self-imposed exile that ultimately leads him to leave home at the young age of eighteen.

Shortly after establishing himself as a taciturn but very competent member of an oil-rig crew, George topples from a 116-foot scaffold. In describing this fall, the narrator tells the reader that George is unconscious of the fall itself: "For him there was only the eighth floor and the earth" (2). He remembers before and after the fall, and the change in himself that takes place, but does not remember the actual four seconds of the fall. Immediately after this fall, George thinks not about the effects that falling will have on his life, but rather about the boards "that had snapped beneath his feet" (3). In his mind's eye, he can see himself walking "to where they [the boards] lay at the side of the derrick and kick[ing] them to splinters" (3).

In the years following, George outwardly "seemed much the same as before the fall . . . you would not have thought he had fallen in his life" (4). Despite this appearance, however, George is plagued by the residual effects of falling. After his physical healing is complete, his sleep becomes haunted by dreams; ironically, these are dreams not of falling but of stillness, the absence of falling. In his dreams he is unable to move, even to escape an encroaching cloud, which the narrator describes as "not the type of cloud from which angels or prophets descend" (5). The Biblical allusion here helps to create a connection to the fall that occurs in the Garden of Eden. Just as Adam and Eve lose their innocence of death and sin when they come to the awful realization that their Fall will bring exile from the garden and from God, George loses his innocence when his brother falls and subsequently dies. Like that of the characters in the traditional garden story, George's experience is both good and bad. On one hand, he is prematurely deprived of his innocence. On the other hand, a consciousness is opened to him that is not available before his fall.

For the rest of his life, George has to deal with the reactions of outsiders who have not fallen. The people who view him demonstrate awe, disbelief, squeamish disgust, or forced reverence. Three of the most telling responses come from evangelists. These men represent both the genuine faithful, striving to do the true work of the Lord, and the quack doctors of the Christian tent, dispensing religious healing with an eye to the applause of their audience and the payoff for their pocketbooks. The first evangelist, Oral Roberts, ignores the effect of the fall itself and focuses on George's recovery. He takes advantage of George's pain, testifying to God's mighty work in George's life; Roberts sees George's almost complete physical healing as a testimony for "the God of his father" (12), whom George actually denies. This is ironic given the fact that Roberts had lectured his followers on the "three kinds of healing": physical, emotional, and spiritual (8). By focusing entirely on his interpretation of the meaning of George's physical healing, Roberts reveals a shallow approach to healing in his failure to see the emotional and spiritual needs of the fallen man in front of him.

Reverend R.T. Shorbach, the second evangelist, offers a charismatic ministry that features falling. Reverend Shorbach slays in the spirit every man and woman who approaches the altar. In so doing, he cheapens the experience of falling; what should be a deeply personal and meaningful experience becomes routine and run-of-the-mill. Like George's wife, Sadie, who attended Reverend Shorbach's meetings any time he was close enough for her to do so, Reverend Shorbach's followers sought some sort of magic formula by which they could fall into a state of grace.

The third evangelist, Leslie Snodgrass, is but fifteen years old—the same age George had been when his brother died. The fantastic claims and the hype surrounding his ministry make him seem to be yet another charlatan; however, there is something mysterious and, perhaps, spiritual about this young man. Unlike Reverend Shorbach, who demonstrates his power by felling everyone who approaches him, Snodgrass seems to deal with each of those who approach him as individuals.

After she had a fall of her own from their back porch, Sadie heard about Snodgrass and convinced George to take her to his services. Sadie attends Snodgrass's meeting with the anticipation of a fall that will lead to her being healed of the injuries received when she fell from her porch, and she is incensed when she realizes that there is no fall in store for her—she will "leave just as she came" (18).

Sadie will not fall at this meeting, even though she desperately wants to; ironically, George, who did not want to come in the first place, will experience his final fall at this meeting. But what are we to make of this last fall? Was George struck down by the wrath of the God whom he had spurned? Or is he finally granted the release that he has been longing for? Or is his death a completely random occurrence that is made to look meaningful by the bizarre situation in which it occurs? We have no conclusive answer to this question, but the description of this final fall offers support for the view that George's fall functions as release.

Unlike his first fall, this one is marked by overwhelming sensory consciousness. After the young Snodgrass places his hand on his chest, George reverts to his childhood, a time untroubled by pain and dreams, when he had never had a brother, had never known guilt or shame. A time when falling meant returning to the earth, assured that he would be caught, safe, and lifted up by his parents. In his last moments, George has time to reason that "if it had always been like that, there would have been point in nothing else but to live in the instant when gravity first took hold and pulled you to its center" (19). Armed with this realization, George "abandoned himself to the fall" (19). By embracing, rather than fighting, the inevitable, George finds the freedom in falling.

Work Cited

Gwyn, Aaron. "Of Falling." *Dog on the Cross*. Chapel Hill, NC: Algonquin Books, 2004.

◆ QUESTIONS FOR REVIEW

1. How does Amy's reading of "Of Falling" help you to understand this short story? How does her reading compare with your own? On what points do you agree with her? Disagree? Explain.
2. Identify the thesis of Amy's essay. Does it appear in her essay? If so where? If not, state it in your own words. How effectively does she support it?
3. In order to explain the meaning she finds in this story, Amy has to present quite a bit of plot detail. Does she use too much plot, or fail to use it as effectively as possible? If so, point out specific passages where the essay could be improved. If not, find a passage where her use of plot is especially effective and explain how she uses plot detail in that passage.
4. How effective are Amy's introduction and conclusion? Could either be improved? If so, how? If not, use information in chapter 2 about introductions and conclusions to explain why her introduction and conclusion are effective.
5. Amy quotes several passages from "Of Falling" in her essay. Is her use of these quotations effective? Could they be more effective in places? If so, explain. If not, choose two or three passages where she uses quotations and explain why the quotations make the paper more effective than it would have been without them.

The third student essay, "No Exceptions" by Kendra Stead, is an example of writing *from* literature.

KENDRA STEAD

NO EXCEPTIONS

Marge Piercy's 1971 poem "A Work of Artifice" was first published in her 1982 book *Circles on the Water*. In 1999, Ms. Piercy's poem was republished in *Women: Issues and Realities*:

> The bonsai tree
> in the attractive pot
> could have grown eighty feet tall
> on the side of a mountain
> till split by lightning.
> But a gardener
> carefully pruned it.
> It is nine inches high.
> Every day as he
> whittles back the branches
> the gardener croons,
> It is your nature to be small and cozy,
> domestic and weak;
> how lucky, little tree,
> to have a pot to grow in.
> With living creatures
> one must begin very early
> to dwarf their growth:
> the bound feet,
> the crippled brain,
> the hair in curlers,
> the hands you
> love to touch.

Piercy's feminist poem presents the idea that what is often called women's "nature" is actually the result of socialization. The upbringing of a woman is made analogous to the careful pruning of a bonsai tree—both products stunted mockeries of their potential.

I discovered this poem in a Women's Studies class during my freshman year. I imagined Piercy sitting through countless experiences similar to my own, and I felt that I understood her motivations and her meaning on a deeper level than I would ever experience a Grecian urn. The poem brought many memories to the surface, particularly the memory of the premarital counseling my husband and I had received during the previous summer.

The two of us had heard a lot about the importance of counseling. Because we wanted to put forth every effort to succeed, I set up an appointment with Father Harrison to talk about the realities of marriage. He began with basics: how people know they are ready for marriage, what newlyweds need, and the importance of money management. But then he moved on to a topic I had always been very sensitive about: differences between men and women. Not biological differences, but behavioral and emotional differences. Father Harrison asked me why I wanted to get married. Before I could get the first two words or my answer out of my mouth he stopped me. "Kendra, I can tell you in one word why you want to get married: security. Am I right?" I nodded blankly, afraid to tell a priest no, but trying desperately to grasp what he meant by security. I thought of security as things like health insurance and smoke detectors, and I knew that I wanted to feel secure in that way. Marrying young gave us several years to save money for a house, money we otherwise would have had to spend on college tuition (one area where married students get a break).

That probably has something to do with security, I thought, having a head start on things like down payments and stock portfolios. But Father Harrison's words quickly corrected my conclusions. While I was pondering his word choices, he was jabbering to Hank about his massive insight into my character. "Now, Hank, you're probably thinking I'm a pretty smart guy because I knew that Kendra was getting married for security. But that's not the case. How do you think I knew that?"

My fiancé gazed blankly at the minister and shrugged. Father Harrison's enthusiasm for his point was not abated by Hank's nonchalance. "I know that because that's what every woman wants from marriage!" he exclaimed. I gave myself an internal slap for ignorantly feeding this ridiculous assertion. Apparently my countenance changed markedly because my generally unobservant husband-to-be looked from me to the priest and quietly added, "I don't think Kendra agrees with you."

If anything was gained from premarital counseling it was in that moment, when I realized that Hank knew me well enough to know that my dumbness was shock and not complicity. Father Harrison was not moved by Hank's comment and continued to speak of me in the third person. "It doesn't matter if she agrees, that's just how it is." He paused and gave Hank the honor of being in the room. "Hank, you being a man, I have no idea why you want to get married."

"That's just how it is." I was seeking out my cozy "pot to grow in." I was weaseling a lifetime contract out of a gardener, thereby insuring that someone would always be there to "whittle back my branches." That was what every woman wanted. It occurred to me that my minister should have a little more insight into what men are seeking to gain from marriage, being a member of that sex, but I suspected he would dismiss that as swiftly as he had Hank's comment.

And I was scared to say it. There I was, the outspoken feminist, afraid to assert myself in the face of blatant sexism. Father Harrison moved on to some other inanity, and I kept my responses to a minimum for the rest of the session.

On our way home I became livid—angry with Father Harrison for failing to live up to my rather biased expectations of an Episcopal minister, and angrier with myself for letting him continue prattling on about something that had offended me so deeply. It occurred to me that I had let him talk to me this way because he was a priest, and somewhere I had developed a notion that priests were different from other people, and therefore shouldn't be questioned. I realized that day that priests are in fact different from other people by virtue of the influence they wield; for that reason they should be questioned extensively. By remaining silent I had let him verbally bind my feet and cripple my brain. How many others were like me? How many couples did Father Harrison counsel every year? How many women mistook him for gospel and fell to his essentialist ramblings about women's "nature"?

Marge Piercy's poem reminded me not only that people learn their roles and their behaviors, but more importantly that no ground is sacred enough to allow it to perpetuate discrimination. By writing "A Work of Artifice" Piercy performed one of the ultimate acts of expression, one that will live on far beyond words uttered in conversation. By writing these thoughts, Piercy made a public statement about her beliefs. When we begin making exceptions and allowances for those we hold in esteemed positions, we ourselves perpetuate the system. In a sense, Father Harrison is the gardener of Piercy's poem. He is cultivating his own collection of bonsai trees in the parish by teaching each couple he marries that women are dependent and weak simply by virtue of being women. Piercy taught me that it is *never* acceptable to play the role of the pruned tree.

Work Cited

Piercy, Marge. "A Work of Artifice." *Circles on the Water*. New York: Random House, 1982.

◆ QUESTIONS FOR REVIEW

1. How has Kendra shown you that she has understood Piercy's poem?
2. Kendra writes with passion about being confronted by sexist attitudes and language. Does her message—what she learned from this experience—apply just to women or to everyone?
3. Kendra incorporates phrases and ideas from Piercy's poem in her essay. How effectively does she do so?

✦ WRITING OPPORTUNITY

1. Read several poems by Marge Piercy or other feminist poets. How effective are these poems in presenting a feminist point of view?
2. Write about a time when you felt oppressed. What was the situation? What was its outcome? ✦

The fourth and last sample essay we present was written by Steve Stoeckel, a professional musician and electronics technician who serves as a "community columnist" for *The Charlotte Observer*. In this essay, Stoeckel recounts an experience from his work in sales and relates it to a poem by Carl Sandburg.

STEVE STOECKEL

WHAT ABOUT THE CUSTOMER?

It Must Be Easy for the Man in the Comfy Leather Chair to Forget

I was on the phone to the president, and it wasn't going well. No, not that president: It was the early '80s, and I was apologizing profusely to the president of Dynamic Organic Recording Corporation.

DORC had just released a product that was revolutionizing the industry, and we were selling tons of them. Their competitor, Young Electronics Hawaiian Amalgamated, had released their own version, and each company was fighting for its format to win. My job was repairing these widgets.

A customer had purchased a DORC product from us and needed a quick repair. Since DORC hadn't set up repair centers, I called to find out how long it would take for factory service.

"Six weeks," the service manager said. I told him that seemed long. "I only have three techs," he said, irritated. "We're servicing the whole country. That's not long at all." I refrained from offering obvious solutions to his problem, and simply told him my customer wouldn't be happy being without his machine. Silence. He makes his living with it, I said. Silence.

Which will they choose?

Then I made my fatal error: Young Electronics Hawaiian Amalgamated provides me with schematics and training to fix their product here, I said. Which product do you think our customers will choose, based on service? He hung up. I sighed and packed my customer's widget up.

Unknown to me, there followed conversations between DORC's service manager, the president, the sales rep, and then my boss, who was informed we were being dropped for pushing YEHA's product over DORC's. My boss listened to my story, and was pleased to see I was fighting for our customer. "Call the president and apologize," he said. "Be nice."

"Convince me we shouldn't yank the line," the president was saying. "Sell me." I began by saying I never implied we were pushing the competitor's line. "Oh, I believe you were, Steve," he said. I felt the blood rushing to my cheeks, and remembered: Be Nice. I took a breath. I'm extremely sorry my words were taken that way, I said. I never meant to suggest we weren't fully supporting your product, which is, by the way, a great design.

"Yes, it is, Steve!" the president said, his voice rising with enthusiasm. "It's going to (revolutionize the industry, I thought) revolutionize the industry! Do you have any idea how many man hours we have just in R&D?" Before I could answer, he launched into the History of The Product, which, frankly, was the first thing in this conversation that interested me. Then his voice got warm, conspiratorial.

"I'm like a bear with her cubs regarding this product. It's my passion. I'd like you to feel the same." I agreed, hoping he meant I was the bear and not the cubs. He was delighted, so I agreed with everything else he said over the next few minutes, which pleased him even more. We left with a vow to keep in touch, and if there was anything I ever needed etc. etc.

Profit, not people, valued

As I hung up, it occurred to me he'd never asked about the customer. If he had, I'd have told him (with all the expletives deleted) that the customer would never in a million years buy a DORC product, that he would tell all his friends not to buy a DORC product and that he bought a YEHA product the next day.

This lesson has stayed with me for over 20 years, and every time I encounter or read about a CEO who cares only about product, profit, or preserving the life of the artificial person that is the Corporation, I'm disgusted. I care about all those things too, but I also care about the person who carries all that on his back – the customer.

Maybe it's because I've been on the front lines for 30 years, facing those customers. Maybe it's because I don't have the comfy leather chair, the walnut desk, the yes-men and whatever else that insulates these Masters of the Universe, that makes them ignore customers. Or play games with accounting. Or, worst of all, make products that injure people.

Name us a king

DORC's president wasn't evil, of course, just clueless, and sort of an apprentice Master of the Universe. For you real Masters, I offer one of my favorite Carl Sandburg poems, "Name Us a King," which goes in part: 12

> Name us a king
> who shall live forever —
> a peanut king, a potato king,
> a gasket king, a brass-tack king. . . .
> Name us a king
> so keen, so fast, so hard,
> he shall last forever —
> and all the yes-men square shooters
> telling the king, "Okay Boss, you shall last forever! and then some!" . . .
> a zipper king or a chewing gum king,
> any consolidated amalgamated syndicate king —
> . . . an okay Boss who shall never bite the dust,
> never go down and be a sandwich for the worms
> like us — the customers,
> like us — the customers.

◆ Questions for Review

1. What is the thesis of Stoeckel's essay? Is there a specific sentence in which he states his thesis? If so, which one?
2. What is the overall purpose (or aim) of this essay? What audience do you imagine it is written for?
3. Assuming the excerpt from Sandburg's poem is sufficient to give you the overall meaning of his poem, briefly state that meaning or significance. What is the connection between that meaning and Stoeckel's thesis? Is the connection clear?
4. Stoeckel frames his essay as a narrative. How effective is this framework for Stoeckel's purpose?

◆ WRITING OPPORTUNITY

1. Have you had a life experience that immeadiately made you think of a literary work—a poem, short story, play. or novel? If so, spend a few minutes writing about what it was in that situation that made you think of that work.
2. Have you ever had a job that required you to sell a product that you would not buy? If not, can you imagine yourself in such a job? Write a brief essay in which you explore your sense of what it means to be an ethical salesperson? Do we honestly believe that all those people attempting to sell us products on television use those products? If they do not, are they being dishonest or unethical? ◆

THE RHETORICAL TRIANGLE

Subject

The most prominent point of the rhetorical triangle in an interpretive essay is the subject, the piece of literature about which the essay is written; thus, the primary focus is on the literary text and what it means. Your written response begins with your understanding of that piece of literature, an understanding you may develop by reading the text closely and then working with it to see what it means to you. To illustrate some of the ways in which you can read, examine, and then respond to a literary text, we'll work with the poem by Robert Frost presented earlier, "For Once, Then, Something," first published in 1923. Try this procedure (which should remind you of several of the reading strategies in Chapter 4):

1. First, read the poem silently. Then, read it again, this time aloud, and listen for the language—that is, listen for natural points of emphasis.
2. Read the poem a third time, marking key terms (words or phrases) as you go. Also mark those passages that you emphasized while reading aloud. Jot a quick note about why these seem important or warrant emphasis.

At times, it's tempting to mark nearly every word in a poem as a key term, because poetry can be so compact and intense that nearly every image seems to figure as important. In looking at key terms in Frost's poem, Bill identified four sets of terms and then clustered other words and images that related to those terms to try to bring some kind of order to his investigation. In addition, Bill raised some questions about some terms and jotted comments on others. He also commented briefly on each set of terms and on the sets as a whole; these comments are underlined.

> Conflict
> *Others taunt* (who are these others? why do they taunt Frost?)
> <u>Taunting speaks of</u> <u>opposition</u>, <u>teasing</u>.

Others' view of Frost as poet
  Always wrong to the light (light = illumination = insight—but he's always wrong)
  shining surface picture (superficial, no insight?)
  Me myself... godlike (Narcissus imagery?)
  <u>Frost says taunters see him as superficial and, perhaps, narcissistic.</u>
Nature imagery
  nowhere
  well   ⎤—(water as life-giving, life-sustaining, place to look for insight?)
  water
  <u>Frost, known for his poetry dealing with nature, creates images of water and wells as suitable places to look for insight. These images say that nature is a place to look for insight.</u>
  Water... rebuke the too clear water (nature won't give up secrets easily?)
  Blurred... blotted
  <u>But nature doesn't always cooperate; it's not easy to find whatever it is that Frost's detractors want him to find and write about.</u>
Something seen
  a something white (symbolic value of white?)
  uncertain (why uncertain?)
  Something more of the depths (literal or symbolic depths? both?)
  What was that... Truth? A pebble of quartz?
  something
  <u>Okay, this is what Frost says his detractors want him to see. But it's not always available—it's uncertain, and Frost doesn't really know what he glimpsed at the bottom of the well. But at least it was something.</u>
<u>Taken together, what these terms show is a conflict between Frost and his taunters—critics of his early poetry? They also suggest that seeing deeply into the well isn't always easy. And even when a poet does see something, he's not always sure of what he's seen. So it's a "maybe" kind of deal—maybe he'll see something insightful, maybe he won't. But at least he tries.</u>

3. Divide the poem into a beginning, middle, and end. Think about why you made the divisions you made. What happens in each part?

   beginning—lines 1–6. Frost talks about being criticized for being superficial or shallow.
   middle—lines 7–14. Story of trying to catch a glimpse of that elusive "something more of the depths." Note that *"Once"* is the only word in the poem that's italicized.
   end—lines 14–15. Frost draws (or at least implies) a conclusion based on his experience of trying to reveal deeper insights in his poetry.

4. Apply the Questions for Analysis (see pages 24–31).
   a. What goes with what? (association)

      associations with Frost as poet—
      Frost (1874–1963), a beloved and popular American poet, many poems dealt with nature but many also explored psychological aspects of people (see "An Old

Man's Winter's Night" and "Tree at My Window," to name but two); he was asked to read at JFK's inaugural in 1960.

associations with key terms—
In lines 1–6, the terms associated with Frost as poet suggest superficiality, Narcissism. There's an image that reminds me of Pan (the Roman god of the forest), which doesn't suggest seriousness at all. Frost reports that "Others" (critics?) say that he sees only himself and reports only that in his poetry.

In lines 7–14, Frost reports a time when he was "trying" to see deeper into a well-curb. The terms here suggest that it's really not possible, that nature just won't give up its secrets very readily.

In lines 14–15, Frost presents a conclusion of sorts that may figure as the poem's theme—Truth isn't knowable in any final sense, but whatever Frost saw was enough for him.

b. What opposes what? (opposition)

There is opposition at work in the poem—the "Others" Frost mentions in the poem's first line. Who are these others? Why do they taunt Frost? What have they said about his poetry? Why does Frost feel it necessary to respond to them? (*Note:* Answering these questions will take some research. Were you to research this, you'd find that Frost was criticized early in his career. For example, an anonymous review published in 1913 said that "many of his verses do not rise above the ordinary [. . .]" [Greiner 71]. Another anonymous review, published in the January 1915 issue of the *Bulletin of the Poetry Society of America,* said, "Mr. Frost has been greatly acclaimed by prophets of new poetic cults in England, but his work could hardly be said to have found sympathizers in the Poetry Society" [Greiner 85]. And in 1917, Amy Lowell closed a critical essay on Frost "with the questionable suggestion that his art, while surely brilliant, is painted on a canvas so 'exceedingly small' that he can never equal the achievement of a man with a wider vision" [Greiner 89]. For a thorough discussion of Frost's reception by such critics as these, see Donald J. Greiner's *Robert Frost: The Poet and His Critics* [Chicago: American Library Association, 1974].)

Because the opening clearly reveals conflict—taunting is hardly conciliatory—there is tension at work in the poem. How is it resolved?

c. What follows what? (sequence)

Although we've already divided the poem into three parts—beginning, middle, and end—we can talk a bit more about its structure by looking at sequence. First, we can examine where the poem divides, where its breaks are, by considering how various lines relate to one another. How do lines 1–6 work to form a unit, lines 7–14 another, and lines 14–15 yet another?

Second, we can examine how individual images follow one another, so that the separate images join to form larger or more comprehensive images. For example, we identified these key terms in lines 1–6 that are associated with Frost as a poet, images he attributes to the "Others" mentioned in line 1: always wrong to the light, shining surface picture, me myself, godlike, [framed by a] wreath of fern and cloud puffs. Individually, each image suggests a bit of the nature of criticism of Frost by the "Others," but as a whole they paint a complete picture of a poet who is so self-centered as to be narcissistic. Further, the Pan image (which derives from "godlike" and the framing wreath) suggests that Frost is not a serious nature poet but one who sees only himself and celebrates only his own assumed divinity.

   d. What follows from what? (consequence)

   What results from the taunting, from the conflict and tension Frost reports? Obviously, the poem. Frost wants to respond to his critics, not only to defend himself as a poet but also to present his view about the nature of truth. Ultimately, Frost says that truth is elusive at best, that it's difficult to know truth, even more difficult to present it in a poem. Such a view would probably run counter to Frost's critics in the Poetry Society of America.

5. Write (a) a sentence or two summarizing or paraphrasing the poem, (b) a sentence or two speculating about Frost's purpose in writing the poem, and (c) a sentence or two saying whether you think he achieved his purpose. Identify specific elements from the poem to support the sentences you wrote for (b) and (c).
   a. "For Once, Then, Something" details Frost's conflict with his critics and reveals his idea that you can't fix truth with a capital "T."
   b. Frost's purpose seems to have been (1) to tell his critics (the "Others" who "taunt" him about their perception of shallowness in his poetry) that they're wrong and (2) to present his own view about discovering and then presenting insights or truth in his poetry.
   c. Yes, he succeeds. In the first section of the poem, he presents the nature of the criticism of his poetry (he's shallow and narcissistic); in the second, he shows how difficult it is to discern truth (or insights) from nature (water imagery); in the third, he gives his own vision of what's discernible (it's uncertain, but whatever he saw was enough for the moment). On one level, this poem shows Frost taunting his critics. On another, it suggests that Frost felt that poetry either couldn't or shouldn't fix truth in ways that his critics called for.

At times, there's an indeterminacy at work in poetry, something that leaves the reader great leeway to read a poem in a highly personal way. This is actually one of the strengths of poetry and speaks to the fact that people read literature from an individual perspective and take from that literature what it says to them. As we'll point out below, serious literature is open to interpretation, and because we read as individuals, each reader may develop her own interpretation of a piece of literature.

Exercise 7.2

Apply this reading procedure to Atwood's and Alexie's poems and to at least one of the short stories presented at the beginning of this chapter. How did your applications enhance your reading and understanding of the poetry? The story?

Elements of Literature Interpreting a piece of literature, whether novel, short story, play, or poem, often requires you to consider particular aspects or elements of the text. What follows is a brief look at some of the major elements of literature, with questions you may answer as you consider each element. Throughout this discussion, we refer to stories, but keep in mind that much of what we say will apply not only to fiction but also to drama and poetry, especially narrative poetry.

Plot   The sequence of events in a piece of literature, sometimes known as the *story line*, is the *plot*. To examine the plot, we have to look at what happens, and we can do so by considering these questions: "What follows what?" (sequence) and "What follows from what?" (consequence). Events in a story follow other events, sometimes because they come later in time (a matter of sequence), at other times because one event causes another to occur (a matter of consequence, or cause and effect). Looking at the questions "What follows what?" and "What follows from what?" provides a starting point for considering the action of a literary text. For Frost's poem, answering these questions gives us this summary and initial interpretation:

> Critics (the "Others" mentioned in line 1) taunt Frost for not finding deeper insights into life than he seems to find in his poetry. This taunting causes Frost to try to see deeper into nature (the "well-curb," lines 1, 7) so as to find deeper insights. And, sure enough, he seems to catch sight of something just by trying to glimpse it. But a brief glimpse is all he gets, for nature won't give up its secrets readily and, taking on human attributes, uses a drop of water from a fern to keep Frost from finding that ultimate insight his critics want him to find (line 12). This teaches Frost that, as far as he's concerned, we can't realize the kinds of insights his critics call for. He tells us this by trying to name the thing he saw: "What was that whiteness?/ Truth? A pebble of quartz?" (lines 14–15). He doesn't really know whether he saw a piece of rock or some kind of insight. He knows only that he looked for it and that it was "For once, then, something" (line 15). This realization causes Frost to write the poem, so that he offers an answer to his critics.

Another way of considering the plot, or story line, is to trace (and perhaps even chart or map) its development as we proceed through the story. Consider how the story opens (begins), how that opening leads to and through the action of the story (its middle), and how the conclusion (end) of the story derives from that action. And consider all of this with an eye toward the eventfulness or significance or quality of the story's parts (i.e., its beginning, middle, and end) and its various events. That is, as you trace the story's sequence of events, you should note the significance of the events, not only what happens but also why it happens and then what it causes.

To begin considering plot, ask questions like these: What happens? How does the story begin? What happens in the story's middle? How does the story end? How does the beginning lead to the middle and the middle to the end? Which events are important or significant? Why?

Conflict   Plot proceeds on the conflict between characters and its resolution. Think about how the action in a situation comedy proceeds. There's an opening situation (a beginning) that at least suggests the sequence of events to follow. Then, as the action unfolds (as it moves through the sitcom's middle), it builds conflict. Most often, two characters (or groups of characters) are at odds with or oppose each other, and their conflict comes to a head right before a commercial, so as to keep viewer interest. After the commercial, that conflict is either resolved or complicated further. This pattern of conflict followed by resolution or further complication continues until the end of the program, when some sort of final resolution is reached. This final resolution is often called the *climax*, the most important moment of the program. In serious literature, the climax often strongly suggests the theme of the piece of literature.

Questions to help you consider conflict include these: What is the conflict? What tension is at work in the story? What is the quality of that tension? How is it resolved? Who resolves it? Are you satisfied with the resolution? Is the resolution consistent with the story itself?

Exercise 7.3

Describe or summarize the plot of any of the short stories or poems you've read in this text. Then describe any conflict you may find in the piece of literature you're working with. How does the conflict drive or advance the plot?

Character   We may define a story's characters in several ways:

Major. Major characters are the primary characters in the story.

Minor. Minor characters are characters on the story's periphery who work to further the plot, oftentimes by serving as foils for the major characters. A *foil* is a character whose interaction with a major character serves primarily to develop or reflect some important trait of the major character.

Protagonist. The protagonist is the main character in a story, the one about whom the story revolves. At times, the protagonist is called the *hero* of the story, but that doesn't mean she always acts heroically (in the idealistic sense of that term). Sometimes, we may not like a protagonist, but like her or not, she still serves as the story's main character.

Antagonist. An antagonist is a character in conflict with the protagonist. At times, this antagonist is a foil, but at other times, an antagonist is a major character who greatly influences the actions of the protagonist and so the outcome of the story.

Questions for thinking about characters include these: Who is the major or primary character? Is there more than one? How would you describe each character physically? Ethically? Emotionally? What kind of turmoil is a character in? What causes it? Is the character's reaction believable? Do you like a given character? Why or why not? What action is each character involved in throughout the story? What is the significance of this action? How do the characters interact with one another? What is the result of this interaction?

Exercise 7.4

For at least one of the short stories in this chapter, make a list of characters. Which are major? Minor? Who is the protagonist? The antagonist? How do the protagonist and the antagonist work against each other? What is the outcome of their conflict?

Setting   Setting is the background in which the story takes place. Think about the set for a movie or television show. Much of *Friends,* a situation comedy, is set in the apartments of this show's six major characters. But the setting expands to include various places of work (e.g., the coffeehouse in which one of them worked and where the six friends often meet) and places in New York City. It also extends beyond these physical scenes to embrace the United States at the beginning of the twenty-first century and the social scene of young, urban professionals in this era. So the setting of a story involves not only its physical scene but also its social or political climate.

Consider such questions as these in looking at setting: Where is the story set—time (e.g., season of the year, time of day, particular year, decade, century), place (e.g., specific town or country)? What influences the setting (e.g., weather, terrain, construction, political or social climate)? How does the setting influence or support the characters' actions? How does the setting comment on the characters' actions? What is the meaning of the setting?

Exercise 7.5

In "Shopping," how does the setting help develop the significance of the story? What is the impact of the contrast between the physical setting, the upscale mall, and the poor bag lady? What does the mall represent or symbolize? How does this setting reflect U.S. culture?

Point of View   What vantage point does the writer take in the story? Through whose eyes do we see the action? Here's a list of possible points of view:

Objective. The narrator (the story's teller) simply describes the action without going into any character's mind; also called *camera eye.*

First person. The narrator of the story is also a character in the story and uses "I" as the focal point. The narrator can tell the reader only what he sees and thinks.

Third person limited omniscience. The narrator of the story tells the tale from the perspective of one character in the story and may enter into the thoughts of only that character. It's as though the narrator sits on the shoulder of that character, telling the reader what that character sees and thinks. ("Shopping" is told from this perspective.)

Third person omniscience. The narrator of the story is free to roam. The narrator may report the thinking of any character and may tell what each character sees. ("The Story of an Hour" is told from this perspective.)

When considering point of view, it's important to remember that not all narrators are equally reliable. A first-person narrator may not be a reliable storyteller, because his perspective is necessarily skewed. Consider, for example, Huck Finn, the narrator of Mark Twain's *The Adventure of Huckleberry Finn*. When Huck tells us that Emmaline Grangerford might have been a great poet had she lived. We have reason to suspect Huck's judgement because we have seen some of her poetry. But even if we had not, we should keep in mind the fact that any information we receive from Huck is filtered through his preconceptions and biases. We must always question the reliability of first-person narrators.

Symbols   A *symbol* is a person, place, thing, or event that has meaning beyond what we might normally expect. Writers use symbols to direct the reader's attention toward the meaning they intended. The reader's job is to identify and examine symbols, considering the attitudes implicit in each and how they support or develop the story's theme. Like a rock thrown into a pool of water, symbols create a ripple effect, and their importance spreads beyond their immediate, literal meaning as the reader connects a particular symbol to a larger theme.

In "That Place Where Ghosts of Salmon Jump," Sherman Alexie presents Coyote (note the capital C) as a major character. But Coyote also has symbolic value, assuming mythic proportions. Alexie alludes to what may be a flood myth taken from his tribe's lore. Given Alexie's statement that the rain Coyote created "lasted for forty days and nights," there are clear, immediate connections to the biblical story of Noah and the ark. Later, Alexie tells Coyote, "you're a liar and I don't trust you." In the lore of many tribes, Coyote is a trickster, a shifty, untrustworthy figure. For anyone familiar with such lore, Coyote brings these associations to mind. The coyote is also a popular motif for jewelry and house decorations in the Southwest. Usually, it's a stylized coyote, benign, almost cute, as it sits back on its haunches, head thrown back, yipping and howling at the moon. Yet another dimension to the coyote is the actual four-legged animal *(Canis latrans),* a cousin of the wolf. A fair number of ranchers in the West consider the coyote a pest to be eradicated, because coyotes are reputed to kill lambs and calves, not to mention pet cats and dogs. Alexie evokes all of these associations by using this term. Do you have to understand or be familiar with all of them to understand or interpret or enjoy the poem? No. But you will take more meaning from your readings as you sensitize yourself to the symbolic meanings they offer you.

> **Exercise 7.6**
>
> 1. What symbols (including colors, objects, and gestures) might represent these concepts?
>
> | innocence | purity | anger | evil |
> |---|---|---|---|
> | life | growth | death | solidarity |
>
> 2. What might these terms symbolize?
>
> | eagle | skyscraper | hawk | open arms |
> |---|---|---|---|
> | dove | snake | river | apple |
> | ocean | baseball | rain | water |
> | house | mountain | hearth | |

Traditional Themes and Patterns   Many pieces of literature rely on themes and structural patterns that have been employed throughout the history of literature. A character goes in search of self, so that gaining self-knowledge figures as the story's theme. Another major motif, initiation, involves a character's moving from one stage of life to another. And how many stories have been written about the conflict between men and women, between parent and child, between one group or culture and another? Look also for conflict generated by reality versus illusion, nature versus technology, justice versus injustice, or the individual versus society, to name but a few possibilities.

In examining literature, you may want to look at the ways in which themes and structural patterns are developed. For example, in examining "Shopping," it would be helpful to look at the conflict between mother and daughter, reflecting on what factors help account for this conflict. What do we reveal by labeling it a "generational conflict"? Is there more to this conflict than can be captured in this phrase? What types of conflict do you find in the poems by Alexie? What causes these conflicts and how are they (or might they be) resolved?

Writer

Your purpose in writing *about* literature is to learn more about the literary texts you are examining. However, as we have said above, the focus in this type of writing is the subject itself, so your primary goal will be to present your findings about the text you're reading. That is not to say that you should attempt to adopt the voice of an expert critic who is teaching others how to read, and understand, literature. Rather, you should strive to adopt the voice of an interested explorer, someone engaged in puzzling meaning from a text. One of your goals in this writing assignment should be to enjoy the experience of reading, hence the explorative nature of your work with the text. An excellent example of this type of exploratory writing is Amy Wright's "A Quest to Return to the Garden: Perception 'Of Falling'" (pages 306–309). Amy does not presume to be an expert on Gwyn's "Of Falling." Rather, she explores the story's meaning. She considers, for example, the meaning of "fall" throughout the story, from the title through the final scene, when George Crider falls dead. In her next-to-last paragraph, Amy asks, "But what are we to make of this last fall?" She then offers three potential readings in answer, which suggests that she considered each of the three interpretations before choosing the one she thinks the fall represents.

As we have noted above, writing *from* literature may involve you in any one of several different types of writing, ranging from the personal to the persuasive. Your role as a writer will depend on the type of writing you are engaged in. For example, one type of writing that often results when we write *from* literature is personal: in this writing, we use a piece of literature as a springboard to a personal reflection explaining how our experiences make it possible for us to understand that piece literature more fully and how that piece of literature increases our abilities to understand our experiences. This is the type of writing we find in Kendra Stead's "No Exceptions" (pages 310–312). In her essay, Kendra uses Marge Piercy's "A Work of Artifice" as a means of reflecting on an unsettling visit with a marriage counselor. Because the writing is personal, what we said earlier about writers of personal essays applies here: the writer becomes the focal point of the essay, since the overall purpose is to reveal what the writer learns about herself by reflecting upon her experiences in light of this piece of literature.

Reader

You should assume that your reader will be interested in what you have to say, will be receptive to your thinking, and won't offer resistance to your ideas. Your job, then, is to prove your point, to support the assertion you make about the text. Although an interpretive essay will have an argumentative edge to it—you will, after all, make a case for the validity of your thesis—it will not be a position or persuasion essay (as we define them in Chapters 9 and 10), because you may assume that your reader isn't predisposed to be hostile or resistant to your interpretation, and because you are not attempting to persuade your reader to take any action.

Nonetheless, you need to consider your reader carefully as you write and revise. For one thing, your understanding of who your reader is will determine how much background information you need to present. If you're writing about "For Once, Then, Something," the amount of attention you give to specific statements critical of Frost will depend on how knowledgeable your reader is about Frost and his reception as a poet. Likewise, if you assume your reader is well read, you may not need to explain the Pan image implicit in lines 5–6, for simply mentioning Pan will be enough to evoke this image in your reader's mind. Although your primary focus in an interpretive essay will be the literary text (the subject corner of the rhetorical triangle), you'll still need to take your reader into account.

DISTINGUISHING FEATURES OF INTERPRETIVE ESSAYS

Interpretation

In writing an interpretive essay, you offer and support your opinion as to what a story means—so you're actually writing an argument. You'll need to make an assertion about the story's meaning in a thesis sentence and then support it with detail from the story itself so that you convince your reader that your interpretation is plausible. What we're after here is not the one and only valid interpretation, because that really doesn't exist. Different people may read the same text and derive differing understandings of it. Your job, then, is to use information from the story to support your thinking about the story, so that you give your reader insight into your thinking—what you think and why you think that way.

Theme

What the writer is trying to say is the story's theme, and part of your job in interpreting a piece of literature is to make an assertion about the story's theme. What is the story really about? What insight into life or people or human actions do you gain from reading the story?

Thesis and Support

As we have noted several times, an interpretive essay makes an argument. You'll write a thesis sentence that makes an assertion about your understanding of the text, and then you'll offer support from the text for that assertion. Look again at Kendra Stead's essay (pages 303–306) about Margaret Atwood's poem "Spelling." Kendra presents a thesis at the end of the first paragraph that makes an assertion about the poem's meaning, or theme, and then supports it with details from the poem. Here is a brief overview of the parts of Kendra's essay:

> ¶1: This paragraph, while only two sentence long, clearly identifies Kendra's thinking about Atwood's poem. The second sentence is the thesis: "Atwood uses structure, word play, and historical allusions to convey her belief that the subordination of women throughout history is closely linked to the

suppresssion of women's words." This thesis lays out the structure of the paper to follow.

¶s 2–6: These paragraphs support Kendra's assertion that the structural elements of Atwood's poem are important.

¶s 7–9: These paragraphs develop the idea that Atwood's word play in the poem is significant.

¶10: This paragraph illustrates Atwood's use of historical allusions, the third element of Kendra's thesis.

¶11: This paragraph is the essay's conclusion. In it, Kendra focuses on the issue of women and power, an idea she has developed throughout the essay, and she returns to the language of her thesis to provide a solid link between the introduction and the conclusion.

Beyond Summary

Although interpreting a story may involve writing a summary of part or all of the story, interpreting is not summarizing. A plot summary is a simple retelling of what happens in a story. An interpretive essay has to move well beyond summary; it has to move past the "what" to the "why." Why does Robert Frost "try" to find "something more of the depths"? Why does Nola cry at the end of "Shopping"? Working to consider the "why" of a story and of its key moments or important parts means working to understand its theme, what it means to you as a reader. And it is precisely your understanding of theme that will form the core of any essay you write about a piece of literature.

In her essay interpreting "Of Falling," Amy Wright provides some plot summary. But she doesn't retell the entire story, nor does she substitute summary for interpretation. Instead, she gives enough of the plot to ground her reader in her essay and then moves beyond summary to exploring and interpreting Gwyn's "Of Falling." Amy's essay thus illustrates that summary is often a necessary but relatively small part of writing *about* literature.

Citing Sources

As the writer of an interpretive essay, you'll need to cite or document any sources you use for your essay. Although you may use other sources, you will begin with your primary source. A *primary source* is the particular text that is the subject of the interpretation and so of the essay. We'll have more to say about documenting sources in Part Three. For now, we'll simply note the format our student writers chose for documenting their use of passages from the texts on which they based their essays. At the end of Kendra's essay "The Making of Spells," you'll find a "Works Cited" section, which gives the source of the texts she used in her essay. Here is her reference to Atwood's poem:

Atwood, Margaret. "Spelling." *True Stories*. New York: Simon and Schuster, 1981. 63–64.

Note that Kendra begins with the author's name (last name first) and then gives the poem's title (in quotation marks), the book it appears in (in italics, also sometimes underlined), the book's publication information (city: publishing firm, year published), and finally the page numbers of the poem (63–64). Then in the text of her essay, Kendra gives parenthetical references to the specific lines of the poem she's quoting. e.g., (line 23). For her other sources, she also uses parenthetical references, e.g., (Guiley 371) to identify the source and page number of the quoted material. Why cite a source? Why list the various sources used in an essay and why list individual page references? For one thing, it's a courtesy to the story's writer to do so; it recognizes the story's status as a publication. For another thing, it's a courtesy to the reader of your interpretive essay. It enables your reader to pursue the story further by reading it himself: The publication data (where and when published) help the reader locate the original text, and the page references guide him quickly to the particular passages you've quoted. Finally, citing sources is required by copyright law.

For more specific information about quoting from and documenting sources, see Chapter 12.

Note: We don't offer distinguishing features for writing *from* literature because these essays can range so broadly—from personal to persuasive. Were we to attempt to offer one key characteristic of all such essays, it might be that they present the reader with some key epiphany or insight that the writer had while reading a piece of literature. This epiphany is that "ah ha" moment the writer has when she realizes that some other human has had experiences similar to her own.

ASSIGNMENT AND GUIDELINES FOR WRITING

Assignment

Below we offer two kinds of writing assignments, those *about* literature and those *from* literature. For either assignment, you may use any of your responses to the Writing Opportunity prompts throughout this chapter as a starting place for writing an essay.

1. Write *about* a piece of literature; that is, write an essay interpreting a piece of literature. For example, write about a short story or poem, presenting your interpretation of the story or poem and using information from that piece of literature to support your interpretation. You may, of course, use sources other than the piece you're dealing with, but you must document them correctly. In presenting your interpretation, focus on any of the following elements of literature, talking about how the author uses them to reveal theme:

    plot
    conflict
    characters (major and minor)
    imagery
    symbolism

2. Write *from* a piece of literature; that is, write about an event you experienced that was informed by your work with a piece of literature or that was similar to an experience described in a piece of literature. The following are examples of topics that derive from some of the stories and poems presented in this text:
   a. "Shopping"—write about a conflict you've had with a member of your family or a close friend. What was its source? Its resolution? How might you apply this story to your situation?
   b. "Of Falling"—write about a crisis you or a friend experienced. How did the crisis occur? What was its outcome? How do you view it now? How might you apply this story to your or your friend's situation?
   c. "That Place Where Ghosts of Salmon Jump"—write about a clash between society and your family's lore or cultural traditions. Describe the lore or traditions and the conflict you felt. What was the outcome? How might you apply this poem to your situation?
   d. "The Powwow at the End of the World"—in one sense, this poem is about the negative impact of progress on society. What questionable instances of progress have you seen? What was their impact? Whom or what did they affect? What was the outcome? Read Julie Titone's essay "Balance of Power" (pages 541–544). In what ways do Sherman Alexie's poem and Titone's essay speak with a unified voice? Write an essay exploring this issue and bring both Alexie's poem and Titone's essay to bear on it.

WRITING *ABOUT* LITERATURE

Collecting Information

If you're writing *about* a piece of literature, you may follow this procedure in your prewriting:

1. Select a piece of literature—one presented in this text or one assigned by or approved by your teacher. Read your selection using the reading strategies presented in this chapter and in Chapter 4.
2. As you read and after you've read, focus on questions the text raises. For example, think about questions beginning with "why": Why was Nola crying at the end of "Shopping"? Why does George's body "strike the floor with a hollow sound" at the end of "Of Falling"? Why does Sherman Alexie repeat "I am told by many of you that I must forgive and so I shall" in "The Powwow at the End of the World"?
3. Relate these questions to theme, because the focus of an interpretive essay (an essay *about* literature) is the story's theme. Define the story's theme, stating it in a single sentence.

Focus Statement

Develop a focus statement by writing an initial statement of theme and making a list of details from the story that reveal or support the theme.

Here's the focus statement written by Kristina Geray, whose essay we present at the end of this chapter:

> Nola and Mrs. Dietrich use each other and use Mr. Dietrich. And both are too much concerned with appearances.
>
> **Support:**
>
> 1. reactions to the bag lady—meet her, talk about her on their way into the mall, see her again at the end, Nola cries (why?)
> 2. Nola's vanity and concern for her weight—her mother's obsessed with her physical appearance also.

Note that Kristina gives her initial interpretation of the story in two sentences. Then she lists very briefly the elements of the story that she'll use to support her assertion that both Mrs. Dietrich and Nola are overly concerned with appearances. Although this focus statement could have been more fully developed, Kristina used it effectively as an initial focus for her writing.

Planning Your Essay's Structure

An interpretative essay—an essay *about* literature—is structured by argument; you'll make and then support an assertion about what the text means. This assertion will be your thesis statement, so you should think of this essay in terms of thesis and support. Here's one structure you might use:

> *Beginning.* Present a brief summary of the text that builds to the thesis statement.
> *Middle.* Present detailed support for your thesis that comes from the text itself. Identify key passages that illustrate some aspect of your thesis, and either summarize or quote them. Each time you cite a passage from the text, be sure to tell what it means and how it supports or develops your thesis.
> *End.* Return to the main idea of your thesis. Define the theme, what the writer has said to you.
>
> Kristina Geray's final draft (pages 341–344) follows this suggested shape.
> *Beginning*—¶1 characterizes Nola and Mrs. Dietrich as unhappy and lonely. The thesis statement is the next-to-the-last sentence, and Kristina then had to support her assertion about these characters' preoccupation with appearances.
> *Middle*—¶s 2–7 offer support. ¶2 focuses on physical appearances. ¶3 shows their inability to communicate. ¶s 4–7 focus on the meaning of the woman in black. In each paragraph, Kristina offers support for her thesis by summarizing or quoting passages from Oates's story and noting their importance. Look at the topic sentence for ¶4: "The most glaring example of this concern over appearances is shown by Nola's and Mrs. Dietrich's reactions to the woman in black, a 'disheveled woman' (52) who is probably a bag

lady." This sentence signals support for the thesis, and it makes an assertion Kristina must support, which she does throughout ¶s 4–7.

End—¶8 is a short paragraph that restates ideas from the introduction and then states very clearly the effect of their obsession with appearances on Nola and Mrs. Dietrich.

Refining Your Writing

As you begin sharpening your essay's focus, make sure that you've paid attention to these aspects of writing about literature:

Interpretation and theme. Does your thesis statement present your interpretation of the story? Does it speak to the story's theme? What details from the story have you discussed to support your interpretation? Are these details the most telling or important elements of the story?

Beyond summary. Remember that although a plot summary may be an essential part of your essay, your job is to interpret the story, to give your view of its theme and then to offer support for that view. Simply retelling the story is not interpreting, so be sure to go beyond summarizing the story. Be sure to focus tightly on why something happens or why a character says something or behaves in a particular way and then on what these events, statements, and actions mean. Writing about what things mean is interpreting.

Citing sources. You must cite all sources you use in writing about a piece of literature. One citation will be for the story itself, the primary source. But you'll also list all secondary sources that you use. These sources include reviews of the story and essays of criticism about the story. Use the documentation and citation formats specified by either the Modern Language Association (MLA) or the American Psychological Association (APA), unless your instructor specifies a different format. (For more information about documenting and citing sources, see Chapter 12.)

WRITING *FROM* LITERATURE

Collecting Information

Begin by thinking about your favorite stories, those that you count as important or that have had an impact on your life. Remember the comments we made at the start of this chapter about this kind of essay: Have you ever read a poem or story and realized that you have had an experience similar to that of one of the characters? Have you found any help from a poem or story in solving a problem that you encountered? Have you applied some aspect of a poem or story to your dealings with other people? An essay written *from* a piece of literature would explore the experience, talk about the problem situation and how it worked out, or offer a narrative account of your dealings with others, and it would tie your experience to that piece of literature.

Try this procedure as you begin to work on your essay:

1. Pick a favorite piece of literature, one that has real significance for you. In completing the first exercise in this chapter, did you write about such a piece of literature as this, one that protected or consoled you? If so, that story just might be a good one for you to base your essay on.
2. Reread the story, using the reading strategies presented in this chapter and in Chapter 4. From your reading, write a short interpretation of the story.
3. Freewrite about the story and its importance to you. Consider such questions as these: When did you read it? In what context, in what circumstances? How did it reflect or help you through a particular period or event, positive or negative, in your life? How does the experience of one of the characters parallel your own experience during this event or period? How did the story influence your dealings with other people?

Focus Statement

Based on your interpretation and your freewriting, write a focus statement. What do you want your reader to understand about the experience that's the topic of your essay? How did the piece of literature relate to that experience? What details will you have to present about the experience and from the story in order for your reader to understand these things? Responding to these questions will help you develop a focus statement for your writing *from* literature.

Planning Your Essay's Structure

An essay *from* literature may be informed by one or more of the writing occasions we presented in Part Two of this text, so it's difficult to offer a single structure for this particular kind of essay. We can say, however, that your essay *from* literature must show that you've read and interpreted the text. You can show this by featuring the text prominently at the beginning and end of your essay so that you establish its relevance to your topic.

Kendra Stead ("No Exceptions") does a particularly good job of making these connections. Kendra gives a very brief interpretation of her poem, "A Work of Artifice," at the beginning of her essay. She then relates it to her life in paragraph 2: "I imagined Piercy sitting through countless experiences similar to my own, and I felt that I understood her motivations and her meaning on a deeper level than I would ever experience a Grecian urn." After narrating most of the experience that she associates with the Piercy's poem, Kendra returns to the poem in paragraph 7: "'That's just how it is.' I was seeking out my cozy 'pot to grow in.' I was weaseling a lifetime contract out of a gardener, thereby insuring that someone would always be there to 'whittle back my branches.'" She then continues her narrative (and her explanation of what she learned from her experience), returning again to Piercy's poem in paragraph 8: "By remaining silent I had let him verbally bind my feet and cripple my brain." And in paragraph 9, the final paragraph, she develops at some length the comparisons she sees between her experience and the meaning of Piercy's poem.

Refining Your Writing

Although an essay *from* literature will focus more on your experience than on the story itself, working with the traits of an interpretive essay can help you sharpen your writing *from* literature.

> *Interpretation and theme.* An essay from literature begins in interpretation, whether you actually give your interpretation as part of your final essay or not. Even if you don't include interpretation in your final draft, you should be sure to work with interpretation and theme as important elements of your prewriting.
>
> *Application to experience.* What event forms the core of your essay, and how does the piece of literature square with or apply to it? Be sure that your essay makes explicit connections between the story and the event.

SAMPLE STUDENT PROCESS

The interpretive essay that follows was written by Kristina Geray, a first-year writing student at NMSU who took Joyce Carol Oates's "Shopping" as her subject. As you work through this essay, compare and contrast it with your own interpretation of Oates's story.

Reading "Shopping" was assigned for class reading and discussion. In an e-mail to Bill, her instructor, Kristina asked whether the class could talk about why Nola cried at the story's end. During that discussion, Kristina decided to explore this story in depth and so began her writing process by reading "Shopping" a second time, making the following dialogue notes as she read.

Response to Notes	**Reading Notes**
	Preview— title: "Shopping" author: Joyce Carol Oates pub.: *Ms.* (March '86) narrator: 3rd pers. ltd (perspective)
What happens to change the positive mood to negative? 2nd ¶ shows potential danger.	Beginning—Mother/daughter to go to "splendid Livingstone Mall." It's an "old ritual." Seems positive—Mrs. D's "interior voice" is "calm, free of irony."

(continued)

Response to Notes	Reading Notes
Why N's tears and Mrs. D's skepticism that they're real?	Ending—not positive. Nola's upset & crying. Very different feeling, mood from 1st ¶. Story breaks into 9 shorter parts by extra spacing between parts. Questions—why does mood change, start to finish? Why does Nola lose control? Why the "ritual" of shopping? Why so many breaks in such a short story?
key terms: old ritual *busy, friends* (why italics?) Harmless conversation monosyllables Nola's smile	1st part—¶s 1–6 conflict between Mrs. D & N—lots of tension. Mrs. D divorced, holds tight to N. ritual elements—trip, parking place (always the same). Mrs. D seems ditzy—bad driver.
why "significant"? Began at time of divorce—Mrs. D holding on to N to keep sense of family?	part 2—¶s 7–8 contrasts mall (bright) with outdoor setting (gritty, acrid air). mall a place of sanctuary ("It's like coming home."). shopping trips "significant."
significance of "disheveled woman"? key terms: disheveled woman surprise N's content, absorbed "Let me go"	3rd part—¶s 9–18 "disheveled woman" enters story Nola's social conscience emerges, but as soon as she gets in the mall she gets "distracted" and forgets the homeless woman. tension again—N tells Mrs. D, "Let me go. Let me go."
family's dysfunctional	4th part—¶s 19–21 background on N as child, normally weird kid—tries to constantly "call attention to herself." father upset, yells at Mrs. D.
key terms: considerable beauty savage dieting fat herself again reborn perfect ironic—N's hardly perfect	part 5—¶s 22–28 more background—Nola sent away to boarding school. grew to become "a girl of considerable beauty." diets. (signs of anorexia?) Shows N's concern w. body appearance—vanity? Also shows Mrs. D's vision of who N would be: "herself again, reborn and this time perfect."

Response to Notes	Reading Notes
key terms: time passing no connection present tense how love ends how love begins	6th part—¶s 29–34 back to shopping at mall. N finds "beautiful" "perfect" sweater. Mrs. D thinks it's ugly real tension—Mrs. D fears time passing, realizes there's no connection between her and Nola. But she can't let go.
key terms: N's tense, moody hate Mrs. D alcoholic? rationalizes 3rd glass of wine away as "celebration"	7th part—¶s 35–67 lunch—things fall apart. They argue. N wants to go to school in France. Mrs. D—3rd glass of wine. N—smokes to defy her mother. father castigated—N's got a trash mouth.
appearances again—Mrs. D notices N's skin—"fair and thin and dry" "wear out before she's 40" (during conversation)	important conversation between N & Mrs. D—Mrs. D doesn't understand "How exhausting it is" (N says this). no real relationship—Nola's hand "limp, ungiving" when Mrs. D squeezes it.
very strong section. Mrs. D understands how hopeless it is. But she's "anxious, immediately repentant"—dependent on N for meaning to her life?	8th part—¶s 68–69 more shopping. Mrs. D feels hatred for N—"cold calm clear unmistakable hatred." Mrs. D thinks she doesn't know Nola, doesn't love Nola.
key terms: disheveled woman N's upset, strangely upset crying cloak	last part—¶s 70–72 leaving mall—shopping's over. see homeless woman again. N may approach her but then doesn't. Mrs. D's condescending. Nola's upset, cries. Mrs. D wants a cloak to hide them—mask reality? keep up appearances? no public embarrassment? Important elements— appearances throughout. no relationship between N and Mrs. D, only conflict. Mrs. D just doesn't get it.

Prewriting   Kristina decided to work with the two primary characters in Oates's story, Nola and Mrs. Dietrich. She continued her prewriting by writing a set of notes in which she listed various attributes of each character, at times contrasting one of Nola's traits with one of her mother's.

Nola	**Mrs. Dietrich**
young	old
never married	divorced
dry skin	oily skin
underweight	overweight
smokes	alcoholic
prep school	thinks she loves Nola
hates father	was happiest when pregnant with Nola
hates to throw things away	feels lonely
spends late nights partying with friends	wants to keep Nola for herself
	thinks Mr. Dietrich owes her something

Nola	**Mrs. Dietrich**
wants to talk to lady in black	wants to ignore the lady in black
liked reciting misc. facts	is a lousy driver
father disliked her	worries about appearances
acts coarsely (i.e., putting cigarette butt out on floor)	
wants to confront mother	

Focus Statement

Nola and Mrs. Dietrich use each other and use Mr. Dietrich. And both are too much concerned with appearances.

Support

1. reactions to the bag lady—meet her, talk about her on their way into the mall, see her again at the end, Nola cries (why?)
2. Nola's vanity and concern for her weight—her mother's obsessed with her physical appearance also.

Based on this statement, Kristina wrote a rough draft for peer review. But as she wrote, the focus shifted, moving away from the initial statement about both Nola and Mrs. Dietrich using Mr. Dietrich, so that the essay takes the concern for appearances as its primary focal point.

Rough Draft for Peer Review

Joyce Carol Oates short story "Shopping" centers around two characters, Mrs. Dietrich and her daughter Nola, and their obsession with shopping. As the story develops so does the readers understanding of Nola and her mother who seem as different as night and day. Nola is a weight-obsessed, prep school brat, smart-mouthed and confrontational. Her mother on the other hand is an alcoholic divorcee, desperately trying to cling to the one thing in life that truly made her happy, Nola. All of these differences are on the surface, however. Underneath it all

Nola and Mrs. Dietrich are as alike as two peas in a pod. They are both very lonely people, unwilling or incapable of taking the right steps to make themselves happy. Nola and Mrs. Dietrich are much more concerned with the way things appear to be bothered with actually trying to change things. This preoccupation with appearance is shown time and time again throughout the short story "Shopping."

The most glaring example of this concern over appearances is shown by Nola's and Mrs. Dietrich's reactions to the woman in black. Mrs. Dietrich seems to see the woman in black as nothing more than an eyesore. She is content to simply ignore her, as the other shoppers do, by walking past her without even acknowledging her presence. She defends her actions by saying, when questioned, that the woman is "harmless... She just sits." As far as Mrs. Dietrich is concerned, the lady in black is simply a flaw in the mall scenery. As long as the lady continues to "just sit" Mrs. Dietrich can keep up the pretense that people such as the lady in black don't exist. In her world of luxury, Mrs. Dietrich's pretense is an important way to keep up appearances and keep from standing out in the crowd.

Nola's reaction to the lady in black is a bit more complex than her mother's. Upon first seeing the lady in black, Nola is horrified that "people like her" are allowed in the mall. At this point, Nola seems more upset that the beautiful and blemish-free interior of her second home has been tarnished, rather than with the idea that the lady in black may be suffering any harm. It is only after speaking with her mother about the lady in black that Nola seems to care about the woman as a person. She bemoans the fact that the lady in black may somehow be harmed by the actions of those who choose not to acknowledge her prescence. It is possible that Nola is honestly concerned about the well-being of the woman in black, however, it is more likely that she is simply paying lip-service to the "tragedy of women like that." By speaking of such things Nola may hope to appear more caring and concerned for the outcasts of an affluent society than she really is. Her concern, real or otherwise, is fleeting and she quickly forgets, moving on to the important business of the day: shopping. It is not until Nola and Mrs. Dietrich are preparing to leave the mall that Nola is reminded of the wretched lady in black. Mrs. Dietrich and the other shoppers continue to file past the woman as if she weren't there. Nola, on the other hand, seems to be getting ready to approach her. This is not because of any real concern on Nola's part. It is more out of a desire to appear as a caring person. It almost seems as if Nola is thinking, "If I were to approach this woman and offer her my help, wouldn't it look good to everyone else? Perhaps they'd all comment on what a lovely young woman I am for helping this wretch out." In the end, though, Nola does not approach the woman in black. Helping her out would mean standing out in the crowd. Even though it is important to appear concerned, it is even more important to fit in and not to stand out.

The story ends with Nola sobbing in her mother's car "as though her heart is broken." It would be easy to assume that Nola is crying out of sorrow for the woman in black or out of shame for not having approached her. Neither is the case, however. Nola's tears are very likely a continuation of her act as a genuinely caring person. The idea that these are crocodile tears is supported by the fact that Mrs. Dietrich has "heard these very sobs before." On the other hand, if Nola's tears are real, they most certainly are not for the woman in black. Nola is much too self-centered and spoiled to truly feel that strongly for anyone else. Nola is crying because she came to the mall to forget how isolated she feels. By choosing not to approach the woman in black Nola only served to reinforce her loneliness. In this way, the woman in black has sabotaged Nola's escape from her self-imposed solitary confinement. If Nola's tears are real, Nola is crying for herself, not for the woman in black.

Another example of Nola's and Mrs. Dietrich's concern over appearances is the way they both seem to obsess over Nola's physical appearance. As they prepare to enter the mall Mrs. Dietrich's breath is taken away by Nola's beautiful smile. Mrs. Dietrich's memories of Nola as a child center around the fact that Nola was "plain, rather chunky . . . (and) . . . unpopular at school." When trying to draw attention to herself as a child, it was Nola's physical appearance that came under fire as her relatives began to criticize her "queer, glassy-pale eyes." After being sent away to school it is stated that Nola "matured into a girl of considerable beauty." From this statement it seems pretty evident that Nola's academic progress and character development mean little when compared to Nola's blossoming into an attractive young woman. When Mrs. Dietrich and Nola argue in La Créperie Mrs. Dietrich puts little effort into understanding what her daughter is trying to say and more effort into noticing her daughter's physical attributes. At this point, Mrs. Dietrich "sees with pity that her daughter's skin is fair and thin and dry . . . it will wear out before she's forty." Nola and Mrs. Dietrich both seem tremendously concerned with Nola's weight. Nola is 5 foot 7 and weighs less than 100 lbs, "the result of constant savage dieting." Despite her slenderness (which, in my opinion, is unhealthy) Nola constantly obsesses about her weight. This is well illustrated in a paragraph on p. 53: "Do you think I'm fat, mother?" The last sentence of this paragraph is especially interesting. "Do you think it shows?" she asks her mother as if it would be acceptable for her to be fat as long as it didn't show. This seems to be Nola's & Mrs. Dietrich's entire philosophy on life. It's okay to feel miserable and hopelessly alone as long as it doesn't show.

5

Kristina's review group members felt that her essay was a good start, that Kristina had done a good job of wrestling with the meaning of the story. One reviewer told her that the paragraphs making up the body of the essay had "great detail; even more would make the essay better." Another reviewer offered mostly positive comments about the essay, but noted two areas that needed revision:

> I think your introduction is a little too long. Maybe use the contrast & comparisons in a paragraph after the introduction. Rather than having them lead up to the thesis have them support it.
>
> I think you need to work on the conclusion. You need to shorten it so that your point is more clear. I don't know if this is a completed essay, but the end leaves you hanging.

Although this draft did form a good start, it was not quite the quality her group thought Kristina capable of. Kristina didn't receive as much help from her group as she had wanted, but, given deadlines and due dates, she had to produce a second draft.

Second Rough Draft

An Interpretation of Joyce Carol Oates "Shopping"

Joyce Carol Oates short story "Shopping" centers around two characters, Mrs. Dietrich and her daughter Nola, and their obsession with shopping. As the story develops so does the readers understanding of Nola and her mother who

1

seem as different as night and day. Nola is a weight-obsessed, smart-mouthed, confrontational, prep-school brat. Her mother, on the other hand, is an alcoholic divorcee, desperately trying to hold on to the only thing in her life that ever came close to making her happy, Nola. All these differences are on the surface, however. Underneath it all, Nola and Mrs. Dietrich are as alike as two peas in a pod. They are both very lonely people, unwilling or incapable of taking the right steps to make themselves happy. Nola and Mrs. Dietrich are much more concerned with the way things appear to really bother with actually trying to change things. This preoccupation with appearance is shown time and time again throughout the short story "Shopping."

2   The most glaring example of this concern over appearances is shown by Nola's and Mrs. Dietrich's reactions to the woman in black. Mrs. Dietrich seems to see the woman as nothing more than an eyesore. She is content to simply ignore her, as the other shoppers do, by walking past her without even acknowledging her presence. She defends her actions by saying, when questioned, that the woman is "harmless . . . she just sits." As far as Mrs. Dietrich is concerned, the lady in black is simply a flaw in the mall scenery. As long as the lady continues to "just sit," Mrs. Dietrich can keep up the pretense that people such as the lady in black don't exist. In her world of luxury, Mrs. Dietrich's pretense is an important way to keep from standing out in the crowd.

3   Nola's reaction to the lady in black is a bit more complex than her mother's. Upon first seeing her, Nola is horrified that "people like her" are allowed in the mall. At this point, Nola seems more upset that the beautiful and blemish-free interior of her second home has been tarnished rather than with the idea that the lady in black may be suffering any harm. It is only after speaking with her mother about the lady in black that Nola expresses any concern for the woman. She bemoans the fact that the lady in black may somehow be harmed by the actions of those who choose not to acknowledge her presence. There is a slight chance that Nola is honestly concerned about the welfare of the woman in black, however, it is more likely that she is simply paying lip-service to the "tragedy of women like that." By speaking of such "tragedy," Nola may hope to appear more caring and concerned for "the outcasts of an affluent society" than she really is.

4   Despite her passionate words, Nola's concern is fleeting and she quickly forgets, moving on to the important business of the day: shopping. It is not until Nola and Mrs. Dietrich are preparing to leave the mall that Nola is reminded of the wretched lady in black. Mrs. Dietrich and the other shoppers continue to file past the woman as if she weren't there. Nola, on the other hand, seems to be getting ready to approach her. This is not because of any real concern on Nola's part. It is more out of a desire to appear as a caring person. It almost seems as if Nola is thinking "If I were to approach this woman and offer her my help wouldn't it look good to everyone else? Perhaps they'd all comment on what a lovely young woman I am for helping this wretch." In the end though, Nola does not approach the woman in black. Nola's offer of help would cause her to stand out in the crowd. Despite the fact that Nola seems to feel it is important to appear concerned, it is even more important not to stand out.

5   The story ends with Nola sobbing in her mother's car "as though her heart is broken." It would be easy to assume that Nola is crying out of sorrow for the woman in black or out of shame for not having approached her. Both of these reactions are unlikely, though. Nola's tears are more likely a continuation of her act as a genuinely caring person. The idea that these are crocodile tears is

supported by the fact that Mrs. Dietrich has "heard these very sobs before." On the other hand, if Nola's tears are real the reader should assume that she is not crying for the woman in black. Nola is much too self-centered and spoiled to truly feel that strongly for anyone else. Nola is crying because she came to the mall to forget how isolated she feels. By choosing not to approach the woman in black Nola only served to reinforce her loneliness. In this way, the woman in black has sabotaged Nola's escape from her self-imposed solitary confinement. If Nola's tears are real, she is crying for herself, not the woman in black.

Another example of Nola's and Mrs. Dietrich's concern over appearances is the way they both seem to obsess over Nola's physical appearance. Mrs. Dietrich's memories of Nola as a child center around the fact that Nola was "plain, rather chunky . . . (and) . . . unpopular at school." When Nola tried to draw attention to herself it was her appearance that came under fire as her relative's began criticizing on "her queer glassy-pale eyes." After being sent away to school it is stated that Nola "matured into a girl of considerable beauty." From this statement is seems pretty evident that Nola's academic progress and character development mean little when compared to Nola's blossoming into an attractive young woman. When Nola and Mrs. Dietrich argue in La Crêperie, Mrs. Dietrich puts little effort into understanding what her daughter is trying to say and more effort into noticing her daughter's physical attributes. At this point, Mrs. Dietrich "sees with pity that her daughter's skin is fair and thin and dry . . . it will wear out before she is forty."

Finally, Nola and Mrs. Dietrich both seem tremendously concerned with Nola's weight. Nola is 5'7" and weighs less than a hundred pounds, "the result of constant savage dieting." Despite her slenderness Nola obsesses about her weight. This is well illustrated in a paragraph on page 53:

> "Do you think I'm fat, Mother?" she asks frequently, worriedly, standing in front of the mirror twisted at the waist to reveal her small round belly which, it seems, can't help being round: she bloats herself on diet Cokes all day long. "Do you think it shows?"

The last sentence of this paragraph is especially interesting. "Do you think it shows?" Nola asks her mother as if it would be acceptable for her to be fat as long as it didn't show. This seems to be Nola's and Mrs. Dietrich's entire philosophy on life. It's okay to be miserable and hopelessly alone as long as it doesn't show.

Nola and Mrs. Dietrich, the characters in Joyce Carol Oates short story "Shopping" seem very different. However, their almost all-consuming obsession with appearances makes them, underneath it all, nearly identical and, despite being surrounded by people, very much alone.

Wanting more advice, Kristina scheduled a conference with Bill. After reading this draft, he offered this advice:

Kristina—your focus on the theme of appearance versus reality (and its relation to loneliness) works, so what's here is a very good start. I especially like the way you set up the rest of the paper with the last 2 sentences of ¶1. You got some good advice from your group, especially the comment about your needing to provide a conclusion. Now, you still have some work to do on this, so let's start with the conclusion and go from there:

1. conclusion—it's a little flat; it's more a summary or restatement than a clincher. One way to strengthen it is to talk about Mrs. D's disappointment in Nola not being her reincarnation (see the end of the paragraph about Mrs. D's pregnancy).
2. what's the best order for your paragraphs—you say "most glaring example" to open ¶2, so should you save this example for last? It's an important event—their seeing the homeless woman—so think about leaving your readers with that as most important.
3. Should you expand discussion of their argument in the restaurant (now in ¶6)?—sets up the fact that Mrs. D doesn't really know who Nola is, which can point to the conclusion.
4. Nola's eyes—did anyone really criticize her for these or just notice that they seemed strange?
5. Nola's crying—in the paragraph in which you talk about this (¶5) you give 2 reasons for her tears. Should you give 2 or 1?
6. gotta use proper documentation of sources. Follow the guidelines from the Writing Center, the ones we talked about in class.
7. Can you find some fresher wordings for "as different as night and day," "as alike as two peas in a pod," and "time and time again" (all in ¶1)?
8. mechanics—check possessives, e.g., "Oates's short story" v. "Oates short story" (1st sentence).

One thing more—can you provide a more colorful title? I suspect the one you have above wouldn't be very competitive for Title of the Week. And one more "one thing more"—how many times do you say either "woman in black" or "lady in black"?

After this conference, Kristina wrote her final draft. How does it compare with the other drafts she wrote for this assignment? How much of her group's and Bill's advice did she take?

Final Draft

KRISTINA GERAY

"HOW EXHAUSTING IT IS" TO KEEP UP APPEARANCES

Joyce Carol Oates's short story "Shopping" centers around two characters, Mrs. Dietrich and her daughter Nola, and their obsession with shopping. As the story develops so does the reader's understanding of Nola and her mother who

1

seem to be complete opposites. Nola is a weight-obsessed, smart-mouthed, confrontational, prep-school brat. Her mother, on the other hand, is an alcoholic divorcee, desperately trying to hold on to the only thing in her life that ever came close to making her happy, Nola. All these differences are on the surface, however. Underneath it all, Nola and Mrs. Dietrich are very much alike. Both are very lonely people, unwilling or incapable of taking the right steps to make themselves happy. Nola and Mrs. Dietrich are much too concerned with the way things appear to really bother with actually trying to change things. This preoccupation with appearance is shown time and time again throughout the short story "Shopping."

Nola and Mrs. Dietrich obsess over Nola's physical appearance. Mrs. Dietrich's memories of Nola as a child center around the fact that Nola was "plain, rather chunky [. . . and . . .] unpopular at school" (Oates, 53. All other references are to this source.). When Nola tries to draw attention to herself, her relatives focus on her appearance: "What a strange child! What queer glassy-pale eyes!" (53). Rather than seeing a lonely child who craved attention, her family sees only her strangeness and her eyes. But after being sent away to school Nola "matured into a girl of considerable beauty" (53). From this statement it seems pretty evident that Nola's academic progress and character development mean little when compared to her blossoming into an attractive young woman. Finally, Nola and Mrs. Dietrich both seem tremendously concerned with Nola's weight. Nola is 5'7" and weighs less than a hundred pounds, "the result of constant savage dieting" (53). Despite her slenderness Nola obsesses about her weight. This is well illustrated in a paragraph on page 53:

> "Do you think I'm fat, Mother?" she asks frequently, worriedly, standing in front of the mirror twisted at the waist to reveal her small round belly which, it seems, can't help being round: she bloats herself on diet Cokes all day long. "Do you think it shows?"

The last sentence of this paragraph is especially interesting. "Do you think it shows?" Nola asks her mother as if it would be acceptable for her to be fat as long as it didn't show. This seems to be Nola's and Mrs. Dietrich's entire philosophy on life. It's okay to be miserable and hopelessly alone as long as it doesn't show.

What does show is that Nola and Mrs. Dietrich are miserable. Mrs. Dietrich makes no effort to understand Nola, and Nola resents it. When they argue in La Crêperie, Mrs. Dietrich puts little effort into understanding what her daughter is trying to say and more effort into noticing her daughter's physical attributes. The argument is important. Nola, not looking at her mother, asks, "Why don't we just talk about it, Mother?" (73). Mrs. Dietrich claims not to know what Nola means by "it," and that frustrates Nola. Eventually, this conversation occurs:

> Nola says, sighing, "How exhausting it is."
> "How *what?*"

"How exhausting it is."
"What is?"
"You and me—"
"What?"
"Being together—"
"Being together how—?"
"The two of us, like this—"
"But we're hardly ever together, Nola," Mrs. Dietrich says. (73)

Either Mrs. Dietrich does not know that Nola means their strained relationship is the exhausting "it," or she pretends not to know because she cannot talk about it. At this point, Nola turns away, and Mrs. Dietrich's only response is to silently pity Nola. She "sees with pity that her daughter's skin is fair and thin and dry [. . .] it will wear out before she is forty" (73). Appearance means everything to Mrs. Dietrich.

The most glaring example of this concern over appearances is shown by Nola's and Mrs. Dietrich's reactions to the woman in black, a "disheveled woman" (52) who is probably a bag lady. Mrs. Dietrich seems to see the woman as nothing more than an eyesore. She is content to simply ignore her, as the other shoppers do, by walking past her without even acknowledging her presence. She defends her actions by saying, when questioned, that the woman is "harmless [. . .] she just *sits*" (52). As far as Mrs. Dietrich is concerned, the lady in black is simply a flaw in the mall scenery. As long as the lady continues to "just sit," Mrs. Dietrich can keep up the pretense that people such as the lady in black don't exist. In her world of luxury, Mrs. Dietrich's pretense is an important way to keep from standing out in the crowd.

Nola's reaction to the bag lady is a bit more complex than her mother's. Upon first seeing her, Nola is horrified that "people like her" are allowed in the mall. At this point, Nola seems more upset that the beautiful and blemish-free interior of her second home has been tarnished rather than with the idea that this woman may be suffering any harm. It is only after speaking with her mother about the lady in black that Nola expresses any concern for the woman. She bemoans the fact that the bag lady may somehow be harmed by the actions of those who choose not to acknowledge her presence. There is a *slight* chance that Nola is honestly concerned about the welfare of the woman in black; however, it is more likely that she is simply paying lip-service to the "tragedy of women like that" (52). By speaking of such "tragedy," Nola appears to be more caring and concerned for "the outcasts of an affluent society" (52) than she really is.

Despite her passionate words, Nola's concern is fleeting and she quickly forgets, moving on to the important business of the day: shopping. It is not until Nola and Mrs. Dietrich are preparing to leave the mall that Nola is reminded of the wretched lady in black. Mrs. Dietrich and the other shoppers continue to file past the woman as if she weren't there. Nola, on the other hand, seems to be getting ready to approach her. This is not because of any real concern on Nola's part. It is more out of a desire to appear as a caring person. It almost seems as if Nola is thinking "If I were to approach this woman and offer her my help wouldn't it look good to everyone else? Perhaps they'd all comment on what a lovely young woman I am for helping this wretch." In the end though, Nola does not approach the bag lady. Nola's offer of help would cause her to stand out in the crowd. Despite the fact that Nola seems to feel it is important to appear concerned, it is even more important not to stand out.

The story ends with Nola sobbing in her mother's car "as though her heart is broken" (73). It would be easy to assume that Nola is crying out of sorrow for the woman in black or out of shame for not having approached her. Both of these reactions are unlikely, though. Nola's tears are more likely a continuation of her pretense as a genuinely caring person. The idea that these are crocodile tears is supported by the fact that Mrs. Dietrich has "heard these very sobs before" (73). On the other hand, if Nola's tears are real the reader should assume that she is not crying for the woman in black. Nola is much too self-centered and spoiled to truly feel that strongly for anyone else. Nola is crying because she came to the mall to forget how isolated she feels. By choosing not to approach the woman Nola only served to reinforce her loneliness. In this way, the bag lady has sabotaged Nola's escape from her self-imposed solitary confinement. If Nola's tears are real, she is crying for herself, not the woman in black.

Nola and Mrs. Dietrich seem very different. However, their almost all-consuming obsession with appearances makes them, underneath it all, nearly identical and, despite being surrounded by people, very much alone.

Work Cited

Oates, Joyce Carol. "Shopping." *Ms.* March 1986: 50+.

CHECKLIST: CRITIQUING AN ESSAY *ABOUT* LITERATURE

1. What piece of literature is the essay about? (*Note:* Hereafter, we'll refer to *story,* whether the piece of literature is a short story, poem, novel, or drama.)
2. Identify the essay's thesis. What interpretation does it carry about the story? What is the basic point of interpretation? How clearly is it stated?
3. How effectively are the topic sentences developed? What kinds of detail support the interpretation? How effectively does the detail from the story itself support the thesis?

4. How has the writer introduced and concluded the essay? How effective are these parts of the essay?
5. Are the documentation and citation of primary and secondary sources correct? (For discussion of proper documentation, see Chapter 12.)
6. Does the paper adhere to conventions of usage, mechanics, and format? Correct any errors you find.

CHECKLIST: CRITIQUING AN ESSAY *FROM* LITERATURE

1. What event forms the basis for the essay? What story has the writer chosen as relating to the event?
2. What is the writer's interpretation of the story? How clearly does the interpretation come through in the essay, even if the writer doesn't explicitly state it?
3. How has the writer developed the paper—for example, as a personal, argumentative, or problem/solution essay? How effectively has the writer followed the conventions for the selected development? (See other chapters in Part Two for help here.)
4. How clearly has the writer related the story to the essay's primary event? That is, how effectively does the writer show how the story related to or informed her actions or her response to the event?
5. Are the documentation and citation of primary and secondary sources correct? (For discussion of proper documentation, see Chapter 12.)
6. Does the paper adhere to conventions of usage, mechanics, and format? Correct any errors you find.

Julian Opie, "Incident in the Library II," 1983. Oil paint on steel. 65 × 39-1/3 × 12 in. Courtesy Lisson Gallery, London.

CHAPTER 8

Evaluation Essays

We evaluate things, events, and ideas every day, making judgments about them. At times, we seem to reach a judgment almost instantaneously. How long, for example, does it take you to decide that a particular blouse or tie looks good? Probably not very long at all. At other times, a judgment may take longer to reach, and we deliberate carefully before making a choice.

Evaluation essays present the writer's opinion about her topic and support for that opinion, so that the reader sees something of the process the writer went through to reach her judgment about the topic. Because this judgment will be a value judgment, evaluation essays are essentially argumentative. That is, the writer makes an assertion—a judgment—involving the worth or value of her topic and then defends that assertion through the detail she presents. The following exercise should help to clarify this point.

Exercise 8.1

List as many traits or characteristics of a good teacher as you can. Then think about the teachers you have had. Which of these were good teachers? List two or three of them by name; then decide how many of the traits you listed these teachers had. For each trait give one or two specific examples of how each teacher exemplified that trait.

This exercise offers a fairly concise overview of one way to make and support an evaluation:

1. *Decide what to evaluate.* In the exercise, we gave you a topic or subject to evaluate—a good teacher. If the topic for your writing isn't specified, pick a topic that interests you—something about which you'd like to know more, or something you like or dislike.

2. *Establish criteria for your evaluation.* The paper you'll write as you work through this chapter is often called a criterion-based evaluation. How will you determine the worth of the subject of your evaluation? In the exercise, we asked you to develop a list of traits or characteristics of a good teacher. In essence, we asked

you to develop a way to measure the quality of a teacher. Once you've listed the criteria for evaluating your topic, you'll be able to compare your topic with the list to see how well it matches up. The criteria that you develop will enable you to formulate and support a carefully deliberated judgment, so that when a reader has finished reading your paper, he will understand why you take the position you do.

3. *Make a value judgment.* How well does your topic match with or fit the criteria you established? In the exercise, we asked you to name two or three teachers who matched up well with the criteria you established; we asked you to make a value judgment by naming Mr. Smith, your seventh-grade English teacher, or Ms. Rodriguez, your eleventh-grade math teacher, as "good." Your assessment constituted an initial judgment. In your evaluation paper, you'll frame the judgment you make about your topic as an assertion of the topic's value. This value may be characterized as good or bad, effective or ineffective, beneficial or detrimental, important or unimportant, worthy or unworthy, successful or unsuccessful, best or worst. You're not limited to just these terms, by any means, but your judgment should begin with them. Eventually, you'll write a thesis sentence that will convey this value judgment to your reader, and it will form the point your writing will prove.

4. *Offer specific support for your judgment.* What details can you provide to help your reader understand how you arrived at your evaluation and whether it's valid? In the exercise, we asked you to give a specific example of how each teacher you evaluated as a good teacher exemplified a particular trait.

If Bill were to evaluate the writer Jean Shepherd, one of his favorite humorists, he would follow the procedure outlined here and produce this prewriting:

1. *Decide what to evaluate.*
   Jean Shepherd, one of my favorite short story writers. Shepherd absolutely cracks me up, and I've used one of his books in a humor course I've taught.
2. *Establish criteria.*
   What makes for a good short story writer? More specifically, what makes for good funny short stories?
   a. exaggeration—one of the humorist's stock devices
   b. dialogue—vivid, at times ironic
   c. humorous situations
   d. universality—serious humor is humor I can identify with. Characters aren't so different from me, however exaggerated their situations and actions may be.
3. *Make a value judgment.*
   Jean Shepherd is absolutely one of the funniest short story writers I've ever read. [*Note:* "Funniest" is a superlative, and we assume that this is a positive (good) judgment.]
4. *Offer specific support for judgment*
   > Criterion 1—exaggeration: The exaggeration Shepherd uses brings characters and situations to always funny and sometimes painful life. (stories to draw details from: "The Grandstand Passion Play of Delbert and the Bumpus Hounds" and "Daphne Bigelow")

Criterion 2—Shepherd's use of dialogue is superb. (stories: "Bumpus" and "The Star-crossed Romance of Josephine Kosznowski")

Criterion 3—Shepherd puts his characters in hilarious conflicts and then lets them squirm their way out. (stories: "County Fair" and "Duel in the Snow, or Red Ryder Meets the Cleveland Street Kid")

Criterion 4—Shepherd's characters and the events of their lives seem not so far removed from me. (stories: "Wanda Hickey's Night of Golden Memories" and "Daphne Bigelow")

By drawing specific examples from specific stories, Bill would support the assertions he derived from his initial listing of criteria, so that the criteria would actually become topic sentences of paragraphs designed to support the evaluation's thesis, the value judgment Bill makes about Shepherd as "one of the funniest" short story writers he's read.

SAMPLE ESSAYS

The following sample essays involve evaluations of a book, political advertisements, a public service advertisement, a state law, and a book and movie. As you read through each, consider first what judgment the writer presents and then the criteria the writer uses as the basis for his or her evaluation.

The first sample essay is a newspaper column by Ellen Goodman, who writes a syndicated column. In it, Goodman evaluates the importance of a new book about girls in the United States.

ELLEN GOODMAN
BEAUTY INDUSTRY ON RAMPAGE

1   There are times when I wonder if the female body isn't part of some vast evolutionary speedup. In less than a generation, the girls I know seem to have acquired all these new body parts to worry about.

2   A glance at any teen magazine is a new anatomy lesson. Eyes are now subdivided into half a dozen distinct areas from brow to lash, each of which needs to be thinned or thickened, shaved or shaded. Teeth demand brightening as well as straightening. Thighs have grown cellulite. Lips require "plumping." Arms bulge for biceps. And every unmentionable inch of the body seems to need perfume of one kind or another.

3   Of course it is not our bodies but the beauty industry on this evolutionary rampage. It's rather like the trend in medicine. As general practitioners splintered

into an array of subspecialists, the beauty market splintered into products for every inch from scalp to toenail, acne to elbow.

The difference of course is that medicine changed to make their patients feel better. The beauty industry changed to make their customers feel worse.

Anyone who spends time with teen-age girls knows that they aren't narcissists. Narcissus, after all, wasted away before a pool of water while constantly admiring his image. Teen-age girls are drowning in words like "I hate my body; I hate my looks. I hate myself."

It is this despairing mantra that Joan Jacobs Brumberg explores in *The Body Project*. Her book, subtitled *An Intimate History of American Girls,* is the third in a triumvirate of works about the crisis in the lives of adolescent girls.

First, Carol Gilligan identified the moment when girls in our culture lose their authentic "voice" and self-confidence. Next Mary Pipher explored this psychological reality of female adolescence in *Reviving Ophelia*. Now Brumberg has filled in the blank, saying that a girl's relationship to her body is "at the heart of the crisis of confidence."

Her delightful and painful history ranges from the days when girls were tied into corsets to the days when girls are corseted by internal voices demanding model-thin perfection. It crosses the century from an era when girls rarely mentioned their bodies at all to an era when the body has become their "project."

Allowing us to eavesdrop on a wonderful assortment of teen-age diaries, she compares the self-improvement plans of a late 19th-century adolescent to a later 20th-century girl. The first girl resolves "not to talk about myself or feelings.... To think before speaking. To work seriously. To be self-restrained in conversation and actions.... To be dignified. Interest myself more in others."

The second girl resolves to "try to make myself better in any way I possibly can with the help of my budget and baby-sitting money. I will lose weight, get new lenses, already got a new haircut, good makeup, new clothes and accessories."

In barely a hundred years, a girl's identity had attached like Velcro to her appearance.

The Body Project is not a lament for the good old days. Brumberg tells the history of everything from menstruation to virginity, from mirrors to training bras, from petting to eating disorders. But she has no nostalgia for the era when 60 percent of high school students in Boston were totally unprepared for menstruation.

Nevertheless she is aware of the trade-offs we've made. Girls who once were held under the Victorian umbrella of protection are "freed" into "a consumer culture that seduces them into thinking that the body and sexual expression are their most important projects." Girls once repressed and chaperoned to adulthood are now more independent and vulnerable in a society sexualizing them at a younger age.

While enlivening the history, *The Body Project* draws the crucial connection 14
between bad body images and bad choices, between how girls feel about their
bodies and what they do with them.

"Girls who do not feel good about themselves need the affirmation of 15
others," Brumberg writes, "and that need, unfortunately, almost always empowers male desire. In other words, girls who hate their bodies do not make
good decisions about partners or about the kind of sexual activity that is in
their best interest."

What is missing today, after a century of change, says Brumberg, is "an in- 16
tergenerational dialogue" between women and girls. Her book is a fine text for
such a conversation. It makes us think seriously about a world in which teen-age
misery is described all too seriously as a bad hair day.

◆ QUESTIONS FOR REVIEW

1. Goodman's essay is not a simple book review; that is, Goodman does not simply present a summary of the book's contents and then say that she liked or didn't like the book. What is Goodman's evaluation of *The Body Project*? How important or effective a book does she think it is?
2. Identify Goodman's thesis sentence, the one in which she presents her evaluation of this book. Where does it appear in the essay? Is this an effective placement? Why or why not?
3. What does Goodman offer to support her evaluation of *The Body Project*?

◆ WRITING OPPORTUNITY

Do you think Goodman is right? Is there too much emphasis in today's society on beauty and appearance? If so, is this emphasis limited to adolescent girls? ◆

In "Shooting to Win; Do Attack Ads Work? You Bet – and That's Not All Bad," Kathleen Hall Jamieson provides an analysis of the phenomenon of political advertising that focuses specifically on the shortcomings of one's political opponent. Although many of Jamieson's examples are from the 2004 Presidential campaign between President George W. Bush and Senator John Kerry, the essay still has currency, for attack ads will always be a major element in political campaigns.

Paul Lachine / Newsart

Kathleen Hall Jamieson

SHOOTING TO WIN

Do Attack Ads Work? You Bet—and That's Not All Bad.

Over the airwaves, the suspect charges fly: John Kerry has voted to raise taxes 98 times in his 20-year Senate career. George W. Bush imposed the biggest Medicare premium increase in history. Kerry is proposing a government-run health care plan. Bush endorses the outsourcing of jobs. Kerry didn't deserve his Vietnam war medals. The war in Iraq has cost U.S. taxpayers $200 billion.

Totally true, or completely false? Well, not entirely one or the other, as it happens. In the modern political ad wars, "truth" is a relative commodity, and admakers tweak our perception of it to gain maximum advantage for their clients. Perhaps, if you live in the current election battleground, political attack ads like the ones I've just described have already subtly influenced your views of Bush and Kerry, cementing impressions, raising questions or sowing doubts.

This year, complaints about advertising distortions seem louder than ever. The media generally sling the word "negative" at attack ads and complain about them, even when they're few in number and the specifics are largely accurate. But this time around, our research shows, the grousing reporters and pundits are on to something. Questionable claims in Republican attack ads abound this year, in part because of the sheer volume of Bush attacks on Kerry's record. And the barrage of attacks on Bush from independent "527" groups supporting Kerry, as well as the Swift boat verterans' claims against Kerry, have multiplied the suspect assertions floating around this campaign season.

Voters caught in the crossfire might well wonder, how do ads deceive or mislead us? When they do, does it matter? Do they work, and why? And who or what protects us from their wiles?

The candidates and their supporters will spend about a billion dollars to produce and distribute ads this year. To the campaigns, the expense is worth it. Though ads alone can't determine the outcome of an election, they can be a decisive factor. And attack ads are especially effective. Surveys repeatedly show that negative ads register with voters more quickly than positive information and are more readily recalled as well.

But are such ads of any value to voters? It depends. Yes, they sometimes resort to ambiguities and even deception to create an impression, but many also hit on the central themes of a campaign. In particular, ads that contrast the views of both candidates in a single spot often provide voters with policy specifics and accurate information that will forecast how a given candidate will govern.

Political ads don't usually spread outright lies. Many of their troubling statements contain an element of truth. It's true that Kerry has voted to raise taxes – but not as often or as much as the Republican ads making that claim would have us believe. Yes, jobs have been lost during the Bush administration – but not as many as Democrats claim. Contrary to a Democratic ad, the war in Iraq has not yet cost $200 billion, although it may in the future.

Such deception is lamentable, even unnecessary – after all, simply stating the truth would make the same points – but campaigns exaggerate or oversimplify the truth because it's effective. It gets the voters' attention, builds on widespread assumptions – Democrats are tax-and-spenders, Republicans are pro-business, pro-defense and against the little guy – and it sticks with people unless it's solidly and conspicuously debunked.

Ads often sin by omission as well. It's true, as Republican ads note, that Kerry has opposed funding some weapons systems. What they don't mention is that both President George H.W. Bush and his Secretary of Defense, Dick Cheney, opposed some of the same weapons. Democrats may try to compare current job losses with those of the Great Depression, but the unemployment rate under Bush today is actually about what it was when Clinton was campaigning for a second

AP Wideworld Photos

term. Some deceptions don't exist in the ads per se but in the meaning the audience takes from them. Admakers know that evocative images short-circuit our ability to analyze them critically. That's what's going on in a MoveOn PAC ad focusing on Kerry's support for extending the assault weapons ban. As an AK-47 rifle materializes on-screen, the announcer intones, "This is an assault weapon." True. "It can fire up to 300 rounds a minute." Also true, for the fully automatic version. "In the hands of terrorists it could kill hundreds." True again. But contrary to the inference the ad invites, the fully automatic weapon it displays and describes was not affected by the assault weapons ban, which applied to semi-automatic weapons only. Access to fully automatic weapons has been restricted since 1934 by the National Firearms Act.

As polls repeatedly report, the public hates negative ads. But refine the question, and the answer changes. An Annenberg survey suggests that voters accept civil, accurate, issue-based attack ads. Such ads not only do exist, they also work. One of Ronald Reagan's effective ads in 1980 asked, "Can we afford four more years of broken promises? In 1976, Jimmy Carter promised to hold inflation to 4 percent. Today it is 14 percent. He promised to fight unemployment. But today there are 8.5 million Americans out of work." All true, and all presented in a factual way, without any twist to make the point sharper. Voters also report that they prefer comparative or contrast ads that provide a reason to vote against one candidate while also justifying a vote for the candidate running the ad.

Attack ads have a bad reputation because reporters and the public believe that a candidate generally uses them to spread deception about his rival. Yet in past presidential elections, more distortions appeared in ads

AP Wideworld Photos

bragging about the candidate running the ad than in those blasting the opponent. Although the jury is still out on 2004, cases of self-inflation include Kerry's advertised claim that he "cast a decisive vote that created 20 million new jobs" and Bush's suggestion that he (not Ronald Reagan) provided "the largest tax relief in history."

When it comes to advertising in general and attack ads in particular, of course, money matters. Our 2000 National Annenberg Election Survey found that by outspending Al Gore and buying attack ads questioning the vice president's credibility in the final weeks of the last campaign, Bush blunted Gore's accurate charge that the GOP's Social Security plan would fall short by $1 trillion of doing what it promised. Had the Republicans not gained that last-minute advantage in the battleground states, Gore might have won the electoral college as well as the popular vote.

Similarly, our April survey of voters in the ad-saturated battleground states found that 61 percent had been gulled by the false claim that Bush "favors sending American jobs overseas," 56 percent by the notion that Kerry "voted for higher taxes 350 times" and 72 percent by the assertion that 3 million jobs have been lost in the Bush presidency (at the depth of the slump, the number was 2.7 million).

In political advertising, truth only has an advantage when a credible source makes it known. That's chiefly the media's job. When reporters hold a candidate accountable for the campaigning done in his name, it works. For instance, during the 2000 primary compaign, when Bush was asked whether he actually believed his ad's claim that his rival, Sen. John McCain, opposed funding breast cancer research, he admitted that he didn't.

When a candidate ducks questions, the journalistic fact check is another line of voter defense. In the 1992 Georgia presidential primary, viewers penalized GOP hopeful Patrick Buchanan for a deceptive attack against incumbent President George H.W. Bush after the ad was widely criticized on the national and local news. A CNN-Gallup poll showed that 23 percent of voters reported that the ad had increased support not for Buchanan, but for Bush.

When presidential ads are bombarded with critiques from news outlets, their sponsors and "unaffiliated" supporters usually change the challenged claim. The Bush campaign did this when it reduced its claim that Kerry had voted for tax increases from 350 times to 98. A MoveOn PAC ad did the same in revising the cost of the Iraq war downward from $200 billion to $150 billion in a critiqued Kerry ad.

But the road to accuracy is one of a thousand steps, and hundreds remain to be taken. As Annenberg FactCheck.org shows, the Republicans' figure of 98 tax-increase votes by Kerry is still an exaggeration, and $150 billion inflates the current cost of the Iraq war, which is still under $120 billion, according to the Office of Management and Budget. Confident that voters will continue to find the claims plausible and convinced that frequent airing will drown out news corrections, those on both sides continue to repeat some misleading claims.

Yet a focus on the distortions in ads and the failure of news organizations to keep the worst tendencies in check can obscure the fact that campaign ads do include useful information. In fact, those who want substance in ads should applaud attack and contrast ads. Our research shows that in every year from 1952 to 2000, there have been more policy specifics in contrast ads than in so-called positive ads.

In 2000, for example, the Bush contrast ads forecast a prescription drug benefit, tax cuts, educational reforms and private investment accounts for Social Security. As president, Bush kept the first three promises and has renewed the fourth. This year, among other things, the candidate ads feature alternative plans to increase access to health insurance. This probably ensures that the next president, whoever he is, will work to increase the number of insured.

In a model election, candidates would stick to the high road, and their declarations and ads on Social Security, health care and Iraq would be scrutinized by news organizations that weren't sidetracked by the political horse race, hurricanes and the fate of Dan Rather. Our country has conducted campaigns worthy of emulation, notably 1960 (Kennedy vs. Nixon) and 1980 (Reagan vs. Carter). It has also suffered through others that serve as negative examples, especially 1964 (Johnson vs. Goldwater) and 1988 (Bush vs. Dukakis). It's not too late for the candidates, campaign consultants and reporters to move this election in the direction of the former and away from the latter.

◆ QUESTIONS FOR REVIEW

1. What is the thesis of Jamieson's essay? Where does it appear in the essay? How clear is the value judgment it presents?
2. How does Jamieson support her thesis? That is, what details does she provide to support the thesis? How effective is this support? Why?
3. We generally see attack ads as being negative, but Jamieson says that such ads can actually be positive. How does she support this assertion?
4. How does the cartoon (on page 352) work with the essay? How accurately does it project the essay's content? Is it an appropriate illustration, or is it ineffective? Why?

◆ WRITING OPPORTUNITY

1. Go to this website: www.factcheck.org. There you'll find discussion of current and past campaigns. (For past campaigns, click on the "archive" link.) Using the information there about a political ad or campaign of your choosing, write an evaluation of the ad or campaign. Is or was it fair? Is or was it effective? Why?
2. Evaluate the factcheck.org site. How reliable do you think it is? How fair and accurate in its assessments of the ads or campaigns it presents? What organization sponsors the site? What is your assessment of the organization's fairness?
3. Write your own attack ad. Select a current issue or political candidate, and develop an ad supporting or attacking the issue or candidate. You must be accurate in your assertions; that is, you may not say anything that can't be verified. Write an evaluation of your ad. ◆

Our next essay, an analysis of a public service advertisement, was written by Bill Bridges. Bill uses this essay in his first-year writing classes to help students learn to look carefully at the various components of an ad and decide how each component contributes to the ad's overall effectiveness.

BILL BRIDGES

"NO THANKS"—A STEP BEYOND "JUST SAY NO"

Seventeen—a magazine that's hip, cool, hot, full of columns and articles for today's teenage girl, offering advice on fashion, beauty, guys, nutrition, music. It's a flashy mag, sporting bright colors and graphics that cry out for the reader's attention. In the February, 2001 issue of *seventeen*, the National Youth Anti-Drug Media Campaign placed an advertisement titled "No Thanks" (see Figure 8.1) as part of a national effort to "[. . .] educate and empower all youth to reject illegal drugs [. . .]" ("About Us"). Every advertisement in a magazine like *seventeen* faces rigorous competition from all other ads, so the Anti-Drug Media Campaign faced quite a challenge: create an ad that would attempt to sell not a product like lipstick or clothes but a concept, the idea that a young girl can actually resist drug use. Thus, the purpose of the ad is to empower that young girl, to help her not do something she doesn't want to do. How successfully this ad, which is titled "No Thanks," fulfills its purpose depends on how well it catches and then holds the reader's attention. As one piece of ammunition in the war on drugs, "No Thanks" is no dud; instead, it is an effective ad.

"No Thanks" is certainly an eye-catcher. Dominated by a stark color—mustard yellow—this ad provides a bright, noticeable contrast to the page it opens with, a fairly busy page titled "in the halls of *seventeen*." That contrasting page uses two background colors—the top half, black, the bottom half, purple. "in the halls of *seventeen*" presents nine photographs, with six of these grouped as something of a collage. Against this, "No Thanks" pits its entire mustard yellow page, with just one model included. Only her head and left shoulder show, and the cold yellow color washes over her, highlighting her blonde hair. The left side of her face is brightly lit, while the right half is so dark that we can hardly see any detail at all, only a slight glint from her right eye. But the look on her face is unmistakable: she is clearly displeased and hurt at having been offered a joint by a boy she's interested in. Her eyes show little emotion, only coldness, and her mouth is set in a straight line. With the mustard wash over the entire page, it's as if the reader sees the model through a yellow haze, so that the reader is separated from the model. She looks at the reader as though the reader had offered her the joint, eye contact pulling the reader into the ad and to the model, the wash of color all the while holding the reader back from fully entering the ad. Such tension is effective in reaching the reader and drawing her into the world of the ad.

"No Thanks" invites the *seventeen* reader to identify readily with the ad's model, an attractive young woman who we assume is approximately the age of the reader. Particularly given the expression on her face—disappointment, hurt,

FIGURE 8.1
Partnership For A Drug-Free America.

coldness—the model invites the reader into the ad's scenario. Very few advertisements in this magazine use models whose expressions show anything less than joy or sexy self-confidence. "No Thanks" is one of those few, and teens who've been in a similar situation could identify with the model. By inviting, no, by actually insisting on this identification, "No Thanks" increases its chances of reaching its reader.

Reinforcing the starkness of the mustard wash, the copy (the words of the ad) is also presented starkly in an uneven, ragged font. It's not a pretty font, not an eye-pleasing font; it signals danger. And this danger is reflected in the copy. "No Thanks" opens with a scenario in red letters at the top of the page: "He's superfly. He wants your digits. But first he wants you to get high. Here's what you say." "Superfly," "wants your digits"—this language is breezy, current. Its breeziness echoes that of other language throughout *seventeen*, thus, this language should catch the reader's attention.

The copy actually dominates the ad, taking up at least two-thirds of the available space. After the opening scenario, which spreads across the top of the entire ad, the copy runs down the left-hand side of the page, displayed in black lettering in smaller and smaller point size, so that it creates something of a running movie credits feel. The suggested responses, starting with "No way. I would rather go to math camp than smoke a joint," make it very clear that this ad is anti-drug. Other language from the copy emphasizes the tension and defensiveness at work in this situation: "I like you. I don't like your question." At the bottom of the page, we find this message, in the same font but in red letters: "Or you can just say: No thanks." The font and point sizes fit well with the ad's message and with the attitude suggested by the expression on the model's face, their starkness reinforcing the distaste for drugs we assume the model holds.

How well does this copy work? It gives the reader ideas for responding to someone offering her a joint. In many situations when drugs are offered, youngsters don't know what to say. They don't want to appear to be afraid or not cool, so they take the drugs offered, whether they really want to or not. By providing at least some ideas of how to respond, "No Thanks" does its job. The suggested responses range widely, beginning with a strong statement of outright refusal ("No way") to turning the tables on that "superfly" young man through an appeal to "ask what kind of person I am." Humor also plays a role in the copy, in that the "math camp" line offers a funny response that verges into sarcasm. And it sounds like a response that a teenager would make. Further, the ad plays on plant imagery: "Instead of shoving weed in my face, try flowers. Make it roses," again sounding like something a teenager might say to deflect an offer of marijuana. By offering a range of responses that can be counted as strategies, "No Thanks" should spark ideas in the reader about how she might respond when confronted with or surprised by pressure to use drugs.

Another important element of the copy is its position on the page. It surrounds the model; it frames her. And like a frame protects a picture, the language presented here offers protection for the model—and that young girl who identifies with her. It's almost as if the copy serves as a buffer or even a shield between the model and her "superfly" dude. The implied message to that young girl seems clear: use your language to prepare for such confrontation; use the language here or rehearse your own responses, but be ready when you meet that "superfly" guy.

In the 1980s, President Ronald Reagan offered America "Just Say No" as a slogan to combat drug use. "No Thanks" goes a step beyond. Its message is unmistakable; it makes its point that smoking marijuana (and, by extension, using any kind of illegal drugs) is not something that anyone should do. And it does so not by preaching but by offering practical responses that a teen could use or at least get her own ideas from. Its message is at once one of encouragement, particularly in its subtle focus on "self-respect" as a counter to drugs, and of empowerment, in suggesting ways for the reader to be prepared for future confrontation. "No Thanks" works.

8

Works Cited

National Youth Anti-Drug Media Campaign. "About Us." Home page. 6 Jan.
    2001 <http://www.theantidrug.com/aboutus.html>.
"No Thanks." *Seventeen* Feb. 2001: no pages.

◆ QUESTIONS FOR REVIEW

1. What is the thesis of Bill's essay? Where does it appear in the essay? How clear is the value judgment it presents?
2. Divide the essay into beginning, middle, and end. What rhetorical and/or stylistic devices help form these divisions?
3. Bill says that the effectiveness of the ad "depends on how well it catches and then holds the reader's attention" (¶1). This assertion presents the criteria on which the essay is based. Are these criteria ("catching" and "holding") supported in the essay? How effectively?

◆ WRITING OPPORTUNITY

1. Go to this website: www.mediacampaign.org/index.html. Under the header "Ad Gallery," click on "Print" to see other advertisements in the series of which "No Thanks" is a part. Pick one or two ads, and compare them to "No Thanks." What elements do they have in common? How do they differ?

2. Write your own anti-drug advertisement, one aimed at recent high school graduates who are now college students. After you've written your ad, speculate about its effectiveness.
3. Pick an advertisement for a product you frequently use. How well does the product stack up against the promises made or implied by the ad? ◆

In our fourth sample essay, Jennifer Pitman, a first-year composition student at UNC Charlotte, evaluates the effectiveness of Booze It & Lose It, North Carolina's initiative to battle drunk drivers.

JENNIFER PITMAN

BOOZE IT? LOSE IT!:
AN EVALUATION OF NORTH CAROLINA'S DRUNK DRIVING LAWS

North Carolina has tough, extensive laws against driving while drunk. Begun in 1994 by Governor Jim Hunt and continuing today, the Booze It & Lose It campaign specifically targets drunk driving. The campaign is an ongoing effort that incorporates tougher DWI laws, increases efforts at educating the public, creates a task force on impaired driving, and improves on existing treatment programs. While the laws that have been enacted and continually strengthened have not solved the drunk driving issue, they have been effective in reducing the number of drunk drivers on the road. Strict punishment and enforcement have made the drunk driving laws successful in protecting the innocent and have cut down on the number of repeat offenders. However, there is still room for improvement. The harsh consequences of driving drunk are not widely enough known, and punishment is all too often delayed for an undue period of time.

The most important purpose of these laws is to make travel safer for everyone in the state. MADD, a group that strives for the protection of innocent people, especially children, from drunk drivers, believes that North Carolina is doing a good job. In 1999, it ranked North Carolina among the top four states in the battle against drunk driving (Shearouse). And for good reason. As noted on the home page of the Governor's Highway Safety Program: "Alcohol-related fatalities in North Carolina have decreased dramatically in the 1990s. In 1990 43.5 percent of all traffic fatalities were alcohol-related. The average for the years 1994 to 1996 shows that number dropped to 30 percent. In 1998, that number reached an all-time low of 29 percent. The number of people killed in alcohol-related crashes had decreased from 602 in 1990 to 469 in 1998—a 22.1

percent decrease" (Booze It & Lose It). The extensive laws that have been passed and the continuing efforts of law enforcement clearly have made for safer conditions for those of us on the road.

North Carolina's laws are incredibly strict—the baseline for DWI is a blood alcohol level of 0.8—and that adds to their effectiveness. A first time offender faces a number of restrictions, many fines, and major inconveniences. A person arrested for driving drunk has his license revoked immediately for 30 days, must appear in court, must pay fines, must find alternative transportation, must be assessed and participate in a treatment program, must perform community service, and loses his license for a minimum of one year after conviction. The cost is prohibitive. "In North Carolina, first-time DWI-offenders pay at least $9,640 in legal fees, court costs and fines" (Booze It & Lose It). But depending on the amount of alcohol in the bloodstream, there can be even stricter sanctions. For example, some repeat offenders will be required to use an ignition interlock system which will prohibit them from starting their vehicles ("Driving and Alcohol"). All of these consequences help to deter people from driving when they are drunk.

As if all the penalties are not enough, the law also establishes regulations that are even more severe for repeat offenders. For someone who has been convicted of one DWI, the legal blood alcohol limit decreases from 0.08 to 0.04. If someone has two DWI convictions, the legal blood alcohol limit is decreased again to 0.00. If someone is found guilty of a DWI while driving with a suspended license due to a previous DWI, his vehicle will be seized and sold at auction ("Driving and Alcohol"). A person with a prior charge also faces longer license suspensions and mandatory jail time. These extensive provisions are aimed at reducing the number of people who repeatedly break the law.

Sobriety checkpoints are set up throughout each county in North Carolina in order to catch people who drive while drunk. Since 1993, 26,000 checkpoints have been set up and more than 44,000 people have been charged with DWI ("Booze It & Lose It"). This effort has made North Carolina's roads much safer. Getting drunk drivers off the road helps to reduce fatalities and injuries both to the drivers and innocent people.

Part of the Booze It & Lose It campaign has included public service announcements designed to further increase awareness of the state's drunk driving laws. In one radio ad, the Governor reminds people to "be prepared to pay the consequences" if they drive under the influence. The first television ad depicted a birthday party scene where the guest of honor learns the consequences of the state's tougher laws. Another television ad featured one of the Carolina Panthers warning people not to drink and drive ("Booze It & Lose It"). While these ads were great for getting the "don't drink and drive" message out to the public, they did not do a sufficient job of informing people of the consequences of such behavior. The public needs to be better educated about the penalties associated with drunk driving. If people were more aware that they would lose their license for a whole year, would be required to complete a treatment plan, and would end up paying almost $10,000 for just one offense, they might think twice before they get in a car and drive after they have been drinking.

Punishment for drunk driving offenses is often delayed. The time it takes for individual cases to reach the court should be shortened. Loopholes and exceptions to the laws enable an offender's lawyer to postpone a case for months, during which time the person is not punished. Offenders do receive an immediate 30-day suspension, but with the help of a lawyer, limited driving privileges may be restored after only 10 days. Until a person goes to court, there are no other restrictions or punishments because the person has not been convicted. In order for the laws to be more effective, the court process should be sped up by limiting the number of postponements that can be filed. Immediate punishment is necessary so that dangerous drivers can learn a lesson and be prevented from breaking the law again. 7

The drunk driving laws in North Carolina are very effective overall. They have been valuable in reducing the number of drivers on the road who are under the influence of alcohol, and they have helped reduce the number of innocent people who are injured and killed by drunk drivers. Unfortunately, there are still drivers who never get caught, do not understand what they are risking, and are not punished immediately. North Carolina has not yet solved the drunk driving issue, but it is ahead of many other states in apprehending and punishing drivers who break the law. 8

Works Cited

"Booze It & Lose It." North Carolina Governor's Highway Safety Program home page. 25 May 2001. <http://www.ncdot.org/secretary/GHSP/BoozeIt>.

"Driving and Alcohol." North Carolina State Highway Patrol Safety Program laws page. 25 May 2001 <http://www.ncshp.org/safety1.html#drinking>.

Shearouse, Robert C. "Preparing for 'Rating the States 2000'." Driven Fall 1999. 25 May 2001 <http://www.madd.org/news/0,1056,4794,00.html>.

◆ QUESTIONS FOR REVIEW

1. What is Jennifer's thesis? What is her judgment about the effectiveness of North Carolina's drunk driving initiative?
2. What reasons does Jennifer offer to support her thesis?
3. What support does she provide? How effective is this support?
4. Divide Jennifer's essay into its beginning, middle, and end. How does she open the essay? How does she conclude it? How effective are the introduction and conclusion?

◆ WRITING OPPORTUNITY

How well does your state deal with such public safety issues as drunk driving? Are there other similar issues that concern you, e.g., spouse abuse, domestic violence, or deadbeat parents? How effectively are the laws concerning these issues enforced? ◆

In our next essay, Amy Wright, a writing student at Sam Houston State University, provides an evaluation of *The Da Vinci Code* (both the novel and the movie).

AMY WRIGHT

THE DA VINCI CODE: A STUDY IN PRINT AND FILM

Dan Brown's novel, *The Da Vinci Code* (New York: Doubleday, 2003), is a modern epic of sweeping cultural, historic, religious, and literary proportions. Telling the story of a symbologist and a detective who together enter unwittingly into a modern quest for the Holy Grail, the novel is well written, thoroughly conceived, and emotionally effective. On one level it is a suspenseful whodunit thriller. Underneath this, it is a skillful player of devil's advocate, offering both fascinating trivia and religious hokum. At its heart it is an ethical tale about truth. The film version of *The Da Vinci Code* (Columbia Pictures, 2006), created by Academy Award-winning director Ron Howard, is full of its own virtues and in possession of its own unique vices. It is artistically striking, but many viewers and critics have expressed great disappointment in it after reading the book. The question of which has the greater merit requires an in-depth examination of both the book and the film. The first consideration is of the pure qualities of each within its own medium—is the book a better book than the movie is a movie? The second consideration addresses the film as an adaptation—is it permissible for a director to take certain liberties with plot or theme? In doing so can he still maintain the original work's artistic integrity, or is it sufficient that the film become a completely independent work? Both Dan Brown's novel and Ron Howard's film of *The Da Vinci Code* are brilliant works technically and artistically, and both possess unique and contrasting merits.

Given the number of major characters and the complexity of the plot, a brief summary seems in order to help clarify the discussion to follow:

The Cast of Characters:

> Robert Langdon—American symbologist, called to a grail quest by Sauniere
> Sophie Neveau—French Police cryptologist, granddaughter of Sauniere
> Jacques Sauniere—Curator of the Louvre Museum, Head of the Priory of Sion
> Captain Bezu Fache—Captain of the French Police
> Bishop Aringarosa—Head of the Opus Dei prelature
> Silas—An albino Opus Dei monk and a pupil of Bishop Aringarosa
> Leigh Teabing—English Grail scholar, also known as the Teacher, who is intent upon protecting the secret of the Grail

A Summary of the Plot:

The story opens with the murder of Jacques Sauniere, committed by Silas and orchestrated by the Teacher. The French police begin an investigation of the act which mistakenly leads them to Robert Langdon through a note left by the dying Sauniere. Sophie and Robert team up to find Sauniere's killer and are led, by means of riddles and clues left by Sauniere himself, on a quest to discover the Priory of Sion, an ancient order descended from the Knights Templar, and the Holy Grail, Mary Magdalene. They flee to Teabing, a friend of Langdon's, not knowing that he is the Teacher, who takes them to London where they encounter Aringarosa and Fache, who are now hunting Silas. In the end, Silas is killed, the Teacher arrested, and Langdon cleared. Sophie discovers that she is directly descended from Christ and Mary Magdalene, and Langdon discovers the Grail.

It is unarguably clear that *The Da Vinci Code* is an expertly crafted work of literature. It possesses all of the basic elements of good fiction—a thorough and clear narrative, gripping language that effectively communicates both action and tone, well-developed characters, and significant and thought-provoking themes. The narrative's third person voice gives unobstructed insight into the characters' problem solving processes and mindsets, which in turn lends believability and humanism to the narrative. Brown's language, combined with the progressive building of the story and the gradual revelation of intertwining plot lines, lends a tone of suspense to a novel that is in turn cynical, urgent, awe-filled, incredulous, didactic, and humorous. The characters are uniquely well developed. They have significant pasts which help illuminate the personal dilemmas that they face and govern their actions and reactions, and all undergo journeys throughout the story that bring them to a personal epiphany—a moral realization and validation of their belief in what they fight for. Finally, the themes that Brown addresses are universal in their scope. Though the story is fictitious, it considers such real-life ideas as the implications of faith or nonbelief in one's life, truth versus the perception of truth, and the ethics of the willingness to kill—or to die—for faith, power, money, or one's perception of the greater good. From a purely literary perspective, *The Da Vinci Code* proves to be of tremendous merit.

One of the real gems in reading the book is the story's intertwining of fiction and fact. Brown doesn't miss an opportunity to include any detail, whether trivial, necessary, or positively quirky. Chances are, previous to reading the book, most readers do not know the native Parisian perspective on the Louvre pyramid or the significance of Pagan symbolism and tradition within the Christian church. Because of this unexpected inclusion of random fact, readers may find that a book written as a work of fiction is surprisingly intellectually rewarding. At the same time, within this rich factual base actually lies a quandary for readers. Despite the novel's home in the fiction section of Barnes & Noble, many readers seem determined to take the story as fact. Many forget that the theories introduced in the book are not as new as they sound; the unfaithful have been intent upon besmirching the good name of the church since its founding and the church itself has been guilty of radical attempts to keep its more unsavory secrets hidden. Even with a strong desire to maintain a healthy reality matrix, the fictional aspects of the story, immersed so deeply in fact and fact-based speculation, may present a problem as readers are left to discern what is to be believed and what is not.

Like the novel, Ron Howard's film version of *The Da Vinci Code* is an artistic treasure, made so by poignant performances, well-designed sound and lighting, and beautiful cinematography. Perhaps the single greatest asset of viewing the movie is the sheer powerful sensuality of experiencing a story through sight and sound rather than imagination alone. Because humans are, by nature, sensory beings, it follows as no surprise that there is a great inherent power in dramatic performance. It is one thing to read about a man, hopelessly immersed in a radical Catholic sect, performing agonizing acts of self-flagellation. It is another matter entirely to see this same man, staring with bloodshot eyes at the image of Christ on his wall, and to hear the guttural sounds of agony issuing from him as he mercilessly whips himself, to cringe at the sight of his raw, scarred back. In the same way, a skilled performance, in this case that of Tom Hanks as Robert Langdon, can make vivid the helplessness of a man on his knees in front of a gunman, confessing that he cannot solve the riddle that could save his life. It is this vicarious experience that connects us to the characters, gives us insight into their strengths and weaknesses, and allows us to share their tragedy, romance, fear, or hope.

The film's technical accomplishments, however, are accompanied by certain pitfalls inherent in the undertaking of adapting a novel to film. The main problem lies in the effort to make necessary changes while maintaining the integrity of the original work. Because the same form of narration cannot be used in a film as in a book, the viewer is deprived of a wealth of trivia, background information, and insight into the characters' thoughts. In addition, in the film's effort to sustain a gripping pace and at the same time maintain a reasonable length, all of the action happens unnaturally fast. In the book, every riddle requires careful thought and a number of obvious but wrong guesses before the right conclusion is reached; in the film, the characters seem vested with a supernatural ability to pull the answer to a riddle from the cosmic void, as if it had been merely lying in wait. This apparently super-smart quality dehumanizes characters that the audience would otherwise strongly empathize with. Finally, many audiences find the nature of dialogue in the film to be problematic; the effort of constantly having to read subtitles may become tedious to viewers who see movies so they don't have to read. While the strongly authentic cultural settings only serve to enhance the film, the strongly authentic cultural interactions may prove to be a barrier that audiences cannot readily surmount.

In addition to discrepancies due to artistic choice and time constraints, the movie includes a number of basic plot deviations from the book. One class of inconsistency, changes that are minor and do not truly affect the story, include certain omissions made in order to simplify the plot. Examples of these omissions include the exclusion of the second cryptex, originally found inside the first, the phone call from Langdon to his editor, in which he learns why Sauniere first contacted him, and the explanation of Teabing's spying methods. The film also excludes the projected romance between Sophie Neveau and Robert Langdon, which, while interesting speculatively, has no real bearing on the events of the story. The second classification of changes goes beyond simple omission to include matters that are more significant but still not crucial. One such change is the alteration of the timeline of Sophie and Sauniere's falling out. In the book, the events that lead to their estrangement happen when Sophie is in college, in the movie, when she is still a child. This change, while it doesn't affect the fact of the relationship, does affect its nature. A second obvious change is in the relationship between Bishop Aringarosa and Captain Fache. In the film, the Bishop tells Fache that Langdon is Sauniere's murderer, an assertion that does not exist in the novel. Not only does Aringarosa not lie about Langdon in the novel, Aringarosa actually works with Fache to find Silas and the Teacher. These changes alter both the development of the plot and the nature of these two characters, Aringarosa and Fache, turning them into men of desperation. The third and final group of discrepancies can only be termed the "Hollywoodization" of *The Da Vinci Code*; these are blatant changes that affect the virtue, principle, or theme of the story. One of the greatest changes from book to movie is the downplay of the Opus Dei/Vatican tensions and the change of the council that Bishop Aringarosa attends. Rather than a meeting with Vatican officials about the severance of Opus Dei from the Church, the council in the movie seems to be instead a council of officials plotting to destroy the Grail and save the faith. Thus, in the film, the plot becomes a plight of the Church rather than of one desperate man, making it much darker and more sinister. The final great change that takes place from book to movie involves the remnant of Sophie's family. Though Sophie is reunited with her grandmother Marie Chauvel in the last scene of the film, one very crucial character is missing—Sophie's brother. This simple alteration of the plot effectively strips Sophie of the family that has had a large part in defining her character. And therein lies the dilemma. To give Sophie her brother back would fulfill one quest of the novel—to tell Sophie the truth about her family. On the other hand, to furnish this minor but cosmically important character would deprive Sophie of her status as sole heir. It seems that it was more important to the film writers to maintain the prominence of their heroine than to let her share the blood line and gain a family. This choice both devalues Sophie's family, whose importance is repeatedly stressed throughout the novel, and comments on the respective weight of values and glory in the film industry and society.

Along with these negative changes, Howard also takes advantage of a number of opportunities to elevate his film from escapism to art by inserting poignant original scenes that deal with ethics or morality. Two such scenes are the encounter with the junkie in the park and the scene in the armored truck in which Sophie heals Langdon of his fear. In these scenes, vested with the as-yet-unknown power of her descent from Christ, Sophie performs simple acts of kindness, acts that, as Langdon later points out, may have changed his life and the junkie's irrevocably. Even though Sophie cannot walk on water, which she cynically attempts in imitation of Christ, she finds in herself a power for good that is entirely her own. The film uses these scenes, which are thought-provoking rather than dogmatic, to communicate the moral truth that the only thing necessary to effect change is to embrace one's inherent power to do good.

The question of artistic merit is one not easily answered. It is far less complicated to address entertainment value or personal appeal. This issue, however, is still a vital one today; it is the question that we can never seem to answer sufficiently. Which has the greater redeeming value, the talking picture or the picture of the mind's eye? Which is more worthy of consideration, the high art of literature or the movie, which has its roots in Vaudevillian frivolity? The most obvious conclusion to draw is that literature, with a greater historical root and a more typically serious tradition, is the more respectable medium, and this judgment could easily hold true in this case. A literary endeavor written with the scope and skill of *The Da Vinci Code* can credibly be counted within the canon of twenty-first century literary art. One must stop and consider, however, the merit of a well-crafted film, such as Howard's *Da Vinci Code*. Like the book, the film is exemplary in its own medium. Where the book's strengths lie in style, theme, and development, the movie is visually beautiful, technically sound, and well-acted. Because of these qualities, each individual work succeeds artistically. As an adaptation, Howard's film closely follows the guidelines of Brown's plot and intent but does not rely solely on Brown's novel for its inspiration. This would be impossible after the remarkable changes made from novel to film. By deleting the content that he found to be unnecessary and adding an original moral take on events, Howard has made the story of *The Da Vinci Code* his own, maintaining the integrity of the novel's purpose while giving the film a life of its own as a legitimate separate work. By doing so and thus surpassing any mediocre adaptation, Ron Howard's *The Da Vinci Code* proves its genuine artistic merit.

Works Consulted

Brown, Dan. *The Da Vinci Code* New York: Doubleday, 2003.
The Da Vinci Code. Dir. Ron Howard. Perf. Tom Hanks, Audrey Tatou, Ian McKellen, Jean Reno, Paul Bettany, Alfred Molina, Jurgen Prochnow, and Jean-Pierre Marielle. Columbia Pictures, 2006.

◆ QUESTIONS FOR REVIEW

1. What is the thesis of Amy's essay? What judgment does Amy offer of *The Da Vinci Code*, both the movie and the book?
2. What reasons does Amy offer to support her judgment?
3. What kinds of support does she provide for her position? How effective are these supporting details?
4. Divide Amy's essay into its beginning, middle, and end. What does she do to introduce you to the topic (the beginning)? How effective is this introduction? How effectively does Amy end her essay?
5. How effective is Amy's title? Can you suggest a more effective title? Explain.

◆ WRITING OPPORTUNITY

1. Reflect for a moment on a book you've read that has been made into a movie. Write a brief analysis of the key differences between the book and the movie. Is one clearly superior to the other? Why or why not?
2. What's your favorite book or movie? Write an evaluation of it, focusing on helping someone who's not read it or seen it decide to do so. ◆

THE RHETORICAL TRIANGLE

Subject

What kinds of topics lend themselves to evaluation? Although we can (and do) evaluate nearly everything in our lives, not all subjects lend themselves readily to evaluation essays. The most suitable topics for evaluation essays are those that, for whatever reasons, may be characterized by some degree of controversy or may be open to debate.

Writing an evaluation will require you to judge whether the topic of your essay is good or bad, effective or ineffective, beneficial or detrimental, important or unimportant, and so on. These descriptors can apply to a number of topics, although not equally well to all. When you look in the mirror just before you leave on a date, you probably think "Lookin' good!" but not "Lookin' effective" or "Lookin' beneficial." Were you to consider a change in policy in your university, you probably would think in terms of effectiveness, benefit, or importance. Here's a list of potential topics for an evaluation essay:

- a performance (play, movie, CD, television show, concert, fiction or poetry reading)
- a policy (campus housing, affirmative action, university admissions, non-graded courses)
- a one-time event (a football, basketball, soccer, volleyball game; a school or political rally)
- a piece of literature (novel, short story, drama, poem, autobiography, nonfiction essay)
- a bureaucracy (campus housing office, juvenile court system)
- a law (concerning drunk driving, underage drinking, education, the environment, child and/or spouse abuse)
- a program (date-rape prevention, drug education, child advocacy)
- a proposal (to institute a flat rate income tax, to change a program or implement a new one on campus, to allow or deny high school students off-campus lunch privileges, to add or drop a varsity-level sports program)
- a campaign (political, advertising, fund-raising)
- a public or professional person (politician, teacher, athlete, writer, artist, performer)
- a website

As you can see from this list, topics for evaluation essays can range widely.

Writer

As an evaluator, you'll need to impress your reader with your fairness and with the thoroughness with which you consider your topic. Because you'll present your opinion about the topic, you cannot avoid your biases, but you must take care not to let any preconceived ideas about your topic go unsupported. That is, if you're evaluating a CD by one of your favorite artists, you may well assume that this CD will be every bit as good as previous ones by this same star. It may be; then again, it may not be. Your job will be to evaluate the new CD as fairly and completely as possible, to proceed as a fan of the artist, but to be willing to criticize when necessary. To convince your reader that your evaluation is worth considering, you'll need to show that you've given serious thought to the topic.

Reader

In thinking about the readers for your evaluation essay, you may find it helpful to contrast them with the readers of an information essay (see Chapter 6) and with those of a position or argumentative essay (see Chapter 9). Readers of an information essay generally assume that, as the writer, you know more than they do about the essay's topic, so that they're likely to be receptive to the information you offer. Readers of a position essay are more likely to be skeptical about your purpose, disagreeing with you from the outset. So your job is to help readers on that opposite side understand why you think as you do.

Readers of evaluation essays reside somewhere on a spectrum between those of information and position essays. They will not likely defer to your knowledge in the ways that readers of information might; thus, they will require support for your claims. On the other hand, they are not likely to hold opposing opinions in the same ways that readers of position essays will. The difference in readers is caused, in part, by the difference in types of subjects one evaluates and argues about. As we'll see in Chapter 9, the writer of a position essay normally argues about topics that are connected to his concept of self, topics such as gun control, abortion, and welfare policies. On the other hand, the writer of an evaluation essay evaluates topics such as music groups, literary works, and literary performances. In general, these topics do not lead to the kinds of polarization that position topics do. Thus, while you will need to offer support for your opinions, you will not have to assume that your readers will approach your writing with their own arguments that have to be countered in your paper. (We will talk more about arguments and counterarguments in Chapter 9.)

DISTINGUISHING FEATURES OF EVALUATION ESSAYS

Evaluation Criteria

Sometimes criteria are referred to as the standards against which you'll judge your topic. Look again at your responses to Exercise 8.1 (page 347). What traits of a good teacher did you list? Those traits form the criteria you used to decide whether Ms. Smith and Mr. Jones fit into the category "good teacher"; they represent the standards you think a good teacher should meet.

Criteria are the standards used in evaluating something, and if you don't establish criteria for your evaluation, then you'll present a statement of personal taste rather than evaluation. In the following essay, Lou Jacobs presents a set of criteria for evaluating a photograph. How complete are the criteria he establishes? How effectively does he define or justify each one?

LOU JACOBS, JR.

WHAT QUALITIES DOES A GOOD PHOTOGRAPH HAVE?

1. When amateur and professional photographers get together they often discuss equipment and techniques at some length, but it is not often that photographers take time to consider what makes a good picture.

2. Many photographic organizations list criteria similar to those described below when judging pictures submitted in a competition. Judges may offer opinions like "The composition is off balance," or "The expressions on peoples' faces tell the story well." But photographic criticism is not an exact art. In the media, critics tend to use esoteric terms that even an "in" group doesn't always grasp.

3. Therefore it's important to the average photographer that he or she develop a basis for understanding and verbalizing how pictures succeed or fail in their visual way, or how they happen to be a near-miss. The latter term describes an image that has some, not enough, of the visual virtues discussed below.

4. Of course "a good picture" is a relative description because it's subjective, as is the judgment of all the qualities mentioned in the list that follows. However, there is enough agreement in the tastes of a variety of people to make certain standards general and valid, though the characteristics of a good picture are subject to flexible interpretation. A little honest controversy about the visual success of a print or slide can be a healthy thing.

5. *Impact:* This descriptive word comprises a collection of the qualities that help make a photograph appealing, interesting, impressive, or memorable. For instance, Ansel Adams's "Moonrise, Hernandez, NM" is a famous image that has been selling for astronomical prices at auctions because it has enormous pictorial or visual impact—among other reasons. The picture's impact evolves from many qualities such as the drama of the light, the mood invoked, and the magic sense of realism.

6. It is possible to translate such qualities into your own photographs when you consider how the subjects were treated, whether landscapes or people. Too

seldom do we meet dramatic opportunities in nature as grand as those in "Moonrise," but with a well developed artistic sensitivity, ideal conditions can be captured on film.

Human Interest: Here is another rather general term to encompass emotional qualities, action, and things that people do which appeal to a lot of viewers. A shot of your children laughing or a picture of vendors in a marketplace might both show outstanding human interest. The success of such a photograph depends on how you compose it, on lighting, on timing to catch vivid expressions, and perhaps on camera angle or choice of lens. All of these ingredients of a good picture are coming up on the list.

There is another aspect of human interest in your own or others' photographs. Sometimes the unusualness of a subject and the way it's presented overshadows adequate technique. For instance, a good sports picture showing peak action in a scrimmage or a definitive play in baseball has intrinsic appeal.

A photograph of a pretty girl, a baby, and a sunset are in the same category, because in each case the subject matter grabs the viewer's attention. As a result, a mediocre composition, inferior lighting, a messy background, or other technical or esthetic weaknesses are ignored or excused because the subject is striking.

It's a good feeling when you can distinguish between the subject in a photograph and the way it was treated.

Galleries and museums often hang photographs that are "different," but they're not necessarily worthy of distinction. Many offbeat photographs we see are likely not to have lasting visual value, while fine photographs like those of Ansel Adams or Cartier-Bresson will still be admired in future decades.

Effective Composition: Like other qualities that underlie a good picture, composition can be controversial. There are somewhat conventional principles of design that we follow because they seem "natural," like placing the horizon line or a figure off-center to avoid a static effect. But really effective composition is usually derived from the subject, and generally the urge to keep composition as simple as possible pays off. That's why plain backgrounds are often best for portraits, and if you relate someone to his/her environment, simplicity is also a virtue. Composition may be dynamic, placid, or somewhere between.

Study the compositional tendencies of fine photographers and painters for guidance. Be daring and experimental at times too, because a "safe" composition may also be dull.

Spontaneity: This characteristic of a good picture is related to human interest, realism and involvement. When you are involved with the subject, as you might be in photographing an aged father or mother, you prize most the images that include spontaneous expressions and emotional reactions. Get people involved with each other, too, so they forget the camera and your pictures are likely to be more believable—and credibility is often a pictorial asset.

If your camera lens is not fast enough to shoot at let's say 1/60th of a second at f/2.8, then you need flash. But you get more spontaneity when people aren't posed, waiting for the flash to go off. Natural light also adds to the realistic impression you capture of people and places, since flash-on-camera has an unavoidably artificial look in most cases.

Lighting: Certainly we have to shoot sometimes when the light is not pictorial, so we do the best we can. A tripod is often the answer to long exposures and exciting photographs. In some situations the light improves if we have the time and patience to wait. Outdoors plan to shoot when the sun is low in the early morning, and at sunset time. Mountains, buildings and people are more dramatic in low-angle light. Details lost in shadows don't seem to matter when the light quality itself is beautiful.

Lighting also helps to create mood, another element of a good picture. Mood is understandably an ethereal quality which includes mystery, gaiety, somberness, and other emotional aspects. Effective photographs may capitalize on the mood of a place especially when it's dramatic.

Color: In a painting a pronounced feeling of light and shadow is called chiaroscuro, and in photographs such effects are augmented by color which may be in strong contrasts, or part of important forms. Outstanding pictures may also be softly colored in pastels that can be as appealing as bright hues.

We tend to take color in photographs for granted, but we don't have to settle for literal color when a colored filter or a switch in film may improve a situation. Next time it rains, shoot some pictures through a car window or windshield, or keep your camera dry and shoot on foot—using indoor color film. The cold blue effects, particularly in slides, are terrific. You may later use an 85B filter to correct the color for normal outdoor or flash use.

Keep in mind that "pretty" or striking color may influence us to take pictures where there really is no worthwhile image. And when you view prints and slides, realize that theatrical color can influence your judgment about the total quality of a picture. A beautiful girl in brightly colored clothes, or an exotic South Seas beach scene may be photographed with creative skill, or insensitively, no matter how appealing the color is.

Contrast: Outstanding pictures may be based on the fact that they contain various contrasting elements, such as large and small, near and far, old and new, bright and subtle color, etc. In taking pictures and evaluating them, keep the contrast range in mind, although these values are often integral with other aspects of the picture.

Camera Angle and Choice of Lens: If someone standing next to you shoots a mid-town Manhattan street with a 50mm lens on a 35mm camera, and you do the same scene with a 35mm or 105mm lens from a crouch rather than standing, you might get a better picture. You can dramatize a subject through your choice of camera angle and lens focal length to alter perspective as well as the relationship of things in the scene. Distortion created this way can be pictorially exciting—or awkward and distracting. You may get good pictures by taking risks in visual ways, and later deciding if what you tried seems to work.

Imagination and Creativity: These two attributes of people who take pictures might have been first on the list if they were not abused words. Look each one up in the dictionary. Ponder how you would apply the definitions to your own pictures and to photographs you see in books or exhibitions.

It takes imagination to see the commonplace in an artistic way, but a certain amount of imagination and creativity should be involved every time we press the shutter button. These human capabilities are basic to understanding the other qualities that make good pictures.

As you explore your topic, you'll need to establish criteria by which to evaluate it. And you may be called on to justify your criteria, to defend them as appropriate and effective in evaluating your topic. To help you think about criteria, complete the following exercise.

Exercise 8.2

1. List the traits or characteristics of two or three of the following: a good restaurant, a good romance novel or technothriller, an effective writing class, an important political announcement, a beneficial self-improvement program (e.g., an exercise or weight-loss program), high-quality children's television programming. After making your lists, name two or three examples that exemplify the traits in each category.
2. Are some of the traits you listed more important or essential than others? For one of the categories, rank your criteria from most to least important. Compare your ranked list with that of one of your classmates for the same category. On what points do you agree? Disagree? Other than personal taste, how can you justify the differences between your list and that of your classmate?

Writer's Judgment

Your essay should present a value judgment about the worthiness of your topic. Once you've made this judgment, your job is to marshal support for it. The criteria you established for evaluating your topic can guide you here, because you can state the criteria as reasons, and reasons must be supported.

As an example, look at Bill's essay again (pages 358–361). In evaluating the "No Thanks" ad, Bill presents a value judgment—the ad is effective—in his thesis, the last sentence of the first paragraph. The criteria he uses in making this judgment are given in the preceding sentences, in which he says that the ad will be seen as successful only insofar as it fulfills its purpose ("to empower that young girl") and as it "catches and then holds the reader's attention." These two criteria, then, drive the essay and are supported by topic sentences that must then, in turn, be supported.

> *Paragraph 2:* "No Thanks" is certainly an eye-catcher.
>
> *Paragraph 3:* "No Thanks" invites the *Seventeen* reader to identify readily with the ad's model, an attractive young woman who we assume is approximately the age of the reader.
>
> *Paragraph 4:* Its breeziness echoes that of other language throughout *Seventeen*; thus, this language should catch the reader's attention. [Note that this sentence is the last of ¶ 4. The first sentence provides transition from ¶ 3 and identifies the topic of ¶ 4, the copy or language of the ad, and the rest of the paragraph leads to the assessment of the effectiveness of the copy.]
>
> *Paragraph 5:* The font and point sizes fit well with the ad's message and with the attitude suggested by the expression on the model's face, their starkness reinforcing the distaste for drugs we assume the model holds. [Note that this is the last sentence of ¶ 5.]
>
> *Paragraph 6:* By offering a range of responses that can be counted as strategies, "No Thanks" should spark ideas in the reader about how she might respond when confronted with or surprised by pressure to use drugs. [Note that this is the last sentence of ¶ 6. How does the first sentence of this paragraph function?]
>
> *Paragraph 7:* And like a frame protects a picture, the language presented here offers protection for the model—and that young girl who identifies with her. [Note that this is the third sentence of ¶ 7.]

With a clearly stated thesis that presents his evaluation of "No Thanks" and then with topic sentences that reflect the criteria he brought to bear on the ad, Bill wrote a tightly structured essay.

Exercise 8.3

1. Look at the sample essays earlier in this chapter and identify the thesis of each. How did the writer structure his or her thesis? What key evaluative terms (such as "good" or "bad") did the writer use? How effectively does the thesis serve to guide the paper? What criteria does each writer use to develop the thesis? What kind of information does the writer use to support each criterion? How effective are the criteria and their support? Why?

2. Below are several thesis statements. How effective do you think each thesis would be in guiding an evaluation essay? Why? What criteria could be developed in support of each thesis?
   a. The Sam Houston State University Department of English is an exceptionally good academic department.
   b. Skateboards should not have been banned from the campus.
   c. The campus libraries are not open enough hours to meet student needs.
   d. Drug-education programs aimed at educating elementary students are clearly not working.
   e. Mark Twain was a great American novelist.
   f. Despite having been first published over a century ago, *Little Women* succeeds today as a girls' book.
   g. In making cartoon versions of fairy tales, Disney Studios has not been faithful to the original versions.

"Because" Support

To support your evaluation, you'll provide details to develop or support the criteria you've chosen. Try framing these details as "because" statements, as in this example:

> Mr. Jones is an effective teacher *because* he makes sure his students understand the subject.

Whether this sentence actually appears in the final paper doesn't matter. What does matter is that you develop such sentences and then add support for them. Each "because" statement may serve as a topic sentence for a paragraph in an essay or as the basis for a given paragraph's topic sentence, as in this example:

> *"Because" statement:* Mr. Jones is an effective teacher *because* he makes sure his students understand the subject.
>
> Mr. Jones amazes his students by the amount of energy he puts into their understanding algebra, the great love of his life. If he needs to explain a concept three or four times before his students get it, he does so. If he needs to work extra sample problems on the board to ensure that his class can successfully complete their homework, he works them. If he needs to establish study groups to give students extra help, he does so, even if it means meeting with them before and after school. Whatever it takes to help his students master algebra, that's what Mr. Jones gives.

EVALUATING VISUAL IMAGES

Because images can be powerful in their emotional and persuasive appeal, it's important to examine them carefully, to evaluate them, especially if you find yourself moved by one. Look back at the picture titled "Ground Zero Spirit" (see page 130). Were you touched emotionally by this photograph? How so? What feelings did it engender in you—patriotism, pride, anger, sorrow? To point the way toward evaluating an image, we'll consider two particular kinds of images, both of which are frequently designed to persuade: political cartoons and political advertising. No matter the kind of image you're evaluating, you may begin by considering the image from the three vantage points we discussed in Chapter 4: image as copy or representation, as viewpoint or perspective, and as association or symbol (see pages 127–128). And the questions you may raise as you look at the image from each of these vantage points should focus on the image's accuracy and fairness; consider asking such questions as these: Is the message of the image accurate? Is it truthful? Is it fair? What distortions seem to be at work? What view of its subject does the image present? What's the effect of this view on you, the viewer?

Political Cartoons

Political cartoons, also called editorial cartoons, have long held a major place in American newspapers. While these cartoons are not an American phenomenon—we can actually trace their roots to graffiti in ancient Greek and Roman times—they have played an important role in forming public opinion in America since the American Colonial era.

Stephen Hess and Sandy Northrup illustrate this role by beginning *Drawn & Quartered: The History of American Political Cartoons* (Montgomery, AL: Elliott & Clark Publishing, 1996), with this anecdote:

> "Stop them damn pictures," demanded William M. Tweed of his cohorts. "I don't care so much what the papers write about me. My constituents can't read. But, damn it, they can see pictures."
>
> "Boss" Tweed was head of Tammany Hall, the political machine that had run the city of New York since 1789. His outburst was inspired by a cartoon in the August 19, 1871, issue of *Harper's Weekly,* in which he and his three chief cronies—Peter B. "Brains" Sweeney, Richard B. "Slippery Dick" Connolly, and New York Mayor A. Oakey "O.K." Hall—are shown pointing to one another in response to the question "Who stole the people's money?" Their theft from the city's treasury was estimated at $200 million.
>
> Tweed wanted to stop the cartoons of Thomas Nast, who for four months had been drawing a scathing series attacking him. (8)

"Boss" Tweed was right to fear Thomas Nast and the potential influence of Nast's cartoons. A well-drawn, well-written political cartoon can have an immediate impact on the reader. And that is at once a major asset of the cartoon, as well as a potential liability for the reader. The impact on the reader derives from the cartoonist's ability to capture the reader's imagination and focus it on the cartoonist's point of view. That point of view is necessarily subjective, for the cartoonist is, after all, a person wanting to present his take on things strongly enough to cause a reader to at least consider whether she agrees or disagrees. Hess and Northrup offer two points of view on the cartoonist's presentation of his point of view. First, they tell us fairly simply that a "cartoonist's job is not to present the news but to interpret it" (14). But then they provide a darker perspective: "'Cartoons claim to be peddling truth,' writes political cartoon analyst Charles Press, 'but what they are giving us are their assumptions of reality. The political cartoon has always been an aesthetic achievement only by accident. Its purpose is propaganda, not art'" (15). Your job as the reader of a political cartoon is to be aware that it is an interpretation of the news and may well figure as propaganda.

In *Politics, Ink: How America's Cartoonists Skewer Politicians, from King George III to George Dubya* (Lanham, MD: Rowman & Littlefield Publishers, Inc., 2006), Edward L. Lordan offers an initial criterion for judging the effectiveness of a political cartoon:

> First and foremost, the cartoonist is attempting to stimulate thought or convince his audience of his position. The primary goal of the editorial cartoon is not aesthetic; artistic expression is subservient to persuasion. If an intricate, graphically balanced approach works, then it is the correct one. If a crude, smudged image works, then that, in turn, is appropriate. The image should be judged not on artistic merit, but on its ability to get the cartoonist's point across. (109)

To get this point across, the cartoonist relies primarily on two elements: caricature and allusion. A caricature is a drawing or sketch in which the cartoonist exaggerates one or more aspects of an individual topic. Because exaggeration involves distortion—making something seem bigger or more prominent than it is—we have to read cartoons carefully, for at times exaggeration in political cartoons can be seen, on the one hand, as humorous but, on the other, vicious. Allusion "creates the situation or context into which the individual is placed" (http://xroads.virginia.edu/~MA96/puck/part1.html). Viewing an image for its symbolic value causes us to consider the associations that image holds for us, and the context of a political cartoon raises associations for us. For example, the cartoon we presented by Steve Nease in Chapter 4 (page 126), shows a commonplace event. Two people are gassing up their vehicles at a service station. What associations does that event hold for you? Is it a chore? A pleasure? A genuine kick in the bank account? Do you think gas prices are too high? Couple this cartoon with that presented in Chapter 4 (page 130) of the four oil company representatives raising an oil derrick, which has a representation of an American flag with "Gas Prices" written where the stars for the states should be. What associations do you have with such companies? Are they taking a fair profit, or are they gouging the American public?

Here's a four-panel cartoon strip from *Doonesbury*, by Gary Trudeau. As you read it, look especially at caricature and allusion or context; then examine it through the lenses of image as representation, image as perspective, and image as symbol.

Chapter 8 | Evaluation Essays 381

DOONESBURY © 2005 G. B. Trudeau. Reprinted with permission of UNIVERSAL PRESS SYNDICATE. All rights reserved.

Image as Representation This particular cartoon is a four-panel strip that appeared in any number of American newspapers following the devastation of New Orleans by Hurricane Katrina in 2006. The strip presents a press conference with President George W. Bush. We never see any of the reporters involved in the press conference; we only read an exchange between Roland (a reporter) and President Bush. We do see a caricature of President Bush, whom Trudeau represents by drawing a helmet that looks like a bedraggled version of a Roman warrior's helmet. The helmet is dented; it looks like it has been battered in battle. The horsehair plume (generally worn by Roman soldiers for ceremonial purposes) is frayed, with much of the plume missing, as though it has been pulled out. The verbal exchange between the President and Roland gives Trudeau's impression of the President's true worry about Katrina's aftermath.

The allusion or context is one that is all too familiar, for the devastation of New Orleans and the misery the storm brought the citizens of New Orleans—in fact, of the Gulf Coast region from New Orleans through Mississippi and on into Alabama—is well known. News reports for well over a year kept Katrina and its aftermath firmly before the American public. Through the vehicle of a press conference, Trudeau gives an exchange that suggests a lack of genuine concern on the part of the Bush administration for New Orleans and its citizens.

Image as Perspective As discussed in Chapter 4 (pages 127–128), perspective involves the particular vantage point the image's creator brings to the viewer. We said above that caricatures deal in distortion. We see this tendency taken to extremes in cartoon strips such as this one. A cartoonist wanting to emphasize the warrior characteristics of a given politician might do so by having that character wear a helmet and then distorting the representation of that person by presenting the helmet as much larger than it would actually be. However, in his cartoon, Trudeau takes the distortion further, reducing Bush to a helmet. It's as if a camera shot of a given politician were taken from a perspective in which the helmet he was wearing was the only part of the character captured in the shot. As he presents this helmet, Trudeau changes the view of the President in each panel by focusing on different views of the left front of the helmet. In each panel, we get different details of the helmet, which Trudeau uses to represent President Bush. In the first panel, we see more of the helmet than in any other panel. We see that it is empty, that is, that it's a shell that represents President Bush. (This is, by the way, how Trudeau presents many governmental figures in his cartoons, with Dan Quayle represented by a feather, Bill Clinton by a saxophone and sunglasses, Arnold Schwarzenegger by a muscular forearm and groping hand, and George W. Bush by a cowboy hat and later by the Roman helmet.) In subsequent panels we see the wear and tear on the helmet, with the horsehair plume looking as though it's been plucked out and with a protective bar across the brow of the helmet broken, as though it had been hit by a severe blow. The various depictions of the helmet suggest that Bush, a warrior, has been battered in battle, though in this case the battle is with reporters in a press conference.

Image as Symbol   As we consider the symbolic value of this image, we focus on the helmet. First, it is a caricature of President Bush. It suggests that he is a warrior, and when the strip was drawn and published, we were at war in Iraq. Many scenes or associations come to mind as we think of Bush as warrior, but none clearer than his landing a jet on the deck of an aircraft carrier which displayed a huge banner proclaiming "Mission Accomplished." This proclamation about the war in Iraq proved to have been premature, for U.S. involvement in Iraq continued for several more years. [Note: as we write this, it is in the middle of February, 2007, and U.S. troops are still in Iraq.] When Trudeau first introduced the helmet as symbolic of President Bush, the helmet was pristine, undented, its horsehair plume full and bushy. The battered helmet depicted in this cartoon shows just how embattled Bush has become. Thus, the symbolic value of the helmet is rich, for it suggests that many of the President's policies and pronouncements have been met with resistance, if not outright opposition.

How effective was this cartoon? As a piece of political satire, it was very effective. The caricature of President Bush as battered warrior symbolized the engagements Bush had had, from which he had come away battered and bruised. And by suggesting in the third panel that the President's primary concern was not for the people of New Orleans but for his image and standing with the American people, Trudeau made a biting indictment of the Bush administration. Through caricature and allusion, Trudeau has drawn an effective satirical cartoon.

Exercise 8.4

1. Enter "political cartoons" as the key terms for an internet search. Pick one or two of the sites that carry a number of political cartoons. What elements of caricature do you find for the following U.S. Presidents: Richard Nixon, Jimmy Carter, Ronald Reagan, Bill Clinton, George W. Bush? How much exaggeration is at work in each caricature? How much distortion? What effect does each caricature have on you as a reader? Why?

2. Examine several political cartoons on both sides of an issue, either single panels or comic strips. Is caricature an important element in any of these? How so? What context does each cartoonist present? To what effect? What message does each cartoonist convey? How effective is the particular cartoon as a piece of political commentary? On what do you base your assessment?

◆ WRITING OPPORTUNITY

Using your computer: the first two of these opportunities call for you to evaluate particular cartoons of your choosing. You can find a very large number of websites by entering "political cartoons" in a search engine.

1. Evaluate the effectiveness of a cartoon or comic strip with a political or social edge. What statement is the cartoonist making? How does the cartoon (the drawing itself) work with any captions, dialogue, or other words given? Do you agree with the cartoonist's point of view? Why or why not?
2. Pick two cartoons that take differing points of view of the same topic. Delineate the topic. How does each cartoonist present his point of view? What elements of the topic does each feature? To what effect? Does this selection of emphasis constitute a distortion of the topic? How so? To what effect? With which point of view do you agree? Why?
3. Pick an issue you're interested in that has a controversial edge to it. Draw a cartoon (either a single panel or a strip) that presents your opinion on the issue. Then evaluate your cartoon, assessing its effectiveness. ◆

Political Advertising

As suggested in "Shooting to Win" (see pages 352–357), political ads don't always present the whole picture. Like political cartoons, these ads may skew a point of view by distortion, focusing so tightly on only one element of a political issue or, more likely, of a political candidate's opponent that a very narrow perspective of the issue or opponent is presented. And sometimes, those ads are deliberately misleading, so accuracy and fairness become two primary criteria to evaluate a political advertisement.

Despite such distortion, attack ads can be effective. One of the more famous—or infamous—attack ads is one titled "Daisy Girl," which aired on national television for only a very short while during the 1964 Presidential campaign. The ad, prepared by President Lyndon B. Johnson's campaign offices, never mentioned by name Johnson's opponent, Senator Barry Goldwater. But when it ran, it created quite a furor in the Goldwater camp, because it cast Goldwater as a proponent of nuclear war. During the early 60s, America and Russia were still engaged in the Cold War, and the threat of nuclear war and nuclear winter was ever present. Despite the fact that the ad never mentions Goldwater by name, never specifically alludes to him, Goldwater objected strenuously, and it was withdrawn. But the ad certainly created an effect, for it was shown and discussed on national news programs. Before we begin our analysis of this ad, view it several times at this website: www.cnn.com/ALLPOLITICS/1996/candidates/ad.archive/daisy_long.mov

We begin with the assessment that the ad was effective. One way to assess how it achieved effectiveness is to examine it through the lenses of image as representation, image as perspective, and image as symbol.

Image as Representation To begin, we describe what the ad represents. The ad, which is actually a short film, opens by showing a beautiful little girl in a white dress, plucking the petals from a daisy and counting. She's probably only four or five years old, an implication we get from her counting. As she plucks the petals, she counts out of sequence: "1, 2, 3, 4, 5, 7, 6, 6, 8, 9." So the scene that is set is a realistic depiction of a young girl engaged in an innocent act of picking and counting daisies.

Image as Perspective To begin interpreting the ad, we examine the perspective or the vantage point shown in the ad. As the little girl reaches "8" in her count, the camera takes a different vantage point, and the perspective changes. As she reaches "8," she freezes (or, rather, she is frozen by the camera) and looks at something in the distance and not at the daisy. She is no longer depicted as moving. She can no longer act, though we still hear her voice. When she counts "9," a man's voice overrides the girl's, and he begins a different count, counting backward from 10 to 0. The camera closes in on the little girl, moving into her face and then into her right eye, until the screen is filled by the reflection of that one eye. When the man's countdown reaches 0, a nuclear blast occurs, reflected in the child's eye. In the span of this one-minute ad, the perspective moves from an opening shot of the little girl as a child to one in which the child becomes a victim of nuclear holocaust.

Image as Symbol Finally, we consider the ad's implications, what its symbolic value is for us. The girl symbolizes both innocence and vulnerability, her life threatened by a nuclear explosion. That symbolism is strengthened by the simple white dress she is wearing and by the activity she is engaged in: counting daisies. Flowers traditionally symbolize peace and tranquility. And where are these flowers? In a peaceful meadow in which we can hear in the background the gentle sound of a bird chirping. The framers of this ad are invoking a whole tradition of symbolism here, often referred to as the pastoral tradition—a tradition in which humans return to nature to find peace and quiet. What could be more peaceful than this young girl? But as our discussion above on perspective makes clear, viewers are not allowed to remain in this peaceful scene. As the perspective takes viewers into the girl's eye, an ominous symbol of war and carnage—a black cloud— appears in the center of our vision. As the explosion boils and roils on screen, President Johnson's voice is heard: "These are the stakes: to make a world in which all of God's children can live or to go into the darkness. We must either learn to love each other, or we must die." The connection is clear—the little girl is a child of God, as are we all; thus, she comes to symbolize all of us, Americans and Russians and anyone else who would be harmed by nuclear warfare. Obviously, she comes to symbolize the whole of humankind.

As the ad closes, we hear another male voice: "Vote for President Johnson on November third. The stakes are too high for you to stay home." This statement becomes a tagline for the rest of Johnson's television ads, which you may view by visiting this website: http://www.pbs.org/30secondcandidate/timeline/years/1964b.html

Was the ad effective? Clearly, we think it was. It created a great deal of talk and publicity for Johnson's campaign. Even though some of the response was negative, for the ad indirectly attacked Goldwater, it still got Johnson's message across: "The stakes are too high for you to stay home." This tagline meant that the stakes were too high for voters to elect Goldwater instead of Johnson; it meant that Johnson stood for world peace and against nuclear war. Was it accurate? Goldwater's reputation was that of a hawk, of one who would, when provoked, use military force as a response. So in this sense, it was accurate and resonated with the public. Was it fair? Not entirely, for it probably misrepresented Goldwater's position; that is, Goldwater probably would have considered nuclear war a last resort, which would have been Johnson's position as well. But the creators of the ad wanted viewers to believe that were Goldwater elected there would be a much greater chance of nuclear war than would be the case were Johnson re-elected. Another instance of unfairness in the ad involves Johnson's voiceover: "These are the stakes: to make a world in which all of God's children can live or to go into the darkness. We must either learn to love each other, or we must die." In this language, Johnson resorted to two instances of a logical fallacy, the false dilemma, sometimes called the either/or fallacy (see pages 464–473 for discussion of logical fallacies). Simply put, this is an all or none kind of statement: either you're for me, or you're against me. Were there alternatives to the dilemmas Johnson presented? Yes, and politicians in the 1960s spent a good bit of time exploring those alternatives. But the ad doesn't present any. The implication, however unfair, is clear: if voters do not elect Johnson, then there will be nuclear war.

Exercise 8.5

A. Listed below are some famous (some may say infamous) attack ads from presidential campaigns ranging from 1952 to 1992. (You may find these and more at the CNN Time website (www.cnn.com/ALLPOLITICS/1996/candidates/ad.archive/). View each of these ads and then respond to the questions that follow. (Note: Because these ads are for political campaigns ranging from 1952 to 1992, you may want to conduct some research on the issues and candidates.)
www.cnn.com/ALLPOLITICS/1996/candidates/ad.archive/eisenhower.abilene.mov
www.cnn.com/ALLPOLITICS/1996/candidates/ad.archive/stevenson.mov
www.cnn.com/ALLPOLITICS/1996/candidates/ad.archive/humphrey.mov
www.cnn.com/ALLPOLITICS/1996/candidates/ad.archive/reagan_bear.mov

1. How accurate is each ad? How fair? On what do you base your assessment?
2. Is there any distortion present in a given ad? If so, what is distorted? To what effect?
3. How effective do you find each ad to be? Why?

B. Review "Shooting to Win" (see pages 352–357) and respond to these questions:
   1. To what extent do the campaign ads presented above ring true with the theme of Jamieson's essay?
   2. Find some of the ads Jamieson refers to. In particular, find one or two of the ads produced by the Swift Boat Veterans for Truth. How accurate were these ads? How fair? How effective? Why?
C. Find political ads for a recent or current campaign. Do they qualify as attack ads? Why or why not? What issues did they focus on? Were the ads accurate? Fair? How effective were they? Why? Note: You may use this website to consider the fairness of various political advertisements: www.factcheck.org.
D. Do a web search for the governor or other elected official of your state. What images are used on this site, and to what effect? Are they accurate? Fair? Effective? Why or why not?

◆ WRITING OPPORTUNITY

1. Write an analysis of an ad or series of ads for a political campaign, either past or current. Analyze them for their accuracy and fairness. Were these ads effective? Why or why not?
2. Pick two ads that take differing points of view of the same topic. Delineate the topic. How does each ad present its point of view? What elements of the topic does each feature? To what effect? Does this selection of emphasis constitute a distortion of the topic? How so? To what effect? Which ad do you think is more effective? Why?
3. Pick an issue you're interested in that has a controversial edge to it. Create an advertisement that presents your opinion on the issue. Then evaluate your ad, assessing its effectiveness. (If you have equipment available, script and produce an ad, and show it to your class, pending, of course, your instructor's approval.) ◆

ASSIGNMENT AND GUIDELINES FOR WRITING

Assignment

Write an evaluation of something. Your job is to pick a topic, decide on its worth (i.e., whether it's good or bad, effective or ineffective, and so on), state your value judgment, and then offer detailed support for your judgment. Consider choosing a topic from one of the Writing Opportunity assignments to which you responded earlier in this chapter. Or, consider evaluating a website. (For more information on evaluating the Internet, see pages 390–395.)

Choosing a Topic

To find a topic for this essay, think initially about things you like and things you don't like. Draw a vertical line down the middle of a sheet of paper, and label one side with a plus (+) and the other with a minus (−). Then, list things you like or feel positively about on the plus side and things you don't like or feel negatively about on the minus side.

Another source of potential topics is the list we presented on page 371. Pick one of the broader general categories given there, and brainstorm a list of memorable examples (positive or negative) for the various entries following the category. Here's a list of specific examples Bill came up with for the "performance" category:

> drama—*Equus, Children of a Lesser God, Kringle's Window, The Grapes of Wrath*
> movie—*Pirates of the Caribbean, The Passion of the Christ, Secondhand Lions*
> CD—*Now That I've Found You: A Collection* (Alison Krause), *Other Voices/Other Rooms* (Nanci Griffith)
> TV show—*The Simpsons, CSI, SportsCenter, Cold Case*
> concert—Matt's spring choir concert, NMSU's production of *Carmen*, St. Paul's Christmas music
> fiction reading—Antonya Nelson's "In the Land of Men," Kevin McIlvoy's excerpt from *The Fifth Station*
> poetry reading—Kathleen West's interview colloquium

Some of Bill's examples are national in scope; others (those in the last three categories) are local. But all are potential topics for an evaluation essay.

Once you settle on a topic, spend at least fifteen minutes freewriting about it. Try to focus on what you like or don't like about the topic so that you begin to develop an opinion or prepare to make a value judgment.

Collecting Information

A good beginning point is to brainstorm a list of criteria that may be appropriate to use in judging the quality of the selected topic. For a movie, the criteria may be obvious. But for something like a political campaign, arriving at the criteria for judging may well be the most difficult part of the process—assuming that you won't settle for "winning the election" as the sole means of evaluating the campaign.

Once you've made a value judgment and established the criteria for evaluating your topic, think in terms of "because" and then of "why?" For example, someone could say of New Mexico, "The state truly lives up to its reputation as the Land of Enchantment." This writer could then offer the following statements as points in support of the assertion:

> New Mexico is the Land of Enchantment because of its unique azure skies.
> New Mexico is the Land of Enchantment because of the quality of light on the mountains as the sun sets each day.

> New Mexico is the Land of Enchantment because of its official state question: "Red or green?"
>
> New Mexico is the Land of Enchantment because of the stark contrasts its landscape offers.

Each of the phrases completing the "because" points to a reason that supports the particular assertion. The third sentence, for example, focuses on the official state question. How does this sentence show enchantment? New Mexicans take their chile seriously. When ordering a plate of enchiladas or any of numerous other entrees, they will be asked whether they want red chile or green chile as the basis for the dish. It's rare for a diner to answer "Either" or "It doesn't matter." It's also rare for a diner who prefers green chile to switch to red chile or vice-versa. Chile lovers have their preferences, and they hold to them steadfastly. Because of this seriousness, New Mexico's 1999 legislature adopted "Red or green?" as the official state question, to go along with the official state mammal (the black bear), and so on. But the state question is also tongue in cheek—just how serious can the decision between red or green chile be? The combination of seriousness and whimsy would need to be explained by the writer in supporting the assertion that "the state truly lives up to its reputation as the Land of Enchantment." Providing such an explanation involves offering reasons that answer the question "Why?"

Focus Statement

Include at least a tentative value judgment in your focus statement. Then provide a brief overview of how you plan to proceed; be sure to present the criteria you'll use in evaluating your topic. Here's the focus statement from Bridget McCollam's essay on the *Spawn* cartoons:

> My topic is an evaluation of the Spawn cartoons, a set of 6 episodes that can be considered controversial due to the extreme violence & crudeness involved. I will defend the cartoons, claiming that they are good, trying to refute the violence. I will also give a brief description and history.
>
> **Criteria**
>   plot
>   money/success
>   morals
>   fans
>   character development & depth

In this statement, Bridget's value judgment is clear; she wants to defend the cartoons against criticism based on their violence. Bridget also lists the criteria she'll use to evaluate *Spawn*, but she would have been better served had she written more about each criterion. (Bridget's essay is featured in the "Sample Student Process" section, pages 404–410.)

Planning Your Essay's Structure

It's a good idea to state your evaluation in a thesis sentence near the beginning of your essay. The body of your essay may be structured by the criteria you use in evaluating your topic. Thus, in an evaluation of a movie, a paragraph (or a block of paragraphs) might be given to acting, a paragraph (or block) to cinematography, and a paragraph (or block) to special effects. Your conclusion may make clear once again what your evaluation is and briefly summarize the evidence you have offered that makes you think your reader should share that evaluation.

Thesis Statement

The thesis sentence for an evaluation essay will make a value judgment couched in such terms as: "good" or "bad," "effective" or "ineffective," "necessary" or "unnecessary," "beneficial" or "detrimental," "important" or "unimportant." When you develop this particular focal point, this value judgment, your job becomes one of marshalling support for it. The criteria you establish for evaluating your topic can guide you here. As you look at your reasons for thinking that something is good or bad, effective or ineffective, and so on, keep asking yourself, "Why?" Answering this question can help you generate the detail you'll need to support your thesis.

Sample Structure

Below is a structure you may wish to use. Each entry in this outline may be developed into more than a single paragraph.

1. Introduction—identifies the topic of your evaluation and its importance; contains the thesis asserting the quality of the topic; sometimes summarizes the topic's contents or describes the topic
2. Presentation of evaluation
    a. first criterion, supported by detail, examples, and reasons
    b. second criterion, supported by detail, examples, and reasons
    c. *n*th criterion, supported by detail, examples, and reasons
3. Conclusion—summary or restatement of your evaluation, restatement of its importance

Exercise 8.6

Apply this structure to the sample essay by Jennifer Pitman. How well does the essay follow this structure?

Refining Your Writing

After you've written your essay and (ideally) taken some time away from it, your next step is revision. To begin honing and polishing your evaluation, keep these principles in mind:

> *Evaluative criteria.* What is the basis of your evaluation? How did you decide that the topic you've evaluated is good or bad, effective or ineffective, and so on? Be sure that the traits or characteristics you've discussed are the most important or telling ones for your topic.
>
> *Writer's judgment.* Give your judgment in clear terms, letting this judgment stand as your thesis sentence. Include the evaluative criteria in or near your thesis statement to guide your reader through the essay.
>
> *Support.* Use supporting details to develop and explain the criteria you've chosen. Think in terms of "because," as in this example: "Drug-education programs in elementary schools aimed at decreasing drug use by children and teens clearly are not working *because.* . . ." Listing reasons to complete a "because" statement can help you generate support for your thesis.

Exercise 8.7

1. Look again at the essays presented earlier in this chapter. For each essay, restate the writer's judgment of the topic and the evaluative criteria on which the judgment is based. How clearly stated is each judgment? How effectively do the criteria support it?
2. How detailed is the support each writer uses to develop his or her essay? How effectively does the support develop "because" statements?

AN EXERCISE IN EVALUATION AND THE INTERNET

In "Beauty Industry on Rampage," Ellen Goodman argues that published images of the female body affect teenage girls' self-image and sense of self-worth. Specifically, she claims that images of girls in popular publications such as magazines promote a definition of beauty as something external that beauty products help create. Such publications then allot a large percentage of their advertising space to segments of the beauty industry selling products for the "improvement" of almost every facet of feminine anatomy. Against this, Goodman presents an overview of Joan Jacobs Brumberg's book, *The Body Project: An Intimate History of American Girls*, which argues that unrealistic or bad images of girls lead to poor self-images and bad decision-making. To research the central claims of this comparison further, we turned to the World Wide Web and searched for websites that could provide evidence for each point of view.

Using Search Engines

We began with one of the major search engines. A giant electronic index to the contents of the World Wide Web, a search engine works by searching for strings of characters. To us, they are words with meanings, but to search engines, they are merely strings of characters. Consequently, typographic errors in a search engine's query box may lead you only to websites where the same typographic errors exist. You should also be aware that different search engines work differently. Some build their electronic indices by looking at web page titles, headings, and the contents of metatags, which are descriptive phrases written into the substance of a web page but that do not display. Some less scrupulous website authors include metatags for commonly searched words or phrases (e.g., "money," "health," "travel") in order to create more hits for their sites, knowing full well that many if not most searchers will be disappointed by what they find on the site itself. So don't be surprised if you pull up unrelated or unwanted sites in a search. Other search engines search the first few paragraphs of text or even the full text of each page they find on the web.

On January 25, 2004, using Google to search for potential sites to evaluate, we entered two queries, one for "teen magazine" and the other for "Brumberg and body and history," a Boolean query that looked for the intersection of all three terms in each search result (see Chapter 1, pages 32–35) for more discussion of Boolean searches). Our search using "teen magazine" yielded a large number of potential sites, and we scrolled down through the first several pages of hits. We wanted as representative a sample as possible, so we clicked on a site sponsored by "All You Can Read" (<www.allyoucanread.com>) because it lists the top 20 magazines by popularity in a number of categories. Browsing that site, we found that the top three teenage girls' magazines are (in order of popularity), first, *Teen Magazine* (<www.teenmag.com>), second, *CosmoGIRL!* (<www.cosmogirl.com>), and third, *seventeen* (<www.seventeen.com>). We encourage you to visit one or all three of these sites as we discuss their general traits to see if Goodman's assessment is on target.

Evaluating a Website

Reading Between the Images   Websites generally contain formatted text, graphics, and links to other electronic documents. They may also contain sound files, movie or animation files, and forms. To read websites well, we must evaluate each type of material they exhibit.

All three of these teen magazine sites feature large blocks in bright, popular colors (e.g., hot pink, purple, lavender, tangerine, lime, turquoise), with the blocks carrying topic headers and links. The headings for these major sections are presented in varying fonts, but each is designed to imitate the contemporary voice and concerns of its intended audience of young girls:

> Who's the **Biggest** Party Animal (*CosmoGIRL!*)
> This Week's Cute Boy (*Teen*)
> 10 Things You Should **Never say to a boy** (*Teen*)
> hot story: get hair with **volume** (*seventeen*)

Each site features pop-up ads for various products—health and beauty aids, fashions, and, of course, the magazine the site represents. "Subscribe now!" is a frequent message.

Each site also prominently displays celebrities and attractive models. *Teen*'s "cute boy" is Nick Cannon, a movie celebrity, and readers are invited to "[g]et to know a little about the hottie who's been in this biz a looong time." *Teen* also offers an article about Paul Walker, another movie celebrity whom *Teen* labels a "yum, yum, yummy surfer dude turned big time star!" *CosmoGIRL!* features Ashton Kutcher, yet another male movie star. Clearly, these sites are rife with appeals to sex, and Goodman's thesis seems to be supported so far by our brief overview of the sites.

Evaluating Interactivity   The economics of commerce on the World Wide Web depend on advertising, the price of which, like television commercials, is based upon rates that vary with the number of viewers, or "hits," a site receives. To encourage repeated visits to a site, website designers use many strategies which include many types of interactivity. Some sites flash a suite of images in a series. Others refresh or exchange images with each mouse click, giving a somewhat inflated sense of newness or animation to each visit to the site, including each click of the "back" button. Yet others include sound files that play repeatedly in the background or video images that cycle in the same ways still images may.

All three of our sites are indeed interactive. Each uses flashing text and images; each invites the reader to take quizzes, complete polls, and/or enter contests that would require her to return to the site to learn of the results. *Teen,* for example, has its "Quick Question: Will you try to see Clay or Kelly on tour?" and then provides a list of clickable options ranging from "I'll do ANYTHING" to "I'd rather eat cow eyes." *CosmoGIRL!* offers "quiz: is he your friend . . . or flame?" and "CosmoGIRL GAMES," featuring "Makeover Madness" and "Fashion Addict."

Evaluating Credibility   The textual links from all three sites to other pages also reinforce Goodman's claim that popular media associate beauty with purchases and cosmetic know-how. On each site the reader can find fashion and beauty tips, with these links often using a picture of an attractive model as a "hot button." All three sites have commercial sponsors with prominent links. For example, the site for *seventeen* gives, down the left-hand side of the page, something of a table of contents headed "the latest." Each of the six entries is represented by an attractive young woman. To see where this would lead us, we clicked on the model to the left of the "fashion" entry and found links to thumbnails of attractive young students (most of them women, a few men) at four universities (the University of Mississippi, the University of Michigan–Ann Arbor, the University of Texas at Austin, and New York University). Clicking on any of the thumbnails enlarged the particular photo, which also carried a quote attributed to the student. These quotes ranged from ideas about fashion to thoughts on their studies, but each was designed to present a breezy take on a given topic. One female student, for example, said she wants to prove that women can be successful engineers. Another said, "I own a 150cc scooter! It's a big toy for a little girl like me." A second link—"trend watch"—took us to a webpage with this header:

> hot stuff
> **underthings**
> Pick your favorite lacy top!

The copy of this page read:

> Slinky, lingerie-inspired looks are the perfect girly accent for this fall's menswear fashions. Paired with frayed denim, tailored tweed, or cuddly knits, these lacy tops are soft and sexy without being scandalous. Choose your favorite from this drool-worthy selection and see how other readers vote!

Readers had seven camisole-like tops to choose from. While appearing to be a quick gloss on a current fashion trend, this page was simply an advertisement inviting young teenage girls to dress like many of today's college students and to be "sexy without being scandalous." And it provided both price and a link to each manufacturer's homepage, so that the reader may order her own lacy top.

All of the product-driven advertising on these and other "dot com" (commercial) websites should be reason enough for us as readers to question the credibility of the website.

Sponsorship, like authorship, lends another kind of credibility to websites. All three of the sites discussed here are part of the Hearst Corporation, a media giant. Its business is selling its products, including *seventeen, Teen Magazine,* and *CosmoGIRL!,* so it's no surprise that each site offers repeated advertisements for the hard-copy magazine to which it's tied. Each site, then, is a commercial enterprise that advertises itself and a great many other products. And those products, understandably, given the purpose of each site and its readership, are aimed primarily at perfecting beauty and body images.

In sum, a close reading of each of the three sites supports Goodman's thesis. Idealized images of young women are presented in ways that tie them to the beauty industry and popular culture. Individual viewers are explicitly and implicity asked to identify with those trends in fashion and popular media that will make them more beautiful, more desirable. Readers whose self-image doesn't match the ones they see projected on these and other teen culture websites may evaluate themselves as undesirable. But within the diversity of the web, we need not look far for a counterpoint to this view.

Evaluating a Counterpoint

In her essay, Goodman points to Joan Jacobs Brumberg's book and assigns to it much more credibility on the issue of feminine beauty than she assigns to popular magazines. In support of her reading of Brumberg's book, Goodman points to the types of convincing examples included. These are not advertisements for products, but rather diary entries, psychologists' texts, and historical information.

Goodman explains and elaborates Brumberg's thesis that there is a connection between "bad body images and bad choices, between how girls feel about their bodies and what they do with them."

These thematic links become literal ones in a website titled "body icon: fear and loathing in the mirror" (http://nm-server.jrn.columbia.edu/projects/masters/bodyimage/index.html). We've reproduced one of this site's pages as Figure 8.2, "Body Image Homepage," but we invite you to browse this website to get the full impact of its graphics.

Created by Kim Dixon, Tiffany Kary, and Dan Maccarone as part of their master's degree project at the Columbia University Graduate School of

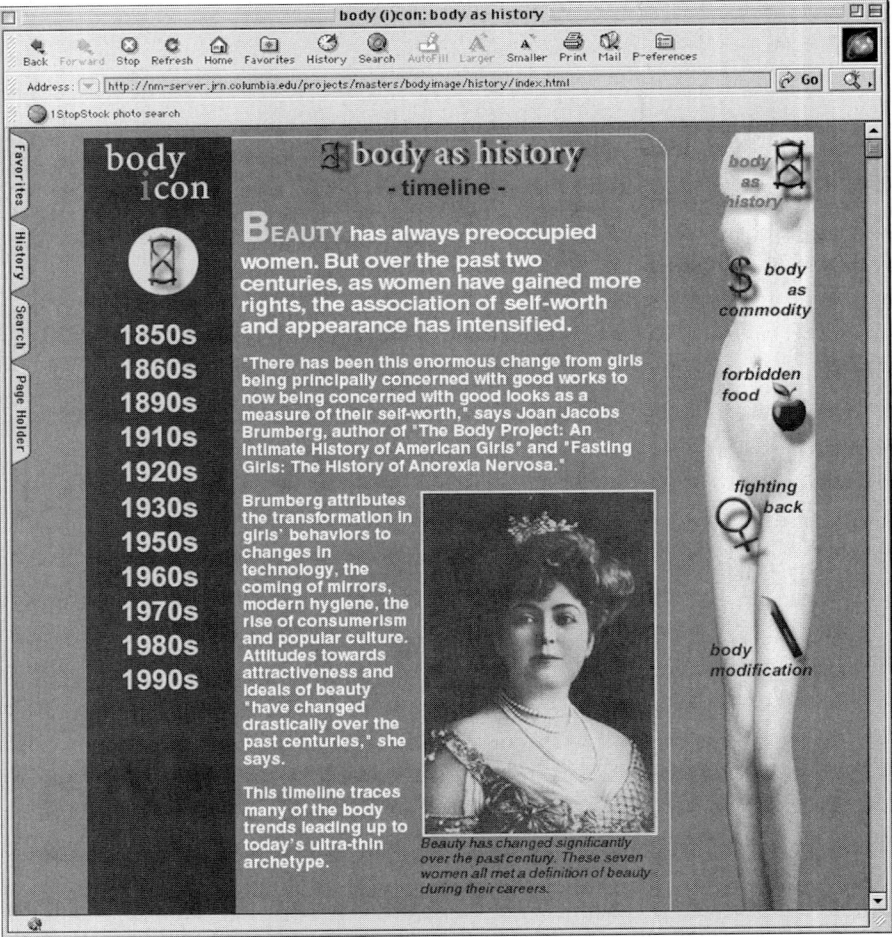

Figure 8.2
Body Image Homepage

Journalism, this site resides on the university's file server (columbia.edu) and provides a web-based interpretation of Brumberg's thesis. The "history" page reproduced here presents images of feminine beauty from the 1850s to the present, with decade by decade discussions and examples. The page is set up in a three-column layout on a blue-green background, presenting us with three ways to begin reading the site. We can access the files historically, by decade, by clicking on the dates in the left-hand column. We can access files thematically, by clicking on the key phrases and icons superimposed over the generalized form of a headless, nude, white female. Here our choices are "body as commodity," "forbidden food," "fighting back," and "body modification." Textual links are signaled by icons—the dark blue dollar sign, the blue apple, and the blue symbol for female. The third way to access the home or index page is to read the text in the center column, while historical images of ideal American beauties, such as Marilyn Monroe, flash up in the large picture placeholder. These images catch our attention, but while they are presented as examples of what has happened in American culture, they are also criticized as damaging ideals for most young women. Dixon, Kary, and Maccarone argue that "BEAUTY has always preoccupied women. But over the past two centuries, as women have gained more rights, the association of self-worth and appearance has intensified." On this site, the authors appropriate the fashion photographs from their original contexts and use them to demonstrate that "ideal" beauty is a socially constructed notion—one that has changed over time, and one that individuals can choose to accept or reject once they become aware of its pervasiveness.

The "body icon" website supports Goodman's contentions in "Beauty Industry on Rampage" by providing more detail than Goodman can about how women's and girls' attitudes about the ideal of beauty have changed over the last 150 years. Thus, careful examination of this site clearly indicates that Goodman's assessment of Blumberg's book is accurate.

Exercise 8.8

1. How effective do you think the four sites referenced above are? On what do you base your assessment?
2. Pick a website for one of your favorite activities and, using the information given in Chapter 1 (pages 32–33) and in Chapter 12 (pages 590–591), evaluate it for its fairness, objectivity, credibility, and effectiveness. On what do you base your assessment?
3. Pick a controversial website and evaluate it, using the same information from Chapters 1 and 12. What is your overall assessment of the site? Note: Be sure that the site you select is one that is in keeping with the guidelines of your Internet server's use policy.

PORTFOLIOS

One of the most important types of evaluation you can undertake involves your own writing. If you've written a self-assessment for each of your essays (see page 95), then you already have pieces of writing that may serve as prewriting for what many writing teachers see as the capstone of a writing course—the reflective essay.

By the end of your writing course, you'll have had a great deal of feedback from your teacher on your writing. And you may have had the opportunity to get your classmates' opinions on your writing. In the long run, however, the person whose opinion matters most when it comes to your development as a writer is you. Your teacher and your classmates will not always be there to suggest ways in which your writing can be improved. Your progress in the future will be directly related to your ability to read your own writing critically; assembling a portfolio gives you the opportunity to hone this important evaluative skill.

Putting the Reflection into Your Reflective Essay

We have used the reflective essay in our own teaching for a good many years now, and we are convinced of its worth as a tool for personal assessment and growth. However, if this process is to work for you, you must not confuse the self evaluation involved in the reflective essay with the evaluation your teacher must perform. You are being asked to reflect on your growth and development as a writer. It is your teacher's task to evaluate your work in the course.

If it is not your task to evaluate your work or your effort in this course, what exactly do you do in reflective writing? Rather than asserting that you have learned a great deal about writing in this course, you should concentrate on what you have learned about your writing. You may begin with a thesis that lists the major things you have learned about your writing over the course of the semester. You are not arguing that your writing has reached the A level, or even that it has gotten better; your argument, should you choose to frame your essay as an argument, is that you have learned something about your writing.

Note that we are suggesting that you discuss what you have learned about your writing, rather than what you have learned about writing in general. We do so because we want to help you resist the temptation to turn your reflective essay into a description of the course you have just taken. Note also that you need not argue that your writing has gotten better during the short time you have been in this writing course. We hope it has. However, starting from a thesis that your writing has improved may well lead to a focus on such empirical evidence as grades: "I was writing C-minus papers at the beginning of the course and by the end I was writing B-plus papers, so I should receive an A for the progress I have made." This is not what we would want from our students, and we suspect it is not what your teacher will be looking for. Improvement in the quality of one's writing is slow and incremental. If you have learned some things about your writing that will allow you to work knowledgeably on improving it in the future, you have achieved a worthy goal.

Just as the reflective essay does not call for evaluation of you or your writing, it does not call for an evaluation of your writing course or your teacher. It is tempting to turn this assignment into what Ron calls a panegyric. (See his reflective essay assignment below.) You may well feel that this has been the best course you have ever taken and that your teacher has made very real contributions to your growth as a writer. If so, that is wonderful. You will probably have the opportunity to write an evaluation or respond to a questionnaire evaluating the course and its teacher. Save that material for that opportunity. Here, your focus should be on what you have learned about your writing.

You may be wondering what is left. "If I can't evaluate myself, if I can't talk about what the course covered, and if I can't talk about how wonderful the course was and what a great teacher I've had in this course, what, then, is a reflective essay?" We may begin an answer to this question by examining what "reflection" means literally. If you look at the surface of water in the proper sunlight, you may well see a reflection of yourself in the water. The first step in reflective learning is the seeing. In the reflective essay, your writing for this course will take the place of the water; that is, you will look for your reflection, as a writer, in that work. This is not to suggest, however, that you should limit your analysis to finished pieces of writing. You can learn much about yourself as a writer by looking carefully at the ways in which your writing developed from draft to draft. And as the essays that follow illustrate, you may well want to reflect on what you have learned about your writing in conversations (and peer-group workshops) with members of your class. Once you begin to look carefully at the work you have done in this class, you will find much on which to reflect.

Sample Portfolio Assignments

Here we present examples of our recent portfolio assignments.

Ron's Portfolio Assignment

Your portfolio should include the following:

- two revisions of papers written during this semester
- a piece of writing done this semester in another class (optional)
- a reflective essay

The two revised papers need not be the two you received the highest marks on. Choose essays that help illustrate your progress as a writer in this course. Since the papers will have already undergone extensive revision, you may well not need to do major revisions on the papers at this point. However, I suspect that you will find that despite the revising you have done, there are local matters that can be attended to in one last polishing. Strive to make the papers as "finished" as you can.

The piece of writing from another course is optional. If you choose to include an outside piece of writing, submit a cover note that gives the writing assignment and other pertinent information. Also, briefly explain what you think you learned in writing this essay and why you like the writing you produced in responding to this assignment.

The reflective essay is the crucial element in this project. In it, you will attempt to chart your course as a writer during the last semester—or longer if you choose. We will discuss this essay in class, but I will answer here a few questions that I anticipate your asking. The essay should be from 1,000 to 1,500 words long. It may be organized as an autobiography in which you detail your progress as a writer in something of a narrative form. In this case, your style of writing is likely to be somewhat informal. On the other hand, you may choose to approach your writing analytically, talking about particular areas that you have worked on during this semester. Such a paper may be a bit more formal than the narrative, but it need not be formal. In either case, you should feel free to address us as a class, to assume the background knowledge that we all have (and to use that knowledge in framing your discussion), and to refer to our class discussions and to interactions you have had with your classmates. Whatever its form, your discussion should include specific references to the writing that you have included in your portfolio. In a sense, these pieces provide the evidence for the claims you are making. Finally, let me urge you not to turn this into a panegyric in which you are the perfect student, I am the perfect teacher, and this is the perfect class. Please strive to take a clear-eyed, honest look at yourself as a writer through the lens of the papers in this portfolio.

Bill's Portfolio Assignment

For your final assignment, you will submit a portfolio that consists of all the writing you have done in this class, together with a reflective essay about your work. [This assignment is based on one in *Paideia,* edited by Kristina Fury and Kimberly Whitehead (New York: Forbes, 1998).]

Reflective Essay For your final essay for this semester, you'll submit an argument about what you've learned as a writer, drawing examples from your experience in the class. This essay is a reflective self-assessment that will involve you in reviewing all of the work you've done this semester so that you can discuss what you've learned about writing, reading, thinking critically, and researching. As you begin thinking about this essay, which should be from three to five pages long, you may respond to these questions:

1. What have I learned? What have I learned that's important? How will it help me academically, personally, and/or professionally?
2. What contributed to my learning? What particular assignments, techniques, and/or activities really helped? How can I demonstrate this? What evidence from my course materials can I use to support my assertions here?
3. Why are these things important to me? What will I be able to do as a result of this course, either as a student or as a professional, once I graduate?
4. How have I developed as a writer, as a student? What specific skills, techniques, and strategies have I learned that will help? What are my strengths as a writer? What do I do well? What are my weaknesses? What do I still need to work on; what skills do I still need to develop as a writer?

Because this essay is an argument, you'll need to support your assertions with detail, with evidence, for example, from your writings and your responses to readings this semester. One way to begin is to look back at the course's purpose statement at the very beginning of your syllabus:

Through a sequence of reading, writing, and workshop exercises, you will

- become familiar with the composing process and learn to adjust it to accomplish various writing tasks,
- develop analytical reading and critical thinking skills,
- develop expository and argumentative writing skills,
- develop research skills, and
- use collaborative learning in various contexts.

Have you done these things? How effectively? To what extent?

Sample Reflective Essays

Here we offer two reflective essays written by students in our classes.

JACQUELINE COTTER
ENGLISH 1103, FALL, 2000
UNC CHARLOTTE

GETTING IT RIGHT: FITTING MESSAGE TO AUDIENCE

1   Sitting back at the closing of my first semester away from home at college, I have come to realize how different I am compared to three months ago. One of the main differences between me as a college student and me as a high school student is the way that I think about writing. I have found that I now consider who I am writing to before I begin my writing. I realize that when I write, the way I say something can be as important as the ideas I am trying to express.

2   When writing an evaluation of the book *Their Eyes Were Watching God* by Zora Neale Hurston, I began with a rough draft explaining what a good story it was and why I saw the heroine as such a great character. After revising and rethinking who my audience might be, I realized that my readers would have read many interesting books with interesting characters but that they would not necessarily call these books good literature. Thus, I had to think about what makes something good literature. I decided to base my discussion on the universal themes and descriptive imagery in the book. I also decided that I had

to re-relearn how to write an evaluation paper; when I made assertions about Hurston's book, I had to give evidence to support my claims.

A big part of developing my skills as a writer also included learning how to take advantage of peer critiques. I started my argument paper with a rough draft explaining why Thanksgiving Day should be a national holiday and why retail stores should close for the holiday. My peer reviewers showed me that my paper did not offer much solid support for my claims and that it lacked awareness for my opponent's position. From these critiques I realized that writing an argument paper on this subject would be very difficult and that I was not going to be able to find support for my argument. I also realized that I would not have been able to find what my opponent's position would be. I soon changed my topic to an argument that there should be cameras in public classrooms, an argument that turned out to be a great deal more successful than the Thanksgiving paper could have been. Even though I did not always look forward to the days that we brought in rough drafts for critiquing, I always walked away more informed about writing a specific type of paper. The first group critique in class, and my first group critique ever, was a workshop on personal papers. I listened to Erin Lowder's and Shari Armstrong's papers being read to me and was impressed that I could see what they saw and hear what they heard in their personal experience. But most importantly I loved the fact that I could feel just how significant Shari's singing experiences were and how much Erin grew from her experience helping out after a hurricane. From reading and critiquing their essays, I learned how personal essays need to be written descriptively and emotionally so that a reader can easily connect with the writer.

As I write, I find it very easy to write on subjects in a personal way, but it is extremely challenging for me to write informatively; in order for me to write these kinds of papers, I had to sit down and do something I have never done before: prewrite. In the process of prewriting, I would begin by thinking about one image or setting that was emotion provoking. Then I would sit down and write on it without stopping for a solid five minutes. The material I got from those freewriting sessions usually gave me enough information, or at least a good start, so that I was able to come up with a topic, thesis, and a very rough outline. Before learning to prewrite, I depended on a planned outline that was always very difficult to follow. However, in my persuasive essay, I used freewriting to come up with ideas about what made me scared; I had no idea what to write about at first, then I imagined how I would feel if I lost someone I love to an accident involving a drunk driver. I wrote:

> I'm scared at the possibility of drunk drivers . . . They could hit the kids playing in the street of my neighborhood . . . if you drive drunk you are just as guilty as the man that killed my brother's best friend.

In the past I would have written a persuasive essay about not drinking and driving and would have said something that had no emotion and was very matter of fact such as: "You should not drink and drive because you could kill someone else and spend the rest of your life in jail." In this essay I was able to appeal to the anger my readers would feel toward those who continually endanger our lives:

> No compassion should be given to those who shadow the streets of the innocent; those that cause our hearts to stop as we read the newspaper should realize that their criminal behavior will not go unpunished, that they are not blameless.

I can see just how much more persuasive I can be when I prewrite and use my raw emotions that I put down on paper before I even begin to write a rough draft.

5   One of the biggest hurdles for me as a writer, if not the biggest hurdle, is deciding on a topic for a given essay. Looking back at my Interest Inventory always gave me some ideas, but ideas aren't good enough to supply the spark that is required for good writing. As I went through English 1103, writing a personal, an informative, an evaluative, an argument, and a persuasion essay, I realized that no matter how much time I put into the essay, if I did not truly care about the subject, my paper would ultimately turn out below my standards as well as my professor's. When coming up with a topic, I had to think about something that I have strong feelings for. For example, in my personal essay, I was able to focus on how much I missed the children that I had served as nanny for during the summer; in my informative essay, I explained why I felt so unprepared for my freshman experience in college. I have learned that I should not choose a subject simply because I can ramble on about it; rather I should write about things that I am willing to put time into because I care about them.

6   My English 1103 class has definitely not been my favorite class of all time because of the amount of time it has required me to put in and because the writing process is not always the most interesting thing to a college freshmen. However, learning to aim for an appropriate audience, learning to prewrite, and learning to critique and revise are some of the most useful skills that I have gained. These skills have helped me to be able to communicate to my readers exactly what I want to say in exactly the way they need to hear it.

Commentary   Jackie organizes her essay around the various principles of good writing that she has begun to master in this course. She focuses on the ways in which she is developing a sense of audience and on the difficulties she has had with expository writing in the past. Here, Jackie comes upon a very important principle for her writing. In the past, she has found expository and argumentative writing much more difficult than personal writing because of her lack of interest in expository and argumentative topics. What she now realizes is that various prewriting strategies can help her discover those topics that she can become personally involved with—and thus be passionate about.

Jackie's reflective essay is a good one because she grounds it in examples of her writing throughout the course. She explains why her personal essay about being a nanny was easy to write and why her initial argument about people working on holidays was difficult. In talking about her persuasive essay, she illustrates the role that prewriting is coming to play in her development as a writer by giving an example of her prewriting for this paper and then showing how that work led to a particularly persuasive passage in her paper.

STEVE DURAN
ENGLISH 111H, FALL, 1998
NEW MEXICO STATE UNIVERSITY

STEVE WANTS AN A

1 Chances are, writing will be a necessary part of life up until the time when the Sun finishes the nuclear reactions of hydrogen in its core and expands its outer layers so far as to encompass the earth, raising all of our body temperatures to well above 5,000 degrees. Since this won't happen for another four or five billion years, I suppose it might be worthwhile to learn some skills in writing.

2 I've always enjoyed writing, ever since the day I learned to write my name with a thick blue crayon. I practiced my new skill extensively, drafting my monosyllabic work on every surface in the house. My earliest work, circa 1984, I believe, was titled "Steve Wants a Cookie" and was first drafted on the wall of the kitchen. Unfortunately, later that day, a vicious case of writer's block struck with such brutality that I was forced to delay future drafts until the next day. Even more unfortunate, upon returning to my work, it had been white-washed, and my proposal had not been appreciated or taken to heart as I received no cookie. It seems my work did not receive favorable reviews from the household critics. I have learned that all writers must accept criticism, and I do believe that my work has substantially progressed. My writing goals have also evolved from "Steve Wants a Cookie" to "Steve Wants an A."

3 With that in mind, let me review what I have learned about my writing. This past semester, I have learned the value of a discovery draft, rough draft, and peer reviews. In the past, I found no use for these nuisances, and I must admit I still look upon them with something less than favor. But whether I like them or not, I now appreciate their value. Before this class, when I had a paper to write I would just wait until the day before the deadline, then spend all day and night writing. I did fine this way, although I spent a good eight or nine hours straight on a paper, which can drive any normal person to the outer perimeters of their

sanity. I would sit in my hard wooden chair, staring at a blank computer screen until an idea popped into my head. Then I'd take the idea, put it into words, think about it, revise it, and finally type it out. This is a lot of work for my little pea-brain, so as you can imagine, this was a time-consuming process. Was there a better way to write? Of course not. There couldn't be.

As painful as this is to admit, I was wrong. As I have learned this semester, there is a better way. With a discovery draft, I could get all my ideas on paper, just to have them out of my head, free from all that other garbage floating around in there. Once down on paper, I could read and evaluate it and see if it made sense. Then, I could organize those ideas into more coherent sentences and paragraphs that might make sense to someone else besides me. Next, I would give it to some other poor slob to find my mistakes for me. Once read by normal people, it becomes clear what I need to do better and what few things I have done right. Then all I have to do is completely overhaul my paper, and I am done. It is amazing how such a simple process has for so long evaded such a simple mind.

In learning to write for different purposes, I also learned how to use language for each purpose. In "Intricacies of an Idiot," I evaluated just what makes Homer Simpson so entertaining. It all boiled down to the fact that Homer is a foolish, lazy, incompetent moron and I, on the other hand, am . . . well, less of a foolish, lazy, incompetent moron and therefore have the right to laugh at his shortcomings. In that essay, I found that use of language that is appropriate to my audience was critical to adequately evaluating Homer. I tried to use as many different descriptive adjectives as I could to keep it colorful, but after a certain point, there simply are no more synonyms for "lazy" and "moron."

Writing with my audience in mind is another important lesson I learned this semester. I never used to think about what my readers would think; I just wrote until I liked what I wrote. But I overlooked an important factor, which I call the B/S factor. Yes, the Boredom/Suicide factor is an important way to measure how well I had written for my audience. If my readers are continually drifting off into Slumberland or threaten to kill themselves (or me), chances are I have not written particularly well for my audience.

In "The Space between Your Ears," an essay about the mental side of golf, I tried to use technical terms for golfers, but still keep it understandable and interesting. In essays where the author presents information or explains a process, most often boredom is almost inescapable. So I tried to use language and humor that even non-golfers could understand. I used references to other sports to let non-golfers relate to my ideas. I tried to write for my main audience (golfers) while keeping a secondary audience (non-golfers) in mind. This creates a balance that is critical in maintaining a low B/S level.

I also learned that I must take my audience into account in controversial papers. In ". . . And Justice for Some," I took a stand that the death penalty is a necessary part of the justice system. Even though I was writing for an audience that strongly disagreed with my ideas, I acknowledged the good points in their arguments, and then respectfully informed them that they were wrong and I was right. Even though I am sure they despise me and my ideas, and desire to see me given a life sentence in prison for that essay, I am sure I convinced them that I actually deserve the death penalty.

In my paper titled "The Deceptive Logic of Math," I approached my readers in a different way. I took the position that math is illogical and useless in real life. By itself, I am sure anyone may be willing to give me five seconds to prove my point, but I also included my belief that anyone who disagreed with my theory should be shipped off to a deserted island where they would be exploited for my own personal gain. I don't think I made any new friends in this essay, but I proved my point.

I learned many important things this semester. First, focusing on reading strategies helped me get through boring or difficult essays by making me pay the right kinds of attention. I also learned that discovery drafts, rough drafts, and peer reviews are not unnecessary wastes of time; they are very necessary wastes of time. I learned that I must keep my audience in mind when writing papers. I don't want my readers to become violent with boredom while reading my paper—unless that is the purpose of my paper; then I hope they become as violent as possible. I've learned to be respectful to my critics. And for my final argument to he who has the power, I believe my work has dramatically improved—as a direct result of this course—from "Steve Wants a Cookie" to "Steve Wants an A." Although my well crafted title states my argument as clear as can be, allow me to sum it all up by saying: Steve wants an A . . . although, he would settle for a cookie.

Commentary   We present Steve's essay as an example of a rather creative approach to the reflective essay. Steve decided to write a humorous essay in which he spoofs the kind of grade consciousness a reflective-essay assignment might seem to encourage. Rather than presenting a thesis such as "I have learned a good deal about my writing in this course," Steve tells his reader outright that his thesis is "Steve wants an A in this course." Within the framework of this spoof, however, Steve lists many important principles of good writing. And, more important, he shows how he has applied these principles in his own writing.

SAMPLE STUDENT PROCESS

This example essay was written by Bridget McCollam, a first-year writing student at NMSU. Bridget began her writing with her topic—HBO's *Spawn* cartoons—already in mind. So her job was to explore that topic, to see whether it would actually serve her as the basis for this paper.

Prewriting Here's Bridget's prewriting:

comic book—so popular, movie deal and cartoon deal—HBO
6 cartoons depending on how popular, depending on popularity
making more now
HBO midnight audience he wanted appeal to, Friday nights—violence

Are the Spawn cartoons good, or does the violence & nudity make them unvaluable?
Are the Spawn cartoons worthy of the airtime they receive, or should they be taken off?
Is the violence & nudity necessary for the Spawn cartoons to give the right effect?

controversial—
good   *bad*
plot   extreme violence
interesting   nudity—xx—dirty
good characters graphic detail

watched it on good night—fun—with Jim—so liked it
now becoming stressed

The Spawn cartoons are exciting, with a plot that captures the attention of the viewer, characters that one can feel empathy for and detail that must be seen, the Spawn cartoons are definitely worth watching.

detail of red cloak, green eyes, clinking of chains, mostly dark burned face
description of clown—repulsive, fat, stomach hanging out, teeth yellow & misshapen.
Wanda—beautiful, in charge, nice
good guy—long white beard, respectable
history must be in there
dance bar—naked women—somewhat crude
general plot—many little
war between heaven & hell
character development as Spawn begins to understand
countdown of energy 9:9:9:9

disgusting—nudity—bar
lesbians & fat guy
audience can't relate
detail such as finger ripping off, blood not necessary

Continued Prewriting The next bit of writing we see from Bridget continues her prewriting and consists of notes she took while watching these cartoons:

"The following program is recommended for mature audiences only. It contains adult situations, adult language, graphic violence, and nudity."

created by Todd McFarlane
9:9:9:9

> narrator/good guy from heaven
> every 400 years (?)
> begin with graphic death, ruthless
> born as clean slate—instincts all drain from past
> first image of Spawn—huge, flowing red cloak, chains, then just glowing green eyes in a dark face, *voice* "what the hell are you?"
> naked lady—"I love you Al"
> from hell—"proper escort" from hell—ugly clown, repulsive
> Spawn—sad green (glowing) eyes & pool of red cloak
> hell spawn—instinct, killer, act upon violence
> Spawn confused, desperate
> takes off mask—burned face, images of fire in alley, homeless help him
> narrator in story gives advice "home—war getting these"
> COP & TWITCH
> images (black & jumbled) of past happiness with Wanda
> Spawn watches as Wanda is married happily with best friend
> Spawn has no idea how long
> narrator—hell tries to keep him (warrior) confused
> clown comes—disgusting
> dead 5 years
> Al Simmons—govt assassin—really good
> where you been all this time
> went to hell, back for Wanda who has child *Al couldn't give her*

Bridget's notes continue along these lines for another two or three pages. But these should be enough to give you a good idea of her strategy.

Focus Statement   Bridget then reviewed her notes and wrote the following statement:

> My topic is an evaluation of the Spawn cartoons, a set of 6 episodes that can be considered controversial due to the extreme violence & crudeness involved. I will defend the cartoons, claiming that they are good. trying to refute the violence. I will also give a brief description and history.
>
> **Criteria**
>   plot
>   money/success
>   morals
>   fans
>   character development & depth

Rough Draft for Peer Review   Using her planning page as a very rough guide, Bridget wrote a draft of her essay, revised it, and then submitted the following rough draft for peer review.

Adult Audiences Only

Every Friday night at midnight millions of viewers tuned in to HBO to watch the Spawn cartoons, a unique creation by Todd McFarlane. These cartoons began as comic books and were so popular that McFarlane was offered both a movie deal and a cartoon deal. HBO was the company to offer the cartoon deal, which was the following: They would make six episodes, and depending on the success of these, more might be made later. These new episodes are in the making right now.

The opening warning sums up the problem of the Spawn cartoons when it flashes on the scene: "The following program is recommended for mature audiences only. It contains adult situations, adult language, graphic violence, and nudity." The Spawn cartoons are extremely violent and involve nudity that may very well be considered crude and disgusting. There is almost an unbelievable amount of blood, including one scene where the viewer actually watches the bullet rip through a man's skin. There may be a question of whether all this blood and gore is necessary. Perhaps it is not, but the other factors of these cartoons are so well done that it makes up for the disgusting bloody parts. With plot that captures the attention of the viewer, characters that one can feel empathy for, and detail that must be seen, the Spawn cartoons are definitely worth watching.

A government assassin who is rather good at his job is murdered, but his love for his wife leads him to make a deal with the devil. The deal: Al Simmons can see his wife, but for the price of his soul, which means he must be a warrior for the devil in the eternal battle between heaven and hell, of which "Earth is the battlefield, and human souls are the prize." Al Simmons returns as a Spawn from hell. There is a war within him between good and bad. There are representatives from heaven and hell to lead him whichever way. An evil clown from hell turns into an insectlike demon periodically, and the story is narrated by a respectable man with the long white beard from heaven. Al, now known as Spawn, realizes his beloved wife, Wanda, is now married to his best friend and has a child; a child that for whatever reasons, Al could not give her. He now lives in an alley with a group of homeless people. Spawn must choose between this evil and the good inside of him, but is confused about what is happening to him. There are political issues, crime scenes, child rape and murder, and everything manages to tie in together at the end. The plot has so many twists and turns that it is impossible to not watch, as it sucks the viewer in, catching his attention time and again.

In a story so crude and violent, it is hard to imagine deep, complex characters, yet McFarlane manages. Viewers can watch the development of spawn as he "grows" in his understanding of this new world he has been thrown into so violently. He starts out angry at everything around him and scared of what is happening to him. However, by the end of the six episodes, he has matured slightly in his understanding of this new world. He has learned some control of these strange powers he has been granted and has come to terms with the changes in the world he left. Although there is little development in other characters, they are never the less quite complex. Viewers get a full picture of many of the characters personalities, making them more than merely a single-minded image with only one purpose. Wanda is a good example of this. She appears to actually love her new husband, although she misses Al still, and of course mourns his death. Viewers get a real idea of why Al Simmons was so in love with this woman.

The detail in these cartoons is almost unbelievable. Spawn is amazingly striking. The first image presented of him is a huge red cloak that he always wears. There are spikes on his knuckles, with red gloves, he wears a red and black mask. The second time Spawn is pictured, it is his face, in darkness except for his glowing green eyes. Spawn's cloak can do many neat tricks, such as reach out and grab someone, strangling them. Spawn also has chains that he can use to grab an enemy and injure them. These chains make a trademark clinking noise to warn viewers of what will happen next. When Spawn takes off his mask, his shriveled, disgusting face is revealed from his death in a fire. The detail is evident in other places. Sound is often important, such as the beating of a fan giving a man flashbacks of a war he once fought. The detail makes it impossible to look away, as viewers get pulled in to watching what will happen next, not wanting to miss anything.

I have to admit, I went into the theater to watch these cartoons only because my male friends dragged me, and I stressed that I was going to leave if I did not enjoy them. The first scene I saw was absolutely repulsive, too much to describe here. But needless to say, the cartoons redeemed themselves, and I walked out of the theater impressed. 6

Bridget's peer group thought she had done a good job with this draft, and they noted that the criteria she had established for her evaluation worked. Bridget evaluated *Spawn* on the basis of its effective plot, depth of characters, and graphic detail. But they suggested that she consider:

1. restructuring the paragraph (3) about the plot. It seemed to jump around a little bit, probably because the topic sentence comes at the end of the paragraph.
2. redoing the description of Spawn in ¶5. That paragraph also seemed to lack coherence, as Bridget presented details describing Spawn's dress, then his face, then more about his dress, then back to his face. So they suggested that this paragraph be restructured.
3. thinking about smoothing out the writing in several places to eliminate unnecessary words and to create a stronger sense of style in the essay.

Following the peer group's suggestions, Bridget rewrote the essay and submitted a revised draft.

Final Draft

Bridget McCollam

ADULT AUDIENCES ONLY

Every Friday night at midnight millions of viewers tune in to HBO to watch the *Spawn* cartoons, a unique creation by Todd McFarlane. These cartoons began as comic books and were so popular that McFarlane was offered both a movie deal and a cartoon deal. Looking for something offbeat that might appeal to a late night adult audience, HBO offered to make six cartoon episodes, and depending on their success, possibly more. These new episodes are in the making right now. 1

2   The opening warning sums up the problem of the *Spawn* cartoons when it flashes on the screen: "The following program is recommended for mature audiences only. It contains adult situations, adult language, graphic violence, and nudity." These cartoons are extremely violent and involve nudity that may very well be considered crude and disgusting. There is almost an unbelievable amount of blood, including one scene in which the viewer actually watches a bullet rip through a man's skin. Is all this blood and gore necessary? Perhaps not. But the other factors of these cartoons are so well done that they make up for the disgusting bloody parts. With plot that captures the attention of the viewer, characters that one can feel empathy for, and detail that must be seen to be believed, the *Spawn* cartoons are definitely worth watching.

3   At first, the plot of *Spawn* seems simple enough. Al Simmons, a government assassin who is rather good at his job, is murdered, but his love for his wife leads him to make a deal with the devil. The deal: Al can see his wife, but for the price of his soul, which means he must become a warrior for the devil in the eternal battle between heaven and hell, where "Earth is the battlefield, and human souls are the prize." Al returns as a spawn from hell, but despite his pact with the devil, within him rages a war between good and evil. This battle is sometimes waged by representatives from hell and heaven who attempt to sway Al. An evil clown from hell turns into an insect-like demon periodically and tries to make Al respond, to do evil and so condemn himself to hell. As counterpoint, the story is narrated by a respectable man from heaven with the long white beard, who advises Al to control himself and to fight against the evil within. But the struggle is difficult. Al realizes his beloved wife, Wanda, is now married to his best friend and has a child, a child that for whatever reasons, Al could not give her. Confused about what is happening to him, Spawn must choose to give in to the evil he sees all around him or to resist it as best he can. His first instinct is to kill his friend, who has replaced him in Wanda's life. Complicating this plot line are political issues and such crimes as child rape and murder. Eventually, these lines manage to tie together at the end. The plot has so many twists and turns that it is impossible to not watch, and it sucks the viewer in, catching his attention time and again.

4   In a story so crude and violent, it is hard to imagine deep, complex characters, yet McFarlane manages. Viewers can watch the development of Spawn as he "grows" in his understanding of this new world he has been thrown into so violently. He starts out angry at everything around him and scared of what is happening to him. However, by the end of the six episodes, he has matured slightly in his understanding of this new world. He has learned some control of these strange powers he has been granted and has come to terms with the changes in the world he left. Although there is little development in other characters, they are nevertheless quite complex. Viewers get a full picture of many of the characters' personalities, making them more than merely single-faceted images with only one purpose. Wanda is a good example of this. While she appears

to actually love her new husband, she misses Al still and of course mourns his death. Viewers get a real idea of why Al Simmons was so in love with this woman.

The detail in these cartoons is almost unbelievable, and Spawn himself is particularly striking. The first image seen of Spawn is a huge red cloak that he always wears, a cloak that can do many neat tricks, such as reach out and strangle a victim. He wears red gloves, with spikes on his knuckles, and a red and black mask. Spawn also has chains that he can use to seize and injure an enemy. These chains make a trademark clanking noise to warn viewers of what will happen next, so sound reinforces the detail of the Spawn's costume and weapons. The second time Spawn is pictured, the viewer sees his face, obscured in darkness except for his glowing green eyes. When Spawn takes off his mask, his shriveled, disgusting face is revealed, charred from his death in a fire. The detail is evident in other places. Sound is often important, such as the beating of a fan that gives a man flashbacks of a war he once fought. The detail makes it impossible to look away, as viewers get pulled in to watching what will happen next, not wanting to miss anything.

I have to admit, I went into the theater to watch these cartoons only because my male friends dragged me, and I stressed that I was going to leave if I did not enjoy them. The first scene I saw contained some of the worst of the gore and nudity, and I very nearly left. Yet as I stayed and watched, I saw the plot unfold in all its complexity. I felt for Spawn and hated the evil clown. I was hooked. Needless to say, the cartoons redeemed themselves, and I walked out of the theater impressed.

CHECKLIST: CRITIQUING AN EVALUATION ESSAY

1. What is the subject of the evaluation?
2. Identify the thesis statement. What evaluation does it make? How effectively is it worded? How should it be strengthened?
3. What criteria and reasons are offered for the evaluation?
4. What support is offered for the reasons? How effective is this support?
5. How effective are the introduction and conclusion? Why?
6. Does the paper adhere to conventions of usage, mechanics, and format? Correct any errors you find.

Vanessa Bell, "A Conversation," 1913–1916. Oil on canvas, 34 × 32 in. The Samuel Courtauld Trust, Courtauld Institute of Art Gallery, London. © 1962 The Estate of Vanessa Bell, courtesy of Henrietta Garnett.

CHAPTER 9

Position Essays

In this chapter, we will ask you to take a stance on an issue, to be ready to qualify your position by considering the opinions of others, and then to write an essay that presents your informed stance or opinion—your position—on that issue.

What does it mean to take a position on an issue? And what is the relationship between taking a position and having an argument? A position essay involves argument in the best sense of that term. What comes to mind when you hear the words "argue" and "argument"? You may think about the last time you stood toe to toe with someone verbally duking it out over something that mattered to you both. In such a situation, you (and your opponent) were probably much more interested in winning the argument than in being sure that you stated your position clearly. You probably didn't pay a great deal of attention to stating your argument in such a way as to avoid misrepresenting your opponent's position. That kind of argument is precisely what this chapter is not about.

Instead, we want you to think of argument in terms of developing an informed position. Such development will involve you in exploring a topic to find out what you think about it and why, but it will also involve you in seriously considering what someone opposed to your stance thinks about the topic and why. You'll use that opponent's thinking as a means of sharpening your own focus. To do this, you'll have to keep an open mind from the outset. You'll have to be willing to modify your stance if you cannot show why you do not accept the arguments your reader is making.

Ultimately, writing a position paper will help you hone your critical-thinking skills. As you explore your topic to discover a stance and ways to support it and then as you consider why and in what ways someone might oppose your stance, you should become a stronger, more logical, and more critical thinker.

SAMPLE ESSAYS

The following sample essays include arguments about students' and teachers' rights in college classrooms, the relationship between religion and science, and euthanasia.

Our first essay by Michael C. Haley, a professor of linguistics at the University of Alaska, Anchorage, argues that students have a right to expect college teachers not to bring their partisan politics into the classroom.

MICHAEL HALEY

THE RIGHT NOT TO LISTEN

Shortly before the U.S. invaded Iraq in the spring of 2003, the director of the composition program in our English department wrote a "cautionary" memo that was sent to all the members of the department faculty. It was a carefully worded document, very low-key and pointedly measured in its advice, yet my first thought was, "This is dynamite!"

The memo began harmlessly enough, by simply informing us that a number of students had complained to the administration about certain (unnamed) teachers' use of the classroom as a forum in which to propound their own political and moral views opposing the U.S. military action in Iraq. Without directly criticizing this classroom practice, the director's memo quietly urged—correctly and courageously, in my opinion—that teachers show respect for the beliefs of all students on all sides of this contentious issue.

A few days later, in a regular meeting of the English Department, our Chair brought up the director's memo, explaining that it had originally been intended only for the composition teachers under the director's immediate supervision, but had somehow mistakenly been distributed to the entire faculty. After apologizing for this mistake, the Chair nevertheless went on to reinforce the memo's basic message with what I thought to be admirable verve and clarity: When leading classroom discussions on controversial issues like the war in Iraq, we should be respectful of students on all sides, including those who might actually support the invasion of Iraq, and we should avoid using either our authority as classroom teachers or our exceptional verbal skills as professionals to bully or intimidate students who do not share our personal political views.

That did it! Tensions that had been boiling under the surface ever since the faculty received the composition director's memo suddenly erupted. Ours being an unusually collegial department (as university departments go), the dialogue never once got nasty or personal, never once came to shouting, but it was nonetheless very emotional. In the middle of the discussion, I looked down at my own hands on the table and saw that my knuckles were white.

Naturally enough, those who vehemently opposed the war in Iraq had the most to say. Whether or not any of them had actually used a classroom as a forum for venting their own personal passions against the war, they all seemed to feel a definite need to defend themselves—or perhaps, in fairness to them, a need to defend certain principles of academic freedom and the rights of free speech—against the complaint of the students. Who were these complaining students, the anti-war faculty wanted to know, and why hadn't they spoken up for themselves in class, if they are so in favor of this war? Why should any students feel "intimidated" by a professor's anti-war sentiments, and why should their feelings of intimidation be used to censor faculty? Were these students so timid and weak in their opinions that they didn't want to talk about the war at all? Didn't they know how important this issue was? (One faculty member asked, "Don't they even realize that people are going to *die* in Iraq?")

6   Some of my colleagues clearly feel there is something fundamental to their role as educators at stake in such matters. Students who make such complaints, these teachers seem to think, simply need to be educated, and it is our job as educators to do just that. From the perspective of these teachers, it isn't merely such current events as the war in Iraq that students need to be educated about; it is also about the importance of standing up for yourself and speaking up for your beliefs on important issues. In short, if the complainers indeed feel intimidated, this is merely proof that they need to grow up. They need to be trained, through vigorous exercise in discussion and writing on hot topics, *not* to be intimidated. According to these teachers, professors who are willing to show the courage of proclaiming their own political beliefs openly in class, especially about such critical issues as the war in Iraq, are merely setting a good example for their students.

7   Who holds the moral high ground here? Should professors be exercising their own freedom of speech in the college classroom, educating students on contemporary issues, perhaps in the cause of demonstrating the importance of open and unapologetic self-expression? Or are the complaining students right in thinking that they should be able to take a required course at a public university without being subjected to their professor's personal political opinions?

8   For the moment putting aside the pedagogical issues, which are profound enough in themselves, I want to think first about a more basic question that has troubled me deeply ever since the Supreme Court of the United States of America opened the way for a group of Neo-Nazis to march with their swastikas and bullhorns through the streets of Skokie, Illinois, a community heavily populated by European Jewish immigrants, some of them survivors of the Holocaust. That question is this: Where does one person's freedom to speak end, and another person's right not to listen begin?

9   *The right not to listen?* Do we Americans really have the right not to listen? If not, should we? Whether we actually have such a right turns out to be a surprisingly complicated question of law and of fact, which I will leave for others, but for me the question of "Should we have this right?" is a rather simple issue of basic fairness.

10   The freedom to speak one's mind and heart is a sacred human right. It is a natural right, a birthright of our species, not merely a Constitutional right. In fact, the U.S. Constitution has got nothing to do with it, except in helping to ensure that Congress will leave it well enough alone. There must have been some reason, however, why the framers of our Constitution listed the freedom of speech among the very first in our Bill of Rights, and surely that reason concerns much more than the general health of the body politic. Indeed, freedom of speech is a vital freedom, vital not just to our social and political health as a people, but to our mental and spiritual health as persons. We exercise no liberty that is more fundamental to our nature, to our quality of life, or to our dignity as human beings than the free use of language to express our thoughts and feelings.

11   Those who rightly champion this marvelous human power of thought and self-expression, however, often forget that it is intrinsically two-sided. Its mode of operation is that of a dialectic, which necessarily involves both a speaker and a listener in communion. Not even the cognitive act of silently formulating an idea can take place without an equal and opposite yet wholly integrated act of interpretation. For this we need, at a minimum, the voluntary attention and cooperation of an inner listener. (Would you bother talking to yourself if you didn't want to hear what you had to say?)

12   Formulating, articulating, expressing, listening to, interpreting, evaluating, embracing or rejecting ideas—all these are not really separate activities, but the necessary and complementary functions of a single great enterprise. They are all equal manifestations of a uniquely human essence: the capacity for language and the freedom of articulate thought that language bestows upon our species. Thus, when we conceive and express ideas—or when we freely receive, interpret, consider, and evaluate ideas—we are exercising, not separate rights, but the same basic right. It is this that motivates and justifies both the freedom to speak and the freedom to listen. To deny human beings either of these freedoms is to deny them an innate prerogative to fulfill an innate potential. The freedom to actualize this potential in both ways, in listening as well as in speaking, is critical not only to the survival of our democracy, but to the survival of our species.

13   None of this is to say, of course, that we *must* expend this great potential on any or every idea or discussion that happens to come up. In fact, that's part of the beauty and freedom of it, one of the most liberated and liberating aspects of its power: We invoke it at will. Natural and habitual as linguistic behavior is to our species, it is no involuntary reflex, but a choice. It is no mere biological response to some physical need or stimulus, but a spiritually ennobling choice that affirms and reaffirms, every time and in every way it is exercised, the ultimate freedom of the human mind and will. It is this fact about the mind, its extraordinary freedom, that gives us the courage of our own ideas. To articulate or to abandon an idea, to consider an idea further or to refuse to consider it at all—if the mind were not at liberty to invoke any and all of these options, then how could we ever have any confidence in the mind as an instrument of ideas? No idea is

trustworthy whose conception, expression, or reception is a matter of compulsion rather than of choice.

Therefore, just as surely as the freedom to speak entails the freedom to listen, so the freedom to speak entails the freedom *not* to speak—and the freedom *not* to listen. The same priceless principle of human dignity and liberty and integrity is at stake in all these freedoms: the right to our own ideas.

What exactly does this mean? It means that I have no more right to make you speak something you don't want to say than you have a right to stop me from listening to something I want to hear. *And* it means that you have no more right to make me listen to something I *don't* want to hear than I have a right to stop you from saying something you want to speak.

In short, you get to decide, not I, which ideas you will advocate. And I get to decide, not you, which ideas I will entertain. The right not to listen is every bit the moral equivalent of the freedom to speak.

Assuming that we could all agree upon this elementary principle of fairness and civility someday, how in a free society might we protect the rights of both speakers and listeners? At first, this might seem to be very difficult, if not impossible. After all, much of what one person in a given community might wish to communicate will invariably turn out to include ideas that another person in the same community would rather not be exposed to at all, and it's difficult to grant the one a suitable platform while totally protecting the other from exposure.

In fact, it's more than difficult. There simply can be no such thing as "hearing protection" in a society populated by beings whose most characteristic faculty is language. It is unrealistic and unreasonable for people to expect that they can or even should be able to live within an open society—where free expression is not only fiercely protected, but actively encouraged—without being exposed to ideas that they find offensive. If there is any such human right as "the right not to hear disagreeable ideas," it must surely be nothing more than the right to withdraw from society altogether and live without the companionship and bother of other humans.

Forcing or even pressuring people to *listen* to ideas they find offensive, however, is an altogether different affair. Hearing is merely an experience, but listening is an act of will; any attempt to force that act upon another is a violation and abuse of the human will. Listening involves deliberate and deliberative hearing, paying attention, giving heed; trying to compel that kind of consideration from another mind is nothing less than an attempt to usurp the mind's finest and most personal and private powers of choice and contemplation.

Unlike the impossible task of protecting citizens from exposure to objectionable ideas, protecting the right of human beings to decide for themselves which ideas deserve serious consideration could turn out to be a very simple task of social management. We could merely limit the advocacy of controversial ideas and the discussion of contentious issues to convenient times and places—convenient for those who want to avoid the discussion, as well as for those who want to participate in it. This solution should not at all be difficult to implement: As soon as it became apparent that a particular question or presentation was divisive, we would simply relegate the demonstration or debate to an open and orderly forum, where anyone and everyone would be free to attend, or to absent themselves; to speak, or not to speak; to sit quietly and listen, or to get up and leave, so as not to listen. An open forum of this sort would not only protect but would maximize *all* the linguistic rights of *all* people.

21   Can a college classroom be structured so as to constitute such an open forum? Perhaps it can, though not without difficulty. Imagine, for instance, an elective course in the art of debate. Using a combination of the course description, syllabus, and opening lecture, the instructor could make it perfectly clear, right from the first, that controversial, often emotional, issues will be argued, noting that students will unavoidably be exposed to ideas and opinions that they may find disagreeable. The list of actual or possible topics to be debated could be provided up front, and it should also be made clear that successful performance in the course will necessarily involve careful *listening* to ideas and arguments on both sides. None of these ideas or arguments, however, would come from the instructor, who would state this provision as a promise and keep it religiously throughout the course. If only for pedagogical reasons, the teacher would remain scrupulously neutral in the debates, putting aside personal biases and offering even-handed critiques of equal candor and rigor to the reasoning and argumentation on all sides of every question.

22   Such careful provisions for the protection of students' rights will surely seem extreme and overly ideal to many, but I offer this model without apology, if only to provide a sharp contrast to the abuses that many faculty in this country are constantly committing in their classrooms. They are routinely, and with impunity, using the classroom as a platform for their personal political ideologies. This is grossly unfair, especially in the case of required courses. Students in a required English composition course, for instance, constitute a captive audience. The option of dropping the class and finding another section is not a viable one in the face of the harsh realities of enrollment on most of college campuses today. Nor is it a viable option for students to practice selective listening, stopping their ears or "tuning out" or just ignoring their professor's political speeches. Few of us have developed a tough enough skin to sit through an impassioned oration by a gifted, articulate speaker—particularly if the orator is attacking or belittling our own cherished beliefs and values—without being deeply disturbed by it.

23   Again, though, the real question is this: Why should any of us *have to* sit through something of that sort, in the first place? No one should have to, and least of all the students in a required college course, who are bound to believe, with plenty of justification, that they *must* listen to what their professor is saying if they wish to succeed and get a good grade, no matter how disturbing that listening experience may be. Unfortunately, the attitude of some professors about this matter seems to be, "If it disturbs my students to hear me criticize this

country and its insane policies, *good!* They *need* to be disturbed! I'll get in their faces and stay there if doing so will make them open their eyes and ears and *think*, for once!" It is difficult for me to imagine that anyone with such an attitude might be able to teach anyone anything at all about the art of thinking or the nature of human thought.

Less strident voices may object, "But people in a healthy, enlightened society do need to listen to ideas that challenge their beliefs, and students need to learn how to listen to ideas they don't like." Ah yes, it all sounds very familiar. I well remember something of the sort coming from the mouths of my parents when I was a child: "You must listen to us, son, and take your medicine, because we know what's best for you. You don't really know what you need. We do." My parents were right, of course, but is this really the sort of stance college professors should take towards the adults, young or old, in their classrooms? Can we have grown so paternalistic towards our students that we believe their complaints about getting a strong dose of our politics (after paying good money for our instruction in composition) are merely evidence of their not really knowing what they need? 24

Our students may indeed not know what is good for them. Or then, again, maybe they do. Regardless, it is clear to me what is good for us, and for the society we are attempting to prepare our students to enter. We must restore civility and fairness to our classrooms. And we can do so rather easily by simply exercising a little self-restraint and some common-sense respect for the feelings and opinions and values of all our students. A little humility wouldn't hurt, either, if only we could acknowledge that we don't really have all the answers. At the very least, such an admission should force us to understand that, with respect to our personal and political views, our students must always enjoy an absolute right not to listen. 25

♦ Questions for Review

1. What is the thesis of Haley's essay? Does it appear in the essay? If so, where? What reasons does he give for accepting his position?
2. Divide the essay into beginning, middle, and end. What rhetorical and/or stylistic devices help form these divisions?
3. What audience might Haley's essay be written for? Is that audience likely to resist his argument? Does Haley show respect for those who might disagree with him? Explain.
4. Does this essay take opposing points of view into consideration? If so, are they represented fairly? Are they effectively countered?
5. How would you characterize your attitude toward this subject before reading Haley's essay? What effect did this essay have on your thinking?

✦ WRITING OPPORTUNITY

Haley's essay raises the issue of just where the line should be drawn between freedom of speech and actions that deny other freedoms people should have. This issue has been complicated by the advent of the internet. Governments world wide are struggling with the question of what constraints can and/or should be placed on what people can communicate via this new technology. Write an essay in which you reflect on what role governments should play in regulating what one can post and read in cyberspace. ✦

Our second essay was written by David Amante, who is an emeritus member of the English faculty at UNC Charlotte. The winner of numerous teaching awards, Amante believes his teaching should help students prepare not only for the professions they will enter but also for the lives they will lead.

DAVID AMANTE

TEACHING IS ALWAYS A POLITICAL ACT

1   Do university professors have an "obligation" to be completely objective and not deal with contemporary or controversial issues in courses where those issues are not central to the announced subject matter? If there is such an "obligation," then is it in some way unethical for a teacher to reveal his or her stance, or beliefs, on a "hot" political issue? Must teachers only speak about issues within their disciplinary areas of expertise and avoid comment on political issues such as the war in Iraq? Do students have a "right not to listen" to professors whose views differ from theirs? Or, do professors have an obligation to teach modes of dissent? Is the act of teaching, in some senses, always "political"? These are the questions to be explored in this essay.

Facts About Facts:

2   First, let's examine some facts about "facts." Things that are facts are often believed to be "real" or "true" in all circumstances. *Webster's New World Dictionary,* 3rd Edition defines this sense of "fact" as follows: "**2** a thing that has actually happened or that is really true; thing that has been or is. **3** the state of things as they are; reality; actuality; truth" (485). Some facts are physical, such

as the speed of falling objects in certain gravitational fields, and their "truth" can be verified through empirical means such as scientific experiments which can be replicated. But other facts are true only within certain institutions, organizations, or conventions. These latter are "Institutional Facts" and are rule bound by social institutions, not physical laws of the universe. Institutional facts are subject to change and a variety of interpretations. For example, it would seem to be a question of fact as to whether two people are married. But what if they are gay men who made a commitment to each other in a ceremony sanctioned by the state in which they lived? Two people could have witnessed the same ceremony and still disagree as to whether it was a fact that the two were married. One might point to the marriage license as evidence of the marriage, while the other might say that regardless of what this state institution says, marriages only occur between two people of different genders. Indeed, should those two people move to another state that does not accept the fact of their marriage, they may find themselves without the rights given to married partners.

Teaching in American State Universities

3   Teachers in universities always have to contend with both empirical and institutional facts and with apparent contradictions that arise when individuals confuse these two types of facts. As teachers, we are usually offering our interpretations of the competing paradigms in our disciplines. For example in my own discipline, a person who reads a Shakespearean play from a New Critical perspective will find meanings in the play that may differ considerably from those found by a reader who approaches that same play from a New Historical perspective. There can be heated arguments between members of a discipline who work in different paradigms. Such disagreement is often uncomfortable to my students; in fact many of the students I teach, at a regional state university in the South, often find disagreements of any kind foreign and unpleasant. To be sure, these students come from diverse backgrounds; however, as a whole the state of North Carolina is somewhat conservative in politics and rather fundamentalist in religious beliefs. Many of my students have been trained to accept authority, to accept the beliefs and ideology of the culture they grew up in as being natural and right. As a part of their upbringing, they have been led to believe that to disagree with others blatantly is bad manners.

4   In such a context, students need to be taught how to dissent, and I believe the English Department plays a crucial role in beginning that part of their education. Instructors of English must teach these students how to begin to think for themselves. The preceding statement would seem wrongheaded to many of my students. If asked they would say that they came to college to prepare themselves for their future work, not to learn to think for themselves. Most would assert that they already do that quite well, thank you. Like most of my colleagues, however, I see the development of students' ability to question their most cherished beliefs as the most important part of my job. That's why we have designed a writing

curriculum that focuses on sound thinking. First-year students receive instruction in writing effective prose; at the same time they are introduced to the various ways different disciplines reason, some governing principles within disciplines, conflicting theories within disciplines, and rudiments of a variety of ways of conducting arguments. The focus of our second-semester first-year writing course is argumentation; in this course, students are taught how to judge and construct reasonable arguments.

The Iraq War

The Iraq war was, and is, a controversial case about public policy and as such has been subject to much debate in the United States. From the beginning, I was against declaring war on a nation that, as far as I could see, posed no physical threat to our country. From my vantage point, the war seemed to be a product of the United States' desire to guarantee a continuing supply of oil to the American economy. I never accepted the assertion that Iraq possessed Weapons of Mass Destruction. Of course, the gassing of thousand of Kurds was a wanton massacre, but it had taken place almost a decade before this war; far more deadly massacres had more recently happened in Africa and the American government had not declared war on any African countries. Perhaps the most compelling argument I had against the Iraq war was my objection to a "first strike" foreign policy that assumed we had the right to attack another nation on the strength of a mere suspicion that it was planning to do harm to the United States. Given my strong feelings about this war, I felt dissent was called for.

Since I believed that our nation was on the wrong track, I thought it was necessary to register some form of protest and start a dissenting dialogue. Just prior to the beginning of the Iraq war—when our military build up clearly showed our national intent to wage war—my university had faculty experts on the Middle East give several public presentations on the history of the region and the culture, in part to defuse the rather alarming anti-Muslim sentiments rising in our community and the growing fear Muslim students expressed in response to several threats, insults, and perceived threats. Several hundred students and a number of faculty members attended, listened, and expressed their views; the event even made the local evening news. I was happy that this forum was held, but I believed the academic community needed to do more.

So a few days later, I proposed in an English Department meeting that the English Department sponsor a real Teach-In about the Iraq war and designate one or two days in which we would suspend classes to let students attend sessions of a Teach-In at our university. My motion was seconded and discussed but my colleagues felt that they needed more clarification about what this meant and, in effect, tabled my motion for "further study." So I called the president of the faculty and emailed the members of the Faculty Executive Committee about my proposal and was assured that it would be discussed at the next meeting in two weeks. The U.S. invaded Iraq several days later and the Teach-In to prevent the war became a moot point.

Did I mention the Iraq war in my classes? Of course I did. I felt it was my duty to share my beliefs and to model how to dissent. In presenting my viewpoint, I attempted to use all three of Aristotle's modes of persuasion: logic, ethos, and emotion. I gave my students a logical analysis of this war in a non-abrasive and non-abusive manner that, I hope, increased my ethical appeal. Of course, my ethos as a speaker rested in great part on all my previous interactions with my students. And finally, I attempted to appeal to their emotions by offering evidence of the terrible toll this war would exact in terms of human life—both American and Iraqi.

How did I incorporate this discussion into my classes? In a typical class, I spent five minutes or so offering my point of view of this war. Then I would serve as moderator, attempting to elicit a variety of responses from the class and especially encouraging opposing arguments. My goal is always to start a dialectic, a search for what the class believes to be true. The rest of the class period would be devoted to more traditional instruction, but the discussion on the war would continue in other class meetings.

Over the course of a couple of days of discussion, I shared my belief that there are some justified wars, such as WWII; I did, however, recount my opposition to the Viet Nam War and the fact that I was drafted during that war and spent most of two years in the US Army in Germany. I emphasized the point that it is a common practice in wartime for a government to "demonize" the enemy—that is, to make the "enemy" into a simplified, dehumanized, imagined being who is wholly evil, so that the citizens/soldiers can more easily see the enemy as "things" to be killed. I pointed out the fact that there are American Muslims and various Arab-Americans and that not all Iraq citizens are car bombing fanatics.

In my literature course, I discussed Dickens' novel *Hard Times*, showing how the antagonist, Bounderby, dehumanizes the workers and simplifies them to fit his gross and materialist view of the world. My goal was to help students see the harm such distortions can do to individuals, such as Stephen Blackpool [the "good" and reasonable worker], and to society in both Dickens' times and our present times. I wanted to show some moral problems in the literature that may also be at issue in contemporary society. To do so, I compared Bounderby's kinds of oversimplifications to the kind of things one can hear on a conservative talk show such as the one hosted by Rush Limbaugh.

In my composition course, my discussion of the Iraq war was part of my students' preparation for an assignment to write arguments having to do with pubic policy. A primary goal of this assignment was to encourage students to reflect upon their beliefs and learn how to conduct cogent and persuasive arguments for their own beliefs. My teaching in this course was designed to help students learn to reason logically, create credibility by the way they represent themselves in writing, and use their passion and emotions to help persuade others to their beliefs. In order to do so, however, students must learn to challenge their own beliefs, to dissent from the ways they have been taught to think.

Let me explain this point more fully. One of the most difficult tasks for a beginning writer is to understand what those on the other side of an argument believe and to engage in a dialogue with the opposition that, at the least, recognizes their rights to their beliefs. Many of my students approach argumentation as if it deals in the kinds of empirical facts that scientists deal with. Their goal, as they see it, is to help those on the other side of an argument to see the "correct" way to think about a topic. They will never be able to write successful arguments that create dialogue with those who take an opposing position until they come to see the "institutional" nature of the facts they are discussing.

This word "institutional" brings us back to my claim above that it is the job of the university professor to teach dissent. The most powerful "institution" in any society is the government. And the number one priority of those in government is to maintain power. In the context of the United States of America, that means that regardless of who holds power, Republicans or Democrats, their top priority is to create an argument for why they should retain power in the next election cycle. If we accept this premise, then it is easy to see why an educated citizenry must learn how to dissent against the government in power. It does not serve the purpose of those who hold power to deal in complexities and shades of grey. They cannot admit that their policies in regard to national and international affairs are flawed, that other ways of conducting these affairs might have been better, that doubt is warranted. I once taught with a teacher who announced in a faculty meeting that her goal was to be sure that students in her first-year writing course would never be completely happy again. We may (and did) all laugh. But her humorous comment spoke to a central role that education plays in all our lives—it makes us aware of complexity; it creates dis-ease; it dispels our notions that simple solutions can produce the happy-ever-after we once loved to believe in.

Let's return then to my opposition to the Iraq War and my belief that I had the obligation to discuss my viewpoint in my classes. What if I had been a supporter of the Iraq War? Would I have had an equal right and obligation to discuss the matter with my students? I'd say I would have had an equal right, but not as strong an obligation. Why? Most of my students were in support of the war. By announcing and explaining my support of the war, I would have done little to help most of my students develop their abilities to reason and think.

In any case and whatever my opinion, I have the right to express it in my teaching. Neither I nor my students check our freedom of speech at the door of a classroom. Attempting to do so would be a disservice to my students in two ways. First, it would be a disservice because they deserve a teacher who is human—especially in a humanities class. We learn from people whom we come to know as people. As long as I attempt to keep my guard up so that students cannot discern how I might feel about an issue as crucial as the Iraq War, there will be a wall between us that precludes the kind of interchange out of which learning grows. And secondly, if I hide my point of view because I think my students will be cowered by my superior status and superior thinking ability, I have assumed an authority-based classroom that would, in itself, preclude the kind of learning I want to encourage. My students learn from the first day of class that dissent is expected and encouraged. In my classroom, I represent an institution, the University. If I can't accept and welcome challenge, then how can I be said to be a teacher (and model) of dissent?

What can one say about a so-called "right not to listen"? Are students' rights violated by having professors espouse views that do not match those of the political party currently in power? Do students have a "right" to avoid dissenting opinions or ideas that seem to challenge their ideological beliefs? No. Rather, students have the "right" to hear any and all points of view, including mine. If I am lucky, they will learn to disagree with me and learn to become dissenters and, thereby, practice the First Amendment of the United States Constitution which reads as follows: 17

> Congress shall make no law respecting an establishment of religion, or prohibiting the free exercise thereof; or abridging the freedom of speech or the press; or the right of the people peaceably to assemble, and to petition the government for a redress of grievances.

Because we have such an amendment, I believe teachers have the right and the obligation to share their beliefs with their students.

◆ QUESTIONS FOR REVIEW

1. What is the thesis of Amante's essay? Does it appear in the essay? If so, where? What reasons does he give for accepting his position?
2. Divide the essay into beginning, middle, and end. What rhetorical and/or stylistic devices help form these divisions?
3. What audience might Amante's essay be written for? Is that audience likely to resist his argument? Does Amante show respect for those who might disagree with him? Explain.
4. Does this essay take opposing points of view into consideration? If so, are they represented fairly? Are they effectively countered?
5. How would you characterize your attitude toward this subject before reading Amante's essay? What effect did this essay have on your thinking?

◆ WRITING OPPORTUNITY

In his essay Amante makes the distinction between empirical and institutional facts. He asserts that "apparent contradictions . . . arise when individuals confuse these types of facts." Think of a time in your own life when you or someone you know dealt with a situation that could fit this description. Write an essay in which you explain the difficulties of that situation. ◆

In our third essay, "Nonoverlapping Magisteria," one of the leading scientists of the last half of the twentieth century, Stephen Jay Gould, argues that science and religion do not have to be mortal enemies.

STEPHEN JAY GOULD

NONOVERLAPPING MAGISTERIA

1   Incongruous places often inspire anomalous stories. In early 1984, I spent several nights at the Vatican housed in a hotel built for itinerant priests. While pondering over such puzzling issues as the intended function of the bidets in each bathroom, and hungering for something other than plum jam on my breakfast rolls (why did the basket only contain hundreds of identical plum packets and not a one of, say, strawberry?), I encountered yet another among the innumerable issues of contrasting cultures that can make life so interesting. Our crowd (present in Rome for a meeting on nuclear winter sponsored by the Pontifical Academy of Sciences) shared the hotel with a group of French and Italian Jesuit priests who were also professional scientists.

2   At lunch, the priests called me over to their table to pose a problem that had been troubling them. What, they wanted to know, was going on in America with all this talk about "scientific creationism"? One asked me: "Is evolution really in some kind of trouble and if so, what could such trouble be? I have always been taught that no doctrinal conflict exists between evolution and Catholic faith, and the evidence for evolution seems both entirely satisfactory and utterly overwhelming. Have I missed something?"

3   A lively pastiche of French, Italian, and English conversation then ensued for half an hour or so, but the priests all seemed reassured by my general answer: Evolution has encountered no intellectual trouble; no new arguments have been offered. Creationism is a homegrown phenomenon of American sociocultural history—a splinter movement (unfortunately rather more of a beam these days) of Protestant fundamentalists who believe that every word of the Bible must be

literally true, whatever such a claim might mean. We all left satisfied, but I certainly felt bemused by the anomaly of my role as a Jewish agnostic, trying to reassure a group of Catholic priests that evolution remained both true and entirely consistent with religious belief.

Another story in the same mold: I am often asked whether I ever encounter creationism as a live issue among my Harvard undergraduate students. I reply that only once, in nearly thirty years of teaching, did I experience such an incident. A very sincere and serious freshman student came to my office hours with the following question that had clearly been troubling him deeply: "I am a devout Christian and have never had any reason to doubt evolution, an idea that seems both exciting and particularly well documented. But my roommate, a proselytizing Evangelical, has been insisting with enormous vigor that I cannot be both a real Christian and an evolutionist. So tell me, can a person believe both in God and evolution?" Again, I gulped hard, did my intellectual duty, and reassured him that evolution was both true and entirely compatible with Christian belief—a position I hold sincerely, but still an odd situation for a Jewish agnostic.

These two stories illustrate a cardinal point, frequently unrecognized but absolutely central to any understanding of the status and impact of the politically potent, fundamentalist doctrine known by its self-proclaimed oxymoron as "scientitic creationism"—the claim that the Bible is literally true, that all organisms were created during six days of twenty-four hours, that the earth is only a few thousand years old, and that evolution must therefore be false. Creationism does not pit science against religion (as my opening stories indicate), for no such conflict exists. Creationism does not raise any unsettled intellectual issues about the nature of biology or the history of life. Creationism is a local and parochial movement, powerful only in the United States among Western nations, and prevalent only among the few sectors of American Protestantism that choose to read the Bible as an inerrant document, literally true in every jot and tittle.

I do not doubt that one could find an occasional nun who could prefer to teach creationism in her parochial school biology class or an occasional orthodox rabbi who does the same in his yeshiva, but creationism based on biblical literalism makes little sense in either Catholicism or Judaism for neither religion maintains any extensive tradition for reading the Bible as literal truth rather than illuminating literature, based partly on metaphor and allegory (essential components of all good writing) and demanding interpretation for proper understanding. Most Protestant groups, of course, take the same position—the fundamentalist fringe notwithstanding.

The position that I have just outlined by personal stories and general statements represents the standard attitude of all major Western religions (and of Western science) today. (I cannot, through ignorance, speak of Eastern religions, although I suspect that the same position would prevail in most cases.) The lack of conflict between science and religion arises from a lack of overlap between their respective domains of professional expertise—science in the empirical constitution of the universe, and religion in the search for proper ethical values and the spiritual meaning of our lives. The attainment of wisdom in a full life requires extensive attention to both domains—for a great book tells us that the truth can make us free and that we will live in optimal harmony with our fellows when we learn to do justly, love mercy, and walk humbly.

In the context of this standard position, I was enormously puzzled by a statement issued by Pope John Paul II on October 22, 1996, to the Pontifical Academy of Sciences, the same body that had sponsored my earlier trip to the Vatican. In this document, entitled "Truth Cannot Contradict Truth," the pope defended both the evidence for evolution and the consistency of the theory with Catholic religious doctrine. Newspapers throughout the world responded with frontpage headlines, as in the *New York Times* for October 25:

"Pope Bolsters Church's Support for Scientific View of Evolution."

Now I know about "slow news days" and I do admit that nothing else was strongly competing for headlines at that particular moment. (The *Times* could muster nothing more exciting for a lead story than Ross Perot's refusal to take Bob Dole's advice and quit the presidential race.) Still, I couldn't help feeling immensely puzzled by all the attention paid to the pope's statement (while being wryly pleased, of course, for we need all the good press we can get, especially from respected outside sources). The Catholic Church had never opposed evolution and had no reason to do so. Why had the pope issued such a statement at all? And why had the press responded with an orgy of worldwide, front-page coverage?

I could only conclude at first, and wrongly as I soon learned, that journalists throughout the world must deeply misunderstand the relationship between science and religion, and must therefore be elevating a minor papal comment to unwarranted notice. Perhaps most people really do think that a war exists between science and religion, and that (to cite a particularly newsworthy case) evolution must be intrinsically opposed to Christianity. In such a context, a papal admission of evolution's legitimate status might be regarded as major news indeed—a sort of modern equivalent for a story that never happened, but would have made the biggest journalistic splash of 1640: Pope Urban VIII releases his most famous prisoner from house arrest and humbly apologizes, "Sorry, Signor Galileo . . . the sun, er, is central."

But I then discovered that the prominent coverage of papal satisfaction with evolution had not been an error of non-Catholic Anglophone journalists. The Vatican itself had issued the statement as a major news release. And Italian newspapers had featured, if anything, even bigger headlines and longer stories. The conservative *Il Giornale*, for example, shouted from its masthead: "Pope Says We May Descend from Monkeys."

Clearly, I was out to lunch. Something novel or surprising must lurk within the papal statement but what could it be?—especially given the accuracy of my primary impression (as I later verified) that the Catholic Church values scientific study, views science as no threat to religion in general or Catholic doctrine in particular, and has long accepted both the legitimacy of evolution as a field of study and the potential harmony of evolutionary conclusions with Catholic faith.

As a former constituent of Tip O'Neill's, I certainly know that "all politics is local"—and that the Vatican undoubtedly has its own internal reasons, quite opaque to me, for announcing papal support of evolution in a major statement. Still, I knew that I was missing some important key, and I felt frustrated. I then remembered the primary rule of intellectual life: when puzzled, it never hurts to read the primary documents—a rather simple and self-evident principle that has, nonetheless, completely disappeared from large sectors of the American experience.

I knew that Pope Pius XII (not one of my favorite figures in twentieth-century history, to say the least) had made the primary statement in a 1950 encyclical entitled *Humani Generis*. I knew the main thrust of his message: Catholics could believe whatever science determined about the evolution of the human body, so long as they accepted that, at some time of his choosing, God had infused the soul into such a creature. I also knew that I had no problem with this statement, for whatever my private beliefs about souls, science cannot touch such a subject and therefore cannot be threatened by any theological position on such a legitimately and intrinsically religious issue. Pope Pius XII, in other words, had properly acknowledged and respected the separate domains of science and theology. Thus, I found myself in total agreement with *Humani Generis*—but I had never read the document in full (not much of an impediment to stating an opinion these days).

I quickly got the relevant writings from, of all places, the Internet. (The pope is prominently on-line, but a Luddite like me is not. So I got a computer-literate associate to dredge up the documents. I do love the fracture of stereotypes implied by finding religion so hep and a scientist so square.) Having now read in full both Pope Pius's *Humani Generis* of 1950 and Pope John Paul's proclamation of October 1996, I finally understand why the recent statement seems so new, revealing, and worthy of all those headlines. And the message could not be more welcome for evolutionists and friends of both science and religion.

The text of *Humani Generis* focuses on the magisterium (or teaching authority) of the Church—a word derived not from any concept of majesty or awe but from the different notion of teaching, for *magister* is Latin for "teacher." We may, I think, adopt this word and concept to express the central point of this essay and the principled resolution of supposed "conflict" or "warfare" between science and religion. No such conflict should exist because each subject has a legitimate magisterium, or domain of teaching authority—and these magisteria do not overlap (the principle that I would like to designate as NOMA, or "nonoverlapping magisteria"). The net of science covers the empirical universe: what is it made of (fact) and why does it work this way (theory). The net of religion extends over questions of moral meaning and value. These two magisteria do not overlap, nor do they encompass all inquiry (consider, for starters, the magisterium of art and the meaning of beauty). To cite the arch cliches, we get the age of rocks, and religion retains the rock of ages; we study how the heavens go, and they determine how to go to heaven.

This resolution might remain all neat and clean if the nonoverlapping magisteria (NOMA) of science and religion were separated by an extensive no man's land. But, in fact, the two magisteria bump right up against each other, interdigitating in wondrously complex ways along their joint border. Many of our deepest questions call upon aspects of both for different parts of a full answer—and the sorting of legitimate domains can become quite complex and difficult. To cite just two broad questions involving both evolutionary facts and moral arguments: Since evolution made us the only earthly creatures with advanced consciousness, what responsibilities are so entailed for our relations with other species? What do our genealogical ties with other organisms imply about the meaning of human life?

Pius XII's *Humani Generis* is a highly traditionalist document by a deeply conservative man forced to face all the "isms" and cynicisms that rode the wake of World War II and informed the struggle to rebuild human decency from the ashes of the Holocaust. The encyclical, subtitled "Concerning some false opinions which threaten to undermine the foundations of Catholic doctrine" begins with a statement of embattlement:

> Disagreement and error among men on moral and religious matters have always been a cause of profound sorrow to all good men, but above all to the true and loyal sons of the Church, especially today, when we see the principles of Christian culture being attacked on all sides.

Pius lashes out, in turn, at various external enemies of the Church: pantheism, existentialism, dialectical materialism, historicism and of course and preeminently, communism. He then notes with sadness that some well-meaning folks within the Church have fallen into a dangerous relativism—"a theological pacifism and egalitarianism, in which all points of view become equally valid"—in order to include people of wavering faith who yearn for the embrace of Christian religion but do not wish to accept the particularly Catholic magisterium.

What is this world coming to when these noxious novelties can so discombobulate a revealed and established order? Speaking as a conservative's conservative, Pius laments:

> Novelties of this kind have already borne their deadly fruit in almost all branches of theology. . . . Some question whether angels are personal beings, and whether matter and spirit differ essentially. . . . Some even say that the doctrine of Transubstantiation, based on an antiquated philosophic

notion of substance, should be so modified that the Real Presence of Christ in the Holy Eucharist be reduced to a kind of symbolism.

Pius first mentions evolution to decry a misuse by overextension often promulgated by zealous supporters of the anathematized "isms":

> Some imprudently and indiscreetly hold that evolution . . . explains the origin of all things. . . . Communists gladly subscribe to this opinion so that, when the souls of men have been deprived of every idea of a personal God, they may the more efficaciously defend and propagate their dialectical materialism.

Pius's major statement on evolution occurs near the end of the encyclical in paragraphs 35 through 37. He accepts the standard model of NOMA and begins by acknowledging that evolution lies in a difficult area where the domains press hard against each other. "It remains for US now to speak about those questions which although they pertain to the positive sciences, are nevertheless more or less connected with the truths of the Christian faith." [Interestingly, the main thrust of these paragraphs does not address evolution in general but lies in refuting a doctrine that Pius calls "polygenism," or the notion of human ancestry from multiple parents—for he regards such an idea as incompatible with the doctrine of original sin, "which proceeds from a sin actually committed by an individual Adam and which, through generation, is passed on to all and is in everyone as his own." In this one instance, Pius may be transgressing the NOMA principle—but I cannot judge, for I do not understand the details of Catholic theology and therefore do not know how symbolically such a statement may be read. If Pius is arguing that we cannot entertain a theory about derivation of all modern humans from an ancestral population rather than through an ancestral individual (a potential fact) because such an idea would question the doctrine of original sin (a theological construct), then I would declare him out of line for letting the magisterium of religion dictate a conclusion within the magisterium of science.]

Pius then writes the well-known words that permit Catholics to entertain the evolution of the human body (a factual issue under the magisterium of science), so long as they accept the divine Creation and infusion of the soul (a theological notion under the magisterium of religion):

> The Teaching Authority of the Church does not forbid that, in conformity with the present state of human sciences and sacred theology, research and discussions, on the part of men experienced in both fields, take place with regard to the doctrine of evolution, in as far as it inquires into the origin of the human body as coming from pre-existent and living matter—for the Catholic faith obliges us to hold that souls are immediately created by God.

I had, up to here, found nothing surprising in *Humani Generis*, and nothing to relieve my puzzlement about the novelty of Pope John Paul's recent statement. But I read further and realized that Pope Pius had said more about evolution, something I had never seen quoted, and that made John Paul's statement most interesting indeed. In short, Pius forcefully proclaimed that while evolution may be legitimate in principle, the theory, in fact, had not been proven and might well be entirely wrong. One gets the strong impression, moreover, that Pius was rooting pretty hard for a verdict of falsity.

Continuing directly from the last quotation, Pius advises us about the proper study of evolution:

> However, this must be done in such a way that the reasons for both opinions, that is, those favorable and those unfavorable to evolution, be weighed and judged with the necessary seriousness, moderation and measure.... Some, however, rashly transgress this liberty of discussion, when they act as if the origin of the human body from pre-existing and living matter were already completely certain and proved by the facts which have been discovered up to now and by reasoning on those facts, and as if there were nothing in the sources of divine revelation which demands the greatest moderation and caution in this question.

To summarize, Pius generally accepts the NOMA principle of nonoverlapping magisteria in permitting Catholics to entertain the hypothesis of evolution for the human body so long as they accept the divine infusion of the soul. But he then offers some (holy) fatherly advice to scientists about the status of evolution as a scientific concept: the idea is not yet proven, and you all need to be especially cautious because evolution raises many troubling issues right on the border of my magisterium. One may read this second theme in two different ways: either as a gratuitous incursion into a different magisterium or as a helpful perspective from an intelligent and concerned outsider. As a man of good will, and in the interest of conciliation, I am happy to embrace the latter reading.

In any case, this rarely quoted second claim (that evolution remains both unproven and a bit dangerous)—and not the familiar first argument for the NOMA principle (that Catholics may accept the evolution of the body so long as they embrace the creation of the soul)—defines the novelty and the interest of John Paul's recent statement.

John Paul begins by summarizing Pius's older encyclical of 1950, and particularly by reaffirming the NOMA principle—nothing new here, and no cause for extended publicity:

> In his encyclical *Humani Generis* (1950), my predecessor Pius XII had already stated that there was no opposition between evolution and the doctrine of the faith about man and his vocation.

To emphasize the power of NOMA, John Paul poses a potential problem and a sound resolution: How can we reconcile science's claim for physical continuity in human evolution with Catholicism's insistence that the soul must enter at a moment of divine infusion:

> *With man, then, we find ourselves in the presence of an ontological difference, an ontological leap, one could say. However, does not the posing of such ontological discontinuity run counter to that physical continuity which seems to be the main thread of research into evolution in the field of physics and chemistry? Consideration of the method used in the various branches of knowledge makes it possible to reconcile two points of view which would seem irreconcilable. The sciences of observation describe and measure the multiple manifestations of life with increasing precision and correlate them with the time line. The moment of transition to the spiritual cannot be the object of this kind of observation.*

The novelty and news value of John Paul's statement lies, rather, in his profound revision of Pius's second and rarely quoted claim that evolution, while conceivable in principle and reconcilable with religion, can cite little persuasive evidence, and may well be false. John Paul states—and I can only say amen, and thanks for noticing—that the half century between Pius's surveying the ruins of World War II and his own pontificate heralding the dawn of a new millennium has witnessed such a growth of data, and such a refinement of theory, that evolution can no longer be doubted by people of good will:

> *Pius XII added . . . that this opinion [evolution] should not be adopted as though it were a certain, proven doctrine. . . . Today, almost half a century after the publication of the encyclical, new knowledge has led to the recognition of more than one hypothesis in the theory of evolution. It is indeed remarkable that this theory has been progressively accepted by researchers, following a series of discoveries in various fields of knowledge. The convergence, neither sought nor fabricated, of the results of work that was conducted independently is in itself a significant argument in favor of the theory.*

In conclusion. Pius had grudgingly admitted evolution as a legitimate hypothesis that he regarded as only tentatively supported and potentially (as I suspect he hoped) untrue. John Paul, nearly fifty years later, reaffirms the legitimacy of evolution under the NOMA principle—no news here—but then adds that additional data and theory have placed the factuality of evolution beyond reasonable doubt. Sincere Christians must now accept evolution not merely as a plausible possibility but also as an effectively proven fact. In other words, official Catholic opinion on evolution has moved from "say it ain't so, but we can deal with it if we have to" (Pius's grudging view of 1950) to John Paul's entirely welcoming "it has been proven true; we always celebrate nature's factuality, and we look forward to interesting discussions of theological implications." I happily endorse this turn of events as gospel—literally "good news." I may represent the magisterium of science, but I welcome the support of a primary leader from the other major magisterium of our complex lives. And I recall the wisdom of King Solomon: "As cold waters to a thirsty soul, so is good news from a far country" (Prov. 25:25).

Just as religion must bear the cross of its hard-liners, I have some scientific colleagues, including a few prominent enough to wield influence by their writings, who view this rapprochement of the separate magisteria with dismay. To colleagues like me—agnostic scientists who welcome and celebrate the rapprochement, especially the pope's latest statement—they say: "C'mon, be honest; you know that religion is addle-pated, superstitious, old-fashioned b.s.; you're only making those welcoming noises because religion is so powerful, and we need to be diplomatic in order to assure public support and funding for science." I do not think that this attitude is common among scientists, but such a position fills me with dismay—and I therefore end this essay with a personal statement about religion, as a testimony to what I regard as a virtual consensus among thoughtful scientists (who support the NOMA principle as firmly as the pope does).

I am not, personally, a believer or a religious man in any sense of institutional commitment or practice. But I have enormous respect for religion, and the subject has always fascinated me, beyond almost all others (with a few exceptions, like evolution, paleontology, and baseball). Much of this fascination lies in the historical paradox that throughout Western history organized religion has fostered both the most unspeakable horrors and the most heart-rending examples of human goodness in the face of personal danger. (The evil, I believe, lies in the occasional confluence of religion with secular power. The Catholic Church has sponsored its share of horrors, from Inquisitions to liquidations—but only because this institution held such secular power during so much of Western history. When my folks held similar power more briefly in Old Testament times, they committed just as many atrocities with many of the same rationales.)

I believe, with all my heart, in a respectful, even loving concordat between our magisteria—the NOMA solution. NOMA represents a principled position on moral and intellectual grounds, not a mere diplomatic stance. NOMA also cuts both ways. If religion can no longer dictate the nature of factual conclusions properly under the magisterium of science, then scientists cannot claim higher insight into moral truth from any superior knowledge of the world's empirical constitution. This mutual humility has important practical consequences in a world of such diverse passions.

Religion is too important to too many people for any dismissal or denigration of the comfort still sought by many folks from theology. I may, for example, privately suspect that papal insistence on divine infusion of the soul represents a sop to our fears, a device for maintaining a belief in human superiority within an evolutionary world offering no privileged position to any creature. But I also know that souls represent a subject outside the magisterium of science. My world cannot prove or disprove such a notion, and the concept of souls cannot threaten or impact my domain. Moreover, while I cannot personally accept the Catholic view of souls, I surely honor the metaphorical value of such a concept both for grounding moral discussion and for expressing what we most value about human potentiality: our decency, care, and all the ethical and intellectual struggles that the evolution of consciousness imposed upon us.

As a moral position (and therefore not as a deduction from my knowledge of nature's factuality), I prefer the "cold bath" theory that nature can be truly "cruel" and "indifferent"—in the utterly inappropriate terms of our ethical discourse—because nature was not constructed as our eventual abode, didn't know we were coming (we are, after all, interlopers of the latest geological microsecond), and doesn't give a damn about us (speaking metaphorically). I regard such a position as liberating, not depressing, because we then become free to conduct moral discourse—and nothing could be more important—in our own terms, spared from the delusion that we might read moral truth passively from nature's factuality.

But I recognize that such a position frightens many people, and that a more spiritual view of nature retains broad appeal (acknowledging the factuality of evolution and other phenomena, but still seeking some intrinsic meaning in human terms, and from the magisterium of religion). I do appreciate, for example, the struggles of a man who wrote to the *New York Times* on November 3, 1996, to state both his pain and his endorsement of John Paul's statement:

> *Pope John Paul II's acceptance of evolution touches the doubt in my heart. The problem of pain and suffering in a world created by a God who is all love and light is hard enough to bear, even if one is a creationist. But at least a creationist can say that the original creation, coming from the hand of God was good, harmonious, innocent and gentle. What can one say about evolution, even a spiritual theory of evolution? Pain and suffering, mindless cruelty and terror are its means of creation. Evolution's engine is the grinding of predatory teeth upon the screaming, living flesh and bones of prey. . . . If evolution be true, my faith has rougher seas to sail.*

I don't agree with this man, but we could have a wonderful argument. I would push the "cold bath" theory: he would (presumably) advocate the theme of inherent spiritual meaning in nature, however opaque the signal. But we would both be enlightened and filled with better understanding of these deep and ultimately unanswerable issues. Here, I believe, lies the greatest strength and necessity of NOMA, the nonoverlapping magisteria of science and religion. NOMA permits—indeed enjoins—the prospect of respectful discourse, of constant input from both magisteria toward the common goal of wisdom. If human beings are anything special, we are the creatures that must ponder and talk. Pope John Paul II would surely point out to me that his magisterium has always recognized this distinction, for "*in principio, erat verbum*"—"In the beginning was the Word."

Postscript

Carl Sagan organized and attended the Vatican meeting that introduces this essay; he also shared my concern for fruitful cooperation between the different but vital realms of science and religion. Carl was also one of my dearest friends. I learned of his untimely death on the same day that I read the proofs for this essay. I could only recall Nehru's observations on Gandhi's death—that the light had gone out, and darkness reigned everywhere. But I then contemplated what Carl had done in his short sixty-two years and remembered John Dryden's ode for Henry Purcell, a great musician who died even younger: "He long ere this had tuned the jarring spheres, and left no hell below."

The days I spent with Carl in Rome were the best of our friendship. We delighted in walking around the Eternal City, feasting on its history and architecture—and its food! Carl took special delight in the anonymity that he still enjoyed in a nation that had not yet aired *Cosmos*, the greatest media work in popular science of all time.

I dedicate this essay to his memory. Carl also shared my personal suspicion about the nonexistence of souls—but I cannot think of a better reason for hoping we are wrong than the prospect of spending eternity roaming the cosmos in friendship and conversation with this wonderful soul.

◆ QUESTIONS FOR REVIEW

1. What is the thesis of Gould's essay? Does it appear in the essay? If so, where? What reasons does he give for accepting his position?
2. Divide the essay into beginning, middle, and end. What rhetorical and/or stylistic devices help form these divisions?
3. What audience might Gould's essay be written for? Is that audience likely to resist his argument? Does Gould show respect for those who might disagree with him? Explain.
4. Does this essay take opposing points of view into consideration? If so, are they represented fairly? Are they effectively countered?
5. How would you characterize your attitude toward this subject before reading Gould's essay? What effect did this essay have on your thinking?

◆ WRITING OPPORTUNITY

In talking about the edict of Pope Pius XII, Gould says: "I knew the main thrust of his message: Catholics could believe whatever science determined about evolution of the human body, so long as they accepted that, at some time of his choosing, God had infused the soul into such a creature. I also knew that I had no problem with this statement, for whatever my private beliefs about souls, science cannot touch such a subject and therefore cannot be threatened by any theological position on such a legitimately and intrinsically religious issue." But assuming an evolutionary perspective, wouldn't it make a difference whether the creature that was to become modern man was endowed with a soul 10,000 years ago or 5 million years ago, in terms of what other creatures in our world today might be thought to possess souls? Write an essay in which you explore the question of whether other creatures have souls in terms of the effect one's answer will have modern scientific research. ◆

Our last sample essay was written by Jennifer Pitman, a first-year writing student at UNC Charlotte. Her essay deals with an issue that has divided U.S. Americans for many years: Euthanasia.

JENNIFER PITMAN

EUTHANASIA AND THE RIGHT TO DIE

1. Euthanasia is the deliberate and painless death of a person suffering from a fatal disease or incapacitating condition. There are two types of euthanasia: passive and active. Passive euthanasia involves altering some form of support to bring about death. For example, the removal of life-supporting equipment would be considered passive euthanasia. As its label suggests, active euthanasia involves taking some direct action to bring about a person's death. This type of euthanasia is often referred to as "mercy killing." Most of us have heard of Dr. Jack Kevorkian, a physician who is now in prison for his role in active euthanasias. He has helped numerous people end their lives when they have been faced with what they saw as unbearable situations. The Supreme Court has supported passive euthanasia, but it has ruled that active euthanasia is an issue that must be dealt with by individual states. Since the euthanasia debate revolves around active euthanasia, I will use the word *euthanasia* to mean "active euthanasia" unless otherwise stated.

2. I believe people should be able to end their lives peacefully if they are suffering from a fatal illness. Euthanasia provides terminally ill patients with the freedom to choose how and when they will die. This freedom should be guaranteed by law to all who choose to exercise their right to a peaceful death.

3. Euthanasia offers terminally ill patients compassion and mercy and allows them to end excruciating pain. People in advanced stages of cancer, AIDS, Lou

Gehrig's disease, and similar illnesses have little hope or joy; they are waiting, often in great pain, to die. Dr. Peter Admiraal, a well-known Dutch physician who supports euthanasia, has said that most patients "ask for euthanasia as a last resort due to agonizing pain" (qtd. in McCuen 72). In some situations, a person can be in so much pain that living becomes indistinguishable from torture. As a society, we would not knowingly allow someone to be tortured, so why would we insist that a terminally ill person endure such torturous pain?

The family of the terminally ill patient is also deeply affected by their loved one's mental, physical, and emotional deterioration. Watching someone you love suffer constantly and knowing their suffering will only be ended by death is both overwhelming and agonizing. It would be difficult to help a loved one die, but it might be more difficult to watch that person suffer so terribly and not be able to provide any relief for them. Families should have the freedom to carry out the last wishes of their loved ones.

Another issue terminally ill patients face is the cost of medical care. Unfortunately, end of life care is very expensive and in most cases will only extend life for a very short while. At times, adequate care (hospice or in-home), medication and treatment are simply not affordable. Opponents of legalizing euthanasia would argue that with death as an option, patients might feel pressure, for financial reasons, to choose death over life. It cannot be denied that money would inevitably play a part in these life and death situations. With euthanasia as an option, however, the patient could continue treatments as long as the quality of life those treatments afforded him was worth the money being spent. The decision to discontinue treatment, however, could not, and would not, become a simple matter of money.

The laws in Oregon provide a good model for how this process can work. Euthanasia first became legal in Oregon in 1994 and was approved by the voting public of that state in 1997. This law requires that a candidate for euthanasia must be terminally ill with no longer than six months to live. Two doctors must agree on this diagnosis. And then, the patient must request life-ending drugs three times, the last request in writing (Robinson). While Oregon is the only state that has passed such legislation at this time, New York and Washington have also had euthanasia referendums on ballots—Washington in 1991 and New York in 1992. Neither was passed, but there was strong support for euthanasia in both states.

Those who oppose euthanasia foresee many problems should euthanasia be legalized. For example, they fear that doctors could prescribe a fatal dose of medicine to a terminally ill patient who has not requested her death. Under Oregon's laws this would not happen because the patient, herself, must request (no fewer than three times) that she be given such life-ending drugs. Another fear is that people with non-fatal diseases such as depression or schizophrenia might receive help in committing suicide. Again, Oregon's law would not allow such legal suicides since at least two doctors must agree that a person's situation is terminal. Oregon's example shows how carefully written laws can allow terminal patients the dignity of ending their lives without extending the rights of euthanasia to those whose conditions do not warrant this drastic action.

Some people fear that if legislation is passed allowing euthanasia, many people will see these laws as statements that it is right to take one's life. Rita Marker, the executive director of the International Anti-Euthanasia Task Force, suggests that legalizing euthanasia "is like giving the household seal of approval. It's telling people: 'If it's legal, it's right'" (Albom 53). Marker bases her argument on the idea that governmental policy determines people's personal decisions. This is simply not true. For example, gun ownership is legal, but not everyone owns a gun or thinks it would be right to do so. The same can be said concerning abortions: many women consider it wrong to have abortions, despite the fact that the law would allow them to do so.

When dealing with intense personal matters such as those surrounding the end of one's life, people do not allow politics and public opinion to determine their values. People have settled the issue of whether it is right to end their lives before they get to this critical juncture. Their decisions are often influenced by their religious beliefs. Jews, Muslims, and Catholic Christians are likely to believe that euthanasia is wrong. However, Anglicans, Methodists, Presbyterians, and Quakers are likely to be more receptive to euthanasia. Buddhists and Hindus accept and approve of euthanasia if it is undertaken when one is terminally ill and if it is undertaken for the correct spiritual reasons, for ending an existence that is causing suffering to the individual and to her family (Campbell 38). Religiously and culturally, America is extremely diverse, and this diversity makes it impossible to determine which set of beliefs is correct. Thus, our government must keep itself separate from our religions. A government that tells a Quaker that he cannot choose euthanasia has set itself against a religious belief, whereas a government that makes euthanasia available to a Catholic is, in no way, telling him that he should take his own life.

The choice of euthanasia should be a personal one, made by the dying patient, not by our government or society. The person who is suffering is the only one who can decide if death is the right choice. Legalizing euthanasia would not force the act on anyone; it would simply offer a choice to those who find it an acceptable means to end their suffering.

Works Cited

Albom, Mitch. "Bringing a Peaceful End to Pain and Suffering." *Los Angeles Business Journal* Dec. 2000: 53.

Campbell, Courtney, "Euthanasia and Religion." *UNESCO Courier.* January 2000, Vol. 53, Issue 1 pp. 37–40.

McCuen, G. E. *Doctor Assisted Suicide and the Euthanasia Movement.* Hudson: Gary E. McCuen Publications, 1994.

Robinson, Bruce A. "Physician Assisted Suicide in the U.S." 22 November 2003 <http://www.religioustolerance.org/euth_us.htm#oregon>.

◆ QUESTIONS FOR REVIEW

1. What is the thesis of Jennifer's essay? Does it appear in the essay? If so, where? What reasons does she give for accepting her position?
2. Divide the essay into beginning, middle, and end. What rhetorical and/or stylistic devices help form these divisions?
3. What audience might Jennifer's essay be written for? Is that audience likely to resist her argument? Does Jennifer show respect for those who might disagree with her? Explain.
4. Does this essay take opposing points of view into consideration? If so, are they represented fairly? Are they effectively countered?
5. How would you characterize your attitude toward this subject before reading Jennifer's essay? What effect did this essay have on your thinking?

◆ WRITING OPPORTUNITY

Do some research on the laws and attitudes regarding euthanasia in another country and then discuss the differences you find between that country and the U.S. in regard to this issue. ◆

THE RHETORICAL TRIANGLE

Reader

A position essay addresses readers who take the other side of the argument. The writer's goal is to show these readers how a reasonable person could take the position the writer is arguing for. Note that we are not suggesting that a writer should aim to convince readers to change their minds and accept the writer's position on an issue. No one changes anybody else's mind, at least not by means of one brief piece of writing. The writer can provide information that may be helpful if the reader is interested in examining a position. In the final analysis, however, any change of mind will take place over a period of time and will involve the reader's will and emotion; it will not occur as the direct result of the power of any arguments a writer may make in one paper. Still, if arguments are couched in such a way as to seem fair and reasonable, they may play a role in the evolution of a reader's thinking. If they seem illogical or strident, they will likely be rejected out of hand—if they are read at all.

We may seem to be undervaluing the power of reason and logic, but there is logic to what we are saying. If reason and logic were sufficient to make people form and change beliefs, then—assuming that all of us are reasonable people—reason would lead us all to the same set of beliefs. Since eminently reasonable and intelligent people disagree about many issues, there must be more involved than reason. Otherwise, we could all reduce our thinking to the kind of formulaic principles used by the famous Spock character in the *Star Trek* movies.

Reader as Opposition Your task in writing a position essay is to lay out your thinking in such a way as to help your readers see how a sensible person could take a point of view different from theirs. In this situation, your readers' role is to resist you and thereby help sharpen your argument. Just as a knife is sharpened by rubbing it against a whetstone, your argument can be strengthened if you make every effort to counter the points you think opposing readers would make against it. In the end, all you ask of readers is that they hear you out and attempt to understand your reasoning.

Subject

The subject for a position paper should be one about which reasonable people can disagree. It would not be worthwhile to write a position paper arguing that human life is precious or that U.S. Americans should enjoy freedom of speech. Most of us can readily agree to these assertions; in fact, most of us would not consider it reasonable for a person to disagree with these positions.

However, a close look at these issues will reveal ways in which you can frame arguable topics dealing with them. For example, you could take the position that in certain cases human life, though precious, should be ended because of the extreme suffering terminal patients would otherwise have to endure. This is essentially the position that Jennifer Pitman takes in her essay, "Euthanasia and the Right to Die." Similarly, you could take the position that even though U.S. Americans have the right to free speech in principle, there are limits to those rights when exercising them would infringe upon the rights of others; this is essentially the position that Michael Haley takes in "The Right Not to Listen."

Exercise 9.1

As you saw in the first section of this chapter, Michael Haley and David Amante take opposing positions on the issue of whether teachers should openly espouse their political opinions in class. Despite their differences, there are matters relating to how teachers should comport themselves in class on which both of these writers would likely agree. For example, both would agree that teachers should not demean students. Both would also likely agree that students should be given ample opportunity to develop their powers of critical thinking. With this in mind, read three other essays that defend an argument (essays you find for yourself or essays provided by your teacher), and then respond to these questions for each essay:

1. What would be the thesis of an essay written in opposition to this essay?
2. What points might the writer of this essay and the writer of an opposing argument agree on?

One final note about topic selection: You do not have to write about a subject of national importance, such as freedom of speech or euthanasia. You may well choose a topic of local interest. For example, you may care about campus issues, such as raising the tuition at your school, increasing the number of parking spaces for students, or increasing (decreasing) support for athletic teams. Other issues may be regional: your state may be considering whether to institute a lottery or to remove unenforced laws (e.g., laws having to do with adultery or homosexuality). Heather Hall's essay, "The Next Big Winner Is . . . !!," is a good example of an essay treating a regional topic, since the citizens of North Carolina, the state in which Heather lives, continue to discuss the merits of a state lottery.

The benefits of dealing with a local or regional issue are obvious: You will no doubt be interested in such issues if they affect you directly, and you should not have much difficulty finding information about them. Be careful, however, to choose issues that are arguable. And find out whether your teacher wishes you to write about a topic that involves issues that help us define ourselves. For example, even though a person might feel very strongly that the parking policies on his university campus should be changed, it is very unlikely that he, or someone who disagreed with his position, would see this as an issue that helps to define who they are. Compare this topic with the one that Heather Hall treats in our sample essay at the end of this chapter. Many of those who oppose a state lottery see gambling as not only wrong but immoral. They could not change their minds about supporting a lottery without, in some sense, changing who they are. And issues such as abortion, capital punishment, and euthanasia are even more emotional.

We are not suggesting that your position paper has to be written about one of these gut wrenching topics. We are saying that the more emotional involvement you and your readers have in a topic, the more challenging you will find it to think and write logically about that topic. The mental stretching that such writing assignments cause will develop muscles that will prove useful in the rest of your academic career and beyond.

Writer

According to Aristotle, there are three basic means of persuading. He labeled them *ethos*, *logos*, and *pathos*. *Ethos*, or ethical appeal, is the writer's credibility; *logos*, or logical appeal, is reasoned argument; *pathos*, or pathetic appeal, is emotional argument. In practice, it is often impossible to separate these types of persuasion. For example, if a writer offers an argument that is seriously flawed in its logic, he at once undermines his rational argument and his credibility. But for purposes of discussion, we will consider these as three different avenues of persuasion.

As we envision the position essay, the writer's credibility (ethical appeal) is very important because the writer's goal in this type of essay is to help the reader gain respect for someone who holds a position diametrically opposed to his. As we will see, the writer's logic is important, but logos without ethos will not be successful in this assignment. To achieve ethos, the writer must prove that he is knowledgeable, engaged, and fair.

Knowledge The writer of a position essay must know a geat deal about her topic. It helps, of course, if the writer has a degree in the field or if her experiences add credibility to her writing. However, you do not need such credentials to speak with authority about the topic you have chosen. Look, for example, at the essay written by Heather Hall (pages 479–482). Heather makes no claims to special expertise in matters of state government and funding, but her obvious interest in the issue of the lottery has caused her to learn enough about the subject to write with authority. Likewise, Jennifer Pitman (pages 437–439) has clearly taken the time to make herself knowledgeable about the issues surrounding euthanasia.

In argumentative writing it is assumed that the writer will get the facts right. Of course, facts do not convince readers by themselves. Two people can agree on the number of people in the United States who are addicted to hard drugs without agreeing on the steps government should take to combat drugs. However, a writer completely undermines himself if he is not in possession of relevant facts or if he presents as fact information with which the reader will disagree.

Exercise 9.2

Look back to three of the essays at the beginning of this chapter (or essays that your instructor chooses). Identify any instances in which the writer presents as fact information with which someone opposing his or her argument might disagree. Also identify instances in which these authors could have used more facts to support their arguments. How would their arguments be strengthened by the use of more facts?

Engagement An engaged writer has a much better chance of drawing readers into her topic. To be engaged in her writing, the writer must care about her subject. Much of the writing that lacks this quality treats subjects we have all seen over and over again. There is nothing wrong with writing about subjects that are often discussed but, if writers aren't really interested in their topics, they tend to speak in general terms, saying the same things that so many other people have said. There is no specific detail and no personal experience.

For an example of the role that personal experience can play in argumentative writing, look at Heather Hall's argument in favor of the lottery (pages 479–482). She draws upon her recent experiences as a college student to point to real problems caused by the economic problems in North Carolina. And, since she is the child of a public school teacher, she can cite specific problems the lack of funding has caused in the public schools. We do not mean to suggest that engagement requires that you have personal experience with the subject, but you must find a way to engage yourself with, and get below the surface of, your subject. Even though Jennifer Pitman ("Euthanasia and the Right to Die," pages 437–439) offers no personal experiences having to do with euthanasia, the clarity with which she presents both the reasons for accepting euthanasia and the objections that those in opposition will have to this practice reflect her genuine interest in her topic. She is not merely reciting arguments she has read in a source.

Fairness   The writer of a position essay must be sure that his involvement with the topic does not impair his ability to see the issue from the perspective of the reader. That is, the writer's interest must not blind him to the work that has to be done in writing about this topic. For example, a writer's interest in affirmative action could grow out of a personal experience of having been denied a certain job. If the pain the writer experienced in that situation makes it impossible for him to imagine why anyone would be in favor of affirmative action, then he is too close to this topic to write about it. To examine your feelings about a possible topic for a position paper, try to sketch what an argument for your opposition might look like. It will be crucial that you counter the arguments the other side is likely to make. If you find that it's impossible to imagine how that side would argue, you may have difficulty writing about the topic.

In countering the arguments of the opposition, it is neither necessary nor desirable to show disdain for either the arguments or those who would offer them. Rather, the writer should let the reader know that he understands that a reasonable person could hold a position on this topic that is different from his. Finally, however, the writer has to show why the opposing argument does not convince him.

Two essays in this chapter illustrate the point we are making. In "The Right Not to Listen," Michael Haley spends much time articulating and responding to the arguments of those who would oppose his point of view. In doing so he is careful to check himself when he is tempted to mis-characterize his opponents. For example, in talking about faculty who objected to his Chair's pronouncement against political content in the classroom, he says: "Whether or not any of them had actually used the classroom as a forum for venting their own personal passions against the war, they all seemed to feel a definite need to defend themselves—or perhaps, in fairness to them a need to defend certain principles of academic freedom and the rights of free speech—against the complaint of the students." Though he is tempted to indict faculty members for what he sees as misconduct, he is careful to point out that they may well not be guilty of any such actions and to indicate that even if they did things he would not have approved of, they would have seen themselves as defending basic principles of free speech. At another point in the essay, he goes on to say of those who oppose him: "Some of my colleagues clearly feel there is something fundamental to their role as educators at stake in such matters." Although his point of view is clear and well argued, Haley treats those on the other side of this argument as "colleagues" who hold different points of view on this important issue.

One of those colleagues, who teaches at a university in a distant part of the United States from Haley, is David Amante. Like Haley, Amante is committed to his point of view on this controversial topic. Also like Haley, he resists name-calling and misrepresentation of his opponents. We get insight into why Amante's essay is so carefully and respectfully written when we examine his comments on what he is attempting to do in his teaching. Amante tells us that "One of the most difficult tasks for a beginning writer is to understand what those on the other side of an argument believe and to engage in a dialogue with the opposition that, at the least, recognizes their rights to their beliefs." Amante's goal is to teach his students how to dissent—even with him. As he puts it, "If I am lucky, they [his students] will learn to disagree with me and learn to become dissenters and, thereby, practice the First Amendment of the United States Constitution. . . ."

Our point here is that Haley and Amante have started a conversation in which they can talk with each other about this important issue. They certainly disagree, but their conversation can start from a place of mutual respect and understanding. When one makes a claim that the other wishes to counter, he can do so in the terms used by his opponent, rather than having to begin by showing how the opponent has completely missed, or willfully ignored, the arguments on the other side of this issue.

We see the same kind of logical clarity and ethical carefulness in the essay by Stephen Gould, "Nonoverlapping Magisteria." Gould definitely believes that those who would create a better world by ousting religion are wrong. However, he makes his case, not by railing at those who disagree with him, but by demonstrating how carefully he attends to the arguments of religious figures such as Pope Pius XII and by telling stories about his interactions with members of the clergy. He acknowledges the fact that there are those "hard-liners" in science who give no quarter to religion. Rather than demeaning those who would disagree with him, Gould says that their position causes him "dismay." And he goes on to argue that "Religion is too important to too many people for any dismissal or denigration of the comfort still sought by many folks from theology."

Gould's reasoned argumentative style will become even clearer if you compare his essay to one dealing with a similar topic in Chapter 10, Richard Dawkins' "When Religion Steps on Science's Toes." Even though the title might suggest that Dawkins will also talk about these ideas in a dispassionate manner, it is clear very early in the essay that the tone and ethos of Dawkins' essay will be very different from that of Gould's. In the first phrase of the essay, Dawkins refers to the "cowardly flabbiness of the intellect" of those, such as S. J. Gould, who disagree with him on the wisdom of attempting to separate religious from scientific matters. In characterizing those who want to pay respect to both of these institutions, Dawkins derisively refers to what he sees as the weak thinking of those who would have these "Nonoverlapping Magisteria . . . snuggle[ing] up together in a respectful and loving concordat." In another place, he refers to a statement made by Pope John Paul II as "casuistical doubletalk." And near the end of his essay he refers to those who would attempt to allow science and religion to co-exist peacefully as "dishonestly self-serving." Our point here is not to depict one of these essays as good and the other as bad, but rather to draw your attention to the very real differences between argumentative essays designed to engage those on the opposing side in conversation and those essays that focus on persuading people on one side of an argument to take actions in support of their beliefs. We will have much more to say about these other essays in Chapter 10.

DISTINGUISHING FEATURES OF POSITION ESSAYS

Logical Arguments

The primary distinguishing feature of a position essay is the writer's logical argumentation. Although you may well write persuasively (in ways we will discuss in Chapter 10), the thrust of your essay will be to offer readers logical support for your position. You will make your argument(s) clear and then offer your readers ample support for the claims you are making.

Types of Argumentative Claims

There are two basic types of argumentative claims you may make in writing a position paper: claims of cause and claims of value.

Claims of Cause   Modern science is built upon the insight that one event that happened before another (chronology) may have, in fact, caused the second event. As our ancestors learned to associate certain illnesses with contact they had had with sick people and/or contaminated water, they began to learn how to prevent, or minimize, certain diseases. Of course for every scientific discovery, there has been the potential for false causal connections. The same thinking that associates disease and previous contact with a diseased person associates bad luck with a cat having crossed one's path or with a failure to go around, rather than under, a ladder. When we decide that these events are related by chronology but not by cause/effect, we see them as examples of the *Post Hoc Propter Hoc* fallacy (see page 468) and label them superstitions.

   Although many cause/effect relationships have been established beyond reasonable doubt, humans continue to debate countless cause/effect relationships. Do state lotteries cause people to gamble more, or in more destructive ways, than would be the case without a state lottery? Do drug laws only serve to cause a larger market for those who would sell illicit drugs? Do gun control laws cause there to be fewer gun-related deaths than would be the case without those laws? These are a few examples of the important arguments we could base on causal reasoning.

Claims of Value   We have already discussed some arguments of value in Chapter 8, Evaluation Essays. When you write an essay supporting your claim that a particular movie, concert, or book is good, you have written one type of argument of value. However, the values we associate with argumentation tend to be more directly tied to our core beliefs of right and wrong than those we write about in evaluation essays. If I am attempting to convince a reader that a particular movie is good (or has value), I do not expect her to mount a counterargument to mine; thus, I do not include counterarguments in my essay. I simply explain the reasons for my belief and hope that the reader will consider my point of view when she decides whether to see this movie. Such is not the case when we appeal to values in an argument essay. If I am arguing that gambling is evil, I must expect that the reader will disagree with me, perhaps arguing that life itself is a gamble. Then, I must be prepared to offer my counterarguments that gambling in a lottery is different from the gambling we have to do when we get into our cars or take out an insurance policy and so forth.

Moving from Arguments to Policy

In writing a position essay, you may elect to base your paper on a claim of cause, such as *legal gambling causes more people to gamble,* or a claim of value, such as *gambling is wrong.* However, in most cases, writers do not want to limit themselves to one of these types of argument, and, in fact, they often find it difficult to separate the two in practice. For example, if a person is arguing that *legal gambling causes harm to a society,* he will likely find himself having to specify what gambling causes and then to show why he assigns a negative value to those things. For this reason, it often makes more sense to state our position in terms of a policy that we would like to advocate and to use the arguments of cause and/or value as supports for that policy. In our example above the writer's position would be framed in terms of the following policy statement: "Gambling should not be legalized." Working from this argument of policy, the writer can then use both claims of cause and claims of value in support of his position. Figures 9.1 and 9.2 illustrate the way in which claims of cause and claims of value may be seen as foundations upon which to build an argument for (or against) a policy.

If we wanted to argue that we should have stronger gun-control laws, we could support our thesis with a claim such as (1) individual safety is a *good* to be chosen over other *goods* (such as individual freedom) or (2) stricter gun-control laws will *cause* an increase in the safety of individuals in this society. Of course, neither statement is a self-evident truth; both need support if the reader is to understand why the writer offers them as reasons for stronger gun-control laws.

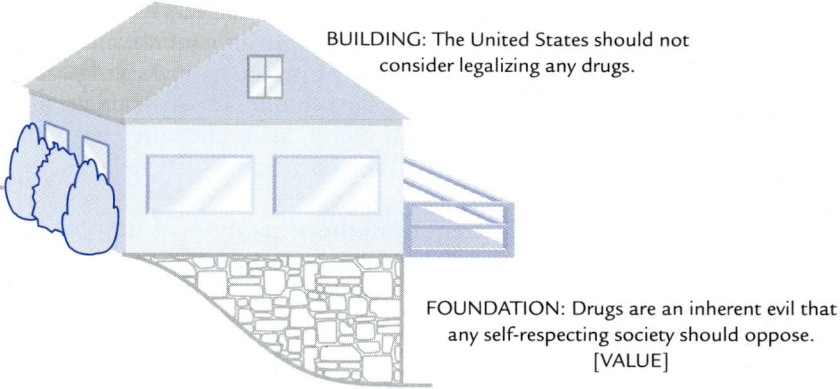

BUILDING: The United States should not consider legalizing any drugs.

FOUNDATION: Drugs are an inherent evil that any self-respecting society should oppose.
[VALUE]

FIGURE 9.1 Policy Argumentative Thesis Supported by a Value Statement

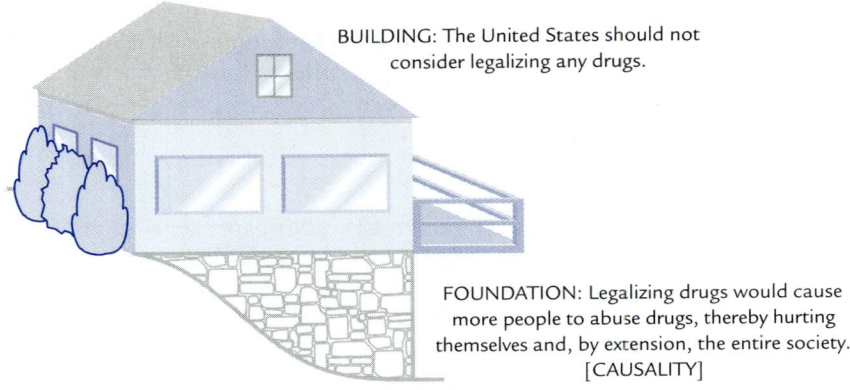

FIGURE 9.2 Policy Argumentative Thesis Supported by an Analysis of Causes

Exercise 9.3

Examine three of the sample essays from the beginning of this chapter (or essays chosen by your teacher). What is the thesis of each essay? What claim(s) does each thesis rest on? Explain.

Types of Logical Supports

Appeals to Authority As children, when we wanted our siblings to understand why they should do what we told them to do, we often resorted to authority: "Mommy said you'd better...." We knew it would mean something to our siblings if we could convince them that what we were saying carried the authority of a parent.

Appeals to authority are also a mainstay of adult argumentation. To support claims that the city council should spend tax dollars on a sports team, proponents offer testimony by an expert economist who explains the potential benefits to the city by projecting increased revenues from fans coming to see the team play. To support claims that drugs should remain illegal, advocates offer testimony of leading religious leaders or quotations from holy books that label these substances as inherently immoral.

Appeals to authority are different from the other types of support we will discuss because they focus not on *why* one is making a claim but on *who* is making this claim. If someone says, for instance, that drugs are immoral and we ask why, that person may well answer with a *who* response: "Because my minister (or spiritual teacher or church or synagogue or holy book) says that drugs are immoral." We entrust a lot of our lives to the assumptions that come with our religious, moral, or ethical heritages. We accept the truths that come to us in this way without empirical or scientific proofs; often, we do not attempt to move beyond these authorities to ask why.

Of course, such reasoning will not be convincing to those who have a different set of religious teachers and values. So, arguments resting on competing authoritative assertions of value and opinion often grind to a halt when these authorities clash with one another.

Arguments in which authority figures are used to establish the accuracy of facts and figures and causal analyses are in danger of suffering the same fate. In what has come to be a cliché, the defense attorney brings in an expert witness to say that the defendant is not responsible for the criminal action because the defendant had a horrible childhood, which led to a type of insanity that ultimately led to the crime's being committed. But the prosecutor brings in an expert witness who says that even though the defendant's childhood was indeed horrible, this childhood was not the *cause* of the criminal action, and thus the defendant should be held responsible for that action.

Will the two lawyers leave it at that? Probably not. Often, when two authorities present differing views of what caused a defendant to behave in a certain way, each side will attempt to show that its authority is more of an expert in these matters than the other. Perhaps one authority teaches at a more prestigious university, has a national following of psychologists who can testify to her expertise, or has been an expert witness in hundreds of similar court cases. In other words, the attorneys can argue over which authority is more likely to assess the situation correctly.

It should be clear that appeals to authority have their limitations. They are most effective when they are used in combination with other types of supporting evidence, such as facts and figures, opinions, examples, and personal experience.

Exercise 9.4

Examine the supports for the two sample essays dealing with politics in the classroom, "The Right Not to Listen" and "Teaching Is Always a Political Act" (see pages 414–425). What kinds of authorities do these two essays appeal to? Which essay makes more use of appeals to authority? Why do you think it does? Is this an effective strategy?

Facts and Figures   By *facts*, we mean events or actions that are verifiable. When we say, "It's a fact," we should be able to offer proof that is undeniable. It is a fact that water boils at 212 degrees Fahrenheit. How do we know? We heat water to 212 degrees Fahrenheit and watch it. In this case, the statement of fact lends itself to what we call *empirical* verification; we can see—or, to use a more scientific term, *observe*—its truth. Other facts have to be verified by means of historical record or statements from authorities. Thus, you can "prove" that there were inhabitants in North America before Columbus arrived by researching the historical record. You can establish the fact that light travels at a speed of 186,000 miles per second by resorting to the testimony of experts who have the resources to do the empirical tests that establish this fact.

Figures or statistics are a bit more complicated than facts. The truism that just about anything can be proved with statistics points to the difficulty involved in connecting statistics to the claims you want to make. You must remember that statistics do not prove anything by themselves. However, with other supports, they can be an important ingredient in argumentative writing. Statistics may be as simple as a listing of the numbers of men and women enrolled in a given college or as complicated as the data given in support of DNA testing in a court of law. But simple statistics are often more effective than complicated statistics. The writer has enough of a burden in helping his readers understand the relevance of statistics to his claim without also having to explain how the statistics were obtained and to convince readers of their correctness.

Nevertheless, statistics can be very useful tools in argumentation. For example, if you know that "the proportion of drivers fifteen to nineteen years of age who were involved in fatal crashes, and were intoxicated, dropped from 26.3 percent in 1983 to 12 percent in 1994 [. . .]" ("Research on Youth," www.charweb.org/organizations/madd/yout_res.htm), you have valuable statistical support for your claim that the legal drinking age should be twenty-one.

Opinion Statements   Although there are various types of opinion statements, as we will see, in general, opinion statements are assertions that cannot be tested empirically or established as fact by reference to historical documentation. It may seem that a position essay should contain only one opinion statement and a host of facts, statistics, and examples in support of that opinion. But that is not the way we argue—or think, for that matter.

As a simple example, imagine that we want to argue that Alfred should be elected class president. We might offer as support for our claim the opinion that Alfred is a disciplined person. If we think it necessary—as it probably is—we can offer facts in support of this opinion: Alfred made the honor roll; he established a record for the mile run at the school; and so forth. Our opinion statement (that he is a disciplined person) connects our facts about his performance in academics and athletics to our predictions about his performance as class president: We predict that the same discipline that led to his achievements in these areas will lead to achievements as class president.

Since opinion statements are crucial in argumentation, it is important that we dispel the myth that one opinion is as good as another. You may hear friends and acquaintances offer their opinions in such a way as to imply that in calling something an opinion, they immediately remove any need or possibility of evaluating that statement. In certain cases, this is true. There are at least three different kinds of opinions, represented by these three statements:

1. Murder is bad.
2. Milk tastes good.
3. Alfred is a disciplined person.

Sentence 1 is the type of opinion statement that needs no support. Anyone who would not accept this statement at face value would likely reject any supports we might offer for it. Such a person would not be the kind of reasonable reader we would be writing for. Sentence 2 is difficult to support. Even though many people like milk, that fact is support only for the assertion that many people think milk tastes good. This is a matter of personal taste—literally—and as such is the type of opinion you will do well to avoid in your arguments.

Sentence 3, about Alfred, is the type of opinion statement that will prove most useful in argumentative writing. It is not a truism, and it is a statement that lends itself to support. If we think Alfred would make a good class president, we may well think it useful to offer the opinion that he is a disciplined person. As noted, we can then offer our supports for this opinion, and the reader is free to evaluate that opinion, to see whether it seems valid or not.

Exercise 9.5

Choose a paragraph from two of the sample essays at the beginning of this chapter. List every opinion you find in these two paragraphs. Then, label them as one of the three types of opinion statements we discussed. What kinds of support for the third type of opinion statements—those needing support—are offered? What insights into these essays do you get from this analysis?

Examples We are all familiar with examples, perhaps so familiar as to sometimes overlook their power. We reason with them all the time. Most of our parents reared us on examples. They told us of horrible things that happened to little boys or girls who didn't do what their parents said. (There was one little boy—remember Pinocchio?—whose proboscis became extremely elongated because he was factually challenged. But that's another story.)

Sometimes facts and examples overlap. For instance, a person arguing for capital punishment may use as an example (and a fact) a state in which capital punishment was reinstated and the violent crime rate went down. We tend to think of something as an example rather than a fact when we view it in some detail. Many examples are stories, or we can make them into stories if we choose to do so. Stories are powerful. For example, look at the stories Jaclyn Talbert uses to introduce "Justice For Those Who Have Shown Us No Mercy." In fact, the narratives here may be labeled as examples, stories or, in the first case, as a personal experience. Regardless of how we label them, Jaclyn uses them very effectively to introduce her essay in a dramatic fashion and, at the same time, provide support for her claim that individuals who commit the most heinous types of crimes should be sentenced to death.

Personal Experience As Jaclyn's essay illustrates, personal experiences can be very effective in argumentative writing. In the past, you may have been reluctatnt to use personal experiences in this type of writing, assuming that arguments must be supported by only logical proofs. It is certainly true that your arguments cannot rest entirely on personal experience; however, personal experience can be a powerful tool in argumentation. One of the most persuasive argumentative essays ever written, Dr. Martin Luther King, Jr.'s "Letter from Birmingham Jail," contains the following powerful passage, built on personal experience:

> [. . .] Perhaps it is easy for those who have never felt the stinging darts of segregation to say, "Wait." But when you have seen vicious mobs lynch your mothers and fathers at will and drown your sisters and brothers at whim; when you have seen hate-filled policemen curse, kick, and even kill your black brothers and sisters; when you see the vast majority of your twenty million Negro brothers smothering in an airtight cage of poverty in the midst of an affluent society; when you suddenly find your tongue twisted and your speech stammering as you seek to explain to your six-year-old daughter why she can't go to the public amusement park that has just been advertised on television, and see tears welling up in her eyes when she is told that Funtown is closed to colored children, and see ominous clouds of inferiority beginning to form in her little mental sky, and see her beginning to distort her personality by developing an unconscious bitterness toward white people, [. . .] then you will understand why we find it difficult to wait.

Ethical Stance

We said that the primary distinguishing feature of a position essay is logical argumentation. A second, and very important, characteristic of a successful position essay is the writer's ethical stance. A key to that is her fairness. She must make it clear that she knows and respects arguments on the other side.

An analogy that comes to mind in thinking about the stance of the writer of a position essay involves the art of fencing. In fencing, the two combatants begin with a ceremonial touching of swords, in which they symbolize respect for the sharpness of their blades and for each other's skill in the art of fencing. They proceed to thrust and parry, each attempting to gain advantage over the other. Unlike a street brawl, however, in which any means of conquering the opponent would be used—kicking, throwing sand in the face, or pulling hair—the fencing contest is carried out under the strictest rules of fairness. The hand not holding the sword is held behind the back to symbolize the contestant's commitment to fair play and honest competition. Each combatant wishes to win the match, but also wants to be sure that in doing so neither she nor her opponent is demeaned.

ASSIGNMENT AND GUIDELINES FOR WRITING

Assignment

Write a paper in which you state and support your position on an issue about which reasonable people can disagree.

Choosing a Topic

The exercises in Part A should help you find and begin to examine your topic. If you think you already know the topic about which you want to write, skip to Part B.

Part A
1. Begin your search for a topic by thinking of two or three issues about which you feel strongly. If issues do not come to mind immediately, consult your responses to the Interest Inventory (pages 11–13), looking especially at the sections dealing with school, work, and society. Or you may find potential topics in your responses to the "Writing Opportunity" assignments in this chapter. For each potential topic you have uncovered, freewrite for ten minutes or so.
2. After you have written about your potential topics, answer the following questions about each one:
   a. What is the topic?
   b. What is your stance on it; what opinion do you hold about it?
   c. How did you come to think this way? How did you develop this stance?

Part B
Pick one topic that you feel strongly about. Think of someone you know and respect who might take an opposing point of view on this topic. Spend a few minutes describing this person, including his or her political leanings, home life (the neighborhood in which the person lives, for example), job, and so on. Then spend ten minutes freewriting on your topic from this person's perspective. After you have finished writing, answer these two questions:

1. Are you sufficiently interested in this topic to write about it?
2. Are you able to look at the topic from the perspective of your opponent?

If you can answer both questions affirmatively, this is probably a good topic for you to write about. You are ready to move on to consider what about the topic interests you most and what the best arguments for the opposing position are. Otherwise, respeat this exercise, using a different potential topic.

Collecting Information

Questions for Analysis If you have selected a topic that you care about, chances are you already know a good deal about it. However, in order to have the credibility you are going to need for this writing situation, you may want to learn more. To see what you already know about your topic, it may be helpful to ask the questions of association, opposition, sequence, and consequence presented in Chapter 1 (pages 24–31); in particular, it may be helpful to focus on issues of definition and cause as they relate to your position.

Key Values As we've discussed above, one way to provide a foundation for your argument is to appeal to key values. You should determine which of your key values are relevant to your argument and what your reader's response will be to those values. In most cases, your reader will not completely dismiss the values you believe in—just as you will not dismiss your reader's values—but he probably will assign different priorities to those values. For example, if you are writing in favor of gun control, those on the other side will agree with you that safety is important.

However, their commitment to freedom and living in a free country will take precedence over their concern for safety. Once you have determined the differences between the two sides by analyzing key values, you will have a better sense of how to proceed in your argument. Below is an analysis of key values for the gun-control example.

> *Topic: Gun Control*
>
> *Thesis:* U.S. citizens should not be allowed to own guns unless they have a need for them in their professions (such as law enforcement) or in hunting activities.
>
> *Values Relevant to My Argument*
>
> *My key values:*
> Freedom—one of many good things that we should strive for. It can be a bad thing when it endangers other individuals.
> Government control—a good thing when it promotes the good of a society. A bad thing when it takes away citizens' rights for no reason.
> Safety and protection—a very desirable goal worth sacrificing for
>
> *My reader's key values:*
> Freedom—a basic human right that is to be guarded with great diligence
> Government control—inherently evil because governments are inherently evil. They take freedoms away from individuals.
> Safety and protection—one of many good things we should strive for. It cannot be allowed to take precedence over freedom.

Key Causal Assertions Our second major foundation for arguments is causal reasoning. You can generate material for your essay by exploring the types of causal statements you might want to use as your foundation and predicting your reader's responses to these causal assertions. Because it is extremely hard to prove that one thing causes another, agreement about causes and effects is difficult to achieve. Still, it is very important to gain insight into disagreements between you and your reader about causes. You may argue that more controls should be placed on the sale of guns because you believe that such controls will cause a decrease in gunshot injuries and deaths. Your reader may disagree. How, you may wonder. It seems obvious that fewer guns would result in fewer accidents and more guns would result in more accidents, right? The problem here may arise because your reader does not agree with a causal claim that you haven't even asserted because it seems so obvious to you. You believe that stricter gun laws will surely result in fewer guns. But your reader may disagree, arguing that guns will always be available to those who want them and that making something illegal only makes people want it more. Once you realize how you and your reader differ on the causal claims you associate with this thesis, you can begin to plan your strategy for supporting your claims.

> *Topic: Gun Control*
>
> *Thesis:* U.S. citizens should not be allowed to own guns unless they have a need for them in their professions (such as law enforcement) or in hunting activities.

Causal Claims Relevant to My Argument

Analysis of My Causal Claims
   A desire to protect citizens causes authority figures to create gun laws
   Gun control laws cause a reduction in accidental deaths
   Gun control laws cause a reduction of violence in our society
   Gun control laws cause a reduction in the number of armed robberies

Analysis of My Reader's Causal Claims
   A desire to control our lives and take away freedoms causes authority figures to create gun laws
   Gun control laws do not cause a reduction in accidental deaths
   Gun control laws do not cause a reduction of violence in our society
   Gun control laws do not cause a reduction in the number of armed robberies

Imaginary Dialogue   Another useful strategy in generating information for a position essay is an *imaginary dialogue,* a conversation you create between two people who disagree about an arguable topic. Below is such a conversation that Ron wrote, imagining what he and his reader might say to each other about gun-control laws.

   Topic: Gun Control
   Imaginary dialogue:
   Me: We certainly need stronger gun laws in this country.
   Counterpart: We already have way too many laws about too many things, and the laws don't do anything but restrict the freedoms of those people who are willing to abide by laws.
   Me: I don't see how you can say that, given the increase in crimes in which guns are used. In this city alone, we have had a tremendous increase in armed robberies in the last few years.
   Counterpart: What makes you think that controlling guns will lower the number of armed robberies? People who are going to rob are not worried about laws against owning guns.
   Me: But the laws will make it harder for them to get guns. It's not that they are trying to obey laws, but laws do control the flow of any product. So laws would make it harder for them to get guns in the first place. And the laws would also make it easier to trace guns used by criminals.
   Counterpart: Why? Given the fact that our borders are absolutely porous and given the fact that making guns illegal will increase the profits to be made on selling guns, why should we think that making guns illegal will make it harder for people to get them? If anything, it might increase the supply of guns. Look at what is happening with drugs. Does anyone think that our laws are keeping drugs out of the hands of those who really want them? And for that matter, look back at the Prohibition saga. All these laws do is to restrict the rights of law-abiding citizens, increase profits for those who want to traffic in illegal goods, and, perhaps, create a nuisance for those who want the contraband. But if they want the contraband badly enough, they will find a way to get it.
   Me: So you are arguing that the government shouldn't control any substance, or good, at all—that the citizens should be able to get anything they want?

Counterpart: Well, I would say there are some things that should be controlled by governments, but not many. I don't like the government protecting me where I don't need protecting.

Me: So where would you say the government should protect citizens?

Counterpart: I'd say that harmful products should be regulated when it comes to children. Children should not be able to buy pornography, to buy drugs that might harm them, and so forth.

Me: So that's all? Governments should not protect us from ourselves otherwise?

Counterpart: No, it's more complicated than that. I'd say that the government should protect us from such things as nuclear devices. The ordinary citizen should not be able to get his hands on a nuclear device that could destroy thousands or millions of people.

Me: So the government should protect us from nuclear destruction, but it should not protect us from a maniac down the street walking into a store and buying a handgun that he can use to kill me the next time he cuts me off in traffic and I object. Won't I be just as dead whether I'm killed by a nuclear device or by a handgun owned by someone who has no business having one? Where do we draw the line? If governments are in the business of protecting citizens, why should they not try to protect me from the idiot down the street?

Counterpart: There are several ways to answer you here. We can start by saying that I am not absolutely sure where to draw this line between what governments should try to accomplish and what they should not try to accomplish. However, that does not mean that there is no such line or that I should not continue to try to find it. I'm reminded of the logical rule of thumb called the argument of the beard. A person asks how many hairs it takes to make a beard. The answer comes back, "I don't know." The questioner then asks, "So you don't know the difference between a man with a beard and a man without one?" To which the second person responds, "The fact that I don't know where exactly to draw a line doesn't mean there is no line." Let me move on to another answer. Surely it would be a good thing to protect your life from both, from the person who would attempt to blow up your whole city with a nuclear device and from the person who would kill you over a traffic disagreement. However, it is much harder to protect you from the kind of random violence represented by the latter case than from the terrorist groups that might try to steal nuclear weapons. The government may be able to keep tabs on certain groups, but it cannot control the behavior of every individual citizen—not and maintain a free country. And that brings me to a third point. The more authority we give governments to protect us, the more of our lives we have to give them in return. If we have a law that says that someone cannot own a gun, how do we enforce it? Do we undertake routine checks like the routine license checks we now have? Would you be willing to submit to an unwarranted search of your car any time you go out for a Sunday afternoon drive?

Me: Well, I might. But I'm not sure. You have given me a good deal to think about. We'll have to continue this conversation later on, since I have to finish writing this chapter. Thanks.

Focus Statement

As you begin to generate information for your essay, look back over your freewriting and write a brief statement about the focal point of your essay. It should include a tentative thesis statement, which simply states the issue and the side you are taking. It should also suggest the claims you will use as the foundation for your thesis and how you will counter major objections to your position. Here is a sample focus statement for a paper on the issue of putting a basketball arena in uptown Charlotte:

> I am in favor of a basketball arena in uptown Charlotte. I believe that cities are healthier when they have a clearly defined center. Since Charlotte already has a major football stadium in its uptown, the addition of the basketball arena will help to solidify the uptown as the center of a major city. I am aware that this project will require some tax dollars and that many people will object to raises in taxes to support this project. I am not sure that we will have to raise taxes, if our priorities are clear—I will look into this question in my paper and see what I think. Even if we do have to raise taxes, I think the benefits in terms of the local economy will offset that—I will look into this matter in some detail. The benefits to the average citizen can be many. A vibrant uptown will make this a much more desirable city to live in—I may want to talk about some cities that have such uptowns and describe them a bit. In addition, the traffic flow of the outerbelt can be designed with this center city in mind, and the positive effect on the daily commute of all commuting citizens will be payoff enough for this project.

Planning Your Essay's Structure

In a position essay, you will assume a reader who takes an opposing point of view. Thus, the overall structure of your essay will be provided by the argument mode, which is based on thesis and support: You make an assertion (which will be the essay's thesis) and then spend the rest of the essay showing *why* that thesis should be accepted or believed. This is very general, of course. As you think about the overall shape of your essay, you may find it useful to look at the argument structure in more detail. To help you do so, we will explore two separate structures—one informal, the other formal.

Informal Argument Structure The informal argument structure includes a thesis, support for that thesis, and answers to the arguments that are put forward by the other side. The following plan for a position essay in favor of raising taxes on tobacco uses this informal argument structure:

   I. A *thesis statement* (with "should"): Taxes should be raised on tobacco products.
  II. A list of reasons (or claims) that indicate why one should accept this thesis
    A. *Cause:* Raising taxes will decrease smoking.
    B. *Value:* Taxing "sins" is a good thing.

III. Supporting information for those reasons
   A. 1. Statistics about drops in smoking in other countries that have increased taxes on tobacco, such as Canada
      2. Statements of opinion from authority figures: psychologists, on failure of health concerns to make people modify behavior
      3. Statistics about the role money plays in causing people to take action
      4. Personal experience as to why the writer quit smoking
   B. 1. Statistics on amount of money the government spends on health problems caused by cigarettes
      2. Statistics on numbers of underage people currently smoking
IV. Counterarguments to the reasons your counterpart will offer for her position
   A. 1. *Argument:* This is another case of the government running our lives.
      2. *Counter:* We run our lives, but if we run them in such a way that the government has to pay for our mistakes, the government has a right to charge us.
   B. 1. *Argument:* This is another tax aimed at the poor.
      2. *Counter:* This is not aimed at the poor, but admittedly will hit them harder—since a larger percentage of their paycheck will be required to keep smoking. It would be good if this did not have to happen. But to put the financial burden on the well-off would not be fair. And if this were done, some would say it is just another example of society's lack of concern for the poor—let them kill themselves if they want to. So, there is no winning this kind of debate. But if lives are saved—as they will be—it is worth it.

The "Should" Thesis We strongly suggest that you include the word "should" when you state your thesis for your position essay. In doing so, you will be stating a policy argument as opposed to an argument supporting a claim of value or a claim of cause. While it is possible to limit yourself to a claim of value or cause, in doing so you run the risk of stopping short of the real point you want to make regarding your position. For example, you could argue that "professional sports teams cause increases in taxes for those cities that have such teams." This is a clear claim of cause and you could spend an entire essay in supporting this claim. However, it would be possible for a reader to understand and accept your argument about this cause/effect relationship yet assert that you haven't made it clear that you oppose any efforts of your city leaders to procure professional sports. Such a reader may agree that the teams cause taxes to rise, yet he may argue that the good that a professional team will bring—increased business for the city, charitable activities of the players and their spouses, and so forth—will cause improvement in the quality of life of citizens in your city. And besides, he may assert, the taxes in your city are really quite low for a major metropolis. If you oppose any attempt to bring a professional sports team to your city, you can make your position absolutely clear with a thesis that states a policy argument: "Our city leaders should oppose acquisition of any major sports teams."

> **Exercise 9.6**
>
> Identify each of the following claims as cause or value and then write a policy statement (with a "should") that each could support. Then identify other claims that could support that policy statement.
>
> *Example:* Lowering taxes in this city will cause an increase in the number of businesses locating here.
>
> Clearly this is a causal claim. The obvious policy statement one would associate with this claim is, "We should lower taxes in this city." Such an argument might include other claims such as, "Our current taxes are too high" (value) and "An increase in the number of businesses will cause an increase in tax revenue" (cause).
>
> 1. Cloning is immoral.
> 2. Prostitution is a sin.
> 3. Cheating on one's taxes is unethical.
> 4. A good system of higher education will improve the economy in this state.
> 5. Car telephones have contributed to a rise in the number of fatal accidents in our state.

Reasons (Claims)   Assuming that you have written a thesis that contains a policy argument, your next step is to identify the claims that explain your reasons for adopting this position. These reasons will be stated as claims of value or claims of cause. For example, you might argue in favor of increasing efforts to rid a city of prostitution because

> prostitution is wrong (evil, or immoral) (*value*)
> and/or
> prostitution has other undesirable consequences (such as increased traffic in drugs or loss of business for uptown merchants) (*cause*)

Of course, these claims will be made in various ways, and in many cases the type of claim being made doesn't become clear until we translate these claims into sentences that have a specific value or causal assertion. For example, you might say that prostitution should not be tolerated because laws should protect us from such things as prostitution. In doing so, you are likely making a claim based on a value assuming that paying for sex is evil by definition. You could have written, "Prostitution should be banned because it is inherently evil." This is a very clear claim of value.

Another possible argument would be that prostitution should not be tolerated because sexually transmitted diseases are on the rise in the community. In this case, you would be making a claim based on a causal argument; your assumption is that prostitution is responsible, at least in part, for the rise in sexually transmitted diseases.

> **Exercise 9.7**
>
> Below we offer several claims that might be given in support of "should" theses. In each case, explain whether the claim is based on value or causality. Are there cases in which both cause and value are implicit in one claim?
>
> 1. *Thesis:* Citizens of this state should not vote for Senator X.
>   *Claim:* He is the pawn of special interests such as the tobacco lobby.
> 2. *Thesis:* We should abolish capital punishment.
>   *Claim:* We do not have the right to play God.
> 3. *Thesis:* Euthanasia should be legal.
>   *Claim:* It is inhumane to make individuals continue to suffer when there is no quality to their lives.
> 4. *Thesis:* You should support the school bond issue.
>   *Claim:* Education is crucial if society is going to make the progress necessary for the survival of the human race.
> 5. *Thesis:* The referendum on a state lottery should be defeated.
>   *Claim:* The state should not encourage gambling.

Support Claims of value and cause may be supported by appeals to authority, facts and statistics, opinion statements, examples, and personal experience. For example, the last claim in Exercise 9.7 is based on causality. The claim is that state lotteries cause people to gamble more than they would if there were no lottery. This is a debatable claim. Those who oppose this argument may believe that gamblers will find a means to gamble, whether they live in a state with a lottery or not. So, how will the writer support her claim? She could search for data on gambling in states with lotteries. She might cite the amount of money collected in lotteries and ask readers to assume that not all of this money would have been spent on gambling had there been no lottery. She could also search to see whether there have been in-depth studies on the matter. If she could find surveys about gambling habits suggesting that people gamble more when states have lotteries, she could bolster her argument greatly. Finally, she might share any personal information she has on gambling and the influence that lotteries have on gambling.

Here is an overview of the types of support Michael Haley offers in his essay, "The Right Not to Listen" (pages 414–419).

Thesis: Students should have the right not to have to listen to teachers' personal political biases in a required college class

Claim 1 *Value*
Freedom of "hearing" is a key value for humans

Support

Opinion: Freedom of Speech and Freedom of Hearing are inextricably bound together—two sides of the same coin.

Opinion: One doesn't have real speech unless one has a listener
Value: We should value freedom of speech as a key part of what it means to be human
Cause: To deprive one of his/her freedom of speech would cause damage to that person's mental health
Cause: If humans lose freedom of speech, it could cause them not to survive as a species
Cause: the freedom to speak of and consider ideas gives rise to human intelligence

Claim 2 *Value*
Forcing people to listen to ideas they find offensive is an abuse of the human will.

Support
Opinion: "Hearing" and "listening" are not the same thing; listening requires an act of free will
Value: It is wrong to keep someone for enacting his/her free will

Claim 3 *Value*
Forcing students to listen to an advocacy for a political opinion they disagree with is grossly unfair.

Support
Fact: Students in required classes in large university have no choice (or little) as to whether to take that particular class or not
Cause: Making a student listen to powerful advocates of points of view they disagree with will do damage to the personality of students
Opinion: Making students listen to ideas they disagree with because it is good for them is paternalistic
Fact: Students in college are adults

Claim 4 *Cause*
Teachers who force students to listen to their political opinions will lose their ability to teach students anything about thinking

Support
Offers none; seems to assume that once they think about his, readers will agree with him

Exercise 9.8

Using as a model our analysis of the types of support offered in Haley's essay, choose one of the other essays in this chapter (or one selected by your instructor) and analyze the types of support the writer uses.

Counterarguments In arguing successfully, it is crucial to understand how your reader would structure her argument. If you want to argue that your city should not support a major sports team ("should" thesis) because doing so would cost the city a lot of money and thus cause an increase in taxes (claim), what will your counterpart say? We know what her thesis will be, since it will be the direct opposite of yours: The city *should* support a major sports team. Now, what kind of reasons can she offer? She can, and in most cases will, disagree with your causal claim. She may believe that although the team will require money from the city, it will also generate increased revenues for the city, which will offset those costs; thus, the team will not cause an increase in taxes—in the most optimistic case, it will allow for a reduction in taxes. Your task is to anticipate the supports your reader will offer for her claim (in this case, that increased revenues will offset the costs). Perhaps you know that she is likely to refer to another city where the acquisition of a new sports team did not cause an increase in taxes for the citizens. Your task in this situation is to show why your city is not like that other city.

However, your reader is not obligated to disagree with your causal claim. She could agree with your assessment that this sports team will cause an increase in taxes but argue that taxes are relatively low at present and that the benefits a team will bring—such as more jobs, more recreational opportunities for citizens, and a sense of pride and identity—will offset this increase in taxes. In a case such as this, your reader is accepting your analysis of cause but is shifting the ground (the foundation) on which the argument is being waged. You want to ground your argument on cost, but your reader is looking to other grounds, such as city pride and increased jobs.

Your argument will be strengthened if you can anticipate such shifts in ground and be prepared to counter them. You may show why cost *is* the crucial ground for the argument. How much do citizens in your city pay in taxes, and how does their tax rate compare with rates in other major cities? You may also want to counter the claims your reader makes in her counter argument. For example, if she claims that sports teams bring about a feeling of pride and unity, you might refer to riots that have broken out when a sports team has won a championship and suggest that your city can do without such "pride."

Exercise 9.9

Choose one of the essays in this chapter or an essay selected by your instructor, and analyze the way in which the writer anticipates and responds to the counterarguments of the other side.

Formal Argument Structure The more formal argument structure we will examine is often called *classical argument*. It comes to us from the classical rhetoricians, who divided argument into six parts:

exordium—the writer captures the reader's attention
narratio—the writer offers background information
partitio—the writer states the argument
confirmatio—the writer makes the case for his position
confutatio—the writer offers refutation of major arguments against his position
peroratio—the writer concludes the argument

In practice, very few writers follow the classical structure completely. The attention they give to the individual sections varies greatly, and at times certain parts are left out. For example a person arguing in favor (or against) capital punishment may spend very little time on the *narratio,* preferring to devote most of his attention to constructing his argument (*confirmatio*) and countering the argument of those who would oppose him (*confutatio*). This structure seems very appropriate in a society that has had the lengthy discussion of this topic that ours has; most readers will need little review of the background. However, a person arguing in favor of a new stadium for a professional basketball team might spend a relatively large portion of her essay in reviewing the background of this team and this city in order to set the stage for her readers. In doing so, she might decide to devote less time to counterarguments, feeling that her readers will be more likely to accept her arguments if she sets a context for those arguments than if she spends her time refuting the arguments of those opposed to an arena.

Writers of argument essays do not follow any model (classical or otherwise) slavishly. Even when they do include all the parts of a classical argument, they do not necessarily present those parts in a prescribed order. For example, let's examine the structure of two arguments at the beginning of this chapter. Michael Haley's essay, "The Right Not to Listen," follows the classical structure very closely. However, David Amante's essay, "Teaching Is Always a Political Act" is very different. He introduces his subject quite clearly in paragraph one. He then spends the next eleven paragraphs setting the context for his argument, with a brief pause at the beginning of paragraph 4 to assert which side of the issue he will defend. Most of his real arguing is done in the story that he tells (*narratio*), which is actually divided into three sections. In paragraphs 2 and 3, he sets a context for his argument by explaining a crucial distinction between empirical and institutional facts; in paragraph 4 he outlines the writing program at his university to provide a background against which to view his teaching goals; and in paragraphs 5–12, he narrates the story of what happened at his university and what he did in his classes at the beginning of the war with Iraq. By the time he gets to his *confirmatio,* he is able to state his argument very briefly. In the last paragraph, he recognizes the fact that there are those who would disagree with him, (*confutation*), but he spends no time in refuting their argument directly, assuming that the story he has told will make it clear why he disagrees with their point of view. He then ends the essay (*peroratio*) with an appeal to the Constitution for the support of his pedagogy.

Below we analyze each of the arguments using the terms of classical argument structure:

Michael Haley, "The Right Not to Listen"
Exordium—paragraph 1
Narratio—paragraphs 2 through 5
Partitio—paragraph 6 through sentence 1 of paragraph 10
Confirmatio—sentence 2 of paragraph 10 through paragraph 23
Confutatio—paragraph 24
Peroratio—paragraph 25

David Amante, "Teaching Is Always a Political Act"
Exordium—paragraph 1
Narratio—paragraphs 2, 3, and paragraph 4, sentence 3 through paragraph 12
Partitio—paragraph 4, sentences 1 and 2
Confirmatio—paragraphs 13 through 16
Confutatio—*paragraph 17, sentences 1 through 5
Peroratio—paragraph 17, sentences 6 and 7

* We are here defining "sentence" as that which comes between periods—so "No." would be a sentence.

Exercise 9.10

After examining the structure of the two essays outlined above, use the formal argument structure as a means of analyzing one of the other sample essays or an essay selected by your instructor. Then discuss how the writer's purpose dictates the essay's structure.

Thesis Statement

Since it is crucial to know your thesis early in the argument process, you should have decided on it by this time. If you are writing a policy argument, be sure you have included "should" as a part of your formal thesis statement.

Checking for Logical Fallacies

Your opponents can challenge your argument in many ways. It isn't possible to write an irrefutable argument if you are dealing with a debatable topic. However, you can avoid discrediting yourself and your position by making sure your argument is valid. Your argument will be valid if you do two things: (1) offer support for claims that need support and (2) connect your claims logically to your thesis. If you say that a new stadium should be built because it will enhance the economy of the uptown, you must support this claim. Your reader will see the logical connection between the claim (that the new stadium will enhance the economy of the uptown) and your thesis (that the stadium should be built). If, however, you argue that a new stadium should be built because professional sports build character in the young people who play them, you have a problem of validity—of connection between claim and thesis. Opponents may argue that even though this is true, it is not reason enough to pay the money that such teams will require. Arguments can go wrong in many ways, but the overriding problem for the writer is a failure to look at arguments from the perspective of the reader. You may think that the only way to have a major sports team in the city is to build a new stadium, but if your reader does not see the connection between a new stadium and getting a sports team, she may well reject your argument that the city should build a new stadium.

Offering an argument that is worthy of your reader's consideration means constructing an argument free of logical fallacies. As you refine your essay, be sure you aren't guilty of any reasoning errors. There are many different ways to categorize such logical fallacies. We choose to group them into three types: fallacies of irrelevance, causal fallacies, and fallacies of definition.

Fallacies of Irrelevance   As we've noted, you may support your claims by reference to authority, facts and figures, examples, opinion statements, and personal experience. However, if these supports are to be effective, they must be clearly connected to the claims you are making. Failure to make this connection will result in one or more of the following logical fallacies: *argumentum ad hominem,* stereotyping, bandwagon fallacy, *argumentum ad ignorantiam,* or hasty generalization.

Argumentum ad Hominem   The fallacy of *argumentum ad hominem* involves name-calling, or arguing by attacking a person instead of an issue. When a speaker attacks a person rather than speaking to the issue at hand, the attack is irrelevant. For example, a politician may argue that her opponent should not be elected because he has been divorced, but if the politician fails to show how this "fact" is related to the thesis—that one should not vote for her opponent—she is making an error of relevance and reducing her chances of convincing her audience.

This is not to suggest that facts concerning a politician are never relevant to questions of whether that politician should serve in an office; the fact that a candidate for county treasurer has been convicted of embezzlement is certainly relevant. Our point is that in writing an argument, you must be sure that your audience sees how the facts you present are relevant to the question at hand.

Stereotyping   We are guilty of stereotyping when we attempt to attribute certain characteristics to an individual by placing her in a certain group—often, but not always, a racial, ethnic, or religious group. Examples of stereotypical thinking include the following: Girls do well in English, whereas boys do well in mathematics; civil servants are plodding, bureaucratic types who do not really care for people. An example of reasoning by stereotype is "I wouldn't hire her; she belongs to some strange religious group." The assumption underlying such a statement is that this person's membership in the group will have some bearing on the way she performs the job. Of course, if the person offering this argument can show that the religious group in question believes that employees should undermine their capitalistic employers, he can show the relevance of this fact. Otherwise, it is irrelevant.

Bandwagon Fallacy   We often see the bandwagon fallacy in advertisements: "Kangaroos have outsold the competition for two consecutive years. When are you going to drive a Kangaroo?" The argument offers no relevant reason for buying this type of car. It could be that many people are buying Kangaroos because they are well-built cars. However, it could also be that many people are buying Kangaroos because they have been convinced that many people are buying Kangaroos. The advertisement asks us to do something without giving us a good reason for doing it.

Argumentum ad Ignorantiam   The phrase *argumentum ad ignorantiam* can be translated as "argument from ignorance." The error occurs when the writer fails to take responsibility for his supporting assertions. Children are noted for this type of reasoning: "My dad is Superman; you can't prove he isn't." The U.S. court system has declared that a defendant's failure to prove his innocence is irrelevant to the question of whether he is in fact innocent—thus the maxim "innocent until proven guilty." When arguing, the one who asserts is responsible for supporting those assertions with relevant information.

Hasty Generalization   The fallacy of hasty generalization results when a writer moves too quickly from specific information—such as facts, figures, and personal experience—to conclusion. For example, consider a person who has never seen a cat. If that person then sees three black cats and generalizes from this personal experience that all cats are black, she will be guilty of hasty generalization. The fact that cats A, B, and C are black does not give the necessary support for the conclusion that all cats are black. That one person happened upon three black cats is irrelevant to the color of cats.

Similarly, consider the argument "Boxing is safer than football, because each year twice as many football players as boxers are injured." A close examination of these statistics would show that they are irrelevant to the question of safety in the two sports because the number of people who play football is much larger than the number of people who box.

It is important to note here that generalizing is indispensable to learning; if we could not generalize, we would not be able to learn anything new. Furthermore, there is no way to be absolutely sure that we always make correct predictions. Consider again the person who has never seen a cat. What if the person now sees a hundred cats and all of them have four legs? Wouldn't she be in a position to generalize that all nondeformed cats are born with four legs? She can't be sure (absolutely) of this generalization, but she would feel relatively confident in making it. Of course, it is conceivable, though highly unlikely, that the first hundred cats this person sees will be black. In this case, although her generalization that all cats are black will still not be correct, at least she will not have made the leap from one or two specific instances to the generalization.

Exercise 9.11

The following is the first paragraph of "For Pollsters, 'More' Doesn't Always Mean 'Better'" by John Shelton Reed:

> Just before the election of 1936, *The Literary Digest*, a widely read and influential magazine, announced the results of its presidential preference poll. The New Deal was going to be repudiated; FDR would be swept out of office. Alf Landon would be the next president, taking nearly 60 percent of the two-party popular vote. The announcement was made with a great deal of hoopla. The Digest quoted a reference to itself as an "oracle, which, since 1920, has foretold with almost uncanny accuracy the choice of the nation's voters...." And, after all, hadn't they mailed out over 10 million "secret ballots" to voters all over the nation, after ransacking tax rolls, telephone directories, automobile registration and magazine subscription lists for names? And hadn't they heard from more than 20 percent of the nation's voters in return?

Of course, President Roosevelt won by a large margin. Explain in a paragraph any logical fallacies you see in the reasoning of those who conducted the poll.

Causal Fallacies   Given how difficult it is to prove that one thing causes another, it is little wonder that many arguments fail because readers cannot accept the causal statements that are offered. When working with causality, you must be careful to give your readers insight into the reasoning that underlies your causal assertions. If you say that Alfred will be a good class president because he earns good grades, you should be aware of the assumptions that led you to accept this causal statement. A spokesperson for another candidate may well argue that Alfred's good grades are a sign that he will work too hard at being a good student to pay the proper attention to his role as president. You could support your statement by providing examples of individuals who have been good presidents (in the opinions of students and faculty) and who have had good grades, by offering your opinion that the same intelligence and discipline that cause Alfred to earn good grades will cause him to be a good president, or, perhaps, by presenting the opinions of authority figures. You cannot simply make this causal statement and expect your audience to accept it at face value.

As this example illustrates, a writer can fall prey to faulty causal reasoning by assuming a cause-and-effect relationship when his audience is unwilling to make such an assumption. Let's examine three specific types of faulty causal reasoning.

Post Hoc, Propter Hoc (After this, because of this)   As the translation of the Latin phrase indicates, this most basic causal fallacy occurs when one assumes that just because event B came after event A, event A is the cause of event B. A black cat may cross one's path and that person may subsequently have bad luck. But why should he think the cat caused the bad luck? Of course, the logic of cause and effect dictates that causes exist prior to (before) effects; thus, we always look for chronological connections to see whether we can establish causal connections. If we become ill soon after we eat at a certain restaurant *every time* we eat at that restaurant, and if we find that that restaurant has a very low health code rating, we may tend to assume a causal connection between the event (eating at the restaurant) and the effect (becoming sick). This reasoning is very different from a *post hoc, propter hoc* statement, such as "I would never go to that restaurant; I went there one time and was sick for the next three days."

Oversimplification   The writer who focuses on one of several causes of a phenomenon as *the* cause of that phenomenon is oversimplifying. A classic example of this error in reasoning occurs when a motorist claims that the motorist in front caused an accident by failing to signal for a turn before she stopped to wait for oncoming traffic. Certainly, failure to signal could be a contributing cause of such an accident. However, would the accident have occurred if the following motorist had been traveling at a proper speed and distance from the first car, had been paying careful attention to his driving, and had been operating a car with no mechanical defects? Probably not. In these circumstances, the following motorist would likely have been able to stop in time even though the leading motorist failed to signal. The person who blames the high price of petroleum on the greed of large oil companies, on conflicts in the Middle East, on the policies of a particular administration, or on any other *one* cause is guilty of the same type of oversimplified causal reasoning.

When framing arguments, you will do well to resist the temptation to find *the* cause of any complicated event or human situation. Things are not usually so simple. We are not suggesting, however, that you must account for all the potential causes of any one event. For example, there is a sense in which the invention of the automobile is a cause for any auto accident, but that cause is so far removed from the effect as not to be a valid factor. How, then, do you decide which causes are appropriate to an analysis? There is no easy way to answer this question, but there are three distinctions among causes that may help you make the decision concerning their relevance. A cause may be seen as necessary, sufficient, or contributory.

A *necessary cause* is one that is essential to produce the effect. In the hypothetical car accident, negligence on the part of the following driver is a necessary cause for the accident. He was driving too fast or too close to the car in front, was not paying proper attention to the situation, or had failed to maintain his car properly. In a more literal sense, both cars are necessary causes for the accident. In this sense, of course, it is also necessary for the car in front to come to a stop.

A *sufficient cause* is one capable of producing the effect. In our example, any of several errors on the part of the following driver is sufficient to cause the accident.

No matter what other factors are present—no matter how carefully the first driver signals or how carefully the second driver is watching the situation—if the second car is too close to the first car, the crash is going to occur. Thus, following too closely is a sufficient cause for the accident. (Of course, there is a sense in which this cause is not sufficient without a stop on the part of the driver in front; however, we are treating the stop of the first car as a given here, because at some time a stop must occur.)

In addition to the necessary and sufficient causes we have examined for our hypothetical accident, there may be *contributing causes.* The brakes of the following car may not be as effective as they were when the car was new, and these less than optimal brakes may be a contributing cause to the accident. If they are not severely deficient, however, they are not a sufficient cause for the accident, because they would have stopped the car if the driver had been thoroughly attentive and driving at a safe speed and at a proper distance.

In sum, you would be well advised not to say what *the* cause of an event or a situation is unless you can show that that cause is necessary for the effect. You must also be aware that any effect will have many more contributing causes than you can possibly treat; thus, you should devote most of your energies to necessary and sufficient causes.

The Either/Or Dilemma   A specific type of oversimplification, the either/or dilemma occurs when a writer pretends that only two causes or two effects exist when multiple causes or effects exist. For example, consider the statement "Either the allocation for education in the state budget must be held at its present level, or the taxpayers are going to have to pay more taxes in the future." This either/or statement is based on the following assumed causal relations: Allocating more money for education causes taxes to be raised to pay for that education budget; not allocating more money for education requires no higher taxes. However, these are not the only possible causes of these effects. Taxes could be raised even if the amount of money spent on education were not increased. Other factors, such as increased expenditures for welfare and unemployment compensation, could cause a need for increased taxation. There may also be other effects of these causes. For example, an increased budget for education will not necessarily increase the overall tax burden of citizens. If the increased expenditure on education produces more people who are capable of assuming jobs and, thus, more people who are paying taxes, individual taxpayers may end up paying lower taxes at some time in the future. Also, if the increased expenditure on education ultimately causes fewer people to need welfare or unemployment compensation, this increase in funds could be balanced by a decrease in the amount of money needed for these services.

Our purpose here is not to prove that the statement given as our example is patently false; it could be that increased monies spent on education will require increases in taxation. Rather, our point is to demonstrate the oversimplification found in either/or statements. Sophisticated readers will not find them convincing.

Exercise 9.12

Find and explain the errors in causal reasoning in the statements below.

Example: Detroit automakers say they are building better cars, and it must be so, for since 1973 the number of highway deaths has decreased significantly.

Explanation: This is a rather obvious case of oversimplification. Automakers may be building better cars, but many other factors may be contributing to the decrease in highway deaths. A very important factor that must be taken into account is the reduction of the maximum highway speed to 55 miles per hour, which occurred in 1974 and continued in most states until 1987. Other factors, such as safe-driving campaigns and reductions in travel due to increased fuel costs, may also have been causes.

1. The spouses of successful business executives wear expensive clothing, so the best way to help your spouse be successful in business is to buy expensive clothing.
2. Mr. Smith will surely support the ERA. After all, he has been active in civil rights work for twenty years.
3. Either you are for an increase in teachers' pay or you prefer your own pocketbook to the welfare of the youth of our society.
4. The federal government should never cut taxes again. It cut them in 1981, and unemployment rose immediately.
5. You were bound to be mugged sooner or later. A person cannot continually be part of crowds the size of those at baseball games without being mugged.
6. If I were you, I would take German from a native German. After all, you do want the best instruction for your money.
7. If I were you, I would take German from a nonnative speaker. After all, you do want to pass the course, don't you?

Exercise 9.13

When we label an assertion as an example of faulty reasoning, we do not mean to imply that it is impossible to treat the topic of that assertion in a reasonable and convincing fashion. For example, there is quite a bit of difference in the basic reasoning at work in statements 1 and 2 in the preceding exercise. Whereas statement 1 is unreasonable to the point of being humorous, there is some degree of reason involved in statement 2, even though we cannot accept the assertion as it stands. If you were going to argue that Smith will back the ERA, how would you develop your argument? Write a paragraph in which you plan a strategy for such an argument.

Fallacies of Definition Fallacies of definition occur when arguments are supported by opinion statements. We call them fallacies of definition because all opinion statements hinge on definitions. If a writer asserts that Joe fought with Bill, readers will probably see little point in arguing the fact. They may not believe the statement; indeed, they may decide to investigate to see whether it is true, but they will not argue it. However, if the speaker goes on to offer the opinion that Joe is brave, readers may be inclined to disagree and to question the speaker's definition of "brave." Opinion statements are so labeled because they include one or more such arguable terms.

To be successful, the writer of an argumentative paper must be sure that the definitions of terms in his opinion statements are clear and that he offers support for those definitions that need support. If he fails in either of these tasks, his argument will be less effective. A failure in clarity is called *equivocation,* and a failure in support is called *begging the question.*

Equivocation   Equivocation is the stuff of the slick advertising slogan. For example, consider the following slogan: "When guns are outlawed, only outlaws will have guns." Here there is a shift in meaning of the word "outlaw." In its verb form, it means simply "to declare illegal or against the law." However, in its noun form, it has come to mean "a habitual criminal," the kind of person who can be shot on sight in some states. Although it is true that when guns are outlawed only people who are going against that law will have guns, it is not true that when guns are outlawed only habitual criminals will have guns.

For another example, suppose a person offers as a supporting premise the assertion that anyone who would commit a premeditated murder is insane and then moves from this premise to the conclusion that such a person should be found "not guilty by reason of insanity." The equivocation here involves the word "insane." In the conclusion, the word must mean "mentally deranged to the point of not knowing the difference between right or wrong and/or not being in sufficient control of oneself to keep from doing wrong things." However, if readers accept the premise, they are probably ascribing a less technical meaning to "insane": "disturbed in thinking, not normal." They might accept the premise that a person who would kill is "disturbed," but they would not necessarily believe that a person who kills lacks the ability to control his actions.

Begging the Question   The fallacy of begging the question occurs when a conclusion is deduced from a premise that masks the same assertion made in the conclusion. For example, the sentence "You should not major in a liberal arts field because it will do you little good" has a pair of assertions that are actually saying the same thing: A liberal arts major is not *good* because it does one little *good.* Both assertions claim that a liberal arts major is not good, but neither helps a reader understand what the writer means by "good."

In many cases, the writer who falls into the trap of begging the question could frame a workable argument by carefully defining terms. For example, the preceding argument could be structured as follows:

> A college education should provide one with marketable skills.
> A liberal arts major does not provide one with marketable skills.
> One should not choose a liberal arts major in college.

Of course, the writer has much work to do in helping her readers accept the two supporting premises, but she is no longer begging the question.

Exercise 9.14

Label the fallacies of definition in the following examples, and explain which word or phrase causes the difficulty.

Example: That film should be given the Academy Award because it was the best picture of the year.

Explanation: This is a simple case of begging the question. There is really only one assertion that is stated twice: The film is the best because it is the best. The writer offers no insight into what "best picture" means or why he considers this the best film.

1. We all agree that each company should be free to set its own price. Therefore, how can we deny companies the freedom to set prices as a group?
2. I wouldn't choose only children to be camp counselors because they are not good in group situations.
3. Dad, how can you say I'm not dependable enough to have the car? Yesterday, you said you could depend on me to ask for the car every weekend.
4. I can't believe you voted for a Democrat.
5. The West wasn't won with a registered gun.

By this time, it should be clear that these three types of reasoning errors remain mutually exclusive only so long as they are viewed from the perspectives we offer. By changing our perspective, we can see the same error as a definitional fallacy, a causal fallacy, or a fallacy of irrelevance. To illustrate the point, consider the fourth statement in the previous exercise: I can't believe you voted for a Democrat. Because this exercise followed our discussion of fallacies of definition, you probably found a definitional problem in it. To reveal the problem, you may have phrased the argument as follows: One should not vote for a Democrat; she is a Democrat; thus, you should not vote for her. Or, to make the question begging even more obvious, the argument could be phrased as follows: Democrats are bad (should not be voted for) because they are Democrats. This makes it clear that no premise is given in support of the assumption that Democrats are bad.

But if this particular example had followed the section on causal fallacies, you could well have discussed its problems in the terminologies we developed there. In order to do so you might have phrased the underlying assumption as follows: The fact that she is a Democrat will cause her to do a bad job in office. Of course, the writer offers no support for this implicit causal assertion.

From a third perspective, the error may be seen as a fallacy of irrelevance—specifically, as a stereotype. The writer is attempting to determine the worth of a certain individual by placing her in a class. No support is offered for the assumption that all Democrats are unworthy candidates. Thus, the sophisticated reader is likely to see the implied premise—the candidate is a Democrat—as irrelevant to the conclusion—you should not vote for her.

Although the three categories of problematic arguments we have devised may be helpful to you, the preceding discussion should make the point that the basic principles of logical argument are much more important than any classification system for fallacious arguments. *The* basic principle is that disagreements arise because of differences in the perceptions of those who are arguing. A corollary to this principle is that whenever there is a real argument, the short, albeit witty, statement will not suffice. Arguments such as "When guns are outlawed, only outlaws will have guns" and "The West wasn't won with a registered gun" will work only for people who already share the point of view of the writer or for people who are not sophisticated enough to see the problems in these statements.

Refining Your Writing

After you've written a draft of your essay and taken some time away from it, revise it, keeping the following principles in mind:

Thesis sentence. Be sure that you and your reader know what your "should" thesis sentence is.

Logical argument. Be sure that your thesis is clearly connected to foundational claims of cause and/or value and that these claims are adequately supported. Be sure that you have countered the major arguments that your counterpart would offer. Check to see that you have not used any logical fallacies.

Ethical appeal. Be sure that you have not misrepresented your counterpart's argument and that you have treated those on the other side fairly.

SAMPLE STUDENT PROCESS

The student example below was written by Heather Hall, a first-year writing student at UNC Charlotte.

Prewriting   Heather first brainstormed possible issues for her position paper:

Paper Ideas
Education
    School choice plan
    Education lottery
    Teachers

Children
    Abuse
    Child care
    Exceptional

Dance Therapy

Psychology
    Psychotherapy
    Overmedication

From this list of possible topics, Heather selected the issue of a state lottery. She then attempted to gain insight into the writing task at hand by examining her key values and those of people opposed to her position:

Value
What are my key values?
   Education (I believe we must find the ways to provide a quality education for all students in our public schools.)
   Fairness (I believe it is fair to let people select the taxes they will pay; this seems fairer than imposing taxes on those who can't afford additional taxes.)
   Honesty and Consistency (There are so many ways that all members of our society "gamble" that to say it is immoral to play a lottery seems a bit dishonest to me.)
   Responsibility and Free Will (I don't like the idea of telling people what kinds of things they can do—unless the state needs to do so for its own protection.)

What are key values for my opponents?
   Morality (This will likely be their most important value. Nothing, no matter what good it seems to offer, can be supported if it is immoral.)
   Education (My opponents will value education as I do, so this will be an area of common ground for us.)
   Planning and Hard Work (I would expect a good many of my opponents to oppose any kind of wealth, or desire for wealth, that doesn't come by hard work. They will see a "something-for-nothing" mentality as bad for a person.)

The next step in Heather's process was a focus statement that would lead her to a rough draft of her paper.

Focus Statement

I'm going to write in favor of a state lottery. I will argue that we have to raise more money for education and that the lottery is the best way to do that at the present time. I am going to do research to see how other states have benefited from lotteries and to determine how a state can be sure that monies from a lottery go for educational purposes. I will not be able to change people's minds who think that all types of gambling are wrong, but I can try to show that this is a type of gambling that doesn't really hurt poor people and that it can, in the end, do much good for everyone in the state.

Heather's next step was to write a discovery draft to bring to class for review.

Discovery Draft

In the past several months, the State of North Carolina has been in a serious "budget crunch." What does that mean you ask? We are almost broke. To fix this problem, the state has started eliminating jobs, cutting funds, and postponing projects that have been planned for years. Among those groups taking the biggest budget cut are the school systems and the universities. Every one at the University of North Carolina at Charlotte knows that we barely have enough money to function. The first sign that showed a problem was the announcement that Spring 2002 report cards would not be mailed home (no complaints here);

instead they would be posted online. Once summer school started we found out that teachers have not been allowed to print off the computers or photo copy for their classes. This has caused many problems at UNCC and this sort of thing is happening all over the state.

People are asking, "What are we going to do?" Well, one thing that we can do is to pass a state lottery bill, since it is clear that most of the citizens here favor such a bill. This has been an option in North Carolina for years. Why has North Carolina ignored this solution, when so many other states around us are benefitting from loteries? Most of these lotteries profits go to education.

Everyone would love to have extra money in the state for education. The funds to run successful school systems in the state have been missing for a long time. As more and more students enter the system, class sizes increase and the budget decreases. Most public elementary, middle and high schools in the state have classes with upwards of thirty students in them. And in addition to the overcrowding problem, there is the problem of not enough money for books and supplies. And there is also a problem with the school buildings themselves. Many of them are very old and in desperate need of repair. The classrooms in these schools are not large enough, the heating and cooling systems are not sufficient, and worst of all, many schools are full of asbestos and lead. Children are getting sick from the asbestos, lead, and the mold that is growing all over the schools. These are just a few of the complaints coming from parents and educators in the state. If the state had extra money, from an educational lottery for example, these things could be fixed without having to worry about funding for other things.

As I have said, many of North Carolina's neighboring states have lotteries. One lottery that has been very helpful to education is Georgia's lottery program, called the Helping Outstanding Pupils Educationally (HOPE) scholarship. This scholarship provides financial assistance to all high schools students who perform well in school and want to attend college at a state supported school. Other states have similar lotteries that are proving very helpful to education.

I know there are also many opponents of a lottery in the state. They have many reasons for opposing a lottery. Their first reason is that a lottery is an inefficient method of raising funds. They argue that too much money is spent on raising the award. That may be true, that a lottery does cost a lot of money to run, but still there is a great deal of profit in the lottery. And people would rather pay their money to a lottery than to be taxed. Secondly they say that lotteries promote the notion that good fortune comes from luck, not hard work. Those opposing lotteries say that they target low-income families that want to "get rich quick" [I have to get an answer to this one.] Thirdly they say that the lottery takes money away from the budgeted money of the thing that the lottery supports. The education budget would be made primarily from the money the lottery raised. The money already budgeted for education in the state would be placed elsewhere. This would be excellent for the state of North Carolina right now because we are in a "budget crunch". The educational system would come out with more money than they had to begin with (even if it was only a few million more) and the rest of the money could go to other state agencies that also need the money right now.

Like it or not, lotteries are going to be around for a long time to come. An educational lottery would be great for the state of North Carolina right now. It would be an optional tax for the citizens but still make millions of dollars for the educational system.

Peer Review Heather's paper was read by a classmate, who offered the following assessment:

> I agree with you about the lottery, so I may not be the best person to help you. I believe what you say in favor of having a lottery—but like I said, I'm on your side. I think you have done a good job of guessing what your opponents will say—but in places you are not sure what you will say back. In other places you say things (such as telling about the amount of lead in the schools, the amount of work needing to be done on schools) that you don't have any support for. I know you still have to look up sources, so this will help make your paper stronger. Good luck.

Heather then produced her second draft, the final draft for her class with Ron. After she had finished the course, however, Ron asked Heather to revise the paper one more time for inclusion in the third edition of *The Longwood Guide to Writing*. At that time, Ron offered extensive comments on Heather's paper. Those comments are presented on this second draft. As you will see, Ron made some corrections and brief comments in the text—those, we have presented in red below. And he also made longer comments suggesting revision problems that Heather should solve on her own—those are presented in comment boxes in the margins of the paper.

Second Draft

THE NEXT BIG WINNER IS...!!

In the past several months, the State of North Carolina has been in a serious "budget crunch." What does that mean you ask? Well, we are almost broke. To fix this problem, the state has started eliminating jobs, cutting funds, and postponing projects that have been planned for years. Among those groups taking the biggest budget cuts are the school systems and the universities. Students and faculty at the University of North Carolina at Charlotte know that the school barely has enough money to function. The first sign that showed the students a problem was the announcement that spring semester report cards would not be mailed home; instead they would be posted online. Since summer school started teachers have not been allowed to print off the computers or photo copy for their classes. This has caused many problems at UNCC and this sort of thing is happening all over the state.

Comment: The preceding sentence needs work. You don't need to say that a "sign" "showed" something. The concept of "showing" is contained in the word "sign." And, can you get rid of this weak "be" verb (was). You might say something like "students first knew there was a problem when they learned that . . ." or perhaps you have a better idea.

> **Comment:** Note that you will want to change the language here—you don't want to use "say" and then follow with a question.

> **Comment:** These first two sentences sound wordy—can you say what you mean in one sentence?

> **Comment:** Here again you need to think about combining sentences. Let me show you what I mean. What if the previous two sentences were combined something like this? "Since many middle school teachers have only one set of books, students must use those books in class and leave them there."

> **Comment:** This is important—so your wording needs to be much more exact. We don't want the Bible "talking." That would give most people the "willies."

> **Comment:** You move rather abruptly into the lottery issue. Why not slow down a bit and offer an answer to your question. That is, people are asking "What are we going to do?" There is a solution to this problem, namely to institute a state lottery for the purpose of supporting education. Then you can move on to say that a recent poll shows that 70% of those surveyed support such a lottery.

> **Comment:** Again, look at the two previous sentences to see if you can combine and tighten your structure.

> **Comment:** Have you already mentioned "other" schools—or can you begin here with "many"?

> **Comment:** Do you have a source for this information—I'm shocked to hear this. I thought most of the lead had been removed. If you can make me (and others) believe that this claim is valid, you will help your argument.

> **Comment:** The "forever" above undermines the seriousness of your argument. Why not say something less colloquial—like, "lotteries can be traced in history as far back as Biblical times" or some such.

People are asking, "What are we going to do?" Seventy percent of the state says, "Why not ratify an educational lottery?" ("Facts"). This has been an option in North Carolina for years. Why not join every Canadian province, 38 U.S. states, the District of Columbia, Mexico, Puerto Rico, and the U.S. Virgin Islands and have a lottery? Most of these lotteries profits [how about: "profits from these lotteries"] go to education, but some [lotteries] support things [is the environment a 'thing'?] like the environment, health care, and tax relief ("Did?"). North Carolina is the only state on the east coast without a lottery. The state should develop an educational lottery so that our school systems have enough money to function properly.

The majority of people would love to have extra money in the state for education. The funds to run successful school systems in the state have been missing for a long time. As more and more students enter the system, class sizes increase and the budget decreases. Most public elementary, middle and high schools in the state have classes with upwards of thirty students in them. Many schools, especially middle schools, have only one set of books per teacher; this means that students have to share books and do not have the advantage of taking books home to work or study from. Other schools in the state are very old and in desperate need of repair; most were built between the 1950's and the 1970's. [does the 'most' refer to the schools in need of repair or to all schools in NC?] The classrooms in these schools are not large enough, the heating and cooling systems are not sufficient, and worst of all, many schools are full of asbestos and lead. [Children are getting sick from the asbestos, the lead, and the mold that is growing all over the schools. These are just a few of the complaints coming from parents and educators in the state. If the state had extra money, from an educational lottery for example, these things could be fixed without having to worry about funding for other things. [you're overworking 'things' here; can you find a more precise word?]

Lotteries have been around forever; there are even references to lotteries in the Bible. It calls them lots and defines them as small tokens used to decide matters. The Bible talks about lots in reference to the selection of warriors (Judges 20:9-10), the choosing of a king (1 Samuel 10:19-21), and in deciding priestly rotation (Luke 1:9). Near the time this country was being founded, [how about: "One of the founding fathers of our country,] Thomas Jefferson called the lottery a "wonderful thing, [because] it [laid] taxation only on the willing" (Brimley and Garfield 132). At that time, [In Jefferson's time? Or if not, say exactly what time] lotteries were used to support colonial soldiers and build schools like Harvard, Princeton, and Yale. Prohibition of lotteries was started in the late 1800's and ran until 1964 when one was established in New Hampshire to support education (132). In 1999, $11,949.44 million were raised in 37 states and Washington, DC alone (134). South Carolina established the most recent lottery in January 2002.

> **Comment:** Okay, look at this sentence—"prohibition" means to disallow or stop something. So do you want to say that prohibition was "started"?

In 2001, North Carolina governor Mike Easley and other lottery supporters said that a lottery could raise $500 million for education in its first year alone. The difference between that, and the projected sales of $933 million in tickets would go toward promotion and expenses. The first thing Easley wants to put the money towards is the reduction of class sizes and the development of a prekindergarten program for the state (Nivens).

> **Comment:** Has Easley officially declared himself a "supporter" of the lottery? I'm wondering if he didn't just offer this as a fact to be used in considering whether we should have a lottery, but maybe I'm wrong.

Later on, as more money is made by the lottery [why the passive voice here?] it could help fund higher education. It [what does this 'it' refer to? What does the 'it' in the previous sentence refer to?] could go toward student scholarships and grants or to general funding in [for?] our colleges and universities. Georgia has the Helping Outstanding Pupils Educationally (HOPE) scholarship. This scholarship provides financial assistance to students attending public and private colleges or universities in the state. [See if you can't combine the two previous sentences.] Since it was established in 1993, the scholarship has provided more than 600,000 students with over $1.5 billion; all of this [what does this 'this' refer to?] was funded by the Georgia Lottery for Education ("Georgia's"). [Are you still talking about Georgia—this is a bit confusing.] Other money could be put towards expanding campuses, improving technologies and lowering tuition in the schools. The cost of a college education rises every year; soon, many students will not be able to afford a good secondary education. [Confusing—college is post-secondary education.] With lottery money, these schools could keep student's [students'] costs down.

There are also [Where does this 'also' come from?] many opponents of a lottery in the state. They have many reasons for opposing a lottery. [How about combining sentences.] Their first reason is that a lottery is an inefficient method of raising funds. They argue that too much money is spent on raising the award. The fact is that states get the same amount as they would if they raised the sales tax one cent (which North Carolina has done recently.) Secondly, it is said that the lottery takes funds away from the budgeted money of the thing that the lottery supports (Honeyman, Wattenbarger, and Westbrook 156). The education budget would be made primarily from the money the lottery raised. The money already budgeted for education in the state would be placed elsewhere. This [This what?] would be excellent for the state of North Carolina right now because we are in a "budget

> **Comment:** Wordy—Get rid of such a phrase as "the reason is." How about something like—"They argue that the lottery is an inefficient method of raising money because too much money is spent on overhead and payouts to winners."

> **Comment:** Whose fact is this? Yours or those who argue against the lottery? Make that clear.

> **Comment:** I understand what you're saying in the previous 3 sentences—but work on saying what you mean more clearly.

crunch." The educational system would come out with more money than they [they who? What does 'they' refer to?] had to begin with (even if it was only a few million dollars more as opposed to $500 million more) and the rest of the money could go to other state agencies that desperately need the money. Lastly those who oppose a lottery say that lotteries prey on the poor by target marketing to those who can least afford to play. Most lottery retailers are based out convenience stores, supermarkets, and gas stations. There are often more of these stores in low-income neighborhoods because of zoning regulations in high-income areas. [combine some sentences in here.] Also keep in mind that players buy tickets where they work and shop, not necessarily where they live. A Minnesota survey found that more than half the players bought tickets in zip codes outside their own home zip codes. A 1999 Gallup Poll on Gambling in America found that fifty-seven percent of Americans had bought a lottery ticket in the past 12 months. It found that: those most likely to play had incomes of $45,000–$75,000 per year, those with incomes less than $25,000 per year were least likely to play, and those with incomes more than $75,000 per year spent three times more on lotteries than those with incomes under $25,000 (Burke). All of these [these what?] are respectable reasons to not have a lottery, but I believe that the reasons to create a lottery out weigh them.

Many speculate that lotteries are going to be around for a long time to come. An educational lottery would be wonderful for the state of North Carolina. It would be an optional tax for the citizens but still make millions of dollars for the educational system.

Comment: You might need to do a little work here or earlier to make it clear that the state's needs in these areas are real.

Comment: This is a very important issue—it probably needs to be in a separate paragraph.

Comment: Look at how you are using "also". It means in addition to. But I get the feeling that you want it to mean "however," or "but." Am I right?

Comment: Your conclusion could be strengthened a bit.

Heather reworked her paper in light of Ron's comments and produced the following final draft.

Final Draft

Heather Hall
THE NEXT BIG WINNER IS . . . . !!

Recently, the state of North Carolina has been in a serious budget crunch. What does that mean, you ask? Well, we are almost broke. To fix this problem, the state has started eliminating jobs, cutting funds, and postponing projects that have been planned for years. Among those groups taking the biggest budget cuts are the school systems and universities. Students and faculty from the University of North Carolina at Charlotte know that the school barely has enough money to function. Students first noticed the problem when they learned that grades would be posted on the internet instead of being mailed out. Professors have not been allowed to make photocopies for their classes. This has caused many problems at UNC Charlotte and this sort of thing is happening all over the state.

What options does the state have for solving this crucial problem? One solution that has been rejected for many years now is the institution of a state lottery. Even though our state legislature is the only one on the East Coast not to have seen the wisdom of this solution, a recent poll shows that seventy percent of those surveyed support such a lottery ("Facts"). Why not join every Canadian province, 38 U.S. states, the District of Columbia, Mexico, Puerto Rico, and the U.S. Virgin Islands and establish a lottery? Most of the profits from these lotteries go towards education, but some support environmental agencies, health care services, and tax relief ("Did you know?"). North Carolina should develop an educational lottery so that our school systems have enough money to function properly.

The majority of people in the state want our schools to have the money they need to operate successfully. As more and more students enter the system, class sizes increase. Many middle and high school teachers have only one set of books, so students must use those books in class and leave them there. Since most schools in North Carolina were built between 1950 and 1980, many schools in the state are very old and in desperate need of repair. The classrooms in these schools are not large enough, and heating and cooling systems are not sufficient for the number of students in these buildings ("Tough Questions"). With additional money from a lottery, the state could make school buildings safe and relatively comfortable while still providing the materials and teachers our students need.

Those who oppose lotteries say they have no place in a moral society. Yet, lotteries can be traced as far back as Biblical times, when "lots," or small tokens, were used to decide important matters. These lots were used to select warriors (Judges 20:9–10), choose a king (1 Samuel 10:19–21), and determine priestly rotation (Luke 1:9). In the early days of this country, lotteries were used to support Colonial soldiers and build schools such as Harvard, Princeton, and Yale. Thomas Jefferson, one of America's founding fathers, called the lottery a "wonderful thing, [because] it [laid] taxation only on the willing" (Brimley and Garfield 132).

Since some early American citizens disapproved of them, lotteries were prohibited from the 1800's until 1964 when New Hampshire established a lottery to support education (132). By 1999, lotteries were contributing significantly to states' economies with over $11,949.44 million raised in 37 states and Washington, DC (134). South Carolina established the most recent lottery in January 2002.

In 2001, North Carolina Governor Mike Easley and groups supporting a lottery said that a lottery could raise $500 million for education in its first year. Easley would like to use the money to reduce class size and develop a statewide pre-kindergarten program (Nivens).

As more money is raised from the lottery, it can be used to increase funding for higher education. North Carolina could implement a college scholarship program for students, similar to the one Georgia's lottery supports. In Georgia, the Helping Outstanding Pupils Educationally (HOPE) Scholarship provides financial assistance to students attending public and private colleges or universities in the state. Since the HOPE scholarship was established in 1993, it has provided nearly one million students with over two billion dollars ("Georgia's HOPE Scholarship Program"). Other money raised in North Carolina could be used to expand campuses, improve technologies and lower tuition in the schools.

Some citizens who oppose the lottery claim that it is an inefficient method of raising funds because too much money is spent on overhead and payouts to winners. But it should be pointed out that a lottery raises the same amount of money that would be produced by a one cent raise in sales tax (Honeyman, Wattenbarger, and Westbrook 156). Since North Carolina has recently raised everyone's sales tax one cent, we should take Jefferson's advice and impose a tax on those who are "willing."

Another objection to lotteries comes from those who argue that the proceeds of a lottery cannot be guaranteed to go to the projects they are earmarked for. That is, if a lottery produces $500 million in profits, our education budget will not see an increase of $500 million. They claim that state legislators would take some of the monies that might otherwise be allocated to education and allocate them to other state-funded projects. There are two important points to be made here. First, even if some of the money from the lottery goes to fund other pressing needs, there will still be more money for education than we have at this time, and second, having additional money to reallocate elsewhere would be excellent for North Carolina right now since we are in a budget crunch.

Finally, some who oppose a lottery say that lotteries prey on the poor by target marketing to those who can least afford to play. They point out that many lottery tickets are sold in convenience stores, supermarkets, and gas stations in low-income neighborhoods because of zoning regulations in high-income areas. However, it is important to remember that players buy tickets where they work and shop, not necessarily where they live. A Minnesota survey found that more than half the players bought tickets in zip codes outside their own home zip code (Burke). And lottery tickets are bought by people in all economic classes. A 1999 Gallup Poll on Gambling in America, which found that fifty-seven percent of Americans had bought a lottery ticket in the past 12 months, produced the following revealing statistics: 65% of people with incomes of $45,000 to $75,000 have played in the last year while only 53% of those with incomes less than $25,000 played, and those with incomes more than $75,000 per year spent three times more on lotteries than those with incomes under $25,000 (Burke).

Those opposing the lottery raise important issues that need to be examined, but lottery supporters in every Canadian province, 38 U.S. states, the District of Columbia, Mexico, Puerto Rico, and the U.S. Virgin Islands believe that the reasons to create a lottery outweigh the reasons not to. Lotteries have helped others all around us, and it is time for the representatives in North Carolina to listen to the seventy percent of their constituents who support a lottery to fund education.

Works Cited

Brimley, Vern Jr., and Rulon R. Garfield. *Financing Education in a Climate of Change, Eighth Edition.* Boston: Allyn and Bacon, 2002.

Burke, Duane V. "Top Ten Myths About Lottery (and Why They Are Not True)." August 20, 1999. North American Association of State and Provincial Lotteries. 19 June 2002. <http://www.naspl.org/burke899.html>.

"Did You Know?" North American Association of State and Provincial Lotteries. 20 June 2002. <http://www.naspl.org/faq.html>.

"Facts." North Carolina Lottery for Education Coalition. 19 June 2002. <http://www.nclotteryforeducation.org/facts.html>.

"Georgia's HOPE Scholarship Program." Georgia Student Finance Commission. 22 Nov. 2003. <http://www.gsfc.org/Hope/Hope_support/html_summary_grant_all_cov_H.htm.>.

Honeyman, David S., James L. Wattenbarger, and Kathleen C. Westbrook, eds. *A Struggle To Survive: Funding Higher Education in the Next Century.* Thousand Oaks, CA: Corwin, 1996.

Nivens, David. "Lottery pros and cons tout dollars." *High Point Enterprise.* 19 Mar. 2001. 20 June 2002. <http://www.hpe.com/2001/03/19/news/319news1.html>.

"Tough Questions on the School Bonds." Charlotte Mecklenburg Schools. 12 Dec. 2003. <http://www.cms.k12.nc.us/departments/publicinformation/bonds0203/toughquestions.asp>.

CHECKLIST: CRITIQUING A POSITION ESSAY

1. State the essay's thesis, being sure to include the word "should." Is this a thesis about which reasonable people will disagree? State the foundational (value and/or causal) assertions that support this sentence. Are they logically connected to the thesis?
2. List the types of support that the writer uses for each causal or value claim made in the argument. Are all claims clearly supported?
3. Briefly sketch the organization of the paper. Does the writer use an informal or a formal structure? Is the organization effective?
4. What is the thesis of those who would oppose this argument? Does the writer present the opposition's point of view fairly, without distortion? Does the writer acknowledge and respond to their counterarguments?
5. Does the paper adhere to conventions of usage, mechanics, and format? Correct any errors you find.

Thomas Hart Benton, "Trial by Jury," 1964. Oil on canvas, 30 × 40 in. The Nelson-Atkins Museum of Art, Kansas City, MO. Bequest of the artist (F75-21/11). © T. H. Benton and R. P. Benton Testamentary Trusts/UMB Bank Trustee/Licensed by VAGA, New York, NY.

CHAPTER 10

Persuasion Essays

In this chapter, we turn to persuasive writing. How does persuasive writing differ from the argumentative writing we discussed in Chapter 9? Your goal in writing a position paper was to make your position clear to someone who disagreed with you on the issue in question. Your goal in this chapter will be to move readers to action.

As we explained in Chapter 9, persuasion is not possible in many situations. Some of our beliefs are central to our concept of self. Thus, when we enter into a discussion about these beliefs, we are not likely to change them. When both sides in an argument are operating from such fixed beliefs, persuasion is not possible. The best that can be hoped for in such situations is a clear presentation of the two sides with the modest hope that each will understand the logic behind the other's position—hence, the position essay.

The goal in a persuasion essay is, in one sense, more ambitious and, in another sense, less ambitious than the goal in a position essay. It is more ambitious in that the goal in persuasion is to cause readers to take some action. It is less ambitious in that the writer assumes an audience that is already sympathetic to her argument. The writer's purpose, then, is not to change the mind of the reader, but to energize and move the reader who already shares (or at least leans toward) her viewpoint.

The key component of persuasive writing is pathos—or emotion. While our reason may help us formulate and solidify our beliefs, it is emotion that acts as the catalyst to bring our actions and our beliefs together. We tend to act because we are moved to do what we have come to understand to be the right course of action—or at least that is the way it should be. Of course, that isn't always the case. We are sometimes moved to do things that we can give no good reasons for doing. When an advertiser persuades us to buy a product that costs more money than we can really afford to spend or one that harms our health, we have been moved to take an action without having been convinced logically that that action is good for us. In such a situation, the advertiser's ability to separate reason and emotion makes his writing effective, even though what he is doing is not ethical.

In analyzing the sample essays in this chapter, we will differentiate between effective and ethical writing. Effective persuasive writing achieves its writer's purpose; ethical persuasive writing weds reason and emotion and does so in a fashion that is fair to those who might take an opposing point of view. Each of the sample writings we present below is effective. In addition, each of these essays meets certain basic requirements of ethical writing, in that none of them encourages an action that could not be supported by reasoned arguments. However, some of these essays are less ethical than others; several of them deal somewhat unfairly with those who might take an opposing point of view. We have chosen to include writing that we see as somewhat problematic from an ethical standpoint because much of the persuasive writing you will face on a daily basis is designed to use emotion as a tool to achieve the writers' ends—sometimes with little or no attempt to connect reason and emotion.

In the writing that you do in this chapter, you should focus on emotion as a way of moving your readers to take action. However, you will advocate actions that you believe to be good for you and your readers. And even though you may not spend as much time developing a logical argument as you would if you were writing for an audience that would resist your reasons, you should still argue your case logically and avoid oversimplifications and distortions of your opponents' arguments.

SAMPLE ESSAYS

The following persuasive essays deal with some of the more important issues facing our society: abortion, discrimination, the relation between religion and science, spousal abuse, and the death penalty. In our first essay, "Dismemberment and Choice," Michael R. Heaphy, a medical doctor, describes abortion in graphic detail that is designed to convince readers to take actions that will lead to the outlawing of abortion.

Michael R. Heaphy

DISMEMBERMENT AND CHOICE

1   For the last few years, it has been commonplace to hear conventionally enlightened people soberly and confidently announce that they are not pro-abortion but, rather, pro-choice. Because of the generality that is implicit in the unqualified word "choice," it is logical to examine the pro-choice argument from a broad perspective.

2   To make a *pro-choice* argument is to assert a liberty to perform an action, X, without bothering to explain why X should be legal, without acknowledging the nature of X, and, sometimes, without permitting the name for X to cross one's

lips. Illogically, "choice" is both the premise and the conclusion. The pro-choice argument for abortion is that abortion should be legal because women have a *right to choose*. The problem with this argument is that an unqualified right purely and simply to *choose* could be used to advocate legal status for drunk driving, cannibalism, insider trading, or anything else. Unless one believes that all conceivable actions should be legal, it is not reasonable to base advocacy of legality for a particular action on *unqualified* choice.

3   To understand what abortion is all about, it is useful to re-direct our attention from the abstract plane down to a more practical level. Such a real-world viewpoint can be achieved by considering the day-to-day work of a physician who does little else with his professional life except abortions. For example, in my own state of Ohio, there is the practice of W. Martin Haskell, M.D.

4   Depending on the size of the unborn child (or should I use one of the sanitized terms—like the "conceptus"?), Dr. Haskell employs various techniques. If the fetus isn't too far along, Haskell can probably use the suction curettage method in which a sharp curette is used to reduce the fetus into chunks small enough to be sucked out of the uterus.

5   Later in pregnancy the fetus is too large for this method. Such cases provide Dr. Haskell with many of his referrals. He is an expert at killing human fetuses at five and six months' gestation. He uses laminaria to dilate the cervix in a three-day procedure, then simply goes in, makes a direct instrument attack on the fetus, kills it, and takes it out.

6   Of course, the head is usually crushed in this D&E (dilation and evacuation) procedure. An unripened cervix just doesn't expand enough to pass a five- or six-month head. If the unborn baby is big enough, then the arms and legs may have to go too. The fetus is typically dismembered and removed piece by piece in a D&E abortion. The parts are often inspected to make sure an arm or a leg hasn't been left in the mother.

7   The news organizations' reticence about mentioning the actual nature of abortion may arise in part from a chink in the gleaming semantic armor that otherwise encases the subject: The abortion advocates forgot to re-name the body parts encountered in abortion.

8   Presumably the "conscientious practitioners" of abortion (as the AMA now calls them—in slight departure from its own earlier description of them as "modern day Herods"), would be loath to admit to killing unborn children. They would rather say that they *terminate pregnancies*, an odd assistance for a process that invariably terminates itself.

9   As long as the discussion is couched in such genteel terms, there isn't much room for primitive, natural words like "arm" and "leg." They are gaucheries. On the other hand, if we could simply introduce a few Choice words into the vocabulary, then our mass media would no longer need to shy away from the topic of abortion techniques. The unborn child won't be called a child but just a "fetus" (Latin for "offspring"), and the arm is only a "potential arm" or, say, a "brachium."

Dr. Haskell operates abortion facilities in Cincinnati and suburban Dayton. When Yvonne Brower, a University of Cincinnati student, called to enquire if she could observe abortions to gather information for a term paper, the clinic manager was magnanimous. On September 21, 1989, Miss Brower observed Dr. Haskell killing fetuses at the Women's Med Center, which he owns, in Kettering, Ohio. The events of that morning prompted Miss Brower to file a complaint with the police.

The following excerpt from the police report is of interest:

> She stated that by 11 o'clock she had already observed two "D&E" three-day procedures on two patients. She stated on the third patient, however, the abortion was different.... The patient's water was already broken and she spontaneously gave birth prematurely before the proper D&E procedure could be done. She stated that the baby was delivered feet first very quickly through the birth canal. The head was on its way out when Dr. Haskell reached over and got his scissors and snipped the right side of the baby's common carotid artery.

Even then, Miss Brower stated, the newborn infant was not exactly dead. The police report again:

> The complainant stated that the baby was still moving when she looked at it once again.... it was breathing shallow breaths, as was evidenced by the chest moving up and down. She stated that she could also observe the baby's hand having slow, controlled, muscular movements, unlike the short jerky twitchy motions she had seen and learned to expect when the baby was already dead before it came out of the birth canal.

The *Dayton Daily News* reported this story on Sunday, December 10, 1989. In the *Daily News* Dr. Haskell described the event in question in this way: "it came out very quickly after I put the scissors up in the cervical canal and pierced the skull and spread the scissors apart. It popped right on out.... the previous two, I had to use the suction to collapse the skull."

Haskell also said Miss Brower "quite possibly" misinterpreted what happened in the abortion. Miss Brower, however, said she saw Dr. Haskell perform fifteen abortions the day before and two others that morning. "So it's not like I hadn't seen any before," she said.

Dr. Haskell was questioned by the police. He maintains that when he does abortions he always causes the death of the fetus to occur just before delivery rather than after. The prosecutor did not bring charges.

Of course, if killing the unborn, at the moment when Haskell *openly admits* to the act, is not merely *not illegal* but rather a "fundamental right," it would be remarkable for virtually the same act to constitute legal homicide a few seconds later. *Legal* homicide or not, however, it would seem clear that a direct, intentional, and lethal assault on a human fetus must constitute a *homicide-in-fact* in that old-fashioned, as-long-as-words-have-meanings sense that even our federal judges are not quite able to change. It would be rather surprising if, here or there, some abortionist did not proceed to act on the logical basis that the result is the same whether one kills the fetus and then takes it out or takes it out and then kills it.

At present, good people in America are working to undo a decree that has transformed an entire class of human beings into constitutional outlaws suitable for discretionary killing. The idea that something so grandiose and Platonic as "choice" will be lost to our people if this killing is prohibited is as ludicrous as suggesting that the American people are already deprived of the same ideal by the prohibition of burglary or rape. The abortion struggle is of pivotal importance for humanity because it is about the value of human life and the value of truth. If that seems too abstract, then consider a more concrete approach: Recall that it is also about crushing unborn babies' skulls and ask whether or not it is OK to do that. 17

♦ QUESTIONS FOR REVIEW

1. What is the thesis of Heaphy's essay? Does it appear in the essay? If so, where? What reasons does he give for accepting his position?
2. Divide the essay into beginning, middle, and end. What rhetorical and/or stylistic devices help form these divisions?
3. What audience might Heaphy's essay be written for? Is that audience likely to resist his argument? Explain.
4. Does Heaphy offer counterarguments to those who would disagree with him? If so, does he represent the opposition's argument fairly? Explain. What counterarguments are offered?
5. In addition to (or instead of) logical argumentation, what kinds of persuasive appeals does Heaphy use in this essay? Would these appeals be likely to work for his intended audience? Why, or why not?
6. How would you characterize your attitude toward this subject before reading Heaphy's essay? What effect did this essay have on your thinking?

♦ WRITING OPPORTUNITY

Write about some other topic that you feel as passionately about as Heaphy feels about abortion. Why is this topic so important to you? What are you doing as a result of your passion for this subject? ♦

Our second essay, "Exposed in the Supreme Court: Lies about 'Partial Birth Abortion'" by Thomas Oliphant, was published in the *Boston Globe* in 2000.

THOMAS OLIPHANT

EXPOSED IN THE SUPREME COURT: LIES ABOUT "PARTIAL BIRTH ABORTION"

The State of Nebraska got caught red-handed here last week.

The exposure was technically legal in nature, and because it was before the Supreme Court there was enough of a veneer of gentility to cushion the blow's humiliating severity.

But in getting caught in several acts of out-and-out deception, Nebraska's effort to argue for its statute banning "partial-birth abortion" was not only unmasked as fraudulent in open court; the equally important politics of "partial-birth abortion" were changed utterly.

From now on, no slogan-spouting antiabortion politician can responsibly say he opposes "partial-birth abortion" without answering the simple question, "What's that?" What was demonstrated last week is that the question cannot be answered, which turns out to have been the deceptive purpose of this six-year political farce all along. George W. Bush, to pick one example, has had a free ride on this dishonest formulation long enough.

The problem poor Donald Stenberg, Nebraska's attorney general, faced in oral argument before the court was how to explain why the statute avoided specifying the act it purported to criminalize.

In fact, in none of the 31 state statutes enacted to date (plus a bill passed twice by Congress and vetoed twice by President Clinton) is "partial-birth abortion" the actual target. By now, presumably a few people have gotten past the evasions to learn that the term is entirely a public relations fabrication and has no medical meaning.

The Nebraska statute at issue is typical, criminalizing any procedure "in which the person performing the abortion partially delivers vaginally a living unborn child before killing the child and completing the delivery."

What tripped Stenberg up and unmasked the nefarious purpose behind the law is the fact that doctors say that the language can cover two kinds of procedures.

One—dilation and extraction—is used very late in pregnancy and involves dilating the cervix so the fetus comes into the vagina feet first. Collapsing the skull and suctioning out the brain allows the head's delivery. This is the stuff of the antiabortion movement's famous cartoons pretending that a "baby" right out of a Good Housekeeping ad is killed on the verge of live birth. In reality, the fetus involved is often brain-dead or otherwise hopelessly flawed, and the procedure protects the woman's health, including her ability to have children in the future.

The other — dilation and evacuation — is used commonly in the second trimester of pregnancy. It involves removing the fetus in sections from the uterus, during which it is common, for example, for the arm or leg of a living fetus to be pulled into the vagina.

Stenberg tried to argue that criminalizing only the former was the state's intent, claiming a valid state interest in "drawing a bright line between infanticide and abortion." He then claimed that it was no big deal anyway because the procedure is used so rarely that banning it would have no impact on the choices of the vast majority of pregnant women. That was the first clue to the deception, since when this fight was just beginning, the antiabortion movement was claiming just the opposite.

But if outlawing dilation and extractions is the intent, as Stenberg claimed, why not specifically outlaw them by name? His failure to answer was bad enough, but the legislative history in Nebraska three years ago is much worse. It turns out that an effort was made in the state Senate to amend the bill to ban dilation and extractions specifically, and it was defeated in a 27–11 vote.

Indeed, the bill's chief sponsor opposed the amendment because, he said, it would change "what the bill is designed to do," namely, to ban both procedures and breach Roe v. Wade's wall between allowable regulations during the second trimester (for safety only) and during the third (when abortions can be banned as long as there are exceptions to protect the life and health of the woman). The absence of a health exception in all the phony antiabortion statutes is flagrant icing on the factual cake.

"That's just glaring here," said Justice Ruth Bader Ginsburg of Stenberg's twisted presentation, for which dissembling would be a mild adjective.

Speaking for his two antiabortion colleagues — Chief Justice William Rehnquist and Clarence Thomas —Antonin Scalia sounded less like a jurist and more like a pol. Since he acknowledges no right to choose under Roe, any pregnancy regulation is permissible.

The collapse of Nebraska's argument foreshadows the collapse of the political case as well after nearly a decade of fraudulent claims.

The issue is not "partial-birth abortion." It's the right to choose, and if he wins the right to make two appointments to the court, Governor Bush is a dagger aimed straight at it.

◆ QUESTIONS FOR REVIEW

1. What is the thesis of Oliphant's essay? Does it appear in the essay? If so, where? What reasons does he give for accepting his position?
2. Divide the essay into beginning, middle, and end. What rhetorical and/or stylistic devices help form these divisions?
3. What audience might Oliphant's essay be written for? Is that audience likely to resist his argument? Explain.
4. Does Oliphant offer counterarguments to those who would disagree with him? If so, what are they? Does he represent the opposition's argument fairly? Explain.
5. In addition to (or instead of) logical argumentation, what kinds of persuasive appeals does Oliphant use in this essay? Would these appeals be likely to work for his intended audience? Why, or why not?
6. How would you characterize your attitude toward this subject before reading Oliphant's essay? What effect did this essay have on your thinking?

◆ WRITING OPPORTUNITY

Since the famous Supreme Court ruling in 1973, *Roe v. Wade,* abortion has been legal in the United States. Do some research into laws regarding abortion in at least three other countries. How do their laws compare to those in the U.S.? How do your findings influence your thinking, if at all? ◆

Our third essay, "I Have a Dream," was delivered by its author, Martin Luther King Jr., on the steps of the Lincoln Memorial in Washington, D.C., on August 28, 1963.

MARTIN LUTHER KING, JR.
I HAVE A DREAM

1   I am happy to join with you today in what will go down in history as the greatest demonstration for freedom in the history of our nation.

2   Five score years ago, a great American, in whose symbolic shadow we stand today, signed the Emancipation Proclamation. This momentous decree came as

a great beacon light of hope to millions of Negro slaves who had been seared in the flames of withering injustice. It came as a joyous daybreak to end the long night of their captivity.

But one hundred years later, the Negro still is not free. One hundred years later, the life of the Negro is still sadly crippled by the manacles of segregation and the chains of discrimination. One hundred years later, the Negro lives on a lonely island of poverty in the midst of a vast ocean of material prosperity. One hundred years later, the Negro is still languished in the corners of American society and finds himself an exile in his own land. And so we've come here today to dramatize a shameful condition.

In a sense we've come to our nation's capital to cash a check. When the architects of our republic wrote the magnificent words of the Constitution and the Declaration of Independence, they were signing a promissory note to which every American was to fall heir. This note was a promise that all men, yes, black men as well as white men, would be guaranteed the "unalienable Rights" of "Life, Liberty and the pursuit of Happiness." It is obvious today that America has defaulted on this promissory note, insofar as her citizens of color are concerned. Instead of honoring this sacred obligation, America has given the Negro people a bad check, a check which has come back marked "insufficient funds."

But we refuse to believe that the bank of justice is bankrupt. We refuse to believe that there are insufficient funds in the great vaults of opportunity of this nation. And so, we've come to cash this check, a check that will give us upon demand the riches of freedom and the security of justice.

We have also come to this hallowed spot to remind America of the fierce urgency of Now. This is no time to engage in the luxury of cooling off or to take the tranquilizing drug of gradualism. Now is the time to make real the promises of democracy. Now is the time to rise from the dark and desolate valley of segregation to the sunlit path of racial justice. Now is the time to lift our nation from the quicksands of racial injustice to the solid rock of brotherhood. Now is the time to make justice a reality for all of God's children.

It would be fatal for the nation to overlook the urgency of the moment. This sweltering summer of the Negro's legitimate discontent will not pass until there is an invigorating autumn of freedom and equality. Nineteen sixty-three is not an end, but a beginning. And those who hope that the Negro needed to blow off steam and will now be content will have a rude awakening if the nation returns to business as usual. And there will be neither rest nor tranquility in America until the Negro is granted his citizenship rights. The whirlwinds of revolt will continue to shake the foundations of our nation until the bright day of justice emerges.

But there is something that I must say to my people, who stand on the warm threshold which leads into the palace of justice: In the process of gaining our rightful place, we must not be guilty of wrongful deeds. Let us not seek to satisfy our thirst for freedom by drinking from the cup of bitterness and hatred. We must forever conduct our struggle on the high plane of dignity and discipline. We must not allow our creative protest to degenerate into physical violence. Again and again, we must rise to the majestic heights of meeting physical force with soul force.

The marvelous new militancy which has engulfed the Negro community must not lead us to a distrust of all white people, for many of our white brothers, as evidenced by their presence here today, have come to realize that their destiny is tied up with our destiny. And they have come to realize that their freedom is inextricably bound to our freedom.

We cannot walk alone.

And as we walk, we must make the pledge that we shall always march ahead.

We cannot turn back.

There are those who are asking the devotees of civil rights, "When will you be satisfied?" We can never be satisfied as long as the Negro is the victim of the unspeakable horrors of police brutality. We can never be satisfied as long as our bodies, heavy with the fatigue of travel, cannot gain lodging in the motels of the highways and the hotels of the cities. We cannot be satisfied as long as the negro's basic mobility is from a smaller ghetto to a larger one. We can never be satisfied as long as our children are stripped of their self-hood and robbed of their dignity by a sign stating: "For Whites Only." We cannot be satisfied as long as a Negro in Mississippi cannot vote and a Negro in New York believes he has nothing for which to vote. No, no, we are not satisfied, and we will not be satisfied until "justice rolls down like waters, and righteousness like a mighty stream."

I am not unmindful that some of you have come here out of great trials and tribulations. Some of you have come fresh from narrow jail cells. And some of you have come from areas where your quest for freedom left you battered by the storms of persecution and staggered by the winds of police brutality. You have been the veterans of creative suffering. Continue to work with the faith that unearned suffering is redemptive.

Go back to Mississippi, go back to Alabama, go back to South Carolina, go back to Georgia, go back to Louisiana, go back to the slums and ghettos of our northern cities, knowing that somehow this situation can and will be changed.

Let us not wallow in the valley of despair, I say to you today, my friends.

And so even though we face the difficulties of today and tomorrow, I still have a dream. It is a dream deeply rooted in the American dream.

I have a dream that one day this nation will rise up and live out the true meaning of its creed: "We hold these truths to be self-evident, that all men are created equal."

I have a dream that one day on the red hills of Georgia, the sons of former slaves and the sons of former slave owners will be able to sit down together at the table of brotherhood.

I have a dream that one day even the state of Mississippi, a state sweltering with the heat of injustice, sweltering with the heat of oppression, will be transformed into an oasis of freedom and justice.

I have a dream that my four little children will one day live in a nation where they will not be judged by the color of their skin but by the content of their character.

I have a *dream* today!

I have a dream that one day, down in Alabama, with its vicious racists, with its governor having his lips dripping with the words of "interposition" and "nullification" — one day right there in Alabama little black boys and black girls will be able to join hands with little white boys and white girls as sisters and brothers.

I have a *dream* today!

I have a dream that one day every valley shall be exalted, and every hill and mountain shall be made low, the rough places will be made plain, and the crooked places will be made straight; "and the glory of the Lord shall be revealed and all flesh shall see it together."

This is our hope, and this is the faith that I go back to the South with.

With this faith, we will be able to hew out of the mountain of despair a stone of hope. With this faith, we will be able to transform the jangling discords of our nation into a beautiful symphony of brotherhood. With this faith, we will be able to work together, to pray together, to struggle together, to go to jail together, to stand up for freedom together, knowing that we will be free one day.

And this will be the day – this will be the day when all of God's children will be able to sing with new meaning:

> *My country 'tis of thee, sweet land of liberty, of thee I sing.*
> *Land where my fathers died, land of the Pilgrim's pride,*
> *From every mountainside, let freedom ring!*

And if America is to be a great nation, this must become true.
And so let freedom ring from the prodigious hilltops of New Hampshire.
Let freedom ring from the mighty mountains of New York.
Let freedom ring from the heightening Alleghenies of Pennsylvania.
Let freedom ring from the snow-capped Rockies of Colorado.
Let freedom ring from the curvaceous slopes of California.
But not only that:
Let freedom ring from Stone Mountain of Georgia.
Let freedom ring from Lookout Mountain of Tennessee.
Let freedom ring from every hill and molehill of Mississippi.
From every mountainside, let freedom ring.

And when this happens, when we allow freedom to ring, when we let it ring from every village and every hamlet, from every state and every city, we will be

> able to speed up that day when *all* of God's children, black men and white men, Jews and Gentiles, Protestants and Catholics, will be able to join hands and sing in the words of the old Negro spiritual:
>
> *Free at last! Free at last!*
> *Thank God Almighty, we are free at last!*

◆ QUESTIONS FOR REVIEW

1. What is the thesis of King's essay? Does it appear in the essay? If so, where? What reasons does he give for accepting his position?
2. What audience was King's essay be written for? Was that audience likely to resist his argument? Explain.
3. Does King offer counterarguments to those who would disagree with him? If so, what are they? Does he represent the opposition's argument fairly? Explain.
4. In addition to (or instead of) logical argumentation, what kinds of persuasive appeals does King use in this essay? Would these appeals be likely to work for his intended audience? Why, or why not?
5. King's essay is particularly interesting because it is in reality a speech that you can hear him deliver at this URL: http://video.google.com/videoplay?docid=1732754907698549493. Listen to the speech and then discuss the role that "delivery" plays in making a speech effective. What types of structures in the speech seem to be written for a speech that is going to be read aloud?

◆ WRITING OPPORTUNITY

King's essay is different from the other essays in this chapter in that it deals with a topic that was once arguable but that is largely decided in his favor today. Think about an argument that is hotly debated today but that you think may well be decided within the next 100 years. What makes you think it may be resolved? What resolution do you foresee? ◆

Next, we offer an essay titled "When Religion Steps on Science's Turf: The Alleged Separation Between the Two Is Not So Tidy," written by Richard Dawkins, one of the world's leading evolutionary biologists.

RICHARD DAWKINS

WHEN RELIGION STEPS ON SCIENCE'S TURF

The Alleged Separation Between the Two Is Not So Tidy

A cowardly flabbiness of the intellect afflicts otherwise rational people confronted with long-established religions (though, significantly, not in the face of younger traditions such as Scientology or the Moonies). S. J. Gould, commenting in his Natural History column on the pope's attitude to evolution, is representative of a dominant strain of conciliatory thought, among believers and nonbelievers alike: "Science and religion are not in conflict, for their teachings occupy distinctly different domains . . . I believe, with all my heart, in a respectful, even *loving* concordat [my emphasis] . . . ."

Well, what are these two distinctly different domains, these "Nonoverlapping Magisteria" that should snuggle up together in a respectful and loving concordat? Gould again: "The net of science covers the empirical universe: what is it made of (fact) and why does it work this way (theory). The net of religion extends over questions of moral meaning and value."

Who Owns Morals?

Would that it were that tidy. In a moment I'll look at what the pope actually says about evolution, and then at other claims of his church, to see if they really are so neatly distinct from the domain of science. First though, a brief aside on the claim that religion has some special expertise to offer us on moral questions. This is often blithely accepted even by the nonreligious, presumably in the course of a civilized "bending over backwards" to concede the best point your opponent has to offer—however weak that best point may be.

The question, "What is right and what is wrong?" is a genuinely difficult question that science certainly cannot answer. Given a moral premise or *a priori* moral belief, the important and rigorous discipline of secular moral philosophy can pursue scientific or logical modes of reasoning to point up hidden implications of such beliefs, and hidden inconsistencies between them. But the absolute moral premises themselves must come from elsewhere, presumably from unargued conviction. Or, it might be hoped, from religion — meaning some combination of authority, revelation, tradition, and scripture.

Unfortunately, the hope that religion might provide a bedrock, from which our otherwise sand-based morals can be derived, is a forlorn one. In practice, no civilized person uses Scripture as ultimate authority for moral reasoning. Instead, we pick and choose the nice bits of Scripture (like the Sermon on the Mount) and blithely ignore the nasty bits (like the obligation to stone adulteresses, execute apostates, and punish the grandchildren of offenders). The God of the Old Testament himself, with his pitilessly vengeful jealousy, his racism, sexism, and terrifying bloodlust, will not be adopted as a literal role model by anybody you or I would wish to know. Yes, *of course* it is unfair to judge the customs of an earlier era by the enlightened standards of our own. But that is precisely my *point*! Evidently, we have some alternative source of ultimate moral conviction that overrides Scripture when it suits us.

That alternative source seems to be some kind of liberal consensus of decency and natural justice that changes over historical time, frequently under the influence of secular reformists. Admittedly, that doesn't sound like bedrock. But in practice we, including the religious among us, give it higher priority than Scripture. In practice we more or less ignore Scripture, quoting it when it supports our liberal consensus, quietly forgetting it when it doesn't. And wherever that liberal consensus comes from, it is available to all of us, whether we are religious or not.

Similarly, great religious teachers like Jesus or Gautama Buddha may inspire us, by their good example, to adopt their personal moral convictions. But again we pick and choose among religious leaders, avoiding the bad examples of Jim Jones or Charles Manson, and we may choose good secular role models such as Jawaharlal Nehru or Nelson Mandela. Traditions too, however anciently followed, may be good or bad, and we use our secular judgment of decency and natural justice to decide which ones to follow, which to give up.

Religion on Science's Turf

But that discussion of moral values was a digression. I now turn to my main topic of evolution and whether the pope lives up to the ideal of keeping off the scientific grass. His "Message on Evolution to the Pontifical Academy of Sciences" begins with some casuistical doubletalk designed to reconcile what John Paul II is about to say with the previous, more equivocal pronouncements of Pius XII, whose acceptance of evolution was comparatively grudging and reluctant. Then the pope comes to the harder task of reconciling scientific evidence with "revelation."

> Revelation teaches us that [man] was created in the image and likeness of God. . . . if the human body takes its origin from pre-existent living matter, the spiritual soul is immediately created by God . . . Consequently, theories of evolution which, in accordance with the philosophies inspiring them, consider the mind as emerging from the forces of living matter, or as a mere epiphenomenon of this matter, are incompatible with the truth about man. . . . With man, then, we find ourselves in the presence of an ontological difference, an ontological leap, one could say.

To do the pope credit, at this point he recognizes the essential contradiction between the two positions he is attempting to reconcile: "However, does not the posing of such ontological discontinuity run counter to that physical continuity which seems to be the main thread of research into evolution in the field of physics and chemistry?"

Never fear. As so often in the past, obscurantism comes to the rescue:

> Consideration of the method used in the various branches of knowledge makes it possible to reconcile two points of view which would seem irreconcilable. The sciences of observation describe and measure the multiple manifestations of life with increasing precision and correlate them with the time line. The moment of transition to the spiritual cannot be the object of this kind of observation, which nevertheless can discover at the experimental level a series of very valuable signs indicating what is specific to the human being.

In plain language, there came a moment in the evolution of hominids when God intervened and injected a human soul into a previously animal lineage. (When? A million years ago? Two million years ago? Between *Homo erectus* and *Homo sapiens?* Between "archaic" *Homo sapiens* and *H. sapiens sapiens?*) The sudden injection is necessary, of course, otherwise there would be no distinction upon which to base Catholic morality, which is speciesist to the core. You can kill adult animals for meat, but abortion and euthanasia are murder because *human* life is involved.

Catholicism's "net" is not limited to moral considerations, if only because Catholic morals have scientific implications. Catholic morality demands the presence of a great gulf between *Homo sapiens* and the rest of the animal kingdom. Such a gulf is fundamentally anti-evolutionary. The sudden injection of an immortal soul in the timeline is an anti-evolutionary intrusion into the domain of science.

More generally it is completely unrealistic to claim, as Gould and many others do, that religion keeps itself away from science's turf, restricting itself to morals and values. A universe with a supernatural presence would be a fundamentally and qualitatively different kind of universe from one without. The difference is, inescapably, a scientific difference. Religions make existence claims, and this means scientific claims.

The same is true of many of the major doctrines of the Roman Catholic Church. The Virgin Birth, the bodily Assumption of the Blessed Virgin Mary, the Resurrection of Jesus, the survival of our own souls after death: these are all claims of a clearly scientific nature. Either Jesus had a corporeal father or he didn't. This is not a question of "values" or "morals"; it is a question of sober fact. We may not have the evidence to answer it, but it is a scientific question, nevertheless. You may be sure that, if any evidence supporting the claim were discovered, the Vatican would not be reticent in promoting it.

Either Mary's body decayed when she died, or it was physically removed from this planet to Heaven. The official Roman Catholic doctrine of Assumption, promulgated as recently as 1950, implies that Heaven has a physical location and exists in the domain of physical reality — how else could the physical body of a woman go there? I am not, here, saying that the doctrine of the Assumption of the Virgin is necessarily false (although of course I think it is). I am simply rebutting the claim that it is outside the domain of science. On the contrary, the Assumption of the Virgin is transparently a scientific theory. So is the theory that our souls survive bodily death, and so are all stories of angelic visitations, Marian manifestations, and miracles of all types.

16 There is something dishonestly self-serving in the tactic of claiming that all religious beliefs are outside the domain of science. On the one hand, miracle stories and the promise of life after death are used to impress simple people, win converts, and swell congregations. It is precisely their scientific power that gives these stories their popular appeal. But at the same time it is considered below the belt to subject the same stories to the ordinary rigors of scientific criticism: these are religious matters and therefore outside the domain of science. But you cannot have it both ways. At least, religious theorists and apologists should not be allowed to get away with having it both ways. Unfortunately all too many of us, including nonreligious people, are unaccountably ready to let them.

17 I suppose it is gratifying to have the pope as an ally in the struggle against fundamentalist creationism. It is certainly amusing to see the rug pulled out from under the feet of Catholic creationists such as Michael Behe. Even so, given a choice between honest-to-goodness fundamentalism on the one hand, and the obscurantist, disingenuous doublethink of the Roman Catholic Church on the other, I know which I prefer.

◆ QUESTIONS FOR REVIEW

1. What is the thesis of Dawkins' essay? Does it appear in the essay? If so, where? What reasons does he give for accepting his position?
2. Divide the essay into beginning, middle, and end. What rhetorical and/or stylistic devices help form these divisions?
3. What audience might Dawkins' essay be written for? Is that audience likely to resist his argument? Explain.
4. Does Dawkins offer counterarguments to those who would disagree with him? If so, what are they? Does he represent the opposition's argument fairly? Explain.
5. In addition to (or instead of) logical argumentation, what kinds of persuasive appeals does Dawkins use in this essay? Would these appeals be likely to work for his intended audience? Why, or why not?
6. How would you characterize your attitude toward this subject before reading Dawkins' essay? What effect did this essay have on your thinking?

✦ WRITING OPPORTUNITY

Dawkins' basic argument is that true science cannot be done without a rejection of religion. If Dawkins' theories came to be generally accepted, how would science be taught in public schools, and how would that instruction impact our freedom of religion? Write a brief exploratory essay examining this question. ✦

Our next persuasive essay, "Zero Tolerance for Abuse," was written by Jaime Sherrill, a first-year writing student at the University of North Carolina at Charlotte. In her essay, Jaime attempts to persuade readers to take action to help those who are abused by their spouses.

JAIME SHERRILL

ZERO TOLERANCE FOR ABUSE

Most injuries were to the head and neck and, in addition to bruises, strangle marks, black eyes, and split lips, resulted in eye damage, fractured jaws, broken noses and permanent hearing loss. Assaults to the trunk of the body were almost as common and produced a broken collarbone, bruised and broken ribs, a fractured tail bone, internal hemorrhaging, and a lacerated liver.

1   Unfortunately these injuries were not inflicted upon a boxer at a boxing match; these were injuries to women as a result of domestic violence. According to Natalie Jaffe's pamphlet, "Assaults on Women: Rape and Wife Beating," this description is typical of the kind of physical harm suffered by battered women surveyed in shelters and treatment centers in California. The fact that men can inflict such physical and emotional harm upon a woman infuriates me.

2   Many women get trapped in abusive relationships that are oftentimes too difficult to get out of. Children are sometimes trapped in these vicious cycles, watching their mothers helpless at the fist of an all too overpowering man. Why are there not more regulations against domestic violence? It seems to me that we are only turning our heads to a problem that will never disappear unless we stand up as women and say, "We are too strong to allow this to happen, and we will not tolerate it under any circumstances."

3   Many times, abuse in relationships goes unacknowledged. The abused may think it is a one-time thing and that it will never happen again. History, however, is destined to repeat itself unless we rally together and tell men we will no longer allow them to get away with this intolerable act. We need stricter laws for the

abusers. They should be behind bars just like any other criminal. They have committed larceny by robbing a woman of her dignity and self-esteem. They have committed murder by killing the hopes and dreams of a woman. They have committed assault, and have left physical and emotional bruises on their victims. They have been labeled repeat offenders and always seem to make bail with simply an apology or a dozen roses.

A woman should be able to wear make-up to make herself feel more beautiful, instead of having to wear make-up to cover up the black eye she received because her husband's or lover's hand "slipped." Make-up can cover up the temporary scars, but permanent scars run much deeper. It takes more than make-up to conceal them. A woman who has been abused is frightened. She is frightened of her partner, and this is a fear that she shares with many other women in all social classes and backgrounds that are abused. An abused woman often times feels guilty. She feels as if she is to blame for her partner's violence and that she has provoked him in some way. She then puts the blame on herself instead of the abuser and thinks of herself as a failure.

A 15-year-old girl lay motionless on the concrete, unable to stand. Her boyfriend, who was about to become a new father, had just violently beaten her in a heated argument. The young female, almost nine months pregnant, lay crying at the hands of a man who supposedly loved her and her unborn child. After this episode the girl and her parents decided that some sort of action must be taken against the man and they decided to press criminal charges. Several weeks later the unwed mother gave birth to a beautiful healthy baby boy and decided after much emotional and physical trauma to list the baby's father "unknown" on the birth certificate and give the baby her last name. Two years later the father of the child is still a part of her life even though they are no longer in a relationship. He has supervised visitation with the child once a week and is now seeking joint custody. Why did the court even allow this violent man supervised visitation with his record? Unfortunately, this is the story of a very close friend of mine who is still struggling with the issue that she was once in this very unhealthy relationship, and now this abuser wants to take this child from her. Anyone can see that this man is an unfit father and does not deserve to be with a child he abused while it was still in the womb. Yet, the judicial system is allowing him visitation with the child and considering joint custody. Is this a sign that society is now almost condoning violence?

Why do men abuse their partners? Many factors may play a role in this behavior. It could be that we live in a society that condones violence. Violence is everywhere, especially in movies, television, and newspapers. Sadly, violence is almost accepted as a part of life. Many of those responsible for this violence grew up watching their fathers abuse their mothers; they are only acting out what was part of their environments as young children. Although these situations are a part of the cause of this violence, there still can be no excuse for this kind of behavior.

The behavior I am talking about is all too predictable. Domestic abuse most of the time follows one specific pattern. There are three phases: the tension-building phase, the explosion or actual beating, and the loving phase. The tension-building phase often occurs or builds as a result of small incidents, such as a woman's failure to comply with her partner's request. The tension is followed by the explosion in which the abuser unfairly takes out all of his anger on his partner, and she becomes the object of his rage. He may violently punch, choke, kick, or even stab his partner. When the beating is complete, the abuser usually feels guilty and apologizes saying it will never happen again. Foolishly, the woman often believes him, and this is one major reason a woman remains in an abusive relationship.

We must find a way to prevent this horrifying pattern. But unless society as a whole refuses to tolerate violence any longer, meaningful changes will not occur. We cannot sit in the dark and let the violence continue; no one deserves to be beaten or threatened with physical harm. There is absolutely no excuse for this type of behavior and society should not tolerate such senseless violence. If the problem continues, it will only get worse. But women must have help to get out of these abusive relationships. We have already begun by opening many shelters and organizations devoted to helping these unfortunate victims seek refuge from abusers. This, however, is not nearly enough; it is only a small step on a long path towards a permanent solution.

Works Consulted

Fleming, Jennifer Baker. *Stopping Wife Abuse: A Guide to the Emotional, Psychological, and Legal Implications for the Abused Woman and Those Helping Her.* New York: Anchor/Doubleday, 1979.

Jaffe, Natalie. *Assaults on Women: Rape and Wife Beating.* New York: Public Affairs Committee, pamphlet no. 579, n.d.

◆ QUESTIONS FOR REVIEW

1. What is the thesis of Jaime's essay? Does it appear in the essay? If so, where? What reasons does she give for accepting her position?
2. What audience might Jaime's essay be written for? Is that audience likely to resist her argument? Explain.
3. What kinds of persuasive appeals does Jaime use in this essay? Would these appeals be likely to work for her intended audience? Why, or why not?
4. One's style of writing is very important in persuasion. A key element in Jaime's style is sentence structure. Find several examples of particularly effective sentences in Jamie's essay. What makes them effective?

◆ WRITING OPPORTUNITY

In her essay, Jaime Sherrill argues that "women must have help to get out of these abusive relationships." Tellingly, Sherrill assumes that it is women, and not men, who are enduring abuse. And statistics on abuse would support her assumption. Do you think this is simply because men are stronger and larger than women? Or, are other there other societal and/or evolutionary causes for the disproportionate violence in males? ◆

Our last essay in this section was written by Jaclyn Talbert, a first-year writing student at UNC Charlotte. In "Justice for Those Who Have Shown Us No Mercy," Jaclyn wants to persuade readers to support efforts to keep capital punishment in our legal system.

JACLYN TALBERT

JUSTICE FOR THOSE WHO HAVE SHOWN US NO MERCY

What do we dream of as children? Some girls dream about their weddings and what they will name their children, and some boys dream about the fame their pro football careers will bring them. Of course the dreams differ from person to person, but there is one milestone in life that all children cannot wait to reach. They can't wait to get their drivers' licenses so that they can cut the cord and experience some freedom from their parents. After reaching this milestone, my cousin had only two more days to dream. She went to the grocery store for her mom one day, and she never returned. A nicely dressed, average looking guy was standing in the middle of a country road a few blocks from her house waving his arms as if he needed help, so she stopped. She rolled down her window, and before she could ask how she could help, he shot her six times in the head and neck. She was the sixth of seven people that he killed that night. The sixth lifeless body he pushed aside so that he could pull her car behind a barn and await his last victim.

He was caught. And my aunt and uncle, and the families of six other victims, sat and listened to him explain the events of that awful night. He explained how each one of these innocent people looked like a demon and how he murdered each one in cold blood. After that day, he went to live in a home for the mentally ill, where he continues to live in peace and quiet. He was diagnosed as insane.

There is no peace for my aunt and uncle. Their lives have been shattered, ripped apart. Not a day goes by when my aunt does not blame herself for sending her daughter to the store that night. Hardly a night passes without her wondering if she could have warned her more clearly about strangers. Driving continues to be a nightmare for my aunt and uncle even now that nine years have passed, and they check and double check their doors to be sure they are locked. Anger and fear fills their hearts because the man who murdered their baby sits in a state supported hotel with his parole date inching closer and closer.

My cousin's death is but one example. There are many more. A young woman named Susan Smith sits comfortably in a North Carolina jail after drowning her two young sons. I still remember the shock and sorrow I felt as I heard about their deaths. At first it appeared that someone had kidnaped the children from Susan and murdered them—that was Susan's story. But then we learned the truth. I can still remember hearing the news as I was riding in the back seat, in busy Charlotte traffic, headed to the funeral of my friend, Brian, a twenty-year-old victim of cancer. The announcer said, "I never dreamed I would be announcing this, but there has been a confession in the Smith case. She did it. She killed her children." The news paralyzed me. How was it possible? What had caused her to lose her senses? Was there some mistake? We all know there was no mistake. Susan killed those precious little boys. The world watched as the car was pulled out of the lake, and as she excused what she had done because her boyfriend did not want to be a father and was going to leave her.

Another example involves a couple, Richard and Dawn Heikkia, who adopted Matthew and loved him as their son. This son murdered Richard and Dawn in cold blood, after planning the murder for months. Police found shotgun shells labeled "mom" and "dad." And in one of many letters written from prison, Matthew told the prosecutor about planning the crime. "My parents loved me, but I still wanted them dead because they pissed me off. [. . .] I did kill my parents for money and the car. I know they loved me. My mother told me that she loved me right before I put the slug through her head." The letters he wrote to his girlfriend included a gruesome, detailed story of the murders, and but one regret: "I am not sorry for what I have done. I just wish that I killed you when I had the chance" (Lang 136–145).

Unfortunately, Matthew was familiar with our system of justice. He mocked the prosecutor, telling him: "I'll cop an insanity plea, be out in twenty or so years, still young and smart enough to find you and Linda [his girlfriend]." He was right—at least about the verdict. He was deemed insane and is now living in a psychiatric hospital (Lang 145).

Does the state not have the right to rid itself of these killers—of people who would stand on the side of the road and methodically murder six strangers, of people who would kill their children because they were an "inconvenience," of people who would kill their parents in cold blood and boast of their intentions to kill others while awaiting trial? Many people argue against capital punishment, but those who would do so are concerned over the rights of the wrong person. When it comes time to deal with these murderers, the innocent victim is already dead. The murderer is not the one who deserves our pity. The victim and the victim's family should be our primary concern.

The murderer should die. It is not we, as a society, who are deciding his fate; he did that himself when he decided to murder, to rape—to torment a fellow human being. A person responsible for stealing someone else's life hardly deserves the chance to live his own. I know there are those who consider it inhumane to take the lives of killers—even confessed killers. They give us arguments full of contortions and misplaced human concern. They argue that our methods of execution are inhumane because the murderer may feel pain. I agree that we should attempt to remove these killers from our society with as little pain as possible; we should not try to make them suffer, since we do not wish to stoop to their level. However, we cannot stop enforcing punishment simply because the killer might feel some pain.

Pain abounds in this situation. Someone has died; someone has lost his daughter, granddaughter, sister, or mother—and someone is responsible. The murderer did not stop to think, or care, how this person would be missed. The murderer did not bother to wonder whether she had reached her goals in life! It is amazing that anyone would speak for these killers. But Nicholas Jenkins argues, in "Dirty Needle," that since it is against the law to electrocute chinchilla in America, we are being inhumane in electrocuting human beings. There is one vital difference between the chinchilla and the murderer, however: the chinchilla has not forfeited its right to live.

The murderer can blame no one but himself for his seat on death row. The person who has no say in this matter is the victim. He did not ask to be murdered. Why should our justice system take the side of the accused? Is it not our duty to punish those who have stolen innocence from our children and the last beat of our hearts?

We have lost touch with the value of human life when we are more concerned for the rights of murderers than the rights of their victims. But this is what has happened. Criminals know that the chances are slim that they will be truly punished for their crimes. In 1987, the Bureau of Justice records indicated that a murderer sentenced to life in prison with a chance of parole would serve an average of 85.3 months (Baird and Rosenbaum 108). We cannot judge just how effective execution is as a deterrent to other criminals, but we do know that it prevents that murderer from being free to murder again in slightly more than seven years.

Works Cited

Baird, Robert M., and Stuart E. Rosenbaum. *Punishment and the Death Penalty: The Current Debate.* New York: Prometheus, 1995.
Jenkins, Nicholas. "Dirty Needle." *New Yorker* 19 Dec. 1994: 5+.
Lang, Denise. *The Dark Son.* New York: Avon, 1995.

◆ QUESTIONS FOR REVIEW

1. What is the thesis of Jaclyn's essay? Does it appear in the essay? If so, where? What reasons does she give for accepting her position?
2. What audience might Jaclyn's essay be written for? Is that audience likely to resist her argument? Explain.
3. Does Jaclyn offer counterarguments to those who would disagree with her? If so, does she represent the opposition's argument fairly? Explain. What counterarguments are offered?
4. In addition to (or instead of) logical argumentation, what kinds of persuasive appeals does Jaclyn use in this essay? Would these appeals be likely to work for her intended audience? Why, or why not?
5. How would you characterize your attitude toward this subject before reading Jaclyn's essay? What effect did this essay have on your thinking?

◆ WRITING OPPORTUNITY

Using Jaclyn's essay as your model, begin a persuasive essay with a personal story that will affect your readers emotionally. ◆

THE RHETORICAL TRIANGLE

Reader

The reader of a persuasion essay is not someone who is opposed to the writer's thesis. At first glance, this seems wrong. Why would a writer attempt to persuade someone who already agrees with him? When we look more carefully, however, we see that the writer is not attempting to persuade the reader to believe something but rather to act on his beliefs. Think for a moment about situations in which an author might present an essay like those at the beginning of this chapter. For example, where might one hear such an essay as "Dismemberment and Choice"? It would be much more likely to be heard at a gathering of people with conservative leanings than at one of people with more liberal views. Liberal thinkers would likely dismiss Michael Heaphy's essay immediately because of the name calling he engages in and the overall tone of his essay. Those predisposed toward an anti-abortion position might well not be bothered by these matters. They are likely to respond emotionally, becoming even more opposed to abortion because of the gruesome details Heaphy provides.

You might be tempted to wonder whether Heaphy is wasting his time in speaking to such an audience. There is a cliché we often use when we think people are trying to convince those who need no convincing—*preaching to the choir*. If we look closely at this cliché, we may come to understand more clearly what type of audience we should be attempting to persuade. A preacher in Ron's youth once explained why the choir is the perfect audience for most sermons. Those who do not come to church would not heed the preacher's message even if they were somehow exposed to his sermon. But if those who are coming to church aren't doing what the preacher is exhorting them to do, they are well suited to hear his message; they know what they should do, and it is the preacher's task to energize them to act on what they already know.

Exercise 10.1

We discussed what kind of readers Heaphy's "Dismemberment and Choice" might have been intended for and speculated on a situation in which the essay might be read. Choose two or three other essays from the beginning of this chapter and discuss the audiences that would be appropriate for them. Then think of specific occasions on which these essays might be read aloud to a particular audience. What new insights can you gain into the relationships of the rhetorical triangle by imagining such situations?

Subject

The subject of a persuasion essay should be something that elicits an emotional response. Such essays often deal with the same types of debatable issues that position essays treat. However, the subject for a persuasive essay does not have to be debatable. Four of the six sample essays treat subjects that are clearly controversial. A fifth, Martin Luther King, Jr.'s, "I Have A Dream," may not be controversial today, but the issue of whether blacks should enjoy all the benefits of citizenship in the U.S. was hotly contested at the time of his writing. The remaining essay, Jaime Sherrill's "Zero Tolerance," seeks to impress upon readers how much spousal abuse there is in our country and to make readers feel the awful pain that is inflicted by this abuse, in hopes of causing them to take actions to help solve this problem. We refer to this topic as "not debatable," since no one is going to argue in favor of spousal abuse.

In saying that a subject isn't debatable, we are not suggesting that the issues involved in and around it do not allow for disagreements. Humans can and will disagree about the details and nuances in any subject. We are suggesting, rather, that with subjects such as spousal abuse, reasonable people will likely agree on the basic issues at hand. How could we not agree with Jaime and Alysia Tucker (whose essay at the end of this chapter also deals with spousal abuse) that we should do more to protect women from abuse? Of course, there are reasons we don't do more, ranging from selfishness with our money (that we might donate to treatment programs dealing with abusers) to lethargy. But no one is likely to speak up in favor of selfishness or lethargy. The writer's task, then, is not to argue against another point of view but rather to appeal to readers to do what they would agree they should do.

Exercise 10.2

Most readers would certainly agree with Jaime Sherrill (in "Zero Tolerance for Abuse," pages 501–503) and Alysia Tucker (in "No More," pages 529–532) that more should be done to protect women from violence, but they may not agree with all the claims on which these writers build their case. Find one or two statements in each essay with which reasonable people may disagree. Do the writers offer support in favor of their points of view on these matters? Explain. Do they acknowledge potential disagreements?

Writer

As the discussion in Chapter 9 indicated, there is a sense in which a writer of a position essay may want to draw attention to herself. The writer wants to be seen as a clear thinker (someone capable of mounting a logical argument for her case) and as ethical (someone who can be trusted to be honest and fair in dealing with the issue). The writer of a persuasive paper is not as likely to draw this kind of attention to herself. She takes the stance that anyone who is thinking clearly on an issue would see things the way they are being presented in her paper. Whereas the writer of a position essay may tend to focus on her beliefs as opposed to the beliefs of potential readers, the writer of a persuasion essay focuses on aspects of the subject on which she and her readers agree, thereby taking attention away from herself.

As we noted earlier, persuasive writing often deals with issues that are not arguable in the way that topics of position papers are. Thus, writers of persuasion essays often do not need to deal with the possibility that they hold opinions differing from those held by others. Writers such as Jaime are free to emphasize the pain and suffering caused by abuse. Even when they deal with topics that are controversial, writers of persuasion essays do not focus on the controversial nature of their topics. For example, Heaphy ("Dismemberment and Choice") writes about abortion as if there were really only one correct point of view on this subject. These kinds of essays are most successful when the reader has the feeling that any right-thinking person would see things in the way this writer sees them.

Exercise 10.3

We mentioned Heaphy's essay as an example of a persuasion essay in which the writer seems to assume that his is the only point of view on a controversial issue. Compare Heaphy's tactics in this essay with those of two or three of the other writers whose essays are featured at the beginning of this chapter. Rank these essays in terms of the degree to which they show awareness of an opposing point of view.

DISTINGUISHING FEATURES OF PERSUASION ESSAYS

Emotional Appeal

The key distinguishing feature of a persuasion essay is emotional appeal. The writer wants to move his readers to action, but humans seldom act on the basis of reason alone. How many former smokers can trace their decision to quit smoking to a presentation of the statistics on the health risks of smoking? Argumentation may have been helpful in laying the groundwork for the change, of course. Most smokers know and accept the argument that smoking is bad for them. Most of those who have quit, however, were moved to action by some emotional appeal or event, such as an appeal from a loved one or the death of someone close to them from a smoking-related illness. Those who wage campaigns against smoking are aware of this fact, as you can see by looking at their campaigns. Although they may offer statistics to show the harmful effects of smoking, the focus of antismoking advertisements is usually on an emotional appeal of some sort.

It is telling that those who would have us smoke also rely on persuasion and emotion as opposed to reason and argument. No cigarette advertiser lists the health benefits of smoking or attempts any other kind of rational argument in favor of smoking. Rather, the advertisements appeal to our emotions—our appetite for the pleasure of a relaxed smoke; our desire to be sexy, cool, and popular; or, if that won't do it, our desire to be seen as daring and defiant, as going our own way, as disdainful of the fears and cautions of the less strong among us.

Exercise 10.4

1. One of the mainstays of cigarette advertising for years was the "Marlboro Man." Find two or three examples of advertisements (from magazines in your library) using this theme. Who was the Marlboro Man? What emotions are being appealed to by the use of this theme?
2. Another long-standing and controversial advertising campaign involved the mascot for Camel cigarettes, Joe Camel. Find two or three advertisements using this theme. What emotions do these advertisements appeal to? What readers would most likely be attracted to these advertisements?
3. Find two or three other advertisements for cigarettes. Analyze the components of these advertisements: the pictures, the words, and the overall composition—that is, the way in which the words and pictures are combined. What emotions do the advertisements arouse in readers? What types of people are likely to be most affected by this type of appeal?

Ethical Persuasion

It may seem that we are picking on cigarette advertisers. We are. They provide us with a clear example of the distinction between effective persuasion and ethical persuasive writing. We think it is unethical to attempt to persuade people to take actions for which it is impossible to offer logical arguments. All of the issues written about in this chapter could be argued logically. Jaime could have made a logical argument for doing more to combat domestic abuse, though she didn't need to; Heaphy could have made a logical argument against abortion, though he did not choose to do so; and so on. However, it would not be possible, at least from the moral foundations on which we build, to argue in favor of smoking or in favor of refinancing one's house at a higher interest rate to buy a vacation or luxury consumer item.

Exercise 10.5

Examine three or four persuasive arguments you encounter in advertisements—in magazines, on radio or television, or in some other medium, such as the Internet. What do the advertisements seek to persuade you to do? What methods of persuasion are employed? How effective are they in persuading you to take the desired action? Given our discussion here, how ethical are these attempts at persuasion—that is, could the advertisers argue their cases logically?

We noted that each of the essays at the beginning of this chapter deals with a topic that could be argued logically. However, when writers decide to dismiss their opposition, they often write in ways that will discredit them with anyone who takes an opposing side. Such is the case in several of our sample essays. Richard Dawkins ("When Religion Steps on Science's Turf") knew that he was not going to convince Christians to accept his point by referring to the God of the Old Testament as "pitilessly vengeful." If opponents did not give up on his essay at that point, they certainly quit listening to him when he accused the pope of using "casuistical doubletalk," or when he labeled those who want to argue for separating science and religion as "dishonestly self-serving." We find similar language in Michael Heaphy's "Dismemberment and Choice." In his attack on those who perform abortions, Heaphy indicates that all those who would disagree with him on this issue are assisting those who commit murder. The tactics these writers use are diametrically opposed to the strategies of ethical argumentation we discussed in Chapter 9. But does that make them unethical? We choose to reserve that term for persuasion that encourages actions that could not be argued for logically. You should be aware, however, that the question of what is, and what is not, ethical persuasion is itself an arguable topic. What is not arguable is whether these types of emotional appeals are effective—they most certainly are.

Exercise 10.6

It should be clear from our discussion that there is no clear-cut line between ethical and unethical persuasion. It is probably best thought of as a continuum, from most ethical to least ethical, on which individual pieces of writing may be placed. Examine three of the essays from this chapter or three essays selected by your instructor, and rank them from most ethical to least ethical. Use as your criteria for this ranking the fairness with which they represent the arguments of those who oppose them and the tendency to insult those who oppose them or to call them names.

Persuasive Language

Once you decide to write persuasively—that is, to concentrate on engaging the emotions of your readers—what tools are available to you to accomplish your task? Put simply, the basic tool of persuasion in writing is the force of your language. Below, we discuss three ways of achieving this forceful language: description, narration, and prose style.

Description In Chapter 5, we talked about the powerful role that description plays in personal writing. The following passage makes it clear that description is also effective in persuasive writing:

> Maudlin viewers of the death penalty call the most wanton slayer a "Child of God" who should not be executed regardless of how heinous his crime may be because "God created man in his own image, in the image of God created he him." (Genesis 1:27) Was not this small, blonde six-year-old girl a child of God? She was choked, beaten, and raped by a sex fiend whose pregnant wife reportedly helped him lure the innocent child into his car and who sat and watched the assault on the screaming youngster. And when he completed his inhumane deed, the wife, herself bringing a life into the world, allegedly killed the child with several savage blows with a tire iron. The husband has been sentenced to death. Words and words and words may be written, but no pleas in favor of the death penalty can be more horribly eloquent than the sight of the battered, sexually assaulted body of this child, truly a "child of God."
>
> J. Edgar Hoover, *Law Enforcement Bulletin.*

In this passage, J. Edgar Hoover, former director of the Federal Bureau of Investigation, illustrates and explains the role that description can play in persuasive writing. Hoover is aware that those who oppose capital punishment appeal to our emotional reaction to the killing of any human being, even one who has taken someone else's life. He counters this appeal to emotion with one of his own—the description of the horrible death of a beautiful and innocent child. Hoover then explains what he is doing, by stating ironically that words cannot be as effective as the sight of a child who has been killed in such an awful fashion. We say "ironically" because words are all that Hoover has at his disposal to create this image for us. The more effective his description, the more effective his argument for the death penalty.

> **Exercise 10.7**
>
> Examine two or three of the sample essays at the beginning of this chapter to determine how they use description to persuade their readers. Select two or three especially effective passages and explain how they engage the reader's emotions.

Narration   It is easy to see why narration is effective in persuasion. Our emotions are engaged when we react personally to the issue at hand, and what better way to engage readers personally than by telling stories that they can relate to? In the following passage from "Crack and the Box," Pete Hamill uses a story of a brief visit with a woman addicted to drugs to introduce his readers to the horrors of addiction:

> One sad, rainy morning last winter, I talked to a woman who was addicted to crack cocaine. She was 22, stiletto-thin, with eyes as old as tombs. She was living in two rooms in a welfare hotel with her children, who were two, three, and five years of age. Her story was the usual tangle of human woe: early pregnancy, dropping out of school, vanished men, smack and then crack, tricks with johns in parked cars to pay for the dope. I asked her why she did drugs. She shrugged in an empty way and couldn't really answer beyond "makes me feel good." While we talked and she told her tale of squalor, the children ignored us. They were watching television.
>
> Walking back to my office in the rain, I brooded about the woman, her zombie-like children, and my own callous indifference. I'd heard so many versions of the same story that I almost never wrote them anymore; the sons of similar women, glimpsed a dozen years ago, are now in Dannemora or Soledad or Joliet; in a hundred cities, their daughters are moving into the same loveless rooms. As I walked, a series of homeless men approached me for change, most of them junkies. Others sat in doorways, staring at nothing. They were additional casualties of our time of plague, demoralized reminders that although this country holds only two percent of the world's population, it consumes 65 percent of the world's supply of hard drugs.

Hamill's story is an attempt to persuade readers not to be indifferent in the face of the tragedy of drug addiction. He tells us about a visit to a specific woman, all the while pointing out that this woman—and her faceless children—are representative of the thousands of people whose lives have been ruined by drugs. If we feel sympathy for this woman, "stiletto-thin, with eyes as old as tombs," and her innocent children forced to live in "squalor" through no fault of their own, we may well be moved to take the action that Hamill proposes later in his essay.

> **Exercise 10.8**
>
> Several of the sample essays at the beginning of this chapter make use of narration. Choose two or three of those narratives, and discuss the role they play in their respective essays. What is the writer attempting to persuade her or his readers of? What emotions do these narratives appeal to? How effective do you imagine they will be in helping the writers achieve their purposes?

Prose Style A final tool for persuasion is much easier to illustrate than to explain. We see it at work in the following excerpt from the powerful essay that Jaime Sherrill wrote against the abuse of women:

> Many times, abuse in relationships goes unacknowledged. The abused may think it is a one time thing and that it will never happen again. History, however, is destined to repeat itself unless we rally together and tell men we will no longer allow them to get away with this intolerable act. We need stricter laws for the abusers. They should be behind bars just like any other criminal. They have committed larceny by robbing a woman of her dignity and self-esteem. They have committed murder by killing the hopes and dreams of a woman. They have committed assault, and have left physical and emotional bruises on their victims. They have been labeled repeat offenders and always seem to make bail with simply an apology or a dozen roses.
>
> A woman should be able to wear make-up to make herself feel more beautiful, instead of having to wear make-up to cover up the black eye she received because her husband's or lover's hand "slipped." Make-up can cover up the temporary scars, but permanent scars run much deeper. It takes more than make-up to conceal them.

We also see a powerful illustration of prose style in the following excerpt from Martin Luther King, Jr.'s "Letter from Birmingham Jail."

> We have waited for more than 340 years for our constitutional and God-given rights. The nations of Asia and Africa are moving with jetlike speed toward gaining political independence, but we still creep at horse-and-buggy pace toward gaining a cup of coffee at a lunch counter. Perhaps it is easy for those who have never felt the stinging darts of segregation to say, "Wait." But when you have seen vicious mobs lynch your mothers and fathers at will and drown your sisters and brothers at whim; when you have seen hate-filled policemen curse, kick and even kill your black brothers and sisters; when you see the vast majority of your twenty million Negro brothers smothering in an airtight cage of poverty in the midst of an affluent society; when you suddenly find your tongue twisted and your speech stammering as you seek to explain to your six-year-old daughter why she can't go to the public amusement park that has just been advertised on television, and see tears welling up in her eyes when she is told that Funtown is closed to colored children, and see ominous clouds of inferiority beginning to form in her little

mental sky, and see her beginning to distort her personality by developing an unconscious bitterness toward white people; when you have to concoct an answer for a five-year-old son who is asking: "Daddy, why do white people treat colored people so mean?"; when you take a cross-country drive and find it necessary to sleep night after night in the uncomfortable corners of your automobile because no motel will accept you; when you are humiliated day in and day out by nagging signs reading "white" and "colored"; when your first name becomes "nigger," your middle name becomes "boy" (however old you are) and your last name becomes "John," and your wife and mother are never given the respected title "Mrs."; when you are harried by day and haunted by night by the fact that you are a Negro, living constantly at tiptoe stance, never quite knowing what to expect next, and are plagued with inner fears and outer resentments; when you are forever fighting a degenerating sense of "nobodiness"—then you will understand why we find it difficult to wait.

In both these essays, one by a student writer and one by an acknowledged master of prose style, we find examples of powerful language that makes each passage persuasive. Note the use of sentence repetition for effect in both pieces. Jaime begins four consecutive sentences with the same pronoun and auxiliary verb: "they have." Martin Luther King, Jr. uses the repetition of an adverbial clause beginning with "when you" to introduce each indignity that blacks have had to suffer. In the passage from her essay, Jaime consciously uses repetition to drive home her point that women have suffered far too often at the hands of violent men; King consciously repeats an adverbial clause structure to reinforce his point that the indignities suffered by blacks have been more numerous and constant than human endurance can be expected to tolerate. These repetitions add power to both pieces of writing.

These are not the only elements that make for effective prose style in these two excerpts. Note the turns of phrase Jaime uses in the second paragraph when she talks about what make-up should be used for as contrasted with what it is used for by battered women. Also note the contrast between the "temporary scars" that make-up can cover and the "permanent scars" that run too deep to be covered over by anything. Note the contrast King draws between the "jetlike speed" at which African nations are moving toward "political independence" and the "horse-and-buggy pace" at which blacks in the United States are moving toward "gaining a cup of coffee at a lunch counter." Note also the way in which King uses figurative language to picture the "clouds of inferiority beginning to form in [his daughter's] little mental sky."

Our discussion of prose style should make it clear that persuasive writing uses the tools of language to help readers identify with their subjects emotionally and remember to act upon what they have felt. It may sound strange to say that language is the key to both of these—emotional impact and memory. But it is. People will feel what we have said only to the degree that we make our subjects vivid and real to them. And they will remember what we say much better if our language is powerful. Humans respond to the way something is said as well as to what is said. That is why we remember President John F. Kennedy's famous admonition, "Ask not what your country can do for you—ask what you can do for your country." How much less effective would his speech have been had he said, "Don't be selfish when it comes to civic matters; see what you can do to make this a better country"? The power and much of the persuasive effect of this part of his speech would be missing.

Exercise 10.9

We have discussed description, narration, and prose style separately. In practice, the three often work together in persuasive writing. To see how this is so, examine "Justice For Those Who Have Shown Us No Mercy" (pages 504–506) by Jaclyn Talbert. Then, discuss the ways Jaclyn uses description, narration, and prose style to craft this very persuasive essay.

ASSIGNMENT AND GUIDELINES FOR WRITING

Assignment

Write a paper in which you persuade readers to take action on a belief you hold. Your readers may already share this belief with you. If they do not, they are at least favorably disposed to the arguments for this belief. Consider choosing a topic from one of the Writing Opportunity assignments to which you responded earlier in this chapter.

Choosing a Topic

If you have written a position essay, you have already uncovered one or more topics that you feel strongly about. If so, consider writing a persuasion essay about one of these topics. If you're undecided about a topic, try any or all of the activities in Part A.

Part A

1. Take a look again at your responses to the Interest Inventory (pages 11–13). Look especially for topics that you feel strongly about, topics that make you angry or frightened. Pick two or three, and freewrite about each for five to ten minutes. Why did you pick these particular potential topics? Why do they arouse such strong feelings?
2. Make a "Bug List," as described by James L. Adams in *Conceptual Blockbusting* (Reading, MA: Perseus, 1986). Develop a list of things that bug you about your school, your community, your friends, your educational system, and the world. Write two or three sentences about each entry on your list.

Then, select those you think are most interesting, and write three or four more sentences about each of these. Why did you select these particular entries as more interesting than the others?

3. Look back over the writings you did in response to the Writing Opportunities in this chapter—perhaps you've been keeping them in a writer's notebook. Write three or four sentences about any particularly interesting topics you find there.

Part B Choose two potential topics, and freewrite for ten minutes about each. Then, determine which topic is more interesting to you. Which involves you more emotionally? Select it as your subject for this essay, or if you do not feel ready to do so, return to some of the activities above.

Collecting Information

Questions for Analysis. Apply the Questions for Analysis (pages 24–31) to your topic. Write a detailed response to each question that seems pertinent to your topic.

Logic. Examine your topic to see whether it lends itself to logical support. To do so, state your position tentatively, and then determine whether it is possible for a reasonable person to take an opposing point of view. If you find that yours is a debatable topic, sketch briefly the argument that you would offer in favor of your point of view. It may be helpful to construct an imaginary dialogue of the type presented in Chapter 9 (pages 455–457).

Emotional appeals. List key emotional appeals you would use in support of your topic. You may want to list key values that you and your reader share (see Chapter 9, pages 453–454) so that you can determine what emotions may be associated with those values. For example, if "fairness" is a key value, then you may well find that appeals to anger (over unfair treatment) are effective. Or, if a key value is "family," then appeals to fear (that something may harm a member of one's family) may be effective.

Reader. Use your reader as a means of generating information. Decide what specific occasion you will use to present your appeal to your reader. Analyze your reader in terms of his knowledge and feelings about your topic. Also reflect on what will be most successful in helping make your reader take the action you propose.

Focus Statement

As you begin to generate information for your essay, look back over your freewriting and write a focus statement. The following focus statement was written by Jaime Sherrill for her essay "Zero Tolerance for Abuse":

I want to convince women to take action against men who are constantly abusing women. I will not need to offer a logical argument, since this isn't a debatable topic. I want to help make my audience, women who care about the world they live in, start doing something about this problem. I will attempt to stir their emotions by telling stories about women who have been beaten.

Jaime's focus statement provided her with a starting place: She did mount an effective emotional appeal by telling the stories of abused women. She probably did not know when she wrote this statement that she would also use prose style effectively to engage the emotions of her reader. Had she known this, she could have listed it as a strategy here in her statement.

Planning Your Essay's Structure

Persuasion essays may be organized by either of the argument structures (formal or informal) introduced in Chapter 9 (pages 460–464). However, they are more likely to assume the informal structure, with relatively little attention given to logical supports and more attention devoted to emotional supports. Michael Heaphy's essay, "Dismemberment and Choice," makes use of an informal argument structure that may be analyzed as follows:

I. *Thesis* (implicit): The pro-choice position on abortion is not defensible (paragraph 1).
II. *Logical support for thesis:* Arguments as to the meaning of pro-choice (paragraph 2)
III. *Emotional support for thesis*:
   A. Description of abortion practices of Dr. Haskell (paragraphs 3–6)
   B. Discussion of euphemisms used in renaming parts of murdered babies (paragraphs 7–9)
   C. Detail from Miss Brower's charges against Dr. Haskell (paragraphs 10–14)
IV. *Refutation of counterargument:* There is no distinction—as the other side would attempt to make—between killing that takes place just before birth and killing immediately after birth (paragraph 15).
V. *Concluding statements* (paragraphs 16–17)

Thesis Statement

The thesis statement for a persuasion essay is often implied rather than stated. For example, Heaphy does not say anywhere in his essay exactly what he wants readers to do. If he were to do so, his thesis might be something like the following:

> You should do all within your power to cause our government to make abortion illegal and to discourage anyone from having an abortion.

Note the difference between what we envision as a thesis sentence for a persuasion essay such as Heaphy's and a thesis sentence for a position essay on the same topic, which might be stated as follows:

> Abortion should be illegal.

To arrive at a possible thesis sentence for your persuasion essay, begin with a thesis for a companion argument. For example, Jaime Sherrill might have begun with this argumentative thesis:

> Our system of justice should do more to combat spousal abuse.

To move to a persuasive thesis, she needs to involve her readers:

> You should take actions to help decrease spousal abuse.

As we've said, your thesis may very well not be included in your essay, because an effective persuasion essay often follows the dictum of "showing" rather "telling." That is, once the writer has graphically described the horrors of abortions, it seems a bit anti-climatic to say, "Now, go out and do all you can to stop this killing." Some things go without saying. However, you should be careful to *say* what your thesis is in your planning stages so that you are clear on just what you want your persuasive language to achieve.

Refining Your Writing

After you've written a draft of your essay and taken some time away from it, revise it, keeping the following principles in mind:

> *Emotional appeal.* Be sure that you have given your readers a way to identify emotionally with your subject. Explore ways to strengthen the emotional impact of your essay.
>
> *Effectiveness of language.* Review your essay to determine whether its prose style plays an important role in its overall effectiveness. Consider the role that narration and description play in your essay, and determine whether additional narratives or more descriptive language would add to the overall effectiveness of your essay.
>
> *Ethical persuasion.* Examine your treatment of those who would oppose your position to be sure that your essay is both effective and ethical—making for what we consider *good* writing.

Using Visuals to Persuade

As we said at the beginning of this chapter, persuasion involves much more than logical reasoning. Our intellectual understanding of and belief in a certain set of facts or logical inferences can certainly contribute to our acceptance or rejection of a given argument. However, in matters that are very important to our sense of self, reason isn't enough. Our emotions also have to be engaged. Although words can certainly appeal to our emotions by means of their connotative force, images prove even more powerful because, unlike words which are abstractions (even when they refer to concrete entities),

Mike Peters Editorial Cartoon © 1988 Mike Peters. All rights reserved. Reprinted with the permission of Mike Peters and the Cartoonist Group.

images have the ability to represent the real world in which we live. When we read a text we must decode a series of abstract words, working out the logic of what those words symbolize, and then understand what those words mean in our everyday lives. If words are like medicine in tablet form, images are like medicine in the form of an IV. Once we see the image, the message (both denotative and connotative) of that image surges through our bloodstream.

As a case in point, let's analyze this cartoon using the tools we discussed in Chapter 4 (pages 127–129).

First, we can view the cartoon as a copy. It represents a reasonably common occurrence in our world, the scene in which a judge delivers a verdict to an individual who has been convicted of a crime.

Next, let's analyze this cartoon as one artist's viewpoint. In fact, as we explained in Chapter 8 (page 380), this cartoon is called a caricature because it purposely distorts to reflect the biases of the artist. Of course, any individual image will be a viewpoint, because no one image can present all the angles from which that scene could have been presented. In a caricature, however, the artist takes this aspect of presentation to the extreme to make people and situations appear in a humorous and satirical light. In this cartoon, the artist has exaggerated the height of the judge's bench so that the woman has to look up to the judge as a child would. The features of the judge are exaggerated; his nose is huge and his mouth is even larger as he pronounces the sentence. The judge, himself, is a very large man, and he is leaning over his desk, peering down at the woman as he issues his sentence. The woman, on the other hand, is short, slightly stooped and without a face—as far as the viewer can tell. Her head is covered in a scarf and only her nose and right eye can be seen. She has no mouth, so she is silent. She has no face, so she has no identity; she is not an individual. In sum, then, the angle from which we are viewing the scene makes it very clear that all the power belongs to this large menacing-looking man.

From the vantage point of association, this cartoon makes use of several very powerful symbols. First there is the conflation of the historically male-dominated court system with the historically male-dominated legislative branch of U.S. government—the Congress. These symbols are given added power by the use of an archetypal symbol of height—that is, to be above another person is to be in a superior position relative to that person. Another way our language captures this symbolism is in the saying that one person may have the "upper-hand" over another. Here we have a case in which the highest branch of legislative government, the Congress, sits in judgment over a poor woman who has already been victimized by a rapist (according to the caption). She is not to be heard—having no voice, of course, is symbolic of lack of power. And she appears before this court not only silent, but also with her head covered, a traditional symbol of women's inferior status.

When we add the caption, "You've been found guilty of being poor, female, and raped and we sentence you to nine months' hard labor," the message is clear. The artist wants us to believe that the male-dominated system of government in the U.S. has historically abused women's rights and that a repeal of *Roe* v. *Wade* would mean a return to that sad condition. That is the underlying argument here. However, that argument is never stated, not even in the words of the caption. Rather, the cartoon taps into a belief that courts have often been unfair in dispensing justice. We are presented with a victim, a poor woman who has been raped; rather than receiving help from this high court, she is victimized a second time by the court which treats her as a criminal. All of this information comes to the viewer instantly and forcefully in the image of this silent woman enduring the harangue of this haughty judge.

The other side of this debate has its own powerful images. As a case in point, examine the cartoon which appears on the following page.

Cagle Cartoons, http://cagle.msnbc.com/news/2004Fairrington/images/abortion.gif.

First, let's look at this image as a copy. Although this is one image, we actually have a representation of two different scenes, one in which a protestor in favor of abortion rights carries a protest sign and another in which a new-born baby is being thrown into a garbage can. These scenes do not occur together (as they are depicted in this caricature), but aspects of the real world are being represented. People do march in protest events, and unsavory-looking trash bins are a part of the world we live in.

What do we find when we examine this image as a viewpoint? As is the case with the first cartoon, this is a caricature in which the artist presents characters who oppose his point of view in a very unrealistic and unfavorable light. The first thing that may leap off the page at the reader is the picture of the helpless baby about to fall into a trash can. From all the perspectives that one might choose regarding babies, the creator of this cartoon has chosen to focus on the baby's helplessness and vulnerability. The baby is extremely small and totally unprotected, without clothes or a blanket around it. What perspectives of the garbage cans are highlighted? Clearly, the artist wants the audience to see the dangerous and unsanitary nature of garbage cans. Of all the things that might be in a garbage can, we see a bottle that will likely shatter and cut the baby; we see old shoes that, like the baby, have been discarded as of no use; we see a board with a nail, a piece of what looks like an old fish carcass, and hovering flies.

And what do we find when we look at the viewpoint being offered in the other scene? Surely many attractive women and men have walked in demonstrations for women's rights, but the woman here is not one of them. She has a disproportionately large head, which consists largely of an open mouth. She has glasses, but no visible eyes. And she is clutching, not simply holding, a protest sign, her hands so tightly fisted that should she decide to, she is ready to punch anyone who gets in her way.

So what is the viewpoint being offered here? Clearly, the creator of this cartoon wants to depict those who would favor legal abortion in a very negative light. The protestor is presented as an unreasonable, combative person who would shout down anyone who disagrees with her. The image of an innocent and vulnerable baby in the process of falling into this nasty garbage can would shock and horrify any right-thinking person.

Finally, what do we find when we examine the symbolism in this image? Any number of items in the cartoon could be looked at for their symbolic value, but we will limit our discussion to four highly emotional symbols: the baby, the garbage can, the beer (or wine) bottle, and the image of the coat-hanger. The baby, beer bottle, and garbage come together in one implied analogy: aborting a fetus is throwing a baby into the garbage. In terms of our everyday use of language, we often talk about people treating other people "like garbage." In this cartoon we have a literal representation of this metaphor. These symbols work on another level also. Even though the picture of the shrill woman and the one of the baby being thrown into a garbage can represent two different scenes, they are telescoped into one in this cartoon. So we have a shrill woman standing right beside a gruesome scene of garbage and alcohol. The association is not a pleasant one.

The final symbol we will discuss is the depiction of the coat-hanger. This one is particularly interesting because it is a case of one side of an issue taking a key symbol used by the other side and turning it against them. For years, those who supported a woman's right to choose have referred to what they have called "coat-hanger abortions." Their argument has been that when legal abortions are impossible, women will resort to illegal abortions which in their most extreme and gruesome depictions would be performed with the use of a coat hanger. Here that argument and symbol are used against the pro-choice proponents. They seem to be in some way condoning, or more likely condoning the threat of, coat-hanger abortions, since this shrill and unattractive woman is waving a sign with a coat-hanger on it.

The argument of the cartoon is made clear by the brief caption—the woman asserting her rights to her body and the baby asserting its separate identity as a human being. However, most of the real impact of this message is to be found in the image itself.

Exercise 10.10

Above we have discussed two cartoons that some might see as arguments related to the issue of abortion. We prefer to call them powerful pieces of persuasion because they are intended for audiences that already accept the argument made in the cartoon. Those who consider themselves pro-choice and believe that a woman's body is hers to control may well resonate with and be further convinced by the first cartoon above. However, those who consider themselves pro-life will only be offended.

Find two cartoons on either side of another controversial issue. Then use the following questions to analyze each of the cartoons:
1. What is the controversial topic being addressed? Which side of the issue is each cartoon taking?
2. What scene(s) does each cartoon represent?
3. What features in the presentation help to reveal and support the artist's point of view?
4. What are the key symbols in each cartoon? How do they function to persuade?
5. How does the caption function to complement and support the message in the image?

Exercise 10.11

Create a cartoon intended to persuade viewers to accept the argument you are writing in this chapter's writing assignment. Then, write an explanation of the cartoon in terms of *representation, perspective,* and *symbol*. Note: If you do not want to attempt the art work, your teacher may suggest that you write a description of the cartoon you would draw, and then explain how it would persuade in terms of its basic elements: *representation, perspective,* and *symbol*.

SAMPLE STUDENT PROCESS

Our example student essay was written by Alysia Tucker, a first-year writing student at New Mexico State University. Alysia knew very early on that she wanted to write about battered women, so her prewriting begins with some responses to the Questions for Analysis.

Prewriting

What do I associate with battering?
- anger, pity, suffering in general
- people who will not help themselves
- frustration

What goes with battering?
- poverty, lack of education
- suffering children

What opposes battering?
- my life and that of most of the people I know (in the sense of being opposite to?)
- legal system (in the sense of being intended to stop battering)

What causes battering?
- power difference between men and women (men are stronger than women)
- poverty of women who can't leave batterers
- weak men who take out frustrations on weaker people
- court system that allows batterers to go free
- women who stay with batterers

What does battering cause?
- suffering for all
- children scarred for life
- death of many women
- shame in our society

Focus Statement

I want my audience to understand abuse and how dangerous it is. I want them to know they can help put a stop to it.

This is a good statement of what Alysia wants to do, but it provides little insight into how she might go about accomplishing her goals. Her discovery draft allows her to experiment with how to develop her paper and leads to an audience analysis.

Discovery Draft

Battering is the establishment of control and fear in a relationship through violence and other forms of abuse. Millions of women were physically abused by their husbands or boyfriends within the last year. Battery is a crime that ~~sometimes~~ *often* goes *unnoticed and* unreported. It results in severe harm and death among our countrys women. (Add stats here.) We must take a stand for victims by encouraging them. (Put in article from Standard Times here.) One woman I know was abused *by her husband*. She had a little girl and he would make her *sit and* watch him beat her mom. He would come home drunk and abuse her until she finally escaped. She is now married to a man who loves her and has never beat her. (Add Stephanie Rodriguez's story here.)

It is never easy *for a battered woman* to leave a batterer. (Add stat here.) They are afraid of reprisal. Authorities should interfere and take action. Some women are afraid of homelessness. (Add stat.) A woman and child shouldn't have to be afraid to leave (Add stat about 1st shelter here.)

(Add stat about murdered women here.) Police think that strangers will do more harm than intimates. But they need to understand that they can do more damage than strangers. Some people say they just "lost it." But then they would be beating other people who angered them.

There are signs you can look for in a battered woman. Low self-esteem and denial is one of them. Another one is taking responsibility of the abuser's actions. She may be very family-oriented in a traditional way and may be over-protected. If you see these signs, take action and help them or she may stay, allowing it to continue.

Audience Analysis   After writing her discovery draft, Alysia wrote the following audience analysis to help her move to a second draft of her essay:

> The projected reader of my essay is people who know abused victims. They probably already know a little about abuse but are unwilling to take the steps necessary to prevent it. The reader is likely to ignore the essay. The reader will most likely respond to the sources and facts. I will try to use shocking facts to get my message across.

Second Audience Analysis   Next, Alysia produced a second audience analysis from a list of questions provided by her teacher, Bill.

1. *What should this paper do for (or to) your readers?*
   I want my readers to gain knowledge of what they can do for abuse victims.

2. *What will the readers' initial reaction to your thesis be?*
   They will probably ignore the essay but hopefully read it and understand.

3. *What do your readers know about the topic at this point?*
   They probably know a little but aren't ready to involve themselves.

4. *What question(s) should your essay raise for readers?*
   How can they take actions, how can they be involved, especially if they are younger?

5. *Ultimately, what do you want your readers to do?*
   I want my readers to speak up for battered women. If they know someone being abused, help her out of the situation.

6. *How will the readers respond to the information you give them?*
   I think all the sources will surprise the reader because they were very shocking to me.

Alysia then wrote her second draft.

Second Draft

Battering—the establishment of control and fear in a relationship through violence and other forms of abuse. The batterer uses acts of violence and a series of behaviors, including intimidation, threats, psychological abuse, isolation, etc. to coerce and to control the other person. Battery is a crime that often goes unnoticed, unreported, and ignored, resulting in severe bodily harm and death among our country's woman today. 1

Our communities allow violence to occur in homes and families too often. People may not think we should interfere in the lives of other people, but in this case we must take a stand for victims of violence. An article from *The Standard Times* reported examples of beaten women: 2

Kathy was beaten when there were dirty dishes in the sink. She was beaten when her live-in boyfriend was drunk. She was beaten when he was sober. Janine's eye was blackened when her fiance disagreed with their wedding plans. Doris was punched when she was pregnant. She was slapped when dinner was a minute late. She was shoved and beaten when dinner was on time. Laura was kicked in the stomach when she tried to break up. She was slapped around when she tried make up. And all were hit at least once because the man in their lives claimed they "pushed their buttons"—brought abuse on themselves by not seeing how stressed their mates were. (1)

One woman I know was abused by her husband repeatedly. She had a little girl and her husband would make the child sit and watch him beat her. He would come home drunk and punch her in the face until it was black and blue with bruises. He would shove her violently against the walls, then kick her in the stomach, enabling her to breath. He would slap her around, while her child cried in the background. This continued for two years. Then she developed the courage to leave him. Now she is remarried to a man who loves her and would never consider hitting her. This woman was lucky to have left her husband before she was severely injured or killed. But leaving isn't always the best alternative. 3

It is never easy for a battered woman to leave her husband. They are often afraid of reprisal from the offender and so they stay, allowing the abuse to proceed. They also fear the thought of being homeless. There are nearly three times as many animal shelters in the United States as there are shelters for battered women and their children (Senate Judiciary Hearings, 1990). Do we put more value on the lives of animals or do we just refuse to think there is a problem with domestic violence? We need to wake up and get back to reality, and realize that the women in our country are being savagely beaten and killed by husbands and boyfriends. The victims need our encouragement and support. They should know they will have a decent shelter to live in if they choose to leave their offenders. A woman and her child should never be homeless because they are beaten. They should be welcomed with open arms 4 to homes that are run with caring people. Although some women are afraid to speak up, those who publicly report their abuse can help women in their situation.

Stephanie Rodriguez, a woman battered by her father and her ex-husband, wrote a powerfully worded book about her survival through her abusive situations. In her book, she retold a story used by her friend, a train engineer, about abuse: One night on a long stretch of track, he noticed a figure far ahead. On the tracks, he thought. For a long time the distance between the train and the figure appeared to remain the same. He wondered if it wasn't some sort of optical illusion. After awhile, however, the train began to gain on the figure, and soon my friend was close enough to see the terrified and exhausted dog, running for all he was worth, looking back over first one shoulder, then the other at the tremendous monster bearing down on him. He blew the whistle. The dog increased his speed, but was unable to maintain his pace. Finally the train ran over him. She stated that she hated that story but came to realize what it meant. That the dog was so involved in the business of staying ahead of the monster on his tail that he couldn't possibly conceive of another thing. He didn't have time to reason that a single step in either direction would save him. It was just like being a victim of abuse. She was so caught up in violence that she couldn't hear her friends and family calling from the other side. When she was a child, her mother committed suicide as a result of years of abuse, thinking it was her only way out. She married an abusive husband but managed to escape from him before she was faced with the same situation. Many abused women are faced with options such as suicide or killing in self-defense.

Currently there are 2,000 battered women in America who are serving prison time for defending their lives against their batterers. (source) These women who killed their aggressors did not kill in cold blood—they were defending themselves and sometimes the children involved in the abusive position. So why did the court system incarcerate them? If women cannot protect themselves from being murdered, the number of female homicide victims will increase. The average prison sentence of men who kill their women partners is two to six years, Women who kill their partners are sentenced on average to fifteen years, despite the fact that most women who kill do so in self-defense. (Source).

Of the 5,745 women murdered in 1991, six out of ten were killed by someone they knew. Half were murdered by a spouse or someone with whom they had been intimate (source). One memorial on an Internet home page tells one woman's story: Linda M. Ponder, a twenty-seven year old, was killed by her ex-boyfriend in a mad rage. He had previously been arrested for beating her and the police had confiscated a gun from him after he threatened her with it. After she was killed, the police wanted the case closed concerning the person who supplied him with both guns (one they took away and one the boyfriend was given before he murdered his girlfriend). The police claimed they didn't have enough evidence. It is a shame that this woman died because the police and those around her, stood by and watched. Police were more likely to respond within five minutes if the offender was a stranger than if an offender was known to the female victim (Bachman 1994). Authorities need to understand that husbands and boyfriends can do just as much damage to females as strangers can.

Reviews

Alysia then presented this draft to a classmate, including a list of questions she had about her paper. Here are Alysia's questions and the reviewer's answers to them:

1. *Does the story in ¶5 fit or should I leave it out?*
   I like the story—it fits very well—maybe elaborate some more on the meaning of the dog not getting off the tracks.

2. *I think I use "should" too many times at the end of ¶4. Can you help with sentences and give ideas on how I can change that?*
   I would definitely switch up ¶3 so that the reader does not encounter so many "should's."

3. *I still need a conclusion para. Any ideas?*
   Well—I like the idea of maybe presenting a case where an institution has been up and running and helping women. Present the idea that it can be done. Your last paragraph is a little weak—sentence structure is not quite there. Maybe use that paragraph with your example and a lead into what can be done (conclusion).

4. *Some of my paragraphs are lacking and I'm still looking up sources to use.*
   No comment on this.

Alysia also sent a copy (by e-mail) to Ron, who offered the following comments, along with some marks in the margins of her draft:

   Hi Alysia, thanks for your paper. You're on your way to writing a very good one, I think—the basic material is here. Below I am using the system that Bill and I use. That is, we make comments in each other's texts in capital letters. Some of the comments just tell what we think about a word, sentence, or section. Other times, we rewrite for each other. So what I've done is to point out some places where I think you might work on your paper.
   As I said above, I think your materials are strong. I would suggest, however, that your overall organization can be stronger in general. In particular, you need something at the beginning to capture your reader. I would suggest seeing if you can't bring the story of the dog running from the train to the beginning. That gives me chills just to think about it—the fear and torment of the animal as the train slowly overtakes it. I think you could move from that to another case or two of battered women and then go into your discussion of just how bad this problem is and what should be done about it.
   Speaking of which, it would be good if you could make it clearer to your readers what you would like them to do (or what anyone can do) about this situation. That brings us to the question of whom you are writing for. I don't think you are writing to battered women. If you are, I take back my suggestion about starting with the dog and the train—that makes them look too helpless. However, if you are talking to others, then that story works as a beginning. But what can (should) your readers do about this situation? Think about what group of people you would like to speak to about this topic; that might help.
   Well, I won't say more now. I'm copying these comments to Bill—he might have something to say about them, and I suspect he'll have some of his own.
   Good luck. It's going to be a good paper.

Alysia then produced the following final draft.

Final Draft

ALYSIA TUCKER
NO MORE

Stephanie Rodriguez tells a story about an incident that happened to a friend of hers, who had been an engineer at one time. Rodriguez recounts this story of the engineer's encounter with a lone figure on the tracks in front of his train:

> For a long time the distance between the train and the figure appeared to remain the same. He wondered if it wasn't some sort of optical illusion. After awhile, however, the train began to gain on the figure, and soon my friend was close enough to see the terrified and exhausted dog, running for all he was worth, looking back over first one shoulder, then the other at the tremendous monster bearing down on him. He blew the whistle. The dog increased his speed, but was unable to maintain the pace. Finally the train ran him over. (4, 5)

Rodriguez tells this frightening story as a way of dramatizing the plight of battered women. According to Rodriguez, the dog "was so involved in the business of staying ahead of the monster on his tail that he couldn't possibly conceive of another thing. He didn't have time to reason that a single step in either direction would save him" (5).

What is domestic violence? In broad terms, it may be defined as "violent acts carried out by persons in a marital, sexual, parental, or caregiving role toward others" (Stith, Williams, and Rosen 1). In this paper, I will concern myself with abuse that men inflict on women they are (or have been) living with. This type of spousal violence is responsible for an unbelievable number of injuries to women each year. In his book *Family Violence,* Henry Wallace estimates that 8.7 million couples experienced some form of spousal abuse (or battering) in 1985 (165). These cases lead to the deaths of thousands of women each year, and these deaths occur in homes where there are other family members and in communities where other people know there is abuse. These people may not think we should interfere in the lives of others, but we must take a stand for the victims of violence by encouraging them to be courageous and leave their abusers before serious injuries occur.

An article from *The Standard Times* reported examples of beaten women.

Kathy was beaten when there were dirty dishes in the sink. She was beaten when her live-in boyfriend was drunk. She was beaten when he was sober. Janine's eye was blackened when her fiancé disagreed with their wedding plans. Doris was punched when she was pregnant. She was slapped when dinner was a minute late. She was shoved and beaten when dinner was on time. Laura was kicked in the stomach when she tried to break up. She was slapped around when she tried to make up. And all were hit at least once because the man in their lives claimed they "pushed their buttons"—brought abuse on themselves by not seeing how stressed their mates were. (par. 1)

There are stories closer to home. One woman I know was abused by her husband repeatedly. She had a little girl and her husband would make the child sit and watch him beat her. He would come home drunk and punch his wife in the face until it was black and blue with bruises. He would shove her violently against the walls, then kick her in the stomach, making it difficult for her to breathe. He would slap her around, while her child cried in the background. This continued for two years. Then she developed the courage to leave him. Now she is remarried to a man who loves her and would never consider hitting her. This woman was lucky to have left her husband before she was severely injured or killed.

But it is never easy for a battered woman to leave her husband. These women are often afraid of reprisal from the offender and so they stay, allowing the abuse to continue. When this is the case, the authorities should act without hesitation for the safety of the victim. Other cases are even more difficult to deal with, however. Many women do not even seem to want to leave their terrible situations. Such women were often abused as children and grow up thinking that abuse is natural in a home. Or, they may depend on their abusive spouses economically. The husband brings in the money that allows the wife to live and have a home, constantly showing the power and control he has over her. This leads the battered women to fear the thought of being homeless, and they have a right to do so. There are nearly three times as many animal shelters in the United States as there are shelters for battered women and their children (Senate Judiciary Hearings 1990). Do we put more value on the lives of animals than on those of these women, or do we just refuse to think there is a problem with domestic violence? Regardless, we need to realize that the women in our country are being savagely beaten and killed by husbands and boyfriends. These victims need our encouragement and support. They should know they will have a decent shelter to live in if they choose to leave their offenders. A battered woman and her child should never be homeless. They should be welcomed with open arms in homes run by caring people.

But in many cases intervention is needed while women are still living with violent abusers. Yet it is very hard for women to get the protection they need. Police are more likely to respond within five minutes if the offender is a stranger than if an offender is known to the female victim (Bachman 1). Authorities need to understand that husbands and boyfriends can do just as much damage to females as strangers can. And we need to stop excusing the violent behavior of these killers. Some batterers excuse their behavior by saying that they just "lost it." If this were true, wouldn't they be hitting and beating on bosses and clients who repeatedly anger them? But they don't. They always find the easy victim, someone who loves, honors, and cherishes them, someone who will accept their apology if given.

We must find a way to help these innocent victims. We can start by learning how to identify them. There are many signs you can look for in a battered woman. The victim will have low self-esteem and will deny the fact that she is being abused. She will often take responsibility for the offender's actions and accept them as right, thinking she was wrong for angering him. The woman may also be very family-oriented in a traditional way, staying close to home, being overly protective of her children. A battered woman may believe that no one can help her situation because they do not understand and that their attempts to help will only cause more problems. If you see any of these signs in a loved one or in someone you know, take action! Get her help! If nothing is done, the problems will only continue. She may claim to love her husband or boyfriend, and show her love by staying, but he will only return this love with a slap in the face or a punch in the stomach, possibly escalating through the years.

The horrible reality is that many women in our country are being hurt and killed by people they love and trust. Innocent women feel alienated and abandoned by their friends and family when they call for help and nobody —responds. The call may be a silent pleading in their eyes or bruises on their bodies, but it is there. Unless abuse is stopped, the only change we will see is an increase in the number of injuries and deaths occurring among battered women every year. If someone is calling out to you for help, take action. Like the frightened dog losing ground to the monster locomotive, these women are too tired and weary to think clearly for themselves. You would help that dog. Won't you help these innocent women?

Works Cited

Bachman, Ronet. *Response from the Criminal Justice System*. US Dept. of Justice. Bureau of Justice. Rept. 0717-R-01. Washington: GPO, 1994.

Rodriguez, Stephanie. *Time to Stop Pretending*. Middlebury, VT: Eriksson, 1994.

Stith, Sandra, Mary Beth Williams, and Karen Rosen. *Violence Hits Home*. New York: Springer, 1990.

United States Senate Committee on the Judiciary. *The Violence against Women Act of 1990*. Rept. 1008-C. Washington: GPO, 1990.

Wallace, Harvey. *Family Violence: Legal, Medical, and Social Perspectives*. Boston: Allyn and Bacon, 1996.

"Why Does Society Allow This to Happen?" *Standard Times*. 4 June 1995. 9 Oct. 1998 <http://www.s-t.com/projects/DomVio/dvwhydoessoc.html>.

Exercise 10.12

You will note that two of the essays in this chapter—Jaime Sherrill's "Zero Tolerance for Abuse" and Alysia Tucker's "No More"—treat the same general topic. Although the topics are the same, the essays are very different. We would argue that both are very effective, however. Analyze these two essays in terms of the criteria for successful persuasion we have developed in this chapter. What makes each essay successful? Then, choose a topic that is treated by one of the other writers in this chapter, and sketch a plan for how an essay you might write on this topic would differ from the one that writer has written.

CHECKLIST: CRITIQUING A PERSUASION ESSAY

1. State the action the writer of the essay would like her audience to take. What "should" thesis is this action connected to? Is that argument debatable?
2. State the audience for the essay. Is this audience likely to be favorably disposed—or at least neutral—to the underlying "should" thesis?
3. If the "should" thesis is debatable, does the writer offer logical arguments in favor of her position? Are they effective?
4. List the types of persuasive arguments the writer uses in the essay. How effective are they?
5. Sketch the basic organization of the essay. Is it effective? Does the introduction capture the reader's attention and draw him into the topic? Does the conclusion leave the reader with a sense of completeness?
6. Does the paper adhere to conventions of usage, mechanics, and format? Correct any errors you find.

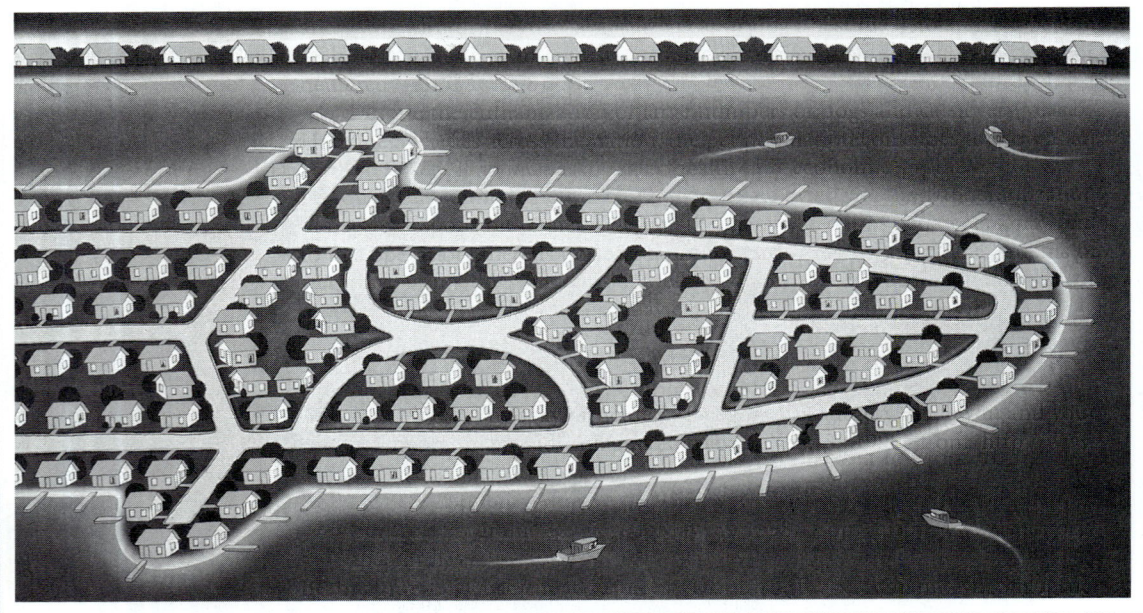

Roger Brown, "Nassau County: A Time-Photo Alteration," 1973. Oil on canvas, 84 × 54 in. © The School of the Art Institute of Chicago and the Brown family.

CHAPTER 11

Problem/Solution Essays

Writing is one of the best means we have for solving problems, especially when we take the time to write through a problem, exploring it thoroughly, speculating about potential solutions, and then selecting and justifying what seems the best of those solutions. Problem solving is something of an art, requiring a willingness on the part of the investigator (the problem solver) to range widely and freely over the whole terrain or scene of the problem, giving serious consideration to every solution that occurs, no matter how frivolous, difficult, obvious, or fantastic it may seem. When more than one solution is possible, it may be difficult to determine what is the very best solution to the problem.

The following story offers an example of an elegant, yet seemingly overdone, solution to a problem. As part of research and development efforts for the U.S. space program, NASA scientists wanted to develop a reliable pen for astronauts to use for recording data and observations while in space. Ordinary pens won't work in outer space, because they need gravity to make ink flow onto the page. So NASA created a pen with a pressurized ink cartridge, at a cost of $1 million. And it worked in outer space; U.S. astronauts had reliable pens for making permanent records. Facing the same problem, Soviet scientists provided their cosmonauts with pencils.

Now, the purpose of this example isn't to denigrate NASA and its efforts to provide U.S. astronauts with the best, most efficient equipment. Ink is more permanent and, therefore, more legible in the long run; pencil tips break and wear down, so pencils have to be sharpened periodically, raising the question of what to do with the shavings in a zero-gravity environment. The point is that you may well find more than one solution to a problem. A more elaborate solution isn't always the best; then again, that more elaborate solution may well be, depending on the investigator's exploration of the problem and evaluation of all the possible solutions that arise.

The problem/solution essay will in many ways be the most comprehensive writing task you'll undertake, for it brings together the skills of evaluation, interpretation, argument, and persuasion. As you work through this assignment, keep in mind that your goal is to convince your audience that you've considered the problem thoroughly and that the solution you propose is the most workable and efficient—the best—solution to it.

SAMPLE ESSAYS

The following sample essays focus on problems and solutions to them. As you read each, try to identify those places where each writer clearly defines a problem and then a solution to it.

Our first essay is "Out of Hurricane's Way" by William E. King, who was the mayor of Kemah, Texas, a Houston suburb that is on the western side of Galveston Bay. King published the essay in 2004, a year before Hurricane Katrina inundated the Mississippi Gulf Coast and destroyed much of New Orleans. Hurricane Rita followed close on Katrina's heels, threatening Houston initially. Before you read King's essay, think back to the impact Katrina and Rita had.

WILLIAM E. KING

OUT OF HURRICANE'S WAY

Would the Texas Gulf Coast, like Florida, be Prepared for a Mass Evacuation? The Mayor of Kemah Doesn't Think So.

1 On Sept. 11, 1900, J.H.W. Stele, H.S. Murray and Rabbi Cohen, all of Galveston, sent the following telegram to Gov. Joseph Sayers:

2 "Gov. Sayers, send military supplies fire arms animal and human food stuff danger food riots any moment. Situation horrible can't describe for god sake help us."

3 Two days before, a wall of seawater had inundated almost all of Galveston Island and for miles inland on the mainland. In its wake, 8,000 people were left dead, thousands more injured. The property damage was inestimable, but most of Galveston was simply gone. To put the enormity of this disaster in perspective, the attack on the World Trade Center killed less than 3,000 people, only about a third of the number lost in the 1900 hurricane.

4 Since Sept. 11, 2001, we have been obsessed with preventing another terror attack. Billions have been spent on homeland security, and we subject ourselves to incredible inconvenience in the name of thwarting terrorism.

5 But the terror that is more likely to be visited on the Houston area is a Category 4 or 5 hurricane. And the damage it will do will dwarf anything al-Qaida

can pull off. However, notwithstanding the virtually meteorological certainty that the big one is going to show up someday, we spend an infinitesimal fraction on hurricane preparedness compared with what we spend on homeland security.

6   First, we need to understand the dimensions of the future calamity. The Texas Division of Emergency Management, or DEM, produces storm surge maps that show how far hurricanes of various strengths will push water onto the mainland. According to these projections, a Category 4-5 storm will flood virtually all of Galveston Country, all of Clear Lake, the East Side to Loop 610, all of Baytown south of I-10 and about half of Brazoria County. The surge will be 20-25 feet high. That means every house in Clear Lake will have water over its roof or up to the second story. The only structures that will be visible in Kemah will be the Boardwalk Tower ride and the roofs of the three-story restaurants. Riding out a Category 4-5 storm within the flood surge area is simply not a survivable option.

7   And that does not count the flooding that will occur upstream from the torrential rains. Tropical Storm Claudette dropped 40 inches of rain on Alvin in 1979 in 24 hours, creating a nightmare. When a 25-foot storm surge dams up that water downstream, the flood stages upstream become almost too fantastic to believe. Some predict that I-45 will be under 20 feet of water at the Clear Creek bridge.

8   The real challenge is: How do we get residents in the surge area out of harm's way? Again, the dimensions of the problem must be considered. The approximate population of the area that will be flooded by a Category 4-5 storm is about 1 million. The thought of trying to evacuate more than 1 million people in the matter of a day or so is simply overwhelming. Computer models estimate that it would take more than 24 hours to evacuate everyone, if everything works perfectly. Of course, it will not. Cars will break down and run out of gas. People will panic.

9   In addition, the models do not take into account the fact that many people will wait too long to leave and find their evacuation routes cut off. The elevation of SH146 and NASA Road 1 is about eight feet. A Category 4-5 storm would flood that intersection as many as two days before the storm hits. The nightmare scenario quietly discussed by many emergency managers foresees thousands of evacuees stranded on highways and being drowned in their cars. Most emergency managers think this could result in tens of thousands of casualties; some talk in excess of 100,000. If readers think these numbers are just fantasy, they should know that on three occasions, hurricanes in India and Pakistan have killed more than 100,000 people, the most recent being in November 1970, when a storm reportedly claimed more than 200,000 lives.

10   There are those who point to recent storms and their relatively low casualties as an indication that hurricanes do not pose a truly calamitous threat. However,

close examination of the storm tracks and intensities distinguishes them from a major storm hitting a major population center. For example, Hurricane Charley, which just hit Florida, was a Category 4 storm, but there were only 27 casualties. However, Charley made landfall just north of Fort Myers, which is a relatively low population area. The population of the three counties where Charley went ashore is less than 1 million, with the brunt of the storm hitting Charlotte County, which has a population of only 150,000. The population of our coastal area is about 5 million.

Similarly, Hurricane Frances, although massive, had played itself out and became a Category 3 storm by the time it hit major population centers in Florida. I happened to be in Florida a few days before Frances made landfall, and it was clear that officials there have done a better job of preparing for a mass evacuation.

Of particular concern here are residents who will not be able to evacuate themselves. One report prepared by DEM estimated that there were 8,000 households in Galveston County alone in which residents did not own a car. With an average of about three persons per household, that means there are about 25,000 people that will need a ride out. Based on my experiences in our area, I think this number could be much higher. Add to that the sick and elderly who physically are not up to driving themselves through 24 hours of rush-hour traffic, and we have a real logistical nightmare.

What I find particularly disheartening about this issue is the fatalistic attitude of emergency managers. They religiously preach the dangers of a major hurricane, but we have gone so long without a major storm that their warnings are now mostly falling on deaf ears, both in the public and in our elected leadership. As a result, many emergency managers have accepted that the next major storm is going to be an apocalyptic disaster. I recall discussing people with substance abuse problems, and alcoholics in particular, at one meeting with emergency managers and the problems that this population presents in an evacuation. One longtime emergency manager, in response, said caustically, "They'll wash up." Of course, it did not reflect his true feelings, but rather the sort of gallows humor one finds in desperate situations.

However, I cannot accept that there is nothing that can be done. A major storm will, no doubt, do incredible damage, and there will be, no doubt, lives lost. But we can act to minimize that loss.

Specifically, the following steps should be taken:

- Priority should be given in highway design and construction to maximize hurricane evacuation routes. SH146 is a prime example. It is virtually worthless as an evacuation route. However, the Texas Department of Transportation has had a plan to expand the highway for some time. Between the Houston-Galveston Area Council favoring other projects and misguided opposition by some local leaders, the project is years behind schedule.

- The DEM, local governments and the media should do a hurricane-education blitzkrieg at the beginning of each hurricane season. We basically have two generations that have grown up in this area without a major storm. The community memory of the devastation has faded. In addition, each year thousands of new residents who are ignorant to the risk move into the area.
- The current structure of each county and city calling its own evacuation is unworkable and should be scrapped. Instead, the state should divide the coastline into hurricane evacuation corridors and establish a regional evacuation task force for each corridor. These task forces should be charged with the responsibility and given the authority to develop a comprehensive plan for the evacuation of all citizens in harm's way, especially those who will be unable to evacuate themselves.
- Once the evacuation plans are put in place, the personnel responsible for executing them should test and train on those plans with annual simulated evacuations. These simulations would make it more likely that the plans would be effective and would be another tool to raise the public awareness of the danger involved.
- Texas law should be changed to authorize mandatory evacuations. Florida already does so. When I was in Florida recently, the hotel management came by and informed me that the area would probably be evacuated the next day and that I would be required to leave. Allowing individuals to stay when there is a clear and present danger is not only dangerous for those individuals, but also the emergency personnel that may be put in the position of attempting rescues.

Yes, a comprehensive plan is going to cost money. But so does fighting terrorism, and we seem to have no problem finding funding for that fight. Notwithstanding the horror and tragedy of the attack on the World Trade Center, it will pale in comparison to a major storm hitting our area if we are unprepared.

Consider this passage from the 1999 book *Issac's Storm* by Erik Larson: "Throughout Galveston, men and women stepped from their homes to find corpses at their doorsteps. Bodies lay everywhere. One hundred corpses hung from a grove of salt cedars at Heards Lane. Some had double-puncture wounds left by snakes. 'There were so many dead,' said Phillip Tipp, 'you would sink into the silt onto a body at every other step.' He had reached Galveston aboard a small sail boat. We kept running into so many dead bodies that I had to go forward with a pike and shove the dead out of the way."

The truth is, we cannot afford to *not* have a comprehensive hurricane evacuation plan. If readers do not believe it, they should imagine for a moment being trapped with their family on a highway with vehicles lined up as far as they can see—while seawater begins to seep into their car as the storm surge rises around them.

◆ QUESTIONS FOR REVIEW

1. How did your experience with Hurricane Katrina and Hurricane Rita affect your reading of King's essay?
2. What problem does King define in his essay? What is the scope of the problem? How many people would possibly be affected by a major hurricane hitting Houston?
3. King published this essay in the *Houston Chronicle,* a major daily newspaper in Southeast Texas. He uses a large number of local place names (e.g., Galveston County, Kemah, Clear Lake) that will likely be familiar to *Chronicle* readers. What details does King present that help a reader unfamiliar with the Houston area understand the problem?
4. What is King's thesis? Identify a sentence that carries his solution to the problem.
5. Divide King's essay into these parts: introduction, discussion of the problem, discussion of the solution, conclusion. Compare the amount of space King gives to the problem with that he gives to the solution. Why do you think he chose this structure? How thorough is the discussion in each section? How effective are the introduction and conclusion? Why?

◆ WRITING OPPORTUNITY

1. Have you experienced a hurricane, earthquake, tornado, ice or snow storm, flood, forest fire, or other natural disaster? What happened? What did you learn from the experience?
2. What emergency plans are in place for your hometown or school in the event of a natural disaster? How adequate do these plans seem to be? Write an analysis of the plans and then a proposal to strengthen them. ◆

Exercise 11.1

On the facing page is a map (a visual image) showing the general threat to areas in the Houston area of hurricanes ranging from Category 1 through Category 5.

1. How effective is this map in helping you understand King's statements about the potential damage a major hurricane could cause were it to hit the Houston area?
2. Are there other visuals that would help you in understanding the scope of potential damage outlined in King's essay? If so, what do you think would have been helpful for King to have included?

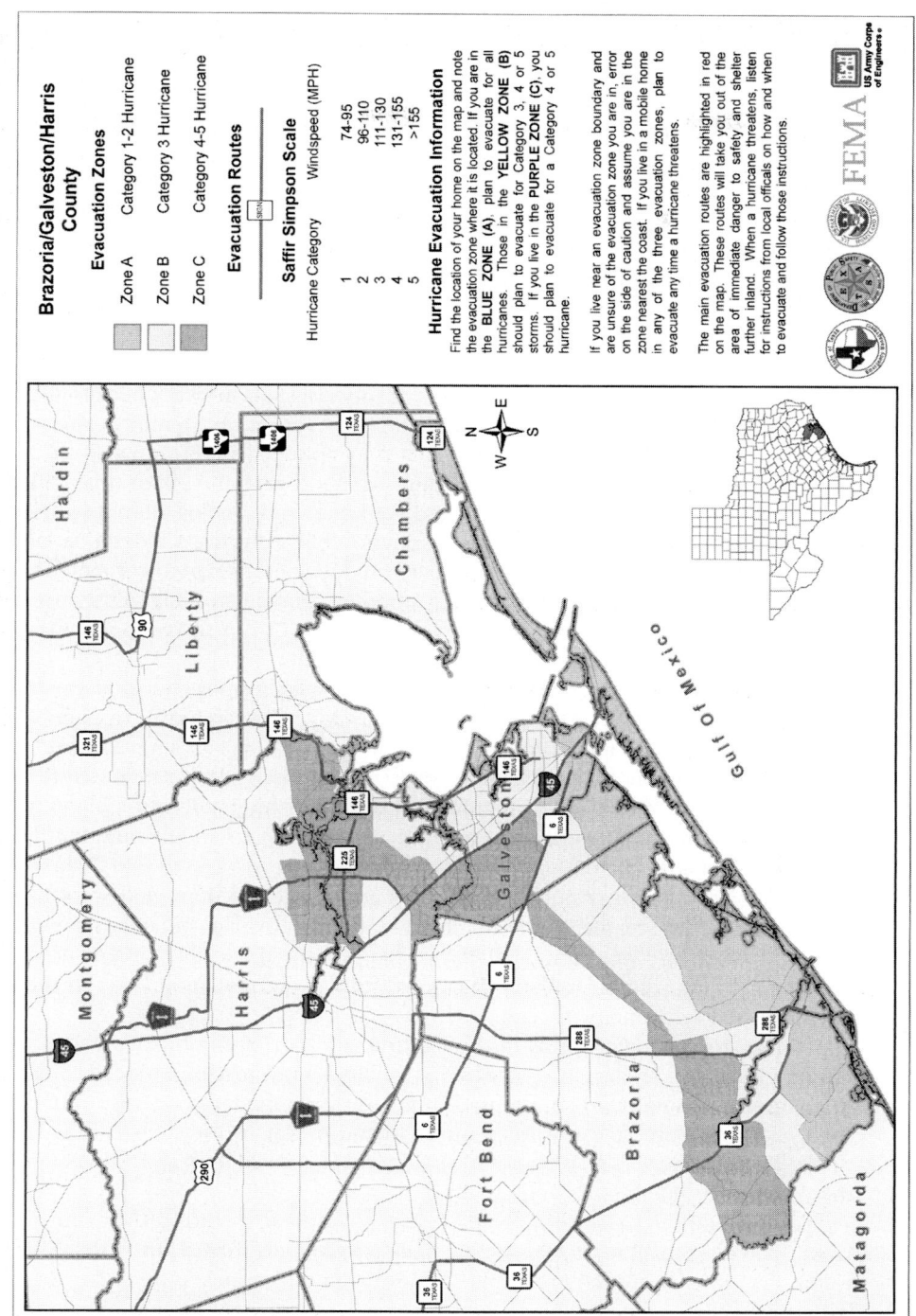

Julie Titone

BALANCE OF POWER: CAN ENDANGERED SALMON AND HYDROELECTRIC PLANTS SHARE THE SAME RIVERS?

At the turn of the century, thousands of sockeye salmon swam back to their central Idaho spawning grounds at Redfish Lake every year. So many crowded the creek that drains the lake, in fact, that they spooked the mounts of riders trying to cross. By last year, however, their numbers had shrunk dramatically: only four sockeye salmon made it to Redfish Lake, only one of them a female.

The sockeye earned the dubious distinction of becoming a federal endangered species last November. They are far from alone in their predicament. This spring, the Snake River stocks of spring, summer, and fall chinook salmon were listed as endangered, and biologists have identified 214 Northwest populations of wild-spawning salmonids threatened with extinction.

In the early 1900s, as many as 16 million wild salmon traveled up the Columbia River and its tributaries each year. Today, there are only 2 million, all but 300,000 of which are from hatcheries. As salmon sport-fishing declined in recent decades, many Idaho riverside communities lost an important source of income. Now the misery is flowing downstream, as fishing communities on the Lower Columbia and along the Pacific coast face up to rough new harvest restrictions. The fish just aren't there anymore.

Genetically weaker hatchery fish, overharvesting, and degraded spawning habitat share some of the blame for the dwindling runs. But biologists say the biggest culprits are the dams, which are blamed for up to 95 percent of the deaths of young salmon making their way from their spawning beds to their adult homes in the Pacific Ocean.

There are 30 major dams in the Columbia Basin. Some of them, such as Grand Coulee Dam, have no fish passage facilities at all and have blocked entire drainages to oceangoing fish. Eight of them—four on the Lower Snake, four on the Columbia—provide a 460-kilometer obstacle course for such fish as the Snake River sockeye. The turbines in each of these dams kill up to 15 percent of the young fish that pass through them.

Young salmon, or smolts, are particularly vulnerable during their journey from spawning grounds to the ocean because the transformation from freshwater fish into saltwater creatures, "smoltification," appears to make them lethargic. Without natural spring freshets to push them downstream, the young salmon must find their way through a series of slack-water reservoirs. The journey from spawning grounds to ocean, which once took a week before the dams were built, now takes up to six weeks.

To help juvenile salmon through the slow, predator-filled reservoirs, since 1977 the U.S. Army Corps of Engineers has collected millions of fish at the first of the eight dams, then barged or trucked them downstream. Critics of that elaborate transportation system note that it has not resulted in an increase in the number of adults coming back upstream to spawn. Quite the opposite has happened.

The Endangered Species Act gives the National Marine Fisheries Service final say in recovering the wild salmon. But the Northwest Power Planning Council has significant authority in managing the Columbia River system, thanks to the Northwest Power Act of 1980. That Act required that fish and wildlife get equal attention with hydropower and other industrial uses of the Columbia. After more than a decade that hasn't happened. The Power Council set a goal of doubling the total salmon population. Instead, the total numbers dropped and numbers of wild species plummeted.

Balancing the loss of these fish against the costs of modifying dozens of dams has put the Pacific Northwest into an all-too-familiar predicament. In 1990, when conservation groups first petitioned for endangered status for some salmon species, the region was already deadlocked over spotted owl protection. Comparisons between the salmon and owl were inevitable and frightening. Protecting the spotted owl and its ancient forest habitat has dealt a major blow to the timber industry, which will have a ripple effect on the economics of Oregon, Washington, and northern California.

Salmon protection will involve tampering with the very lifeblood of the four-state region: the Columbia River and its tributaries. Improving fish passage could mean blasting new fish tunnels through the dams. It means changing the amount of water that goes through hydropower turbines, and the timing of that water's release from reservoirs. For example, allowing spring "drawdowns" will turn reservoirs into rivers and flush the fish to the ocean. Such changes could have a dramatic impact on reservoir levels, which would drop as much as 11 meters during the drawdowns. That eliminates barge traffic, leaves marina docks high and dry, and can cause embankments to slough and crack.

Salmon protection would thus raise utility rates for residents and industries, such as aluminum factories, grown reliant upon cheap hydropower. It would affect inland ports and the businesses that depend on them, because the reservoirs would no longer be high enough year-round to float barges. It would force irrigators to lengthen pipes they use to suck water from the rivers.

At first glance, the salmon may seem to have even more sociopolitical cards stacked against it than the spotted owl.

But unlike the spotted owl, the salmon has economic value. More than one far-reaching law protects it, and no one says salmon are expendable. There's no fish equivalent of the bumper sticker "Save a logger. Eat an owl."

Efforts to recover the endangered salmon would boost all salmon and steelhead populations, both in the wild and in hatcheries (wild populations supply the varied genetic stock that keeps hatchery populations healthy). Therefore, salmon protection could actually be an enormous boon to the economy. Furthermore, the impact of more salmon for canning or as a lure for tourists has not been calculated. The focus has been on the short-term costs of recovering the endangered populations, not the long-term benefits of bolstering all the salmon runs. According to the Northwest Resource Information Center, one conservative 1992 estimate held that 44 million adult salmon and steelhead trout were lost to Northwest fisheries in the years 1960–1980. The estimated commercial and recreational loss to the region: $6.5 billion.

Annual drawdowns could well be part of the Snake River sockeye recovery plan currently being written by a team of biologists for the National Marine Fisheries Service. The team is building upon work done by the Northwest Power Planning Council. Last December the Power Council gave a qualified endorsement to drawdowns as part of its own complex plan for reestablishing salmon runs.

Officials of the Bonneville Power Administration, which markets most of the region's hydropower, often note that the effort to restore salmon runs has cost its ratepayers a billion dollars in lost power sales and physical improvements to the river system. But they no longer contend that annual drawdowns to help the fish would increase consumers' power costs by a third; that estimate is down to about 4 percent. The Northwest would still have some of the cheapest electricity in the country.

This March the U.S. Army Corps of Engineers took its first reluctant but well-orchestrated step toward changing river operations. The corps conducted a month-long experiment to see how the reservoir system would respond to lower, faster flows. It dramatically dropped the reservoirs behind Lower Granite and Little Goose dams, the first ones that young Idaho salmon confront on their way down the Snake River. Official results of the drawdown test are still being written, but no major physical failures were observed. The dams' turbines didn't vibrate wildly when their power generation was cut in half; the levees protecting the upstream city of Lewiston, Idaho, didn't collapse.

Hydropower interests and communities that would suffer most from drawdowns demand proof that drawdowns, by pushing the juvenile salmon downstream, will result in more adults coming up to spawn. Biologists have no proof, only strong evidence.

Unfortunately, because the dams haven't been reconstructed to pass fish through at low water levels, the test had to be done before juvenile fish were actually traveling to the sea. So the March experiment does not prove that drawdowns would actually move fish quickly through the reservoirs.

According to a new report prepared for Idaho Governor Cecil Andrus, 20 drawdowns would be 5 to 20 times cheaper than the other salmon protection plans that have been proposed. Although there is no guarantee that drawdowns will save any of the Columbia Basin's wild salmon, they remain an expensive gamble worth taking. Without help, the Northwest's remaining wild salmon—and eventually the hatchery fish that depend on those wild stocks for genetic diversity—will surely swim to extinction.

◆ QUESTIONS FOR REVIEW

1. Titone writes about the decline of the salmon population. How does she help her readers understand the scale of this problem?
2. What causes of this decline does Titone acknowledge as contributing to the problem? What does she identify as the major causes of the problem?
3. How effectively does Titone discuss the effect of dams on the salmon population? What details does she provide that you think are effective?
4. What solution does Titone offer? How effectively does she support it?
5. How effectively does Titone address such concerns as the economic impact of dam restructuring, the effects of drawdowns, and the protection of the spotted owl?
6. How effective is the title of this piece? How does Titone use the term "power" in it? Identify and comment on other instances of word play that you think particularly effective.
7. What is the thesis of this essay? Where does it appear?

◆ WRITING OPPORTUNITY

1. Write about a local environmental issue that concerns you. What is the issue? What is its significance?
2. Read Sherman Alexie's "That Place Where Ghosts of Salmon Jump" (pages 298–299). How do Titone's essay and Alexie's poem complement each other? ◆

Andrew Overton, a first-year writing student at New Mexico State University, wrote the following problem/solution essay, which shows that not all problems addressed in an essay need to be as serious as natural disasters and environmental issues.

ANDREW OVERTON

CHANGE

Pepsi. Not Coke, but Pepsi. No other selection of soda will do for Jay Burmac. Everyone at the factory in which he works knows his preference; his wife knows what brand to buy on shopping day, and most importantly all the vendors in Baltimore's metro area know what kind to stock in their machines. Every Friday at 2:00 in the afternoon, the Pepsi guy can be seen pulling his truck in and unloading fresh cases of Pepsis to stock in the vending machine. And every Friday at 2:05, Jay can be seen leaving his office for his Pepsi break.

This Friday has been especially hard on Jay, and nothing would ease his tension like a cold Pepsi. Silently walking up to the machine, not to disturb the sanctity of his shrine, Jay checks the front pockets of his Dockers khakis for change. Finding only thirty-some-odd cents, he checks his wallet. Whew, one last dollar. It's not like him to be without the necessary change at hand. Not the greatest dollar bill, either. It seems to have changed hands a thousand, no, a million times, and each time someone hastily crammed it in a billfold, he folded and creased the corners, or he worked off some nervous tension by tearing it a couple of times. Making it as flat as he can, Jay attempts to slide it into the vending machine's bill acceptor. Nope, rejected. "I knew that was going to happen," Jay mutters as he begins rubbing it on the corner of the machine to make the bill smooth and even. He feeds the bill in again. It slides right back out. Much like feeding an infant applesauce, time and time again Jay slides in the bill only to have it spat back at him, his anger increasing with each rejection. Realizing it won't work, his frustration gives him only one option, to go man-to-man or, in this case, man-to-machine. Pounding his adversary with his fists, he demands his Pepsi. "Give it up, give it up!" he yells. "Please just give me my Pepsi!" Two of his coworkers hastily drag Jay off the machine, consoling him all the way, "You'll get him next time, Jay, wait till next time."

An epidemic of inconvenience grips our nation. Its signs can be found everywhere, in wallets and purses, in the clenched fists of little children. The dollar bill, the most inconvenient convenience around. Many do not see the problem the dollar bill poses, because the problem is not what it is or what its value is, but what it is made of. Using paper for a one-dollar amount is no longer necessary or prudent. Too many problems arise from the fact that it is made of paper, problems that will be solved, for "on December 1, 1997 President Clinton signed legislation calling for a new $1 coin, which will be placed into circulation during the year 2000" (Coin Coalition, 1998, par. 1).

Who has not come across the problem of putting a dollar bill into a vending machine? It is an inconvenience to not receive the candy bar from the machine despite having the cash. All of these crumpled problems could be solved if the dollar were in the form of a coin instead of paper. It would be as easy as inserting a quarter into the coin slot, something most machines will gracefully take. Imagine reaching into your pocket and pulling out a single coin that more than covers the cost of your snack of choice. No more fumbling in your pockets to find one more nickel, no more hassle with a paper dollar the machine will not take. Your favorite snack would only be a drop and not a shove, grumble, and pound away.

Not only would the dollar coin save vending machine customers a lot of grief, but it would also save vending machine companies a lot of money. Vending machines are equipped with dollar changers that can cost $300 dollars each. Additional costs include service calls and repairing machines with jammed bill changers. According to a 1991 University of Chicago study, the vending industry would save an estimated $142 million dollars a year (Kapner, 1995). Saving this much money a year could then be translated into greater savings for the consumer, possibly curbing rising vending costs.

Vending machine companies are not the only ones who would save money using the dollar coin. Other businesses, which don't necessarily make as many transactions involving the dollar bill, would save money if the dollar coin were implemented. Using a coin instead of a cumbersome bill would speed up transactions and would reduce the number of bills employees would have to count at the end of the work shifts. According to a study performed by the Walgreen's Drug Store chain, changing from the bill to the coin would save the company $500,000 a year (Kapner, 1995).

Switching from the dollar bill to the dollar coin would not only improve profit margins of businesses, but it would save the government money, too. Dollar bills last on average only 17 months; coins, on the other hand, can remain in circulation for 30 years. Although cheaper to produce (four cents compared to eight cents), the dollar bill costs more to maintain in circulation because of its short life span. According to estimates made by the Federal Reserve and General Accounting Office, if the dollar coin replaced the dollar bill it would mean a savings to the United States government of $2.28 billion dollars over the first five years (Coin Coalition, 1998, par. 2). Just one more way for the Federal government to curb unnecessary spending of taxpayer dollars.

A loud whistle blows. Startled by the sudden noise, Jay looks up from his desk at the old circular clock hanging on his wall. Five o'clock. "The best time in the world," Jay points out as he gathers a loose bundle of papers into a somewhat manageable pile to be stuffed into his briefcase. With his mind set on reaching the bus stop on time, Jay doesn't hesitate as he exits the large red brick building. He has little time between five o'clock closing and the bus that delivers him home. Shuffling quickly, he entertains the same thoughts he has a thousand times before while making the walk—never understanding why his wife must be so Earth conscious, disallowing an automobile. Arriving at the stop he looks at his watch, noticing he has made better time than usual. Pulling a one out of his wallet, he slides it into a vending machine, hesitating slightly at the remembrance of the earlier events of the day. Right as the bus pulls up to the stop, the machine finally accepts his cash and gives him a Susan B. Anthony dollar coin to be used as the token allowing him to ride.

Today's destination isn't like others, because instead of riding straight home Jay is on a mission, charged by his wife to buy a new shirt she saw in a shop downtown for their infant. Stepping onto the bus, handing over the coin he just received, Jay finds just the right seat. The bus goes from stop to stop, leaving people behind at each one, until it reaches Jay's stop. He steps onto the curb and heads straight into the Baby Gap. Browsing for just the right shirt (anything different and he would catch hell at home), Jay notices the sickly condition of the sales clerk. He picks up the little shirt his wife had in mind and lines up at the cash register. As he stands in line, he notices the woman in front of him is carrying a white cane. "That will be 75 cents, Ma'am," the cashier announces to the lady in between several sneezes. She fumbles in her purse, and Jay sees that she has handed the clerk a ten dollar bill. The cashier deposits it in the cash tray and returns only a quarter in change. Assuming nothing is wrong, the lady replaces the quarter into her purse, takes the baby shoe laces she bought, and makes her way tapping side to side out the door of the store.

Jay steps forward, ready to come to the woman's aid. He clears his throat. "You want something, Jack?" the clerk asks. "You got a problem or something?" Jay hears menace in the voice and steps back. "Uh, no. No, I don't at all. Nope, not me." Bad neighborhood, bad neighborhood, he thinks, best to not get involved.

The clerk sneezes, then asks for $17.93. Jay hands him a twenty. The clerk stifles another sneeze with his hand and reaches into the cash register, pulling out $2.07 in change. Stuffing the moist bills into his wallet, Jay grabs his bag and briefcase and leaves the store, mumbling under his breath the whole way, "Filthy, filthy town."

Every day in several large cities around the country, mass transit systems use the Susan B. Anthony dollar coin as their tokens. Dollar bills are expensive to process and count for the large mass transit systems that must carry thousands of people a day. Since the dollar coin is already used by several systems, it would be much easier to just use a new dollar coin. Rather than having to exchange a dollar bill for a dollar coin and to put up with all the hassle of making that exchange, people would already have dollar coins. Having coins instead of bills would also save money; making the switch would save an estimated $124 million dollars annually for nationwide mass transit systems (Feulner, 1995, par. 8). How? Processing dollar bills is expensive. Edwin Feulner, President of the Heritage Foundation, gives Chicago as an example of how money could be saved: "The Chicago Transit Authority (CTA) handles about 410,000 dollar bills a day. The cost of sorting these bills is about $22 per thousand. But coins can be counted for just $2. Switching to a dollar coin could save the CTA $2.4 million per year in bill-processing costs" (par. 10).

Coins are also healthier than currency. How many times have those old dollar bills been handled by a guy with a bad cold, who probably has blown his nose several times? How disease ridden are those dollar bills? A paper dollar bill is very susceptible to collecting dirt, filth, or anything else that touches it, compared to its coin counterparts. In a recent examination of two twenty dollar bills, a one dollar bill, and one quarter performed by *Discover* magazine, the dollar bill was found to be the most bacteria ridden of the bunch. The one with least bacteria was the quarter ("On the money," 1998, p. 78).

By now you may be thinking that the legislation President Clinton signed into law will fail. After all, the government tried to replace paper dollars with the Susan B. Anthony dollar coin in the 1970s. They failed to catch on with the public then; why should they gain approval now? Opponents of the legislation flatly state that "coins are cumbersome, inconvenient, and [. . .] tend to get lost" (Poulson, par. 3). Rep. Thomas Davis of Virginia said, "About the only people who benefit are the tailors as we wear out our pockets with more coins" (Geier, 1995, p. 14). Not gaining popularity would lead a new dollar coin towards the same outcome as the Anthonys—sitting in vaults at the U.S. mint.

One of the biggest reasons for the failure of the 1979 Susan B. Anthony dollar coin was its close resemblance to the quarter. Not only in its silver color, but its ridged edge was very similar, too. Having similar characteristics can make it confusing for the blind which coin to choose when attempting to make a transaction. Despite this earlier botched attempt, switching to a coin from a bill can make it easier on the blind. Bills can be indistinguishable from each other. This shouldn't matter because if a blind person hands a higher denomination bill to someone, the correct change should be returned, but because dishonest people exist the system is very unfair for them. Switching to a different colored, smooth edged dollar coin would make it easy on all. People with sight could quickly distinguish the coin from others in their pocket, and those without wouldn't be taken advantage of in smaller exchanges.

Ultimately, the problem to be solved is how to gain public acceptance of the new coin. One way to do this is by publicizing Canada's success with its own coin. In 1987 despite initial public resistance, Canada introduced a dollar coin that has become so popular there are now calls for a two-dollar coin (Geier, 1995). A second step is just to stop making paper bills, so that eventually the dollar bill would become an increasingly rare collector's item, too valuable to spend on candy or gum. Finally, the government will have to mount an advertising campaign to help the public get used to the idea. Infomercials are everywhere on late night TV, and Americans are used to having as much as one-third of their favorite sitcom taken up by commercials. Some smart ad agency is bound to be able to sell the public on the convenience of the new coin.

And that's what switching from a bill to a coin is about—convenience. Convenience for the vendor when accepting money for their goods. Convenience for the businesses that must employ people to deal with counting. Convenience for the blind who decide which is the right amount to give. Convenience for every individual involved in making one dollar transactions. Switching to a dollar coin would make life much more convenient and easier for everyone; it just makes sense.

References

Coin Coalition. (1998). Why a $1 coin? Retrieved November 16, 1998, from http://www.coincoalition.org/why/htm

Feulner, E. (1995, November 30). Time to say goodbye to dollar bill. *Heritage Foundation Commentary.* Retrieved from http://www.heritage.org/Press/Commentary/ED113095a.cfm

Geier, T. (1995, May 1). The buck's farewell? *U.S. News & World Report,* 14.

Kapner, S. (1995, May 1). To coin or not to coin: Chains, vendors debate dollar's fate. *Nation's Restaurant News,* 4.

On the money. (1998, October). *Discover,* 78–80.

Poulson, B. (1997, June 18). The one dollar coin act. *Independence Institute Opinion-Editorial.* Retrieved from http://www.i2i.org/main/article.php?article_id=421

◆ QUESTIONS FOR REVIEW

1. Andrew begins his essay with a narrative and then returns to it about halfway through the paper. What do you think is the purpose of this narrative? How effective is it?
2. What is Andrew's problem statement? His thesis? Where does each come in the essay? How effectively is each worded?
3. What solution does Andrew offer? How effectively does he support it?
4. What opposition is there likely to be to Andrew's solution? How effectively has he considered such opposition?
5. How effective is the title of this essay? In how many contexts does this one-word title work?

◆ WRITING OPPORTUNITY

1. Identify a university or local, state, or national governmental policy that needs changing. What is the policy? Why is it a bad one? How would you change it?
2. Write a brief essay in which you discuss how the introduction of the dollar coin has affected our currency system. What's your opinion of the paper dollar versus the coin? ◆

THE RHETORICAL TRIANGLE

Reader

The audience for a problem/solution essay should be someone who cares about (or can be made to care about) the problem. Your task is at once to inform and persuade. You want to make sure that the reader understands the problem and its significance. In addition, you want to persuade the reader that yours is the best solution to this problem and that he should take appropriate action to help solve the problem. The questions that follow should help you determine just who this reader is and what you need to do to convince him to accept your position.

1. Who can solve the problem? Who has the power or authority to change things?
2. What is this person's role in the problem? Did he create the problem? Is his role one of oversight—of being responsible for, say, enforcing a policy that you may argue against? Or is he a concerned individual who has no particular official involvement with the problem, but who might be able to influence the eventual outcome—for example, a taxpayer and voter who is living in a city that is in the process of deciding how to solve the problem of traffic congestion?
3. What does he already know about the problem? Is he likely to see it as a problem?
4. What does he need to know to take the action you think he should?
5. How opposed is he likely to be to your solution? Why?

Determining a specific audience for your paper can help you sharpen its focus from the outset, and you may use your responses to such questions as those above to guide you in exploring the problem and then in writing a discovery draft and subsequent drafts of your essay.

Exercise 11.2

Speculate about the intended readers for two of the essays at the beginning of this chapter. How effectively did the writers of these essays seem to have considered their respective audiences? Identify any details that you think are particularly effective for their readers. What makes them effective?

Subject

What topics are appropriate for an essay that explores a problem and then poses a solution to it? Problems range widely, from the very personal to the global, and some are not solvable in the kind of argumentative essay this chapter presents.

In the list of problems that follows, identify those for which you think you could offer a workable or feasible solution.

> world hunger
> financial aid snafus on your campus
> the U.S. budget deficit
> mudslinging political campaigns
> a dangerous intersection near your home
> lighting on your campus
> gangs
> racism
> sexism
> your study habits
> your less-than-ideal grades
> favorable or unfavorable treatment of one of the following groups on your campus: women, minorities, students with disabilities, athletes
> inner-city unemployment rates
> clear-cutting in national forests
> environmentalists' interference with legal logging operations in national forests

Although each of these problems could be solved, at least theoretically, the problems that are closer to your immediate world are often easier for you to think about solving in tangible ways. As you seek a topic for this paper, consider those that are closer to you and your interests and that lend themselves to argument. For example, a topic such as sexism would be too broad for the scope of this essay. But you could narrow that topic to sexism on your campus so that you deal with specific instances of sexist behavior, with your essay offering specific solutions for the situation at your school.

Writer

As a writer of a problem/solution essay, you must present yourself as both informed and fair. It must be clear that you have examined the problem and its solutions thoroughly. If you demonstrate that you understand the complexity of a situation, you are much more likely to be perceived as fair. Thus, it is important that you show that you have explored the topic thoroughly, examining such aspects as why the problem truly is a problem, how it came to be a problem, what it causes or creates, and whether major causes of the problem may actually provide benefits for certain people. For example, were you to write about the pollution caused by a particular industry, you would consider such questions as these: What is beneficial about this industry? What product does it produce? How many people does it employ? If your solution would negate these benefits, what could you offer as an alternative, so that, for example, workers would not lose jobs?

> **Exercise 11.3**
>
> Look again at two or three of the essays presented at the beginning of this chapter. How knowledgeable and fair does the writer of each seem to be? Point to specific places in each essay that demonstrate these two elements of the writer's ethos. What do those examples show you about the writers?

DISTINGUISHING FEATURES OF PROBLEM/SOLUTION ESSAYS

Well-Defined Problem

Problems may be defined in any number of ways, and how we define a problem helps shape the solution. Here's an example that illustrates this point:

> Oftentimes, patients in hospitals or nursing homes are physically restrained as a means of protecting workers and the patients themselves. These restraints most often take the form of tie-downs, with a patient strapped into a bed by ties around his wrists and ankles, and occasionally around his chest. But many times, patients do not need such restraints to be applied.

Below are four possible problem statements dealing with this issue. Which seems most accurate, most clearly defined?

1. Restraints are unnecessary for many patients; thus, their use should be banned.
2. The problem is restraints.
3. Indiscriminate use of physical restraints is unnecessary and oftentimes detrimental to a patient's well-being.
4. The use of restraints is unnecessary and harmful.

Of these, the third forms the best problem statement. It details the writer's value judgment about the use of restraints and points to indiscriminate use as the primary problem. The problem is not with the restraints themselves, but with how they're used.

The first statement offers a blanket indictment of restraints, saying that all use of restraints should be banned no matter the circumstances. But at times, restraints are called for. An emergency-room patient who is violent because of drug-induced hallucinations, for example, may need to be physically restrained. The second statement is too broad to be of much help. Does the problem with restraints lie in their design and construction, allowing patients to slip out of them easily? Or are they too constrictive, again a design and construction problem? The fourth statement, like the first, offers a judgment about using restraints but, like the second, is too broad to be of much help.

Developing a detailed problem statement is important, because in defining the problem specifically, you may point toward a solution and, subsequently, to the development of the paper as a whole. Were you to select the third statement to use in a paper, you would give examples of instances when physical restraints should be used and when they were used but weren't necessary. Such development is at least implied by the problem statement.

We must point out that, however important the problem statement will be in guiding your investigation of the problem and potential solutions, it will not stand as your essay's thesis. Instead, the thesis sentence will present your stance on the topic and, in many cases, issue a call to action on the part of your readers. (We'll have more to say on this matter in the section on structuring your essay.)

Exercise 11.4

For at least two of the essays presented at the beginning of this chapter, identify the problem statement. How effectively does the problem statement for a particular essay help shape that essay's structure? If you don't find a specific problem statement, write one. How might such a statement as the one you wrote have helped the writer during prewriting and drafting?

Thorough Exploration of the Problem

To explore the problem, consider each aspect of it, answering such questions as these:

1. What is your definition of the problem? How specifically have you defined it? Is this definition the most accurate? How would changing the definition refocus the problem statement?
2. What caused or causes the problem? What are its effects? For example, what does it cost? How damaging is it?
3. Who is affected by the problem? Why is it a problem for them? To what extent are they affected?
4. Who or what is responsible for the problem?
5. What changes need to be made? Why?

Exercise 11.5

In "Balance of Power," Julie Titone discusses the potential economic impact of saving the salmon, contrasting that with the feared negative impact on local and regional economies. Why did she spend several paragraphs talking about economic matters? How effectively does her speculation about economic benefits counter the fears that an economic downturn would result if her plan were adopted?

Best Solution

As the example of the space pen at the beginning of this chapter illustrates, a problem may well have more than one solution. In writing this essay, you may consider three or even four possible solutions, each of which may solve the problem. If such is the case, then you'll need to pick the best solution, the one that seems most effective or fair or cost-efficient. Making this selection will require you to evaluate the various solutions you've developed, so you need to establish criteria for evaluating them. (For a discussion of using criteria to evaluate a topic, see Chapter 8.)

ASSIGNMENT AND GUIDELINES FOR WRITING

Assignment

Identify a problem, something that bothers you. Explore it, and offer a possible solution. The first part of your job is to identify a specific problem, define it clearly, and explore its implications. The second part is to consider potential solutions, evaluate those solutions, and then make an argument for the one you think is best. As you think about potential topics for this essay, consider using one of your responses to a Writing Opportunity prompt in this chapter.

Choosing a Topic

What bothers you? What problems can you identify that irritate you or that make you shake your head in dismay or that give you cause for real concern? To select a topic, try writing a "Bug List" (as described in James L. Adams's, *Conceptual Blockbusting*). This list is just what its name implies—a list of things that disturb, anger, irritate, vex, or rankle you, no matter how big or small. As an example, here are the first several entries of a list that Bill wrote:

> soccer refs who don't
> attitude
> "Little League" parents (whatever the level)
> no stoplights where Stern Drive and Sam Steel Way intersect Union Ave.
> students who don't study
> wooden-headed administrators
> irresponsible parents
> child and spouse abuse
> treatment of divorced women in our legal system
> weeds forever in my lawn
> my golf swing
> the apparent idiocy of too many elected officials

As these entries indicate, a Bug List is a list of whatever bothers you, whatever you think is problematic. Some of the issues Bill listed are personal and fairly solvable. For example, the irritation with his golf swing wouldn't be a topic with enough depth for this paper, nor would it lend itself to argument. On the other end of the spectrum, can we expect to solve a problem like "attitude"? What is "attitude," and what tangible solutions might we find to solve it? Such a topic is too broad and too vague to be the topic for a problem/solution essay. Another problem that Bill can't solve is that of child and spouse abuse. But this topic could be narrowed to something like this: the inadequacy of efforts in the United States to make deadbeat parents pay child support. This revised topic is more workable because it focuses on a specific problem—what is and is not being done to make deadbeat parents pay up—and could lead to an argument for specific actions to be taken by officials with the power to enforce court-decreed child support.

Exercise 11.6

Respond to at least one of these options:

1. Write a Bug List. Spend at least ten minutes making a list of anything that irritates you, no matter how big or small or serious or frivolous it may seem. Pick two of your entries and freewrite about each for ten minutes.
2. What problems do you confront or know about that you'd like to see solved? Spend at least ten minutes developing a list of all such problems that come to mind. Then pick two of your entries and freewrite about each for ten minutes.
3. Look at your Interest Inventory for less-than-ideal situations that could be potential topics. Although any section could hold potential topics for this essay, take a close look at the "education," "jobs," and "attitudes and issues" sections. Pick two topics and freewrite about each for ten minutes.

After you've completed this exercise, look over what you wrote, and identify two or three topics that you think have potential. Continue freewriting about just these topics, focusing on why you think each is a problem and how it might be solved. If one of these topics seems workable and captures your interest, then proceed to the next step (collecting information). If not, keep freewriting about the problems you uncovered in any of the lists you generated.

Collecting Information

As you begin to collect information, look back to the assignment, which lists three parts to your job as a writer. What kinds of questions does each part bring to mind? Consider responding to such questions as the following:

Defining and exploring the problem. What is the problem? Why is it a problem? Just how dire or big is this problem? How did it come to be; what or who caused it? What are its effects, consequences, or ramifications? What will happen if it isn't solved? Whom does it affect, to what extent, how positively or negatively? Why hasn't this problem been solved yet; what obstacles stand in the way?

Finding a solution. What are possible solutions? What aspect(s) of the problem would each potential solution solve? How effectively? What benefits does each solution hold? Which seems the best or most workable or most feasible solution? Why?

Defining an audience. Who can solve the problem; who has the power, authority, or funding necessary to solve it? What opposition is your audience likely to have to your solution? How can you most effectively counter those points of opposition? (Once you've defined your reader, write a dialogue between you and the reader about the problem.)

In addition to considering these questions, look again at the Questions for Analysis (pages 24–31) and ask those that seem most applicable. Look particularly at questions of sequence and consequence and at those involving both support for and opposition to the problem you're working with.

Gathering information may also involve you in research, interviews, or observation.

Research   If your topic is one that's been in the news, that's been written about in professional or popular journals, or that involves questions of legality, you may need to conduct research in your library or on the Internet. Just remember that you must document any sources you use. (For more discussion of researching and documenting sources, see pages 582–585, 590–598, and 598–621.)

Interviews   Are there people you know or can identify who are involved in some way with the problem? What is their connection to the problem? Be as specific as possible. In considering interviews, you'll need to establish a set of questions to ask each person so that you get the information you need. Your job is not to challenge but to gather information. (For more discussion of interviewing, see pages 585–587.)

Observation   It may be helpful for you to spend time observing some part of the problem. For example, if Bill decided to write about the lack of stoplights at the two intersections he named in his Bug List, he could gather some information by observing traffic patterns during peak-use hours, counting cars, accidents, near accidents, and so on. What aspects of your problem are observable? What might you gain by spending some time on-site, seeing what goes on as part of the problem? (For more discussion of observing to gather information, see page 589.)

Focus Statement

Your focus statement for this essay should consist of two parts: (1) a statement of the problem and (2) a statement of the solution you think best or most effective. Then, for each of these statements, you should list the kinds of supporting information you can or will need to offer to convince your reader that the problem truly is a problem and that your proposed solution is the best. Here's a template you could use for your focus statement:

> *Problem.* Your statement of the problem. Support: statistics? examples? impact on people, environment, animals?
> *Solution.* Your solution and rationale for choosing it. Alternate solutions with rationale for not choosing them.
> *Audience.* Write at least an initial definition of your intended audience. How will you convince its members that your assessments of the problem and the proposed solution are accurate?

Use these categories as headings and then list support under each category. If you find that you don't have any support listed in a particular category, that may point you toward the necessity of conducting some research into the topic.

Planning Your Essay's Structure

This particular essay readily lends itself to blocking (see pages 49–50); that is, the essay form can divide fairly neatly into a problem block and a solution block. Think of these blocks as bins into which you can put the information you generated while exploring the problem and possible solutions. Or look back over that information, and mark various entries with a "P" for "problem" and an "S" for "solution." These bins or blocks can form the two major sections of your paper.

> *Problem block—defining the problem.* In presenting the problem section, you'll need to define the problem clearly and explore it in depth so that you convince your reader that it really is a problem. This section of the essay will contain the problem statement (the definition of the problem) and discussion of the problem's importance, significance, costs, harm, and so on.
> *Solution block—finding a solution.* In presenting the solution section, you have a number of options. If your solution is detailed, you should make it the focal point of the entire section, discussing thoroughly the implications of the solution and why it's workable or feasible. If several solutions occur to you or seem workable, you may want to treat each solution in turn, considering its strengths and weaknesses, and then settle on the one you think best. From there, your job is to argue the merits of this best solution so that you convince your reader of its worth.

Julie Titone's "Balance of Power" offers a good look at both problem and solution blocks. We can divide this essay into the following sections:

I. Beginning—¶s 1–3
Here, Titone uses some startling statistics to alert the reader to the problem of salmon population decline, and she focuses on the impact of this decline, labeling it a "misery."

II. Problem block—¶s 4–13
In this section, Titone explores the impact of dams as the primary reason for the decline. Specifically, these paragraphs do the following:
¶4—acknowledges various causes for decline, naming dams as biggest problem
¶s 5–7—show how dams impede the migration of salmon
¶8—shows legal aspects of the power struggle
¶9—offers spotted owl comparison
¶10—shows impact of salmon protection on reservoirs
¶11—shows impact of salmon protection on economy
¶s 12–13—debunk spotted owl comparison
III. Solution block—¶s 14–19
In this section, Titone discusses the potential benefits of restructuring dams and salmon runs:
¶14—potential positive economic impact
¶15—plan for study to be conducted
¶16—revised estimates of costliness to power companies and their customers
¶s 17–19—Corps of Engineers experiment, potential positive results
IV. Ending—¶20
This paragraph serves as an effective conclusion for Titone's essay, focusing on potential benefits and the need to protect the salmon.

Thesis Statement

Earlier in this chapter, we noted the importance of a well-defined problem, and we advised you to write a clear, detailed problem statement. But even though your problem statement will be important in guiding your investigation of the problem and its solutions, this statement will not serve as your essay's thesis. Because you're writing an argument, your thesis should urge your reader to take a particular action or stance on your topic. Where may a thesis occur in a problem/solution essay? As with other types of essays, it may appear anywhere. Generally, however, a problem/solution thesis appears in one of two places: at the beginning of the solution section, so that the writer outlines the direction the rest of the essay will take, or at the end of the essay, so that the thesis functions to drive the writer's point home. The essays by Kristina Geray and Julie Titone provide useful illustrations.

Kristina presents her thesis at the beginning of the solution section of her essay, "The Pet Overpopulation Problem" (pages 567–571). Her thesis—"The most obvious and effective of these methods of accomplishing this goal is the sterilization of pets"—opens paragraph 10 and appears about two-thirds of the way through the paper.

Titone takes a different tack, presenting her thesis in the final paragraph of her essay. That thesis—"Although there is no guarantee that drawdowns will save any of the Columbia Basin's wild salmon, they remain an expensive gamble worth taking"—presents Titone's stance on the topic. She spends the first nineteen paragraphs of her essay discussing the problem thoroughly and then speculating about the potential benefits of her proposed solution. But it isn't until the final paragraph that we see her definitive stance on the issue.

Refining Your Writing

As you begin revising your essay, consider the following characteristics of a successful problem/solution essay.

Well-defined problem. Define the problem as clearly and specifically as you can. Keep in mind that your definition of the problem may well point toward a solution—inherent in the problem is the solution.

Thorough exploration of the problem. What is the problem? Why is it a problem? Whom does it affect? What are its costs? Who caused it? Remember that part of your job is to convince your reader that the problem truly is a problem.

Best solution. Not all solutions are created equal. In exploring and selecting the best solution, you should consider alternative solutions; generally, a problem will have more than one possible solution. As you reconsider how effectively you've presented your solution, use such questions as these to sharpen your response to the problem: What is your solution? What are its elements? Which aspects of the problem will it solve? What alternative solutions exist? Why are these not as good as the one you've selected as best?

Audience consideration. In your prewriting, you should have written at least an initial audience analysis, and you may well have written a second, more detailed analysis of your intended reader. Who is your reader? Why did you select this reader; that is, what is the reader's relation to or involvement with the problem? How effectively have you considered your reader's possible objections to or doubts about your solution?

SAMPLE STUDENT PROCESS

The sample student essay is by Kristina Geray, a first-year writing student at NMSU, who decided to write about a problem with some immediacy for her—unwanted stray pets. Kristina's interest in the topic derives from her personal experience. As she notes in the essay's introduction, a lot of stray dogs wander by her home, but she can't take every one in.

Prewriting

I'm so tired of this—another dog dropped off, pretty reddish color. She'll probably grow up to be a big dog, if she lives. That's—how many? At least 4 or 5 since December. Can we keep her? I doubt it. We have too many now as it is. Can't afford another one. It's hard. If she leaves, she'll just get run over if she gets on the highway. Or maybe coyotes will get her if she tries to run in the desert. Or she'll get picked up. Maybe she'll get to Arthur's house—he takes in every stray that comes along. I wonder what his feed bills are. I really admire him for trying to save every animal that comes his way.

Focus Statement

I want to write about the problem of stray pets (mostly dogs and cats).

Problem. We have an overpopulation of pets. There are too many strays that nobody wants, so they end up living a short, lousy life. Strays get euthanized by county agents or humane society—how many? What's the cost?

Solution. What solutions will work? Euthanization is not humane, and it does not work anyway, not if the number of strays at my house means anything. Sterilization makes more sense, but that would be like legislating morality—how do you get pet owners to neuter their pets?

Audience. My audience would be those people affected most by the problem of pet overpopulation. The people most affected would be pet owners since they are most directly impacted by anything involving their pets. Any solution to this problem would involve pet owners since it would be up to them to actually start using the solution.

Research Strategies

Kristina knew that she would need statistics to illustrate the magnitude of the problem with strays, so she searched the Internet, using such key terms as "American Society for the Prevention of Cruelty to Animals (ASPCA)," "spaying," and "neutering" as a start. She quickly found three sites that carried information she could use. At http://www.aspca.org, she found two documents: "Why Spay or Neuter?" at http://www.aspca.org/spay.htm and "New York State Animal Population Control Program" at http://www.aspca.org/apcp.htm. At an environmental site—http://www.geocities.com/CollegePark/6280—she found a link to a site covering a number of issues, including animal abuse. One article she found there, titled "Have You Ever Tortured an Animal?" included information about strays.

To gather still more information, Kristina interviewed two people directly involved with pet care in Doña Ana County: Pamela Angell, director of the Doña Ana Humane Society Animal Shelter, and Alice Lewis, an employee of a local veterinary clinic. Further, while at the animal shelter Kristina picked up a Humane Society pamphlet, which figured as another source. During her conversations with both Angell and Lewis, Kristina took these few notes that show the severity of the problem of too many strays in the county, focusing on the number of animals and the costs associated with them:

> *Personal communication—Pamela Angell, May 7, 1998*
> numbers are incredible—13K+ dogs & cats in county (13,157)
> 10,208 euthanized—killed
> 1,554 adopted
> 1,359 back to owners
> cost—$321,762 ($\frac{1}{2}$ from taxes, rest from adoption charges and donations)
> numbers on the rise—23% increase, last 10 years
> Angell says 1 female dog & girl pups produce min. of 13,120 puppies in 6-year span
> spaying best—county humane society sponsors low cost neutering & spaying, available to pet owners with low income

> *Personal communication, Alice Lewis, May 14, 1998*
> male cat $35 under 5
> kidney & blood work is more expensive after 5
> test kidneys liver, red & white blood cells
> male dog 90 lbs. $90
> girl cat $65
> $120 for heavy female, $75 for lighter female
> c-section $350 for *small* dog
> uterus 5–10 times larger—blood supplied is greater
> $200–300 for pyemetra
> male prostate—requires extra blood work, EKG & possibly X-rays

Discovery Draft

Having taken notes and thought through her topic, Kristina began writing a discovery draft. When you read the final draft, note which information in this initial draft appears in that final draft and which does not.

> ~~He is the poster~~ ~~He can't save the world but he tries.~~
>
> As I write this I'm contemplating a problem. She's a very pretty, red-haired problem with a muscular body and big, warm, brown eyes. She's also the ~~sixth~~ seventh stray dog to wander by my home in fourteen months. She's the fourth one ~~I've decided~~ my mother and I have decided we can't keep. She'll have to go to the pound. She might be adopted. More likely she'll be euthanized. With 5 dogs allready in our care we can't afford to take on another one.
>
> She's an example of a problem faced by every person in this nation at one point or another, the problem of pet overpopulation. It is estimated that seven to thirteen hundred animals are abandoned per county per year in the U.S. In 1997 in Dona Ana county alone over 13000 dogs and cats ~~are abandoned~~ are picked up by or given into the care of the Doña Ana County Humane society.
>
> Some people may argue that it is not their problem ~~if~~ that the number of unwanted pets has reached such high levels. They are sadly mistaken. The pet overpopulation problem affects everyone which makes it everyone's problem. Aside from the obvious annoyances that stray animals cause, such as fighting with

wanted animals and knocking over trash containers in pursuit of a meal, they are a health hazard and an economic drain. Stray animals do not recieve shots or any other type of veterinary care. As a result of this stray animals can carry *fleas, ticks,* rabies, parvo, ~~and~~ heartworm ~~Stray cats~~ and distemper. They ~~defecate~~ in public places and on private lawns. ~~They live in~~ and obtaining their meals by rummaging in dumps and trash cans. These ~~del~~ problems *have adverse* affects on both wanted animals and humans ~~as well~~. spread these diseases by biting humans & animals, defecating

The economic drain these animals cause is absorbed by individuals as well as by the taxpayers. Some individuals, such as Father Lon Ashley, an Episcopalian preacher *living in Chaparral*, take it upon themselves to care for the numerous strays that ~~find their way to the homes of these caring people every day~~ roam New Mexico streets. At this point in time Father Ashley cares for over 70 dogs and many more cats, goats, and horses. He pays about $? a day to feed all the animals that have been abandoned on his doorstep.

More often than not, however, stray ~~animals~~ and abandoned animals end up in the local Humane Society where the tax payers pick up the tab for their care and eventual euthanization. In 1997, 13157 cats and dogs ~~wound up~~ were left in the care of the Doña Ana County Humane Society. Of these 78%, 10208 animals, were euthanized, 12%, 1554 animals, were adopted, and 10%, 1395 were returned to their owners. The total cost ~~to the taxpayers~~ for care of these animals was $321,762, half of which was payed by the taxpayers. The other half was made up by donations and service charges.

Rough Draft for Peer Review Kristina stopped writing before completing an initial draft; in fact, she had written only about the problem. But she had started. A day or two later, she returned to her writing and produced this draft. Other than the obvious one of length, what differences do you see between this draft and her discovery draft?

As I write this I am contemplating a problem. She's a very pretty, red-haired problem with a muscular body and big, warm, brown eyes. She's also the seventh stray dog to wander by my home in the last fourteen months. She's the fourth dog my mother and I have decided we can't keep. With five dogs already in our care, we cannot afford to take another into our home. She will have to go to the pound. Hopefully, she'll be adopted. More likely, though, she will be euthanized.

This pretty, rust-colored pup is an example of a problem faced by every person in this country at one time or another: pet overpopulation. It is estimated that seven to thirteen hundred animals are abandoned per county per year in the United States (Berthiaume et al., 1996). In 1997 in Doña Ana County alone over 13,000 dogs and cats were picked up by or given into the care of the Doña Ana County Humane Society (P. Angell, Animal Shelter Director DACHS, personal communication, May 7, 1998).

Some people may argue that it is not their problem that the number of unwanted pets has reached such disastrously high levels. They are sadly mistaken. The problem of pet overpopulation affects everyone. It is *everyone's* problem.

Aside from the obvious annoyances that stray animals cause, fighting with wanted animals, for example, they are a health hazard and an economic drain. Stray animals do not receive shots or any other form of veterinary care. As a result, stray pets may carry fleas, ticks, rabies, parvo, heartworm, and/or distemper. They spread these diseases by biting humans and other animals, by defecating in public places as well as on private lawns, and by rummaging in dumps and trash cans (Be a PAL, 1989). The health of strays has an adverse effect on the health of both humans and wanted animals.

The economic drain these animals cause is, more often than not, absorbed by taxpayers. Humane Societies, where most strays and abandoned animals end up, use tax money to defray the expense of caring for and eventually euthanizing these pets. In 1997, 13,157 dogs and cats were left in the care of the Doña Ana County Humane Society. Of these 78 percent, 10,208 animals, were euthanized. Twelve percent, 1,554 animals, were adopted and ten percent, 1,395 animals, were returned to their owners. The total cost for the care of these animals was $321,762, half of which was paid by taxpayers. The other half was made up by donations and service charges.

The most popular method of solving the problem of pet overpopulation, the euthanization of strays, has proved inefficient. Over the past ten years there has been a 23 percent increase in the number of animals impounded by the Doña Ana County Humane Society (P. Angell, 1998). It can be assumed that this increase reflects a trend in the overall population of pets in Doña Ana County as well as throughout the nation. Euthanization has only served to slow the rate of growth of the pet population, not to keep it down. Another, more successful method is greatly needed.

The best solution to this problem is prevention. It is estimated that in six years one female dog and her female offspring can produce 13,120 puppies. (This is a low estimate). This number is nearly equivalent to the number of animals (cats and dogs) taken care of by the Doña Ana County Humane Society in 1997 (P. Angell, 1998).

8   Others make the claim that 70,000 puppies and kittens are born every day in the United States (Be a PAL, 1989). At this rate an estimated 25.5 million puppies and kittens are born in the United States in a year. Only 7.5 million animals are destroyed, nationwide, by Humane Societies every year (Be a PAL, 1989). Assuming that in one year Humane Societies euthanized only those animals born in that same year, there would still be a *whopping 18 million puppies and kittens* needing loving homes in our nation. Even if half of these animals die from disease or neglect during the first few months of their lives, taxpayers will still be responsible for the care of *nine million animals*. Let's make a few more assumptions here. Let's assume that half (4.5 million) of these animals were kept from breeding and the other half were allowed to breed at the rate mentioned earlier in this paper (13,120 animals produced by one female pet and her female offspring in six years). Only half of the breeding animals would be female, so we need only concern ourselves with 2.25 million animals, less than one-tenth of the original 25.5 million dogs and cats born in one year. If this small fraction of all the animals born in a single year and their offspring are allowed to breed unchecked for six years, our nation will be faced with the responsibility of caring for *over 29.5 billion (mostly unwanted) pets!*

9   These numbers show how important it is to find some way of preventing these animals from breeding as soon as *possible!*

10   The most obvious and effective of these methods of accomplishing this goal is the sterilization of pets. Two operations are involved in the sterilization of animals. The first of these is spaying in which the ovaries are removed from a female dog or cat. The second is castration, or neutering, in which a male animal's testes are removed.

11   The chief objection most people have to this form of population control is the expense, which can run from $35 for a small male cat to $120 for a very large female dog. The cost goes even higher if the female animal is in heat at the time of the operation. However, this cost is nothing when compared to the amount the owner may pay if complications arise during a beloved female pet's pregnancy. An emergency cesarean section for a small dog costs about $350. This price increases for larger animals. Treatment for prostate cancer, a condition that may affect unsterilized male dogs or cats, also costs several hundreds of dollars (A. Lewis, Solano Animal Clinic employee, personal communication, May 14, 1998).

12   In addition to these high veterinary costs, numerous incentive programs exist to encourage people to sterilize their pets. Many animal welfare programs offer spay/neuter operations at a reduced price. The Doña Ana County Humane Society has a financial aid program set up to assist low income families who want to have their pets sterilized (P. Angell, 1998). Many states also offer reduced licensing fees to owners of spayed or neutered animals (ASPCA Government Affairs, 1998). For these reasons, cost is not a legitimate excuse for anyone to avoid sterilizing their animals.

13   Another reason people often refuse to have their female pets spayed is the myth that a female dog or cat must have at least one litter in order to lead a healthy life. Nothing could be further from the truth. The earlier a female pet is spayed, the healthier she will be as she ages. A female pet spayed before the age of sexual maturity, at about six to nine months, faces only one-seventh the risk that a full female faces of developing mammary cancer. Spaying a pet also reduces the animal's risk of developing other expensive to treat and potentially fatal conditions such as breast cancer and pyometra (a pus-filled uterus) (ASPCA, 1998).

Other popular myths that prevent people from sterilizing their pets are that the operation will be dangerous and painful for the pet, that after the surgery the animal will become fat and lazy, and that the operation will cause the animal's personality to change.

The first of these should be taken with a grain of salt. There is only a very slight risk to any animal undergoing this common procedure, and it takes only two to three days for a dog or cat to recover if given proper care (ASPCA, 1998).

Second, sterilization cannot make an animal fat or lazy. Only lack of exercise and an unhealthy diet can cause that. Responsible owners can prevent a pet from becoming obese by monitoring food intake and exercising the pet regularly (ASPCA, 1998).

Finally, any changes that take place in an animal's personality after sterilization will be to the owner's benefit. Spaying or neutering a pet destroys its desire to mate, causing it to wander from home less frequently. The animal will be less territorial, making it less eager to fight or to mark its territory (the owner's home and yard) with urine. Also, a sterilized cat or dog is less likely to attack a person without provocation and is just as loyal as an animal that has not been spayed or neutered (ASPCA, 1998).

Despite the euthanization of large numbers of dogs and cats every year by Humane Societies across the nation, the pet population continues to grow at an alarming rate. This increase creates health and economic problems for every person in this country and can best be controlled by one method: the sterilization of pets by responsible owners. Despite the many objections pet owners may find to this operation, there is no reason not to spay or neuter a pet. The benefits of sterilization, for dogs and cats as well as for owners, far outweigh any risk or inconvenience the pet or owner may experience.

References

ASPCA. (1998). Why spay or neuter?: This low cost surgery offers you and your pet many, many advantages. Retrieved May 8, 1998, from http://www.aspca.org/spay.htm

ASPCA Government Affairs. (1998). New York State Animal Population Control Program. Retrieved May 8, 1998, from http://www.aspca.org/apcp.htm

Berthiaume, B., Cornielle, C., Forrest, K., Funai, D., Nachmann, M., Shrugrue, T., & Tisdale, C. (1996). Have you ever tortured an animal?: Are you sure? There are many ways in which we indirectly abuse animals. Retrieved May 8, 1998, from http://www.geocities.com/College Park/6280

Humane Society of the United States. (1989). *Be a PAL: Pet Overpopulation Fact Sheet.* [Brochure]. Washington, DC: Author.

Reviews Kristina's essay was reviewed by a classmate in a one-on-one reading session. The reviewer thought that the essay worked, in the main. Among her comments to Kristina about the draft were these:

1. The problem is very clearly stated and gives very good reasons for why animal overpopulation is such a big problem.

2. By talking about how spaying/neutering animals will help decrease the problems people face as well as the benefits to the animals' well-being, the writer's solution is convincing.
3. The use of statistics throughout is very good. The writer did the math, and the number of animals and the cost to us all really worked.
4. The thesis is stated at the end of the essay and is effective in relating the problem and solution clearly.
5. By addressing concerns as taxpayers (which we all are), the writer relates to her readers that the problem does indeed involve everyone.

The reviewer also offered some suggestions for revision:

1. I like the introduction, but it could hit harder. At the end of ¶1, the writer says the dog "will be euthanized." Why not just say "killed"? "Euthanized" doesn't carry as much impact as "killed."
2. Can you incorporate some sources more smoothly? On p. 1, that long reference to "P. Angell" gets in the way. What does the "P" stand for? Same with "A. Lewis."
3. At the end of ¶6 I was a little confused by the idea that euthanization has slowed the rate of growth. Most of what the writer said about euthanization so far is that it doesn't work.
4. In the next ¶ (7), I don't think the first sentence fits with the other 2.

Before she began her final draft, Kristina asked Bill, her instructor, to look over her rough draft. Bill found the reviewer's comments to be on target, but he did make two suggestions dealing with format:

1. Your reviewer is right about the topic sentence of ¶7. Why not delete that sentence and write a new one? You could also insert the statistical information and use either numbers or bullets of some kind to feature or emphasize the numbers here.
2. Near the end, you talk about myths that some pet owners believe. That section has a fair number of short, choppy paragraphs. How might you put them together to smooth things out?

With advice, then, from two readers, Kristina reviewed her essay and produced a final draft. What differences do you see between this draft and the review rough draft? How much of her readers' advice did she take?

Final Draft

KRISTINA GERAY

THE PET OVERPOPULATION PROBLEM

As I write this I am contemplating a problem. She's a very pretty, red-haired problem with a muscular body and big, warm, brown eyes. She's also the seventh stray dog to wander by my home in the last fourteen months. She's the fourth dog my mother and I have decided we can't keep. With five dogs already in our care, we cannot afford to take another into our home. She will have to go to the pound. Hopefully, she'll be adopted. More likely, though, she will be killed. She'll be picked up by a dog catcher, taken to an animal shelter, and put up for adoption. Odds are she won't be adopted and, after a short period—only three days—she'll be euthanized. She'll be killed.

This pretty, rust-colored pup is an example of a problem faced by every person in this country at one time or another: pet overpopulation. So many dogs and cats are running loose that they simply cannot be controlled. Many of these strays once were pets but are abandoned by their owners. And they are abandoned in alarming numbers. It is estimated that seven to thirteen hundred animals are abandoned per county, per year in the U.S. (Berthiaume et al., 1996). The problem locally is even worse. According to Pamela Angell, Animal Shelter Director for the Doña Ana County Humane Society, last year over 13,000 dogs and cats were picked up by or given into the care of the Doña Ana County Humane Society (personal communication, May 7, 1998).

Why are so many pets abandoned? For one, people move and either can't take their pet with them or just don't want the hassle of moving Rover with them. For another, Fluffy, that cuddly little furball somebody's child brought home, became a walking allergen. And then there's always that litter of puppies somebody intends to find homes for but somehow never does (Berthiaume et al., 1996). In each of these instances, abandonment provides an easy way out.

Some people may argue that it is not their problem that the number of unwanted pets has reached such disastrously high levels. They are sadly mistaken. The problem of pet overpopulation affects everyone. It is *everyone's* problem.

Aside from the obvious annoyances that stray animals cause, fighting with wanted animals, for example, they are a health hazard and an economic drain. Stray animals do not receive shots or any other form of veterinary care. As a result, strays may carry fleas, ticks, rabies, parvo, heartworm, and/or distemper.

They spread these diseases by biting humans and other animals, by defecating in public places as well as on private lawns, and by rummaging in dumps and trash cans (Humane Society of the United States, 1989). The health of strays has an adverse effect on the health of both humans and wanted animals.

The economic drain these animals cause is, more often than not, absorbed by taxpayers. Humane Societies, where most strays and abandoned animals end up, use tax money to defray the expense of caring for and eventually euthanizing these pets. In 1997, 13,157 dogs and cats were left in the care of the Doña Ana County Humane Society. Of these, 78 percent, 10,208 animals, were euthanized. Twelve percent, 1,554 animals, were adopted, and ten percent, 1,395 animals, were returned to their owners. The total cost for the care of these animals was $321,762, half of which was paid by taxpayers. The other half was made up by donations and service charges. Over the past ten years, there has been a 23 percent increase in the number of animals impounded by the Doña Ana County Humane Society (P. Angell, personal communication, May 7, 1998). It can be assumed that this increase reflects a trend in the overall population of pets in Doña Ana County as well as throughout the nation. Despite the number of animals euthanized, the number of strays just keeps growing.

Nationwide, the numbers are staggering:

- In six years, one female dog and her female offspring can produce 13,120 puppies, and this is a conservative estimate (P. Angell, personal communication, May 7, 1998).
- Some 70,000 puppies and kittens are born every day in the United States. At this rate an estimated 25.5 million puppies and kittens are born in the United States in a year (Humane Society of the United States, 1989).
- Only 7.5 million animals are destroyed, nationwide, by Humane Societies every year (Humane Society of the United States, 1989).

Assuming that in one year Humane Societies euthanized only those animals born in that same year, there would still be a *whopping 18 million puppies and kittens* needing loving homes in our nation. Even if half of these animals die from disease or neglect during the first few months of their lives, taxpayers will still be responsible for the care of *nine million animals.* Let's make a few more assumptions here. Let's assume that half (4.5 million) of these animals were kept from breeding, leaving the other half to breed at that rate of 13,120 animals every six years. Only half of the breeding animals would be female, so we need only concern ourselves with 2.25 million animals, less than one-tenth of the original 25.5 million dogs and cats born in one year. If this small fraction of all the animals born in a single year and their offspring are allowed to breed unchecked for six years, our nation will be faced with the responsibility of caring for *over 29.5 billion (mostly unwanted) pets!* How much clearer can it be that euthanization can't solve this problem?

These numbers show how important it is to find some way of preventing these animals from breeding as soon as *possible!*

The most obvious and effective of these methods of accomplishing this goal is the sterilization of pets. Two operations are involved in the sterilization of animals. The first of these is spaying, in which the ovaries are removed from a female dog or cat. The second is castration, or neutering, in which a male animal's testes are removed.

The chief objection most people have to this form of population control is the expense, which can run from $35 for a small male cat to $120 for a very large female dog. The cost goes even higher if the female animal is in heat at the time of the operation. However, this cost is nothing when compared to the amount the owner may pay if complications arise during a beloved female pet's pregnancy. An emergency cesarean section for a small dog costs about $350. This price increases for larger animals. Treatment for prostate cancer, a condition that may affect unsterilized male dogs or cats, also costs several hundreds of dollars (A. Lewis, personal communication, May 14, 1998).

In addition to these high veterinary costs, numerous incentive programs exist to encourage people to sterilize their pets. Many animal welfare programs offer spay/neuter operations at a reduced price. The Doña Ana County Humane Society has a financial aid program set up to assist low income families who want to have their pets sterilized (P. Angell, personal communication, May 7, 1998). Further, many states offer reduced spaying and neutering costs to make the procedure more affordable (American Society for the Prevention of Cruelty to Animals [ASPCA], Government Affairs, 1998). For these reasons, cost is not a legitimate excuse for anyone to avoid sterilizing their animals.

Another reason people often refuse to have their female pets spayed is the myth that a female dog or cat must have at least one litter in order to lead a healthy life. Nothing could be further from the truth. The earlier a female pet is spayed, the healthier she will be as she ages. According to the American Society for the Prevention of Cruelty to Animals (ASPCA), a female pet spayed before the age of sexual maturity, at about six to nine months, faces only one-seventh the risk that a full female faces of developing mammary cancer. Spaying a pet also reduces the animal's risk of developing other expensive to treat and potentially fatal conditions such as breast cancer and pyometra (a pus-filled uterus) (ASPCA, 1998).

Other popular myths that prevent people from sterilizing their pets are that the operation will be dangerous and painful for the pet, that after the surgery the animal will become fat and lazy, and that the operation will cause the animal's personality to change. The first of these should be taken with a grain of salt. There is only a very slight risk to any animal undergoing this common procedure, and it takes only two to three days for a dog or cat to recover if given proper care. Second, sterilization cannot make an animal fat or lazy. Only lack of exercise and an unhealthy diet can cause that. Responsible owners can prevent a pet from becoming obese by monitoring food intake and exercising the pet regularly. Finally, any changes that take place in an animal's personality after sterilization will be to the owner's benefit. Spaying or neutering a pet destroys its desire to mate, causing it to wander from home less frequently. The animal will be less territorial, making it less eager to fight or to mark its territory (the owner's home and yard) with urine. Also, a sterilized cat or dog is less likely to attack a person without provocation and is just as loyal as an animal that has not been spayed or neutered (ASPCA, 1998).

Despite the euthanization of large numbers of dogs and cats every year by Humane Societies across the nation, the pet population continues to grow at an alarming rate. This increase creates health and economic problems for every person in this country and can best be controlled by one method: the sterilization of pets by responsible owners. Despite the many objections pet owners may find to this operation, there is no reason not to spay or neuter a pet. The benefits of sterilization, for dogs and cats as well as for owners, far outweigh any risk or inconvenience the pet or owner may experience.

References

American Society for the Prevention of Cruelty to Animals. (1998). Why spay or neuter?: This low cost surgery offers you and your pet many, many advantages. Retrieved May 8, 1998, from http://www.aspca.org/spay.htm

American Society for the Prevention of Cruelty to Animals, Government Affairs. (1998). New York State Animal Population Control Program. Retrieved May 8, 1998, from http://www.aspca.org/apcp.htm

Berthiaume, B., Cornielle, C., Forrest, K., Funai, D., Nachmann, M., Shrugrue, T., & Tisdale, C. (1996). Have you ever tortured an animal?: Are you sure? There are many ways in which we indirectly abuse animals. Retrieved May 8, 1998, from http://www.geocities.com/College Park/6280

Humane Society of the United States. (1989). *Be a PAL: Pet Overpopulation Fact Sheet* [Brochure]. Washington, DC: Author.

CHECKLIST: CRITIQUING A PROBLEM/SOLUTION ESSAY

1. In a sentence, state the problem the essay addresses. In another, state the solution. How clearly are both the problem and the solution stated?
2. How is the problem developed or explained? What examples or details does the writer give to show that the problem truly is a problem?
3. How has the solution been justified or supported? What alternative solutions are considered and discussed? How has the writer shown that the proposed solution is better than any alternatives discussed?
4. How likely is the introduction to catch the reader's attention?

5. How effectively does the conclusion finish the paper?
6. At what points is the reader likely to disagree with or be resistant to the argument presented? How has the writer addressed these concerns?
7. What ethos has the writer presented in this paper; that is, how does the writer appear to be knowledgeable and fair?
8. How effectively is any material quoted from an outside source incorporated into the flow of the paper? Is the documentation (both in-text and bibliography) correct?
9. Does the paper adhere to conventions of usage, mechanics, and format? Correct any errors you find.

PART III

Research

In *Searching Writing,* Ken Macrorie comments on the researcher's natural curiosity in examining a topic:

> Look at a two-year-old grabbing books off a shelf, seeing how they open, ripping pages, finding out how they taste. Not much different from a kitten first time out of his box. Apparently, we're all born curious. Inside or outside school, research should be like that, but usually isn't.

Macrorie touches on several important points concerning research. First, humans really are curious; we're more than willing to look into things and do so frequently, because we want to know more about them. Although it's true that we make snap decisions about some things, more often than not we consider our options; we examine an idea or a topic or a product to make up our minds about it, especially when what we're considering is of major consequence. Futhermore, research permeates our lives. If you're a comparison shopper, you're a researcher. When you contemplate a major purchase (e.g., a car or a guitar) and read brochures or check on the reliability or reputation of what you want to buy, then you're a researcher. Whatever its purpose, research should be as explorative and even as messy a process as that which Macrorie attributes to his two-year-old "reader."

Admittedly, looking into things and comparison shopping aren't the kinds of activities that drive most academic research. Students usually engage in research projects because they've been assigned. A biology student, for example, may be required to study the behavior of burrowing owls. He may sit under a tree at various times over a period of weeks, watching a burrow and taking notes on such matters as when the owls emerge from it, what they feed on, and how they interact with each other as well as with other animals, including the researcher himself. Those notes then inform the research report, in which the writer interprets the notes and uses them to support any generalizations he may make about the behavior of burrowing owls. A chemical engineering student may be required to conduct a lab experiment to determine the viscosity of various fluids; she conducts the experiment under controlled conditions and then writes a report presenting her findings and her interpretation of them. A student in a literature class may be asked to write an essay about the importance of a particular theme in a given poet's work. He will read several of her poems, but he will also read what other critics have said about her and her poetry. The research paper this student writes will include not only his interpretation of the poems but also his consideration of the critics' comments.

Note that interpretation figures prominently in the three examples of research writing just described. Ideally, research writing embodies the writer's interpretation of the topic. It should entail in-depth inquiry into a subject of the writer's choosing. It should be a springboard to discovery as the writer attempts to find new information to help her make up her own mind about a topic or support or modify a tentative position on the topic. The best research writing, then, should begin in curiosity and convey the excitement the writer feels in interpreting and making discoveries about the topic and, perhaps, about herself.

At times, student research papers seem to resemble a collection of facts and quotes, strung together in some semblance of order but not really making any particular point. Such papers have no definite shape; they have no discernible beginning, middle, and end. Because they have been written for no particular purpose or audience, they lack direction. At least part of the the problem students have with research writing stems from misconceptions about what a research paper should be and about what it means to conduct research. Research writing, even when assigned, should begin as a question the writer has about a particular topic. Thus, the writer's initial job is to probe the topic in search of an answer. The paper becomes an account of the writer's exploration of the topic; it presents her understanding of its importance and her stance on it.

Research writing, even when driven by a teacher's assignment, need not be drudgery, need not be boring for either the student writer or the teacher. Our goal in Chapter 12 is to present strategies that will help you engage with and manage a research project, which is one of the most comprehensive yet natural uses of writing that you may make.

As you'll learn in working through Chapter 12, Researching and Writing, we present the two major systems of documentation in use in American schools and universities today: that of the Modern Language Association (MLA) and that of the American Psychological Association (APA). The student sample research paper we give in Chapter 12 is documented in APA style. But throughout our text, we have presented documented essays, several of them illustrating the MLA style. As you develop the documentation for your researched essay, you may wish to refer to any of the essays listed below to see how the writer handled documentation.

MLA Documentation

Chapter 6

Elizabeth Gardner, "Transforming a Nation, Transforming an Enemy" (pages 227–233)

Chapter 7

    Kendra Stead, "The Making of Spells" (pages 303–306)
    Kendra Stead, "No Exceptions" (pages 310–313)
    Amy Wright, "A Quest to Return to the Garden: Perception 'Of Falling'" (pages 306–309)
    Kristina Geray, "'How Exhausting It Is' to Keep Up Appearances" (pages 341–345)

Chapter 8

    Bill Bridges, "'No Thanks'—A Step Beyond 'Just Say No'" (pages 358–361)
    Jennifer Pitman, "Booze It? Lose It!: An Evaluation of North Carolina's Drunk Driving Laws" (pages 362–364)

Chapter 9

    Jennifer Pitman, "Euthanasia and the Right to Die" (pages 437–439)
    Heather Hall, "The Next Big Winner Is . . . . !!" (pages 479–482)

Chapter 10

    Jaime Sherrill, "Zero Tolerance for Abuse" (pages 501–503)
    Jaclyn Talbert, "Justice for Those Who Have Shown Us No Mercy" (pages 504–507)
    Alysia Tucker, "No More" (pages 530–532)

Chapter 12

    Clarita Brown, "The American Indian Movement as a Counterculture" (pages 618–623)

APA Documentation

Chapter 11

    Andrew Overton, "Change" (pages 546–550)
    Kristina Geray, "The Pet Overpopulation Problem" (pages 567–571)

Chapter 12

    Gardiner Rhoderick, "Yes, It's Graffiti, But Is It Art?" (pages 630–637)

Patrick Hughes, "Book Look," 1997. Oil on board construction, 31 × 56 × 12-1/2 in. Courtesy of Flowers Gallery.

CHAPTER 12

Researching and Writing

What comes to mind when you think of writing a research paper? Beginning an assigned research project, many students groan as they envision themselves seated in a library until late at night, slaving away at huge piles of books, picking a pithy quotation from one source, taking a telling statistic from another. But research should not entail this kind of drudgery. Although it is true that research requires you to use outside sources, your research should begin in curiosity. You should begin by asking a question about a particular topic, so that your initial job is to probe the topic in search of an answer. Once you have found at least a tentative answer to your question and have adopted a stance on the topic, you may structure your writing to achieve one of the aims we talked about in Part Two.

> *Inform.* Is there a topic you want to know more about? Use a research assignment to investigate the topic and then to inform others of what you learn.
> *Evaluate.* Do you have to choose the better of two options? How will you make that choice? Use a research assignment to examine both options thoroughly, compare them, and then make an informed choice.
> *Argue.* Do you have a topic you feel strongly about or a position you want to convince others about? Use a research assignment to develop support for your position.
> *Solve a problem.* Do you know of something that needs to be fixed or needs to be changed? Use a research assignment to consider the problem, weigh various potential solutions, and then present what you think is the best solution.

A research paper written to fulfill one of these purposes will not be a mere rehashing of other writers' ideas. By presenting *your* investigation, *your* serious, comprehensive look into a topic, you'll move away from the research paper as a simple collection of facts and quotations.

At the same time, you'll need to follow certain conventions. Research writing necessarily involves using sources. Using someone else's work can be fruitful, for it lets you

> expand your own knowledge and so present a more comprehensive essay to a reader,
> engage another writer in a "discussion" to develop your own perspective,

marshal support for your perspective, so that your reader may see you as a more informed, more convincing authority than he might otherwise, and sharpen your research and interpretive skills, which will be required in much of the work you'll be asked to do as a college student.

When you use sources, you must avoid plagiarism. You must also report the results of your inquiry in such a way that other researchers can use your findings if they so desire. As you follow the guidelines in this chapter, you should achieve a necessary balance between content and convention in research writing.

Exercise 12.1

What is the best experience you've had with writing a research paper to date? The worst? Write a paragraph about each of these experiences. Next, develop a list of traits for a good research paper or research process. Then, compare your list with those of your classmates to help you clarify and expand your list. Finally, use the expanded list as a checklist to help guide your research writing.

WRITING STRATEGY

Research Notebook

A research project requires that you keep an accurate record of all you do to complete it, from start to finish. One of the best ways to create and maintain this record is with a research notebook—a notebook that is separate from any learning or reading log your instructor may have you keep. In your research notebook, you should

- make a timeline of important dates, including the project's final due date and your own schedule for major elements, such as the date for completing a first rough draft and the date your review group will meet to discuss one another's drafts,
- keep dialogue notes for everything you read,
- make complete bibliographical entries for all the materials you research,
- keep all of your notes from other activities you undertake, such as conducting interviews, and
- keep all your prewriting and drafts.

A research notebook will help organize your entire project by holding all related materials together in one place.

TOPIC SELECTION

What makes a research topic workable? For our purposes, we'll assume that the essay you submit will be 1,500 to 2,500 words, about 6–10 double-spaced pages, so you'll have to pick a topic you can develop in those limits. Your topic may be something close to you and thus personal, it may have to do with a local issue, or it may be as broad as a national problem. Whether personal or global, your topic needs to be one about which you can find information, whether you find it in a library, through field work, or on the Internet.

Sometimes you will have a free choice of topics for your writing, so your task becomes one of finding the right topic, one you want to spend a good bit of time with. But how do you find this topic? Identifying your interests is the most logical starting point. When you begin a research assignment, you may know, or at least have some idea of, a topic. If you're blank, however, look through your Interest Inventory (see pages 11–13) to see if any topic appeals to you immediately. Your inventory should reveal your expertise on several subjects. It should also tell you that you feel strongly about a number of issues. From such topics as these, ones in which you have expertise and about which you feel strongly, can come strong research papers.

Although you will at times be free to choose any subject you wish, at other times you will not. Either your instructor will ask you to find a subject in a specific context (e.g., the American colonial period) or will limit you to an even narrower subject (e.g., George Washington's battle strategies in several important battles during the American Revolution). In such instances, your job is to make the subject your own, that is, to find a topic of significance in it so that your paper reveals your thinking about the topic.

One of the best ways to begin searching for a topic is to freewrite, so that you uncover what you do and do not know. You may already know a good deal about such subjects as the colonial period or Washington's battle plans if such subjects have been assigned in the context of the course you are taking on early American history. If you are free to choose your own subject, then we suspect you will pick one you are familiar with or want to know more about. Whichever the case, begin by freewriting. Ask such questions as "What interests me about this topic?" and "What do I know about this topic?" Then work toward answering those questions as you freewrite.

Exercise 12.2

1. If you have even a tentative topic for a research project, then use it as you complete this exercise. If you don't have a topic, pick one of the following subjects and freewrite on it for ten minutes, asking questions you think are appropriate. Then read back over your freewriting and look for a focal point, something that might serve as the basis of a research project. If you find such a point, consider why you think it might work for a research paper.

nuclear energy
alternatives to nuclear energy
good (bad) study habits
history of a favorite sport or hobby
buying something (e.g., the best camera or microcomputer)
benefits of some kind of exercise (e.g., running, swimming, biking)
job opportunities for college students
a social issue (e.g., drunk driving)
a national, regional, or local environmental issue
a campus issue

2. If your teacher has assigned your research topic, use it in the freewriting exercise offered here. If you are free to choose your own topic, begin thinking now about potential topics. Pick one, and freewrite on it for ten minutes, asking appropriate questions. Then read back over your freewriting and look for a focal point, something that might serve as the basis of a research project. If you do not find one, freewrite for another ten minutes; then look again. Continue working with this process until you find at least a tentative topic. Why do you think it might work into a research paper?

SEARCHING A TOPIC

We assume at this point that you have found at least a tentative topic, one you are curious enough about to spend some time exploring. How can you search the topic? How can you find, record, and make sense of information about the topic?

Sources of Information

Once you've found a tentative topic, your next step is to survey sources to see what information is available. Depending on your topic, you may rely wholly on your library to support your research, or you may find it necessary or desirable to do some kind of field search. Or you may use the Internet to investigate your topic. Then again, you may use a combination of two or even all three of these. After you have identified your sources, your task is to create meaning from the information they provide. Your paper must be much more than a listing of facts and quotations found in your sources. These sources are the raw materials from which you shape your finished product.

Taking Notes   As you read through your sources, look for ways to respond to them. With what in those sources do you agree or disagree? At what points are the thoughts of others consistent or inconsistent with your experience? What do you find of consequence in the information? Is there some action you think should be taken, or was some action taken that should not have been? Answering such questions as these as you explore sources can help you focus your thinking.

As you work with your sources, you'll need to find some way to organize their information so that you can access it easily at any point during the research process. One convenient way to organize is the traditional note-card system. When you take notes, use 3-by-5-inch index or note cards, recording one bit of information (e.g., a summary of a certain passage or a direct quotation) per card. Listing one bit per card makes it easy for you later on as you shuffle notes and move various citations around to find the most effective way to use the information. Note-card formats vary, but each card should carry at least this information:

1. The last name of the person you are citing (e.g., author or interviewee) or some other identification of the source (e.g., keyword or the title),
2. The source's call number, if it has one, or the web address or the database in which you located the source if the source comes from the Internet,
3. The note itself,
4. The page number you took the note from.

Figure 12.1 shows a sample note card containing a direct quotation and a brief introduction to it. This note card refers to David Guterson's article, "No Longer a Fringe Movement," which appeared in the October 5, 1998 issue of *Newsweek*. We identified the passage for future reference by citing Guterson as its author. Were we working with an unsigned or anonymous article, we would have identified the passage using a key word from the article's title.

If you find organizing note cards burdensome, then keep a notebook dedicated solely to your research project. As you read various sources, use dialogue notes to help you determine a given source's importance to your project. If you're using a computer, keep your notes in files organized by author or topic. Whatever

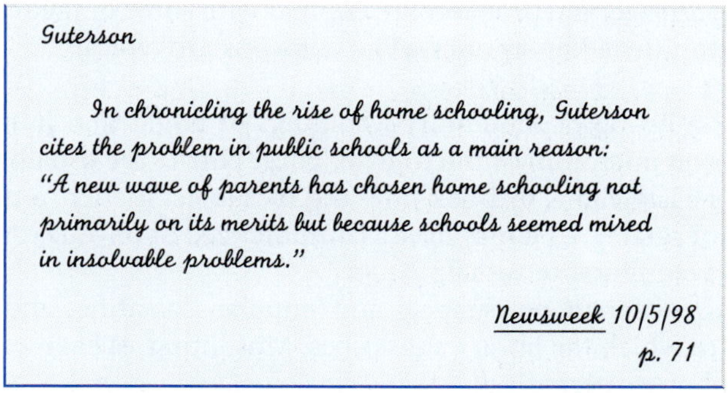

> Guterson
>
> In chronicling the rise of home schooling, Guterson cites the problem in public schools as a main reason: "A new wave of parents has chosen home schooling not primarily on its merits but because schools seemed mired in insolvable problems."
>
> *Newsweek* 10/5/98
> p. 71

FIGURE 12.1 Note Card with Direct Quotation and Introduction

method you use—note cards, research notebook, or computer—be sure to include complete bibliographical information about each piece you read. If you need to return to a particular source, you'll be able to locate it readily; if you decide to use it in your paper, you'll have the documentation you'll need to provide.

Summarizing and Paraphrasing   At times, a source will not contain specific facts, statistics, or language you want to quote directly, or it will be too long for you to quote directly. Still, it may contain ideas you wish to use. If this is the case, you'll need to summarize those ideas, putting in your own words what you interpret as the passage's main point or points. If you incorporate a paraphrase or a summary in your research essay, you must document it, as we will explain in the next section. (For a discussion of writing summaries and paraphrases, see pages 121, 132–140)

Plagiarism   Incorporating another person's words or ideas into your writing as your own is plagiarism. Even using short phrases and parts of sentences written by someone else constitutes plagiarism, unless you document those pieces properly. Documentation includes clearly identifying paraphrased and summarized materials in your text, with a reference to the appropriate source. It also includes identifying quoted materials in the text by placing a direct quote in quotation marks and providing a reference to its source. And it includes in-text citations, notes (such as explanatory footnotes, footnotes identifying sources, and endnotes), and a reference list (a bibliography or "Works Cited" list). Further, if someone helps you (perhaps as an editor), you must acknowledge that person's contribution to your writing on an acknowledgments page either immediately following your essay's title page or as the last page of your essay.

Any failure to document sources properly, whether intentional or accidental, can lead to a charge of plagiarism. Because plagiarism is a matter of academic dishonesty, the penalty for plagiarism can be severe. (Ask your instructor to define your university's policy concerning plagiarism.)

Library Search

From past experience, you probably are familiar with some of the services and research opportunities a library offers. The following are typical:

1. *Catalog*—a listing of the library's holdings of books and journals that are bound or on microfilm or microfiche. These entries are usually alphabetized by author's last name, by book title, and by subject matter. Your library may have a card catalog, or it may have a computerized or on-line catalog accessed through a computer terminal.
2. *Periodicals*—current newspapers and popular, scientific, and professional journals to which the library subscribes. Most libraries have a reference section that houses periodicals.
3. *Interlibrary loan*—a system enabling a library to borrow books and periodicals it does not have from other libraries. If you cannot find a source you need, consider using interlibrary loan.

4. *Micromaterials*—collections of various materials (e.g., back issues of the *New York Times*) on microfilm or microfiche. Most libraries have microreaders available for patrons' use.
5. *Government documents*—collections of studies commissioned by agencies of the U.S. government. Certain libraries across the United States are designated document repositories and make these documents available to the public.
6. *Guides to periodicals and reference works*—indexes, bibliographies, or summaries of various reference works. The most widely used of these guides is the *Readers' Guide to Periodical Literature,* which lists articles in magazines and journals arranged alphabetically by subject matter and by author's last name.
7. *CD-ROM databases*—subject-specific databases typically dedicated to particular topics.
8. *Recent articles index*—a computerized index to articles published within the last three or four years on a range of topics. You may search such an index by subject area, by author, and by title.

Computer Tip

SAMPLE LISTING OF CD-ROM DATABASES

Although the following list is not exhaustive, it should give you an idea of the range of materials available to you through various electronic media in your library.

ABI/Inform (business)
Agricola (agriculture)
America, History & Life
Compendex (engineering)
Computer Select (computers)
Congressional Masterfile
Criminal Justice Abstracts
Econlit (economics)
ERIC (education)
Ethnic NewsWatch
GPO (U.S. government documents)
Medline (medicine)
MLA (literature and languages)
National Trade Bank Data
NTIS (technical reports)
PAIS (public affairs)
PsycLit (psychology)
Science Citation Index
Social Work Abstracts
U.S. Government Periodicals Index
Water Resources Abstracts ✦

Another valuable source of information and assistance is the reference librarian, who can help you find what you're having trouble finding, become an independent user of the library, and learn to use such resources as a CD-ROM database. If you're having a particular problem in using your library, ask the reference librarian for help.

Identifying Potentially Helpful Sources   One of the more difficult tasks students face in conducting research is determining the relevance to their research project of the printed information they find. To discover what you think is important in a printed source, use the following strategies:

1. Preview a book by scanning the title, subtitle, table of contents, foreword, introduction, and conclusion. What was the author's purpose in writing the book? How pertinent is that purpose to your topic? Similarly, preview an essay or news item, scanning the title, introduction, conclusion, headings, and any graphics (tables, charts, or pictures).
2. Use the index of a book to locate particular information about your topic.
3. Use the bibliography of a book or article to locate additional sources relevant to your topic.

Reliability of Printed Sources   Not all printed sources of information are equally reliable, and part of your job as a researcher is to determine just how reliable your sources are. But how? Traditionally, the reliability of printed texts has been evaluated based on these five criteria:

Accuracy. What are the text's major premises? How well researched, supported, and documented do they seem to be? Does the text have an editor? Is the publisher likely to have employees whose job it is to check the facts of publications?

Authority. Who is the author? What are her credentials? What is her standing in the field? Who published the text? Both national and university presses generally require their publications to be well-researched and well-written, so that books from such houses are usually thought of as constituting reliable sources. Where does the essay or news item appear—in a national, regional, state, or local publication? We do not mean to imply that national sources are necessarily better than local sources. A statewide publication such as *Texas Monthly* (a well-written magazine concerning issues and topics in Texas) is generally considered to be a more reliable source of information on a particular topic than a nationally circulated gossip tabloid.

Objectivity. What biases are evident in the text? How fair does the writer's use of language seem? What is the nature of the text? Is it a political, social, or religious tract? A scholarly investigation of a particular topic? A piece of propaganda? What is its purpose, to sway a reader or to invite him to make up his own mind?

Currency. What is the publication date? Are the text's information and sources up-to-date?

Coverage. What is included or covered in the text? In how much depth? Are some topics given more thorough or more preferential treatment than others? Is such treatment warranted?

Whatever the kind of publication, your job is to determine the quality of the writer's treatment of the subject. The better that quality, the more reliable the source is likely to be.

> **Exercise 12.3**
>
> Using the topic you wrote about in an exercise earlier in this chapter or the tentative topic you have chosen for your research paper, locate in your library the following sources relating to your topic, listing the title, author, and call number for each:
>
> two books
> two essays in popular journals (e.g., *Time, Newsweek, Better Homes and Gardens, Popular Mechanics, National Geographic*), if applicable
> two essays in scholarly or professional journals, if applicable
> two items from a newspaper, including one from the *New York Times*
> two items from a CD-ROM database
> two government documents, if applicable
>
> How reliable is each potential source? On what do you base your opinion?

Field Search

Oftentimes, students overlook the value and appropriateness of using sources beyond those they find in a library. Field sources can be especially important for current community or campus issues, even for topics of national scope. If you have such a topic, you should not limit yourself to searching a library for information. Similarly, if one of your teachers is a noted authority on your topic, you should try to interview him, even though his writings may be available in your library.

Survey your campus or local community to locate potential sources. Use a local telephone book to find businesses or chapters of local and national civic organizations and special interest groups (e.g., environmental protection groups) that may be able to provide information about your topic. Many groups can furnish trade publications, pamphlets, brochures, and newsletters relevant to your search. To discover who is most concerned with your topic, read local and campus newspapers. Many individuals will be willing to talk with you about their points of view. Whereas using printed materials from groups is a relatively easy task, preparing to talk with someone is more difficult.

Interviews An interview is a face-to-face meeting in which some topic is discussed. Interviews vary in formality, from discussion limited to questions submitted by the interviewer prior to the interview, to discussion that is not so limited, sometimes becoming an informal talk between two people who are interested in the same subject. Whatever the circumstances, follow these general guidelines to prepare for and conduct an interview:

1. Contact the person you want to interview as far in advance as possible to set up the interview. Identify yourself and your purpose clearly so that the interviewee will have some time to think about the general subject of the interview.
2. Prepare questions ahead of time to help you think your way through the interview. Decide what information you would like to receive, and frame questions to elicit it. Although you may use only some of these questions in the actual interview, preparing them will help you focus the interview. Ask pertinent, relevant questions; stick to the subject.
3. Include questions designed to establish the interviewee's credentials, such as who she is and how she came to be an expert on your subject.
4. Ask open-ended questions, those designed to elicit the interviewee's ideas and whatever facts she may know that you need. Ask for definition of terms or for clarification of points that are not clear to you. Open-ended questions let the interviewee talk at length about the subject and should elicit the information you seek.
5. In drafting and asking questions, remember that you are not an investigative reporter out to champion a cause or expose criminal activity. Questions should ask for information; they should not be of the "Do you still beat your wife?" ilk.
6. Take notes or use a tape recorder, but do not record secretly. Get the interviewee's permission to record ahead of time. If the interviewee seems hesitant about being audio-taped, just talk with her and jot notes immediately after the interview.
7. At appropriate intervals and at the end, summarize the interview. Tell the interviewee what you have understood her to say so that she can clarify her position if need be.
8. As a courtesy, offer to provide the interviewee with a transcript of the interview and a copy of your paper—before the paper is due—so that she can see how you plan to use the interview. At that time, the interviewee can check facts and quotations for accuracy, thereby strengthening your paper.

Reliability   What is the person's status as an authority on your topic? Is she a nationally known figure? What is her background or education in the field? If your topic is more local than national in scope, what standing does your source have with respect to your topic? What qualifies her as an expert or authority? The more expertise your source has, the more reliable she may be.

Exercise 12.4

1. Find a topic of current interest in your local or campus community. What is at issue? Identify the thoughts of people on both sides. Summarize at least two published sources for each side. Identify at least one person on

each side of the issue, and prepare a list of questions you would ask in an interview. If possible, interview these people, and summarize the results of your interviews. How reliable do you think the sources you have uncovered are? Why?

2. In a news magazine such as *Newsweek, Time,* or *U.S. News and World Report,* find an interview of a national business, political, or religious leader. Summarize the interview's content and key points. How would you characterize the questions asked? The answers? Are there any questions you wish the interviewer had asked? If so, what are they? Why would you have asked them?

3. Arrange to interview one of your classmates. Prior to the interview, prepare a list of questions that ask things you would like to know about this person. After the interview, write a brief character sketch or biography of your classmate, and have him or her check your writing for accuracy.

Questionnaires   Sometimes your topic will call for a survey of a sizable group of people. In such a case, interviewing will not be feasible. Instead, to reach this group, you may want to devise a questionnaire. Questionnaires may take two different forms. In the first type, a person chooses from a list of possible answers to a set of questions. For example, a survey at a fast food restaurant may ask us to judge whether the service was "excellent," "satisfactory," or "poor." The second type of questionnaire consists of a set of questions with spaces set aside for the recipients' responses. We see questionnaires often. For example, political pollsters use questionnaires to ascertain voter attitudes and then to predict a candidate's chances of winning, and advertising executives use them to ascertain consumer preferences before marketing a product.

Questionnaires survey primarily for two kinds of responses:

1. Factual information, such as frequency of product or facility use or kind of products or services used
2. Opinion, such as statements of agreement or disagreement with particular people (perhaps politicians or celebrities), respondents' perspectives on particular issues, a short statement about topics of particular interest or concern

Figure 12.2 shows an example of a questionnaire that could be part of a research project on how well a school library functions. Questions 1–3 ask for factual information, and questions 4–8 seek an opinion.

As you frame questions for a survey, try not to bias the responses; that is, try not to direct the respondents' responses to fit any preconceived notions you may have. As an example, look at question 7 in the library questionnaire. If the question read, "What should the library change its hours to?", it would reflect the writer's bias that the hours should be changed.

SURVEY OF SMITHSON LIBRARY

To respond to the following questions, circle or mark the most appropriate response.

1. How often do you use the library?
   Daily   Seldom
     1   2   3   4   5   6

2. What time of day do you most often use the library?
   Morning   Afternoon   Evening

3. For what purposes do you most often use the library? (Circle all that apply.)
   Reading   Studying   Typing   Researching   Other

4. How helpful are the following library personnel?

	Very helpful					Not helpful	
Reference librarians	1	2	3	4	5	6	No opinion
Reading room librarians	1	2	3	4	5	6	No opinion
Circulation librarians	1	2	3	4	5	6	No opinion
Interlibrary-loan staff	1	2	3	4	5	6	No opinion

5. To what extent are you able to find the resources you need in the library?
   Always   Seldom
     1   2   3   4   5   6

6. How adequate are the library hours for your needs?
   Adequate   Inadequate   Undecided

7. Should the library change its hours of operation?
   Yes _____   No _____
   If yes, should the library *increase* or *decrease* its hours? (Circle one.)

8. In the space below (and continuing on the back of this sheet, if necessary), please discuss your overall opinion of the library. Consider, for example, what its two primary strengths and weaknesses are. How would you address the weaknesses?

FIGURE 12.2   Sample Research Questionnaire

In addition to posing topical questions to respondents, pollsters may also seek demographic information in an attempt to identify particular characteristics of the group being surveyed. In a political race, pollsters might ask respondents their age, gender, race, income level, education level, religious preference, status as homeowner or renter, marital status, and political affiliation. For our hypothetical library survey, appropriate demographic information would include the respondent's age, class (e.g., freshman), and major. Such information allows pollsters to describe a "typical" respondent so as to see trends or patterns in the responses and thereby enhance their analysis of the information. A researcher might find, for example, that 85 percent of the freshmen and 80 percent of the sophomores surveyed feel the library is something of a maze in which they have trouble finding what they need, but only 5 percent of the graduate students surveyed feel this way. The researcher could conclude from such responses that a comprehensive library orientation program is needed to help undergraduates learn how to use the library.

A final note about administering a survey: Your university may require that a researcher wishing to involve human subjects in any way get permission to do so from an appropriate university administrator. Before you distribute a survey, ask your instructor about your university's policy concerning such matters.

Exercise 12.5

Identify a current issue about which you are concerned. Devise a questionnaire of at least five questions to ascertain opinions of others on this issue. Administer the questionnaire to at least twenty people, drawing on as broad a range of respondents as possible. Summarize and analyze the results. How did your questions help shape the results?

Observation   The last form of field search we will discuss is firsthand observation. If your topic is about something of a physical nature (e.g., an environmental issue, campus parking facilities, campus bike traffic), one of the best ways of conducting research is to watch. If possible, observe the scene of your topic several times at different times of the day. Draw a sketch of the scene, if doing so will help clarify your observation. Take notes; jot down your impressions of what you see; describe what you see; try to discern patterns in what you see. What is important about what you're observing? What does it mean?

Exercise 12.6

Spend an hour at a busy spot on campus. Describe the scene before you. Who is there? For what purpose? Are there any dominant patterns that emerge, things that are striking about what you see? If so, identify them. What makes them dominant or striking? What conclusions do you draw from your observation?

Internet Search

One of the most promising and, at the same time, potentially frustrating avenues for research is the information superhighway—the Internet. It is promising because of the vast amount of information it holds, ready for you as researcher to read, print out, and incorporate into an essay. Further, the Net opens lines of research that stretch beyond your local library. And you may use the Net for your research whenever a computer terminal is available to you, so you're not necessarily limited by the hours your library is open. But the Internet is potentially frustrating as well. First, it holds a vast amount of information, so much that you cannot possibly hope to review it all. Sometimes, the Net crashes and may be down for several minutes, several hours, or even several days as computer technicians work to restore service. But the biggest liability of the Internet as a ground for research involves the reliability of the sources available on it. Anyone can post anything on the Net, as evidenced by the websites of hate groups and pornographers.

Reliability of Internet Sources Because of the ease with which items can be posted on the Internet, you must consider the reliability of any Internet sources you want to use. The following questions for judging the reliability of Internet sources are based on the five criteria we listed for evaluating printed sources:

> *Accuracy.* Does the information seem error-free? Is there any evidence of documentation of ideas? Is an editor or fact checker listed in the article? (Given the availability of the Internet and the ease of publishing on it, authors seldom rely on editors and/or fact checkers.)
> **Comment:** There are no universally accepted standards for ensuring accuracy on the Internet.
> *Authority.* Is the article signed—that is, is the author identified? If so, who is the author? What are his credentials? What is his standing in the field? Is the author someone you've heard of? Who sponsors the page on which the article appears? How reputable is this sponsor? Does the article offer links to information about the author and/or the sponsor?
> **Comment:** It's often difficult to determine who has written an article on a web page; even when an article is signed, it's difficult to determine the writer's credentials. Further, the sponsor, if there is one, generally isn't listed, and it's often difficult to determine sponsorship from the web page's address.
> *Objectivity.* What biases are evident in the text? How fair does the writer's use of language seem? What is the nature of the text? Is it a political, social, or religious tract? A scholarly treatment of a topic? A piece of propaganda? What is its purpose? To allow the writer to rant and rave about a particular topic? To sway the reader? To invite the reader to make up his own mind about the topic?
> **Comment:** The Internet carries a lot of potentially useful information for a researcher. At the same time, it carries a lot of propaganda, some of which

ventures into such realms as racism and hate. You must attempt to determine the writer's objectivity.

Currency. Is the web page dated? If so, what does the date mean; that is, is it the date the piece was originally posted on the Internet or when it was updated? How current are any links the text includes? Are the links still active, or have they moved or expired?

Coverage. What is included or covered in the text? In how much depth? Are some topics given more thorough or more preferential treatment than others? Is such treatment warranted? What does the web page carry that you can't find in potentially more reliable sources?

Our goal here is not to discourage you from using the Internet as a potential source for your research. But what you must keep in mind as you consider using information from websites is this: *Anyone can post anything on the web.* You have to approach using such information just as you would buying a used car—with *caveat emptor,* "Let the buyer beware," as your motto.

Using the Internet Your way into the Internet is your computer terminal and a web browser such as Netscape. Either use a specific command to open your browser or click on its icon. Once you have accessed your browser, you may use any of several search engines, which can help organize your search. Popular engines include Yahoo!, Google, Excite, Infoseek, AltaVista, and LookSmart. Each engine will give you different results because of its organization, so it may be helpful for you to use more than one engine, especially if you're not satisfied with the results that a given engine generates. Once you select a particular engine, you may use its subject index to begin, or you may use a keyword search.

A *subject index* is a listing of various topics or subjects that enables you to move quickly to a specific part of the Net. When you click on a subject heading, subtopics are displayed, and as you move deeper into the subject, you find increasingly narrow subtopics. For example, a search into the subject heading Education led to instructions for a specific line dance via this route:

> Clicking on Education led to a departments heading that included K–12 and Universities and Colleges. Under the K–12 heading were three subtopics: Homework Help, Teacher Resources, and Special Education. Under the Universities and Colleges heading were three subtopics: Financial Aid, Fields of Study, and Graduate Schools. Clicking on Fields of Study led to a listing of a large number of fields of study offered by colleges and universities. Clicking on Dance led to a listing of types of dance, including Ballet, Jazz, and Country & Western. Clicking on Country & Western led to a listing of various home pages devoted to various kinds of country and western dances, and clicking on Kickit Line Dancing led to an alphabetized organizing grid for different line dances. Clicking on the Sh–Sj grid led to a list of dances in that range of the alphabet, and, finally, clicking on Shaggin' (Evelyn Young) led to step-by-step instructions for doing this particular dance.

What does all of this show? That there's a wide range of information available and that one very good search strategy is to browse, that is, to go into a particular topic area in which you may be interested, select promising or interesting sites, and see what's there.

A *keyword search* requires you to locate a box labeled something like Search the Web. Click on this box to place the cursor in it; type in one or two keywords, and either press Enter or click on the button labeled something like Search or Go Get It! In most cases, you'll be given the total number of hits generated by your search (a *hit* is a reference that includes at least one of your keywords) and then a listing of the sources. Usually, you can click on the title of an individual source to connect to it or call it up on your screen for review.

As noted, different engines are organized differently and so produce different results. A recent search for articles using the keyword "graffiti" generated these results: Excite, 32,798 hits; Infoseek, 29,860 hits; AltaVista, 273,710 hits. Not only does the number of hits vary, but the first several articles listed are not the same, so you'll probably want to use at least two engines for your search. Why so many hits? The Net is a web, so making connections is very easy. Every article with even the most remote tie to your keywords will be accessible. Hits will be displayed in groups of ten, with each entry carrying the article's title, its size (in kilobytes, Kb), a percentage indicating the relevancy of the article to your keywords (the higher the percentage, the more relevance), and either the first few words of the text or a brief description of the article's contents. You can't possibly read or even scan a large number of articles, so plan on looking closely at only the first twenty or thirty, as these are likely to be the ones most germane to your search.

If the articles your search generated don't seem to be what you're looking for, try different keywords. If you've gotten an incredibly large listing of articles, then try narrowing the scope of your keywords (e.g., "lifesaving techniques" instead of "water safety"). If the number of articles seems too small, then try broadening the scope of your keywords. (Most search engines are designed to let you conduct a Boolean search, which lets you narrow the scope of your keywords by using "and" or "+" between terms. See the Help function of your search engine for more information on the correct format for a Boolean search.)

Sample Search To give you an idea of what form an Internet search might take, let's follow Gardiner Rhoderick as he looks for information about the topic of his research paper, graffiti. You'll find a copy of Gardiner's paper in the Sample Student Process section at the end of this chapter (pages 624–637).

Part of Gardiner's assignment was to incorporate at least two sources from the Internet, so he decided to conduct a keyword search. He logged on to the Internet and selected Netscape's search engine for his search (see Figure 12.3). In the box labeled Search the Web, Gardiner typed in the keyword "graffiti" and clicked on the Search bar. Netscape went to work, locating 138 potential websites for Gardiner to consider and then listing them in order of likely relevance (see Figure 12.4).

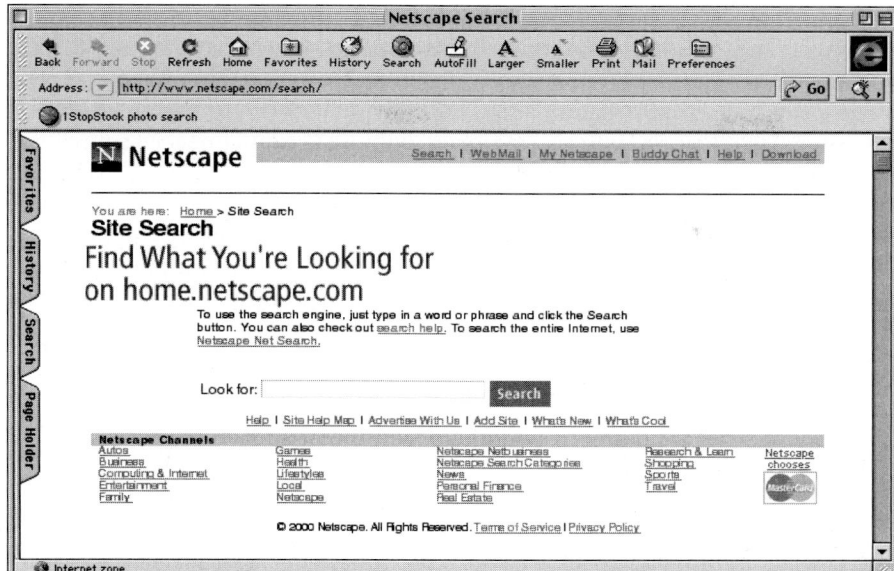

FIGURE 12.3
Netscape Search Engine Screen

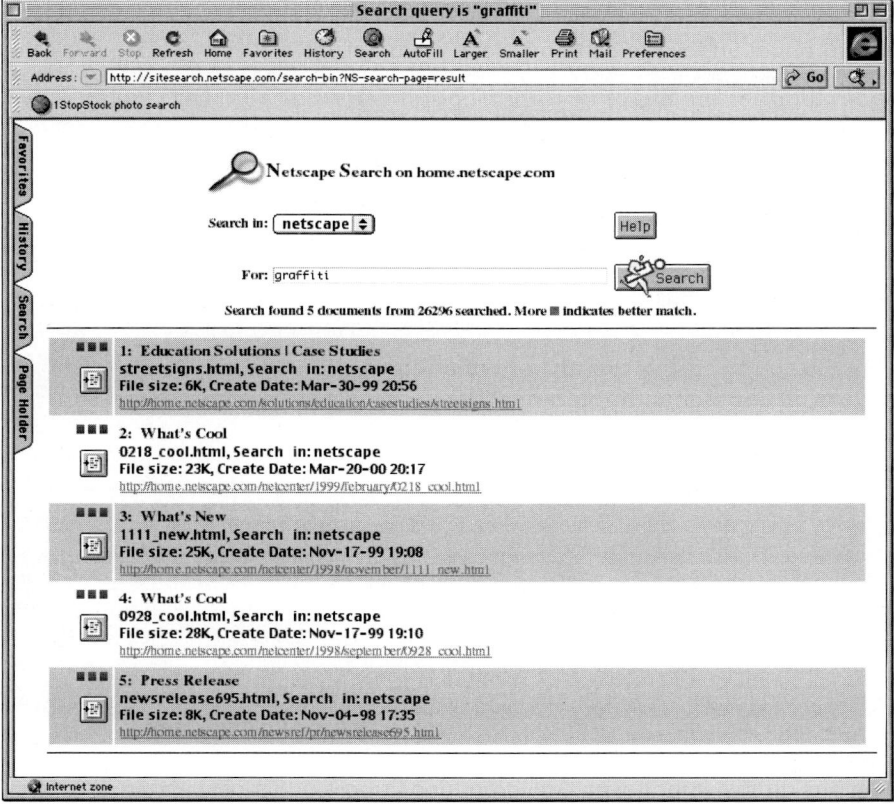

FIGURE 12.4
Internet Search Results

One of the sites listed on the second Search Results page, Art Crimes, looked promising, so Gardiner clicked on it and worked his way back to the Art Crimes home page (see Figure 12.5). Sponsored by Susan Farrell and Brett Webb, this site offers a good bit of information about graffiti. You'll note that Farrell and Webb have organized their site into six categories. Because Gardiner needed sources for an academic paper, he decided to browse the Interviews & Articles section listed under Information & Resources. There, he found a listing of twenty-eight interviews of graffiti artists, twenty-six articles, and twenty-five researched discussions of graffiti. Scrolling through the researched discussions, Gardiner browsed several entries, deciding to use two as sources for his essay: Sherri Cavan's "The Great Graffiti Wars of the Late 20th Century" and Killian Tobin's "A Modern Perspective on Graffiti."

Gardiner's search was profitable. If he hadn't found the Art Crimes site as quickly as he did, he could have used Netscape's keyword feature to send the search engine on a different but related track. We noted that Gardiner's first keyword, "graffiti," yielded 138 potential sources. Of the first ten of those hits, about half viewed graffiti positively, and the other half saw it in a negative light.

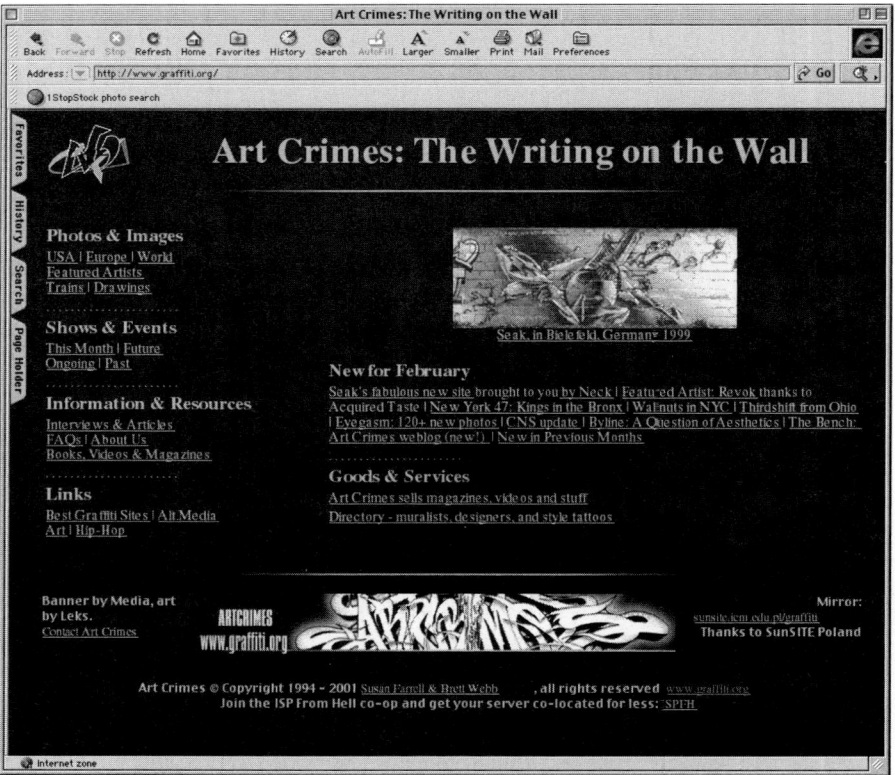

FIGURE 12.5 Art Crimes Home Page <www.graffiti.org>

A different search yielded very different results. We decided to add "vandals" to "graffiti," so that "graffiti vandals" appeared in the Search box. That search identified about 150 potential sources; of the first 10 sites listed, all were negative about graffiti. The Internet offers you a wealth of sources to support your research, if you'll just log on and go exploring.

Exercise 12.7

1. Using the search engine of your choice, base an Internet search on any of the following keywords: skateboards, grammar, the name of your favorite celebrity (e.g., singer or actor), president, skiing (snow or water), your home state, your hometown. Click on two of the first ten hits listed and read them. How reliable do these sites seem? On what do you base this assessment? Next, record the number of total hits your search generated and bibliographical information about the two sites you visited, including the relevancy rating.
2. Select either of the two sites you visited. Click on the More Like This link. Scan the first ten sites that come up and decide how similar to or different from your selected site they are.

COMPUTER TIP

RESEARCH TOOL

Computers can be incredibly helpful research tools because of the access they offer to the Internet and because of their editing and storage capabilities. To use your computer more efficiently, try these strategies:

Bookmarking a site. Your search engine will allow you to identify a site for future reference and then store that site's Internet address in a file labeled Bookmarks. To enter a site as a bookmark, go to the site. Click on Bookmarks and then on Add Bookmark. Then, when you want to return to that site, all you need do is click on Bookmarks and then select the site you wish to retrieve.

Downloading a file. You may download or transfer a web page from the Internet to your computer. To download a page, click on File, then select Save As. At the prompt, type in the drive you wish the page to go to, add a colon and then enter a file name (e.g., a:graffiti2). Hit the Enter key, and the file will be transferred to the drive you've designated.

Copying and pasting. You may copy part of a Net file to another file. Let's assume that you're working in Windows on your research paper. Keeping that file open, you may go to the Internet at the same time to find

 a source there that you need. When you locate that source, highlight the part you wish to copy and then click on the Edit heading. Under Edit, click on Copy. Then diminish the Internet screen by clicking on the minus (–) icon in the upper right-hand corner of the screen. Place the cursor in the still open research paper where you want the passage to appear; then click on Edit and then on Paste. The passage should appear. *Note: Be sure to document any material you import from any source to avoid plagiarism.* ◆

Helpful Internet Sites The Internet offers an incredible range of materials and sites to support your research. At times, it will be more practical for you to begin your search for information by accessing a site that is directly related to your topic. The sites listed below offer a range of materials, are easy to access, and provide links to other relevant sites.

ERIC (Educational Resources Information Center) <http://www.eric.ed.gov> ERIC provides a bibliographical database for documents and journal articles related to education published since 1966.

Government Documents The Government Printing Office (GPO) is responsible for printing reports from the various agencies funded by Congress and so by U.S. tax dollars. As you can well imagine, the GPO prints a tremendous number of reports and other materials that you may need to access during your research. The best way for you to do this is by going to your library's website and searching for the GPO database. In all likelihood, your library will have links to these materials.

Indexes, Abstracts, Bibliographies, and Table of Contents Services <http://info.lib.uh.edu/research/websubs/indexes.html> Maintained by the University of Houston libraries, this site lists a wide range of links to indexes, abstracts, bibliographies, and table of contents services to help the researcher find such materials as journal, magazine, and newspaper articles, book chapters, and conference proceedings.

Library of Congress <http://www.lcweb.loc.gov> This site affords access to the holdings and exhibits of the Library of Congress as well as links to other libraries, special topics databases, and other Library of Congress Internet resources.

The Modern English Collection <http://etext.lib.virginia.edu> A collection of fiction, nonfiction, poetry, drama, letters, newspapers, manuscripts, and illustrations published from 1500 to the present. The site is sponsored by the Electronic Text Center at the University of Virginia.

The *New York Times* <http://www.nytimes.com> The *New York Times* online, including archival materials. You'll have to register to use this site, but there's no cost, and registration is very easy.

Longman Publishers <www.ablongman.com/compsite/> This site contains very useful information about using the Internet to support your research. When you reach the Compsite home page, click on the Resources icon (a flashlight with the word "resources" written below it). You'll then be able to access information under these headings:

> Evaluating sources
> Citation and documentation
> Search strategies
> Research sites and search engines
> Writing resources (including links to on-line writing centers)
> Research resources
> Web authoring
> Internet information

Purdue University Online Writing Lab <http://owl.english.purdue.edu> This site is a comprehensive resource for writers. For example, it has over 130 handouts available on topics ranging from general writing concerns to spelling. It also includes sections on grammatical concerns and English as a second language.

In addition, a number of publications have their own websites. The best way to locate these sites is by using a search engine and conducting a keyword search using the name of the publication. For example, you may access *Newsweek* by entering the magazine's name in an engine's Search box. Your search will take you to <www.Newsweek.com>.

COMPUTER TIP

MORE USEFUL INTERNET SITES

The Electric Library	http://www.elibrary.com
The Internet Public Library	http://ipl.org
The WWW Virtual Library	http://ulib.org
Inter-Links Journal List	http://www.nova.edu/Inter-Links/start.html
HYTELNET	http://library.usask.ca/hytelnet ◆

Exercise 12.8

1. Use a search engine to locate the following sources about a topic you're working on. List the title, author, and web address for each.

   two books
   two essays in popular journals (e.g., *Time, Newsweek, Better Homes and Gardens, Popular Mechanics, National Geographic*), if applicable

two essays in scholarly or professional journals, if applicable
two items from a newspaper, including one from the *New York Times*
an item you locate through the Library of Congress
a government document, if applicable

How reliable is each potential source? On what do you base your opinion?

2. Visit the Longman Publishers Compsite, and locate information on the following:

documenting information
evaluating information from the Internet
problems with grammar and mechanics
links to two search engines

INCORPORATING MATERIAL FROM SOURCES

To use your sources as effectively as possible, you need to be sure that each piece of information you use is clearly set in a context. Your reader needs to see just how you are using that information, for example, how particular information supports your ideas or how your interpretation of information fits with other material in your paper.

You can help the reader see how things fit by introducing passages smoothly. Passages that are not introduced are often problematic: either they intrude on the reader, interrupting the paper's flow, or they simply don't make sense because they aren't clearly connected to the rest of the paper. You can use a number of strategies to introduce passages, as these hypothetical examples illustrate.

1. Preview the passage by identifying its main idea.

> [Strong disagreement = main idea]
>
> A. B. Smith does not agree with the current criticism of President Gumbody's economic policies and vehemently attacks critics, saying, "Senator Jones can criticize our policies all he wishes—where are his alternatives? It's time for him to put up or shut up."
>
> ["Vehemently" shows writer's interpretation of Smith's comments]

2. Connect the quoted material to information that precedes it.

> "This" refers to previously-given information.

Of this perspective, A. B. Smith states, "Now is not the time for divisiveness but for unity."

> Quotation marks signal direct quote of someone else's words.

A. B. Smith comments on this criticism: "Let those who criticize our policies submit workable alternatives. So far, no one has, though we've continually challenged our detractors to do so."

A. B. Smith says that "to date, no suitable alternatives have been submitted," thus denying his opponent's claims to the contrary.

> Last part of the sentence forms writer's comment on previously-given information.

3. Make the passage an integral part of your own ideas.

> Writer interprets supporters' actions as loyalty.

Despite intense criticism, President Gumbody's supporters remain loyal because "the opposition has offered no workable alternatives."

> "Because" introduces support for author's opinion about the loyalty of Gumbody's supporters.

The examples above involve shorter passages that fit within the boundaries of a sentence. If you quote longer passages, you'll need to inset them, and the format you'll employ will depend on the style guide you're using as the authority for your format. Below are examples in both MLA and APA format.

MLA

Author identified to help introduce passage to be quoted.

Book title (underlined) used to help introduce the passage to be quoted.

Publication date and edition number appear to provide complete information about the book.

Joseph Gibaldi, author of the <u>MLA Handbook for Writers of Research Papers</u> (2003, 6th ed.), states:

> If a quotation runs to more than four lines in your paper, set it off from your text by beginning a new line, indenting one inch (or ten spaces if you are using a typewriter) from the left margin, and typing it double-spaced, without adding quotation marks. A colon generally introduces a quotation displayed in this way, though sometimes the content may require a different mark of punctuation or none at all. [. . .] A parenthetical reference to a prose quotation set off from the text follows the last line of the quotation. (110–111)

Left margin set by one-inch indent.

Note that the quoted passage is not given in quotation marks.

The ellipsis (3 spaced periods) indicates that part of the passage has been omitted. Place an ellipsis in brackets, as in this example, to indicate words that you have decided to omit. Otherwise, the reader will assume that the quoted author inserted the ellipsis.

Page number of quoted passage. Appears in parentheses, without the designation "p." (which stands for "page") following the quotation. Note that the quoted material is not in quotation marks. The page reference follows the closing period because it is not part of the quoted passage.

APA

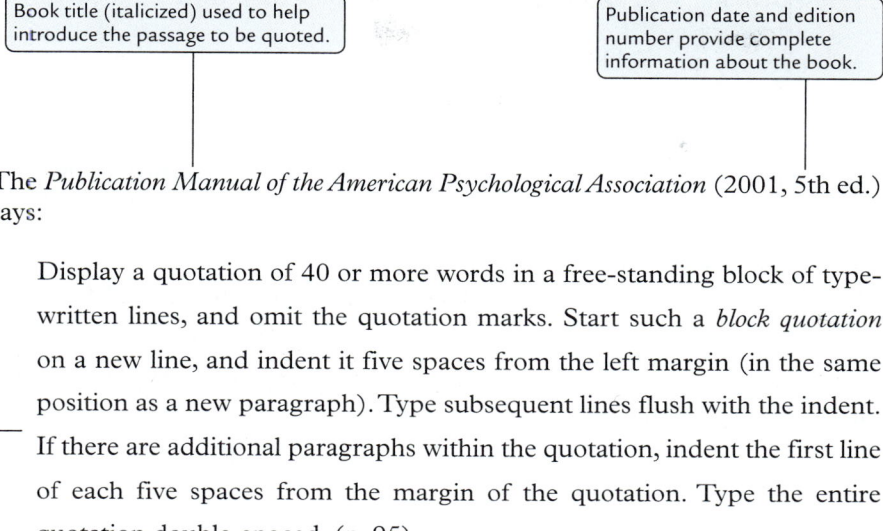

The *Publication Manual of the American Psychological Association* (2001, 5th ed.) says:

> Display a quotation of 40 or more words in a free-standing block of typewritten lines, and omit the quotation marks. Start such a *block quotation* on a new line, and indent it five spaces from the left margin (in the same position as a new paragraph). Type subsequent lines flush with the indent. If there are additional paragraphs within the quotation, indent the first line of each five spaces from the margin of the quotation. Type the entire quotation double-spaced. (p. 95)

Note the differences between these two. First, the MLA recommends a bigger indentation than does the APA. Second, although both formats carry a page reference, the MLA format does not use "p." for page, whereas the APA format does. Which of these formats should you use? If your instructor doesn't specify a particular format, choose the format likely to be used in your discipline.

DOCUMENTING INFORMATION

Documentation, an essential part of any research project, involves both honesty and courtesy. You will use sources other than yourself in preparing a research paper, and you should credit those outside sources for the information you borrowed. Documentation, from start to finish, does at least these things:

1. Gives credit where it is due (a courtesy to the author you borrow from),
2. Provides readers with points for departure should they wish to use your research and your sources as the beginnings of their own work (a second courtesy),
3. Takes away any problem of plagiarism—that is, of your using someone else's words or thoughts without giving credit (a matter of honesty).

Documentation begins with an initial, or working, bibliography and includes citations in the text as well as a formal bibliography in the paper's final draft.

Initial Bibliography

An initial bibliography is a list of potential sources, which you may keep in a computer file or on note cards, one source to a card, as a matter of convenience. A bibliographical note card should carry such information as the author's name (last name first, to make alphabetizing the final bibliography easy), the source's title, publication data, library call number (if applicable), and a very brief summary of the work's contents. A typical bibliography card is shown in Figure 12.6.

You probably will not use every source you survey initially, and your initial bibliography makes it convenient for you to retrieve more useful sources later. Just as you may not use all your initial sources, you may augment your bibliography as you find pertinent sources later in your project.

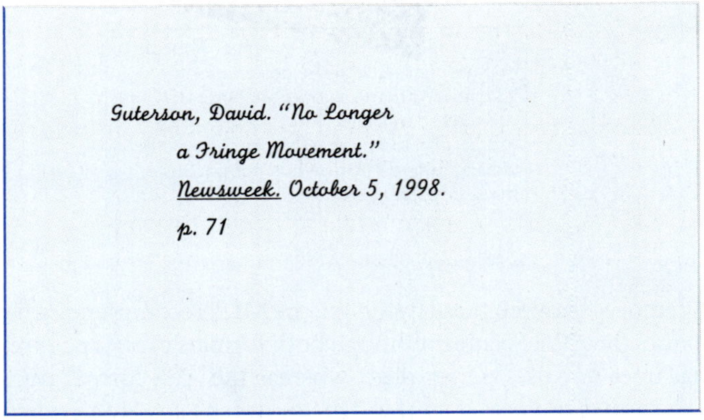

> Guterson, David. "No Longer
> a Fringe Movement."
> Newsweek. October 5, 1998.
> p. 71

FIGURE 12.6 Typical Bibliography Card

Final Bibliography

The final bibliography, which you submit on a separate page as part of the final paper, may be either a list of only the works you cite in your paper itself or a list of all the works you surveyed in preparing your paper. If the former, you should title the page Works Cited, Bibliography, Literature Cited, or References. If the latter, you should title the page Works Consulted, which indicates that your list includes all works you surveyed during your research, whether your paper actually uses information from them or not. In any case, alphabetize each section of your bibliography by author's last name, and use the same entry format as that of your initial bibliography.

The following are sample entries for the kinds of sources you will be most likely to use. You'll note that two different formats are listed. The first is used by the Modern Language Association, and the second by the American Psychological Association.

Gibaldi, Joseph. <u>MLA Handbook for Writers of Research Papers</u>. 6th ed. New York:
  Modern Language Association, 2003.

American Psychological Association. (2001). *Publication manual of the American
  Psychological Association* (5th ed.). Washington, DC: Author.

These two manuals, two of the most widely used in the United States, carry information about various aspects of research writing, including documentation, manuscript preparation (e.g., spacing, margins, pagination, and binding), and mechanics of writing (e.g., spelling and punctuation). For writing papers in a particular discipline (e.g., agriculture, biology, or anthropology), consult the style manual adopted by experts in the field. If you do not know which manual is recommended for your discipline (the field of your major), consult one of your teachers for advice. Once you have chosen a style manual, become familiar with its conventions, and then be consistent in your use of it.

Some features of the MLA and APA styles are the same. Both specify double-spacing within and between entries. Both require that the first line be placed at the left-hand margin, with subsequent lines indented half an inch (or five spaces).

Moving beyond the basic layout, you'll notice several differences between the MLA and APA styles in the following entries. For example, although both formats require an alphabetical listing of authors by last name, the MLA format specifies that the author's name be given as it appears on the work's title page, whereas the APA format requires that only the initials of the author's first and middle names be used. Also, the MLA format specifies that the publication date be placed at the end, whereas the APA format specifies that it be placed in parentheses following the author's name. Here's how a book written by three writers would be documented in both these formats:

MLA Young, Richard E., Alton L. Becker, and Kenneth L. Pike. <u>Rhetoric:
  Discovery and Change</u>. New York: Harcourt, 1970.

APA Young, R. E., Becker, A. L., & Pike, K. L. (1970). *Rhetoric:
  Discovery and change.* New York: Harcourt.

Why the difference? Each style manual follows the traditional format established for its discipline.

The basic information that either format delivers includes the author's name, the title of the piece, and publication information (i.e., the date and place the piece was published). A correctly documented source should enable another researcher to locate that source with ease. If you have any questions concerning the elements of an entry, consult the style manual you are using.

604 Part Three | Research

The following examples provide a quick guide to the kinds of information and its placement in MLA and APA bibliographical entries for printed and electronic sources.

MLA—WORKS CITED ENTRIES

From Printed Sources

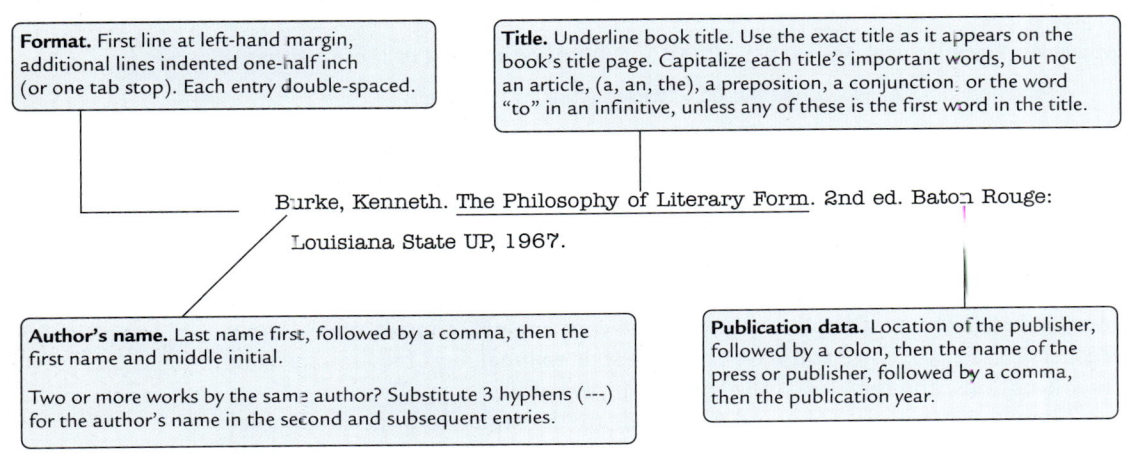

From Electronic Sources

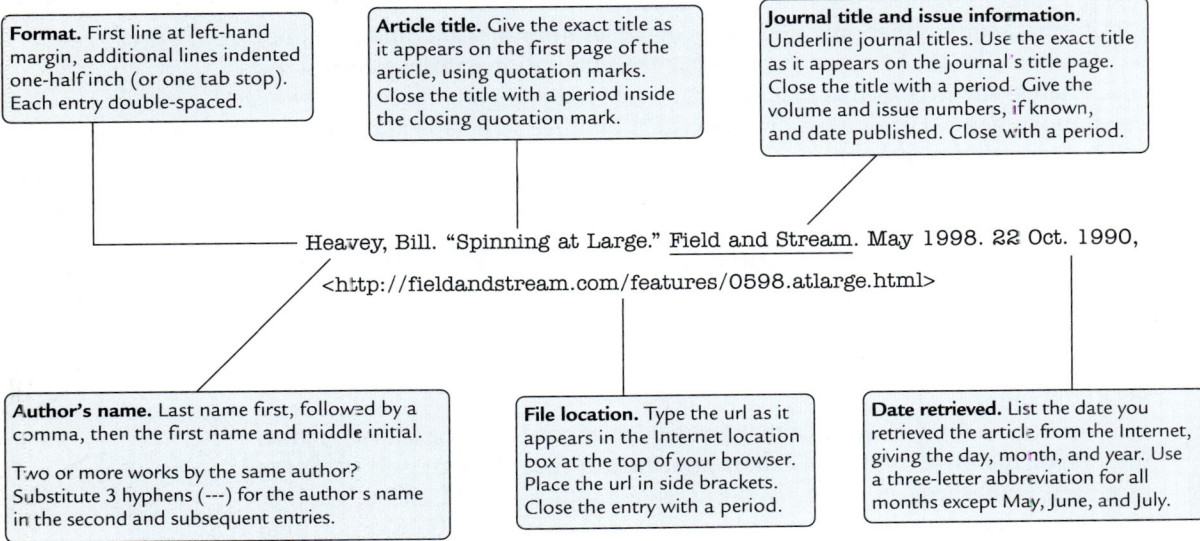

APA—REFERENCES ENTRIES

From Printed Sources

Author's name. Last name first, followed by a comma, then initials of first and middle names.

More than one author: follow initials of first author with a comma, then list the initials and last name of subsequent authors, their names separated by commas. Close the entry with a period.

Title. Give the title exactly as it appears on the title page, using italics. Capitalize only the first word of the title, unless the title has proper nouns. If the title has a colon followed by a subtitle, capitalize the first word following the colon. Close the title with a period.

List the edition of the work in parentheses following the title, closing the entry with a period.

Burke, K. (1967). *The philosophy of literary form.* (2nd ed.). Baton Rouge: Louisiana State University Press.

Format. First line at left-hand margin, additional lines indented one-half inch (or one tab stop). Each entry double-spaced.

Date published. List date published in parentheses following the author(s). Close the date with a period.

Publication data. Location of the publisher, followed by a colon, then the complete name of the press.

From Electronic Sources

Author's name. Last name first, followed by a comma, then initials of first and middle names.

More than one author: follow initials of first author with a comma, then list the initials and last name of subsequent authors, their names separated by commas. Close the entry with a period.

Title. Give the article's title exactly as it appears on the first page, capitalizing only the first word, unless the title has proper nouns. If the title has a colon followed by a subtitle, capitalize the first word following the colon. Close the title with a period.

Give the journal title exactly as it appears, using italics. Capitalize major words. Close the entry with a period.

Heavey, B. (1998, May). Spinning at large. *Field and Stream.* Retrieved from http://fieldandstream.com/features/0598.atlarge.html

Format. First line at left-hand margin, additional lines indented one-half inch (or one tab stop). Each entry double-spaced.

Date published. List date in parentheses following the author(s). Close the date with a period.

Retrieval data. List the site from which you retrieved the article, unless it is a well-known database. List the retrieval date only if the item is likely to be changed or updated. Note there is no period following the url, and there are no angle brackets.

Below we've provided sample bibliographical entries, in MLA and APA formats, of the most common sources you're likely to use in writing a research paper. For additional documentation examples, consult the style manual you're using.

BOOKS

1. **Single author**

   MLA Burke, Kenneth. The Philosophy of Literary Form. 2nd ed. Baton Rouge: Louisiana State UP, 1967.

   APA Burke, K. (1967). *The philosophy of literary form.* (2nd ed.). Baton Rouge: Louisiana State University Press.

2. **Two or more books by the same author**

   MLA Burke, Kenneth. A Grammar of Motives. Berkeley: U of California P, 1969.

   ---. Language as Symbolic Action. Berkeley: U of California P, 1966.

   APA Burke, K. (1966). *Language as symbolic action.* Berkeley: University of California Press.

   Burke, K. (1969). *A grammar of motives.* Berkeley: University of California Press.

3. **Two or three authors**

   MLA Young, Richard E., Alton L. Becker, and Kenneth L. Pike. Rhetoric: Discovery and Change. New York: Harcourt, 1970.

   APA Young, R. E., Becker, A. L., & Pike, K. L. (1970). *Rhetoric: Discovery and change.* New York: Harcourt.

4. **More than three authors**

   MLA Britton, James, et al. The Development of Writing Abilities (11-18). London: Macmillan, 1975.

   APA Britton, J., Burgess, T., Martin, N., McLeod, A., & Rosen, H. (1975). *The development of writing abilities (11-18).* London: Macmillan.

5. **Translation**

    MLA   Aristotle. Poetics. Trans. Hippocrates G. Apostle, Elizabeth A. Dobbs, and Morris A. Parslow. Grinnell, IA: Peripatetic, 1990.

    APA   Aristotle. (1990). *Poetics*. (H. G. Apostle, E. A. Dobbs, & M. A. Parslow, Trans.). Grinnell, IA: Peripatetic.

6. **Author and editor**

    MLA   Burke, Kenneth. On Symbols and Society. Ed. Joseph R. Gusfield. Chicago: U of Chicago P, 1989.

    APA   Burke, K. (1989). *On symbols and society*. (J. R. Gusfield, Ed.). Chicago: University of Chicago Press.

7. **Edited collection**

    MLA   Skaggs, Calvin, ed. The American Short Story. 2 vols. New York: Dell, 1985.

    APA   Skaggs, C. (Ed.). (1985). *The American short story*. (Vols. 1-2). New York: Dell.

8. **Government document**

    MLA   Rohman, D. Gordon, and Albert O. Wlecke. Pre-Writing: The Construction and Application of Models for Concept Formation in Writing. Cooperative Research Programs of the Office of Education, U.S. Department of Health, Education, and Welfare, Project No. 2174, 1974.

    APA   Rohman, D. G., and Wlecke, A. O. (1974). *Pre-Writing: The construction and application of models for concept formation in writing* (Cooperative Research Program of the Office of Education, U.S. Department of Health, Education, and Welfare, Project No. 2174).

9. **Author unknown**

    MLA   Exploring Your World: The Adventure of Geography. Washington: National Geographic, 1995.

    APA   *Exploring your world: The adventure of geography*. (1995). Washington, DC: National Geographic Society.

ARTICLES

1. **Article in a scholarly journal with continuous pagination**

    MLA Schutz, Aaron, and Anne Ruggles Gere. "Service Learning and English Studies: Rethinking 'Public Service.'" College English 60 (1998): 129-49.

    APA Schutz, A., & Gere, A. R. (1998). Service learning and English studies: Rethinking "public service." College English, 60, 129-149.

2. **Article in a scholarly journal without continuous pagination**

    MLA Davis, Sherri Heckler. "The Zen Art of Prewriting." New Mexico English Journal 12.1 (1998): 21-23.

    APA Davis, S. H. (1998). The Zen art of prewriting. New Mexico English Journal, 12(1), 21-23.

3. **Article in an anthology or collection**

    MLA Britton, James N. "Language and Experience." Explorations in Children's Writing. Ed. Eldonna L. Evertts. Urbana: NCTE, 1970. 49-64.

    APA Britton, J. N. (1970). Language and experience. In E. L. Evertts (Ed.), Explorations in children's writing (pp. 49–64). Urbana, IL: National Council of Teachers of English.

4. **Article in a newspaper**

    MLA Dooley, Martha. "New Mexico's Welfare Plan Is 'All about Jobs.'" Las Cruces Sun-News 7 Aug. 1998: A1+.

    APA Dooley, M. (1998, August 7). New Mexico's welfare plan is "all about jobs." Las Cruces Sun-News, pp. A1, A3.

5. **Editorial**

    MLA "Highway Roadblocks Need Early Warning." Editorial. Las Cruces Sun-News 7 Aug. 1998: B7.

    APA Highway roadblocks need early warning [Editorial]. (1998, August 7). Las Cruces Sun-News, p. B7.

6. **Letter to the editor**

    MLA Fry, Thomas E. Letter. Las Cruces Sun-News 11 Dec. 1998: B7.

APA	Fry, T. E. (1998, December 11). Water wrongs [Letter to the editor]. *Las Cruces Sun-News*, p. B7.	

7. Article in a magazine published weekly or biweekly

MLA	Chambers, Veronica, and Devin Gordon. "The Mommy Track." <u>Newsweek</u> 10 Aug. 1998: 62-63.
APA	Chambers, V., & Gordon, D. (1998, August 10). The mommy track. *Newsweek*, 62-63.

8. Article in a magazine published monthly or bimonthly

MLA	Howe, Steve. "Doing the Wild Thing." <u>Backpacker</u> Sept. 1998: 58+.
APA	Howe, S. (1998, September). Doing the wild thing. *Backpacker*, pp. 58-62, 147.

9. Review

MLA	Petersen, Carol. "Composition and Campus Diversity: Testing Academic and Social Values." Rev. of <u>Academic Advancement in Composition Studies: Scholarship, Publication, Promotion, Tenure</u>, ed. Richard C. Gebhardt and Barbara Genelle Smith Gebhardt, and <u>Gender Roles and Faculty Lives in Rhetoric and Composition</u>, ed. Theresa Enos. <u>CCC</u> 50 (1998): 277-91.
APA	Petersen, C. (1998). Composition and campus diversity: Testing academic and social values [Review of the books *Academic advancement in composition studies: Scholarship, publication, promotion, tenure* and *Gender roles and faculty lives in rhetoric and composition*]. College Composition and Communication, 50, 277-291.

10. Article in a reference work (e.g., an encyclopedia)

MLA	Burns, Edward McNall. "Marshall Plan." <u>The World Book Encyclopedia</u>. 1965 ed.
APA	Burns, E. M. (1965). Marshall plan. In *The world book encyclopedia* (Vol. 13, pp. 186-187). Chicago: Field Enterprises Educational.

11. Anonymous article in a magazine

MLA	"Recruiters at the Gates." <u>Sports Illustrated</u> 10 Aug. 1998: 29.
APA	Recruiters at the gates. (1998, August 10). *Sports Illustrated*, 29.

ELECTRONIC SOURCES

1. CD-ROM database

MLA Stewart, Ian B., and George G. Sleivert. "The Effect of Warm-up Intensity on Range of Motion and Anaerobic Performance." Journal of Orthopaedic and Sports Physical Therapy 27.2 (1998): 154-61. Abstract. CD-ROM. SilverPlatter. Mar. 1998.

APA Stewart, I. B., & Sleivert, G. G. (1998). The effect of warm-up intensity on range of motion and anaerobic performance [CD-ROM]. *The Journal of Orthopaedic and Sports Physical Therapy, 27*(2), 154-161. Abstract retrieved from SilverPlatter File: Sport Discus Item: 454824.

2. Web page

MLA Cavan, Sherri. "The Great Graffiti Wars of the Late 20th Century." Home page. 14 Apr. 1998 <http://userwww.sfsu.edu/~kazbeki/grafwars.html>.

APA Cavan, S. The great graffiti wars of the late 20th century. Retrieved April 14, 1998, from http://userwww.sfsu.edu/~kazbeki/grafwars.html

3. On-line book

MLA Crane, Stephen. The Red Badge of Courage. 1895. 7 Nov. 1998 <http://etext.lib.virginia.edu/etcbin/browse-mixed-new?id=CraCour&tag=public&images=images/mode>.

APA Crane, S. (1895). *The red badge of courage.* Available from http://etext.lib.virginia.edu/etcbin/browse-mixed-new?id=CraCour&tag=public&images=images/mode

4. On-line journal article

MLA Heavey, Bill. "Spinning at Large." Field and Stream May 1998. 22 Oct. 1998 <http://www.fieldandstream.com/features/0598.atlarge.html>.

APA Heavey, B. (1998, May). Spinning at large. *Field and Stream.* Retrieved from http://www.fieldandstream.com/features/0598.atlarge.html

5. On-line review

MLA Soergel, Dagobert. Rev. of WordNet: An Electronic Lexical Database, ed. Christine Fellbaum. D-Lib Magazine Oct. 1998. 17 Oct. 1998 <http://www.dlib.org/dlib/october98/10bookreview.html>.

APA Soergel, D. (1998, October). [Review of the book *WordNet: An electronic lexical database*]. *D-Lib Magazine.* Retrieved from http://www.dlib.org/dlib/october98/10bookreview.html

6. On-line newspaper article

MLA Erlanger, Steven. "Clinton Reopens Mideast Talks; Hopes to Wrap Up Agreement." New York Times on the Web 22 Oct. 1998. 22 Oct. 1998 <http://www.nytimes.com/library/world/mideast/102298mideast-talks.html>

APA Erlanger, S. (1998, October 22). Clinton reopens Mideast talks; Hopes to wrap up agreement. *The New York Times.* Retrieved from http://www.nytimes.com

7. E-mail

MLA Dent, Nancy Burns. E-mail to the author. 8 Aug. 1998.

Note: The *Publication Manual of the American Psychological Association* (5th ed., 2001, page 214) stipulates that personal communications, whether letters, e-mail, or memoranda, not be included in a reference list because these "do not provide recoverable data." However, such communications should be cited in the body of your essay in a parenthetical expression like this one, for example: (N. B. Dent, personal communication, August 8, 1998).

8. MOO or MUD

MLA "Finding Time for Your Own Professional Development." Online posting. The Netoric Project's Tuesday Cafe. 25 Aug. 1998. ConnectionsMOO. 11 Dec. 1998 <http://bsuvc.bsu.edu/~00gjsiering/netoric/logs/TC082598.TXT>.

Note: This citation is for the archived log of a discussion that took place on August 25, 1998.

APA	Finding time for your own professional development. (1998, August 25). Message posted to *The Netoric Project's Tuesday Cafe*, ConnectionsMOO, archived at http://bsuvc.bsu.edu/~00gjsiering/netoric/logs/TC082598.TXT

9. **On-line bulletin board**

MLA	"Families, 4-H, Nutrition News--Feb. 1996." 2 Jan. 1999 <http://www.bbpages.psu.edu/penpages_reference/28603/286031000.html>.
APA	Families, 4-H, nutrition news. (1996, February). Message posted to http://www.bbpages.psu.edu/penpages_reference/28603/286031000.html

OTHER SOURCES

1. **Music recording**

MLA	Griffith, Nanci. *Other Voices/Other Rooms*. Elektra, 1993.
APA	Griffith, N. (1993). *Other voices/other rooms* [CD]. Nashville: Elektra Entertainment.

2. **Film or video recording**

MLA	*Camelot*. Dir. Joshua L. Logan. Perf. Richard Harris, Vanessa Redgrave, Franco Nero, David Hemmings, Lionel Jeffries, and Laurence Naismith. Warner Bros., 1967.
APA	Warner, J. L. (Producer), & Logan, J. L. (Director). (1967). *Camelot* [Videotape]. Burbank, CA: Warner Bros.

3. **Interview that you conducted**

MLA	Williams, Jennifer A. Personal interview. 26 June 2004.

Note: The *Publication Manual of the American Psychological Association* (5th ed., 2001) does not list a format for a personal interview, presumably because an interview would not yield "recoverable data" (see page 214). However, you should cite a personal interview in the body of your essay in a parenthetical expression. The format for such a citation is this: (interviewee's name, personal communication, date). For an example of such a citation, see Kristina Geray's essay "The Pet Overpopulation Problem" in Chapter 11 (pages 567–571).

4. **Advertisement**

   MLA   ComforTemp DCC. Advertisement. Backpacker Sept. 1998: 12-13.

   Note: The *Publication Manual of the American Psychological Association* (5th ed., 2001) does not list a format for citing an advertisement.

5. **Television program**

   MLA   "The Triumph of Evil." Frontline. PBS. WGBH, Boston. 26 Jan. 1999.

   APA   Robinson, M. (Producer). (1999, January 26). The triumph of evil. *Frontline* [Television series]. Boston: WGBH.

6. **Performance**

   MLA   Chavez, Denise, perf. Women in the State of Grace. National Museum of Women in the Arts, Washington. 20 Apr. 1996.

   APA   Chavez, D. (Performer). (1996, April 20). *Women in the state of grace.* [One-woman show]. Washington, DC: National Museum of Women in the Arts.

Note: This list of sample references is not exhaustive. If you need to cite a source we have not listed here, consult the style manual you're using for the proper format.

CITATIONS

Citation formats vary as widely as bibliographical formats, and yours will depend on the style manual you choose as your guide. In all but a few disciplines, *in-text citations* are accepted as the standard citation format because they provide a quick and easy form of notation. An in-text citation consists of a parenthetical reference to the complete bibliographical reference, which will appear in the Works Cited or References listing at the paper's end. In the following examples, we present first the MLA citation form, then the APA form.

In the first set of citations, the source is identified in the sentence by title and author, and the page from which the quote was taken appears in parentheses at the end of the passage.

MLA

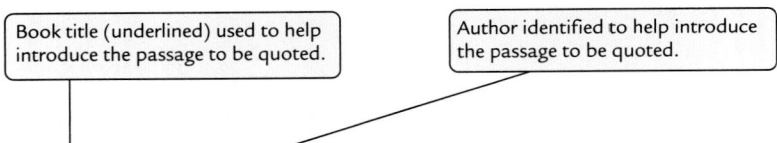

In <u>Language</u>, Leonard Bloomfield advocates a commonsensical or utilitarian approach to questions of grammar, stating, "Grammatical doctrine should be accepted only where it passes a test of usefulness, and even then it should be re-shaped to suit the actual needs" (506).

> Page number of quoted passage. Appears in parentheses, without any designation (e.g., "p." or "pp."), following the quotation. Note that the quoted material is in quotation marks, and the page reference follows the closing quotation mark, with a period to end the sentence following the page reference. Because it is not part of the quoted passage, the page reference does not appear inside the quotation marks.

A Works Cited entry for this passage would read as follows:

Bloomfield, Leonard. <u>Language</u>. Chicago: U Chicago P, 1933.

APA

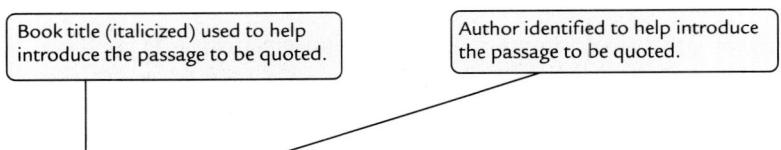

In *Language,* Leonard Bloomfield advocates a commonsensical or utilitarian approach to questions of grammar, stating, "Grammatical doctrine should be accepted only where it passes a test of usefulness, and even then it should be re-shaped to suit the actual needs" (p. 506).

> Page number of quoted passage. Appears in parentheses, with the designation "p." (which stands for "page"), following the quotation. Note that the quoted material is in quotation marks, and the page reference follows the closing quotation mark, with a period to end the sentence following the page reference. Because it is not part of the quoted passage, the page reference does not appear inside the quotation marks.

A References entry for this passage would read as follows:

Bloomfield, L. (1933). *Language.* Chicago: University of Chicago Press.

In the next example, the source is identified in the sentence, and the author and page reference are listed in parentheses following the passage:

MLA

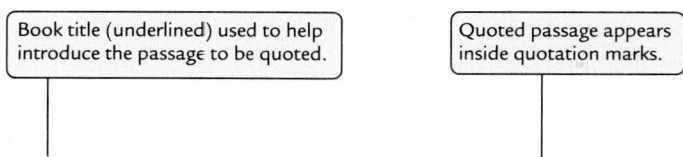

In Language, we find the idea that "grammatical doctrine should be accepted only where it passes a test of usefulness, and even then it should be re-shaped to suit the actual needs" (Bloomfield 506).

APA

In *Language,* we find the idea that "grammatical doctrine should be accepted only where it passes a test of usefulness, and even then it should be re-shaped to suit the actual needs" (Bloomfield, 1933, p. 506).

Our final example involves two or more works published by the same author. We draw on Bloomfield again and assume that we have written as essay in which we have used at least two of his works.

MLA

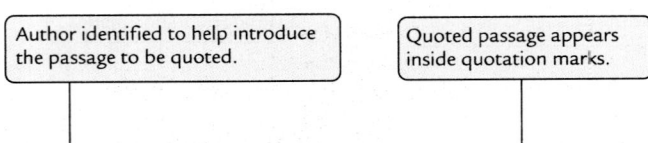

> Author identified to help introduce the passage to be quoted.

> Quoted passage appears inside quotation marks.

Bloomfield states that "grammatical doctrine should be accepted only where it passes a test of usefulness, and even then it should be re-shaped to suit the actual needs" (Language 506).

> Book title (underlined) and page number appear in parentheses. The page reference appears without designation as "p." and there is no comma separating the page number from the book title. MLA style calls for abbreviating a title by using an identifiable key term, but not the entire title, if it is longer than one word. Listing the book title in this reference directs the reader to the bibliographical entry for the work by Bloomfield with "language" as the identifiable key term. Because it is not part of the quoted passage, the page reference does not appear inside the quotation marks.

APA

> The parenthetical 1933a refers the reader to the reference list for the work's complete bibliographical information. APA style specifies that two or more works by an author in the same year be listed alphabetically by title in the reference list. The suffixes "a," "b," and so on are added to the publication date for identification in in-text citations. Because APA style includes the publication date in the text, it readily differentiates between works by the same author published in different years.

Bloomfield (1933a) states that "grammatical doctrine should be accepted only where it passes a test of usefulness, and even then it should be re-shaped to suit the actual needs" (p. 506).

> Quoted passage appears in quotation marks.

> Page number of quoted passage. Appears in parentheses, with the designation "p." (which stands for "page), following the quotation. Note that the quoted material is in quotation marks, and the page reference follows the closing quotation mark, with a period to end the sentence following the page reference. Because it is not part of the quoted passage, the page reference does not appear inside the quotation marks.

If the work you're citing has more than one author, the general format for the in-text citation is the same as for a work by only one author. However, you'll need to list multiple authors as indicated below:

MLA *two or three authors*—give the last name of each person listed, following the order listed on the bibliography page (e.g., Young, Becker, and Pike 39–43).

more than three authors—either give the first author's last name followed by "et al." (e.g., Allison et al. 27) or give all the authors' names in the order listed on the bibliography page.

APA *two authors*—give the last names of both authors every time you refer to their work (e.g., Stewart and Slievert 1998).

three, four, or five authors—give the last names of all authors in the first citation, but include only the last name of the first author followed by "et al." in subsequent citations [e.g., Young, Becker, and Pike 1970 (first reference) and Young et al. 1970 (subsequent reference)].

six or more authors—give only the last name of the first author followed by "et al." (e.g., Allison, et al. 1983).

For a source from the Internet, the basic format of your in-text citation will remain the same. If your source is formatted like a journal, that is, with separate pages and page numbers, then give the page number on which the material you're quoting appears. Some Internet sources don't number pages but do number paragraphs. If that's the case with your source, then include the paragraph number in your citation. For APA format, use either the paragraph symbol —¶— or abbreviate it as "para." For MLA format, use either "par." or "pars." If your Internet source doesn't number either pages or paragraphs, then you're not required to include either.

In-text references are easier for the writer to use than footnotes because the latter require the writer to gauge how much space to leave at the bottom of the page. However, in-text references do not provide as much immediate information as *footnotes* or *endnotes,* which are complete references placed either at the bottom of the page on which the referenced materials appear (footnotes) or on a separate note page at the end of the paper (endnotes). If you are studying in a discipline that specifies either footnotes or endnotes in research papers, refer to that discipline's standard or recommended style manual for format information.

At times when you're using a source, you may find it necessary to shorten the original passage by omitting what you think are less-than-essential words from the passage. To do so, you must insert an ellipsis (three spaced periods) to show that you've edited the passage you're quoting. This is accepted practice, so long as you don't distort the author's original intent. For example, were you to use this passage—"Gloria was chosen primarily because of her abilities to work with the rest of the cast, but for other reasons as well"—but delete the middle part of the sentence so that your quote read "Gloria was chosen primarily . . . for other reasons," then you would have distorted the writer's meaning.

If you omit words at the first or in the middle of a sentence, then you should show that by using an ellipsis—three spaced periods. If the part you're omitting comes at the end of the sentence and includes the last word of the sentence, then you should use four spaced periods. MLA style specifies that an ellipsis that does not appear in the original text (that is, one that signals that you, the writer quoting from a source, has omitted material) should be placed in brackets, thus: [. . .] . APA style does not specify that brackets be used. For an example of the use of the ellipsis with brackets, see "The American Indian Movement as a Counterculture" in the next section of this chapter.

SAMPLE ANNOTATED ESSAYS

We've included two sample essays that we've annotated to point out particular features of the documentation style each uses. The first, "The American Indian Movement as a Counterculture," by Clarita Brown, uses MLA style and appears immediately below. The second, "Yes, It's Graffiti, But Is It Art?" by Gardiner Rhoderick, uses APA style and appears on pages 630–637.

> [Title centered, no quotation marks used, unless there's a quote in the title]
>
> [Author's name centered NOTE: check with your instructor for specific instructions about essay headings.]

Clarita Brown

The American Indian Movement as a Counterculture

There are many definitions of what people consider a "counterculture" to be. If a counterculture is a group of people that goes against the normal system of society in order to voice their ideas and thoughts on changing problems in that society, then the American Indian Movement (AIM) is a strong, proud counterculture. Like the Civil Rights Movement, AIM fights against federal oppression and societal mistreatment and helps Native Americans find a sense of unity, empowerment and support. As AIM co-founder Dennis Banks put it,

> [Quote incorporated by identifying speaker]

"AIM's position has always been to create the seed, plant the seed, develop it a little, and then move on" (qtd. in Record and Hocker 21). This seed consists of

> [2 authors: both last names and page reference]

unity, power, and support.

The American Indian Movement was founded in 1968 in Minneapolis by Dennis Banks and George Mitchell. It was a small organization that did not get any national recognition until it took several actions to let everyone know Native American struggles are not over.

The first event was in November, 1969, when a group of students, including some AIM members, protested on Alcatraz Island. They demanded the land be used for Indian schools, basing their demand on the "provision of an act passed on July 31, 1882 (*22 Stat.* 181)" (Churchill and Wall 119).

> Citation in original source listed as part of quoted material, followed by MLA format citation for 2 authors: both last names and page reference

The second event happened in 1972 in Washington, DC, when AIM organized a protest called "The Trail of Broken Treaties" to protest unjust treatment by the government. More than 1,000 Native Americans traveled to Washington, where they took over the Bureau of Indian Affairs (BIA) headquarters for a few days. Before leaving Washington following negotiations, "the occupiers packed away twelve tons of BIA files to take back to their respective reservations" (Weyler 54). These files exposed shady connections between the BIA and some corporations and corrupt deals to take over Indian land by unscrupulous resource developers. Among the artifacts was a letter to the BIA regarding two elderly women who had been beaten to death on a Wisconsin reservation. The BIA had only filed the letter and refused to set out an investigation (Weyler 55). AIM members wanted documentation of BIA abuse, and they found it.

The third and most important event was a 71-day standoff at Wounded Knee, South Dakota, on the Pine Ridge Reservation. "In 1973, the federally installed regime of tribal president Richard 'Dickie' Wilson was attempting to transfer the barren but uranium-laden northwestern eighth of the reservation—an area known as the Gunnery Range—to the Interior Department" (Churchill 40). Spurred by this and by the Pine Ridge people's struggle to survive in nearly third-world conditions, AIM stepped in to give the people a voice. Confronting AIM were the FBI, the US army, US marshals, and local law enforcement. In the end, two AIM members were killed by gunfire, AIM leaders surrendered, and the federal government proclaimed victory. But it was an empty victory, because AIM did what it set out to do, which was to give Native Americans a national voice. They became a counterculture to be dealt with.

AIM, like some countercultures, uses actions of protest to let people know what is wrong with the way society treats them, or in the case of Pine Ridge Reservation, how society lacks concern for Native American well-being. Pine Ridge is a third-world in the United States' backyard. People there live in shack-like homes, drink contaminated water, and try hard just to live day to day. These are only a few of the reservation's problems; in addition, "close to half of all Pine Ridge residents—including a growing number of teenagers—battle alcoholism, which contributes to high rates of suicide and Sudden Infant Death Syndrome, and an increasing incidence of abuse of the elderly" (Record and Hocker 22). People on reservations do not have the resources or money to take care of these problems, and society remains blind and does not help. AIM, like the Civil Rights Movement, tries to spread awareness of these problems to the public through protests and other actions.

Like all countercultures, AIM finds itself out of the mainstream society when its members decide to take up a cause and protest. What they want to do is cause change, and sometimes yelling, misconduct, and going against the societal norm form the only way to do it. As J. Milton Yinger says in <u>Countercultures</u>, "[Such actions] represent efforts to create a cultural world in which new identities can be formed or tenuous ones validated and strengthened around congenial values and norms" (38).

AIM is trying to get society's attention focused on the problems Native Americans face on their reservations, and if they need to shout or even break the law, then so be it.

Besides the problem of getting society's attention, the United States government has unfairly treated AIM and its members, because of their strong voice. The standoff at Wounded Knee would have never escalated to a 71-day standoff or to gunfire if the government had not flexed its muscles in an attempt to show who was boss. A counterculture becomes a target when it becomes a threat to the status quo, and the US government made AIM its target. Witnesses at Wounded Knee reported that the "federal army" brought automatic weapons, snipers, armored personnel carriers, and about 130,000 rounds of ammunition (Record and Hocker 17). AIM responded by fighting back with a ragtag group of individuals armed with old 30-30's. Whether coming up with their own arsenal and using it was illegal or a form of self-defense, AIM resisted and two members died.

From Wounded Knee came a national understanding of Native American struggles and mistreatment. Famous supporters, like Robert Redford, joined their cause. An AIM leader in the stand-off, Russell Means, became an actor and has starred in major motion pictures, but still strongly and actively supports AIM. "What Wounded Knee told the world was that John Wayne hadn't killed us all [. . .]. Suddenly billions of people knew we were still alive, still resisting" (White 39).

[Note: El ipsis appears in brackets, indicates material has been deleted from original quote.]

Another outcome of the Wounded Knee siege was the making of the move Thunderheart. This movie, set in the poor Pine Ridge Reservation, tells of AIM's cause and shows how intertribal war continued after the siege. Mysteriously, "more than sixty other American Indian Movement supporters were killed on Pine Ridge during the next thirty months" after Wounded Knee (Churchill 41). Thunderheart,

[Note: Movie title, underscored]

telling the story of a Native American FBI agent trying to solve these killings, captured on film the poverty of Pine Ridge and the terrible living conditions there, and it served to spread the word about AIM and the problems of Native Americans.

Unlike some countercultures that come and go, AIM thrives. Today there are chapters of AIM in several states, which include New Mexico, Arizona, and California. AIM is very well organized and has created specifications for its members to follow. Members are expected to follow six principles, which include requiring them to be drug and alcohol free, to fight for their cause, and to fight for as long as they can. The most important principle is the sixth, which reads, in part, "AIM is for everyone [. . . .] AIM philosophy [. . .] is that you work with the people not above the people [. . .] AIM is willing to risk their reputation even when it is unpopular at the time [. . . .] And AIM is ready to battle and risk their lives for the people" (Means par. 7). Members are not asked to pay a fee or fill out a membership card; they show their membership by becoming and remaining active in AIM.

["par. 7" lists the 7th paragraph of Means' online article as the source of the quoted material]

AIM's sixth principle is one which mainstream society has the most difficulty understanding. It is hard to imagine that a group of people would be willing to give their lives for a cause that society looks upon blindly. But members must risk losing their jobs and even their families when they are asked to leave for a cause in any part of the United States, at any time (Means par. 7). In mainstream society the family is a key part, and someone in this society could never visualize leaving their family for a group of activists.

Mainstream society looks down on AIM and most countercultures because they don't see the importance of fighting for change and what one truly believes in, so AIM keeps shouting. Some people, even Native Americans, believe AIM has put their own people in danger and caused mayhem within the Native American community. But others say with AIM's help there is a sense of togetherness and power within Native American communities. Elmer Bear Eagle, a veteran of Wounded Knee, said, "What I took away from Wounded Knee 1973 was a feeling of freedom, a feeling of real pride, being here with the people, with everybody" (qtd. in Record and Hocker 17). Even as a Native American not directly involved with AIM, I always feel a sense of pride come over me when I see videos of AIM members sitting in front of the BIA building with their red berets and red AIM clothing. I used to think I would not do anything like that, but now I don't know what I would do in a situation like that. I am thankful for the American Indian Movement because they give me a voice, make me proud, and fight for a better way of life for all Native Americans in the United States.

Works Cited

Churchill, Ward. "A Force, Briefly, to Reckon With." The Progressive 61.6 (1997): 39–41. Online. Proquest Direct. 17 July 1998 <http://lib.NMSU.EDU/resources/dbpqd.html>.

> Journal title (underlined), followed by issue volume and number (61.6), year published and inclusive pages of article.

> Online data base listed as source, followed by data accessed and url

Churchill, Ward, and Jim Vander Wall. Agents of Repression: The FBI's Secret Wars against the Black Panther Party and the American Indian Movement. Boston: South End, 1988.

Means, Sherry. "Introduction to the American Indian Movement: 101." American Indian Movement Website. 17 July 1998 <http://www.dickshovel.com/ aim101.html>.

Record, Ian, and Anne Pearse Hocker. "A Fire That Burns: The Legacy of Wounded Knee." Native Americas: Akwe:kon's Journal of Indigenous Issues Spring 1998: 14–25.

Weyler, Rex. Blood of the Land: The Government and Corporate War against the American Indian Movement. New York: Everest, 1982.

White, Richard. "The Return of the Natives." The New Republic 215.2 (1996): 37–44. Online: Proquest Direct. 20 July 1998 <http://lib.NMSU.EDU/resources/dbpqd.html>.

Yinger, J. Milton. Countercultures: The Promise and Peril of a World Turned Upside Down. New York: Free, 19.

WRITING ASSIGNMENT

Find a subject you are or can become curious about; then, to begin, ask several questions that you think your research might answer or that you want it to answer. As you explore your topic, keep in mind our discussion of the reliability of sources. To help organize your project, keep a research notebook in which you place all notes, drafts, and photocopies you may make. Your instructor may want you to submit all such materials with your final draft. And keep in mind the four potential purposes for a research paper listed at the start of this chapter: to inform, to evaluate, to argue, or to solve a problem.

SAMPLE STUDENT PROCESS

The essay we'll follow in our discussion of a sample student research project was written by Gardiner Rhoderick, a first-year student at NMSU. Gardiner chose a problem/solution framework for his paper, a decision that guided not only the format for the paper but his research as well.

Prewriting   Gardiner began by jotting this very quick Bug List (see page 555):

>   no skate park in Las Cruces
>   too much control—police, school
>   graffiti paintovers
>   no respect for artists
>   too much emphasis on winning
>   writing classes at 8:30 in the morning
>   specified writing process—too many drafts
>   too many restrictions on doing my thing

From here, he decided to write about graffiti. His interest in this topic was timely, for during the semester in which he wrote the essay, a number of articles about the Las Cruces program to paint over graffiti were published in the local paper. Gardiner framed a fairly broad statement of the problem and then responded to questions designed to help him explore the problem statement with an initial audience firmly in mind.

Audience Analysis 1

Problem statement: Graffiti artists are misunderstood because graffiti is associated with gang problems.

1. *Who can solve the problem you're dealing with? Who has the authority or power to change things?*

    The general public is capable of solving the problem, but the true authority to change the problem lies in the hands of law enforcement officials.

2. *What is this person's role in the problem? Did he create the problem? Or is his role one of oversight, of being responsible for, say, enforcing a policy or practice that you may argue against? Or is he a concerned individual who has no particular*

official involvement with the problem but might be able to influence the eventual outcome—for example, a taxpayer and a voter living in a city that is in the process of deciding how to solve the problem of traffic congestion.

> The public really doesn't have a role, but is more of a victim concerning the problem.
> They are more like concerned citizens who could immediately influence the outcomes of the problem.

3. *What does he already know about the problem? Is he likely to see it as a problem?*

> They understand the basic underlying fault of the problem, but not the reasons or the motivation for it.

4. *What does he need to know to take the action you think he should take?*

> The public needs to go through a thorough educating process to understand all the background concerning the problem.

5. *How opposed is he likely to be to your solution? Why?*

> The acceptance of the solution is likely to be ignored, seeing as how there is a tremendous bias towards the people who partake in the problem.

Research Strategies   The assignment specified that Gardiner use at least four sources to support his writing and that two of those were to be Internet sources. His final bibliography has five entries: three books and two articles he found on the Internet. Because the books were published by reputable publishers and accepted by the NMSU library, Gardiner felt there was little question of their reliability. And he decided that the Internet sources were reliable as well. Unlike many Internet articles, both of these were signed by their authors, so it would be possible to check further into their credentials as authorities on the topic of graffiti. Further, Sherri Cavan, author of "The Great Graffiti Wars of the Late 20th Century," has a home page through San Francisco State University and signs her article in this way:

> Sherri Cavan, Ph.D.
> Department of Sociology
> San Francisco State University

These credentials show that Dr. Sherri Cavan is a university faculty member.

Initially, Gardiner might have questioned the reliability of the essay by Killian Tobin, "A Modern Perspective on Graffiti." Gardiner found it on a website promoting graffiti, so there's a question of potential bias. The website has as the first part of its address http://graffiti.org. The "org" portion of the address indicates that the site is sponsored by a private organization (rather than a government agency or an educational institution)—in this case, one with commercial interests, listing graffiti-related items such as videotapes for sale. Further, in promoting graffiti, the site is promoting an activity that's illegal in most, if not all, communities. As noted earlier in this chapter, Gardiner found Tobin's article by browsing the site. He settled on the article because it offered support for his position that what society needs is a new way of looking at graffiti. Further, the tone of the article is not shrill, and the essay's primary purpose is to report about problems surrounding graffiti and how graffiti has come to be seen as less than desirable by the public. Only the last paragraph offers Tobin's opinion, but even that paragraph is written with a very controlled, scholarly tone. And the article is only not signed but also lists a 1995 copyright date. Although the article does not list any research references, Gardiner judged it to be reliable enough to support his writing.

Rough Draft   With his research notes in hand, Gardiner wrote and then revised the following draft for an in-class peer review session:

> For the past 20 years graffiti has been evolving into a problem of insurmountable circumstance. Scrawls and messages adorn a spot in every city in the country (maybe the world) and is costing the United States billions of dollars every year to eliminate. Whether made by the stroke of a marker or the spew of a spraycan, the marks left on dumpsters, back alleys, business walls, bathrooms, rooftops and road signs are considered by the majority of the US population to be a sign of decay and hostility.   1
>
> Graffiti is seen as a threat to the general public. The appearance of graffiti shows signs of supposed gang activity, therefore promoting gangs, and ultimately promoting violence. Graffiti is to blame for the decrease in general property value, neighborhood deterioration, and poor business development. These consequences of graffiti are more than disturbing, but are made worse by the misconception of what graffiti actually is. The context in which the word has fallen into (and the media created) has evoked a mood of disgrace, disgust and anger among the public community.   2
>
> Modern graffiti as we know it began in 1973 by a man who wrote "Taki 183" (his moniker and the street on which he lived) on every flat surface in New York City. His graffiti, or "tag," became somewhat of a novelty, and local New Yorkers were amused when they caught a glimpse of the moniker. He was given media coverage, an article in the New York Post, and quickly became somewhat of a celebrity. Soon, as others saw what Taki was doing, more and more graffiti began to emerge. Other doers of graffiti, or "writers" as they have come to be called, began mimicking Taki's actions. As the graffiti population increased, the diversity among the forms of graffiti did also. Simple tags gave way to calligraphic signatures. When this was out done, stylized letters began to emerge, soon murals began to pop out all over the city of New York, and finally graffiti took its form: as a stylistic interpretation of the alphabet. Graffiti ignited across the country and the world, and a sub-culture of thousands were soon taking to the streets, armed with a spraycan.   3
>
> The actual date of the prohibiting of graffiti is unclear. Although at first enjoyed by many, by the early eighties, graffiti suddenly became an eyesore. Abatement programs were started across the country to eliminate the problem. The media stepped in, and this is where the war on graffiti began.   4
>
> On one hand, we have the anti-graffitist, which accounts for the majority of the population (including the media). They condemn graffiti, stereotype its members, believe in harsh punishment for offenders, and are quick to neglect the qualities inherent in graffiti.   5
>
> On the other hand, we have a sub-culture consisting of tens of thousands of members. They embrace graffiti. They believe in the artistic merit of graffiti, but   6

also realize the illegal aspect of it. They offer no explanation as to why they do it, and at the same time, have a hard time understanding why themselves.

Graffiti has been mistaken for nothing but a scrawl on a wall. Its members have been stereotyped to oblivion and their "art" has been misconstrued among the public. Writers continue to produce graffiti, no matter what the consequence, knowing that what they do is wrong. So the problem arises: How do we stop graffiti? The answer is: you don't.

It is a known fact that graffiti will never be eliminated completely. There will always be someone engraving a tree, writing their name in concrete, or taking to the streets. The solution to the problem of graffiti is lessening its occurrence. In order to do this, the public must be educated. Misconceptions of graffiti and its creators need to be addressed and properly cleared up. Ideas of gangs, violence, and hostility need to be dealt with as well as informing who and what writers are all about. Acceptance of the art must also be pushed. Local businesses have endorsed graffiti projects on their walls, and although completely legal, the appearance of it still scares and shocks the public. More effort must be placed on opening up the people's eye to the artistic aspect of graffiti.

The concept of graffiti as an accepted art form is highly radical. But so is spending billions of dollars a year to cover it up. When a balance is reached between the toleration and prohibiting of graffiti, the problem itself will decline, and so will the cost of controlling it. If graffiti goes unnoticed and no action is taken, the walls of the country will be full of graffiti, while the pocketbooks of its citizens will be empty.

One of Gardiner's classmates responded to the draft by answering the questions on a peer review sheet.

1. What problem has the writer taken on? How clearly worded is the problem statement?

Legalizing graffiti. It is not very clear. You can easily make an assumption, but it is not said in the essay. It is not: "legalize graffiti."

2. How effectively has the writer explored the problem? Consider such questions as these: Why is the problem a problem? How widespread is it? Who is affected by it? What is its impact?

The writer explores the problem well, however, you need a few more details, figures, and etc., how much does it cost to cover graffiti, how much does it cost to have police take care of taggers, how many cops are on task forces? What about laws that say residents must clean-up graffiti w/in two weeks of it being there? How much property is affected? How many homes, businesses, and other buildings?

3. What solution or solutions does the writer offer? How clearly stated is the essay's thesis, that is, the solution? Has the writer cast it as an argumentative thesis? If not, make suggestions for revision.

How will you educate people about graffiti? How can you prove graffiti does not promote violence and gang activity? You need to state your thesis a lot more clearly.

4. What support has the writer offered for the solution? How effective is this support? Are you convinced that the solution is feasible or workable?

You need to show how an educated community could deal with and understand graffiti. Is education the only solution or just a start?

5. Who is the reader for this essay; what audience has the writer chosen? How effectively has the writer addressed that reader's potential concerns? What other audience concerns can you identify that the writer has either chosen to ignore or simply didn't know should be addressed? Make specific suggestions for revision.

I feel the reader is already involved with graffiti. You need to work on addressing those who know very little of graffiti. Show how you can save money and raise property values with the art work being displayed in the neighborhood. Maybe discuss designated tagging areas or even tagging licenses. You may also want to explore the tagger's view of his art a little more.

6. Pay particular attention to each paragraph's development. Identify the topic sentence for each paragraph. How does that topic sentence support or develop either the problem or solution section of the paper? How effectively does each paragraph support or develop its topic sentence? Make specific suggestions for revision.

The topic sentences are very good. However, there needs to be more support. In ¶4, how was it enjoyed? What made it an eyesore? It is just like that throughout the essay.

7. How many sources has the writer used? Are these documented correctly? To what extent has the writer incorporated and introduced quoted material smoothly and effectively? Make specific suggestions for revision.

Sources are not clearly documented. There are not many quotes. You may want to look at local graffiti—the mural across from Baskin Robbins.

Gardiner also had a conference on the draft with Bill, his instructor, who raised the following points:

1. Where are your sources? Remember that you have to include them, introduce any quoted material, and then document them correctly. I'm really concerned about this, because your draft doesn't show any notations or references at all.
2. Can you smooth out the introduction a bit? You make it seem that graffiti is a very recent phenomenon, but it's been around just about forever.
3. 2nd ¶—this seems out of place. You may want either to move it somewhere else in the paper or just delete it altogether. What does it add?
4. Taki ¶—opening sentence seems too broad and sweeping to me. This paragraph is one, by the way, that must be documented, because it contains specific materials that you took from somewhere—where?
5. You make a lot of unsupported assertions in this paper. The best way to strengthen these is to provide material from sources. Here's an example: you say at one point (¶7) that graffiti art has been "misconstrued" among the

public. Why not quote somebody on this? Look at the source you're using about Denver's attempts to stamp out graffiti.

Overall, if you're going to convince a reader like me that there's a value in certain styles of graffiti and that it's not all gang-related, you need to define terms more clearly so that I can understand what you mean by the kind of graffiti we as a society ought to value as legitimate art. A final note—what title will you give this piece?

After reviewing both his classmate's and Bill's comments, Gardiner wrote this summary assessment of the draft, focusing on what he thought worked well and what needed more work:

The purpose of this essay is to help educate those that see graffiti as a harmful crime done out of violence. My paper goes into the explanation of why graffiti exists, why some do it, and what it should be seen as. The essay has a basic, overall strong-point. That is its ability to bring in the average Joe of sorts, those that want to see graffiti abolished, and suddenly realize the essay is pro-graffiti, although still addressing the issues that are pertinent to them. The work serves as more of an educational tool. It informs those who are unclear about the aspects of graffiti of the false bias they are more than familiar with. The language is intended for a mature audience, mostly because this is the audience that needs to make the difference, or rather, the change. The conclusion seems the most weak to me. Next time, I plan on developing a smoother, more "resolving" type of ending. I feel the conclusion ends too abruptly. And obviously I have to do the sources thing.

Gardiner also wrote a second, more focused audience analysis.

Audience Analysis 2

1. What do you want your readers to understand or gain from reading your paper?

I would like my readers to take what I've said into consideration and thoroughly comprehend the aspects of graffiti which are commendable and should be given at least some form of acceptance.

2. What attitudes are your readers likely to have toward your topic? What aspects of that attitude have you addressed in your paper?

Most readers will have an attitude of negativity towards the topic. Maybe not so much with the ideas the essay addresses, but with the problem we're dealing with in general. I have tried to include the main reason for the bias in the essay, as well as sharing new information that they might not have known.

3. What do your readers already know about your topic? What do they need to know?

The reader already understands the basic principle behind the problem. What they need to know is the separation between the two forms of graffiti, understanding the artistic value of true graffiti, and learning about the bias that they themselves practice.

4. What questions are your readers likely to have about your topic? How effectively have you answered them?

I feel that the questions they would ask are far and few in number. This problem deals with more of informing what the people have never heard of.

5. What particular action do you want your readers to take, if any? Is your writing compelling enough to make them want to take this action? Why or why not?

I would like my readers to open their minds a little more and be willing to accept graffiti for its artistic merit. I feel that no matter what kind of motivation my paper has, people care so little about the problem, or listening to solutions, that any attempt would be in vain.

6. Is there any part of your paper that may make your readers reject your thinking? If so, how effectively have you prepared them for this material?

I should hope not.

7. Is there any aspect of your paper that is likely to surprise your readers? If so, does this surprise serve your purpose? If not, how may you more effectively prepare your readers for this material?

I would hope the fact that I am not looking for legalization of graffiti would cause somewhat of a surprise. In a reflective way it serves a purpose, but not in dealing with the situation.

With all this advice and planning at work, Gardiner produced the draft that follows.

Final Draft

> Title centered, no quotation marks used, unless there's a quote in the title
>
> Author's name centered NOTE: check with your instructor for specific instructions about essay headings.

Gardiner Rhoderick

Yes, It's Graffiti, But Is It Art?

The history of graffiti is a long one. Petroglyphs carved in rock and figures painted on the walls of caves stand as reminders that ever since humans learned that they could inscribe something on a wall, somebody has had the desire to leave his mark. Today these marks—graffiti—have evolved into a problem of insurmountable circumstance. Scrawls and messages adorn every city in the country and cost the

United States billions of dollars every year to eliminate, four billion in 1995 alone (Walsh, 1996). Whether made by the stroke of a marker or the spew of a spray can, the marks left on dumpsters, back alleys, business walls, bathrooms, rooftops and road signs are considered by the majority of the United States population to be a sign of decay and hostility.

Modern graffiti emerged in the late 1960s or early 1970s by people like "Taki 183" (his moniker and the street on which he lived). "Taki 183" appeared on nearly every flat surface in New York City. Taki's graffiti, or "tag," became somewhat of a novelty, and local New Yorkers were amused when they caught a glimpse of the moniker. He was given media coverage, was the focus of an article in the *New York Times*, and quickly became somewhat of a celebrity. Soon, as others saw what Taki was doing, more and more graffiti began to emerge. Other perpetrators of graffiti, or "writers" as they have come to be called, began mimicking Taki's actions.

As the number of graffiti writers increased, the forms of graffiti became diverse. Simple tags gave way to calligraphic signatures. When writers became bored with simple tags, stylized letters began to emerge. These consisted of two-dimensional letters, usually filled with two to three different colors. Eventually, they grew into complex multicolored masterpieces, and soon murals began to pop out all over the city of New York. Graffiti became a form of rebellious self-expression, a way for anyone to say "I'm here and I count." The graffiti artist as rebel held great appeal, and a subculture of thousands soon took to the streets, armed with spray cans, creating street art.

Art and popular culture scholars began to analyze and discuss graffiti in the context of street art. In 1975, Robert Sommer classified street art as: ⎯⎯⎯ *Colon indicates inset quote to follow*

⎯⎯⎯ Professional art. Art legally introduced into a public place.

Indent inset material ½" spaces

Folk art. Created by nonprofessionals according to a traditional pattern to be displayed in their own spaces, e.g., harvest figures or a crèche.

Naïve art. Created by nonprofessionals according to individual inclination to be displayed in their own places.

People's art. Anonymous art in a public space.

Chance art. The unintended creation of an attractive display, e.g., paint peeling on a building wall which reveals interesting hues and textures, or the accidental formation of rocks at Delaware Water Gap that resembles an Indian head.

Graffiti. Inscriptions on rocks, walls, etc. Most graffiti are not art. (p. 13)

People's art and graffiti are both "extralegal" (Sommer, 1975, p. 15) and are often confused. Tobin defines "artistic graffiti" as a new art form that "is a modern day offspring of traditional graffiti that has elevated itself from just scrawling words or phrases on a wall, to a complex artistic form of personal expression" (para. 1). Most people, however, do not make this distinction, and the confusion concerning graffiti begins here.

Graffiti has been mistaken for nothing but a scrawl on a wall. Its writers have been stereotyped to oblivion as society's outcasts (gangsters and dopers), and their art has been misconstrued among the public. Supposedly, graffiti shows signs of gang activity, therefore promoting gangs, and ultimately promoting violence. The context which the word has fallen into (and the media created) has evoked a mood of disgrace, disgust and anger among the public.

The actual date of the prohibiting of graffiti is unclear. Although at first enjoyed by many, by the early eighties, graffiti had become an eyesore. Abatement programs were started across the country to eliminate the problem. The media stepped in, correlating modern graffiti with gang members and violent overtones. News stories focused on costs and property damage, never once revealing the essence of artistic graffiti, and this is where the war on graffiti began.

Typical of anti-graffiti programs was one begun in Denver, Colorado, during the 1980s. It involved an extensive article and ad campaign to alert Denver's citizens of the graffiti blighting their city. Farrell (1993) characterizes this campaign as biased and aggressive:

> To maximize the sense of threat and violation, verbs such as "attack," "destroy," and "rob" are frequently paired with "graffiti vandal" and "graffiti vandalism." In a public service announcement aired on local television, Mayor Frederico Peña claims that "each day the citizens of Denver are being robbed, robbed by graffiti vandalism on their public and private property" (*In The Public Eye,* 1989). . . . Significantly, such phrasing implies not only violent assault, but an aggressive intentionality on the part of the "graffiti vandal," who doesn't "write" or "paint," but "attacks" and "robs." (p. 138)

[Citation appears as given in original text.]

Because most people associate it with gang activity, graffiti has been greatly misunderstood. And the war only continues.

On the one hand, we have the anti-graffitist, which accounts for the majority of the population (including the media). They condemn graffiti, stereotype its members, believe in harsh punishment for offenders, and are quick to ignore the qualities inherent in graffiti. Anti-graffitists have been known to respond violently. Dr. Sherri Cavan, a sociologist at San Francisco State University, reports that "a youthful tagger [was] shot and killed by an armed citizen intent on projecting public property from enemy attack. The Los Angeles County district attorney's office declined to file charges against the gunman . . ." (para.14).

On the other hand, we have a subculture that Cavan calls the "aerosol nation" (para. 3) consisting of tens of thousands of members. They embrace graffiti. They believe in the artistic merits of graffiti, but also realize the illegal aspect of it. They offer no explanation as to why they do it, and at the same time, have a hard time understanding why themselves. Writers continue to produce graffiti, no matter what the consequence, knowing that what they do is wrong. So the problem arises: How do we stop graffiti? The answer: we don't.

Graffiti will never be eliminated. Someone will always engrave a tree, write his name in concrete, or use a spray can to mark the streets. The solution to the problem is not legalization. Nor is it a complete lockdown on graffiti and its perpetrators. The solution is tied to how artistic graffiti is defined. Misconceptions of artistic graffiti and its creators need to be addressed and properly cleared up, so the public must be educated about it. Ideas of gangs, violence, and hostility need to be dealt with, as well as informing who and what writers are all about. Acceptance of this art form must also be pushed. Local businesses have endorsed graffiti projects on their walls, but, although completely legal, the appearance of graffiti on business-sponsored walls still scares and shocks the public. More effort must be placed on opening up the people's eye to the artistic aspect of graffiti.

The first step in keeping the streets clean is making a delineation between what artistic graffiti actually is and isn't. A simple marking, made with a pen, marker, or spray paint, has been the traditional definition of graffiti for years. What hasn't been given attention is the new strand of artistic graffiti we have today. This complex and intricate style of painting has never been addressed, and most have no idea it exists. This is why, when we speak in terms of graffiti, many have their mind made up, quickly taking a solid stance on the issue. This is where the problem of an uninformed society comes into play.

The second step is a tolerance of sorts. Those who continue to scar the streets, making an ugly mess for the public to see, are more than worthy of being the target of mainstream America. Their useless marks do nothing but create an eyesore, and the activities of these individuals should be stopped. What should be tolerated (perhaps not legalized, but at least tolerated) is the unprecedented artistic version of graffiti. Although technically violating the law, the motives and skill behind the current movement is in no way lethal, in no way a direct sign of hostility, in no way a gang-instigated crime.

Contrary to popular belief, the average graffiti artist comes from a white middle- to upper-middle-class family. Their ages range between twelve and thirty years old, and they are never involved in gangs or gang violence (Walsh, 1996, p. 10). They do what they do, not to instill fear, but to inform the public, maybe as indirectly as possible, of the problems they have experienced in their upbringing and culture. Even though some may be politically motivated, while others are in it for themselves, their common goal is to share what they create with the rest of the world. They retreat to dilapidated urban areas, the forgotten areas of society, and add life with bold color, design, and complexity. Unfortunately, their efforts are usually unnoticed or, when noticed, misunderstood, leaving viewers with nothing but a negative response. The murals that can take hours on end to produce are all too quickly blotted out in a matter of minutes.

Even when graffiti makes a positive contribution to society, authorities work to stamp it out. A large mural (a piece of "people's art" or "artistic graffiti") painted on a drugstore wall by a group of art students under the direction of their teacher was almost immediately "painted over by the building owner as a 'routine maintenance procedure'" (Sommer, 1975, p. 94). Farrell (1993) tells a more troublesome incident in Denver. In 1989, an AIDS outreach group had commissioned a group of Denver's more famous graffiti artists to paint a series of murals about AIDS prevention measures, including a hotline number. The positive impact was immediate as officials saw a marked increase in the number of calls to the hotline. These murals were promptly attacked by anti-graffitists, and officials declared them signs, not art, that were illegal because the artists did not have permits to paint them. The ploy worked, and the murals were painted over (pp. 182–183). People who see artistic graffiti as non-art need to take another look.

The third step is to push the acceptance of artistic graffiti. More businesses using it as a type of advertising or decoration will help the public come to accept and enjoy it. Cities have found that if they endorse a city-sponsored wall, "tagger" graffiti declines dramatically. Sommer (1975) cites several examples of the respect artistic graffiti has enjoyed:

> Artist Arnold Belkin painted a large mural for a playground in the Hell's Kitchen of New York City. Belkin was able to develop a large amount of community support for the mural; a year afterward, there was not a single extraneous spot, line or number defacing the mural. . . . Jerry and Salla Romotsky, an artist-writer team in Los Angeles who have followed the activities of Chicano street gangs in decorating neighborhood walls, found that gangs rarely disturb actual works of art. While many barrio walls have literally been covered with script, genuine murals have been spared. There have been a few instances where murals have been hit, but these are the exceptions rather than the rule. (pp. 21–22)

Walls decorated with artistic graffiti are respected and devoid of useless scribbles. The more that artistic graffiti is seen in a dignified manner, well-done and completed, the more the public will begin to understand what it really is: art.

The concept of graffiti as an accepted art form is highly radical. But so is spending billions of dollars a year to cover it up. When a balance is reached between tolerating artistic graffiti and prohibiting tagging, the problem itself will decline, and so will the cost of controlling it. Art needs to be valued, not painted over because of unwarranted fear of gangs and drug dealers.

References

Cavan, S. The great graffiti wars of the late 20th century. Retrieved April 14, 1998, from http://userwww.sfsu.edu/~kazbeki/grafwars.html

Farrell, J. (1993). *Crimes of style: Urban graffiti and the politics of criminality.* New York: Garland.

Sommer, R. (1975). *Street art.* New York: Links Books.

Tobin, K. (1995). "A modern perspective on graffiti." 1995. *Art crimes: The writing on the wall.* S. Farrell and B. Webb (Eds.). Retrieved April 12, 1998, from http://graffiti.org/faq/tobin.html

Walsh, M. (1996). *Graffito.* Berkeley, CA: North Atlantic Books.

CHECKLIST:
CRITIQUING A RESEARCH ESSAY

1. What is the purpose of the research essay—to inform, evaluate, argue, or solve a problem?
2. What is the thesis? How effectively does it fulfill the purpose you identified above?
3. Who is the intended audience? At what points in the essay is the reader likely to disagree with the writer? How effectively has the writer anticipated and addressed those disagreements? Are there any places in the essay that are likely to surprise the reader? If so, how well has the writer prepared the reader for them?

4. How does the paper begin? What did the writer intend the introduction to do, specifically? How effective is the introduction in identifying the topic, establishing the writer's stance or position on it, and bringing the reader into the paper?
5. What support is offered for the thesis? In what order? How convincing are the examples, statistics, illustrations, and other kinds of support? How appropriate is the support for the audience?
6. How appropriate for the reader is the language used in the paper? Is it too formal? Too colloquial? How appropriate is it for the subject?
7. How does the essay end? What did the writer intend the conclusion to do, specifically? How effectively does it close or round out the essay?
8. What is the essay's title? How effectively does it represent the paper to the reader? How appropriate is it for the topic?
9. Which style manual has the writer used? Are outside sources used and documented correctly? How effectively are materials from sources introduced? How effectively is information (e.g., quotations and summaries) from those sources integrated into the text?
10. Does the paper adhere to conventions of usage, mechanics, and format? Correct any errors you find.

PART IV

Writing and Assessing

Writing and assessing are almost inseparable. Every time we put words on paper, we invite evaluation or criticism. But the more we come to think of writing as a process, the more we can push that kind of assessment into the background. As we do so, we move from a one-sided view in which writing is seen as a product to be assessed, or judged, to a broader perspective that includes the role writing can play in helping us become assessors or evaluators.

Assessment via Essay Exams

Chapter 13 deals with a type of writing that many students dread—the essay examination. We have often heard arguments (from both students and teachers) against this type of writing. They suggest that if a teacher uses students' writing *only* to find out whether they have learned the course material, no *real* writing has been done. Such arguments often characterize the essay exam as an exercise in which students are asked to regurgitate information given by a teacher rather than to do any real thinking (or composing). Those who hold this view often advocate that essay exams be replaced by objective tests that measure what students know but inflict far less pain on teachers and students.

We will answer these arguments in some detail in Chapter 13. For now, we focus on one of the chief benefits of the essay exam: It allows students to use writing to show what they know. Students literally answer questions in their own words. In doing so, they connect things in ways that show their understanding of the subject matter at hand. It makes an important difference whether a writer says

> Japan bombed Pearl Harbor, and the United States declared war on Japan immediately.

or

> Because Japan bombed Pearl Harbor, the United States declared war on Japan.

The second sentence makes a stronger causal link. As another example, consider the following two sentences having to do with slavery and the U.S. Civil War:

> The Civil War was about slavery.

or

> The Civil War cannot be discussed without reference to the question of slavery.

The second sentence suggests that the writer understands the complexity of the connection between slavery and that war, an understanding that is not evident in the first sentence.

Our claim here, then, is that the writing done on essay exams allows a type of assessment that can be achieved in no other way. An objective test can indicate whether a student has learned facts and rote definitions. However, essay exams allow students to show their grasp of ideas and concepts better than objective tests, because ideas and concepts are not reducible to the types of words and phrases used in objective tests.

Jais Nielsen, "Exit!," 1918. Oil on canvas, 47-1/4 × 40 in. Lolland-Falsters Kunstmuseum, Maribo, Denmark. Photo: Lolland-Falsters Kunstmuseum/Bridgeman Art Library © 2008 Artists Rights Society (ARS), New York/COPY-DAN, Copenhagen.

CHAPTER 13

Essay Examinations

You will likely take many essay examinations in your college career. Given the amount of time and effort these essays require, you may wonder why so many teachers continue to make them an integral part of their examinations. They do so because they believe preparing for and writing essays fosters a different kind of learning than objective testing. Consider your own reaction to essay examinations. How does it change your behavior in a classroom when a teacher informs you that a test, or at least a part of a test, will require you to write an essay? As teachers who give essay examinations in our language and literature classes, we hope these exams encourage students to take notes in class, read and take notes on the assigned readings, and, in general, prepare themselves to explain and reflect on the course materials. It is one thing to know that you will be responsible for determining which item in a list of potential causes of World War I should be excluded (in a multiple-choice test); it is quite another to know that you could be asked to write an essay in which you discuss the historical period in question.

What difference, you may ask, does it make how I am tested if the result is to ensure that I know the causes of World War I? That's a good question. In a sense, the rest of this chapter will serve as our complete answer to it. But let's begin with a brief answer first.

As we've stressed throughout this text, writing is a powerful learning tool. In preparing for an exam, you should write summaries and paraphrases, in which you translate information you have been given into your own words. In doing so, you should come to know that information in a way that you would not if you were preparing for a multiple-choice test, because essay exams require you to interact with and think about the information you have been given and thereby add depth to your learning.

To explore this point more fully, let's think about what happens when we listen to a set of directions for finding a place in a rather large city. We know we should write them down, but sometimes we aren't able to do so. What happens? After two or three turns, we find that we can't play back (that is, "say back") the directions we have been given. In effect, we didn't learn the material. However, if someone were to give us a test in which they listed the various roads we would need to take to get to the location, we might well be able to recognize the roads that were mentioned and to label as wrong any roads that were not mentioned. That knowledge, however, will not get us to our location.

But what if we had drawn a map at the time we were given the directions? Even if we mislaid that map, the chances of our getting to the right place would increase if we had taken the time to draw it. In a sense, we would have imprinted the map (with various relationships among the roads we would be traveling) in our minds as we were drawing it. When we write things down (or draw pictures that represent relationships), we come to own that information in ways that we do not otherwise.

We believe there is a similar process at work when writing is used in academic settings. Think of the hypothetical history course we referred to. If you have memorized the list of causes of World War I, you will be able to list them on an objective test or exclude a wrong answer on a multiple-choice test. However, an essay examination on this material might ask you to discuss why most historians agree that one event was a cause of the war, but many disagree about the cause/effect relationship between another event and the war. You wouldn't be well prepared for such an examination if all you had done was memorize a list of causes. Now, suppose a year or two later you are studying the history of art during the pre–World War I period. If you studied for an essay examination in your previous history class and thus had to construct your own "map" of that historical period, you may well have a backdrop of historical information on which to build your new knowledge about the art movements of this period. A listing of the causes of World War I, even if you remembered the list, would likely be of little value to you in this new course of study.

If this were the only benefit of writing essay examinations, it would be a significant one, but there is more. Writing actually encourages you to think for yourself. We have been talking about the causes of World War I as if there were some official list of these causes in history books. Of course, that is not the case. Every historian of the period has his own list of causes. Historians will certainly agree on many of the causes, but they will disagree on various other causes, and even when they do agree on items in the list, they will differ as to the relative importance they assign these causes. As you become an active learner in your history class, you will read what the writers of your texts have to say on the matter, you will listen to the comments of your teacher, and, if you are truly interested in the subject, you may do other reading on your own. After engaging in this type of learning, you may actually be excited by the prospect of answering an essay question that asks you to evaluate potential causes of this war. Your study of this subject and the actual writing of this essay will allow you to develop your own insights about this subject. In such a situation, your writing will allow you to enter into the process by which knowledge is made.

PACKAGING THE PROCESS

At the outset of this chapter, we need to say a bit about the type of writing required in essay examinations, as compared with the writing we have been encouraging you to do to this point. From the beginning of this text, we have emphasized writing as process. Although there is no correct number of drafts that a piece of writing should go through and no prescribed amount of time that should elapse between the beginning and completion of that writing, we have encouraged you to engage in activities that require you to take more, rather than less, time in your writing process. In Chapter 1, we suggested various ways of exploring your topics and finding different angles from which to approach topics. In Chapter 3, we offered advice on ways to improve your writing by reseeing it after getting it on the page. As its name makes clear, however, the essay examination does not allow you the luxury of reflecting on what you have said and reconceptualizing your essay. But that does not mean that you cannot bring a process approach to essay-exam writing. In fact, if anything, your writing process in this situation is even more important than in other, less stressful writing situations.

The process of writing an essay examination begins long before you sit down to write it. Your approach to a course requiring essay examinations is a part of this process. As you read materials for this course and as you attend class sessions, you should reflect on the issues introduced in the course. As you do, you should ask yourself what kinds of information your teacher stresses. Your teacher will have her own ways of signaling what are particularly significant ideas. The headings in your textbook should also give you insight into the writer's judgments as to what is important and how important concepts are linked to each other. You will remember that Chapter 4 introduced dialogue notes as a way of reading materials actively. You may find this reading strategy particularly helpful as you reflect on the materials in your texts and on the class notes you take. At first, it may seem strange to think about using your classroom notes as a springboard to writing; when you think about it, however, you may see how your classroom notes can become a kind of text you can explore as you seek to understand the major concepts being presented in class.

Assuming that you have developed a basic understanding of the course material, you are ready to write the essay exam. As we noted, you will benefit greatly by developing a process approach to this type of writing. The in-class process begins with careful reading of the questions to determine *what* the teacher wants in your answer and *how* you may best structure your response. Once you have decided what is being asked and how you want to structure your answer, you can construct a thesis sentence and an outline for your essay. Then, *and only then*, should you begin writing your essay.

We cannot emphasize this last point too strongly. There are important differences between in-class writing and out-of-class writing. Some writers may find it helpful to begin writing out-of-class assignments before they have a clear idea of what information will be included. Writers who are willing and able to discard major portions of a rough draft may use this kind of freewriting to help them find what they want to say. There is no time, however, for such extensive prewriting in an essay examination. Although you may usually feel free to cross out and write over a line here and there, to polish your writing by striking over a word and inserting a more precise one, and to make any editorial changes you have time for, you probably will not have time to reconceptualize your essay once you have begun. You are committed to following the course that you charted before beginning to write the essay.

It is crucial, as you write your essay, that you have confidence in your plan; there is no time for wondering whether you have read the question correctly and whether the material you are offering later in the answer is connected to material earlier in the answer. To put it positively, if you have a clear sense of where you are heading in an essay and how the various parts of the answer fit together to fulfill the requirements of the assignment, you will find that you can produce a reasonably well-developed answer in a short time. Therefore, you can afford to take the time you need at the beginning to plan your essay. It isn't possible to say just how much time you should take for planning, but a rule of thumb we have found useful is to allow around one-fourth of your time for planning. If you have fifteen minutes for an essay, you can afford three or four minutes for planning; a thirty-minute period may allow for seven or eight minutes of planning; and with an hour, you may plan for up to fifteen minutes. Your planning times may vary, but if you are taking considerably more or less than one-fourth of your time for planning, you may benefit by attempting to move closer to this guideline.

WRITING STRATEGY

Summary of the Essay-Exam Process

Before the Exam

1. Take careful notes on readings, class lectures, and class discussions. Review them daily.
2. Use your notes from class and readings as springboards for entries in your dialogue notebook. In this notebook, you might also attempt to devise and answer questions your teacher could ask on an exam.

During the Exam

1. Read the exam question carefully, determining *what* type of information the teacher is asking for and *how* you can structure your essay.
2. Construct a thesis for your essay.
3. Outline your essay.
4. Write the essay.
5. Reread the essay, if there is time, making local corrections.

PLANNING YOUR ESSAY'S CONTENT

Most teachers do not set out to write a specific type of essay question. However, nearly all of the questions we have seen in college classroom situations make use of one or more of the following four processes: summary, synthesis, evaluation, and interpretation. Both summary and synthesis are ways of informing a reader about a given topic. Evaluation introduces the writer's value judgments concerning that subject. And interpretation focuses on the meaning a writer finds in a subject. It is no accident that these four processes are closely related to Chapters 6 through 8 in Part Two. On rare occasions, teachers may offer you the opportunity to make a personal response to course material (with a focus on you as writer) or ask you to write a persuasive essay (which spotlights a reader's reaction to what you have to say about the subject). In most essay-examination situations, however, teachers will want you to focus on the subject in question or your evaluation or interpretation of that subject.

For purposes of discussion, we will treat each of the four processes separately. But, as we shall see later, many, if not most, of the essays you'll encounter in actual exam situations will combine two or more of them.

Summary

On the surface, summary would seem to be no more than saying back to the teacher what the teacher or a source such as a textbook has said. It is not that simple, however. In summarizing, you are responsible for putting other people's thoughts into your own words. But summary is made more difficult by the need for brevity. Unlike a paraphrase, which allows you the luxury of a word-for-word translation, summary requires you to put others' ideas into your own words and to condense their thoughts into a form that will suit your purposes without misrepresenting what they have said. Deciding what to include and what to leave out requires mastery of your source. (For more on summary, see pages 135–140 in Chapter 4.)

Here are examples of essay-exam questions that ask students for summaries:

1. According to the writers of our textbook, what is the evidence that the language used by animals (even when humans work with animals extensively) is different in kind (not just in degree) from human language?
2. What is a linguistic universal? What are some examples of linguistic universals? Why is the concept of linguistic universal important to modern grammarians like Noam Chomsky?
3. What is whole language instruction? Why do the authors of our textbook oppose it?
4. In class we talked about several "first generation" modern dancers. Write a brief discussion of two of these. Be sure to talk about what these dancers see as the purpose of dance and how they view the relationship between dance and musical accompaniment.

Sample Summary Essay The following essay was written by Sybil Huskey, a professor of Dance and Theatre at the University of North Carolina at Charlotte as a sample for the students in her introductory dance classes. It answers question 4 above.

Two of the most important early modern dancers were Isadora Duncan, an American dancer, and Mary Wigman, a German dancer. Duncan helped establish a new kind of dance by means of her artistic daring. She was the first to express the inner feelings of human beings without the artifices, the contrived invention, the traditional methods and the vocabularies used in the ballet. Duncan's movement allowed the natural gestures of the body, freed from acrobatic exaggeration, to express themselves from an inner compulsion. She did not use the traditional costume of the ballet, but instead danced barefooted in a simple Greek-style tunic. She did not interpret or visualize the music in movement, but used music as the impetus to express the feelings that came from her soul, where (she believed) movement had its origins.

In Germany, Mary Wigman developed a form of modern dance influenced by Dalcroze and Rudolph von Laban. Her dances were introspective. She was determined to free dance from its bondage with music and often danced with no musical accompaniment at all. She felt that the dance should determine its own structural form; thus she often had music composed to fit her dances. She was very concerned with the concept of "space." She did not believe that dancers should ever see themselves as working in a vacuum; rather, they should see the space around them as symbolic of the human environment. Wigman rejected no movements, however odd or superficially ugly, if she felt they expressed what she wanted to communicate.

Duncan and Wigman, then, contributed much to the development of modern dance. Both dancers helped to free dance from its attachment to outward form—preferring to see it as arising from meaning that came from within the dancer—and both saw music as serving the needs of dance.

Commentary   This sample provides the information the question asks for, and it does so in the terms used in the question—what the dancers saw as *the purpose of dance* and the dancers' views of *the relationship between dance and musical accompaniment.* Note also that the essay begins with a very brief, one-sentence preview of the content and ends with a brief summary that captures the similarities between the contributions of these dancers. The simple structure reflects the question, which asks for a discussion of two dancers. The writer provides a paragraph of information on each dancer and then closes the essay with a paragraph describing each dancer's impact on modern dance.

Synthesis

Often a teacher will ask you to draw together and put into your own words other people's thoughts, and to do so in a condensed form. The teacher who asks you to synthesize two different sources assumes that although the sources may have differing things to say about a subject, an astute reader can see useful ways of bringing them together.

Synthesis does not have to be restricted to discussion of information that comes from sources, however. Any question that asks you to look at two or more things from a perspective that brings them together is calling for synthesis. For example, question 7 below asks the essay writer to consider Chomsky's theory of language development and Piaget's theory of language development from the perspective of language theory itself. In doing so, it requires synthesis as the writer sorts through the various issues involved in language development and compares and contrasts the approaches of these two philosophers. Similarly, question 5 asks the writer to build a frame that will help bring together—perhaps by means of comparison and contrast—the various problems European countries face today. The question could have called for a simple listing of countries' individual problems; however, in asking for a discussion of the various "types" of problems the countries face, the question calls for a synthesis.

These essay-exam questions ask for synthesis:

5. According to the various articles we have read on the United Kingdom, France, Spain, and Germany, what are the major types of problems that modern-day Europe must contend with? Illustrate these types by discussing specific problems in individual European countries.
6. Edelman talks about politics being a series of pictures from which a pattern emerges or on which a pattern is imposed. Would Hedrick Smith ("The Image Game") agree or disagree with Edelman? Be specific in justifying your answer.
7. In what ways do Noam Chomsky and Jean Piaget seem to agree about language development in humans? What would seem to be important areas of disagreement between the two?

Sample Synthesis Essay   The following essay was constructed by Ron from several written in response to question 7 above. He uses it as a model for students in his Introduction to Language course.

> Noam Chomsky and Jean Piaget do agree about several aspects of how humans develop their language abilities; however, there is a crucial difference in their theories about language development. Let's look at similarities first. Both Chomsky and Piaget recognize the importance of nature in the development of speech. Both men believe that humans are born with innate structures in the brain that allow for language development. Just as a bird has an instinct for how to build a nest, a human is born with innate abilities when it comes to language. Here Chomsky and Piaget could be contrasted with the most extreme behavioristic position (as explained by Skinner in *Verbal Behavior*), in which the human being is seen as a *tabula rasa*, or blank slate, when it comes to language. While they discount this behavioristic position, Chomsky and Piaget would agree with Skinner (and with each other) that nurture plays a role in language development. Both would point to feral children as examples of the importance of one's environment and would agree that young children must have some interaction with speakers of language if they are to develop their own abilities to speak. However, when we get to the exact role that this interaction plays and to what is going on in the brain of the child as it develops its language ability, we see important differences between the theories of Chomsky and Piaget. Piaget agreed with some aspects of the behaviorists' stimulus-response approach to learning.

Chomsky does not believe in language learning per se. Rather, he believes that a child "grows" his language abilities much like a tree grows from a seed. Except in those matters that are language specific, the child does not try various language moves and see what the responses to those moves are. A bird does not "learn" how to collect twigs for a nest; it knows that instinctively. Similarly, the human child knows which moves are possible in language and which are not. This leads to two other very important differences between Chomsky and Piaget. Chomsky believes that there is likely a specific language learning component in the brain—what he has sometimes referred to as a language organ. Piaget subscribed to a much more general learning mechanism in which various abilities are developed. Chomsky also believes in a universal grammar, which captures the ways in which all human languages are alike. The shape of the language organ would be determined by this universal grammar. Piaget's theories did not include such a grammar. Thus, we can see that while there are some important similarities between the theories of Chomsky and Piaget, when it comes to language development, their differences are striking—since Chomsky does not really believe that language is learned.

Commentary Since Ron put together the best parts of several good essays he received, this sample is likely a more complete answer than most teachers would require in an essay examination. However, it does illustrate some characteristics that all teachers will be looking for in questions that ask for a synthesis. Since a synthesis is a blend, it will include both likenesses and differences. Note that this sample essay devotes approximately equal time to the ways in which Chomsky and Piaget are alike and the ways in which they differ. These comparisons and contrasts provide the basic structure of the essay, as the introduction (the first sentence) announces. Note the ways in which this comparison/contrast structure is alluded to by the transitions within the essay. The end of the essay is signaled by the word "thus" at the beginning of the last sentence. In this sentence, we are told again that there are important similarities in these two philosophers' theories and we are reminded of the one crucial difference in their theories—the question of whether humans actually *learn* language.

There are a few other important points to make about this sample essay. Since this is a technical subject, Ron must deal with such specialized terms as "feral child," "behaviorism," "innate," "universal grammar," and "learning" (in the sense in which "learning" is used in this essay). Although the essay should make it clear that the writer understands these terms (as it does), it is not necessary for each term to be defined as it is used. Doing so would slow down the process of writing (and reading) the essay too much. As a second point, note that Ron is presented with a ticklish problem in that Chomsky and Piaget technically disagree about whether humans actually learn language. It would be tempting to talk about the ways in which Chomsky and Piaget differ (and are similar) in their views of "language learning." But since the viability of this term is one of the issues on which they differ, Ron is careful to talk about the differences (and similarities) in their views of the "development of language abilities." Note also that since Piaget died in 1980 but Chomsky is still alive, Ron decided to use the past tense in discussing Piaget's views and the present tense in discussing Chomsky's.

Evaluation

In Chapter 8, we noted that evaluation requires a writer to judge a subject in terms of such qualities as its worth (good or bad), effectiveness (effective or ineffective), usefulness (beneficial or not beneficial), or significance (important or unimportant). We stressed the importance of developing criteria for evaluation in an evaluation process. For example, if you want to say that a given work of art is excellent, it is crucial that you first establish the criteria to use in judging a work of art and then measure that work by means of those criteria.

Evaluative criteria are no less important in an essay examination. However, in this writing situation, the criteria are often supplied for you, and your success will depend on how well you use them. For example, if a teacher asks whether Jimmy Carter was an effective president and you respond by listing only the many admirable personal qualities of President Carter, you are not likely to receive a high mark on the exam. In some very open assignments, you may well develop your own criteria for evaluation, but in a history class that has focused on the effectiveness of various U.S. presidents, you would not have this freedom. Your judgments must be offered in the context of the criteria developed in that class.

Here are examples of essay-exam questions that ask for evaluations:

8. In this course, we have read several novels written in the last half of the twentieth century. If you had to choose one of these as the best novel written in this historical period, which would it be? What criteria would your choice be based on?
9. It could be argued that no two religious leaders have had more impact on twentieth-century U.S. politics than Dr. Martin Luther King, Jr., and Dr. Billy Graham. As our readings have helped us see, Dr. King affected public policy by means of public campaigns in which he openly called for connection between faith and public policy, whereas Dr. Graham avoided direct public statements about matters of state, instead implicitly supporting the candidacy of certain politicians by means of his private associations and talks with these candidates. In your opinion, which of these clergymen will prove to have had the most significant impact on public policy in twentieth-century United States? Why?
10. During the health-care reform campaign (in President Clinton's first term), were the Harry and Louise ads effective? Why or why not? Be specific in your explanation.

Sample Evaluative Essay   Jason Wise, a student enrolled in a course titled Communication and Public Advocacy, wrote the following essay in response to question 10.

> I believe the "Harry and Louise" advertisements were effective. They met several of the characteristics that successful television advertisements must meet.
>
> They were personal. Each viewer took something a little different away from their viewing. Even people as close as husband and wife would see the advertisements differently. The husband would identify more closely with Harry, the wife with Louise.

The ads were self-disclosive and relied on autobiographical evidence. What we knew about Harry and Louise was what they told us in the ads. Each ad became a vignette, shedding a little more light on just who these people were, making them seem more real. We ended up feeling as if we really knew them.

The ads were visual and made good use of associational grammar. We saw shots of these two people sitting at their kitchen table paying bills, something most of us could identify with. The ads didn't dwell on linear arguments to make their point; rather they made quick references to topics that pointed to problems in the Clinton plan, such as uninsured or underinsured illnesses and not being able to take a new job for fear of losing insurance coverage.

An additional proof of the ads' effectiveness is the interest they created about this topic. The ads spawned spoofs; they were mentioned in monologues by Letterman and Leno, and they generated ad bites that were broadcast on national news. All in all, then, these were very effective advertisements, and helped defeat the Clinton health plan.

Commentary   While there is nothing flashy about this essay, it is successful because it shows that Jason knows some of the major criteria that should be used in evaluating the effectiveness of advertisements. Note also that Jason begins and ends his essay in very straightforward ways, making his evaluation of the ads very clear. The structure of the essay is provided by the basic criteria that Jason uses to evaluate these ads—their personal nature, their ability to make viewers identify with these people, their visual qualities, and their ability to generate interest. It is worth noting that Jason disagreed with the author of the textbook used in the course, who had evaluated the ads as ineffective. Jason chose to write in support of his own opinion that the ads were effective; because he supported his opinion, his essay was seen as satisfactory. Had he chosen to agree with the textbook's author, Jason could have structured his response as a summary, much like Sybil Huskey's essay comparing two modern dancers (page 648). In such an essay, Jason would have been presenting evaluations, but they would have been summaries of the evaluative statements provided in the text. Jason's essay fails to deal with all of the evaluative criteria introduced by his text, but his essay deserves credit for demonstrating his ability to think about this issue for himself and for using some of the criteria mentioned in the text and in class.

Interpretation

When we interpret, we say what a text, an event, an artifact, or an object means; we derive this meaning in indirect rather than direct ways. For example, when we attempt to say what a certain character's actions in a novel mean, we have to look at those actions in the context of other factors such as the character's other actions, the actions of other characters in the novel, and the themes the author is working with in the novel.

It may not be so obvious that interpretation of a text involves more than simply decoding the words of that text. For example, if a character in a novel says,

"These bags are heavy," you can arrive at a literal meaning for those words by reading them and understanding that they mean the bags weigh a lot. However, in order to know what these words mean in the context of the novel, you must know much more. If the character who says them is carrying three bags and walking with another person who is not carrying anything and who is healthy and strong and kindly disposed toward the speaker, you'll likely interpret the words as a request for assistance in carrying the bags. If, on the other hand, both characters are equally burdened and if there has been something of an uneasy silence between the two speakers, you may well interpret the words as an attempt to establish some sort of rapport and to indicate general goodwill.

Context will play a crucial role in the kinds of interpretation you will be asked to do in essay examinations. Consider, for example, question 12 below, which calls for a discussion of how U.S. actions in Iran in the 1970s might be seen as a cause for the taking of U.S. hostages in 1979. To answer this question, the writer probably would begin by listing actions taken by the United States. But that list would not be a sufficient answer. An interpretation requires an examination of the actions in light of what was taking place in Iran and, perhaps, in various other parts of the world in which the United States was involved. An interpretation of U.S. actions in Iran during this historical period could involve an insightful look into the many events and actions that provide the context in which these actions occurred.

This discussion should make it clear that evaluation involves interpretation, since evaluation requires making judgments about a given topic in light of certain criteria for making those judgments. In a sense, the criteria provide the context we have been talking about. We have separated evaluation from interpretation, however, because of the frequency with which students are called on to make evaluations and because of the formal nature in which the context (that is, the evaluative criteria) is set out in evaluation.

Here are examples of essay-exam questions that ask for interpretation:

11. One of the most striking scenes in *The Great Gatsby* occurs when Nick first meets Daisy as she and Jordan Baker sit on (or seem to float above) the couch in Tom Buchanan's living room. Briefly explain the significance of this scene in relation to the novel as a whole.
12. What was the role of the United States in Iran during the rule of the Shah? How might that role be seen as a cause for the taking of U.S. hostages in Iran in 1979?
13. As we have seen, one of the most frequent themes in literature is the quest motif. Analyze the ways in which this motif is used in at least two of the following novels: *The Adventures of Huckleberry Finn; Moby Dick; The Great Gatsby; Ulysses; Invisible Man; Henderson, the Rain King.*
14. In "Revolution in Grammar," Nelson Francis offers three definitions of "grammar," distinguishing between what he labels as Grammar 1, Grammar 2, and Grammar 3. If you had to classify our two textbooks by means of these

categories, where would you put them? Is this easy or hard? That is, does one (or both) of them seem to belong in more than one category? Is one of the books harder to classify than the other? Why?

15. Geography, government, social structure, and economics are all factors that mold historical development. Which one of these areas was the major factor molding North Carolina's development during the period from 1670 to 1770? Why? How did the factor you chose mold developments in the other areas mentioned? Be sure to use specific events in your essay to support your opinion.

Sample Interpretation Essay   The following essay by Matthew Reep, a UNC Charlotte student, was written for his class in North Carolina history, in response to question 15.

> The geography of North Carolina was the most important factor in molding its history. North Carolina's geography played an important role in shaping its government, its social structure, and its economic development.
> North Carolina history began with exploration of the North Carolina coast, by early explorers such as Ralph Lane and John White. The North Carolina coast was a frequent landing point for English ships; thus, the first settlers to North Carolina arrived, and settled, there.
> Later on, Black Beard played an important role in the development of North Carolina. From his base on the North Carolina coast, Black Beard intercepted trade ships traveling between Norfolk and Charleston. Although not officially sanctioned by the North Carolina government, Black Beard had a relationship with Governor Eaton that allowed him to store his loot in the governor's barns and store houses.
> For many years to follow, the majority of North Carolina's trade and commerce were centered at the North Carolina coast. As one might imagine, this trade affected North Carolina's social structure. The rich and powerful men of North Carolina lived and held offices in the eastern part of the state. While the East continued to prosper, the western part of the state was undeveloped frontier country. Citizens of western North Carolina were seen as backward and awkward, while the eastern citizens were educated and polished.
> Of course this geographical dominance by the East led to economic dominance as well. Many eastern citizens were made wealthy by the trade and commerce that were taking place there, while the western citizens were poor in comparison. The North Carolina government was also affected by eastern geographical dominance. Nearly all early North Carolina governors came from the eastern part of the state. Likewise, most of the members of the Legislature of the Royal Colony lived in the eastern part of the state. The number of counties in the East, as compared to the west, reflected, and perpetuated, the power base in the East. The geographical, social, and economic dominance of the East led to its central political role. When England began to put pressure on its colonies, through trade embargos and so forth, the eastern part of the state felt this pressure much more keenly than the west. It is no wonder, then, that the resistance to England, in the Revolutionary War, was centered in the East.

In conclusion, the geography of North Carolina was the most important factor in its development. North Carolina's geography greatly influenced its economic development, its social structure, and its government.

Commentary   Matthew understands that the essay question calls for an interpretation. He knows that he can choose whatever factor he wishes (geographical, economic, social, or political) and make a case in support of it. He also knows that he must connect whichever factor he chooses to the other factors. In fact, the other three factors—economics, social issues, and politics—provide the context that allows him to interpret (that is, to show the meaning of) geography.

Matthew begins his essay with a one-sentence thesis that is set up for him by the essay question. He adds another sentence in which he lets the reader know that he will look at geography in terms of the other factors, thereby creating a very brief introduction for the essay. Note also that since this essay is several paragraphs long, Matthew uses a separate concluding paragraph of two sentences to sum up his argument.

PLANNING YOUR ESSAY'S STRUCTURE

After you decide what your teacher is asking for—summary, synthesis, evaluation, interpretation, or some combination of these—you should decide how to structure your essay. As we saw in Part Two, essays that spotlight the subject will employ one or more of the expository modes: process, comparison, definition, causality, analysis, and classification. You will probably find in the wording of the question itself some indication of what structuring devices are available to you.

Below we categorize some of the essay-exam questions presented earlier, along with some additional questions, according to the expository modes that provide their organization. The type of question in terms of the four processes discussed above is indicated in the second column.

Process

What are the main stages in language learning?	Summary
What are the various stages of the life cycle of a honeybee?	Summary
Describe the process by which a federal law is enacted in the United States.	Summary

Comparison

According to the writers of our textbook, what is the evidence that the language used by animals (even when humans work with animals extensively) is different in kind (not just in degree) from human language?	Summary
In what ways do Noam Chomsky and Jean Piaget seem to agree about language development in humans? What would seem to be important areas of disagreement between the two?	Synthesis

Explain the difference between phonemic and phonetic transcription.	Summary
It could be argued that no two religious leaders have had more impact on twentieth-century U.S. politics than Dr. Martin Luther King, Jr., and Dr. Billy Graham. As our readings have helped us see, Dr. King affected public policy by means of public campaigns in which he openly called for connection between faith and public policy, whereas Dr. Graham avoided direct public statements about matters of state, instead implicitly supporting the candidacy of certain politicians by means of his private associations and talks with these candidates. In your opinion, which of these clergymen will prove to have had the most significant impact on public policy in twentieth-century United States?	Evaluation

Definition

What is a linguistic universal? What are some examples of linguistic universals? Why is the concept of linguistic universal important to modern grammarians like Noam Chomsky?	Summary
What is whole language instruction? Why do the authors of our textbook oppose it?	Summary

Causality

According to the authorities we have read in this class, what were the main causes of World War I?	Summary
What was the role of the United States in Iran during the rule of the Shah? How might that role be seen as a cause for the taking of U.S. hostages in Iran in 1979?	Interpretation

Analysis

As we have seen, one of the most frequent themes in literature is the quest motif. Analyze the ways in which this motif is used in at least two of the following novels: *The Adventures of Huckleberry Finn; Moby Dick; The Great Gatsby; Ulysses; Invisible Man; Henderson, the Rain King*.	Interpretation
One of the most striking scenes in *The Great Gatsby* occurs when Nick first meets Daisy as she and Jordan Baker sit on (or seem to float above) the couch in Tom Buchanan's living room. Briefly explain the significance of this scene in relation to the novel as a whole.	Interpretation

Classification

According to the various articles we have read on the United Kingdom, France, Spain, and Germany, what are the major types of problems that modern-day Europe must contend with? Illustrate these types by discussing specific problems in individual European countries.	Synthesis
In "Revolution in Grammar," Nelson Francis offers definitions of "grammar," distinguishing between what he labels as Grammar 1,	Interpretation

Grammar 2, and Grammar 3. If you had to classify our two textbooks by means of these categories, where would you put them? Is this easy or hard? That is, does one (or do both) of them seem to belong in more than one category? Is one of the books harder to classify than the other? Why?

OVERLAPPING TERMINOLOGIES

The previous list might seem to indicate that the four processes are separable, but they actually overlap, as the following essay-exam question illustrates:

> Our readings and class discussions have made it clear that television has had an impact on nearly every area of our lives, from values of children raised on television to the choice of detergents one has in a supermarket. One area in which television has had tremendous impact is sports. Discuss the significance of television's role in making modern-day professional sports what they are.

From one perspective, this essay could be structured as a causal analysis. You could discuss the various effects that television (the cause) has had on modern-day professional sports. Viewed from another perspective, the topic could be structured using comparison. That is, you could choose to compare modern-day sports with sports in an earlier time and show the tremendous differences caused by television. Clearly, in answering this question, you would include both causal analysis and comparison. The choice of which to use as an overriding structuring device would be up to you.

Similarly, deciding in which category to place a given essay topic is complicated. The following essay-exam question was categorized as "Summary":

> What is a linguistic universal? What are some examples of linguistic universals? Why is the concept of linguistic universal important to modern grammarians like Noam Chomsky?

The first two sentences in this question ask the writer to summarize information that has been given in sources; they ask how the sources define "linguistic universal" and what examples they offer. But in answering why this concept is important, the writer moves into the realm of evaluation. So why have we identified this question as a summary? We have done so because we see it as asking the writer to summarize an evaluation made by a linguistic authority. If the writer were being asked to come up with this judgment on his own, we would call this an evaluation.

As another example, consider the following question, which was also categorized as calling for summary:

> According to the writers of our textbook, what is the evidence that the language used by animals (even when humans work with animals extensively) is different in kind (not just in degree) from human language?

In this case, it is clear that an interpretation was made by an authority on language. This authority studied evidence (i.e., characteristics of animal language and characteristics of human language) and interpreted this evidence to mean that animal language and human language are different in kind. The question, however, does not call for the student writer to interpret the material but rather to summarize the main points made in a source.

The key difference between summaries and syntheses, on the one hand, and evaluations and interpretations, on the other, is the degree to which they ask you to take an active role in interpretation and evaluation. Clearly, any information the teacher asks you to summarize or synthesize is likely to contain evaluations and interpretations; if it did not, the teacher would not deem it worth including on an examination. However, in more advanced classes, you will often be asked to be an active participant in the making of knowledge by doing your own evaluating and interpreting. That is why it is crucial for you to know the difference between these processes. If a question asks for evaluation or interpretation, but you offer only summary, you will not satisfy the requirements of the assignment.

ESSAYS THAT ASK FOR PRACTICAL APPLICATIONS

One specific type of interpretation that students often encounter in essay examinations is the practical application essay. Many teachers like these essays because they allow students to show that they see connections between what they have studied in class and everyday activities and events. We have already seen an essay that could have easily been turned into a practical application essay. Jason Wise wrote an essay in which he evaluated the effectiveness of certain advertisements in a health-care campaign. In doing so, he used the principles for creating effective ads as a framework for his evaluation. A practical application assignment might have asked him to create an advertisement and then to show why it would be effective in achieving the ends it was designed to achieve. Here are additional questions asking for practical application essays:

16. If the media shifted from using a strategy schema to a problem-policy-performance schema, do you think their metaphors would change? Why or why not? If they did, in what ways? Give specific examples in explaining your answer.
17. You're the President of the United States, and you've decided to stop all funding to the National Endowment of the Arts because of obscenity in publicly funded art. What arguments of legitimacy would you use to support your decision? Why? Which arguments would you avoid using? Why?
18. As you know, the normal pronunciation of the "s" in the plural "boys" is "z." Explain why this is the case. If a native speaker of English did not use this form, would he be more likely to leave the "s" off entirely or to pronounce the "s" as "s"? Explain your answer.

19. A successful architectural design must combine form, space, and site in such a way that the building on the site seems to be a logical outcome of that site. Choose a site and describe it in terms of the site characteristics we have been discussing in class. Then discuss some basic outlines of a building that would be appropriate for that site.
20. You're the challenger running against the incumbent in an eastern North Carolina district that includes several large hog-farming operations. The incumbent, an ardent environmentalist, has attacked you in a television ad for accepting contributions from the hog industry. The wording of the television ad suggests that the industry has bought your vote. The visuals are of filthy hog-farming operations and a dirty stream. It is true that you have accepted some sizable contributions from the groups the ad mentions. The ad is hurting you in the polls, so you have decided that you are going to respond. How will you respond to that ad? Use Kathleen H. Jamieson's discussion of counterattack in *Dirty Politics, Deception, Distraction and Democracy* (New York: Oxford UP, 1992) to explain your response.

Sample Practical Application Essay Robbie Grier, a UNC Charlotte student enrolled in the course Communication and Public Advocacy, wrote the following essay in answer to question 20.

There are three key ways of responding to attack ads:

1. Attack with a similar type ad;
2. Use a propositional ad—one that uses many words to counter the claim of an attack ad;
3. Reframe the attack by

—redefining the context or examples given;
—forewarning of manipulation;
—distancing yourself from the attacker with humor;
—citing credible sources to counter the attack;
—dissociating oneself from the attack;
—admitting one's mistake.

In this example, I might try to redefine the context in which the contribution has been made. I would show that my support for the issues surrounding hog farming existed prior to this contribution. Thus, rather than buying my vote, the contribution was an exercise of their right to support a candidate whose views tend to match theirs.

I would also use humor to diffuse the situation. If my opponent referred to unnamed sources, for example, I could use an ad depicting one of my opponent's "campaign workers" interviewing hogs for their opinions.

I might cite credible sources to show that the hog industry does not have the negative environmental impact attributed to it. In doing so, I could change the issue from my acceptance of a contribution to the hog farming industry itself, an issue on which most voters would side with me.

By means of such strategies as these, I might be able to turn an attack on me into a negative for my opponent and a positive for me.

Commentary   Robbie charts a straightforward plan for his essay at the beginning by summarizing the principles he has learned about countering attack ads. From there, he has only to show how he will implement his plan.

PLANNING SAMPLE ESSAYS

Below are several possible essay questions. For each, determine what process or processes the question calls for—summary, synthesis, evaluation, interpretation, and/or application. Then determine what expository modes you would likely use in writing this essay and which of those modes you would use to provide the essay's overall structure.

21. Pick two of the following decades and discuss what course of action you would have taken to deal with the problems faced by the colonists of North Carolina during that time. Be sure to identify the problems and use facts: (a) 1675–1684; (b) 1720–1729; (c) 1760–1769.
22. Contrast the theatrical conventions, themes, and audiences of the Restoration theater of late-seventeenth-century England with those of the bourgeois tragedy of eighteenth-century England.
23. Leadership has always been a problem for North Carolina. During the period from 1660 to 1775, what individuals provided the best leadership for the colony? Be sure to discuss their accomplishments and the obstacles they had to overcome.
24. Explain the relationship between the terms "enthymeme," "responsive chord," "nonverbal communication," and "electronic media." In what way(s) are these concepts important for political communication?
25. What are ad bites? Why have they become popular? Why is Jamieson concerned about them?
26. You've decided to run for mayor of Las Cruces, New Mexico, and you've decided to make an appeal based on myth. Which American myth would you use for your appeal? Using the general characteristics of myths, explain your choice.
27. In many works we have studied, characters experience an initiation or illumination—a recognition about themselves, a situation, or another person. Choose three pieces of literature we have studied and show how they depict this experience. What is the nature of the illumination? Does the recognition promise change for the better or is it presented as coming too late, or as ironic?
28. How has the media's notion of newsworthiness given rise to the pseudo-event? Be very specific in your explanation. Use an example to illustrate your answer.

29. Using as your examples a play by Shaw, a story by Lawrence or Mansfield, and a story from Joyce's *Dubliners,* discuss how these writers represent various social classes. What conflicts and problems do their characters experience? Who has power? Who is powerless and why?
30. North Carolina's early history has been dictated by series of conflicts and their resolutions. Culpeper's Rebellion, the North Carolina Regulator movement, and the American Revolution were major conflicts influencing North Carolina's development. Compare the causes of these events, show their similarities and differences, and indicate how the results aided or hindered North Carolina's unity.
31. Hugh Lefler writes, "Geographical factors contributed to economic differences in agriculture, industry, and trade in the various regions. Economic differences created social distinctions. Racial and social factors were involved in religious rivalries. And all of these factors contributed to political controversies." From your knowledge of North Carolina history, comment on the validity of the above quotation. Be sure to describe the political controversies and relate the statement to them. Which factor had the greatest impact on political controversies? Why? Be sure to use facts.

WRITING STRATEGY

Planning Essay-Exam Answers

Ask yourself these questions as you plan an essay to answer an examination item:

1. Is this primarily a summary, synthesis, evaluation, interpretation, or application essay?
2. If it is a summary or synthesis essay, are evaluative or interpretive issues being summarized or synthesized? If so, what are they?
3. If it is an evaluation essay, are you free to choose your own criteria for evaluation? If so what criteria will you use? If criteria are assumed, what are they?
4. What expository mode provides the overriding structure for your essay?

PART V

Preparing for Publication

As you can see, we have elected to call this part "Preparing for Publication" rather than giving it the traditional title, "Handbook." We do so, in part, to call attention to our belief that the issues usually included in a handbook need not concern you in many parts of the writing process. In fact, your ability to use writing to generate and explore ideas may well be hindered if you attend to issues of editing and usage too early in the process. Our title here reflects our belief that these matters should concern you only as you think about publishing your writing.

Of course, we are using the word "publication" rather loosely. With the exception of journals or dialogue notebooks, which you may keep private, your writing is intended for other people, and whenever you present your writing to others, you're publishing. Before you do so, your writing will require both local revision and editing.

In Chapter 3, we differentiated between global issues, such as a paper's overall content and organization, and local issues, such as the structure of individual sentences and the choice of specific words. We will deal with these local matters in this part. But before doing so, we need to offer a brief discussion of English grammar, because grammar provides us with the terminology we'll use to talk about local revision and editing. For example, in discussing the use of the passive voice, we'll refer to the concepts of *subject* and *object* and *noun* and *verb*. In talking about how to use commas, we'll refer to such grammatical terms as *phrases*, *clauses*, and *modification*. Obviously, our discussion of grammar will be brief, and you may well want to consult a more complete grammar text. However, our brief discussion will allow you to start learning about these important matters.

If local revisions have to do with matters of sentence structure and word choice, what exactly do we mean by "editing"? We are using this word to refer to all of the changes a writer makes in a text to suit it to its intended audience. When editing, a writer checks such things as spelling, verb tenses and subject/verb agreement, punctuation, and manuscript mechanics (ellipses, brackets, parentheses, paragraph indentation, and abbreviations) to be sure that the appropriate rules and conventions have been followed.

Note that we have avoided the word "correct." We do so because it tends to give the impression that there is a logic for editing that is separable from the expectations of readers. No such logic exists. To see what we mean, consider a mathematical example. It is correct to say $2 + 2 = 4$. Likewise, it is incorrect to say $2 + 2 = 5$. Why? Because the underlying logic of the mathematical system dictates one answer and not the other. Those reading the equation $2 + 2 = 4$ are fully expecting the answer 4, but their expectation is not what makes 4 the correct, or right, answer. It is right because it is consistent with the logic of the system on which the equation is built.

Such is not the case in editing. If we say that the sentence "I don't have no marbles" is incorrect, we do so because we know that it fails to meet the usage expectations of those we are writing for. There is nothing in the underlying logic of language that makes this double negative incorrect. In fact, many languages use double negatives for emphasis. And even English speakers have no trouble understanding what "I don't have no marbles" means. No one really believes that it means "I have some marbles." As another example, consider the sentence "They knowed he had failed the test." Most readers will see "knowed" as a breach of Standard English, preferring the standard past-tense verb, "knew." However, this nonstandard verb works within the system of language to convey the writer's meaning just as exactly as the standard verb would.

Thus, we talk about following appropriate rules and conventions when editing. In doing so, we maintain the rhetorical focus used throughout this textbook. Writers use certain editing conventions and follow certain rules, not because these are "correct" in the sense that mathematical answers are correct, but because they meet the expectations of readers and, thus, help writers achieve their purposes in writing. To do otherwise would draw attention to something other than the message and undermine writers' credibility with those on whom they have rhetorical designs.

In most writing situations, readers will expect writers to follow the conventions of Edited American English (EAE). These are the conventions that are set forth in this part. Writing and speaking that does not follow these conventions are usually referred to as nonstandard. It is not "wrong" or "inferior" in any meaningful sense of these words. It is simply not what is expected.

Basic Grammar

PARTS OF SPEECH

Semantic Categories

The first five parts of speech—nouns, pronouns, verbs, adjectives, and adverbs—are often referred to as *semantic parts of speech,* or as *form class words.* They differ from the other traditional parts of speech in that their meanings represent things and concepts outside the sentences in which they appear. This distinction will probably be clearer after you have examined the other parts of speech, the *function words.*

Nouns

Nouns are words that name something—a person, a place, a thing, a state of being, an abstract idea, or a quality. In the following sentence, all the nouns are italicized.

The *scholar* sat on the *bench* thinking about *truth* and *beauty.*

Depending on its function in a sentence, a noun may be said to be in one of three cases: *subjective, objective,* or *possessive.* (For more information on case and sentence functions, see pages 675–680.) Each of the italicized nouns in the following sentences is in the subjective case:

Frank wants to enter the competition next year.
It was the *goal* of the team to win a trophy.

Each of the italicized nouns in these sentences is in the objective case:

That girl likes the *boy* with the red *hair.*
That boy gave the *girl* a furtive *glance.*

Each of the italicized nouns in the next sentences is in the possessive case:

The *boy's* attitude toward authority caused him much difficulty.
It wasn't clear how much attendance would count in the new *teacher's* grading policy.

Note that nouns in English change their form in the possessive case.

Pronouns

Pronouns are words that stand for, or take the place of, nouns. The noun to which a pronoun refers and from which the pronoun takes its specific meaning is called the pronoun's *antecedent.* The phrase *pronoun reference* is used by grammarians to describe the relationship between a pronoun and its antecedent.

Following is a summary of the various forms of English pronouns.

Personal pronouns

	Singular			Plural		
	Subjective	Objective	Possessive	Subjective	Objective	Possessive
First person	I	me	my, mine	we	us	our, ours
Second person	you	you	your, yours	you	you	your, yours
Third person	he	him	his	they	them	their, theirs
	she	her	her, hers			
	it	it	its			

Relative pronouns

Subjective	Objective	Possessive
who	whom	whose
that	that	
which	which	whose

Interrogative pronouns

Subjective	Objective	Possessive
who	whom	whose
which	which	whose
what	what	

Demonstrative pronouns

this   that   these   those

Indefinite pronouns

all	each	most	other
another	either	neither	several
any	everybody	nobody	some

anybody	everyone	none	somebody
anyone	everything	no one	someone
anything	few	nothing	something
both	many	one	such

Reflexive (intensive) pronouns

	Singular	**Plural**
First person	myself	ourselves
Second person	yourself	yourselves
Third person	himself	themselves
	herself	
	itself	
	oneself	

Reciprocal pronouns

each other   one another

Note that the first three types of pronouns—personal, relative, and interrogative—have the same cases nouns do—subjective, objective, and possessive. Unlike nouns, however, most pronouns exhibit different forms that depend on their case.

Verbs

Verbs have often been defined as action words. In a sentence such as "The child ran," the verb "ran" describes the child's action. Not all verbs, however, are action words; many express a state of being, a process, or a condition. One way of categorizing verbs is to divide them into two types: transitive and intransitive. *Transitive verbs* usually take a direct object, but *intransitive verbs* do not. Depending on the context, some verbs can be either transitive or intransitive.

	Verb	*Direct object*
Transitive	Fred paid	the bill.

	Verb	*Modifier*
Intransitive	Fred paid	for his mistakes.

Principal Parts of Verbs   There are four principal parts to all verbs: *present infinitive, past, present participle,* and *past participle.* Regular verbs simply add *ed* to the present infinitive to form the past and the past participle. They add *ing* to the present infinitive to form the present participle. Here are the four parts of some regular verbs:

Present Infinitive	Past	Present Participle	Past Participle
to talk	talked	talking	talked
to live	lived	living	lived
to love	loved	loving	loved
to walk	walked	walking	walked

Many verbs in English, however, are not regular. The principal parts of these verbs must be memorized. The following list presents some of the more frequently used irregular verbs:

Present Infinitive	Past	Present Participle	Past Participle
to be	was	being	been
to go	went	going	gone
to do	did	doing	done
to lie	lay	lying	lain
to lay	laid	laying	laid
to sit	sat	sitting	sat
to set	set	setting	set
to cut	cut	cutting	cut
to give	gave	giving	given
to take	took	taking	taken
to speak	spoke	speaking	spoken
to begin	began	beginning	begun
to drink	drank	drinking	drunk
to throw	threw	throwing	thrown

Verb Tenses There are six tenses in English: *present, past, future, present perfect, past perfect,* and *future perfect*. Each of these tenses has a *simple* and a *progressive form*. In addition, transitive verbs have both *active* and *passive forms*. The following conjugations are for a very irregular verb, an intransitive regular verb, and a transitive irregular verb. For progressives and passives, we present only first-person singular forms.

Here is the conjugation of "to be," which is very irregular:

Present

I am, we are
I am being *(progressive)*
you are, you are
he/she/it is, they are

Past

I was, we were
I was being *(progressive)*
you were, you were
he/she/it was, they were

Future

I will be, we will be
I will be being *(progressive)*
you will be, you will be
he/she/it will be, they will be

Past Perfect

I had been, we had been
I had been being *(progressive)*
you had been, you had been
he/she/it had been, they had been

Present Perfect

I have been, we have been
I have been being *(progressive)*
you have been, you have been
he/she/it has been, they have been

Future Perfect

I will have been, we will have been
I will have been being *(progressive)*
you will have been, you will have been
he/she/it will have been, they will have been

The conjugation of "to talk" is regular.

Present

I talk, we talk
I am talking *(progressive)*
you talk, you talk
he/she/it talks, they talk

Future

I will talk, we will talk
I will be talking *(progressive)*
you will talk, you will talk
he/she/it will talk, they will talk

Past Perfect

I had talked, we had talked
I had been talking *(progressive)*
you had talked, you had talked
he/she/it had talked, they had talked

Past

I talked, we talked
I was talking *(progressive)*
you talked, you talked
he/she/it talked, they talked

Present Perfect

I have talked, we have talked
I have been talking *(progressive)*
you have talked, you have talked
he/she/it has talked, they have talked

Future Perfect

I will have talked, we will have talked
I will have been talking *(progressive)*
you will have talked, you will have talked
he/she/it will have talked, they will have talked

The verb "to begin" has an irregular conjugation.

Present

I begin, we begin
I am beginning *(progressive)*
you begin, you begin
he/she/it begins, they begin
it is begun *(passive)*

Past

I began, we began
I was beginning *(progressive)*
you began, you began
he/she/it began, they began
it was begun *(passive)*

Future

I will begin, we will begin
I will be beginning (*progressive*)
you will begin, you will begin
he/she/it will begin, they will begin
it will be begun (*passive*)

Present Perfect

I have begun, we have begun
I have been beginning (*progressive*)
you have begun, you have begun
he/she/it has begun, they have begun
it has been begun (*passive*)

Past Perfect

I had begun, we had begun
I had been beginning (*progressive*)
you had begun, you had begun
he/she/it had begun, they had begun
it had been begun (*passive*)

Future Perfect

I will have begun, we will have begun
I will have been beginning (*progressive*)
you will have begun, you will have begun
he/she/it will have begun, they will have begun
it will have been begun (*passive*)

Adjectives

Adjectives modify nouns and pronouns. In the following sentence, the adjectives are italicized:

The *old, green* car sat on the *dusty* road.

In many cases, demonstrative, indefinite, and interrogative pronouns may perform the modifying functions of adjectives: *that* coat, *all* coats, *which* coat. In general, the form of an adjective is fixed regardless of how the adjective is used in a sentence. However, adjectives do take different forms when used in comparative structures.

Positive	Comparative	Superlative
quick	quicker	quickest
beautiful	more beautiful	most beautiful

Adverbs

Adverbs modify verbs, adjectives, and other adverbs. The adverbs in the following sentences are italicized:

They walked *slowly* down the street.
The sunset is *perfectly* beautiful *tonight*.
The team played *particularly* well in its last game.

Adverbs are most commonly used to express time, place, manner, negation, affirmation, or degree. Many adverbs end in *ly*; these are usually formed by adding *ly* to adjectives: clear/clearly, lawful/lawfully, quick/quickly. However, some adverbs, such as "fast," "very," and "slow," do not end in *ly*. As "fast" and "slow" indicate, some adjective and adverb forms are identical. As adverbs, these form their comparative and superlative degrees by adding *er* and *est:* fast, faster, fastest. Other adverbs use "more" and "most" to show degree: more slowly, most slowly.

Function Categories

The next two parts of speech, prepositions and conjunctions, are often referred to as *function words,* because their primary duty is to show relationships between the semantic parts of speech. Whatever we call these two types of words, it is relatively easy to see the difference. For example, consider the following sentence:

> The company painted the walls and the ceiling with blue paint.

Such words as "painted," "walls," and "blue" refer to actions, things and qualities in the real world. But what do words such as "and" and "with" do? As we'll see, they tell us something about how the semantic parts of speech are connected to each other.

Prepositions

Prepositions are words that show the relationship between a noun or pronoun (the object of the preposition) and some other word in the sentence. Among the most common prepositions are these:

in	down	through	until
out	under	after	among
on	around	above	below
up	beneath	between	behind

In the following sentences, the prepositions are italicized and the nouns they introduce (and connect to other elements in the sentence) are underlined.

> The tall man was *in* the house he had just bought.
> They all wanted to throw the bomb *out* the window.
> The dog that had bitten the boy ran *around* the corner.
> *Among* the candidates was a man *of* unusual ability.

Conjunctions

Conjunctions, like prepositions, join elements of a sentence—words, phrases, or clauses—to each other and show relationships in the sentence. Unlike prepositions, conjunctions do not take objects. There are two kinds of conjunctions: *coordinating conjunctions* are used to join equal grammatical elements and *subordinating conjunctions* are used to join a subordinate or dependent grammatical part of a sentence to a main clause. The coordinating conjunctions include

and	but	or	nor	for	yet	so

Correlative conjunctions, which can be used to join words, phrases, or clauses, are also coordinating:

both/and   neither/nor   either/or   not/but   not only/but also

Among the most common subordinating conjunctions, which appear at the beginning of the dependent phrase or clause they introduce, are

that	whether	if	when	though	although
while	whereas	because	since	unless	in order that
after					

Interjections

Interjections are like the semantic parts of speech in that they represent meanings outside the sentence. However, they have no forms, as the semantic parts of speech do, since they are essentially separate from the sentence structures around them. Interjections are words that exist only to express strong feeling. Even though they have no syntactical connection with other parts of the sentences in which they appear, they are sometimes punctuated as part of a sentence. Most often, however, they stand alone, punctuated by an exclamation point.

Ouch, I cut my finger!
Ouch! That limb flew in my face!

Some words, such as "ouch," "whew," and "oh," exist only as interjections. But many words that are commonly used as other parts of speech can also be used as interjections; these include "great," "well," "goodness," and "my."

Great! We'll have to do it ourselves.
My! You have a lovely home.

PHRASES AND MODIFICATION

It is difficult to talk about either of these concepts—*phrases* and *modification*—without doing so in terms of the other. Consider the following pairings:

1. tree/green tree
2. walk/walk slowly
3. tired/very tired
4. quickly/very quickly

The first word in each pair is one of the semantic parts of speech: noun ("tree"), verb ("walk"), adjective ("tired"), or adverb ("quickly"). The second part of each pair is a phrase formed by adding to the first word another word that modifies (or tells us something about) the first word. In the first pair, the adjective "green" adds color to the tree; in the second pair, the adverb "slowly" gives us insight into the pace of the walk; in the third pair, the adverb "very" informs us of the degree of tiredness; and, finally, in the last pair, the adverb "very" makes "quickly" even quicker.

It is useful to think of the second part in each pair as a phrase because the two items have formed a unit; that is, they no longer act separately. To see what we mean, consider the following examples (the asterisk before the last sentence in each set indicates that it is *not* one we would write or speak):

1. They cut down the green tree.
   The green tree was cut down by them.
   *The tree was cut down green by them.
2. The little boy walked slowly by his mother.
   The little boy smiled and walked slowly by his mother.
   *The little boy walked and smiled slowly by his mother.
3. The players, very tired, filed into the locker room.
   Very tired, the players filed into the locker room.
   *Very, the tired players filed into the locker room.
4. The young woman very quickly let the young man know that she liked him.
   Very quickly, the young woman let the young man know that she liked him.
   *Quickly, the young woman very let the young man know that she liked him.

We build sentences in modules, or parts. For instance, the sentence "Small boys laugh loudly" is composed of four parts. If we want to break the sentence into its parts, we can do so, but the first break will not produce four parts. We pull on the sentence (metaphorically, that is), and it breaks into two parts: "Small boys" and "laugh loudly." If we then pull on each of these parts, we can break each one into two parts. We can see how this works when we try to pry these parts (or modules) apart within a sentence. As the second sentence in each set above indicates, we can move some of the parts of the sentence around. As the third sentence in each set illustrates, however, there are some very real limitations on what can be separated from what. Each of the phrases must be moved as a whole. We cannot break a phrase apart once it has been formed.

Modifiers

We are now ready to look at the ways in which phrases function as modifiers. Let's begin with a simple definition. A *phrase* is a group of words (i.e., more than one word) that acts as a unit. How many different types of phrases are there? This is a complicated question because its answer depends on our perspective. We can define a phrase according to what its focus is (the part of speech of its main element) or what it does (its role as a modifier). This matter becomes even more complicated when we realize that the various types of modification are defined in terms of the five semantic parts of speech: nouns, pronouns, verbs, adjectives, and adverbs. So we must begin there. There are two basic types of modifiers: adjectival and adverbial.

Adjectival modifiers are elements that provide more information about a noun or a pronoun. The italicized words in this sentence are adjectival modifiers:

The *cracked* plate looked new after the *expert* craftsman had worked *his* magic.

Adverbial modifiers are elements that provide more information about verbs, adjectives, or adverbs. The italicized words in the following sentences are adverbial modifiers that add information about the verb:

> Leonora *slowly* and *carefully* tested the platform to be sure it was steady.
> *Hesitantly,* the rest of the party followed Leonora onto the platform.

The italicized words in the next sentence are adverbial modifiers that add information about adjectives:

> The boy was *quite* happy to see his dad, who arrived in a *pale* blue sedan.

The italicized word in this sentence is an adverbial modifier that adds information about an adverb:

> The boy spoke *rather* quickly and then left the room.

Types of Phrases

The second perspective from which to view phrases identifies them according to the part of speech that acts as the focus of the phrase. This perspective yields five types of phrases: noun phrases, verb phrases, adjective phrases, adverb phrases and prepositional phrases.

Noun Phrases

The focus for each of the italicized phrases below is a noun; thus, these are *noun phrases.*

> *The tall, handsome man* looked tired.
> They praised *the brave young boy* effusively.

Verb Phrases

The focus for the italicized phrases in the sentences below is a verb; thus, these are *verb phrases.*

> She *sang beautifully.*
> He *slept quietly.*

Adjective Phrases

In the following sentences, the focus of each italicized phrase is an adjective. Thus, these are *adjective phrases.*

> He looked *extremely tired.*
> He drove a *very old* car.

Adverb Phrases
In the following sentences, the focus of each italicized phrase is an adverb.

> He asked *very quietly* if he could be excused.
> She worked her way to the front of the line *very deliberately*.

Prepositional Phrases
Since a preposition is a function word, a prepositional phrase works differently than the other types of phrases. Rather than being modified by other words, the preposition introduces a noun or a noun phrase. The italicized phrases in these sentences are all prepositional phrases:

> Theo played ball *with the three boys*.
> He didn't know what to do *about his grades*.
> Maria left home *without her overcoat*.

SENTENCE FUNCTIONS
There are two ways to analyze the parts of a sentence. The first is by determining the various parts of speech of its individual words. The second is by analyzing the various functions that one part of speech, the noun, can perform in a simple sentence. (For definitions of simple, complex, and compound sentences, see pages 680–681.)

Subjects
Nouns are commonly found as subjects of simple sentences, as indicated by the italicized words here:

> The *boys* like all their presents.
> *Ice cream* is their favorite dessert.
> Afterward, the *players* were tired but happy.

Predicate Nominatives
Transitive verbs require some form of completion. Transitive linking verbs are often completed by a *predicate nominative*, a noun that renames the subject of the sentence. Each of the italicized words in these sentences is a predicate nominative:

> Colette is the *person* with the most vision for the project.
> The players are the *ones* who must decide to win the game.
> Leaving town was an *option* they had not considered.

Of course, not all completers of transitive verbs are nouns. Here is an example in which a verb is completed with a *predicate adjective:*

Franco is exceptionally *talented.*

Direct Objects

Active transitive verbs are completed by nouns acting as *direct objects.* Each of the italicized nouns in the following sentences functions as the direct object of its verb:

Elena hit the *ball.*
The boy called the *girl.*
They didn't want that *answer.*

How do we know that these italicized nouns are direct objects? You may have been told that a direct object answers the question "What?" Using this test, we readily see that each of the preceding nouns is a direct object. However, the following italicized nouns would also be labeled as direct objects using this method of identification:

Moises is the *captain* of the team.
The girls were *winners* in their division.
Her actions constituted a *threat* to his masculinity.
The package weighs ten *pounds.*

But we know that the italicized nouns in the first two sentences ("captain" and "winners") are predicate nominatives, since they rename the subject. It may not be quite as obvious, but the italicized noun in the third sentence ("threat") is also a predicate nominative, renaming the subject ("actions"). But what about "pounds" in the last sentence? This noun also seems to answer the question "What?": What does the package weigh? Ten pounds. And "pounds" certainly doesn't rename "package"; so it is not a predicate nominative. Grammarians disagree as to what to call "pounds" in this sentence, but they agree that it is different in crucial ways from direct objects. Then what is a direct object? It is a noun that completes the verb and that can be moved to the subject slot in the passive version of the sentence. This test tells us which of our earlier sentences have a direct object and which do not. (The asterisks identify sentences that are unacceptable to native speakers of English.)

Elena hit the *ball.*
The ball was hit by Elena.

The boy called the *girl.*
The girl was called by the boy.

They didn't want that *answer*.
That answer was not wanted by them.

Moises is the *captain* of the team.
*The captain of the team is been by Moises.

The girls were *winners* in their division.
*The winners in their division were been by the girls.

Her actions constituted a *threat* to his masculinity.
*A threat to his masculinity was constituted by her actions.

The package weighs ten pounds.
*Ten pounds are weighed by the package.

Indirect Objects

Certain transitive verbs, such as "give," "make," "leave," and "take," can be completed by both a direct object and an indirect object. When both objects are present, the verbs indicate motion from the direct object to the indirect object. In some cases, the motion is literal. For example, in the following sentence, there is physical movement of the direct object (the apple) to the indirect object (the teacher):

The boy gave the teacher an apple.

In other sentences, such as the following, the movement is not literal:

The boy gave the car a whirl.

However, our understanding that there is some metaphorical movement is made clear when the two objects are reversed. Whenever the indirect object comes after the direct object, it is preceded by "to." Thus, the two sentences above would be transformed to these:

The boy gave an apple to the teacher.
The boy gave a whirl to the car.

The indirect object may appear before or after the direct object. Note, however, that although it is possible to have a direct object without an indirect object, it is not possible to have an indirect object without a direct object. This principle makes it possible to determine which of two nouns is the direct object and which is the indirect object. For example, consider the following sentence:

The man made the homeowner an offer.

We are not able to determine which of the nouns functioning as objects is the direct object by making the sentence passive, since both of the objects can become subjects of passive versions of the sentence.

> The homeowner was made an offer by the man.
> An offer was made the homeowner by the man.

However, only one of these objects—the direct object—can complete the sentence by itself.

> The man made an offer.
> *The man made the homeowner.

Secondary Objects

Another set of transitive verbs can be completed by two objects. Such verbs as "call," "name," "appoint," and "christen" show a dynamic relationship between a direct object and a secondary object—the direct object becomes, or comes to be seen as, the secondary object. Thus, we have such sentences as the following, in which the italicized words are secondary objects:

> Julia called the members of the team *winners*.
> The mayor appointed Tom as *chief of police*.
> The clever woman named her daughter *executor* of her will.

Note the similarity between the predicate nominative, "captain," in the sentence "Hans became the *captain*" and the secondary object in the sentence "The team named Hans its *captain*." In both cases, "captain" renames "Hans." In the first case, "Hans" is the subject of the sentence; thus, the word renaming "Hans" is in the nominative case. In the second, since "Hans" is the direct object, the word renaming him is a secondary object.

Very similar in structure to the secondary object is the *objective complement*. In this structure, a direct object is followed by a describing adjective.

> The men painted the barn *red*.

Again, note the similarity between this objective complement and the predicate adjective in the sentence "The barn was *red*."

Objects of Prepositions

There is one final type of object in simple sentences. Each of the italicized words in these examples is the object of a preposition:

> Petra gave the letter to the *man*.
> The clerk was waiting inside the *house*.
> Against the *door* was a desk that seemed to be filled with *lead*.

Substantives

We have been careful thus far to limit our examples in the various functional slots of a sentence to nouns. But these slots can be filled in many ways. For example, three of the slots can be filled by pronouns.

Pronoun as subject	*They* called for a meeting of the stockholders.
Pronoun as direct object	The ball hit *him* in the knee.
Pronoun as indirect object	They gave *him* a season pass.

In such sentences, we say that the pronoun is serving in the slot that would normally be occupied by a noun. A word, phrase, or clause that can take the place of a noun is called a *substantive*. The italicized words and phrases in the following sentences are all substantives:

They liked apples.
They liked *living near the city*.
He was right.
Whatever he says is usually right.
They said *that they liked apples*.
To ease their pain was his chief goal.

Verbals

Several of the italicized words and phrases in the examples just given are *verbals*. A *verbal* is a nonfinite form (i.e., a form without tense) of a verb. There are three types of verbals: infinitives, gerunds, and participles.

Infinitives   The *infinitive form* of a verb appears with "to," often referred to as the *sign* of the infinitive. Infinitive phrases can serve as subjects, direct objects, and modifiers. Each infinitive phrase is italicized in these sentences:

Subject	*To eat ice cream* was his idea of fun.
Direct object	Tanya wanted *to eat ice cream*.
Modifier	*To get a better look,* they stood on tiptoe.

Note: The infinitive in the last example functions as an adverbial modifier of the verb and thus is not an example of a substantive.

Gerunds   *Gerunds* are formed with the present participle of the verb. Gerunds or gerund phrases can serve as subjects, direct objects, and objects of prepositions. The following sentences illustrate these functions with italicized gerund phrases:

Subject	*Winning the game* was his chief goal.
Direct object	They discussed *leaving on Friday.*
Object of preposition	He was eager to know their thoughts on *beginning a new business.*

Participles   Like gerunds, participles are formed by using the present participle form of the verb. Participles may also be formed with the past participle form of the verb. Unlike gerunds, however, participles may not serve as substantives. Rather, they function as adjectival modifiers, that is, they modify nouns or substantives. Each of the italicized phrases is a participial phrase.

Falling short of the target, the arrow nearly hit a bystander.
He stopped suddenly, *looking around the crowd intently.*
The young boy showed great promise, *working long hours on his studies.*

Clauses as Substantives

A *clause* is a group of words with a subject and a predicate. A simple sentence may contain only one clause, as does the sentence below. (The next section provides more information on types of sentences.)

Sean hit the ball.

A complex sentence may include a clause as subject, direct object, indirect object, object of an infinitive or gerund, or object of a preposition.

Subject	*That he left early* surprised no one.
Direct object	Andreas said *that he would leave early.*
Indirect object	Give *whoever wants it the most* the ticket.
Object of infinitive	He wanted to choose *what he would read.*
Object of gerund	He liked believing *that he would win the election.*
Object of preposition	Give the ticket to *whoever wants it the most.*

SENTENCE TYPES

One of the most prevalent means of classifying sentences is on the basis of the number and kinds of clauses they contain. In this system, there are four basic types of sentences: simple, compound, complex, and compound-complex.

Simple Sentences

A *simple sentence* contains only one clause. There is no one-to-one correlation between a sentence's type and its length. Each of the following is a simple sentence:

He likes ice cream.

Arriving on Sunday and feeling very rested, the team needed little effort to defeat an obviously inferior team from a school in an adjacent state.

To launch the project, we need a small amount of cash up front.

Complex Sentences

A complex sentence contains one independent clause and one or more dependent clauses. In the following examples, independent clauses are boldfaced, and dependent clauses are italicized:

Because I hate surprises, **I generally try to keep my birthday a secret.**

The man *who found that problem in the system* **received a sizable raise.**

Please take a seat in the waiting room, *if you want to see the doctor.*

Compound Sentences

A *compound sentence* contains at least two independent clauses. In these examples, independent clauses are in boldface type:

They examined the property carefully, and then **they asked for more time to make their decision.**

Upon arriving home, **Jules put the car in the garage,** and **Maurica went around to the back of the house to look for the key.**

The leaves began to fall in early October, and **he sat at the window and watched them collect in his yard.**

Compound-Complex Sentences

A *compound-complex sentence* contains at least two independent clauses and at least one dependent clause. In the following sentences, independent clauses are boldfaced and dependent clauses are italicized:

If you will give me a few days, **I can analyze your problem,** and *if it needs it,* **I'll overhaul your car's engine.**

They finally settled on a price *that Nguyen could live with;* then **they began negotiations as to** *when the deal could be made final.*

The old house stood majestically across the street from the window of her office, and **she would begin each day by taking a long, admiring look at a structure** *that spoke volumes about a simpler time.*

Punctuation, Spelling, and Manuscript Mechanics

The mechanics of writing involve grammatical correctness and the actual appearance of the manuscript. Because mechanics are more readily codified than are other aspects of writing, we outline in this section how you should use punctuation, how you may check your spelling, and how you may prepare a final-draft manuscript to hand in to your instructor.

END PUNCTUATION

The Period (.)

1. The period is used at the end of a statement (declarative sentence) and at the end of a command (imperative sentence).

    Declarative   Olaf wrote to tell me of his new job.
    Declarative   School will be out in three weeks.
    Imperative   Shut the window.

2. A period is also used within or after abbreviations.

Titles	Months	Names	States	Degrees
Dr.	Feb.	R. M. Williams	N.M.	Ph.D.
Mr.	Dec.	D. Charles Smith		M.A.
Ms.		Janis F. Lunstand		M.D.
Rev.				

3. A period is used in numbers, as a decimal point.

    $5.98 $1,352.54

The Question Mark (?)

1. The question mark is used to mark the end of a direct question (interrogative sentence).

    Where are you going?

    Do you know what your goals are?

2. The question mark is also used to punctuate a question that is quoted directly.

"Which way do I turn?" she asked.

If a quoted question comes at the end of a sentence, the question mark appears within the quotation mark, and no other end punctuation is necessary.

Looking puzzled, she asked, "What am I supposed to do with all these forms?"

If quoted material appears in a question but is not itself a question, the question mark appears outside the quotation marks.

Did Bert say, "Today we should go to New York"?

The Exclamation Mark (!)

1. The exclamation mark, or point, is used to end an emphatic (exclamatory) sentence.

    I refuse to listen to this garbage!
    The house is on fire!
    Run for your life!

2. An exclamation mark is sometimes used to set an interjection off from the rest of a sentence.

    Ouch! Something bit me!
    Help! I don't know what to do!

Exercise 1

Place periods, question marks, and exclamation marks where they belong in the following sentences.

1. The boy shouted, "Help" as he ran away from the dog
2. "Why do I always let you get me into such messes" were his first words to his brother when he escaped the dog
3. "Me" exclaimed his brother "Whose idea was it to come here in the first place"
4. When told that the man should be addressed as Dr, the woman asked: "Is he an MD or a PhD"
5. The clerk rang up the groceries and turned to the two men: "Which one of you is paying the $9926 bill" she asked Then she added: "That's a lot of money Almost a hundred dollars for one small shopping cart full of groceries"

PUNCTUATION WITHIN SENTENCES

The Comma (,)

The comma is the most versatile and commonly used mark of punctuation within the sentence. It is often the most confusing as well. In writing, commas usually correspond with a brief pause; in speech, they correspond with some change in voice inflection. However, the ear is not always a reliable guide to the conventions of comma placement. The comma makes the structure of a sentence clear by separating elements that might otherwise be confusing to readers. The following rules and examples demonstrate how commas are used to clarify sentence elements.

1. **Commas are used to separate the parts of a series, whether the series consists of words, phrases, or clauses.**

   Campers shall need pillows, linens, towels, rain gear, hiking boots, playclothes, and a small amount of spending money.
   When the orchestra begins the overture, when the curtain rises, and when the soprano steps slightly forward for a major aria—these are times when the opera has a special kind of excitement.

2. **A comma is used to set off a long introductory phrase from the rest of the sentence.**

   Wearily carrying his knapsack in his hands rather than on his aching back, he climbed the last section of the mountain.
   In the house on the hill, I saw people moving slowly, as if in a dream.

3. **A comma is used after an introductory *yes* or *no*.**

   Yes, I will go to the hospital with you.

4. **A comma is used to separate an introductory adverbial clause from an independent clause.**

   As soon as I finish my paper, I'll join you for dinner.
   If you have any questions, please call me before noon tomorrow.

   If the main clause precedes the adverbial clause, no comma is necessary.

   Please call me before noon tomorrow if you have any questions.

5. **A comma is used before a coordinating conjunction that joins two independent clauses.**

   The moving van led the way, and we followed in the car.
   I'll join you in Florida as soon as I can, but I have a week's worth of work to do first.

6. Commas are used to set off a nonrestrictive adjective clause. Nonrestrictive clauses give additional but unnecessary information and must be set off by commas. A *nonrestrictive clause* is one that could be left out of the sentence without substantially altering its meaning.

> His father, who ran a grocery store for thirty years, retired this week.
> Joe's remark, which was not meant to be unkind, offended Jan.

7. Commas are used to set off an appositive.

> Gerald, her husband, works for the company that designed the new engine.
> They decided on a Japanese car, the only one that gets more gas mileage than their present car.

Most appositives interrupt a clause and give additional information that is not necessary for the sentence to make sense. For example, consider the following:

> Her daughter, Dixie, said she was coming for the weekend.

In this case, the writer (and presumably the reader as well) knows that Dixie is an only daughter, so her name is not really needed; the writer could leave the name out of the sentence with no loss of clarity, which is why the name is set off by commas. However, some appositives give information that is necessary to the meaning of the sentence. Suppose, for example, that Dixie is one of several daughters. In such a situation, the appositive ("Dixie") provides information necessary for the identification of the noun ("daughter")—otherwise the reader wouldn't know which daughter was being referred to. Thus, in this case the appositive is not set off with commas.

> Her daughter Dixie said she was coming for the weekend.

8. Commas are used with transitional connectives (conjunctive adverbs such as *however, therefore,* and *moreover*) when they do not help to join two independent clauses.

> I disagree strongly. I plan, moreover, to speak against your proposal in the meeting. However, I wanted to tell you of my objection personally.

9. Commas are used to set off contrasting or repeated elements in a sentence.

> Many students are interested only in a degree, not in an education.
> Hurry, hurry, hurry. That's all I ever hear.

10. Commas are used to separate direct quotations from phrases that join them to the rest of the sentence.

> After a pause, he said, "I'll join you in a minute."
> "Not that complaint again," she protested.

Note that when the quotation comes first, the comma appears inside the quotation marks.

11. **Commas are used to set off interrupting constructions, such as *I believe* and *you say*.**

    Spring, I believe, has finally come to stay.
    The modern audience, according to Flannery O'Connor, presents special problems for the religious writer.

12. **Commas are used to separate coordinate adjectives that separately modify a following noun.**

    On a dark, cold, gray day, the rescue workers began their search for the missing child.

13. **Commas are used before and after nouns of direct address.**

    There is one way to make this work, Charlotte, but it will require careful planning on your part.

There are a number of other uses for the comma as well.

14. **Commas are used to separate the day from the year in dates:**

    The examination will be given on April 8, 2001.

15. **Commas are used to separate parts of addresses and place names.**

    She lives at 413 South Harper Street, Lauens, South Carolina.
    Steve has a job in Dubuque, Iowa.

16. **A comma is used after the salutation in an informal letter.**

    Dear Mary,

17. **A comma is used to separate sets of three digits in numbers with five or more digits.**

    55,000
    150,000
    275,583,439

The comma is optional with four-digit numbers.

Exercise 2

Insert any commas needed in the following sentences.

1. Neil likes hiking and snow skiing but his favorite sport according to his mother is tennis.

2. If you are going to succeed in business you must focus on what your customers want and need not on what you think they should want.
3. Miska who has to be one of the most easygoing people I know gets rather excited. When she makes up her mind to take action however she is quick to follow through on her intentions.
4. Watching an exciting football game on a cold winter afternoon playing pool into the night matching wits with friends in a game of Trivial Pursuit—these are some of the simple pleasures that I enjoy.
5. Yes she did say she would visit us during the holidays. However I suspect she has been busier than even she expected to be.
6. Just as Bernard was about to speak Delia interjected "I don't think I would put my two cents worth in if I were you Bernard."
7. Her cousin Stan was the last to arrive at the party and when he walked into the room every woman there stopped what she was doing for a brief moment took a deep breath and tried to continue the conversation she had been engaged in.
8. The dark empty street caused a shiver to run up his back. He paused for a minute before whispering "Hurry hurry hurry. Let's get out of here."

Exercise 3

Place commas where they are needed in the following sentences.

1. The letter was dated January 10 2000 and it informed John that a long-lost relative had left him $75000 in his will.
2. She was born November 11 1947 in a large frame house in what was known as Cascade a mill village in Mooresville North Carolina.
3. When they finally arrived in Taos New Mexico the snow suddenly stopped and they could see blue skies in the distance.

The Semicolon (;)

The semicolon is a stronger mark of punctuation than the comma. Its uses are limited and can easily be learned. The following is a list of occasions when it is appropriate to use a semicolon.

1. **A semicolon is used to join independent clauses that are not joined by a comma plus a coordinating conjunction.**

    I'm dropping out of school this semester; I'll be back in the fall.

2. **A semicolon is used to join independent clauses that are connected by a transitional connective.**

    The content of your paper is excellent; however, you need some help with punctuation.

3. A semicolon is used to separate elements in a series when the elements already contain commas.

> Dr. Jackson, the president of the college; Dr. Page, the academic dean; and Jean Brown, the student-body president, all support the change in rules.

The Colon (:)

The colon, an even stronger mark of punctuation than the semicolon, signals a strong separation between what precedes and what follows it. The meaning usually carried by a colon is that of emphatic introduction to something that follows.

1. A colon is used to signal a list or series that follows.

> In her room were all the accumulations of a typical teenager's life: the secondhand guitar, the stereo with oversized speakers, the posters of animals and movie stars, the stuffed animals, and the piles of dirty clothes.

2. A colon is used to separate a long quotation from its introduction.

> Describing the power of a thunderstorm through the poetic vernacular of his character, Huckleberry Finn, Mark Twain writes:
>
>> [. . .] it would get so dark that it looked all blue-black outside, and lovely; and the rain would thrash along by so thick that the trees off a little ways looked dim and spider-webby; and here would come a blast of wind that would bend the trees down and turn up the pale underside of the leaves [. . .]

3. A colon is used to separate independent clauses when the second clause restates, amplifies, or explains the first clause or when the second clause gives an example of what was stated in the first.

> This last statement brings up important considerations for the shaper of any argument: He must ask himself what audience he is directing the argument to and how he wishes to interact with that audience.
>
> There is one excuse that we must not be bullied into accepting: We must not accept laziness.

4. A colon is sometimes used to introduce appositives.

> The House of Representatives faces a difficult decision: whether or not to raise state income taxes.

There are a number of other uses of the colon, including the following.

5. A colon separates the hour and minutes in time indications.

> 4:15 P.M.

6. A colon appears after salutations in formal business letters.

> Dear Sirs: Dear Ms. Simpson:

7. A colon separates chapter and verse of biblical citations.

   John 3:16

8. A colon appears between the city of publication and the publisher in bibliographical entries.

   New York: Longman Publishing Co.

> **Exercise 4**
>
> Place semicolons and colons where they are needed in the following sentences.
>
> 1. The committee consisted of five members Dr. Philip Singer, Chancellor Dr. Fred Smith, Chair of English Dr. Elaine Horton, Professor of Music Dr. Nancy Perkins, Professor of French and Dr. Michael Doyle, Chair of Foreign Languages.
> 2. As the team assembled to begin work on the project, all members wanted to avoid one trap allowing their desire for a quick solution to cause hasty action.
> 3. At precisely 915, the members of the city council assembled and prepared to begin. A local minister read a brief passage from the Bible, John 146, and said a prayer before the meeting began.
> 4. The council faced a difficult decision what to do about funding for the arts.
> 5. The new highway seems to have done a great deal to alleviate traffic jams during rush hour however, it remains to be seen whether it will prove sufficient to handle holiday traffic.

The Dash (—)

The dash usually signals an interruption in thought or a dramatic pause. Sometimes it is necessary for clarity, especially when setting off a series from the rest of the sentence.

1. A dash is used to mark the limits of a series when a nearby noun might be mistaken for a part of the series.

   The conference brought together various professionals—teachers, doctors, lawyers, scientists, and artists.

2. A pair of dashes is used to set off a parenthetical independent clause that interrupts the flow of another clause.

   He quit his job—he had hated it anyway—in order to devote all his time to his study.

3. A pair of dashes is also used to indicate interruption or hesitation in dialogue.

> "I don't know how—I mean, I guess it—oh, I don't know why I took the money," she confessed.

4. A dash is used for an emphatic pause before a word or phrase at the end of a sentence.

> He stole the bread for only one reason—to save his child.
> There was only one thing she needed now—a job.

5. A dash is used to set off a summarizing or concluding main clause.

> The complexities of dormitory living, the exhilaration and the temptations of new-found freedom, the demands of a new level of study—all these make the life of a freshman both exciting and frustrating.

Parentheses ( )

Parentheses are most commonly used to enclose material that is only loosely related to the rest of a sentence—qualifications, asides, examples, explanations, and additional but unnecessary information.

1. Parentheses are used to introduce a qualification.

> That her pleasure in Indianhood and her passion for car travel might be incongruous if not mutually exclusive never occurred to Sissy (as it was to occur to Julian and Dr. Goldman).
>
> Tom Robbins, *Even Cowgirls Get the Blues*

2. Parentheses are used to add nonessential information.

> Specific words or phrases in your paper "go with" (and thus help to develop) the topic you have chosen.

3. Parentheses are used to enclose page numbers of in-text references in documented essays and research papers.

> As Mina Shaughnessy put it in *Errors and Expectations*, "We cannot tell how many needless circumlocutions or imprecise phrasings result from the fear of misspellings, but the number is undoubtedly high" (162).

Note: The closing set of quotation marks comes first, then the page number in parentheses, and finally the period ending the sentence.

Brackets [ ]

Brackets should be clearly distinguished from parentheses. Their uses are much more limited than those of parentheses; most often they are used within quoted material.

1. Brackets are used to insert material not in an original text. Using brackets allows you to fit a quotation into your sentence's structure rather than having the structure of the quoted material take over.

   According to X. J. Kennedy, "His [King Kong's] simian nature gives him one huge advantage over giant ants and walking vegetables in that an audience may conceivably identify with him."

   According to Linda Flower, "a problem is a situation that occurs when [there is] an obstacle in your way." We often find an association between "obstacles" and "problems."

2. Brackets are used with the Latin word *sic* (which means "thus") to indicate that a mistake in quoted material is there because it was in the original.

   One evaluator wrote of the course proposal, "It's [sic] goals were never made clear, so I was never sure what the students were supposed to be learning."

Exercise 5

Place dashes, parentheses, and brackets in the appropriate places in the following sentences.

1. Is his failure to call her a problem of nerve can't make himself pick up the phone, or is there another reason for his action fear of a long-term relationship?
2. The student essay although it had some errors to be sure made important points about the city's failure to support the arts: "The members of the City Council are going to be directly responsible for its the city's like sic of growth in this area."
3. If you want to be sure that your children will develop strong bodies and enjoy the many benefits that come with these bodies, you must see to it that they exercise regularly.
4. Hiking, swimming, jogging these are all activities that promote good cardiovascular health.

Exercise 6

1. Read the following passage from an essay by Theodore Sizer titled "Public Literacy."

   To visit among American high schools is to be struck by how similar these venerable social institutions are. Certainly, there is variety, best explained by differences in social class and, to a small extent, the race and the ethnicity of the students. The feel of a school serving the poor is profoundly different from the feel of its cousin in a Gold Coast suburb. However, it is the similarities that impress—the ubiquitous routines, the seven-period day, the bells, homecoming, school defined as English-math-science-social studies-language, each purveyed to students in isolation from every other. There are the texts, the sequence of topics, the testing, and, most important, the assumptions about learning and teaching and schooling that undergird these practices and the wry, usually genial cynicism of the teachers. In a nation priding itself on its local schooling, the consistencies are surprising. And the consistencies are exhibited by the students themselves—their clothing, lingo, enthusiasms, symbols. Again, class counts here, as does geography. But the wonder is why the differences are not far greater. Americans are mesmerized by their differences. Perhaps they should reflect a bit more on their similarities.

Write three sentences in which you quote from the material above. In each sentence, use brackets to make the quoted material conform to your syntax. Here is an example you may use as a model:

American schools are certainly different in many respects, but they are similar in regard to the "assumptions about learning and teaching and schooling that undergird [the very similar] practices" one finds in very different schools.

2. Review your use of quoted materials in a paper you have written for this course. Then, rewrite one or two passages using brackets to help you incorporate the quoted material more effectively into your text.

Quotation Marks (" ")

Quotation marks are most often used to indicate direct quotations. They are also used to enclose certain kinds of titles.

1. Quotation marks are used to indicate the spoken words in a written dialogue. Study this passage from Flannery O'Connor's "A Good Man Is Hard to Find" and the generalizations that follow it:

   "Good afternoon," he said. "I see you all had you a little spill."
   "We turned over twice!" said the grandmother.
   "Oncet," he corrected. "We seen it happen. Try their car and see will it run, Hiram," he said quietly to the boy with the gray hat.
   "What you got that gun for?" John Wesley asked. "Whatcha gonna do with that gun?"
   "Lady," the man said to the children's mother, "would you mind calling them children to sit down by you? Children make me nervous. I want all you all to sit down right together there where you're at."

From the example, we can deduce the following principles about quotation marks:

Quotation marks always come in pairs.
A new paragraph begins every time the speaker changes.

Only what is actually spoken by one of the characters is enclosed in quotation marks.

A phrase such as "he said," which interrupts a sentence of direct quotation (as in the first sentence of the passage), requires that the sentence contain two sets of quotation marks. The second part of the quotation in this case does not begin with a capital letter because it is not the beginning of a new sentence.

2. Quotation marks are used to indicate a direct quotation from another writer in a documented essay or research paper. Any sentences, clauses, phrases, or key words that are copied directly from a source must be placed within quotation marks.

Wilbur S. Howell identifies "a third great change in the theory of communication since the Renaissance" as the change of thought about "invention," which Howell defines as "the devising of subject matter for a particular speech and, by extension, the providing of content in discourse."

Note: Use quotation marks only for quotations of four or fewer lines. For longer quoted passages, use the block quotation style, in which quoted material is introduced by a colon and indented.

Other rhetoricians have cited the need for the reemphasis of invention. As James McCrimmon points out in "Toward More Rewarding Emphases in the Teaching of Composition":

What is needed in the teaching of composition at any instructional level is an emphasis on what is most important in composition. What is most important is the rhetorical sequence of invention, arrangement or organization, and style. Since both the arrangement and the style are suggested by and dependent on invention, the emphasis is most rewarding when it is concentrated in the first element of the traditional sequence.

3. Quotation marks are used to set off titles of short poems, essays, chapters or sections of books, articles in magazines or journals, graduate theses or dissertations, and short musical compositions.

Robert Frost's poem "Choose Something Like a Star" has been beautifully set to music by Randall Thompson.

Hawthorne's story "The Birthmark" suggests that all human beings are flawed and that attempting to perfect human nature is dangerous and prideful.

In our chapter "Creating Order," we discuss the fact that invention and arrangement are inseparable.

Note: Titles of such works as books, plays, long poems, magazines, films, and long musical compositions are set in italic type. In a typed manuscript, they are underlined.

Special problems that come up with quotation marks are covered by the following rules.

4. Commas and periods always go inside the closing set of quotation marks.

   "I agree with your position," she said.

5. Question marks and exclamation marks are placed inside the quotation marks if the quotation itself is a question or exclamation.

   "Are you ready to eat dinner now?" she asked.
   With a snort, he exclaimed, "You'd do that over my dead body!"

6. Question marks and exclamation marks are placed outside the quotation marks if the whole sentence is a question or an exclamation and the quotation itself is not.

   Did he say, "I'll accept the job"?
   No, I positively did not say, "Call me at home after midnight"!

7. If one quoted element appears within another quoted element, use single quotation marks (' ') for the inner quotation.

   The teacher said, "Please, Lily, begin again with 'The fault, dear Brutus, is not in our stars,' and finish the speech."

The Ellipsis (. . .)

1. An ellipsis, three spaced periods, indicates that something in a passage has been omitted. If you're quoting a source and you decide to omit part of a passage, then you should use an ellipsis to indicate that you have done so. MLA style requires that you enclose the ellipsis you insert with brackets to indicate that you have created the omission.

   But if the writer herself used an ellipsis in the passage and you keep that ellipsis as part of the quote, then you do not use brackets. If the deleted material comes at the end of a sentence, add a fourth period, the fourth being the end punctuation mark of the sentence. Speaking of varying interpretations of the Bible by Christians, Clarence Darrow says, "Yet there are some people who claim to be Christians [. . .] who give more credence to some portions of the book than others."

   Kurt Vonnegut is, above all else, a humanist. Perhaps Robert Scholes puts it best: "Vonnegut, in his fiction, is doing what the most serious writers do. He is helping, in Joyce's phrase, 'to create the conscience of the race.' What race? Human [. . .] ."

2. In informal writing, the ellipsis is used to indicate a thought that trails off.

   I started thinking about those long, lazy days on the vast sandy beaches. . . .

The Apostrophe (')

1. The apostrophe is used primarily to form the possessive case of nouns and some pronouns.

   the teacher's assignment
   the Browns' vacation
   one's name (*but* its name)

2. An apostrophe is used to indicate an omission of letters or numbers in contractions and dates.

   hasn't   has not
   o'clock   of the clock
   don't   do not
   '83   1983

3. An apostrophe is used to form the plural of letters, figures, or words used as words.

   Please write more plainly; I can't tell the difference between your *I*'s and your *e*'s.
   Your papers will be rated on a scale of 1 through 4, with 1's meaning poor and 4's meaning excellent.
   Your writing style would be stronger if you would eliminate some of the vague *this*'s and *that*'s.

Exercise 7

Place quotation marks, ellipses, and apostrophes where they are needed in the following sentences.

1. Get away from me, she said.
2. We soon learned that the teachers as es and os were virtually impossible to tell apart.
3. Pipe down, the judge said, Or Ill give you all 1s and end the process here.
4. The slightly drunk writer turned to the young man and asked, what is your favorite piece of literature? The young man thought a minute and replied, I guess I would have to say it is Wallace Stevenss poem Sunday Morning. Then the writer probed further: which of my writings have you found to have the most impact on you? The young man seemed uncomfortable, but eventually responded: I dont think Ive had the pleasure of coming across anything youve written to date.

Exercise 8

In their book *Linguistics for Students of Literature,* Elizabeth Closs Traugott and Mary Louise Pratt discuss the differences between speech and language. They use as an example the following passage from James Joyce's *Finnegans Wake:*

> And this is why any simple philadolphus of a fool you like to dress, an athemisthued lowtownian, exlegged phatrisight, may be awfully green to one side of him and fruitfully blue on the other which will not screen him however from appealing to my gropesarching eyes; through the strongholes of my acropoll, as a

boosted blasted bleating blatant bloaten blasphorus blesphorous idiot who kennot tail a bomb from a painapple when he steals one and wannot psing his psalmen with the cong in our gregational pompoms with the canting crew.

Traugott and Pratt make the following comment on this passage:

Notice that in this passage Joyce also exploits the fact that writing does not always distinguish homonyms. The word *canting* in the last line, for example, obviously alludes to Latin *cantare*, to sing, from which we get English *chant* and the literary term *canto*; but in conjunction with *kennot* and *wannot*, *canting* also alludes to Modern English *can't,* as well as to *cant* as a derogatory term for jargon, as a verb meaning to whine, as a verb meaning lean (especially with ships—hence the word *crew*), and possibly to Irish English *cant* meaning to sell at auction.

Place any quotation marks needed in the passage from Traugott and Pratt.

SPELLING

Probably no writing skill gives more trouble to the average writer than spelling. Although there are many reasons for spelling difficulties, the primary one is that there is no one-to-one correspondence between the sounds of the English language and the letters of the alphabet that represent those sounds. The English language presents particular spelling difficulties; it has undergone at least two major sound shifts, and there are nearly twice as many distinctive sounds in the language as there are letters. For these reasons, writers cannot depend on phonics alone. To account for all the various sounds in the language, the letters of the alphabet, particularly those representing vowel sounds, often represent several different sounds. For example, the letter *a* may have the vowel sound in "cave," the first vowel sounds in "about" and "absence," or the vowel sound in "all." Similarly, the sound *sh* may be represented by as many as fourteen different spellings, including *sh*ow, *s*ure, trac*ti*on, suspi*ci*on, and man*si*on.

Before the advent of the printing press and the beginning of publication as we know it today, variations in spelling were common. Apparently, they were not seen as a terribly serious problem. Writers often spelled the same word and even names in two or three different ways within a page or two. However, mass publication led to a desire for some agreement as to the correct ways to spell words. For whatever reason—perhaps it was the uniformity of the copies themselves—uniformity in spelling became desirable. Correct spelling eventually became a standard of literacy. That is, those who cannot spell are looked on as less than adequate writers.

Why has spelling remained an important indicator of literacy? One reason may be the ease with which spelling errors can be identified. They virtually "jump off the page." Even poor spellers will often notice misspellings that they themselves would not be guilty of. Furthermore, no real uncertainty is involved in spelling errors; doubt about almost any word's spelling can be immediately resolved by referring to a dictionary. On finding misspellings, the reader can immediately label the writer as incompetent.

A more positive reason for the emphasis on spelling ability is that it allows writers to communicate more effectively. As Mina Shaughnessy says in *Errors and Expectations,* "We cannot tell how many needless circumlocutions or imprecise phrasings result from the fear of misspellings, but the number is undoubtedly high!" Just as it is hard to tell how much inexact writing results from a fear of misspelling something, it is often quite difficult to draw the line between spelling errors and other more serious communication problems. Obviously, the person who writes "recieve" for "receive" has made a simple spelling error. But other problems—sometimes mistakenly labeled spelling errors—are actually more serious communication problems. "Indignation" and "implication" have some phonological similarity, but the person who writes "I don't like your indignation that I did something wrong" has obviously mistaken one word for another, not misspelled a word. And what do we say about the writer who explains that his absence was "do to a flat tire"? Does he know what "due" means? Thus, if you care about your writing and the impression it leaves, you cannot afford to ignore spelling.

We cannot offer any magic formulas for avoiding spelling errors. Obviously, you cannot memorize all the words in the English language, and just as obviously, you cannot check every word of every composition you write in a dictionary. What, then, can you do? Below we offer some suggestions for improving your spelling.

Assuming you are using a word processor, the first line of defense against misspellings is to use your software's spell checker at the end of every writing process. As you know, however, a spell checker will not find all errors; thus, you may well benefit from some of these suggestions:

1. Pay particular attention to *homophones,* words that sound alike but are spelled differently. Examples include *altar, alter; base, bass; cell, sell.*
2. Pay attention to the following pairs of suffixes: *able/ible, ance/ence, ant/ent, ary/ery.* Be sure to check any of these that you are unsure of.
3. Notice silent letters in words such as *debt, doubt, indict, know, scene, subtle;* such letters are vestiges from a time when the word was pronounced differently. You will often be able to remember the spelling of a word having a silent letter by pairing it with a related word that retains the letter in question in its pronunciation: *muscle/muscular, sign/signal.*
4. Pay attention to vowels that are in unstressed positions. Most of these are pronounced as the "colorless" sound "uh," which offers no help in spelling these words. Examples are the first vowels in "abbreviate," "occasion," and "undoubtedly"; the second vowels in "adequately," "beneficial," "bulletin," "carburetor," "dormitory," and "governor"; the last vowels in "destruction," "illusion," "orchestra," and "persistent."

Although no single set of rules will explain the spelling system of the English language, some rules can help you with the most troublesome words. You should know these rules and some of the most common exceptions to them.

1. The letter *i* comes before *e* except after *c* or when the combination is pronounced *ey*.

   receive   believe   weigh

   Exceptions
   counterfeit   either   leisure   foreign
   forfeit   height   weird   neither
   seize   sovereign

2. Singular nouns and third-person singular verbs that end with a consonant and a *y*, change the *y* to *i* and add *es* to form the plural.

   rally/rallies   baby/babies   cry/cries

Words with a vowel immediately preceding the *y* simply add an *s* in the plural form: *boy, boys.*

3. Singular nouns that end in *o* form the plural by adding *es*.

   cargo/cargoes   veto/vetoes

   Exceptions
   alto/altos   piano/pianos

4. Singular nouns that end in *s, ss, ch, sh, x,* or *z* form the plural by adding *es*.

   ash/ashes   match/matches   loss/losses
   birch/birches   tax/taxes   buzz/buzzes

   Exceptions
   fish/fish   series/series   ox/oxen

5. When adding a suffix to a monosyllabic word, if the suffix begins with a vowel and the word ends in a single consonant and contains only one vowel, the end consonant is doubled.

   can/canned   ship/shipped   whip/whipped

The end consonant is not doubled if the last syllable of the original word contains two consonants or two vowels:

   ask/asked   part/parting   *(Two consonants)*
   clean/cleaned   creep/creeping   *(Two vowels)*

6. When adding a suffix to a multisyllabic word, if the suffix begins with a vowel, the word ends in a vowel-consonant cluster, and the accent is on the final syllable, the end consonant is doubled.

   admit/admitted   compel/compelled   occur/occurred

7. Words that end in silent *e* drop the *e* when a suffix beginning with a vowel is added.

   cycle/cycling   judge/judging   dine/dining

   Exceptions

   dye/dyeing   hoe/hoeing

8. Words that end in a silent *e* preceded by *c* or *g* retain the *e* when a suffix beginning with *a* or *o* is added if the sound of the consonant is soft.

   advantage/advantageous   manage/manageable

9. If a prefix ends with a letter that also begins the word it is being added to, both letters are kept.

   dissatisfied   illogical   misspelled   override

10. If a suffix begins with a letter that also ends the word it is being added to, both letters are kept.

    common/commonness   physical/physically

Our final piece of advice in regard to spelling is to check a dictionary whenever you are in doubt. In many cases, this will not be easy to do when you do not know how to spell a word in the first place. However, if you keep some of the principles we discussed in mind, you may find it easier to locate words in the dictionary. Once you realize that an unstressed vowel sound may be represented by any one of the vowel letters, you have freed yourself from some preconceptions that could keep you from finding certain words. Also, as you become increasingly aware of word families (groups of words that derive from the same root), you will be better able to spell words with silent letters or unstressed sounds. For example, from its pronunciation, "abəlishən," you may not know how to spell the word "abolition," but if you recognize its relation to the word "abolish," you will know immediately to look for an *o* in the unstressed middle position. The following list should give you a feel for the various ways in which vowel sounds appearing at the beginning of words may be spelled.

Vowel/Diphthong	Sound	Example
a	ā	ate
	ĭ	any
	ə	about
e	ĕ	every, ember
	ē	eject
i	ī	hide
o	ō	okay
u	ū	use, unique

ai	ā	aim
	ī	aisle
ea	ē	each
ei	ē	either
ey	ī	eye
oa	ō	oat
oh	ō	oh
oi	oi	noise
oy	oi	oyster
ou	ow	out
yu	ū	yule

Similarly, you will find the dictionary more useful if you become aware of the letters that represent consonant sounds. Many consonants, such as *b, d, f, j, k, l, m, n, p, q, r, t, v, w, y,* and *z* correspond (more or less) with one sound. However, other consonants represent more than one sound, as the following list illustrates.

Consonant	Sound	Example
c	s	ceiling
	k	creep
	(silent)	scent
g	g	give
	j	gene
h	h	hole
	(silent)	ghost
s	s	stay
	sh	sure
t	t	tall
ti	sh	condition
w	w	wet
	(silent)	write
x	ks	exit
	z	Xerox

MANUSCRIPT MECHANICS

Instructors have varying requirements for preparing final-draft manuscripts. For example, many require that papers be typed, whereas others accept handwritten manuscripts. No matter what your instructor's standards regarding a paper's final appearance, you should recognize the value of submitting a neat, attractive paper that follows the conventions of manuscript presentation. The audience for a piece of writing (whether a composition instructor or other readers) is more likely to give the paper's content careful attention if the appearance of the paper is pleasing.

1. *Materials.* Use high-quality white bond paper whose size is the standard $8\frac{1}{2}$ by 11 inches. To make corrections, use correction fluid or tape whenever possible. Do not strike over letters. For handwritten papers, use white lined paper, but not torn out of a notebook. Double-space the manuscript whether you type or write.
2. *Margins.* Leave margins of 1 to $1\frac{1}{2}$ inches at the top and left of the page and margins of at least 1 inch on the right and bottom. Make the right margin as even as possible.
3. *Ink.* If you handwrite your papers, write with dark blue or black pen, not a pencil.
4. *Titles.* Do not underline or place in quotation marks the title of your own essay. Do not use a period after your title. It is acceptable, however, to use a question mark or an exclamation mark if the title is a question or an exclamation.
5. *Handwritten corrections.* Most instructors accept infrequent handwritten corrections even on final drafts. Draw a neat, single line through a word to be omitted. If another word is to replace it or if you are correcting a spelling error, write the correct word neatly above the lined-out one. Avoid lining out only parts of words. If you have inadvertently left out a word, use a caret (^) to show where the omitted word should go, and write the word above the caret. Use the symbol ¶ to begin a new paragraph or *no* ¶ to indicate that you have made an error and there should be no new paragraph.

CAPITALIZATION

Observe the following capitalization rules in editing your final draft:

1. Capitalize the first word of every sentence or of a fragment deliberately punctuated as a sentence.
2. In a title, do not capitalize articles (*a, an, the*), prepositions, or conjunctions of less than five letters unless these words begin or end the title or follow a semicolon or a colon. Capitalize all other words in the title.
3. Capitalize proper nouns and adjectives made from proper nouns. Examples of proper nouns are names of people, towns, cities, states, countries, continents, geographical regions, planets, monuments, days of the week, months, holidays, historical events and movements, organizations, associations, government departments, races and nationalities, languages, and religions and their followers, and the word "God" or references to specific gods. Treat such words as *mother, father, grandmother,* and *grandfather* as proper nouns when they are used as names, but not when they are in phrases, such as "my mother." Capitalize *uncle* and *aunt* when they precede a name, as in "Uncle

Jack" or "Aunt Carolyn," but again, not in phrases like "my uncle Jack" or "my aunt Carolyn."
4. Capitalize titles (professor, doctor, and so forth) when they precede the name of the specific person:

Professor Rhame   Dr. Stewart

Abbreviations

Use only recognized, standard abbreviations. In general, abbreviations should be avoided in papers. The following kinds of abbreviations are acceptable, however:

1. Abbreviations of titles when they occur with names:

   Dr. Smith   Mrs. Jones   James Knots, D.D.S.

2. Abbreviations of academic degrees:

   She is working on her Ph.D.

3. Abbreviations having to do with time, provided they appear with specific times and dates:

   7 A.M.   400 B.C.
   10 P.M.   876 C.E.

4. Abbreviations or acronyms for names of countries, organizations, and corporations:

   USA   CBS   FBI   YWCA   NATO

5. Latin abbreviations used in footnotes and bibliographies and in parenthetical comments:

   cf. (compare)   et al. (and others)   i.e. (that is)
   e.g. (for example)   etc. (and so forth)   viz. (namely)

Numbers

1. Spell out numbers that begin sentences.

   Two hundred people attended the barbecue.

2. Spell out numbers that can be written in one or two words.

   The robbers escaped with five million dollars.

3. Use figures in scientific and technical writing. Consult a style manual in your field for advice on using numbers in scientific or technical writing, because conventions vary from one discipline to another.

Italics

Italic type is slanted type that appears in printed material for emphasis. In typed or handwritten manuscripts, italics are indicated by underlining. Use the following guidelines for italicizing words or phrases:

1. Italicize titles of books, magazines, newspapers, journals, plays, films, long poems, long musical compositions, radio and television programs, and works of art. (See the section on quotation marks, page 685, for treatment of shorter works.)
2. Italicize names of specific ships, planes, spacecraft, and trains.
3. Italicize foreign words and expressions.

Hyphens

The hyphen (-), a shorter horizontal mark than the dash, is used in many compound words. The following rules govern hyphens in such words:

1. Hyphenate compound adjectives before a noun:

   well-dressed man   well-bred dog   heart-to-heart talk

2. Hyphenate compounds and compound adjectives made with the prefixes *self, all, quasi,* and *half,* even when they do not precede a noun.

   self-government   all-encompassing   quasi-legal   half-done

Hyphens are also used for dividing words at the ends of lines. Most word processors avoid end-of-line hyphenation automatically. Whenever possible, avoid word division by planning typed or written lines carefully. When dividing a word at the end of the line is necessary, follow these guidelines.

1. Do not divide one-syllable words.
2. Divide words only between syllables.
3. Do not hyphenate after a one-letter prefix (for example, do not hyphenate "a-bout").
4. Avoid dividing a two-letter suffix *(ly, al, le,* and so on) from the rest of a word.
5. Divide compound words only between the two parts.
6. Generally, hyphenate between the prefix and the root or the root and the suffix.

Literary Credits

Lee K. Abbott, "The True Story of Why I Do What I Do." Puerto del Sol: New Mexico State University. Reprinted by permission of the author.

Sherman Alexie, "Evolution." Reprinted from *The Business of Fancydancing*. Copyright © 1992 by Sherman Alexie, by permission of Hanging Loose Press.

Sherman Alexie, "That Place Where Ghosts of Salmon Jump" and "The Powwow at the End of the World" from *The Summer of Black Widows*. Copyright © 1996 by Sherman Alexie. Reprinted with permission of Hanging Loose Press.

Margaret Atwood, "Spelling" from *True Stories*. Reprinted by permission of Margaret Atwood. Copyright © 1995 by Margaret Atwood. Originally published in Canada by Oxford University Press and in the United States by Simon and Schuster.

Jay Chiat, "Illusions Are Forever" from *Forbes ASAP* Magazine, October 2, 2000. Reprinted by permission of *Forbes ASAP* Magazine. Copyright © 2007 Forbes Media LLC.

Judith Ortiz Cofer, "The Myth of the Latin Woman: I Just Met a Girl Named María" from *The Latin Deli: Prose and Poetry*. Copyright © 1993 by Judith Ortiz Cofer. Reprinted with permission of The University of Georgia Press.

Richard Dawkins, "When Religion Steps on Science's Turf: The Alleged Separation Between the Two Is Not So Tidy." Copyright © 1998 by the Council for Secular Humanism (CSH). This article originally appeared in Free Inquiry Magazine, Volume 18, Number 2 (Spring 1998), published by the CSH in Amherst, New York. Reprinted by permission.

Selection by Kim Dixon, Tiffany Kary, and Dan Maccarone Copyright © 2001. All rights reserved.

Screen capture Copyright © 1994–1998 by Susan Farrell & Brett Webb. All rights reserved.

Robert Frost, "For Once, Then Something," and excerpt from "Putting in the Seed" from *The Poetry of Robert Frost*, edited by Edward Connery Lathem. Copyright © 1923, 1969 by Henry Holt and Company. Copyright 1951 by Robert Frost. Reprinted by permission of Henry Holt and Company, LLC.

Ellen Goodman, "Beauty Industry on Rampage," *Las Cruces Sun-News*, October 21, 1997, A-10. Copyright © 1997 by The Boston Globe Newspaper Co./Washington Post Writers Group. Reprinted with permission.

Stephen Jay Gould, "Nonoverlapping Magisteria," *Natural History Magazine 106* (Mar. 1997), pp. 16-22. Reprinted with permission from Rhonda R. Shearer on behalf of the Estate of Stephen Jay Gould.

Aaron Gwyn, "Of Falling," from *Dog on the Cross*. Copyright © 2004 by Aaron Gwyn. Reprinted by permission of Algonquin Books of Chapel Hill.

Michael R. Heaphy, "Dismemberment and Choice" from *National Review*, November 2, 1992, pp. 44–45. Copyright © 1992 by National Review, Inc. 215 Lexington Avenue, New York, NY 10016. Reprinted by permission.

Lou Jacobs, Jr., "What Qualities Does a Good Photograph Have?" from the *New York Times*, February 8, 1981. Copyright © 1981 by The New York Times Company. Reprinted by permission of the *New York Times*.

Kathleen Hall Jamieson, "Shooting to Win; Do Attack Ads Work? You Bet – and That's Not All Bad," the *Washington Post*, September 26, 2004, Outlook Section, B01. Reprinted with permission of Kathleen Hall Jamieson, Ph.D.

William E. King, "Out of Hurricane's Way," *Houston Chronicle*, September 12, 2004. Reprinted with permission of William E. King.

Literary Credits

Martin Luther King, Jr., "I Have A Dream." Reprinted by arrangement with The Heirs to the Estate of Marin Luther King, Jr. c/o Writers House as agent for the proprietor, New York, NY. Copyright © 1963 Martin Luther King Jr.; Copyright renewed 1991 Coretta Scott King.

Elisabeth Kubler-Ross, "On the Fear of Dying", reprinted with the permission of Scribner, an imprint of Simon & Schuster Adult Publishing Group, from *On Death and Dying*. Copyright © 1969 by Elisabeth Kubler-Ross, Copyright renewed © 1997 by Elisabeth Kubler-Ross. All rights reserved.

Excerpt from Charles McNair, "Southern Journal," *Southern Living,* June 2000, p. 228. Copyright © 2000 by Southern Living, Inc. Reprinted with permission.

Gloria Naylor, "Mommy, What Does Nigger Mean?" Reprinted by permission of Sterling Lord Literistic, Inc. Copyright © 1986 by Gloria Naylor.

Netscape search engine screens. Portions Copyright © Netscape Communications Corporation, 1998. All Rights Reserved. Netscape, Netscape Navigator, and the Netscape N Logo are registered trademarks of Netscape in the United States and other countries.

Joyce Carol Oates, "Shopping," *Ms.*, March 1986. Copyright © 1986 by Ontario Review Inc. Reprinted by permission of John Hawkins & Associates, Inc.

Thomas Oliphant, "Exposed in the Supreme Court: Lies About 'Partial Birth Abortion'," *Boston Globe*, May 1, 2000, A19. Reprinted with permission of Boston Daily Globe.

Marge Piercy, "A Work of Artifice," Copyright © 1970, *Circles on the Water* by Marge Piercy. Used by permission of Alfred A. Knopf, a division of Random House, Inc.

Datus Proper, "Dark Hollow," *Field and Stream* Magazine, July 1993. Reprinted by permission.

Arthur Rosenfeld, "Should Anyone Have To Live in Pain?" from *Parade* Magazine, July 20, 2003. Reprinted by permission of the author and the author's agents, Scovil Chichak Galen Literary Agency, Inc.

Meir Shalev, "If Bosnians Were Whales," *New York Times,* August 29, 1992. Copyright © 1992 by The New York Times Inc. Reprinted by permission.

Suzanne Smally, "The Perfect Crime," *Newsweek,* February 3, 2003. Copyright © 2003 by Newsweek, Inc. All rights reserved. Reprinted by permission.

Steve Stoeckel, "What About the Customer?" *The Charlotte Observer,* June 13, 2006. Reprinted with permission from the Charlotte Observer. Copyright owned by the Charlotte Observer.

Julie Titone, "Balance of Power." Copyright © by Julie Titone. Reprinted by permission of the author.

INDEX

Abbott, Lee K. ("The True Story of Why I Do What I Do"), 106–110, 111–123, 131–132
Abbreviations, 702
Absolute phrases, 84, 85–86
Action form, of verb tenses, 667
Action words. *See* Verbs
Adams, James L. (*Conceptual Blockbusting*), 516, 555
Adjectival, 673–674
Adjective phrases, 674
Adjectives, 670
Adler, Mortimer J. ("How to Mark a Book"), 105, 111, 135
"Adult Audiences Only," 388, 404–410
Adverb phrases, 675
Adverbial modifiers, 674
Adverbs, 670
Aims of discourse, 147–151
  and modes, 150–151
Alexie, Sherman, 298–302, 319, 323, 545
  "Evolution," 301–302
  "Powwow at the End of the World, The," 300–301
  "That Place Where Ghosts of Salmon Jump," 298–299, 323, 545
"All in a Day's Work: Generalizing, Profiling, and Stereotyping," 235, 247–248, 258–259, 260–269
Amante, David ("Teaching Is Always a Political Act"), 420–425, 444–445, 464
"American Indian Movement as a Counterculture, The," 618–623
American Psychological Association (APA) documentation format, 574, 575, 600, 601–618
Analysis, audience. *See* Audience, sample analysis of
Analysis mode, 150, 256
  in essay exam, 656

APA. *See* American Psychological Association
Apostrophe, 694–695
Appositives, 84–85
Argument
  logical, 446–452
  structure of, 457–464
  validity of, 464–473
Argumentum ad hominem, fallacy of, 465
Argumentum ad ignorantiam, fallacy of, 466
Aristotle, 442
"Art Crimes: The Writing on the Wall," 594
Assessment
  and essay exams, 639–640, 643–661
  self-assessment, 95
Association. *See also* Clustering
  questions of, 24–28
Atwood, Margaret ("Spelling"), 296–297, 319, 326–327
Audience. *See also* Reader
  revising for, 75–77
  sample analysis of, 44, 75–77
Audience analysis. *See* Audience, sample analysis of
Authority, appeals to, 448–449

"Balance of Power: Can Endangered Salmon and Hydroelectric Plants Share the Same Rivers?" 61–62, 301, 329, 541–545, 554, 558–559
Bandwagon fallacy, 466
Barbash, Louis, 59–60, 62
"Beauty Industry on Rampage," 349–351, 390, 393–395
"Because" statements, 378, 390
Begging the question, fallacy of, 471
Bibliography, format of, 601–613
Birch, Stacey, 56–57, 67–68
Blocking, as shaping strategy, 50–51, 519–520

"Body Image," 394–395
Bookmarking, 595
Bookshelf drawing, as shaping strategy, 53
Boolean search, 37–38, 391
"Booze It? Lose It!: An Evaluation of North Carolina's Drunk Driving Laws," 357–361, 377
Brackets, 690–691
Brainstorming, 16–17
Bridges, Bill ("'No Thanks'—A Step Beyond 'Just Say No'"), 357–361, 377
Brown, Clarita ("The American Indian Movement as a Counterculture"), 618–623
Bug list, 516, 555, 557
Burke, Kenneth, xiii, xvi, 273
Burnett, Frances Hodgson (*The Secret Garden*), 22

Capitalization, 701–703
Case
  noun, 665–666
  pronoun, 666–667
Castoreno, Adam, 42, 43, 53
Catalogs, 180–181
Causal fallacy, 467–470
Causal reasoning, 454–455
Causality mode, 150, 254–255
  claims of, 446
  in essay exam, 655
Cause, in argument
  contributing, 468
  necessary, 467
  sufficient, 467
Cavan, Sherri ("The Great Graffiti Wars of the Late 20th Century"), 594, 625
CD-ROM databases, 583
"Change," 545–550
Character, in literature, 321–322

I-1

Chiat, Jay ("Illusions Are Forever"), 211–213
Chomsky, Noam, 647, 648–650
Chronology, use of, in personal essay, 186–188
Citations, in-text, 613–618
Claims, argumentative, 391–394, 405–406
Clark, Christian ("Emotion and the Death Penalty: An Analysis of Jaclyn Talbert's 'Justice for Those Who Have Shown Us No Mercy'"), 143–145
Clarity, in informative essay, 239–241
Classification mode, 150, 256–257
  in essay exam, 660–661
Clauses as substantives, 684
Clichés, 82–83
Clustering, 20–22. *See also* Association
Cohesion, paragraph, 63–65
Cofer, Judith Ortiz ("The Myth of the Latin Woman: I Just Met a Girl Named María"), 68, 158–163, 177
Colon, 688–689
Comma, 684–646
Comma splices, 92
Comparison mode, 249–254
  in essay exam, 655–656
Complex sentence, 681
Compound-complex sentence, 681
Compound sentence, 681
Computer facilities, 6
Computers, 5–7
  and brainstorming, 15
  and discovery draft, 46
  and end-of-line hyphenation, 703
  and exploratory questions, 31
  and fonts, 94
  and footers, 94
  and formatting text, 94
  and freewriting, 19
  and global revision, 71–72, 78
  and headers, 94
  and interest inventory, 13
  and margins, 94
  and revising text, 71–72, 78
  as research tool, 32–35
  search and replace function, 93–94
Conceptual Blockbusting, 516, 555
Conclusion, as element of essay, 65–68
Conflict
  in literature, 321
  in personal essay, 178–179

Conjunctions, 671–672
  coordinating, 84, 671
  correlative, 671–672
  subordinating, 83, 672
Connotation, 79
Consequence, questions of, 27, 30–31
Consonants, 696–700
Contributing cause, 468
Coordinating conjunctions, 84, 671
Coordination, of ideas, 84
Copying and pasting, as research tool, 595
CosmoGIRL!, 391–393
Corder, Danielle, 18–19
Correlative conjunctions, 671–672
Cotter, Jacqueline ("Getting It Right: Fitting Message to Audience"), 399–402
Counterarguments, 462
Criterion-based evaluation, 347–349, 372–376, 390
Cumulative sentence, 84–86

Dangling modifiers, using Search function to find, 95
"Dark Hollow," 55–56, 57, 58, 66, 68, 153–157, 187, 188
Dash, 689–690
Databases, CD-ROM, 583
"*Da Vinci Code, The*: A Study in Print and Film," 365–370
Dawkins, Richard ("When Religion Steps on Science's Turf"), 445, 496–501, 511
Definition, fallacies of, 470–473
Definition mode, 150, 258
  in essay exams, 656
Demonstrative pronouns, 666
Denotation, 79
Dependent clause, 680–681
Description mode, 150
  in essay exams, 660
  in persuasion essay, 512–513
Detail, in personal essay, 180–181
Dialogue
  as feature of personal essay, 179–180
  imaginary, 455–456
  use of quotation marks with, 692–693
Dialogue notes, 129–132, 333–335
Direct objects, 676–677
Discourse
  aims of, 147–151
  modes of, 140–141, 213–225
  analysis, 150,

as tool for shaping, 224–225
  causality, 140, 220–221
  classification, 140, 222–223
  comparison, 140, 232–237
  definition, 140, 223–224
  description, 140
  narration, 140
  in essay exams, 655–657
  process, 214–215
Discovery draft, 45–46
"Dismemberment and Choice," 486–489, 507–508, 509, 511, 518
Dixon, Kim ("Body Image"), 394–395
Documentation, 292, 296, 601–618
Douglas, Susan, 64–65
Downloading, as research strategy, 595
Draft, discovery. *See* Discovery draft
Drafting, 5, 6. *See also* Discovery draft; Shaping strategies
  for evaluation essay, 406–408
  for information essay, 262–267
  for interpretive essay (*about literature*), 336–341
  for personal essay, 168–179
  for persuasion essay, 524–529
  for position essay, 474–479
  for problem/solution essay, 561–566
Drawing, as shaping strategy, 50–52
Du Bois, W.E.B. (*The Souls of Black Folk*), 219–226
Duran, Steve ("Steve Wants an A"), 74–75, 402–404

EAE. *See* Edited American English
-*ed*/-*ing* phrases, 86
Edited American English (EAE), 664
Editing
  definition of, 94, 663–664
  strategies for, 94–96
Eiseley, Loren, 62
Either/or dilemma, fallacy of, 469
Ellipsis, 573, 694
Embedding, as sentence combining strategy, 83
"Emotion and the Death Penalty: An Analysis of Jaclyn Talbert's 'Justice for Those Who Have Shown Us No Mercy,'" 143–145
Emotional appeal, 510, 519
End-of-line hyphenation, 703
Endnotes, 617
Equivocation, fallacy of, 471
Errors and Expectations, 697

Essay
　developing structure of, 45–53
　elements of, 53–68
　evaluation, 347–410
　information, 203–270
　interpretive (*about* literature), 273–345
　personal, 153–200
　persuasion, 485–533
　position, 413–482
　practical application, as essay exam response, 658–660
　problem/solution, 535–571
　reflective, 396–397
　research, 577–638
Essay examinations, 639–640, 643–661
　and assessment, 639–640
　content of, 646–655
　practical application in, 658–660
　processes used in, 644–646
　structure of answers to, 655–687
Ethical appeal, 442
Ethical persuasion, 511–512, 519
Ethical stance, 452
Ethos, 442. *See also* Ethical appeal
"Euthanasia and the Right to Die," 437–440, 443
Evaluation. *See also* Evaluation essays
　criteria for, 372–376, 387–388, 390
　in essay exam, 651–652
Evaluation essays, 347–410
　versus argumentative writing, 372
　critiquing, 410
　features of, 372–378
　guidelines for writing, 386–390
　samples of, 349–370, 404–410
Evaluation of Internet, 390–395
"Evolution," 301–302
Examples, in position essay, 451
Exclamation mark, 683
Experience
　application to, in essay *from* literature, 274–275
　use of personal, in position essay, 451–452
"Exposed in the Supreme Court," 490–492

Facts and figures, in position essay, 449–45
Fairrington, Brian (cartoon), 521
Fallacies, logical, 464–473
　causal, 467–470
　of definition, 470–473
　of irrelevance, 465–46

Farrell, Susan ("Art Crimes: The Writing on the Wall"), 594
Field search, 585–589
Figures and tables, 242–247
Figures (and facts), in position essay, 449–450
Fish skeleton drawing, as shaping strategy, 50, 52
Fisher, Christopher ("Scars"), 165–176, 187
Focus statements, 41–44, 45
　in essay *from* literature, 332
　in evaluation essay, 338
　in information essay, 247–248
　in interpretive essay (*about* literature), 336
　in personal essay, 186
　in persuasion essay, 524
　in position essay, 457
　in problem/solution essay, 500
Fonts, computer tip for, 94
Footers, computer tip for, 94
Footnotes, 617
"For Once, Then, Something," 295, 316–319, 325–326
Form class words, 665–671
Formatting, computer tip for, 94
Freewriting, 15–20, 36–37
Frost, Robert ("For Once, Then, Something"), 295, 316–319, 325–326
Function words, 671–672
Fury, Kristina, 185
Future perfect tense, 668–670
Future tense, 668–670

Gardner, Elizabeth C. ("Transforming a Nation, Transforming an Enemy"), 227–234, 265
Gates, Henry Louis, Jr. ("Change of Life"), 122
Geray, Kristina,
　"'How Exhausting It Is to Keep Up Appearances," 333–345
　"The Pet Overpopulation Problem," 559, 560–571
Gerund, 679–680
"Getting It Right: Fitting Message to Audience," 399–402
Gibaldi, Joseph (*MLA Handbook for Writers of Research Papers*), 600, 603
Global revision, 74–78, 89–91

Goodman, Ellen ("Beauty Industry on Rampage"), 349–351, 390, 393–395
Gould, Stephen Jay ("Nonoverlapping Magisteria"), 426–437, 445
Govan, Sandra Y. ("Listening to the Word, or, 21st Century Readers and *The Souls of Black Folk*), 219–226
Graham, Michael ("All in a Day's Work: Generalizing, Profiling, and Stereotyping"), 235, 247–248, 258–259, 260–269
"Great Graffiti Wars of the Late 20th Century, The," 594, 625
Grier, Robbie, 659–660
"Gringos on Safari," 189–199
Gwyn, Aaron ("Of Falling"), 289–294, 306–309

Haley, Michael ("The Right Not to Listen"), 414–420, 441, 444–445, 461, 464
Hall, Heather ("The Next Big Winner Is....!!"), 442, 443, 473–482
Hamill, Pete, 513
Hasty generalization, fallacy of, 466–467
Headers, computer tip for, 94
Heaphy, Michael R. ("Dismemberment and Choice"), 486–489, 507, 509, 511, 518
Highet, Gilbert, 77
Holt, John, 248–249
Homophones, 697
Hoover, J. Edgar, 512–513
"'How Exhausting It Is' to Keep Up Appearances," 333–345
Huskey, Sybil, 647–648
Huxley, Aldous, 72
Hyphens, 703

"I Have a Dream," 492–496, 508
"If Bosnians Were Whales," 252–253
"Illusions Are Forever," 211–213
Images. *See* Visual rhetoric
Indefinite pronouns, 666–667
Independent clauses, 680–681
Indirect objects, 677–678
Infinitives, 679
Information, collecting
　for essay *from* literature, 331–332
　for evaluation essay, 387–388
　for information essay, 242–247

Information, collecting (*continued*)
   for interpretive essay (*about* literature), 329
   for personal essay, 185–186
   for persuasion essay, 517
   for position essay, 453–456
   for problem/solution essay, 556–557
Information essays, 203–227
   critiquing, 270
   features of, 238–241
   guidelines for writing, 241–260
   samples of, 204–233, 267–269
Information sources,
   for research, 580–582
-*ing*/-*ed* phrases, 84
Intensive (reflexive) pronouns, 667
Interest inventory, 11–13
Interjections, 672
Internet
   as source, 32–35, 590–598
   evaluation of, 390–395
   reliability of, 590–591
Interpretation, in essay exam, 652–655
   in interpretive essay (*about* literature), 326
Interpretive essays (*about* literature), 273–345
   and personal essay, 274–275
   critiquing, 345
   features of, 326–328
   guidelines for writing, 331–333
   samples of, 303–309, 333–345
Interrogative pronouns, 666
Interviews, 547–549, 585–586
Intransitive verbs, 667
"Intricacies of an Idiot, The," 74–75
Introduction, as element of essay, 55–58
Irrelevance, fallacy of, 465–467
Italics, 703

Jacobs, Lou, Jr. ("What Qualities Does a Good Photograph Have?"), 373–376
Jacoby, Susan, 59
Jamieson, Kathleen Hall ("Shooting to Win"), 351–357, 383
Jargon, 80
Johnson, Louanne (*My Posse Don't Do Homework*), 274
Jones, James, 72
"Justice for Those Who Have Shown Us No Mercy," 143–145, 504–507, 516

Kary, Tiffany ("Body Image"), 394–395
Kennedy, John F., 515–516
Key causal assertions, in position essay, 454–455
Key terms, 62
Key values, appeal to, in position essay, 453–454
Keyword search, 33–35
King, Martin Luther, Jr.
   "I Have a Dream," 492–496
   "Letter from Birmingham Jail," 452, 514–515
King, William E. ("Out of Hurricane's Way"), 536–540
Kozol, Jonathan, 221–222, 250–251
Kübler-Ross, Elisabeth ("On the Fear of Dying"), 204–208, 236–237, 259, 260

Language
   general and specific, 80
   persuasive, 512–513, 519
   technical, 80
"Letter from Birmingham Jail," 452, 514–515
Library, as source, 582–585
"Listening to the Word, or, 21st Century Readers and (*The Souls of Black Folk*)," 219–226
Listing, as shaping strategy, 47–48
Literary texts. *see also* Interpretive essays (*about* literature)
   elements of, 320–324
   samples of, 275–302
   writing *about*, 274, 303–309, 341–344
   writing *from*, 274, 309–315
Local revision, 78–91
Logical appeal, 442
Logical argument, 446–452, 517
Logical fallacies, 464–473
Logos, 442. *see also* Logical appeal
Lunsford, Ronald F. (*Twelve Readers Reading*), 243, 245–246

Maccarone, Dan ("Body Image"), 394–395
Macrorie, Ken (*Searching Writing*), 535
"Making of Spells, The," 303–306, 326, 327–328
Manuscript
   mechanics, 700–701
   preparation, 94
Mapping, as shaping strategy, 50, 51
Margins, computer tip for, 94

Martinez, Daniel, 50–51
McCollam, Bridget ("Adult Audiences Only"), 388, 404–410
McCrimmon, James M., xiii, xv
McNair, Charles ("My Father's Cabin"), 163–165, 177
Meaning, revising for, 74–75
Miller, Chris ("Gringos on Safari"), 86–89, 189–199
"Mirror Image," 36–37, 44–46, 95–102
MLA. *See* Modern Language Association
MLA Handbook for Writers of Research Papers, 600
Modern Language Association (MLA), documentation format, 574–575, 600, 601–618
"Modern Perspective on Graffiti, A," 594, 625–626
Modes of discourse, 150, 249–258
   analysis, 256
   as tool for shaping, 258
   causality, 254–255
   classification, 256–257
   comparison, 249–254
   definition, 258
   description, 150
   in essay exams, 655–657
   narration, 150
   process, 248–249
Modifiers, 673–674
   adjectival, 673
   adverbial, 674
   dangling, 95
"Mommy, What Does 'Nigger' Mean?" 56, 57, 67, 139–140, 216–218, 236, 260
Murray, Donald M., 71
"My Father's Cabin," 163–165, 177
My Posse Don't Do Homework, 274
"Myth of the Latin Woman, The: I Just Met a Girl Named María," 158–163

"Name Us a King," 315
Narration mode, 150
   in persuasion essay, 513–514
Naylor, Gloria ("Mommy, What Does 'Nigger' Mean?"), 56, 57, 67, 139–140, 216–218, 236, 260
Nease, Steve (cartoon), 126–128, 380
Necessary cause, 468
"Next Big Winner Is . . . . !!, The," 442, 443, 479–482
"No Exceptions," 309–312, 325, 332

"No More," 508, 524–532
"'No Thanks'–A Step Beyond 'Just Say No,'" 357–361, 377
"Nonoverlapping Magisteria," 426–437, 445
Note-cards, in research, 581
Noun case, 665
Noun phrases, 674
Nouns, 665–666
Numbers, 702–705

Oates, Joyce Carol ("Shopping"), 275–285
Objective case
  for nouns, 665
  for pronouns, 666
Objects
  direct, 676–677
  indirect, 677–678
  of prepositions, 678
  secondary, 678
Observation, as research strategy, 587, 589
Occasions, writing, 147–151. *see also* Evaluation essays, Information essays, Interpretive essays (*about* literature), Personal essays, Persuasion essays, Position essays, Problem/solution essays, Research essays
"Of Falling," 285–294, 306–309, 329
Oliphant, Thomas ("Exposed in the Supreme Court"), 490–492
"On the Fear of Dying," 204–208, 236–237, 259
Opinion statements, in position essay, 450–451
Opposition
  questions of, 25–27, 28–29
  reader as, 441
"Out of Hurricane's Way," 536–540
Outline, topic, as shaping strategy, 48–49
Oversimplification, fallacy of, 468–469
Overton, Andrew ("Change"), 545–550
Ozment, Katherine, 42–43, 53

Paglia, Camille, 56, 57, 66–67
Paragraphs, as element of essay, 60–66
Paraphrasing, 120–121, 132–135, 582
Parentheses, 690
Participles, 680
Parts of speech, 665–672
  adjectives, 670
  adverbs, 670–671

conjunctions, 671–672
interjections, 672
nouns, 665–666
prepositions, 671
pronouns, 666–667
verbs, 667–670
Passive voice, 668
Past perfect tense, 668–670
Past tense, 678–670
Pathetic appeal, 442
Pathos, 442. *see also* Pathetic appeal
Patterns, structural, of literary texts, 324
Pearl necklace drawing, as shaping strategy, 50, 52
Peer review, 89–91, 95–98, 193–197,
"Perfect Crime, The," 208–210
Period, 682
Periodic sentence, 84–86
Personal essays, 153–200
  critiquing, 200
  features of, 178–181
  guidelines for writing, 184–189
  samples of, 153–176, 187–199
Personal pronouns, 666
Persuasion. *see also* Persuasion essays
  ethical, 511–512
  means of, 442
Persuasion essays, 485–533
  critiquing, 533
  features of, 510–516
  guidelines for, 516–523
  key component of, 485
  samples of, 486–507, 524–532
Persuasive language, 512–516
  description, 512–513
  narration, 513–514
  prose style, 514–516
"Pet Overpopulation Problem, The," 559, 560–571
Peters, Mike (cartoon), 520
Philosophy of Literary Form, The, 273
Phrases
  absolute, 84, 85–86
  and modification, 672–673
  transitional, 64–65
Piaget, Jean, 649–650
Piercy, Marge ("A Work of Artifice"), 310, 325, 332
Pinker, Steven ("Racist Language, Real and Imagined"), 136–139
Pitman, Jennifer
  "Booze It? Lose It!: An Evaluation of North Carolina's Drunk Driving Laws," 362–364, 389

"Euthanasia and the Right to Die," 437–440, 443
Plagiarism, 582
Plot, in literary texts, 320
Point of view, in literary texts, 322–323
"Politics and the English Language," 61
Portfolios, 396–404
Position essays, 413–482
  and argument, 413
  critiquing, 482
  features of, 446–452
  guidelines for, 452–473
  samples of, 413–440, 473–482
Possessive case
  for nouns, 666
  for pronouns, 667
Post Hoc, Propter Hoc, fallacy of, 468
"Powwow at the End of the World, The," 300–301, 329
Practical application essay, as essay exam, 658–660
Predicate adjective, 676
Predicate nominative, 675–676
Prepositional phrases, 676
Prepositions
  definition of, 671
  objects of, 678
Present infinitive, 668
Present participle, 668
Present perfect tense, 668–670
Present tense, 668–670
Prewriting, 4–5, 36–37. *see also* Information, collecting
  for essay *from* literature, 331–332
  for evaluation essay, 387–389
  for information essay, 242–247
  for interpretive essay (*about* literature), 329
  for personal essay, 184–186
  for persuasion essay, 517
  for position essay, 453–456
  for problem/solution essay, 555–557
Primary source, 327–328
Problem/solution essays
  critiquing, 571
  features of, 552–554
  guidelines for, 554–560
  samples of, 536–549, 560–571
Process mode, 150, 248–249
  in essay exam, 655
Progressive form, of verb tenses, 668
Pronoun case, 666
Pronouns, 666–667
  as paragraph connectors, 63

Pronouns, (*continued*)
  as substantives, 670–680
  case, 666
  demonstrative, 666
  indefinite, 666–667
  intensive, 667
  interrogative, 666
  personal, 666
  reciprocal, 667
  reflexive (intensive), 667
  relative, 666
Proofreading, 92–93
Proper, Datus ("Dark Hollow"),
  55–56, 57, 58, 66, 68, 153–157,
  187, 188
Prose style, use of, in persuasion essay,
  514–516
*Publication Manual of the American
  Psychological Association,* 561,
  563–567
Punctuation
  end, 682–683
  within sentences, 684–688

"Quest to Return to the Garden, A:
  Perception 'Of Falling,'"
  306–309, 325, 327
Question begging, fallacy of, 471
Question mark, 682–683
Questionnaires, 587–589
Questions for Analysis, 24–32
Quotation marks, 692–694

"Racist Language, Real and Imagined,"
  136–139
Reader, 41–44. *see also* Audience
  counterarguments from, 462
  of evaluation essay, 372
  of information essay, 237–238
  of interpretive essay (*about* literature),
    325–326
  of personal essay, 177–178
  of persuasion essay, 507–508
  of position essay, 462
  of problem/solution essay, 550–551
  writing for, 41
Readers' Guide to Periodical Literature,
  583
Reading
  importance of, to writing, 5, 105–106
  sample response to, 122, 141–142
  strategies for, 110–123
Reciprocal pronouns, 667
Reed, John Shelton, 467

Reep, Matthew, 654–655
Reflective essay, 396–404
  samples of, 399–404
Reflexive pronouns, 667
Relative pronouns, 666
Reliability of sources, 584–585, 586,
  590–591
Research essays, 577–638
  aims of, 577
  critiquing, 637–638
  exploring topic for, 580–598
  sample student process of, 624–637
  selecting topic for, 579–580
  student samples of
    Brown, Clarita ("The American
      Indian Movement as a
      Counterculture"), 618–623
    Gardner, Elizabeth ("Transforming
      a Nation, Transforming an
      Enemy"), 227–233
    Geray, Kristina ("The Pet
      Overpopulation Problem"),
      567–571
    Hall, Heather ("The Next Big
      Winner Is . . . . !!"), 479–482
    Overton, Andrew ("Change"),
      545–549
    Pitman, Jennifer
  "Booze It? Lose It!: An Evaluation of
    North Carolina's Drunk
    Driving Laws," 362–364
  "Euthanasia and the Right to Die,"
    437–439
    Rhoderick, Gardiner ("Yes, It's
      Graffiti, But Is It Art?"),
      630–637
    Sherrill, Jaime ("Zero Tolerance for
      Abuse"), 501–503
    Stead, Kendra
  "Making of Spells, The," 303–306
  "No Exceptions," 310–313
    Talbert, Jaclyn ("Justice for Those
      Who Have Shown Us No
      Mercy"), 504–507
    Tucker, Alysia ("No More"),
      529–532
    Wright, Amy ("Quest to Return to
      the Garden, A: Perception 'Of
      Falling'"), 341–345
Research notebook, 578
Research strategies, sample, 625–626
Response, writing a, 141–142
Revising, 4–5. *see also* Global revision
  and Local revision

and peer review, 89–91
for audience, 75–77
for meaning, 74–75
for sentences, 81–89
for structure, 77–78
for words, 78–81
getting distance, 73–74
of evaluation essay, 390
of information essay, 260
of interpretive essay (*about* literature),
  336–341
of personal essay, 188–189
of persuasion essay, 525–526, 528–529
of position essay, 473
of problem/solution essay, 550–551,
  566–567
questions for, 74–78, 81, 86, 90–91, 95
sample of, 95–102
strategies for, 73–91
tips for, 102
versus editing, 92
Rhetorical triangle, xic–xv, 147–151
  in evaluation essay, 371–372
  in information essay, 234–238
  in interpretive essays (*about*
    literature), 316–326
  in personal essay, 176–178
  in persuasion essay, 507–509
  in position essay, 440–446
  in problem/solution essay, 550–552
Rhoderick, Gardiner ("Yes, It's Graffiti,
  But Is It Art?"), 592–594,
  624–637
Rico, Gabriele L., 20
"Right Not to Listen, The," 414–420, 441,
  444, 464
Rosenfeld, Arthur ("Should Anyone
  Have to Live in Pain?"),
  213–215, 260

Sandberg, Carl ("Name Us a King"), 315
"Scars," 165–176, 187
Schiffrin, Deborah, 209
Search engines, Internet, 33–34,
Search function, 93–94,
Searching Writing, 535
Secondary objects, 678
Secret Garden, The, 20
Self-assessment of writing, 95
Semantic parts of speech, 665–672
Semicolon, 687–688
Sentence combining, 82–83
Sentences, 81–89
  combining, 82–83

cumulative, 84–86
functions of, 675–680
periodic, 84–86
punctuation
  end, 682–683
  within a sentence, 683–684
repetition of, 62–63
revising, 81–89
thesis, 53–56
topic, 60–63
types of, 680–681
Sequence, questions of, 25, 26, 29–30
Setting, in literary texts, 322
seventeen, 391–393
Shalev, Meir ("If Bosnians Were Whales"), 252–253
Shaping strategies, 47–52
  initial, 41–44
  modes of discourse as, 258
Shaughnessy, Mina (*Errors and Expectations*), 687
Shepherd, Jean, 348–349
Sherrill, Jaime ("Zero Tolerance for Abuse"), 501–504, 508, 509, 514, 517–518, 532
"Shooting to Win," 351–357, 383
"Shopping," 275–284, 322, 329
"Should Anyone Have to Live in Pain?" 213–215, 260
"Should" thesis, 458
Silent letters, 697
Simple form of verb tenses, 668–670
Simple sentence, 680–685
Smalley, Suzanne ("The Perfect Crime"), 208–210
Souls of Black Folk, The, 219–226
Sources
  citing, 327–328, 601–618
  incorporating material from, 598–601
  potential, 580–598
  reliability of, 584–585, 586, 590–591
Spawn cartoons, 404–410
Spellcheck function, 94
Spelling, 696–700
"Spelling," 296–297, 326–328
Statistics, in position essay, 449–450
Stead, Kendra,
  "Making of Spells, The," 303–306, 326, 327–328
  "No Exceptions," 310–313, 325, 332
Stereotyping, fallacy of, 465–466
"Steve Wants an A," 402–404
Stoeckel, Steve ("What about the Customer?") 313–315

Story line (plot), in literary texts, 320
Straub, Richard (*Twelve Readers Reading*), 243, 245–246
Structure
  development of, 41–44, 47–52
  of essay *from* literature, 332–333
  of evaluation essay, 389
  of information essay, 248–259
  of interpretive essay (*about* literature), 330–331
  of personal essay, 186–188
  of persuasion essay, 518–519
  of position essay, 457–464
  of problem/solution essay, 558–559
  revising for, 77–78
Study time, 112
Subject
  of evaluation essay, 371
  of information essay, 234–235
  of interpretive essay (*about* literature), 316–324
  of personal essay, 176–177
  of persuasion essay, 508–509
  of position essay, 441–442
  of problem/solution essay, 551–552
  of simple sentence, 675
Subject index, of search engine, 33–34
Subjective case
  of nouns, 665
  of pronouns, 666–667
Subordinating conjunctions, 85, 672
Subordination of ideas, 84–85
Substantives, 679–680
Sufficient cause, 468–469
Suffixes, 698–699
Summary
  in essay exam, 647–648
  in research essay, 582
  moving beyond, in interpretive essay, 327
  sample, 135–140, 143–145
Symbols, in literature, 323–324
Synthesis, in essay exam, 648–650

Tables and figures, 242–247
Talbert, Jaclyn ("Justice for Those Who Have Shown Us No Mercy"), 143–145, 451, 504–507, 516
"Teaching Is Always a Political Act," 420–426, 444–445, 464
Technical language, 80
Teen, 391–393
Tenses, verb, 668–669

"That Place Where Ghosts of Salmon Jump," 298–299, 506
Themes
  of interpretive essays (*about* literature), 326
  in literature, 324
Thesis sentence, 53–56
  in evaluation essay, 389
  in information essay, 259–260
  in interpretive essay (*about* literature), 326–327
  in persuasion essay, 518–519
  in position essay, 464
  in problem/solution essay, 559
Thesis statement. *see* Thesis sentence
Tietsworth, Mike, 50
Titone, Julie ("Balance of Power: Can Endangered Salmon and Hydroelectric Plants Share the Same Rivers?"), 60–61, 301, 329, 541–545, 554, 558–559
Tobin, Killian ("A Modern Perspective on Graffiti"), 594, 625–626
Topic sentence, 58–61. *See also* Thesis sentence
Topics
  assigned, 13–14
  exploring, 14–32
  finding, 9–13
  outlining, 48–49
  searching, in research essay, 580–598
    field search, 585–589
    Internet search, 590–598
    library search, 582–585
    sources of information, 580–582
  selecting
    for essay *from* literature, 329
    for evaluation essay, 387
    for information essay, 241–242
    for interpretive essay (*about* literature), 328
    for personal essay, 185
    for persuasion essay, 516–517
    for position essay, 452–453
    for problem/solution essay, 555–556
    for research essay, 579–580
"Transforming a Nation, Transforming an Enemy," 227–234, 235
Transitional words/phrases, 63–64
Transitive verbs, 667
Triangle, rhetorical. *see* Rhetorical triangle
Trite expressions, 80–81

Trudeau, Gary (*Doonesbury* cartoon), 380–382
"True Story of Why I Do What I Do, The," 106–110, 111–123, 131–132, 180–181
Tucker, Alysia ("No More"), 508, 524–532
Twelve Readers Reading, 243, 245–246

Umbrella drawing, as shaping strategy, 50; 52

Value, claims of, 446–447
Vargas, Marisol, 36–37, 44–46, 76–77, 95–102
Verb phrases, 674
Verbals, 679–680
Verbs, 667–670
   action words, 667
   intransitive, 667
   tenses of, 668–670
   transitive, 667
Visual rhetoric
   and evaluation essay, 378–386
   and information essay, 242–247
   and personal essay, 181–184
   and persuasion essay, 519–523
   strategies for reading, 123–129

Visualizing, 22–24
Vowels, 796–700

Webb, Brett ("Art Crimes: The Writing on the Wall"), 594
"What Qualities Does a Good Photograph Have?" 373–376
"When Religion Steps on Science's Turf," 445, 496–501
Whitehead, Kimberly, 185
Wise, Jason, 651–652
World Wide Web. *See* Internet
Word processing. *See* Computers
"Work of Artifice, A," 310, 325, 332
Wright, Amy
   "*Da Vinci Code, The*: A Study in Print and Film," 365–370
   "Quest to Return to the Garden, A: Perception 'Of Falling,'" 306–309, 325, 327
Writer
   judgment of (in evaluation essay), 376–377, 390
   of evaluation essay, 371–372
   of information essay, 235–236
   of interpretive essay (about literature), 324–325
   of personal essay, 176
   of persuasion essay, 509
   of position essay, 442–443
   of problem/solution essay, 552
   point of view of, 322–323
Writer's block, overcoming, 68
Writer's notebook, 10–11
   and dialogue notes, 131–132,
   and responding to readersí comments, 92
Writing
   and assessment, 95, 639–640
   and visuals, 5
   importance of computers in, 5–6
   importance of reading to, 5,
   purposes of, 1–2. *See also* Focus statements
   stages in process of, 3–5
Writing center, 6–7
Writing occasions. *see* Occasions, writing
Writing portfolios. *see* Portfolios

"Yes, It's Graffiti, But Is It Art?" 624–637
Yusnukis, Arlene, 16–18, 19

"Zero Tolerance for Abuse," 501–504, 509, 514, 517–518, 532